Religion and Human Rights

Volume 11

Series Editors
Hans-Georg Ziebertz, University of Würzburg, Würzburg, Germany
Carl Sterkens, Radboud University, Nijmegen, The Netherlands

To the extent that modern societies are characterised by centrifugal forces like pluralization of norms, economic globalization, nationalism, political populism and claims of regional autonomy, the question of how to hold this society together becomes increasingly important. Democratic institutions proof to be vulnerable in such context. Even the possibility and desirability of democracy as it developed in Western countries after the Second World War is being questioned. Societal cohesion can no longer be achieved through shared religious beliefs, and common values seem to be scarce. Human rights are regarded as an important instrument to guarantee freedom and equality of citizens. This series investigates how religion can both challenge and contribute to a democratic society shaped by the culture of human rights in different national and cross-national contexts. Volumes address these questions by means of a theoretical, empirical and comparative approach.

Modestus Chiedozie Adimekwe

The Impact of Religion, Personality, Values and Worldviews on Attitudes Towards Human Rights

An Empirical-theological Study Among Nigerian Youth

Springer

Modestus Chiedozie Adimekwe
Universität Würzburg
Bamberg, Bayern, Germany

ISSN 2510-4306 ISSN 2510-4314 (electronic)
Religion and Human Rights
ISBN 978-3-031-65748-1 ISBN 978-3-031-65749-8 (eBook)
https://doi.org/10.1007/978-3-031-65749-8

This Springer imprint is published by the registered company Springer Nature Switzerland AG
The registered company address is: Gewerbestrasse 11, 6330 Cham, Switzerland

Dedicated to HRH, Eze A.E. Adimekwe and Ugoeze M.C. Adimekwe, who first taught me the social virtue of justice

and

to all engaged in the struggle for a just society.

Acknowledgements

"No man is an island"! This famous saying by John Donne expresses the fact that as humans we need each other to survive. The making of this book is a testament to the credibility of these words. Many people were helpful to me at various stages of writing, some of whom deserve special mention. My special thanks go first to my mentor Prof. Dr. Dr. Hans-Georg Ziebertz for his amazing input and patience, but also Prof. Dr. Michelle Becka, who read the manuscript carefully. Dr. Boris Kalbheim was very helpful in the development phase of the work, while Ms. Sylvia Scheller was a good facilitator throughout the project. For that I owe them a word of thanks.

My Bishop, Most Rev. Dr. Solomon A. Amatu, also deserves special thanks for his fatherly support, as does Msgr. Prof. Simon O. Anyanwu, former Chancellor of the Catholic Diocese of Okigwe, for his encouragements. I sincerely thank the Archdiocese of Bamberg for providing me with all the logistics I needed for the academic marathon that led to the birth of this book. In this connection, I mention particularly the Archbishop Emeritus of Bamberg, Prof. Dr. Ludwig Schick and the Vicar General Mgr. Georg Kestel. Also worth mentioning here are Pfr. Anton Heinz and the good people of St. Martin and St. Josef in Hain, Bamberg. The same applies to the Sisters of the Congregatio Jesu, Bamberg.

My thanks also go to Prof. Dr. Chibueze Udeani for the interesting conversations with him, which helped sharpen my view of certain topics regarding the context of study. The following friends of mine were very helpful in the data collection: Frs. Jude Nwigwe, John Agim, Michael C. Nwosu, Mr. Lukman Nwokeyi, Ms. Laetitia Okorie and a host of friends from Kafanchan, as well as the staff and students of all the secondary schools that made up my research group.

I had many brainstorming sessions with several of my colleagues, which I found enriching and had a positive impact on the work. Among them are Frs. Matthew Anyanwu, Obinna Kurumeh, Chidi Ekpendu, Anthony Chimaka, Anthony Iromenu, Bona Uke, Rowland Nwokocha, Kizito Nweke, Mark Odah, John Ekeogu, Joseph

Anumnu, Joseph M. Raja, Chidi Obiodu, Patrick Osuji, Ms. Nina Monowski, Srs. Karin Ebirim and Chidinma Ogbonna, to name a few.

Last but not the least, my family was a huge source of inspiration. The same goes for my godfather, Rev. Dr. Kevin O. Madu, as well as Sr. M. Christa Biesinger, Sr. Humbline Nwaokoro, Sr. Chibugo Lebechi, Sr. Cecilia Aladu, Sr. Ijeoma Madu and Ms. Ozioma Okechukwu. I really appreciate all your contributions!

Contents

1 General Introduction . . . 1
References . . . 10

Part I Religion and Human Rights in Nigeria

2 Nigeria's Human Rights System . . . 15
2.1 Historical Overviews of Human Rights in Nigeria . . . 16
2.2 Mechanisms for the Protection of Human Rights in Nigeria . . . 22
2.2.1 National Human Rights Legal Framework . . . 22
2.2.2 Human Rights Declarations and Treaties . . . 25
2.2.3 Constitutional Democracy . . . 30
2.2.4 National Human Rights Institutions . . . 34
2.2.5 Limitations of Nigeria's Human Rights System . . . 40
References . . . 44

3 Legal, Social and Religious Perspectives on the Status of Human Rights in Nigeria . . . 49
3.1 Right to Freedom of Religion . . . 50
3.1.1 The Context of Freedom of Religion in Nigeria . . . 54
3.1.2 Freedom of Religion in Nigerian Law . . . 61
3.1.3 Recurrent Issues in the Practice of Freedom of Religion in Nigeria . . . 67
3.1.4 Religion and Freedom of Religion . . . 76
3.2 Right to Freedom from Discrimination Based on Sexual Orientation . . . 83
3.2.1 The Legal Status of Homosexuality in Nigeria . . . 85
3.2.2 Social Implications of Nigeria's Anti-homosexuality Laws . . . 90
3.2.3 Religion and Homosexuality . . . 91
3.3 The Right to Life . . . 95
3.3.1 Right to Life in the Global Context . . . 95
3.3.2 Right to Life in Nigeria . . . 98

3.4 Political Rights. 130
3.4.1 Political Rights Provisions in Nigerian Law 132
3.4.2 Contentious Issues in the Exercise of Political Rights in Nigeria 135
3.4.3 Religion and Political Rights 150
3.5 Judicial Rights 157
3.5.1 Right to a Fair Trial in Nigerian Law. 159
3.5.2 Topical Issues in the Right to a Fair Trial in Nigeria 166
3.5.3 Religion and the Right to a Fair Trial 175
3.6 Socio-economic Rights 178
3.6.1 Socio-economic Rights in Nigerian Law. 181
3.6.2 Topical Issues in Socio-economic Rights in Nigeria 183
3.6.3 Religion and Socio-economic Rights. 206
References. 212

4 Explaining Human Rights Attitudes 235
4.1 Human Rights Attitudes Defined 236
4.2 Social Significance of Religion 238
4.3 Theories of Empathy 241
4.4 Theory of Basic Human Values 243
4.5 Theory of Human Dignity 246
4.6 The Integrative Theory of the Quality of Life 249
4.7 Social Identity Theory 252
4.8 Socialisation Theory 254
4.9 State of Research 255
References. 257

Part II Empirical Study

5 Research Design 267
5.1 Differentiated Research Questions and Hypotheses 268
5.2 Data Collection and Sample. 270
5.3 Conceptual Model 271
5.4 Measuring Instruments. 272
5.5 Method of Analysis 283
References. 286

6 Empirical Findings 289
6.1 Evaluations of Human Rights by Students 290
6.2 Differences in Human Rights Evaluations by Religious Affiliation 297
6.3 Nexuses Between Human Rights Attitudes and Explanatory Factors 301
6.4 Predictors of Human Rights Attitudes of Students 307
6.5 Are the Findings as Expected?. 314
References. 317

Part III Discussion of Salient Findings

7 The Quest for an Authentic Culture of Human Rights 321
7.1 Determinants of Human Rights Attitudes in Nigeria. 323
7.1.1 The Salience of Religion 323
7.1.2 The Significant Impact of Value Orientations 334
7.2 Significance of Study for Practical Theology 337
7.3 Significance of Study for the Pastoral Mission of the Church. 339
7.4 Significance of Study for the Global Discourse on Human Rights 341
References. 344

General Conclusion. 349

Appendices. 353

References 359

List of Abbreviations

ACHPR	African Charter on Human and Peoples' Rights
ACJA	Administration of Criminal Justice Act
ACRWC	African Charter on the Rights and Welfare of the Child
Anor.	Another
APPGN	All-Party Parliamentary Group on Nigeria
ATR	African Traditional Religion
C.A.	Court of Appeal
Can.	Code of Canon Law
Cap.	Chapter
CAT	Convention Against Torture and Other Cruel, Inhuman or Degrading Treatment or Punishment
CAT-OP	Optional Protocol of the Convention against Torture
CCC	Catechism of the Catholic Church
CDF	Congregation for the Doctrine of the Faith
CEDAW	Convention on the Elimination of All Forms of Discrimination against Women
CESAC	Comparative Education Study and Adaptation Centre
Cf.	Confer
CFRN	Constitution of the Federal Republic of Nigeria
CRA	Child Rights Act
CRC	Convention on the Rights of the Child
CRC-OP-AC	Optional Protocols on the Involvement of Children in Armed Conflict
CRC-OP-SC	Optional Protocols to the CRC on the Sale of Children, Child Prostitution and Child Pornography
CRPD	Convention on the Rights of Persons with Disabilities
CTITF	Counter-Terrorism Implementation Task Force
CYPA	Children and Young Persons Act
CYPL	Children and Young Persons Laws
DICE	Database for Institutional Comparisons in Europe
EASO	European Asylum Support Office

EMCC	Erga Migrantes Caritas Christi
FGN	Federal Government of Nigeria
FSCA	Federal Sharia Court of Appeal
GANHRI	Global Alliance of National Human Rights Institutions
HRC	Human Rights Committee
HTS	Hervormde Teologiese Studies (Afrikaans)
IACHR	Inter-American Commission on Human Rights
ICCPR	International Convention on Civil and Political Rights
ICCPR-OP1	First Optional Protocols to the ICCPR on Individual Communications
ICCPROP2-DP	Second Protocol to the ICCPR Aiming at Abolishing the Death Penalty
ICERD	International Convention on the Elimination of All Forms of Racial Discrimination
ICESCR	International Convention on Economic, Social and Cultural Rights
ICJ	International Commission of Jurists
ICPPED	International Convention for the Protection of All Persons from Enforced Disappearance
ICRMW	International Convention on the Protection of the Rights of All Migrant Workers and Members of their Families
ICTR	International Criminal Tribunal for Rwanda
ICTY	International Criminal Tribunal for the Former Yugoslavia
IDPs	Internally Displaced Persons
IFRA-Nigeria	Institut Français de Recherche en Afrique, Nigeria
ILC	International Labour Conference
ILO	International Labour Organization
Inc.	Incorporated
INCRESE	International Centre for Reproductive Sexual Rights
IPEC	International Programme on the Elimination of Child Labour
LACON	Legal Aid Council of Nigeria
LFN	Laws of the Federation of Nigeria
LGA	Local Government Area
Ltd	Limited
MLR	Multiple Linear Regression
N.d.	No Date
NACA	National Agency for the Control of AIDS
NAP	National Action Plan
NAPTIP	National Agency for the Prohibition of Trafficking in Persons and Other Related Matters
NBS	National Bureau of Statistics
NCFR	National Commission for Refugees
NCL	(Nigeria) National Child Labour
NCLR	Nigerian Constitutional Law Report.
NDHS	National Demographical Health Survey
NGOs	Non-Governmental Organisations

NHRC	National Human Rights Commission
NICN	National Industrial Court of Nigeria
NLC	Nigeria Labour Congress
NMLR	Nigerian Monthly Law Reports
NPC	National Population Commission
NSCCL	National Steering Committee on Child Labour
NT	New Testament
NWLR	Nigerian Weekly Law Report
OAS	Organization of American States
OAU	Organisation of African Unity
OHCHR	Office of the High Commissioner for Human Rights
OIC	Organisation of Islamic Cooperation
OP-CEDAW:	Optional Protocol to the CEDAW
OP-CRPD	Optional Protocol to the CRPD
Ors.	Others
OSCE	Organisation for Security and Co-operation in Europe
OT	Old Testament
P. / pp.	Page / pages
PROAP	Principal Regional Office for Asia and the Pacific
Pt.	Part
READY	Religious Education and Diversity
RfP	Religions for Peace
RHR	Religion and Human Rights
SDGs	Sustainable Development Goals
SDN	Stakeholder Democracy Network
SSMPA	Same Sex Marriage Prohibition Act
The US	United States of America
The UK	United Kingdom
UBEC	Universal Basic Education Commission
UN	United Nations
UNDESA	United Nations Department of Economic and Social Affairs
UNDP	United Nations Development Programme
UNFPA	United Nations Population Fund
UNHCR	United Nations High Commissioner for Refugees
UNICEF	United Nations Children's Fund
UNPD	UN Population Division
V.	Versus
VAPP Act	Violence Against Persons (Prohibition) Act
VEH	Voter Education Handbook
WACA	West African Court of Appeal.
WEF	World Economic Forum.

Chapter 1
General Introduction

Contents

References.. 10

The term 'human rights' is arguably the most frequently used expression in international politics today. Since entering the political lexicon of late, the term has seeped into everyday parlance like no other term in recent memory. Yet despite being common and part of our everyday language, it is not easy to define due to ideological differences among scholars. So, to understand the term properly, it may be helpful to start by clarifying the meaning of the word '*right*'. In literature, the latter is often employed in two senses: first, it is used to refer to ethical or moral rectitude; and secondly, it is also used in the sense of entitlement and claims. Each of these senses has a specific theoretical grammar showing substantial differences in the two. While it is not the burden of this paper to go into all that, suffice it to say that human rights belong to the category of entitlement and claims, and that it is these features that differentiate them from other forms of rights (Donnelly, 1985).

Not all rights held by human beings are human rights. Constitutional rights are held by humans as rights, but they do not qualify as human rights. For instance, the right to own firearms is guaranteed in the constitutions of many countries, such as the United States of America (hereinafter the US), Colombia, Liberia, etc., but it is not a human right. The same is truer of contractual rights, which refer to legal privileges vested in persons or people upon entering a valid contract with one another. Contractual rights usually concern, but are not limited to, business matters. The right to purchase a product or service, right to be the only seller or buyer, and rights to refunds or repairs are all good examples of contractual rights,[1] but these are no human rights. Human rights surpass the common understanding of rights as legal privileges. In fact, they are no privileges guaranteed by law, nor some form of

[1] What Are Contractual Rights? Available at https://www.legalmatch.com/law-library/article/what-are-contractual-rights.html. Accessed 14.09.2019.

M. C. Adimekwe, *The Impact of Religion, Personality, Values and Worldviews on Attitudes Towards Human Rights*, Religion and Human Rights 11,
https://doi.org/10.1007/978-3-031-65749-8_1

favours to be bestowed on people at the mercy of the whims of some persons, authorities or the state. Instead, they are entitlements and claims made by people relying on a different principle of legitimation which is not necessarily the law. The claims in question are not mere *frivolous* claims, but genuine demands about the dynamic conditions which embody the intrinsic value and dignity of human beings (Moskowitz, 1974). For this reason, Webb et al. (2012: 178) consider human rights to "be part of the life goals and projects of individuals and groups." Similarly, Santuraki (2016: 54) describes them as "social ideals", while Benn (1967) defines them as statements of basic needs and interests of persons or groups of persons. The concept of basic needs here does not necessarily refer to the catalogue of classic basic human needs because human rights are not merely designed to satisfy the immediate basic needs of human beings. On the contrary, human rights refer to those things which every individual needs to live as a human being and to participate fully in society (Donnelly, 1985). They are entitlements and claims based on the humanity of the claimant. By entitlements we mean that human rights are owed equally to everyone without discrimination insofar as (s)he is a human being, whereas as claims they are regarded as just or valid demands made by people based on their human dignity, the denial of which is a sign of disrespect to their humanity (Nelson Mandela, in Aduku et al., 2015).

Both the United Nations' Universal Declaration of Human Rights (1948) and the African Charter on Human and Peoples' Rights (1981) as well as other international human rights documents, all recognise human rights as rights that are inherent in all persons by virtue of their being human (BAOBAB Report, 2003). Here, being human is not the same as being a "creature of a particular species and genus, [because] human rights are the rights of man—not as homo sapiens but as animale rationalis" (Donnelly, 1985: 9). It may be wrong then to regard them as products of nature, as if to say they were given to human beings by, or are directly drawn from, nature in a simplistic fashion; human rights are no 'heaven-sent packages' (Botvar, 2013; Kirchschlaeger, 2014). Of course, they develop over time as responses to nature-based needs of individuals or groups of people, but they are essentially a product of socio-cultural processes and can literally be traced to political struggles of people against particular experiences of injustice, oppression, slavery, fascism, genocide, etc. (Wronka, 1992; Santuraki, 2016). They arose out of the history of these struggles as a political solution aimed at "securing a decent life … in the perspective of the common good" (van der Ven, 2013: 177f).

From the foregoing thesis, one perceives the attributes of "possession paradox"[2] inhering in the notion of human rights. That means, they are portrayed as something which every human being already possesses in virtue of his or her humanness. Yet they have to be constantly demanded because their scope is wide, and the entire list of rights is usually not recognised as such in the statute books of most nation-states (Felix & Akujobi, 2018). So, to realise them requires strong, practical-oriented

[2] Donnelly (1985: 17) describes the "possession paradox" in terms of 'having' and 'not having' a right, simultaneously. According to him, this paradox is at the heart of the practice of rights and a special characteristic of human rights.

political institutions, otherwise they become mere empty words devoid of any practical value. Recently, a compilation of these rights has been done in a codified form by the international community. In this paper, therefore, human rights refer to the corpus of lifegoals, social ideals and values that have been crafted in the form of entitlements and claims that individuals or groups are justified to make based on their humanity in order to secure a life that befits their dignity as humans. In their entirety, human rights embrace all liberties that are preserved by society on ethical grounds. However, from a legal point of view, they refer to a set of specific individual and collective rights that are enshrined in objective law. These rights apply equally to every human being everywhere, irrespective of his or her social attributes and are inalienable "because being human cannot be renounced, lost or forfeited" (Verschraegen, 2002: 268). The sum of these rights forms a complementary whole, such that the abuse of one adversely affects the exercise of others.

The concern of human rights may have always existed from times immemorial, but the global practice of human rights is a recent development. Opinions do not easily converge as to their exact origin. Some scholars consider them to be a patrimony of the West, and by that they mean that human rights originated in the West, from where they were recently universalised (cf. Santuraki, 2016). Others dismiss this position as based on insufficient historical and theoretical evidence, and instead posited that the concept of human rights is part of the intellectual patrimony of humankind, which developed over time as societies and civilisations interact with one another. To buttress their point, this group presented several pieces of evidence to show that the notion of rights existed in the thought frames and belief systems of cultures around the globe (Ramcharan, 1998; Shiman, 1993). Advocates of the pro-Western view acknowledged this position to some extent, but still maintained that while some traces of rights could be found in the cultures of non-Western societies, these cultures lacked the practice of human rights (Santuraki, 2016). Be that as it may, historical evidence shows that the practice of universal human rights never existed before the eighteenth century (Compasito, in Aduku et al., 2015). It began in earnest after World War II, especially with the formation of the United Nations (hereinafter the UN) in 1945 and reached its zenith in 1948 with the drafting of the Universal Declaration of Human Rights (hereinafter Universal Declaration). Granted considerable efforts had been made earlier on in history to assert the rights of the individual,[3] yet it was with the introduction of this document that the era committed to the institutionalisation of the global practice of human rights was inaugurated.

The Universal Declaration is commonly regarded as the international Magna Carta for sustaining the paradigm shift in international law which the UN Charter had initiated, a shift in which governments' obligations to their citizens would henceforth be considered as a matter of legitimate international concern, and no

[3] Notable among these are the Magna Carta (1215), the Petition of Right (1628), the English Bill of Rights (1689), the US Declaration of Independence (1776), the French Declaration on the Rights of Man and Citizen (1789), and the US Constitution (1787) and Bill of Rights (1791) (see Shiman, 1993).

longer sheer domestic affairs (Shiman, 1993; Verschraegen, 2002). The framework of rights embodied in the Universal Declaration accords largely with the common values of societies, civilisations and belief patterns worldwide. In consequence, the document was unanimously endorsed by UN member states when it was introduced in 1948[4] and its catalogue of rights has gone on since to achieve the status of customary international law. However, this universal code—the Universal Declaration—is only a soft law that does not establish enforceable obligations. Hence, to enforce compliance with its provisions, twin treaties were later developed, namely the International Covenant on Civil and Political Rights (1966) and the International Covenant on Economic, Social and Cultural Rights (1966), both of which came into force in 1976. These treaties have binding status in international law, making them binding on state parties (Brown, 2016). Conjointly, the three documents form what is now known as the International Bill of Human Rights. This bill of rights is further complemented by numerous international conventions and protocols dealing with specific human rights concerns, most of which have been endorsed by UN member states.[5] Furthermore, the Universal Declaration has inspired a lot of regional and sub-regional mechanisms worldwide for the protection of human rights.[6] It is on

[4]The document was adopted by the UN General Assembly at its 3rd meeting in Paris on 10th December 1948 as Resolution 217 A (III). Despite controversies concerning the universality of human rights, voting was unanimous. Of the then 58 members of the UN, 48 voted in favour, 8 abstained and 2 did not vote. The 8 countries that abstained are the Soviet Union, Ukrainian SSR, Byelorussian SSR, Yugoslavia, Poland, Czechoslovakia, South Africa, and Saudi Arabia. Honduras and Yemen failed to vote. However, none of the member states dissented or voted against adoption of the document (Brown, 2016; Shiman, 1993).

[5]The UN has passed several international human rights treaties. Notable among them are: the International Convention on the Elimination of All Forms of Racial Discrimination (ICERD), 1965; the Convention on the Elimination of All Forms of Discrimination against Women (CEDAW), 1979; the Convention against Torture and Other Cruel, Inhuman or Degrading Treatment or Punishment (CAT), 1984; the Convention on the Rights of the Child (CRC), 1989; the International Convention on the Protection of the Rights of All Migrant Workers and Members of their Families (ICRMW), 1990; the International Convention on the Rights of Persons with Disabilities (ICRPD), 2006; and the International Convention for the Protection of All Persons from Enforced Disappearance (ICPPED), 2006. Together with the International Covenant on Civil and Political Rights (ICCPR) and the International Covenant on Economic, Social and Cultural Rights (ICESCR)—both of which were drafted in 1966—these documents constitute the core human rights conventions on which global efforts to protect human rights rest. In addition to these nine instruments, there are presently nine optional protocols that are attached to them. Most of these instruments have been endorsed by member states of the UN. The current rate of ratification was recently put at circa 81 percent. See Human Rights Law (n.d.). Available at: https://www.un.org/en/sections/universal-declaration/human-rights-law/ Accessed 01.09.2019.

[6]The Council of Europe (CoE)—founded on 5th May 1949 by the Treaty of London—is Europe's leading human rights organisation and has an observer status at the UN. Its American equivalent—the Organisation of American States (OAS)—was founded on 30th April 1948 in Bogotá, Colombia, with the signing of the OAS Charter which later came into force in December 1951. As far as Africa is concerned, the Organisation of African Unity (OAU)—which was established on 25th May 1963 in Addis Ababa, Ethiopia, but took off in earnest on 13th September 1963, when its Charter entered into force—is the continent's leading human rights organisation. It was dissolved in 2002 and replaced by the African Union (AU). All these regional bodies have their

record that over 80 human rights declarations, treaties and domestic legal proposals have so far been generated across all levels.[7] The Universal Declaration itself has been translated into over 360 languages, giving it a wide reach (Ban Ki-moon, cited in Al Hussein & Kaci, 2015). All these have in turn contributed to creating a sure basis for the institutionalisation of the practice of human rights on a global scale. In sum, the introduction of the Universal Declaration can be rightly regarded as a momentous event in the history of human rights because, since then, human rights have become a subject with global appeal and recognition (Macfarlane, 1985; Santuraki, 2016).

Global recognition of the human rights system does not necessarily mean full acceptance of its framework at international and national levels. In fact, the validity and content of certain rights continue to generate controversies in philosophy and politics. Perhaps the most intense controversy within the international community concerns the issue of the universality of human rights provisions versus cultural relativism. Despite the many achievements recorded in the field of human rights, this issue is still being revisited in various quarters of the globe, including in our context of study. Apart from that, there are also some apprehensions about the concept of rights with no transcendental appeal. For this reason, human rights are sometimes looked at with suspicion in most of Africa as a superficial value system and a piece of foreign cultural imposition. African scholars often attribute this attitude to the salience of religion, which is a common feature of African cultures (see Egede, 2007; Mbiti, 1989; Van der Tuin & Fumbo, 2012). Another genuine concern here borders on the individualistic cast of the human rights provisions, which again does not fit well with the typical communitarian lifestyle of the African people (Mbiti, 1989; Van der Tuin & Fumbo, 2012). That being the case, the concept of human rights with an emphasis on individual autonomy often tends to elicit some form of resistance, especially from our context of study. Despite these controversies, the importance of a system of human rights in the structural organisation of modern society cannot be overemphasised (Ziebertz & Ziebertz, 2016). Modern society has become increasingly complex due to decolonisation and the emergence of new independent states. There are also fresh concerns arising from the fast-paced globalisation which, on the one side, promotes interconnectedness and interdependence between nations, but which on the flip side has serious implications for politics, culture, commerce, communications, and technology. Besides, intense pressures are being felt from more recent challenges, such as climate change, the

respective human rights documents, e.g., the European Convention on Human Rights, 1950/1953, the American Convention on Human Rights, 1969/1978, and the African Charter on Human and Peoples Rights, 1981/1986. All these documents sustain the vision of human rights proclaimed by the Universal Declaration. Likewise, the Muslim States have drafted many instruments that showcase their support for human rights, e.g., the Universal Islamic Declaration of Human Rights (1981), the Cairo Declaration on Human Rights in Islam (1990), the Arab Charter on Human Rights (1994/2004/2008), and the Charter of the Organisation of the Islamic Conference (2008). These are modelled after the Universal Declaration, though their provisions are adapted to the language of Islamic legal system (Brems, 2001).

[7] See Human Rights Law (n.d.), above at no. 5.

changing patterns of international migration, and terrorism (Brown, 2016). In the light of these societal transformations, the practice of human rights emerges as the basis of peaceful coexistence, security and development (FDFA, 2008, in Aduku et al., 2015). For this reason, the Universal Declaration solemnly proclaims in its preamble that the "recognition of the inherent dignity and of the equal and inalienable rights of all members of the human family is the foundation of freedom, justice and peace in the world" (cf. Al Hussein & Kaci, 2015). Therefore, modern society requires human rights as a basic principle of interactions at all levels of society. Today, human rights are entrenched in virtually all constitutions of nations around the world and as such have come to stay as the mainstay of modern democratic societies (Dada, 2012).

It is now over seven decades since the global practice of human rights was institutionalised through the introduction of the Universal Declaration, yet the ideals of human rights are far from being realised because a wide gap persists between their promise and its actualisation in the lives of people. Systemic abuses of human rights continue to prevail at worrisome rates in all corners of the world—sometimes in nation-states that are parties to the charters or solemn treaties of human rights. In 2012 alone, for instance, Amnesty International reports on human rights abuses in 159 countries of the world. The abuses include, inter alia, torture, unlawful killings, forced evictions, disappearances, and violence against women. The Nigerian State joined the UN at independence from the British colonial rule in 1960 and shortly afterwards endorsed the trending practice of human rights. Over the years, the country has ratified and/or acceded to most of the major international and regional human rights instruments as a result. Quite remarkably, the country played a pivotal role in the realisation of the African Charter on Human and Peoples Rights (hereinafter African Charter) and was among the first, if not the first to incorporate the resultant instrument of human rights into domestic law. Other relevant legal and institutional infrastructures for securing the modern practice of rights have also been put in place in accordance with international standards. Now, the important question here is whether this impressive record of endorsement of human rights instruments has also amounted to an impressive record in terms of human rights praxis. In other words, has the enthusiastic subscriptions to the extant international instruments of human rights helped a culture of human rights to develop in Nigeria? Paradoxically, the answer seems to be 'no', as the country's historic track record of human rights has severally been portrayed in strong negative terms, such as "dismal" (Birnbaum, 1995: 23), and "abysmal" (Dada, 2013: 8). She has also been described as having a "culture of violation of human rights" (International Federation for Human Rights, 2010: 6). Despite the accidents of her political history in which she transited from civil rule in 1966 to military dictatorship and then luckily back to democracy in 1999, it is still being suggested that the country's human rights record has remained "consistently poor and unimpressive" (Onwuazombe, 2017: 116)—in short, "a far cry from general expectation "(Ojo, 2006: 26). Hence, the inability to ensure respect for human rights is believed to be the Achilles' heel, or the main weak point, responsible for the "legacy of underdevelopment" in a country reputed as Africa's largest economy (International Federation for Human Rights, 2010: 6).

It is against this backdrop that this study undertakes to explore the human rights attitudes of Nigerian people, and it argues that the human rights practice in the country has largely remained at the level of mere rhetoric, meaning that the guarantees of human rights instruments are yet to be fully implemented. In other words, the aim of this work is to investigate the trends that emerge among Nigerians, especially the youth, in relation to human rights as defined by the UN. This also includes identifying the factors that trigger the possible tendencies. We therefore ask the question: how do young people in Nigeria evaluate human rights and what factors emerge as predictors of their human rights attitudes? We assume that Nigerians' human rights attitudes are biased and that their evaluations, whether positive or negative, are primarily determined by their religious beliefs. Religion plays an important role in the public sphere in Nigeria, even though the constitution seems to indicate that the country is a secular state. Islam and Christianity are the main religious groups in the country, but there is also the African Traditional Religion (hereinafter ATR).[8]

Nigerian libraries are filled with scholarly papers dealing with human rights practice in the country, but to the best of our knowledge none of these papers has sought to unravel the factors that trigger these attitudes using a quantitative approach. What is special about this study is that it seeks to test the above claims about Nigeria's human rights record as well as the predictors of Nigerians' human rights attitudes using data generated from the context. Hence, it is expected that the study will provide firsthand information on this phenomenon as it pertains to Nigeria. Furthermore, Nigerian scholars have tended to approach this subject only from the vertical dimension, as if human rights were limited to state-individual relations. On the contrary, human rights apply in both horizontal and vertical relations in the sense that the recognition and protection of human rights is the common duty of all—the state, individuals, and other entities alike—and not just the state alone (Brown, 2016). The existing literature on the topic shows that the report on the human rights record of any society can be obtained from a two-pronged analysis using the top-down and bottom-up approaches. The latter is a neglected category of human rights analysis in our context, as very few publications have dared to use it. This study adopts the said approach as part of its analytical strategy and therefore focuses on the people, based on the conviction that it is through their recognition of the rights that a human rights culture can develop (Ziebertz & Ziebertz, 2016). In order to identify the predictors of their human rights attitudes, a number of relevant factors such as religion and religiosity are taken into account. This study posits that Nigerians' human rights attitudes are strongly influenced by their religious worldviews, given the importance of religion in the country. For this reason, special

[8]The ATR is the religious and cultural tradition indigenous to the Nigerian peoples. It was the dominant religion on the African continent before the coming of Europeans to Africa (Nwafor, 2010). This religion had been designated as animistic, totemistic, polytheistic, etc. (Magesa, 2002) in a haste, but its main characteristics include, among others, "belief in a Supreme Being, the realm of spirits", and "a unified community" (Krüger et al., 2009: 35ff). The ATR is a relevant minority religion in contemporary Nigeria.

attention is paid to the 'religion factor', and an attempt is made to further investigate the variances in the human rights attitudes of the study population based on their religious affiliation. Other important explanatory factors considered are the psychological trait of empathy, value systems, the perception of socio-political context, and the socio-demographic characteristics of the study population. The complex relationship between human rights and these concepts usually has policy implications. As such, policymakers, stakeholders, managers and administrators will find the findings of the study handy for the kind of work they do.

The importance of an authentic culture of human rights in modern society has already been highlighted above. Human rights culture here refers to the acquisition of a disposition towards human rights through "the formation of consciences and the gradual strengthening of ways of thinking and styles of behaviour" (Odeme, 2011: 239; see Macfarlane, 1985). One of the objectives of studying the human rights attitudes of the Nigerian people is to show the implications of this analysis in the formation of an appropriate culture in Nigeria. The reference to the word 'formation' explains the choice of young people, particularly secondary school adolescents, as our research population. This group represents the most realistic stage in which formation can still take place. These young people are the future of their society and constitute a relevant subgroup of their country's population. They are also active in human rights issues in their country; sometimes, they are used as instruments of human rights violations, for instance, as political thugs, kidnappers, etc. In any case, they are like a window through which one can glimpse the future of human rights in their country. Thus, this study is future-oriented due to the choice of such a research population. It shares this future perspective with the International Programme on Religion and Human Rights, whose research instrument it used to collect data. Through this choice, the school system is indirectly identified as a springboard for social orientation and change.

Discussions about human rights in the Nigerian context can hardly dispense with legal analysis, as Nigeria's Constitution is her foremost human rights instrument. Nevertheless, this study does not engage in deep 'legalistic analysis" as this may not be necessary, as Alston (1985: 512) puts it, "[v]oluntary acceptance of such a positivistic strait-jacket will cause us all too often to find ourselves at the mercy of the vagaries of legal interpretation." Thus, it is not the legality, but rather the legitimacy, of human rights that interests us. All the guarantees in the country's human rights laws are taken as 'given', and then the study will focus on people's acceptance of the rights because it is the extent of such popular acceptance that will lead to the emergence of human rights culture. Ziebertz and Ziebertz (2016: 46) have this to say:

> ... the development of a human rights culture is not only a matter of law. A society depends on the motivation of the people to agree with human rights and to support them. In [an] explorative empirical analysis on the attitudes ... towards [human] rights, the focus is on the legitimacy and not on the legality of these rights. ... The question of legitimacy is highly relevant since people need to recognise the importance of human rights, adopt them and identify with them in order for a human rights culture to develop.

It must also be added at this point that a legal analysis alone would be completely inadequate for a study of this magnitude. The study instead favours an interdisciplinary approach that involves incorporating useful insights from other disciplines such as history, religion, philosophy, theology, and social sciences (Ziebertz, 2002; Wronka, 1992). Even so, the study does not pretend to provide very conclusive answers to human rights issues in Nigeria, as that would amount to nothing but sheer arrogance. All the same, it is to be expected that this will introduce a new way of reading this social phenomenon in our context.

In order to answer the research question systematically, an empirical-theological research design was chosen for this study. Following John Dewey's recipe for empirical research, we distinguish three main sections or operational contexts with unequal number of chapters, namely context of discovery, context of justification, and context of application (cf. Erdmann & Petersen, 1979). The context of discovery is more or less an enlarged form of the theoretical introduction. It is composed of three chapters of unequal sizes that focus on the complex relationship between human rights and religion in Nigeria. The Chap. 2 opens with a historical excursus on the human rights system in Nigeria. Then, to give a clearer background information, the existing mechanisms for the protection of human rights in the system such as the Constitution, human rights treaties, democracy, human rights institutions and civil society organisations are presented. The chapter concludes by highlighting the limitations of the said human rights system.

This is followed by Chap. 3 which deals with the legal, social and religious perspectives on the status of human rights in Nigeria. The study does not cover the entire spectrum of human rights within the framework of the UN but focuses on civil, political, judicial and socio-economic rights. These include the right to freedom of religion, the right to non-discrimination on the basis of sexual orientation, the right to life under the classic questions of the death penalty, abortion and euthanasia as possible restrictions to the right. Others are political rights such as the right to political participation, the right to protest and the right of refugees, as well as the judicial right to a fair trial, operationalised here with two of its safeguards, namely the right to remain silent and the right to defence. Others still are labour rights, the rights of women and children and the right to social security. These are mostly first- and second-generation rights.[9] Their choice is based on the consideration that they largely represent the areas of conflict and tension in human rights practice in Nigeria.

[9] The division of human rights into generations was introduced by the Czech jurist Karel Vasak in 1979. Using the three tenets of the French Revolution, which are liberty, equality, and fraternity, he divided human rights in three basic categories, namely first, second, and third generations. The Universal Declaration does not follow the categories, but the academia adopted and has continued to use them. Based on this classification, first generation comprises the civil-political rights, also known as the blue rights. Examples are the right to personal liberty, freedom of expression and the right to a fair hearing. From observation, the first-generation rights deal with negative rights. By contrast, the second-generation rights, which are the socio-economic rights (i.e., red rights), concerns mostly positive rights, with social security rights, right to work and fair wages, shelter, health care, education, and rights of women and children as good examples. The third generation or green rights consist of the solidarity rights, e.g., the rights to development, environment, and self-determination. Comparatively, the first two represent potential claims of individuals against the state, whereas the third represents potential claims of groups against the state (see Nowak, 2005).

The context of discovery closes with Chap. 4, which provides the pool of theoretical perspectives used for the study. Relevant socio-psychological theories that can be used to explain attitudes towards human rights are outlined here. The theory of the social significance of religion was chosen as the main theory. Additional explanatory factors such as psychological trait of empathy, value systems, and the perception of social context are presented. Socialisation theory is included as an alternative explanation. These theoretical frameworks are clarified in view of the research hypotheses. This study tries to demonstrate the relevance of all these theories for the analysis of attitudes towards human rights.

Next is the context of justification, which takes care of the empirical section. This part is descriptive and contains all the empirical analyses. It has two chapters, namely Chaps. 5 and 6. Chapter 5 deals with the research design, which begins with the presentation of the differentiated research questions and hypotheses, followed by the description of the data collection method, sampling and the conceptual model. The measurement instruments and research analytical strategies are then clarified. The latter describes all statistical analyses carried out as part of the study, including a homogeneity test, factor, descriptive, variance, correlation and regression analyses. These analyses are conducted in view of the differentiated research questions and hypotheses.

In Chap. 6, the findings of the study are presented. The results of the descriptive, variance, correlations and regression analyses are comprehensively reported here. The results show how the sampled students evaluated the human rights issues and which factors shaped their evaluations. Subgroup differences, such as the difference between students' evaluation of human rights issues based on their religious affiliation, constitute an interesting part of this chapter. Before concluding this chapter, efforts are made to answer the research questions and confirm or reject the hypotheses in the light of the overall research outcomes. This is a crucial part of the study and serves as a launch pad for the subsequent discussion in the context of application.

The context of application has only one chapter, Chap. 7. In this chapter, attempts are made to apply the research findings to the issues raised in the context of discovery to see what tentative relevant conclusions can be drawn for the development of an authentic culture of human rights, especially among the young people of Nigeria. The study then concludes with a recapitulation of important findings and research insights as well as a general evaluation of the research methodology.

References

A. Books and Journals

Aduku, A. A., Maduagwu, M., Olabamiji, O., & Udeoji, E. A. (Eds.). (2015). *Human rights*. National Open University of Nigeria.

Alston, P. (1985). The shortcomings of a "Garfield the Cat" approach to the right to development. *California Western International Law Journal, 15*, 510–518.

Benn, S. I. (1967). Rights. In P. Edwards (Ed.), *The Encyclopaedia of Philosophy* (Vol. 7, pp. 195–199). Macmillan.
Birnbaum, M. (1995). *Nigeria: Fundamental rights denied: Report of the Trial of Ken Saro-Wiwa and Others*. University of Michigan.
Botvar, P. K. (2013). Religion and attitudes towards socio-economic human rights. An empirical study of young adults in Norway. In J. A. van der Ven & H.-G. Ziebertz (Eds.), *Human rights and the impact of religion* (pp. 245–263). Brill.
Brems, E. (2001). *Human Rights: Universality and diversity*. Martinus Nijhoff Publishers.
Brown, G. (Ed.). (2016). *The universal declaration of human rights in the 21st century: A living document in a changing world*. Open Book Publishers.
Dada, J. A. (2012). Human rights under the Nigerian constitution: Issues and problems. *International Journal of Humanities and Social Science, 2*(12), 33–43.
Dada, J. A. (2013). The significance and limits of NGOs in human rights protection in Nigeria. *Journal of Law, Policy and Globalization, 19*, 82–91.
Donnelly, J. (1985). *The concept of human rights*. Croom Helm Ltd.
Egede, E. (2007). Bringing human rights home: An examination of the domestication of human rights treaties in Nigeria. *Journal of African Law, 51*(2), 249–284.
Erdmann, H. W., & Petersen, J. (1979). *Strukturen empirischer Forschungsprozesse, I*. A. Henn Verlag.
Felix, O., & Akujobi, A. (2018). Enforcement of fundamental rights in national constitutions: Resolving the conflict of jurisdiction between the Federal High Court and State High Court in Nigeria. *Beijing Law Review, 9*, 53–66.
International Federation for Human Rights. (2010, April). *Defending human rights – Not everywhere not every right: International fact-finding mission report on Nigeria*. Available at: https://www.refworld.org/docid/4bed03412.html. Accessed 16 July 2014.
Kirchschlaeger, P. G. (2014). The relation between democracy and human rights. *Globalistics and Globalization Studies*, 112–125.
Krüger, J. S., Lubbe, G. J. A., & Steyn, H. C. (2009). *The human search for meaning: A multireligion introduction to the religions of humankind*. Van Schaik Publishers.
Macfarlane, L. J. (1985). *The theory and practice of human rights*. Maurice Temple Smith Ltd.
Magesa, L. (2002). *African religion: The moral traditions of abundant life*. Orbis Books.
Mbiti, J. S. (1989). *African religions and philosophy*. Heinemann Educational Publishers.
Moskowitz, M. (1974). *International concern with human rights*. Sijthoff.
Nwafor, A. O. (2010). Comparative perspectives on Euthanasia in Nigeria and Ethiopia. *African Journal of International and Comparative Law, 18*(2), 170–191.
Ojo, E. O. (2006). Human rights and sustainable democracy in Nigeria (1999–2003). *Journal of Social Science, 13*(1), 15–29.
Onwuazombe, I. I. (2017). Human rights abuse and violations in Nigeria: A case study of the oil-producing communities in the Niger Delta region. *Annual Survey of International and Comparative Law, 22*(1/8), 115–160.
Santuraki, S. U. (2016). Reflections on the concept and foundational convictions of human rights. *Uni-Maid Journal of Private and Property Law, 1*(1), 52–62.
Shiman, D. (1993). *Teaching human rights*. University of Denver.
Van der Tuin, L. W. J. M., & Fumbo, C. D. (2012). Women rights and religion among Christian and Islamic students in Tanzania. In J. A. van der Ven & H.-G. Ziebertz (Eds.), *Tensions within and between religions and human rights* (pp. 203–222). Brill.
Van der Ven, J. A. (2013). Towards a legitimate role of religion in the domain of socio-economic rights. An empirical study among adolescents in North-West European countries. In J. A. van der Ven & H.-G. Ziebertz (Eds.), *Human rights and the impact of religion* (pp. 165–202). Brill.
Verschraegen, G. (2002). Human rights and modern society: A sociological analysis from the perspective of systems theory. *Journal of Law and Society, 29*(2), 258–281.

Webb, R. J., Ziebertz, H.-G., Curran, J., & Reindl, M. (2012). Human rights among Muslims and Christians in Palestine and Germany. In J. A. van der Ven & H.-G. Ziebertz (Eds.), *Tensions within and between religions and human rights* (pp. 177–201). Brill.
Wronka, J. (1992). *Human rights and social policy in the 21st century*. University Press of America.
Ziebertz, H.-G. (2002). Normativity and empirical research in practical theology. *Journal of Empirical Theology, 15*(1), 5–18.
Ziebertz, H.-G., & Ziebertz, C. M. (2016). Labour rights and the impact of human dignity, Religious belief and perception of society. An empirical study among youth in Germany. *Journal of Empirical Theology, 29*(1), 45–77. https://doi.org/10.1163/15709256-12341337

International Human Rights Instruments

Al Hussein, Z. R., & Kaci, Y. A. (Eds.). (2015). *Universal Declaration of Human Rights 1948*. UN Publication.
Nowak, M. (2005). *Human rights: A handbook for parliamentarians*, No. 8. OHCHR.

National Human Rights Instruments

BAOBAB Report. (2003). *Women's Human Rights*. Available at: http://iknowpolitics.org/sites/default/files/sharia_nigeria_baobab.pdf. Accessed 01 Apr 2019.

Other Internet Sources

Human Rights Law. (n.d.). Available at: https://www.un.org/en/sections/universal-declaration/human-rights-law/. Accessed 01 Sept 2019.
Ramcharan, B. G. (1998). A Debate about power rather than rights. In: A. Pfaller (Ed.), Debatte/debate – How universal are human rights? *International Politics and Society, 4*, 423–428. Available at: https://www.fes.de/ipg/sets_d/arc_d.htm. Accessed 01 Feb 2020.
What are Contractual Rights? (n.d.). Available at https://www.legalmatch.com/law-library/article/what-are-contractualrights.html. Accessed 14 Sept 2019.

Part I
Religion and Human Rights in Nigeria

Chapter 2
Nigeria's Human Rights System

Contents

2.1 Historical Overviews of Human Rights in Nigeria 16
2.2 Mechanisms for the Protection of Human Rights in Nigeria 22
2.2.1 National Human Rights Legal Framework 22
2.2.2 Human Rights Declarations and Treaties 25
2.2.3 Constitutional Democracy 30
2.2.4 National Human Rights Institutions 34
2.2.5 Limitations of Nigeria's Human Rights System 40
References 44

Introduction

Human rights are arguably the intellectual patrimony of humankind. All societies and civilisations of the world had some idea of the inalienable rights prior to the formation of political systems. Even the social contract philosophers—Thomas Hobbes (1588–1679), John Locke (1632–1704) and Jean-Jacques Rousseau (1712–1778)—all attest to this fact. In pre-colonial Africa, for instance, a system of human rights existed alongside institutionalised derogations such as discrimination, gender inequalities, etc. It is therefore a misunderstanding of history to deny the universality of the concept of human rights. As Baxi (2003: 12f) beautifully puts it:

> … every societal culture has traditions of understanding concerning what rights human beings ought to have. No culture then is devoid of notions about human rights, even when that which constitutes these rights varies within the same culture in time and place, and these vary across comparable cultures. … All available evidence, however, point to the reality that the global human rights culture, far from being a culture of no cultures, is intensely multicultural, a culture of many cultures.

Granted the roots of inalienable rights may be traced to the ancient traditions of societies across the world, the practice of human rights is a recent phenomenon. This practice assumed the status of a global culture only after the gory events of World War II, and it gained access into Nigeria during the European expansion into

M. C. Adimekwe, *The Impact of Religion, Personality, Values and Worldviews on Attitudes Towards Human Rights*, Religion and Human Rights 11,
https://doi.org/10.1007/978-3-031-65749-8_2

the African continent. In this chapter, we try to situate the Nigerian human rights system within the global system of human rights by tracing its history. To achieve this objective, we draw information from a lot of available sources. But it is important to point out that there is no official history of human rights in Nigeria yet. Therefore, our account is tentative but largely reliable.

That said, this chapter begins with historical overviews of the practice of human rights in Nigeria (Sect. 2.1). This is followed by the mechanisms for the protection of human rights (Sect. 2.2), and finally the limitations of Nigeria's human rights apparatus. The aim of this chapter is to highlight some milestones in the history of human rights in the country. This information can help shed more light on the current state of human rights in the same context.

2.1 Historical Overviews of Human Rights in Nigeria

Human rights are not one of those packages brought to Nigeria by the colonialists. In fact, the notion of inalienable rights existed among the diverse traditional socio-political formations in pre-colonial Nigeria. The ancient empires of Benin, Kanem-Bornu, and Oyo, the sultanate of Sokoto, the Emirates of Kano and Katsina, the princedoms of Efik, and the decentralised system of Igboland, etc., all had systems of rights. The catalogue of human rights that existed under these traditional systems includes the right to life, the right to family and clan membership, the freedom of religion, the right of association with kin and age groups, the right of private property, the right to political participation, and the rights to self-determination (Dada, 2013a; Ojo, 2006; Santuraki, 2016). The existence of these rights cannot be denied, but the idea thereof was not conceived in the modern sense of the term. In some cases, their enjoyment depended on certain social attributes such as sex, age, social status, race, colour, etc. Thus, the practice of universal, inalienable human rights is completely new in Nigeria.

There is no consensus as to the exact entry date of the term 'human rights' in Nigeria, though a lot of hypotheses have been advanced in this regard. According to most of these hypotheses, the standard account of the notion of modern human rights in the country can be traced to around the mid-twentieth century, meaning that it filtered into the socio-political space of Nigeria in the colonial era (cf. Federal Republic of Nigeria, n.d.). During colonial rule, Nigerians were denied their political and economic rights. Examples include the violation of the miners' right to take industrial action in the Enugu coal mine in the southeastern part in 1949, and the practice of forced and cheap labour, a common strategy used by the colonial masters to reduce administrative costs. Most importantly, the colonial system subjugated the natives to a foreign power, thereby denying them their fundamental right to self-rule. While there is no denying that colonialism had some positive impact on the development of human rights via provision of legal and institutional infrastructures that contributed hugely to the abolition of certain uncivilised customary practices prevalent in traditional Nigerian societies such as slavery, human sacrifice, Osu caste system, killing of twins, etc., human rights scholars still insist that it was not the colonialists who introduced the concept in Nigeria because colonialism was essentially incompatible with human rights protection (Dada, 2013a). The clamour for human rights can be traced to the colonial period, but it was the globalisation processes activated by European expansion into Africa that brought the term to the consciousness of the largely abroad-trained Nigerian elites and nationalists, as the basic principle of the emerging global order of the post-World War II era. They embraced it as the trending concept and used it as a banner for their own struggle for independence, and it achieved success. First, an elective principle, albeit with limited suffrage, was introduced in the country for the first time through the Clifford Constitution of 1922. This provision disenfranchised the majority of the population but created room for greater indigenous participation in colonial administration. The continued increase led to improvements in indigenous political rights in subsequent pre-independence constitutions, culminating in the 1954 Lyttleton Constitution (Federal Republic of Nigeria, n.d.).

The real project of human rights began in earnest at independence in 1960, with the entrenchment of a bill of rights in the Independence Constitution. This provision marks out the Independence Constitution from those that preceded it.[1] Much unlike it, the pre-independence constitutions did not include the bill of rights in their provisions, as they were not primarily designed to safeguard human rights but "to achieve specific political objectives of the colonialists" (Dada, 2012b: 35). Even so, it has to be reiterated that while the colonialists did not show notable commitments to the cause of human rights, the motion to include the bill of rights in future constitutions was made in that era. In fact, it was proposed in a series of constitutional conferences beginning from 1953, as a measure to assuage the fear of marginalisation expressed by ethnic minorities in the nation on the path to self-determination.[2] The proposal was eventually adopted and the bill of rights included in the Constitution, thus making Nigeria the first African country to incorporate this provision into her Constitution. Since then, the bill of rights has become a permanent feature of Nigeria's Constitution. It was reproduced verbatim in Chapter III of the 1963 Republican Constitution and the 1979 Draft Constitution but was slightly modified

[1] Before her independence in 1960, the country has had the following constitutions: the Clifford Constitution of 1922, the Richard Constitution of 1946, the McPherson Constitution of 1951, and the Lyttleton Constitution of 1954.

[2] In 1953, the minority ethnic groups raised the concerns of marginalisation by the three major ethnic groups (i.e., Hausa/Fulani, Yoruba, and Igbo) in the build-up to the nation's independence. To this the colonial government commissioned a panel of inquiry, otherwise known as the Willink Minority Commission in 1957, to investigate the matter and thereupon proffer possible solutions. In its Report of July 1958, the commission recognised the fears and recommended, among other things, the introduction of the tenets of human rights in future constitutions to guarantee the protection of minority rights. The report was first adopted as the sixth schedule to the Nigerian (constitution) order-in-council, 1954–1958 (Aremu, 2011). It was, therefore, thanks to the recommendation of the Willink Minority Commission that the bill of rights found its way into the Chapter III of the 1960 Independence Constitution (Willink Commission Report, 1958; see Dada, 2012b; Izuagie, 2015).

in the 1999 Constitution. In the 1979 and 1999 Constitutions, the rights were further sorted into two categories and placed in two chapters. While the first category, the so-called fundamental rights, is contained in Chapter IV, the rest are contained in Chapter II entitled 'Fundamental Objectives and Directive Principles of State Policy'. The aim of introducing the tenets of human rights into the Constitution is to create a society that safeguards the political freedom and socio-economic well-being of citizens (Federal Republic of Nigeria, n.d.).

Upon gaining independence on 1st October 1960, Nigeria was admitted into the international human rights community six days later, that is, on 7th October 1960[3] as its 100th member. She became signatory to the Universal Declaration as well as several other international human rights treaties and optional protocols.[4] The West African country has been a member of the Organisation of African Unity (hereinafter OAU) since its inception in 1963 (later replaced by the African Union in 2002) and is actively involved at the regional level. She is a party to the most relevant human rights instrument in the region, namely the African Charter on Human and Peoples' Rights (hereinafter African Charter). In fact, she played a leading role in the realisation of this instrument. Apart from hosting the 1961 Lagos conference of the International Commission of Jurists (ICJ), which serves as an important starting point for the history of the African Charter, history also credits Dr. Nnamdi Azikiwe, Nigeria's first president, with the first proposal of the idea of an African Convention on Human Rights (Mbaiye, 1986: 20). The document itself, the African Charter, was eventually adopted by the 18th Assembly of the OAU in Nairobi, Kenya in 1981 and entered into force in 1986. As expected, Nigeria ratified it in 1983 and was among the first countries to incorporate it into domestic law (International Federation for Human Rights, 2010; Nigeria, 2017). Over the years, relevant institutional infrastructures have been set up for the enforcement of human rights. These include: the Public Complaints Commission (or the Ombudsperson), set up in 1975[5] to redress complaints lodged by aggrieved citizens or residents in Nigeria against administrative injustice; the Legal Aid Council (LACON), established in 1976[6] to provide pro bono services to indigent Nigerians; the National Commission for Refugees (NCFR), established in 1989[7] to manage refugees, asylum seekers and internally displaced persons (IDPs) in Nigeria; and last but not the least, the National Human Rights Commission (NHRC), created in 1995[8] with the mandate to promote and protect human rights in the light of the country's human rights obligations. The establishment of these institutions is in accordance with the UN resolution calling

[3] UN (n.d.). Member States. Available at: http://www.un.org/en/member-states/. Accessed 01.07.2019. See also Amnesty International Nigeria, 2019.

[4] UN Office of the High Commissioner for Human Rights (hereinafter OHCHR) (n.d.). Status of Ratification of 18 International Human Rights Treaties. Available at: http://indicators. ohchr.org/. Accessed 01.07.2019. See also Amnesty International Nigeria, 2019.

[5] See Cap. N37 Laws of the Federation of Nigeria (hereinafter LFN) 2004.

[6] Ibid., Cap. L9.

[7] Ibid., Cap. N21.

[8] Ibid., Cap. N46 Vol. II.

on all member states to set up context-specific institutions for the protection of human rights. But this was also premised on the principle that the safeguard of the rights of the individual depends largely on the domestic machinery of the state. The state alone cannot achieve this objective. Hence, human rights non-governmental organisations (hereinafter NGOs) were also established by citizens to assist the State and governmental entities in the protection and promotion of human rights. Some of the NGOs can be distinguished, namely the Civil Liberties Organisation (CLO)—formed in Nigeria in 1987 perhaps as the first of its kind—Amnesty International (AI), Campaign for Democracy (CD), Committee for the Defence of Human Rights (CDHR), and Centre for Human Rights and Development (CHRD).

From the foregoing reports, it is easy to conclude that the country has been committed to the human rights project since independence. Although this may not be untrue, the existing literature on the subject shows that the formal endorsement of the appropriate instruments is not an adequate measure of the degree of respect for human rights in any given country. This can be historically illustrated using the example of Nigeria. From her independence in 1960–1999, the country was ruled by different military regimes for almost twenty-nine years. During these years, the Nigerian society was essentially militarised. The "militarisation of the Nigerian society", as Ojo (2006: 15) puts it, had several dimensions such as the centralisation of power, suspension of the constitution and its replacement with military decrees and edicts, the weakening of the authority of the court and the deployment of special military tribunals, disregard for the rule of law and due process, adoption of retroactive penal legislation, shifting of the burden of proof in a criminal trial to the defendant, and the use of excessive force by state security apparatuses, etc. (cf. Aduba, 1999, cited in Dada, 2012a). These dimensions had very serious implications for the safeguard of human rights and democratic values. Based on these, successive military juntas systematically infringed on the rights and freedoms of Nigerians, ultimately leading to a culture of impunity in the system. Some of the recurring abuses during that period include torture, lengthy detentions, extrajudicial executions, use of excessive force, disregard of court orders, and abuse of due process (Dada, 2012a; International Federation for Human Rights, 2010). The military era was also characterised by the suppression of freedom of expression or freedom of speech through autocratic decrees and edicts. The State Security (Detention of Persons) Decree no. 2 of 1984, which allows the indefinite detention of citizens in solitary confinement, deserves special mention here. Other examples include the Public Officers (Protection Against False Accusation) Decree no. 4 of 1984 and the Newspapers Registration Decree no. 43 of 1993, both of which criminalised free speech directed against the government. With these provisions, the military government cracked down on the activities of the press and its perceived critics. Media houses were shut down in consequence and a lot of journalists harassed. The murder of Dele Giwa, a front-line Nigerian journalist, via a parcel bomb in 1986 is perhaps the gravest assault on the freedom of the Nigerian press. Be that as it may, clamping down on freedom of expression, or of speech, in any form amounts to a disrespect for human rights, since this right is not only a crucial end in itself, but also an important vehicle for ensuring the protection of all other rights (Macfarlane, 1985).

Besides, Nigerians were denied their basic economic and social rights due to corruption, mismanagement of public resources, weak institutional infrastructures, and lack of political will to tackle issues of gender inequality (Dada, 2012a). In the area of political rights, the country did not fare any better either, as freedom of association was suppressed by the military. The activities of trade and labour unions came under severe surveillance. Here, one remembers the objectionable Trade Disputes Decree no. 7 of 1976,[9] which subtly criminalised recourse to strikes and lockouts in collective bargaining. Later in the same year, the labour union movement in Nigeria was severely restricted from linking with the international labour movement via another decree, namely the Trade Unions (Central Labour Organisation) (Special Provisions) Decree no. 44 of 1976. In 1988, the Nigerian Labour Congress was suppressed[10] and workers' gatherings such as May Day rallies, etc. were outlawed.[11] The ban on the link with the international labour movement became stricter.[12] In order to control union activities of academics and university teachers, the Academic Staff Union of Universities (ASUU) was forcibly split from the labour movement[13] and students' protests were criminalised.[14] Several leading unionists were assaulted and placed under administrative detention. Many, especially among the students and lecturers, were either rusticated from universities and detained or lost their job (Odinkalu, 2001). Excessive force was used to disperse protests or other forms of civil unrests and participants were killed in the process by the state security operatives. This depressing human rights situation under military rule worsened in 1993 with the annulment of the presidential election that truncated the budding 3rd Republic[15] and reached its peak between 1994 and 1998 (Birnbaum, 1995; Federal Republic of Nigeria, n.d.; Ojo, 2006). The country became a pariah state, was put on the agenda of the UN Human Rights Commission for five years and confined to the back seat in the comity of nations.

In 1999, the nation returned once again to the path of constitutional democracy with the hope of a better life, in terms of human rights protection. Recent reports, however, continue to show that the human rights situation in the country has not improved significantly from what it used to be (see Amnesty International Nigeria, 2019; Onwuazombe, 2017). Abuses of basic rights and fundamental freedoms, such as arbitrary arrests and illegal detentions, torture, use of excessive force, summary

[9] It is now Trade Disputes Act Cap. T8 LFN 2004.

[10] See Nigerian Labour Congress (Proscription) Decree No. 22 of 1988.

[11] See Trade Unions Decree no. 25 of 1989.

[12] See Trade Unions (International Affiliation) Decree no. 35 of 1989.

[13] See Trade Unions (Miscellaneous Provisions) Decree no. 17 of 1986.

[14] See section 4(1) of the Students Union Activities (Control and Regulation) Decree No. 47 of 1989.

[15] After independence in 1960, the country became a republic in 1963. The first republic ran from 1963 to 1966, followed by the second republic which lasted for a short-lived period between 1979 and 1983. The third republic (1992–1993), an attempt to return the country to democratic rule, was truncated with the annulment of the 1993 presidential elections. The fourth republic kicked-off in 1999 to date.

executions, curtailment of freedom of expression and association, disregard of court orders, discriminations and gender inequality, continued imposition of the death penalty and wanton killing of citizens, are still commonplace in alarming proportion. A typical example of the latter is the massacre of civilians in Odi, Bayelsa State by the Nigerian military on 20th November 1999, right after the return to civilian rule. The incident took place in the context of a recurring conflict in the Niger Delta over indigenous rights to oil resources and environmental protection and was carried out in retaliation for the alleged killing of 19 soldiers by the natives. About 2500 civilians lost their lives in the incident. In a similar circumstance, the army also massacred hundreds of inhabitants of Zaki Biam in Benue State on 22nd October 2001, in response to the alleged killing of 12 police officers. Between 2015 and 2017, it was reported that the use of lethal force by the army resulted in extra-judicial killings of supporters of the Indigenous People of Biafra (IPOB) movement—a secessionist group located largely in the southeast—and the Islamic Movement of Nigeria (IMN) in Zaria, Kaduna State (Amnesty International Nigeria, 2019; OHCHR, 2018b). Perhaps the biggest assaults on human rights in the country today are the Boko Harām insurgence[16] and the herder-farmer crisis in the middle-belt region.[17] Since the emergence of the Boko Harām sect in 2009, a lot of lives have been lost and property worth millions of dollars destroyed. For these reasons, the country was named one of the countries with particular concern (CPC) by the US Commission on International Religious Freedom in its 2014 Annual Report. The inability of the government to deal with these challenges typifies the general atmosphere of human rights protection in the country.

Overall, in the twenty-plus years since the inauguration of the 4th republic, the practice of human rights in Nigeria has largely remained in the realm of rhetoric. On the brighter side, however, it is significant to note that in spite of the challenges of the country's political past, including the civil war (1967–1970), human rights have survived in her statute books, an indication that they are and remain an acceptable standard of behaviour in the country (Ajomo, 1992; Dada, 2012a).

---

[16]The term 'Boko Harām' is used to describe a local radical Salafist group that emerged in the northeastern region of Nigeria at the beginning of the millennium. Its main motive is to wage a war against what it described as a corrupt political structure in northern Nigeria and the country in general, in order to create a purely Islamic state governed by Sharia law. This group was brutally repressed by the Nigerian government in 2009 and became a violent group in response. Since then, on the surface, the group has been driven by a desire for revenge against state security forces and Islamic authorities for their role in the incident. Under the surface, however, there appears to be evidence that the movement is being driven by a combination of factors, including economic, political and religious. Boko Harām is shaped by its context—that of Nigeria's north and Nigeria—of poor governance and extreme poverty (Campbell, 2014; Imasuen, 2015; Schwartz, 2010).

[17]There used to be minor pastoral tensions in the past between nomadic cattle herders from Nigeria's north and the more settled farming communities in the middle belt. These conflicts have presently escalated to full-blown violent crisis. Some reports liken it to ethnic cleansing against some groups in the nation (Ogunbode et al., 2023), while in popular opinion it is alleged to be a subtle programme of islamisation.

2.2 Mechanisms for the Protection of Human Rights in Nigeria

Human rights are claims that an individual is justified to make as "an abstract member of a common human race", regardless of his or her social attributes (Verschraegen, 2002: 263). They arose from the experience of human struggle against all kinds of injustice as a political solution aimed at protecting the individual from abuse of power by the state, in order to secure respect for a life that befits their dignity as humans. Human rights are, by their very nature, fragile social institutions that require constant work; they are both 'real and utopian'. To stand a chance of being implemented, there is need for both a conducive social order and a set of institutionalised mechanisms of protection (OHCHR, 2018a). Without these, they are practically inexistent.

Since the adoption of the Universal Declaration in 1948, an impressive array of human rights mechanisms have been established at the international and regional levels. On the national level, virtually all political systems across the globe have instituted some human rights machineries in line with the UN General Assembly Resolution no. 48/134 of 20th December 1993. Though the strength and efficacy of these mechanisms may differ from state to state according to their levels of political development, their establishment and modus operandi have to conform to the appropriate UN Principles known as the Paris Principles (Ojo, 2006: 21). On a domestic note, Nigeria has also set up and/or adopted mechanisms—legal and institutional—aimed at ensuring respect for human rights. Prominent among these are national laws and policies, human rights treaties and covenants, democracy, and human rights institutions. These constitute the key for the enforcement of human rights in the country, and their existence is premised on the fact that the protection of human rights is a common duty of all and not just that of the state alone (Brown, 2016). Furthermore, experience has shown that national mechanisms of human rights have a more direct influence on the human rights of individuals than those at the regional and international levels.

Now, we take a closer look at the existing mechanisms for the promotion and protection of human rights in Nigeria.

2.2.1 National Human Rights Legal Framework

In Nigeria, the Constitution is the basic law and anchor of the national legal system. It is the supreme law of the land,[18] meaning that all other legislations must be consistent with it.[19] The 1999 Constitution of the Federal Republic of Nigeria

[18] In section 1(1), the 1999 Constitution of the Federal Republic of Nigeria (CFRN) states thus: "[t]his Constitution is supreme, and its provisions shall have binding force on the authorities and persons throughout the Federal Republic of Nigeria."

[19] It states further in section 1(3): "[i]f any other law is inconsistent with the provisions of this Constitution, this Constitution shall prevail, and that other law shall, to the extent of the inconsistency, be void."

(hereinafter Constitution) as amended is the current constitution of the country. Further references to the constitution in this paper refer to this Constitution unless otherwise stated. Any consideration of the practice of rights in Nigeria must look primarily to the Constitution because it is the country's front-line instrument of human rights. Its opening preamble solemnly proclaims that the Nigerian people have given themselves "a Constitution for the purpose of promoting the good government and welfare of all persons in our country, on the principles of freedom, equality and justice, and for the purpose of consolidating the unity of our people". In this document, human rights issues are extensively covered in two chapters, namely Chapter II and Chapter IV. While the need to incorporate human rights provisions in Nigeria's constitutions was informed by the belief that the State's responsibility to safeguard the rights of its citizens is primary, the provisions themselves are incorporated with the aim of creating a society which upholds the political right and socio-economic well-being of the said persons (Dada, 2012b; Federal Republic of Nigeria, n.d.).

The body of enforceable rights of citizens is contained in chapter IV sections 33–44 as Fundamental Rights. The catalogue of rights here includes the right to life, the right to dignity of the human person, the right to personal liberty, the right to a fair hearing including the right to defence or legal representation, the right to private and family life, the right to freedom of thought, conscience and religion including freedom to change religion or belief, the right to freedom of expression and freedom of the press, the right to assembly and association, the right to freedom of movement, the right to freedom from discrimination, the right to acquire and own immovable property, and the rights accruing from compulsory acquisition of property. These fundamental rights do not cover the entire spectrum of human rights, but mainly the rights of the first generation consisting of civil and political rights, as found in existing international human rights instruments. Moreover, many of these rights are not cast in absolute terms, such as the right to life, which has legal derogations or exceptions under section 33(2) of the Constitution, and the right to strike.[20] The permissible restrictions to the enjoyment of some of the fundamental rights are comprehensively outlined in section 45. These include: (a) situations "where the interest of defence, public safety, public order, public morality or public health so demands"; or (b) "for the purpose of protecting the rights and freedom of other persons"; and (c) for the purpose of dealing with situations of emergency. Then in section 46, the Constitution establishes the specific jurisdiction of the high courts to enforce these rights. The possibility to seek legal redress in the event of abuse is a distinctive feature of human rights (Nowak, 2005). Some consider this constitutional provision to be the most concrete expression of Nigeria's endorsement of the global practice of human rights (Dada & Ibanga, 2011). Generally, constitutions do not create human rights, they only positivise and enforce them. The incorporation of these human rights into the Constitution confers on them the tag of justiciability

[20] The right to strike is part and parcel of the right to peaceful assembly and association under section 40 of the Constitution, but solidarity strikes are prohibited under section 6 of the Trade Union Amendment Act 2005. See also International Federation for Human Rights (2010).

and, as constitutional rights, they protect all within the geopolitical sphere of the Constitution from injustice and abuse of powers.

In contrast to Chapter IV, Chapter II Sections 13–21 of the 1999 Constitution guarantee an additional set of rights entitled "Fundamental Objectives and Directive Principles of State Policy". This chapter outlines the constitutional provisions on the classic economic, social and cultural rights (ESCR). They are guaranteed here not as rights but as legal moral principles that should guide the exercise of public power. The fundamental objectives and directive principles are policy statements that establish broad economic, social and cultural guidelines to aid the realisation of these national ideals. Thus, the government is required to direct its policies towards providing the following for all citizens: suitable and adequate shelter, suitable and adequate food, old age care and pensions; unemployment benefits; sick benefits and welfare of the disabled; opportunity for securing adequate means of livelihood and suitable employment; just and fair conditions of work; protection of workers' welfare; a reasonable national minimum living wage; adequate facilities for leisure and for social, religious and cultural life; adequate medical and health facilities for all citizens; equal pay for equal work without discrimination; equal and adequate educational opportunities; free, compulsory and universal education, and free adult literacy programme. Furthermore, the State is obliged to channel its policies towards ensuring the right of all citizens to engage in legitimate economic activities, a fair distribution of material resources, and the protection and promotion of Nigerian cultures (see also Amnesty International Nigeria, 2019). These fundamental objectives have been included in the Constitution because they are considered very important for the well-being of citizens. They largely cover the second-generation rights and as such constitute the juridical basis for the clamour for the enforcement of socio-economic rights in Nigeria. However, the Constitution in section 6(6)(c) qualifies them as non-justiciable, meaning that they are provisions for whose enforcement one cannot press claims especially against the State nor seek legal redress in case of infraction.

In addition to these constitutional guarantees, a vast array of domestic legislations have been enacted to enhance human rights protection in the country.[21] Prominent among these is the African Charter on Human and Peoples' Rights (Ratification and Enforcement) Act. The latter is particularly important because it reinforces the need for judicial enforcement of socio-economic rights in the country. A handful of policy measures also exist that have been drafted to give effect to

[21] The extant national human rights laws include the 2009 Fundamental Rights (Enforcement Procedure) Rules, the 2019 Nigerian Correctional Service Act 2019, Discrimination Against Persons with Disabilities (Prohibition) Act 2018, Anti-Torture Act 2017, Electoral (Amendment) Act 2015, Violence Against Persons (Prohibition) Act 2015, Administration of Criminal Justice Act 2015, Trafficking in Persons (Prohibition) Law Enforcement and Administration Acts 2015, HIV/AIDS (Anti-Discrimination) Act 2014, Nigeria's Pension Reform Act 2014, National Human Rights Commission (Amendment) Act 2011, Nigerian Legal Aid Act 2011, Employees/Workmen's Compensation Act 2011, Freedom of Information Act 2011, Evidence Act 2011, National Minimum Wage (Amendment) Act 2011, Trade Union (Amendment) Act 2005, National Commission for Refugees Act 2004, the Universal Basic Education (UBE) Act 2003, as amended and the Child Rights Act of 2003, to mention just a few.

Nigeria's vision of human rights. The list is endless, for example, National Gender Policy 2007, National Policy on Child Labour 2013, National Policy on Education 2013, and National Policy on Internally Displaced Persons (IDPs) 2017, among many others. These legislations and policy measures serve as complements to the constitutional provisions on human rights.

2.2.2 *Human Rights Declarations and Treaties*

Nigeria's legal mechanisms for the protection of human rights is not limited to her domestic legal frameworks. There are other equally important legal instruments at international and regional levels that deserve to be given attention here.

International and Regional Human Rights Obligations

Nigeria has acceded to and/or ratified several human rights treaties since joining the UN. Some scholars put the number of the overall human rights instruments endorsed by Nigeria at roughly thirty-five (HRLJ, 2007, cited in Igwe, 2015). Among these are all nine core international human rights treaties as well as five of the nine adjoining optional protocols. Of these core treaties and protocols, the following six were endorsed by accession: the International Convention on the Elimination of All Forms of Racial Discrimination (ICERD 1967[22]), the International Convention on Civil and Political Rights (ICCPR 1993), the International Convention on Economic, Social and Cultural Rights (ICESCR 1993), the Optional Protocol of the Convention against Torture (CAT-OP 2009), the International Convention on the Protection of the Rights of All Migrant Workers and Members of their Families (ICRMW 2009), and the International Convention for the Protection of All Persons from Enforced Disappearance (ICPPED 2009). The remaining eight were ratified, and these include the Convention on the Elimination of All Forms of Discrimination against Women (CEDAW 1985) and its Optional Protocol (OP-CEDAW 2004), the Convention on the Rights of the Child (CRC 1991), its Optional Protocols on the involvement of children in armed conflict (CRC-OP-AC 2012) and on the sale of children, child prostitution and child pornography (CRC-OP-SC 2010), the Convention against Torture and Other Cruel, Inhuman or Degrading Treatment or Punishment (CAT 2001), the Convention on the Rights of Persons with Disabilities (CRPD 2010), and its Optional Protocol (OP-CRPD 2010). These treaties oblige states parties to imbibe the vision of human rights embodied in them and to enact legislations for the purpose of implementing this at the national level.

Among the four international human rights treaties that are yet to be ratified are the two optional protocols to the International Convention on Civil and Political Rights, namely the first protocol on individual communications (ICCPR-OP1) and the second protocol aiming at abolishing the death penalty (ICCPR-OP2-DP).

[22] Here (in Sect. 2.2.2), the figures in parenthesis represent, unless otherwise stated, the date, or years, of accession to or ratification of the respective human rights instruments by Nigeria.

While the protocol on individual communications is meant to empower the relevant human rights monitoring committees to entertain and address complaints from individuals or groups of individuals who allege to be victims of civil and political rights abuses, the protocol aiming at abolishing the death penalty simply requires state parties to put an end to the practice of the death penalty within their territories. The next is the Optional Protocol to the International Covenant on Economic, Social and Cultural Rights (ICESCR-OP), which, if ratified, will enable alleged victims of socio-economic rights or ICESCR abuses to bring their complaints with the UN Committee on Economic, Social and Cultural Rights, for redress. Lastly, the Optional Protocol to the Convention on the Rights of the Child on a communications procedure (OP3-CRC) is also yet to be ratified by Nigeria. This protocol empowers children to have recourse to the UN Committee in the event of specific violations of their rights, especially if domestic remedies have been exhausted (Amnesty International Nigeria, 2019). The reasons for not endorsing these treaties have been attributed to several factors, ranging from "bureaucratic inertia" to the lack of political will on the part of the government to make serious commitments towards ensuring the protection of these rights (Egede, 2007: 273).

In terms of regional obligations, the country has ratified quite a lot of treaties, including the African Charter on Human and Peoples' Rights (ACHPR 1983), the Organisation of African Unity (OAU) Convention Governing the Specific Aspects of Refugee Problems in Africa (1986), the African Charter on the Rights and Welfare of the Child (ACRWC 2001), the protocols to the African Charter on Human and Peoples' Rights on the Rights of Women in Africa (Maputo Protocol) and on the Establishment of the African Court on Human and Peoples' Rights (both of them in 2004), the African Youth Charter (2009), the African Charter on Democracy, Elections and Governance (2011), and the African Union Convention for the Protection and Assistance of Internally Displaced Persons in Africa (2012). For the same reasons mentioned shortly, the country is not yet a party to the Protocol to the African Charter on Human and Peoples' Rights on the Rights of Older Persons and the Protocol to the African Charter on Human and Peoples' Rights on the Rights of Persons with Disabilities in Africa. She has signed the Protocol on the Statute of the African Court of Justice and Human Rights since 2008 but has yet to ratify it to date. In international law, signature alone does not establish the consent to be bound.[23] Unlike ratification[24] and accession,[25] the signing of a treaty represents a mere expression of intent to comply with the provisions of the treaty. Therefore, by mere signing of these and other treaties, the Nigerian State is legally not bound by them. But on the contrast, by ratifying or acceding to the ones she did, the country has committed herself under international law to comply with the international and regional standards enshrined in those instruments. This includes presenting progress reports on the implementation of the provisions of the instruments at periodic intervals

[23] Vienna Convention on the Law of Treaties 1969, articles. 10 and 18.

[24] Ibid., articles 2(1)(b), 14(1) and 16.

[25] Ibid., articles 2(1)(b) and 15.

(BAOBAB Report, 2003; OHCHR, 2018a). The last time Nigeria fulfilled such a reporting obligation was in 2018 at the 31st Session of the UN Universal Periodic Review Working Group.[26] Amnesty International (2019) indicates that the report was eventually adopted at the 40th session of the Human Rights Council in 2019.

In sum, endorsed international and regional human rights treaties and covenants are international law and establish legally binding obligations on state parties. But are they directly enforceable in the legal systems of state parties as such? How do these function in Nigeria?

The Status of International Human Rights Treaties in Nigerian Law

Treaties in Nigeria do not automatically transform into domestic law upon ratification or accession. Nigeria operates a dualist system whereby validly concluded treaties are not enforceable in the national legal system unless they are re-enacted into domestic law by the municipal legislative authority. This process is known as domestication. It is a common feature of common law systems where a distinction is made between international law and municipal law, and the relationship between the two is constructed on the distinction between the making and application of a treaty. The typical example of a common law country is Great Britain which clearly follows a dualist tradition and the US with a partial dualist model. In these systems, ratified treaties do not apply directly within the domestic system, instead they undergo some form of domestication in most cases before application. This indirect approach contrasts sharply with the more direct monist model of civil law systems, which obtains in many countries of continental Europe whereby international and domestic laws are regarded as constituting one unified legal whole (see Dada, 2012a; Egede, 2007). In Nigeria, the dualist model holds sway by virtue of the provisions of the Constitution. The latter is not specific about whose power it is to make treaties. But it reserves external affairs to the federal government, which by implication confers the treaty-making power of the country on the President. This power appears not to be limited by the division of powers in the Constitution; it extends even to matters on the concurrent and residual lists.

In terms of implementing a treaty, however, the Constitution has elaborate provisions. First, it requires all treaties validly entered into by Nigeria to be specifically (re-)enacted into domestic law before they can have the force of law. This requirement is in accordance with section 12(1) which states that: "[n]o treaty between the Federation and any other country shall have force of law except to the extent to which any such treaty has been enacted into law by the National Assembly." In other words, the efficacy of a treaty in Nigeria depends on its domestication via the Act of the federal legislative authority. The Supreme Court of Nigeria gave a judicial interpretation to this constitutional provision in the case of *Abacha v Fawehinmi*,[27] when it held inter alia that: "[a]n international treaty to which Nigeria is a signatory does not ipso facto become a law enforceable as such in Nigeria. Such a treaty would have the force of law and therefore justiciable only if the same has been enacted into

[26] UN Doc. A/HRC/WG.6/31/NGA/1, 27th August 2018.

[27] (2000) 6 NWLR (pt. 660) p. 228.

law by the National Assembly". Second, the Constitution reserves to the National Assembly the power to enact legislation for the purpose of implementing treaties. This point is clear from subsection 2 of the same section 12. The role of the National Assembly in the domestication of treaties in Nigeria is both primary and exclusive, as it includes the power to make laws with respect to matters not included in the Exclusive Legislative List,[28] in other words, for matters on the Concurrent and Residual Legislative Lists. However, a bill for the implementation of a treaty for matters on these lists shall not be presented to the President for assent, but at the same time it shall not be enacted into law unless ratified by a majority of all the State Assemblies in the federation.[29] That simply means, if the matter on which the President has made a treaty on behalf of the nation is one laying on the concurrent list or is reserved for the States, the National Assembly has the power to pass the law for the application of the treaty at the federal level, but then it requires the adoption by the legislative houses of the federating States to be effective. This provision is premised on the fact that Nigeria is a federation with autonomous levels of government.

The domestication of a treaty in Nigeria involves a massive bureaucracy. This leads to delays in the local implementation of already endorsed treaties. Over the years, several treaties are yet to be passed into law many years after their ratification (Okeke & Anushiem, 2018). Some have been domesticated but with limited application, in that they have not been adopted by all the States of the federation. A typical example of such treaties is the Rights of the Child Act (2003). The Act is a fair attempt by the National Assembly to simultaneously domesticate the guarantees relating to the rights of the child in the CRC and its African Union equivalent, the African Charter on the Rights and Welfare of the Child.[30] According to recent

[28] Nigeria embraced federalism in 1954 through the Lyttleton Constitution. Based on this system, the country has a two-tier legislative system, namely the federal and state levels. At the federal level is the National Assembly, which consists of the Senate and the House of Representatives, whereas the state level has the Houses of Assembly. Accordingly, the Constitution divides legislative powers between the federal and the state legislative organs by creating two lists, Exclusive and Concurrent Lists. The National Assembly has exclusive competence over matters in the Exclusive Legislative List, as contained in Part 1 of the Second Schedule to the Constitution. This list contains 66 items that appear to be of common concern to the federation and on which the National Assembly is empowered to make laws. These include issues such as aviation, citizenship, extradition, etc. The national and state legislatures have concurrent powers to make laws on matters in the Concurrent Legislative List, as set out in the first column of Part II of the Second Schedule to the Constitution. But there are also matters which are neither contained in the Exclusive Legislative List nor the Concurrent Legislative List. These matters give rise to a third legislative list, known as 'residual legislative list', which is within the exclusive legislative competence of the House of Assembly of the States. An example of such matters would be issues concerning the establishment, structure, composition, finance, and functions of democratically elected local government councils (see section 7 of the 1999 CFRN). The Constitution does not specifically place treaty-making powers under the Exclusive List; it is in the concurrent list (cf. Egede, 2007; Okeke & Anushiem, 2018).

[29] See section 12(3) of the 1999 CFRN.

[30] The Rights of the Child Act was promulgated by the National Assembly on 16th July 2003. See also Egede (2007).

reports, only about 24 of the 36 State Assemblies have adopted the Act (OHCHR, 2018b). Apart from the aforementioned factors, another reason for the refusal of States to adopt the Act is attributed to oppositions to some of its provisions based on socio-cultural considerations (APPGN Report, 2013; Egede, 2007). So, of the validly concluded human rights treaties, only the African Charter has been properly incorporated into domestic law in line with the Constitution. The resultant law[31] was promulgated in 1983, thus making it enforceable domestically (Nigeria, 2017).

Now, the status of the African Charter and by extension all domesticated treaties in the hierarchy of the Nigerian law had been a source of controversy for quite some time. The controversy arose over some provisions of the African Charter that contradict the Constitution, such as the right to education, which is a justiciable right under the African Charter[32] but is not enforceable in court under the Constitution.[33] At face value, this controversy was specifically about whether the provisions of the African Charter on economic, social and cultural rights are justiciable in Nigeria vis-a-vis the constitutional provisions of Chap. 2. But it bordered ultimately on the place of domesticated treaties and covenants in the national legal framework. Earlier on in 1996, the Court of Appeal ruled in *Fawehinmi v Abacha,*[34] inter alia, that the African Charter supersedes all domestic laws of the country—including the decrees of the military government in power at the time and, by extension, the Constitution—because it is a legislation with an international flavour. Many other cases later endorsed *Fawehinmi v Abacha* on the point of international flavour of the domesticated African Charter.[35] But in the year 2000 under a democratic dispensation, the Supreme Court finally revisited the issue of the status of a domesticated treaty legislation vis-a-vis the Constitution in the Abacha case.[36] This time, the Supreme Court overruled the statement of the Court of Appeal in *Fawehinmi v Abacha* on the superiority of the African Charter and held instead that the Constitution is superior to the Charter. Hence, conflicts between the two (or any other international law) will have to be resolved in favour of the Constitution, by virtue of its supremacy.[37] Having said that, the Supreme Court still maintained that the African Charter takes precedence over other domestic statutes (Dada, 2012a; Nigeria, 2017).

---

[31] The African Charter on Human and Peoples' Right (Ratification and Enforcement) Act no. 2, 1983. It was contained in Cap. 10 LFN 1990 (now Cap. A9 LFN 2004).

[32] Article 17(1) of the African Charter.

[33] See Chapter II, section 18, and section 6(6)(c) of 1999 CFRN.

[34] *Fawehinmi v Abacha* (1996) 9 NWLR (pt. 475) 710.

[35] *Chima Ubani v Director of State Security Services* (1999) 11 NWLR (pt. 265) 129; see also *Comptroller Nigerian Prisons Service v Dr. Femi Adekanye & others* (1999) 10 NWLR (pt. 623) 400.

[36] *Abacha v. Fawehinmi* [2000] 6 NWLR (pt. 660) 228.

[37] *Ibid.* Once again, the Supreme Court gave a judicial interpretation to the supremacy principle of the Constitution, as contained in section 1(3) of the 1999 CFRN.

Lastly, a further implication of the dualist model in Nigeria is the unenviable status of ratified but undomesticated treaties and covenants. In very concrete terms, such treaties do not apply domestically in accordance with section 12(1) of the Constitution. At most, they become part of the national case laws, whereby they can be used by the courts in prosecutions, but only in persuasive capacity (BAOBAB Report, 2003). This has been the position of unincorporated treaties in Nigerian law since the Abacha case.[38] However, the debate on the subject appears to have been recently reignited by the Constitution of the Federal Republic of Nigeria (Third Alteration) Act 2010, which tends to consider ratified but undomesticated labour-related treaties as enforceable in the country without the requisite enabling legislation (Okeke & Anushiem, 2018).

2.2.3 Constitutional Democracy

Democracy[39] has no absolute definition. It is an elastic term that embraces political processes, values, attitudes, and practices that can take different forms in cultures and societies around the world. In everyday parlance, democracy refers to that form of government in which the people have the authority to take part in the decisions that affect the running of their society. Thus, Roser (no date) defines it as "a political system with institutions that allows citizens to express their political preferences, has constraints on the power of the executive, and provides a guarantee of civil liberties." There are as many variants of democracy as there are democratic nations in the world, but the basic feature of this system of government is the ability of the electorate to participate freely and fully in the life of their society. The Vienna Declaration and Programme of Action of the World Conference on Human Rights (1993c) affirms this when it stated that democracy is "based on the freely expressed will of the people to determine their own political, economic, social and cultural systems and their full participation in all aspects of their lives."[40] In other words, every authentic democracy bases its legitimacy on the freely expressed will of people and their full participation in political processes, irrespective of their social attributes. In today's increasingly globalised world, democracy and democratic governance are widely recognised as an 'ideal political system' that allows people to live with dignity. The beauty thereof lies in the fact that it is, among other things, the ideal for "creating and sustaining an environment for inclusive and responsive political processes and settlements".[41] Democracy is one of the core values of the

[38] See *Abacha v Fawehinmi*, above at no. 36.

[39] For the treatment of the term 'democracy' under this subheading, we made extensive use of the following site: Democracy. Available at: available at: https://www.un.org/en/sections/issues-depth/democracy/index.html. Accessed 01.11.2019.

[40] UN Doc A/CONF.157/23, 12th July 1993, para. 8.

[41] Democracy and the United Nations. The Youth Café. Available at: https://www.theyouthcafe.com/un-democracy-day-information-kit/2019/9/democracy-and-the-united-nations-the-youth-

UN. It was adopted by the UN as one of the means to achieve the three main pillars of its work as set forth in the Charter,[42] namely peace and security, development, and human rights. Since the 1990s, the term has received considerable attention in major conferences and summits of the international community. For instance, member states to the 2005 World Summit described it in unequivocal terms as "a universal value."[43] As a result, while assenting to the outcome document of the UN summit for the adoption of the post-2015 development agenda in 2015, the World leaders pledged their commitment to promote a world in which democracy and the rule of law are essential for sustainable development.[44]

Democracy is not just about a political structure; it is also a system of human rights (OHCHR, 2018a). In fact, there is a close link between democracy and human rights, which goes in both directions. The 1993 Vienna Declaration captures this relationship when it described both terms as interdependent and mutually reinforcing.[45] This perspective has been reaffirmed in subsequent UN conferences and summits.[46] Democracy has its foundation in human rights. It is based on the rights of individuals to participate in the political decision-making process as expounded in the relevant human rights treaties. Therefore, one can boldly claim that having rights is the source of democracy (Kirchschlaeger, 2014). For its part, democracy also contributes to human rights via creating the enabling social environment for their realisation. The protection and promotion of human rights requires a conducive social order to succeed. The legal and institutional frameworks of democracy play a particularly important role in establishing this (OHCHR, 2018a). This association between democracy and human rights is captured in article 21 of the Universal Declaration. The latter spells out the political rights of citizens in a democratic polity, as follows: (1) everyone has the right to take part in the government of his/her country directly or indirectly, that is, through freely chosen representatives; (2) everyone has the right of equal access to public service in his/her country; and (3) the will of the people shall be the basis of the authority of government, and this will shall be expressed in periodic and genuine elections by universal suffrage (cf. Kirchschlaeger, 2014). These are regarded today as the principles of democracy and have been further developed in other human rights instruments. The International Covenant on Civil and Political Rights (1966), for instance, formulated the international legal basis for these principles. This includes, among other things, the respect for individual freedoms (arts. 19, 21 and 22) and human rights, especially the right

cafe. Accessed 09.09.2019.

[42] The word itself democracy was not mentioned in the UN Charter, but the preamble to that document begins with the solemn proclamation "We the Peoples", which reflects the fundamental principle of democracy. This implies, among other things, that the will of the people is also the source of legitimacy of the UN. See Democracy, above at no. 39.

[43] UN Doc A/RES/60/1, 24th October 2005, para. 135.

[44] UN Doc A/RES/70/1, 21st October 2015, para. 9.

[45] See UN Doc A/CONF.157/23, 12th July 1993, para. 8.

[46] See, for instance, UN Doc A/RES/60/1, 24th October 2005, para. 135; UN Doc A/HRC/RES/19/36, 19th April 2012, preamble; UN Doc A/HRC/RES/28/14, 9th April 2015, preamble.

to political participation, as well as the principle of holding periodic free and fair elections by universal and equal suffrage (article 25). To these, the Convention on the Elimination of All Forms of Discrimination against Women added the principle of political and legal equality with specific reference to women (arts. 7 and 8), while the International Covenant on Economic, Social and Cultural Rights (1966) along with other treaties that address the rights of certain groups—such as indigenous peoples, minorities, people with disabilities, migrant workers and their family members—added the principle of inclusivity. Over the years, the UN General Assembly and the Commission on Human Rights (now the Human Rights Council)[47] have drawn ideas from these instruments to promote a democratic culture, especially among member states.

Democracy is not a cure-all for social ills. Of course, it has its own weaknesses and does not necessarily guarantee human rights. That hideous human rights abuses persist even in advanced democracies is not debatable. Yet human rights protection thrives the most in a democratic context grounded in the rule of law (Dada, 2013a). One institutional feature of democracy that contributes significantly to this is the separation of powers, whereby the political authority of a state is divided into legislative, executive and judicial powers. This division serves to ensure that each of these three power holders restricts its activities to its constitutional mandate. The aim of this arrangement is to prevent the monopoly of authority by any branch of government and to provide for checks and balances. Again, this principle guarantees the principal role of the legislative as the representative of the people and as the institution empowered to make laws for the state. The legislature does several other functions that have enormous implications for the protection of human rights. For instance, it enacts laws for the implementation of fundamental rights and freedoms, especially in most common law systems. Furthermore, it contributes to human rights through establishing and/or collaborating closely with statutory and non-governmental protective mechanisms and through the exercise of its statutory oversight functions. The protection of human rights is not the exclusive domain of legislative power. The judiciary also plays a vital role in this regard (Nnamani, 2011). But to do this effectively, the judiciary needs to be independent from other power holders. In fact, judiciary independence is the basic tool for the protection of fundamental rights in a functional democracy (OHCHR, 2018a) and a 'sine qua non' for that same form of government. The fact that only a fully independent judiciary can deliver justice impartially based on law is well documented.[48] The independence of the judiciary is also one of the things the principle of divided power guarantees.

Another essential component of democracy that is relevant for the protection of human rights is the media.[49] The role of the media in upholding the rights of

[47] The Human Rights Council was created by the UN General Assembly on 15th March 2006, as a replacement for the UN Commission on Human Rights. See UN Doc A/RES/60/251, 3rd April 2006, para. 1.

[48] See article 14 of the ICCPR; see also Brown, 2016.

[49] UN Doc. E/CN.4/RES/2002/46, 23rd April 2002.

individuals in a democratic society cannot be overemphasised. As already stated above, democracy is about the people's participation in the policy and decision-making processes of their society. In functional democracies, these processes are consensus-oriented because consultations and public opinions are usually sought in order to determine what is in the best interest of the nation. The media can be a potential facilitator in these processes, in that it provides the forum for public debates, discussions and dialogue on a range of issues and can also mobilise or even influence the public participation in the said processes. Furthermore, the media acts as a bridge between the rest of society and the state. It provides the public with information about the state, including the performance of government. In this way, it contributes to creating an accountable system of government, while also facilitating the effective participation of citizens in democratic processes (Wanyande, 1996). However, much like the judiciary, it is only a free, independent and pluralistic media[50] that can play such a crucial role in the democratic process.

Nigeria embraced democracy at her independence from the British rule in 1960. Though the form has been slightly modified over the years, the basic structure of Nigeria's democracy is a presidential system, with a precise definition of functions between the three powers. The executive powers are vested in the President of the federation and the Governors of the federating States. The legislative powers for the federation are conferred on the bicameral National Assembly (Nigeria's federal legislature) consisting of the Senate and House of Representatives,[51] whereas the same power at the state level is bestowed on the State Houses of Assembly. The judicial powers are entrusted to the federal and state courts. The equality of States is the underlying principle for the organisation of the Senate. Based on this, all 36 States of the federation have three Senators each. The same is not applicable for the House of Representatives which has a different principle of arrangement based on population. Nigeria has 360 State Constituencies, which are assumed to have as close to equal populations as possible in accordance with the Constitution.[52] This means that 360 members represent these State Constituencies. The State Houses of Assembly share the same organisation principle of nearly equal population as the House of Representatives, but in the former the members represent their respective Local Government Councils. The review of the State Constituencies takes place every ten years, courtesy of the Independent National Electoral Commission (INEC).[53] This structure serves to ensure an indirect but effective participation of the people in both policy and decision-making processes.

[50] UN Doc. A/RES/59/201, 23rd March 2005, para. 1.

[51] See section 4(1) of the 1999 CFRN.

[52] Ibid., section 49.

[53] Ibid., section 114(1).

2.2.4 National Human Rights Institutions

Apart from the institutional frameworks of democracy, there are concrete institutions created specifically to ensure the realisation of human rights in the country. National human rights institutions (hereinafter NHRIs) is the generic name for that sort of institution. NHRIs refer to independent statutory bodies set up by states with the legal mandate to promote and protect human rights at the national level. Their establishment is premised on the recognition of the fact that the laws alone cannot guarantee the adequate protection of individual rights and fundamental freedoms within society. However, the NHRIs are not equivalent to regular courts because they are not granted judicial or law-making powers. They are administrative in nature and have been designed to function as complements to the law courts within the societal framework. The idea of creating national institutions to promote and protect human rights is an initiative that the UN and human rights treaty bodies have proposed to member states to ensure that human rights are effectively protected in their respective countries. The initiative was endorsed by the UN General Assembly through the adoption of the resolution on the Principles Relating to the Status of National Institutions—better known as the Paris Principles[54]—on 20th December 1993. The principles have since been embraced by the international community as a benchmark for assessing the legitimacy and credibility of NHRIs.

NHRIs cover a range of bodies with structural and functional diversity reflecting the vast differences in national contexts,[55] since states have considerable latitude to establish context-specific human rights institutions. The diversity notwithstanding, one major characteristic of all such institutions is that they are primarily state-owned enterprises. Their establishment by states themselves is perfectly in order because the latter remains the primary actors in international law through which human rights aspirations must be realised at the national level (Dada, 2013b). But then, there is always the concern that the integrity of these institutions can be compromised on account of this relationship with the state. For this reason, they receive a globally recognised seal of quality based on their level of conformity with the Paris Principles, and only those that meet the required international standard upon assessment are granted full membership status in the International Coordinating Committee of the National Institutions for the Promotion and Protection of Human Rights (ICC). That said, functional NHRIs are unique governmental bodies with a legal mandate to operate independently for the purpose of promoting and protecting human rights. They play a crucial role in ensuring respect for human rights in many ways. First, they help to ensure that states adhere to their human rights' commitments via persuasion and constantly pressing for the concrete application of those obligations. In addition, they monitor and report about human rights, propose policy

[54] UN Doc A/RES/48/134, 20th December 1993, annex, para. 1ff.

[55] Regarding diversity, Pinheiro and Baluarte (2000: 2) in their seminal work distinguished three broad categories of NHRIs as Human Rights Commissions, Ombudsmen and other Parliamentary Human Rights Bodies, and Specialised Human Rights Agencies.

options to legislatures and governments, attend to complaints from alleged victims of human rights violations, among other things. In fact, NHRIs are regarded as the best mechanism to ensure the best possible realisation of human rights at the national level because they focus on the entire spectrum of human rights.

In the last two decades, there has been an upsurge in the establishment and reinforcement of NHRIs in nation-states worldwide. As of 27th November 2019, 80 of the 193 UN member states have established a Paris Principles compliant NHRI (GANHRI, 2019). This growing interest can be understood as the recognition of the importance of independent and effective NHRIs in the promotion and protection of human rights among states. The trend is further demonstrated by the strengthening of cooperation between NHRIs in the regions, as exemplified in the recent activities of the Network of African National Human Rights Institutions.[56] NHRIs are an integral part of the human rights system in Nigeria. The following can be distinguished: the Public Complaints Commission,[57] the Legal Aid Council of Nigeria (LACON),[58] the State Directorates for Citizens' Rights, the Truth and Reconciliation Commission,[59] the National Commission for Refugees (NCFR),[60] and most importantly the National Human Rights Commission (NHRC).

[56] The Network of African National Human Rights Institutions (hereinafter NANHRI) is a non-profit-oriented regional umbrella organisation that brings together 44 national human rights institutions in Africa. The Organisation was founded in 2007 and has its permanent Secretariat in Nairobi, Kenya. It seeks to support and strengthen NHRIs to effectively undertake their mandate of human rights protection, monitoring, promotion, and advocacy (NANHRI Report, 2020).

[57] The Public Complaint Commission was established by the Public Complaints Commission Act 1975. The Commission is synonymous with the Ombudsman in Nigeria. Its powers and duties are well set out in section 5 of the Public Complaints Commission Act (see PCC Act Cap. P37 Volume 14, LFN 2004).

[58] The Legal Aid Council of Nigeria (LACON) was established by the Legal Aid Decree or Legal Aid Act no. 56 of 1976. The Decree was repealed and later re-enacted as Legal Aid Act (Cap L9, Volume 8, LFN 2004). The latter was recently replaced by the Legal Aid Act 2011, as the current enabling law. LACON, a statutory body under the supervision of the Federal Ministry of Justice, is charged with the responsibility of providing pro bono services to indigent Nigerians (see Nigeria, 2017).

[59] Under the auspices of this Commission, a Judicial Commission known as Human Rights Violations Investigation Panel was inaugurated on 7th June 1999 at the return to civil rule. However, unlike the Ombudsman, the National Human Rights Commission and other commissions which are permanent standing institutions, the Truth and Reconciliation Commission was only of an ad hoc arrangement (Nnamani, 2011).

[60] The National Commission for Refugees (NCFR) was established by Decree no. 52 of 1989 (now Cap. N21 LFN 2004). The Commission draws from the provisions of the 1951 UN Convention relating to the Status of Refugees, its 1967 Protocol and the 1969 Organisation of African Unity Convention governing specific aspects of refugees' problems in Africa, as guide to manage issues relating to refugees and asylum seekers in Nigeria. In 2002, the government expanded the duty of the Commission in 2002 to include the management of the affairs of internally displaced persons (IDPs) in the country (see Nigeria, 2017).

National Human Rights Commission

The National Human Rights Commission of Nigeria (hereinafter Commission) was established pursuant to the 1995 National Human Rights Commission Act (hereinafter NHRC Act).[61] Despite its chequered history,[62] it can be said that the Commission was set up in response to the recommendation of the UN General Assembly to all member states to establish national institutions for the promotion and protection of human rights in their respective countries.[63] The current enabling Act of the Commission is the NHRC Act 2010, as amended. Its mandate is national and rests on a bipod of promotion and protection of human rights based on the constitutional provisions and the country's international human rights obligations.[64] The Commission is the country's highest national human rights body and as such is empowered to deal with all human rights issues. The indigent citizens constitute its prime target group, to whom it offers simple, non-technical, quick but quality services at no cost. What is more, it is also easily accessible to the public. These features make the Commission attractive to the poor, the vulnerable and victimised individuals as a genuine alternative to the often-capital-intensive procedures of normal courts (Okafor & Agbakwa, 2002). The Commission is not a rival to the courts. Rather, it was designed to complement the work of the courts, to which the Constitution gives power to enforce fundamental rights (NHRC, 2007). However, the Commission was granted some quasi-judicial powers in 2010 with the amended NHRC Act and under this expanded statute it has the powers to investigate and adjudicate complaints. It can also enforce its decisions, which now carries the same status as an order of a high court in Nigeria. The Act also grants the Commission financial and administrative autonomy to enable it to discharge its mandate accordingly (Nigeria, 2017; NHRC Report, 2013). The Commission currently has an Affiliate Status with the African Commission on Human and Peoples' Rights. And with an "A" Status at the International Coordinating Committee (ICC) of the National Human Rights Institutions according to the 2019 accreditation by the Global Alliance of National Human Rights Institutions (GANHRI, 2019), it may not be wrong to say that the National Human Rights Commission of Nigeria is in good standing with the Paris Principles.

Since being established, the Commission has been active in issues of human rights in the country in accordance with its statutory mandate. In all, its main

[61] See Cap. N46 Volume 11 LFN 2004. This principal Act has since been amended in 2011.

[62] The National Human Rights Commission of Nigeria was set up by the military junta of the day at the height of human rights violations in Nigeria. Hence, its establishment was widely viewed as a design by the government to hoodwink people, especially the international community, into thinking that it was human rights friendly. Because of this, the Commission was viewed with "skepticism and cynicism as a mere propaganda tool in the hands of a junta seeking international relevance" (Okafor & Agbakwa, 2002: 665).

[63] See UN Doc A/RES/48/134, 20th December 1993.

[64] See section 5(a) of the NHRC Act 2004. Under section 5, the functions and powers of the Commission are elaborately laid out. See also NHRC (2007); NHRC Report (2013); Nnamani (2011).

objective is to ensure that the laws and regulations concerning the promotion and protection of human rights are effectively applied. The Commission tries to do this using a wide variety of strategies, such as education and public enlightenment, community-specific training programmes, and research advocacy (Nnamani, 2011), to mention just a few. Human rights education is carried out in line with the provisions of article 26 of the African Charter (NHRC Report, 2013). Enlightenment programmes such as workshops, seminars, conferences, summits, and rallies are avenues it uses to sensitise the communities and improve their human rights awareness. These also include the production and distribution of human rights publications. Besides, interactive sessions and meetings such as village square or town hall meetings are organised across the length and breadth of the country, piloted by the Commission. These provide the platform not only to inform the largely semi-literate and illiterate Nigerian populace about the Commission's *raison d'être*, but also inform them about their rights, which will certainly enable them to seek legal redress in the event of violations (Dada, 2013a; Nnamani, 2011).

Regarding the protection of human rights, the investigation of complaints is one of the most important functions of the Commission. It receives and investigates complaints of human rights abuses and assists alleged victims via programmes such as counselling, or by offering other preventive services. Under investigation and resolution of complaints, its main role revolves around mediation, reconciliation, and peacebuilding. Monitoring of human rights situations in the country is another important role of the Commission. The amended Act empowers it to visit places of detention with a view to ensuring that detainees' rights are not violated. Its ability to create awareness of incidents and areas of human rights abuses in the country is not in doubt. All the same, effective monitoring of the situation of human rights in the country cannot be achieved in isolation, but rather in a collaborative manner with all the stakeholders. Aware of this, the Commission accelerated the establishment of the Network for Monitoring and Documentation of Human Rights situations in Nigeria for this purpose. The network consists of the Commission itself and civil society organisations from the six geopolitical zones of the country (NHRC, 2007). Through their collaboration, a National Action Plan (hereinafter NAP) for the advancement of the goals of human rights in the country is drafted and/or updated every three years. Summarily, the NAP represents an integrated and systematic national strategy to contribute to the realisation of human rights in Nigeria. It has been described as "a commitment to concrete measures that can be adopted to entrench a culture of human rights in the country" (Nigeria, 2017). As such, it can serve as a reality gauge of the country's human rights records (Dada & Ibanga, 2011; Nnamani 2011; Federal Republic of Nigeria, n.d.). Lastly, the NAP also offers the opportunity to identify and agree on areas of cooperation for all stakeholders. In this way, the Commission helps in the formulation of the government's human rights policy.

From the foregoing, it is evident that the National Human Rights Commission commands a massive presence in the Nigerian human rights apparatus. It is all the same important to note that while the government, through its institutions and agencies, plays a huge role in ensuring the full realisation of the goals of human rights in the country, the same target cannot be met without the involvement of other stakeholders, including for example civil societies as represented by non-governmental organisations. This is because experience has consistently shown that governments are both protector and predator of human rights (Dada, 2013a).

Human Rights Non-Governmental Organisations

A non-governmental organisation (hereinafter NGO) is defined as "a private, independent, non-profit, goal-oriented group not founded or controlled by a government" (Edwards, 2010: 170). NGOs are important actors in world politics. In the last few decades, they have increasingly become an important force in human rights issues as well. This trend has largely been attributed to their modus operandi and reach. As some have noted, they are innovative, flexible, independent, and address the problems of poor people at the grassroots level (cf. Bagci, 2003). Human rights NGOs are primarily concerned with upholding internationally recognised human rights. Though these organisations have a wider range of forms, they are extra-governmental and private enterprises much unlike the statutory NHRIs. The need for their involvement in the quest for the optimal implementation of human rights is premised on the lack of commitment to this goal by the governmental and quasi-governmental bodies of most nation-states worldwide (Dada, 2013b).

NGOs have played an important role in the overall development of the human rights movement since the early 1800s. Special reference is consistently made in this connection to the Anti-Slavery Society (1836), the International Committee of the Red Cross (1863), and the International Workers' Association (1864). But it was only after the adoption of the UN Charter in 1945 that human rights NGOs gained formal global recognition. The relationship of NGOs with the international human rights community was formalised for the first time in article 71 of the Charter which grants NGOs a consultative status with Economic and Social Council (hereinafter ECOSOC) (Mayrhofer et al., 2014). Ever since then, human rights NGOs have been actively involved in ensuring international protection of human rights. The last three decades have witnessed a dramatic increase in the size and value of human rights NGOs. Their emergence was always in direct response to the urgent need to promote human rights. Today, there are several thousands of such organisations worldwide. In Africa alone, it was reported that over 400 NGOs have observer status with the African Commission on Human and Peoples' Rights in 2019 (Murray, 2019), whereas on the global level, 5161 NGOs had attained consultative status with the UN as of September 2018.[65] Human rights NGOs play a crucial role at all levels, with the focus on ensuring that governments and other power holders uphold human rights and fulfil their human rights obligations. They pursue this objective through a wide range of activities. For instance, they provide information to international and national institutions. Under the universal periodical report (UPR) arrangement, they furnish reliable information concerning the state of human rights in their respective countries. By so doing, they raise awareness of grave violations by state parties and help to halt ongoing violations. Besides, they monitor the activities of governments

[65] See UN Doc. E/2018/INF/5, 31st October 2018.

with regard to their level of compliance with international human rights standards and contribute to human rights policy-making (Mayrhofer et al., 2014).

Human rights NGOs appeared for the first time in Nigeria in the 1980s. As on the international stage, they arose as a reaction to the dictatorial military regimes that trampled on the rights of the Nigerian people. The military dictatorship provoked the formation of the first group of human rights NGOs in the country, prominent among which are the Civil Liberties Organisation (CLO), Committee for the Defence of Human Rights (CDHR), National Association of Democratic Lawyers (NADL), Human Rights Africa (HRA), Women in Nigeria (WIN), Constitutional Rights Project (CRP), Nigerian Foundation for Legal Aid and Human Rights (NIFLAHR), Campaign for Democracy (CD), and United Action for Democracy (UAD) (see Aduku et al., 2015). These organisations fought for the termination of the dictatorship, the protection of human rights and the restoration of democratic rule in the country. Soon after the military rule many other human rights NGOs sprang up. This later trend, it has been claimed, was informed by the continued unimpressive situation of human rights in the country (Dada, 2013b). Currently, there are over 200 human rights NGOs in Nigeria (Nzarga, 2014). Notable among these are Amnesty International (AI), BAOBAB for Women's Rights, Centre for Law Enforcement Education (CLEEN), Human Rights Law Services (HURILAWS), Human Rights Monitor (HRM), Human Rights Watch (HRW), National Institute for Advanced Legal Studies (NIALS), Prisoners' Rights and Welfare Action (PRAWA), Social and Economic Rights Action Centre (SERAC), and Women's Rights Advancement and Protection Alternative (WRAPA). These organisations have different approaches to the one mission of promoting and protecting human rights. Some concentrate on just one human right, while others pay attention to a category of rights. There are also some that focus on the protection of the so-called group rights. All these agencies are actively and broadly committed to human rights issues. As independent entities, they help to fight against human rights violations and assist alleged indigent victims of those violations. Because much of their work involves opposing, criticising or challenging the opinions and actions of power holders in Nigeria, they are often seen by them as anti-governmental rather than non-governmental bodies. They are not safe from the Nigerian populace either, who often perceive them as a threat because their advocacy touches on some of the most controversial areas of private and public life, including, for example, abortion, sexuality, the status of women, minority rights, self-determination, child rights, religious rights and freedoms, and some long-standing cultural practices. These challenges notwithstanding, they are champions of human rights in Nigeria (cf. Aduku et al., 2015).

2.2.5 *Limitations of Nigeria's Human Rights System*

It is proper to conclude this chapter with a brief critical look at Nigeria's human rights system. It is clear that the latter is firmly anchored in international and regional human rights systems. Domestically, the country also has appropriate mechanisms to promote and protect human rights. In this chapter, attention has been paid to the mechanisms mentioned, based on the assumption that the domestic mechanisms of the state are relevant to the cause of human rights, as Donnelly (1995, cited in Okafor & Agbakwa, 2002: 662) aptly puts it: "[t]he struggle for human rights … [is] won or lost at the national level." While there is no denying that the establishment of these mechanisms represents a serious attempt to entrench the culture of human rights throughout the country, Nigeria's human rights system has been criticised for some inherent deficiencies that have serious negative implications on the optimal realisation of human rights objectives.

The first shortcoming concerns the national legal framework, especially the Constitution, which has been criticised for a cluster of inconsistent human rights provisions. Critics easily point to the constitutional principle of non-justiciability in relation to socio-economic rights to begin with. In other words, the Constitution contains provisions on civil and political rights (CPRs) and social, economic and cultural rights (ESCRs). But in Section 6(6)(c) it classifies the latter as unenforceable provisions, in contrast to the former, which it regards as enforceable rights. This dichotomy not only contradicts international and regional instruments guaranteeing these rights, most of which the country has endorsed,[66] but also creates room for the systemic infraction of these rights without the possibility of redress (International Federation for Human Rights, 2008, 2010). Next, the Constitution has also been criticised for the wide amplitude of some of its lawful exceptions to human rights. Take, for instance, the provision of section 33(2) which allows deprivation of one's life in order to effect lawful arrest or to prevent the escape of a suspect from custody, irrespective of the nature or gravity of the offence warranting the arrest or even the detention. This provision is widely considered to be a licence to summary execution given to the state security operatives by the Constitution (Dada, 2012a). Furthermore, the Constitution has been accused of being verbose (cf. Odoeme, 2011) or of a lack of concise language. This has sometimes led to unfriendly outcomes for human rights. For instance, in sections 46(1) and (2) the high court is vested with the jurisdictional competence to entertain cases for the enforcement of fundamental human rights in the country, but the Constitution fails to designate in clear terms which of the high court it meant, given the existence of the federal and state high courts. This confusion is exacerbated by the

[66] For instance, the ICESCR (1966) and the African Charter (1981) have been endorsed by Nigeria.

interpretations of sections 272(1)[67] and 251(1)[68] of the same Constitution. The inherent gap in these constitutional provisions has sometimes led to conflicting decisions[69] by judicial authorities regarding the competence of the two high courts to enforce fundamental human rights in Nigeria. Lastly, it has also been suggested that the Constitution contains provisions that are discriminatory in nature. For example, the right to private and family life,[70] the right to freedom of movement[71] and the right to acquire immovable property anywhere in the country[72] are all guaranteed to Nigerian citizens alone (Dada, 2012b). These provisions sharply contrast with the universal nature of human rights, as prescribed in article 2 of the Universal Declaration.[73] Besides, the Constitution is also criticised for the recurrent sexist overtones of some of its provisions. In other words, some constitutional provisions are written in the masculine gender which gives the unfortunate impression that the provisions in question are for men only.[74] In this context, critics highlight the

---

[67] Section 272 (1) states thus: "[s]ubject to the provisions of section 251 and other provisions of this Constitution, the High Court of a State shall have jurisdiction to hear and determine any civil proceedings in which the existence or extent of a legal right, power, duty, liability, privilege, interest, obligation or claim is in issue or to hear and determine any criminal proceedings involving or relating to any penalty, forfeiture, punishment or other liability in respect of an offence committed by any person."

[68] Section 251 (1) states thus: "[n]otwithstanding anything to the contained in this Constitution and in addition to such other jurisdiction as may be conferred upon it by an Act of the National Assembly, the Federal High Court shall have and exercise jurisdiction to the exclusion of any other court in civil causes and matters".

[69] In both cases, *Bronik Motors Ltd. v. Wema Bank Ltd.* [(1983)1 FWR 463] and *Jack v. University of Agriculture, Makurdi* [(2004) 5 NWLR (pt. 865) 208, the Supreme Court of Nigeria held that both the federal high court and the high court of a state have concurrent jurisdiction in case of enforcement of fundamental right allegedly violated, whereas in the case of *Turkur v. Government of Gongola State* [(1989) 4 NWLR (pt.117) 517 at 547], the Supreme Court of Nigeria in a seemingly contradictory judgment held, among other things, that the enforcement of the fundamental rights in matters outside the jurisdiction of the Federal High Court is not within and cannot be in the contemplation of the section. See Felix and Akujobi (2018).

[70] Section 37 of the Constitution states, thus: "[t]he privacy of ***citizens***, their homes, correspondence, telephone conversations and telegraphic communications is hereby guaranteed and protected."

[71] Section 41(1) provides thus: "[e]very *citizen* of Nigeria is entitled to move freely throughout Nigeria and to reside in any part thereof, and no citizen of Nigeria shall be expelled from Nigeria or refused entry thereby or exit therefrom."

[72] Section 43 states that "[s]ubject to the provisions of this Constitution, every *citizen* of Nigeria shall have the right to acquire and own immovable property anywhere in Nigeria."

[73] For instance, according to the article 2: "*[e]veryone* is entitled to all the rights and freedoms set forth in this Declaration without distinction of any kind, such as race, colour sex, language, religion, political or other opinion, national or social origin, property, birth or other status," inter alia.

[74] The constitutional provision on equal opportunity in section 42(1) begins as follows: "[a] citizen of Nigeria of a particular community, ethnic group, place of origin, sex, religion or political opinion shall not, by reason only that ***he*** is such a person (…)"; similarly, section 42(2) reads: (2) "[n]o citizen of Nigeria shall be subjected to any disability or deprivation merely by reason of the circumstances of ***his*** birth." We see similar formulations in sections 33–35, etc. (cf. BAOBAB Report, 2003).

citizenship rights provision[75]—a provision which allows men to grant automatic citizenship to their non-Nigerian wives while denying the same rights to women married to non-Nigerian husbands. Thus, they argue that the Constitution is male-centred and cannot adequately protect women and group rights (BAOBAB Report, 2003; Ojo, 2006).

Sequel to these, there are issues about the relationship between the Constitution and human rights treaties to which the country is a party. The dualist approach of the Nigerian legal system has some negative implications for the protection of human rights in the country. The domestic law barring the domestic application of endorsed treaties pending their domestication is inconsistent with article 26 of the 1969 Vienna Convention on the Law of Treaties, which specifies that a domestic law shall not be used as a pretext for non-implementation of international human rights obligations. Therefore, this existing constitutional arrangement tends to defeat the main goal of such treaties, which is to protect the individual from the excesses of the government and its agencies. This is because a treaty can be straitjacketed and curtailed according to the whims of the government in the process of domestication (Egede, 2007). Apart from that, the arrangement creates a loophole that the State can exploit to renege on its international obligations. Again, the process of domestication in Nigeria is complex and the constraints thereof account for the very limited instances of the domestic application of long endorsed international human rights instruments. Thus, a lot of treaties that would have been beneficial to the citizens remain unenforceable. This is exactly the case with treaties dealing with women's rights, since most of these are yet to be incorporated into domestic law. The national legal system itself is deprived of the complementary support it ought to get from the treaties upon incorporation (Okeke & Anushiem, 2018). For these shortcomings, some think that the national legal framework constitutes "a formidable clog to the international jurisprudence and goals of human rights" (Dada, 2012b: 39).

Concerning democracy, the transition to democracy is indeed progress, at least from a human rights perspective, since civil liberties thrive the most in a democratic dispensation. However, if there is anything to be learned from history, it is that the transition to democratic rule does not guarantee human rights. Nigeria's nascent democracy is currently bedevilled by several challenges, such as the lack of social cohesion among the federating ethnic nationalities, regional inequality and discrimination against minority groups. Other reasons include abuse of power by elected government officials, widespread poverty, lack of quality education, and the failure to deal adequately with the legacy of the country's authoritarian, military past. In all these human rights are seriously affected.

Fourthly, a cursory look at the institutional infrastructures for the safeguard of human rights reveals that the country has set up an impressive array of machineries to ensure the realisation of the goals of human rights. But whether these institutions can provide the required platform for the effective enforcement of human rights is

[75] In section 26(2) on citizenship rights, the Constitution says: "the provisions of this section shall apply to—(a) any woman who is or has been married to a citizen of Nigeria"; inter alia.

another question. Unfortunately, the quasi- and extra-judicial national bodies are perceived as weak entities incapable of delivering on their mandates (Dada, 2012a). This assessment is due to the fact that most of these infrastructures do not have the much-needed financial and administrative autonomy for their kind of work. The same goes for the NGOs community in the country. It has also been pointed out that their emergence and exponential growth do not coincide with the respect for human rights in the country. Their alleged role abdication is often attributed to factors such as an unfriendly political climate, lack of proper funding, inadequate publicity and the crisis of confidence in the organisations. The result is that they are unable to discharge their duties as champions and virile watchdogs of human rights (Dada, 2013b).

Summary
The chapter shows that the notion of inalienable rights was not alien to traditional Nigerian societies prior to colonial rule. In fact, the idea existed since time immemorial, although not in the modern sense of the term. The earliest use of the term in the present-day Nigeria can probably be traced back to the late 1940s, when Nigerian elites used the term in their struggle for independence. But the institutionalisation of the system of human rights in the country began with the entrenchment of the Bill of Rights in the Independence Constitution in 1960. Since then, human rights have been formally accepted as the common standard of behaviour and a beacon for a better Nigeria.

Nigeria's human rights system is not limited to domestic legal regulations. Apart from the constitutional provisions on human rights, the country has endorsed an impressive number of international and regional human rights treaties for upholding human rights. These also establish legally binding obligations to protect human rights. Relevant institutional infrastructures have also been set up to ensure the best possible realisation of human rights goals in the country. As such, Nigeria's national human rights system comprises a thick web of human rights instruments and institutional frameworks. In spite of these, Nigeria's national human rights system has been criticised for some serious inherent limitations. The shortcomings described are likely to have an impact on the implementation of human rights in the country.

The overall aim of this chapter is, first, to situate the practice of human rights in Nigeria within the larger global context of human rights and, second, to provide some important background information that could potentially help interpret or better understand not only the human rights attitudes of Nigerians, but also the general human rights situation in Nigeria.

References

A. Books and Journals

Aduku, A. A., Maduagwu, M., Olabamiji, O., & Udeoji, E. A. (Eds.). (2015). *Human rights*. National Open University of Nigeria.

Ajomo, M. A. (1992). *Fundamental human right under the Nigerian Constitution*. Nigerian Institute of International Affairs.

Amnesty International Nigeria. (2019). *Human rights agenda*. Index No.: AFR 44/0431/2019. Amnesty International Publications.

Aremu, T. O. (2011). *The right of an accused person under the Nigerian legal system*. LL.B. thesis, University of Ilorin, Ilorin.

Bagci, C. (2003). Historical evolution of NGOs: NGO Proliferation in the Post-Cold War Era. *Avrupa Gunlugu, 2*(4), 299–326.

Baxi, U. (2003). *The future of human rights*. Oxford University Press.

Birnbaum, M. (1995). *Nigeria: Fundamental rights denied: Report of the Trial of Ken Saro-Wiwa and Others*. University of Michigan.

Brown, G. (Ed.). (2016). *The universal declaration of human rights in the 21st century: A living document in a changing world*. Open Book Publishers.

Campbell, J. (2014). Boko Haram: Origins, challenges and responses. *Norwegian Peacebuilding Resource Centre Policy Brief*, 1–4.

Dada, J. A. (2012a). Impediments to human rights protection in Nigeria. *Annual Survey of International and Comparative Law, 18*(1/6), 67–92.

Dada, J. A. (2012b). Human rights under the Nigerian constitution: Issues and problems. *International Journal of Humanities and Social Science, 2*(12), 33–43.

Dada, J. A. (2013a). Human rights protection in Nigeria: The past, the present and goals for role actors for the future. *Journal of Law, Policy and Globalization, 14*, 1–13.

Dada, J. A. (2013b). The significance and limits of NGOs in human rights protection in Nigeria. *Journal of Law, Policy and Globalization, 19*, 82–91.

Dada, J. A., & Ibanga, M. E. (2011). Human rights protection in Nigeria: From Rhetoric to Pragmatic Agenda. *African Journal of Law and Criminology, 1*(2), 70–81.

Edwards, G. E. (2010). Assessing the effectiveness of human rights non-governmental organizations (NGOs) from the birth of the United Nations to the 21st century: Ten attributes of highly successful human rights NGOs. *Michigan State Journal of International Law, 18*(2), 165–228.

Egede, E. (2007). Bringing human rights home: An examination of the domestication of human rights treaties in Nigeria. *Journal of African Law, 51*(2), 249–284.

Federal Republic of Nigeria. (n.d.). *National Action Plan (NAP) for the promotion and protection of human rights in Nigeria 2009–2013*. Available at: https://www.ohchr.org/sites/default/files/Documents/Issues/Education/Training/actionsplans/Excerpts/Nigeria09_13.pdf. Accessed 1 May 2015.

Felix, O., & Akujobi, A. (2018). Enforcement of fundamental rights in national constitutions: Resolving the conflict of jurisdiction between the Federal High Court and State High Court in Nigeria. *Beijing Law Review, 9*, 53–66.

Igwe, O. W. (2015). The challenges of domesticating the African Charter on human and peoples' rights Holus Bolus: The case of Nigeria. *Australian Journal of Management, Policy and Law, 2*, 19–27.

Imasuen, E. (2015). Insurgency and humanitarian crises in Northern Nigeria: The case of Boko Haram. *African Journal of Political Science and International Relations, 9*(7), 284–296.

International Federation for Human Rights. (2008). *Nigeria: NGO coalition shadow report to the CEDAW committee, 31st July 2008*. Available at: https://www.refworld.org/docid/48a0007a2.html. Accessed 16 July 2014.

International Federation for Human Rights. (2010, April). *Defending human rights – Not everywhere not every right: International fact-finding mission report on Nigeria, April 2010.* Available at: https://www.refworld.org/docid/4bed03412.html. Accessed 16 July 2014.

Izuagie, L. (2015). The Willink Minority Commission and Minority Rights in Nigeria. *Ekpoma Journal of Theatre and Media Arts, 5*(1–2), 206–223.

Kirchschlaeger, P. G. (2014). The relation between democracy and human rights. *Globalistics and Globalization Studies*, 112–125.

Macfarlane, L. J. (1985). *The theory and practice of human rights*. Maurice Temple Smith Ltd.

Murray, R. (2019). *The African Charter on human and peoples' rights: A commentary*. Oxford University Press.

Nigeria. (2017). *6th periodic country report 2015–2016 on the implementation of the African Charter on human and peoples' rights in Nigeria*. Federal Ministry of Justice.

Nnamani, S. O. (2011). Institutional mechanisms for human rights protection in Nigeria: An appraisal. *Nnamdi Azikiwe University Journal of International Law and Jurisprudence, 2*, 128–137.

Nzarga, F. D. (2014). Appraisal of human right non-governmental organizations (NGOs) in Nigeria. *Journal of Law, Policy and Globalization, 28*, 145–154.

Odinkalu, C. A. (2001). The management of transition to Civil Rule by the military in Nigeria (1966–1996). In K. Amuwo, D. C. Bach, & Y. Lebeau (Eds.), *Nigeria during the Abacha years (1993–1998)* (pp. 57–99). IFRA-Nigeria.

Odoeme, P. C. (2011). *Human rights and the mission of the Church in Nigeria*. Lit Verlag.

Ogunbode, T. O., Ayodele, I.-O. A., Oyebamiji, V. O., & Faboro, O. O. (2023). A review of farmers/herders clashes in Nigerian environment: Consequences and the way forward. *Journal of African Conflicts and Peace Studies, 5*(1), 120.

Ojo, E. O. (2006). Human rights and sustainable democracy in Nigeria (1999–2003). *Journal of Social Science, 13*(1), 15–29.

Okafor, O. C., & Agbakwa, S. C. (2002). On legalism, popular agency and 'voices of suffering': The Nigerian national human rights commission in context. *Human Rights Quarterly, 24*(3), 662–720.

Okeke, C. E., & Anushiem, M. I. (2018). Implementation of treaties in Nigeria: Issues, challenges and the way forward. *Nnamdi Azikiwe University Journal of International Law and Jurisprudence, 9*(2), 219–229.

Onwuazombe, I. I. (2017). Human rights abuse and violations in Nigeria: A case study of the oil-producing communities in the Niger Delta region. *Annual Survey of International and Comparative Law, 22*(1/8), 115–160.

Pinheiro, P. S., & Baluarte, D. C. (2000). *National strategies – Human rights commissions, Ombudsmen, and National Action Plans*. UNDP.

Santuraki, S. U. (2016). Reflections on the concept and foundational convictions of human rights. *Uni-Maid Journal of Private and Property Law, 1*(1), 52–62.

Schwartz, S. (2010). Is Nigeria a Hotbed of Islamic extremism? *Peace Brief, 27*, 1–5.

Verschraegen, G. (2002). Human rights and modern society: A sociological analysis from the perspective of systems theory. *Journal of Law and Society, 29*(2), 258–281.

Wanyande, P. (1996). The media as civil society and its role in democratic transition in Kenya. *Africa Media Review, 10*(3), 1–20.

Willink, H., Hadow, G., Mason, P., & Shearer, J. B. (1958). *Nigeria: Report of the commission appointed to enquire into the fears of minorities and the means of allaying them.* Her Majesty's Stationary Office.

Islamic Documents

The Quran, with Surah Introductions and Appendices. (2013). Saheeh International Translation. Edited by A.B. al-Mehri. Maktabah Booksellers and Publishers.

International Human Rights Instruments

Global Alliance of National Human Rights Institutions (GANHRI). (2019). *Chart of the Status of National Institutions*. Available at: https://www.ohchr.org/sites/default/files/Documents/Countries/Cooperation/StatusAccreditationChart.pdf. Accessed 06 Dec 2019.

Human Rights Council. (2012). *Human rights, democracy and the Rule of Law, UN Doc A/HRC/RES/19/36 19th April 2012*. Available at: https://www.right-docs.org/doc/a-hrc-res-19-36/. Accessed 01 July 2017.

Human Rights Council. (2015). *Human rights, democracy and the Rule of Law, UN Doc A/HRC/RES/28/14, 9th April 2015*. Available at: https://ap.ohchr.org/documents/dpage_e.aspx?si=A/HRC/RES/28/14. Accessed 01 July 2017.

Nowak, M. (2005). *Human rights: A handbook for parliamentarians*, No. 8. OHCHR.

OHCHR. (n.d.). *Status of Ratification of 18 International Human Rights Treaties*. Available at: http://indicators.ohchr.org/. Accessed 01 July 2019.

OHCHR. (2018a). *Human Rights and Constitution making*. UN Publications.

OHCHR. (2018b). *UN Human Rights Report 2017*. Available at: https://www2.ohchr.org/english/OHCHRreport2017/allegati/Downloads/1_Whole_Report_2017.pdf. Accessed 01 July 2019

UN. (n.d.). *Member States*. Available at: http://www.un.org/en/member-states/. Accessed 01 July 2019. See also Amnesty Report 2019.

UN ECOSOC. (2018). *List of non-governmental organizations in consultative status as of 1st September 2018, UN Doc. E/2018/INF/5, 31st October 2018*. Available at: https://documents.un.org/doc/undoc/gen/n18/352/55/pdf/n1835255.pdf. Accessed 01 Dec 2018.

UN General Assembly. (1966). *International Covenant on Economic, Social and Cultural Rights (ICESCR), International Covenant on Civil and Political Rights (ICCPR) and Optional Protocol to the International Covenant on Civil and Political Rights, UN Doc. A/RES/2200, 16th December 1966*. Available at: https://www.refworld.org/docid/3b00f47924.html. Accessed 10 Oct 2017.

UN General Assembly. (1993b). *National institutions for the Promotion and Protection of Human Rights, UN Doc. A/RES/48/134, 20th December 1993*. Available at: https://www.refworld.org/docid/3b00f25e14.html. Accessed 05 Dec 2019.

UN General Assembly. (1993c). *The World Conference on Human Rights: Vienna Declaration and Programme of Action, A/CONF.157/23, 12 July 1993*. Available at: https://www.refworld.org/legal/resolution/unga/1993/en/14730. Accessed 01 Aug 2018.

UN General Assembly. (2005a). *Enhancing the role of regional, subregional and other organizations and arrangements in promoting and consolidating democracy, UN Doc. A/RES/59/201, 23rd March 2005*. Available at: https://www.refworld.org/docid/43f3122f6.html. Accessed 28 Nov 2019.

UN General Assembly. (2005b). *World Summit Outcome: Resolution, UN Doc. A/RES/60/1, 24th October 2005*. Available at: https://www.refworld.org/docid/44168a910.html. Accessed 19 Nov 2019.

UN General Assembly. (2006). *Human Rights Council: Resolution, UN Doc. A/RES/60/251, 3rd April 2006*. Available at: https://www.refworld.org/docid/4537814814.html. Accessed 05 Dec 2019.

UN General Assembly. (2015). *Transforming our world: The 2030 Agenda for sustainable development, UN Doc. A/RES/70/1, 21st October 2015*. Available at: http://www.refworld.org/docid/57b6e3e44.html. Accessed 10 Oct 2017.

Regional Human Rights Instruments

Network of African National Human Rights Institutions NANHRI. (2020). *A Guide for African National Human Rights Institutions for Implementing Resolution 275 in Africa*. Available at: https://www.chr.up.ac.za/images/researchunits/sogie/documents/NANHRI_Guide_for_NHRIs_on_Implementing_Resolution_275V002.pdf. Accessed 01 Apr 2020.

OAU. (1982). *African Charter on human and peoples' rights ("Banjul Charter"), CAB/LEG/67/3 rev. 5, 21 I.L.M. 58, 27th June 1981*. Available at: https://www.refworld.org/docid/3ae6b3630.html. Accessed 24 Mar 2021.

National Human Rights Instruments

All-Party Parliamentary Group on Nigeria (APPGN) Report. (2013). *Too many to count? Human rights, justice and accountability in Nigeria*. Chatham House.

BAOBAB Report. (2003). *Women's Human Rights*. Available at: http://iknowpolitics.org/sites/default/files/sharia_nigeria_baobab.pdf. Accessed 01 Apr 2019.

Federal Republic of Nigeria. (n.d.). *National Action Plan (NAP) for the Promotion and Protection of Human Rights in Nigeria 2009–2013*. Available at: https://www.ohchr.org/sites/default/files/Documents/Issues/Education/Training/actions-plans/Excerpts/Nigeria09_13.pdf. Accessed 01 May 2015.

Human Rights Council. (2018). *National report submitted in Accordance with Paragraph 5 of the Annex to HRC Resolution 16/21: Nigeria, UN Doc. A/HRC/WG.6/31/NGA/1, 27th August 2018*. Available at: https://documents-dds-ny.un.org/doc/UNDOC/GEN/182/589/9X/PDF/1825899.pdf?OpenElement. Accessed 01 Oct 2019.

International Federation for Human Rights. (2010, April). *Defending human rights – Not everywhere not every right: International fact-finding mission report on Nigeria, April 2010*. Available at: https://www.refworld.org/docid/4bed03412.html. Accessed 16 July 2014.

Mbaiye, K. (1986). *Keynote address: Introduction to the African Charter on human and peoples' rights. Report of a conference held in Nairobi from 2nd to 4th December 1985*. International Commission of Jurists. Available at: https://www.icj.org/wp-content/uploads/1986/04/Africa-human-and-peoples-rights-conference-report-1986-eng.pdf. Accessed 01 July 2015.

National Human Rights Commission (NHRC). (2007). *A report on the state of human rights in Nigeria*. Bluesland Communications Ltd.

Nigeria. (2017). *6th periodic country report 2015–2016 on the implementation of the African Charter on human and peoples' rights in Nigeria*. Federal Ministry of Justice.

Nigeria: *Constitution of the Federal Republic of Nigeria (CFRN)*. (1999). *Updated with the First, Second and Third Alterations (2010) and the Fourth Alteration (2017)*. Federal Ministry of Justice.

Nigeria: *Trade Disputes Act, Cap. T8 LFN 2004*. Available at: https://laws.lawnigeria.com/2020/06/19/index-lfn-laws-of-the-federation-of-nigeria-3/. Accessed 01 Jan 2020.

NHRC. (2013). *Report on State of compliance with international minimum standards of human rights by Nigeria under the universal periodic review mechanism*. Available at: http://www.upr-info.org/sites/default/files/document/nigeria/session_17_-_october_2013/nhrc-nigeria_upr17_nga_e_main.pdf. Accessed 10 Dec 2019.

Other Internet Sources

Democracy. (n.d.). Available at: https://www.un.org/en/sections/issues-depth/democracy/index.html. Accessed 01 Nov 2019.

Democracy and the United Nations. The Youth Café. (n.d.). Available at https://www.theyouthcafe.com/un-democracy-day-information-kit/2019/9/democracy-and-the-united-nations-the-youth-cafe. Accessed 09 Sept 2019.

Mayrhofer, M., Chavez, C., Hegde, V., Killander, M., Larik, J., Nkrumah, B., Salmón, E., & Yigen, K. (2014). International Human Rights Protection: Institutions and Instruments. *Frame, 4*(1). Available at: https://www.fp7-frame.eu/wp-content/uploads/2016/08/02-Deliverable-4.1.pdf. Accessed 02 Feb 2017.

Roser, M. (n.d.). *Democracy.* Available at: https://ourworldindata.org/democracy. Accessed 01 Nov 2019.

Chapter 3
Legal, Social and Religious Perspectives on the Status of Human Rights in Nigeria

Contents

3.1 Right to Freedom of Religion 50
3.1.1 The Context of Freedom of Religion in Nigeria 54
3.1.2 Freedom of Religion in Nigerian Law 61
3.1.3 Recurrent Issues in the Practice of Freedom of Religion in Nigeria 67
3.1.4 Religion and Freedom of Religion 76
3.2 Right to Freedom from Discrimination Based on Sexual Orientation 83
3.2.1 The Legal Status of Homosexuality in Nigeria 85
3.2.2 Social Implications of Nigeria's Anti-homosexuality Laws 90
3.2.3 Religion and Homosexuality 91
3.3 The Right to Life 95
3.3.1 Right to Life in the Global Context 95
3.3.2 Right to Life in Nigeria 98
3.4 Political Rights 130
3.4.1 Political Rights Provisions in Nigerian Law 132
3.4.2 Contentious Issues in the Exercise of Political Rights in Nigeria 135
3.4.3 Religion and Political Rights 150
3.5 Judicial Rights 157
3.5.1 Right to a Fair Trial in Nigerian Law 159
3.5.2 Topical Issues in the Right to a Fair Trial in Nigeria 166
3.5.3 Religion and the Right to a Fair Trial 175
3.6 Socio-economic Rights 178
3.6.1 Socio-economic Rights in Nigerian Law 181
3.6.2 Topical Issues in Socio-economic Rights in Nigeria 183
3.6.3 Religion and Socio-economic Rights 206
References 212

Introduction

Article 2 of the Universal Declaration states: "[e]veryone is entitled to all the rights and freedoms set forth in this Declaration, without distinction of any kind." The idea that a set of rights apply equally and universally to all persons is revolutionary, as such a concept never really existed before the eighteenth century. The eventual institutionalisation of this concept of rights on a global scale is considered one of the

M. C. Adimekwe, *The Impact of Religion, Personality, Values and Worldviews on Attitudes Towards Human Rights*, Religion and Human Rights 11,
https://doi.org/10.1007/978-3-031-65749-8_3

greatest accomplishments of the twentieth century. Today, human rights have assumed the status of a global culture. Nigeria being a member of the UN has also adopted them as a national standard of behaviour. The preceding chapter dealt with her human rights architecture, highlighting the existing legal and institutional mechanisms for protecting human rights. The essence of these mechanisms is to ensure the effective realisation of the goals of human rights. Human rights standards are the same everywhere, but the actual practice of human rights varies widely across UN member states worldwide due to contextual factors. For Nigeria, such factors would necessarily include the country's socio-cultural background, reflected in the religious beliefs of the citizens and their local customs, etc. Nigeria is a country where religion plays a significant role in both private and public domains, regardless of her secular status.

Having dealt with the system of human rights in Chap. 2, this chapter now addresses the actual practice of the rights in Nigeria, paying special attention to the religious, legal and social perspectives. This approach will lead to a more holistic portrayal of the status quo as well as a better understanding of the complex relationships between law, religion and human rights in the same context. As far as this study is concerned, it will help us answer concrete questions about the human rights attitudes of the sampled Nigerian people. For this reason, not the entire spectrum of human rights under the UN framework is covered here, but just a select few. The list of the selected rights includes freedom of religion, non-discrimination against homosexuals, right to life under the three instances of the prohibition of death penalty, and the permissibility of abortion and euthanasia. Others are political, judicial and socio-economic rights. Their selection is based on practical considerations, meaning that the rights represent the domains of Nigeria's everyday life where the discrepancies between the endorsed human rights principles and actual practice are considered so glaring. The rights are presented here as listed.

3.1 Right to Freedom of Religion

Freedom of religion[1] is central to the theme of human rights. In fact, it is coeval with the human rights endeavour itself. As an expression, it means freedom from coercion in matters of conscience, religious beliefs, and practices. As a right, it refers here to a political principle guaranteeing the liberty to choose a religion or no religion without any interference. In recent times, this topic has generated enormous

[1] For the historical perspectives on religious freedom, we used almost exclusively the following two sources: Van der Ven, J.A. (2010). *Human Rights or Religious Rules?* Leiden: Brill Publishers; and Freedom of Religion – History. *Democracy Web*. Available at: https://democracyweb.org/freedom-of-religion-history. Accessed 01.02.2020. But for more contemporary perspectives we turned to Ziebertz, H.-G. (2016). Freedom of Religion as Challenge for Religion and Society. In: T.-M. Courau, M. Babić and J.J. Vila-Chã (eds.). *Religious Freedom*. London: SCM Press, pp. 87–96.

interest on the international stage due to the sudden re-emergence of religion in the public sphere of human life and the pervasiveness of religious conflicts within and between nations across the globe.

Centuries ago, the state and religion existed as a single entity which reinforced each other in terms of administration and expansion. That was the case with ancient kingdoms such as Egypt, Rome, and Greece. These great empires usually sought divine assistance in their campaigns and religious adherence was regarded as an essential part of loyalty to the state. They never lacked an official religion. Similarly, the nation-states that succeeded these empires also had official religions, which served as a vital component of their legitimacy and practice. Their rulers also wielded both temporal and spiritual powers in a single power arrangement. In most cases, the basic tenet of the relation between state and religion was expressed in the age-old Latin phrase of *cuius regio, eius religio*, meaning the ruler determines the religion of his subjects. Under that arrangement, rulers had the power to ban other religions and to banish their adherents. Religious oppression was thus entrenched in the social system of the time and was pervasive (Muehlhof, 2000). Religious diversity was not recognised, as well as the right to unfettered practice of one's religion. It is only recently that states began to allow people to choose their religion, or to abstain from such, without any interference.

The introduction of religious freedom as an entitlement of the individual was directly linked with the traumatic experiences of the many years of religious wars in Europe. But it was also a product of the Enlightenment of the seventeenth and eighteenth centuries, which promoted inter alia the principle of separation. The wars gave rise to several groundbreaking treaties. Examples include: the Treaty of Augsburg in 1555, which formally recognised religious pluralism in that German State; the Union of Utrecht (1579) in the Netherlands, which was one of the first edicts to allow a complete personal religious freedom; the Edict of Nantes (1598), which granted civil and religious rights to Protestants in Catholic France; the Peace of Westphalia of 1648, which built on the provisions of the Treaty of Augsburg to institute religious freedom for minorities; and lastly the French Revolution (1791), which led to the extension of religious freedom to members of all other sects in France. In 1786, the Virginia Statute for Religious Freedom was enacted into state law. The statute was incorporated into the Establishment Clause and Free Exercise Clause of the First Amendment to the US Constitution of 1791. This statute is important because it marks the first formal separation of church and state in history. This separation principle, a precondition for the freedom of religion, was later universalised in the Universal Declaration of 1948 (Van der Ven, 2010). In the same document, the UN General Assembly defined freedom of religion as a universal human right.

Freedom of Religion as a Universal Human Right

The right to freedom of religion is defined in article 18 of the Universal Declaration as follows: "[e]veryone has the right to freedom of thought, conscience and religion; this right includes freedom to change his religion or belief, and freedom, either alone or in community with others and in public or private, to manifest his religion or belief in teaching, practice, worship and observance." This is the primary definition of the right. It has since been further developed in article 18 of the ICCPR. But for minor adjustments in the wording, the latter is very similar to the provision above. It guarantees all persons the right to think freely and to entertain ideas and hold opinions based on religious or other beliefs. This includes the freedom to have or adopt a religion or belief of one's choice.

It is not easy to determine exactly what is meant here by "religion" and "belief" as they are used in the formulation of the right. The ICCPR does not specify their respective scopes, nor does the Universal Declaration or any of the subsequent core international instruments guaranteeing the right. This may be due to the apparent illusiveness of an all-encompassing definition of the terms, as has already been expressed by scholars (cf. Donald & Howard, 2015; Weissbrodt & Hutchinson, 2016; Ziebertz, 2016). Whatever the reason, the 1993 Human Rights Committee, in its General Comment no. 22 on Article 18 of the ICCPR, interpreted the terms broadly enough to include theistic, non-theistic and atheistic beliefs, as well as irreligion (e.g., humanism, existentialism, etc.).[2] These were further expanded by the European Court of Human Rights (hereinafter ECHR) in *Arrowsmith v. UK*[3] and *W v. UK*[4] to include non-religious beliefs such as pacifism and veganism. All these worldviews are protected by freedom of religion. However, to be protected under this provision as a general principle, a belief must be serious, relate to important aspects of human life or behaviour, be sincerely held, be compatible with human dignity and fundamental rights, and be respected in a democratic society.[5] The use of the terms "religion" and "belief" therefore implies support for the right to the said beliefs as well as the right not to profess any religion or belief.

Freedom of religion includes the right of an individual or group of individuals to manifest their thoughts and religion or beliefs in action, in teaching, practice, worship and observance. This can take the form of the liberty to engage in evangelism, to produce and distribute publications promoting their beliefs, non-belief, or worldviews, and to establish faith-based schools for this purpose, or the freedom to exercise religious duties (e.g., performance of ceremonial acts, traveling for pilgrimages, use and display of religious symbols, etc.), or the freedom to participate in religious worship, which implies the right of public gatherings and meetings for religious purposes, the establishment and use of places of worship, and so on, as well as the freedom to observe one's religious customs (e.g., fasting, observing other dietary regulations, wearing special religious dresses, observing religious holidays and rest periods, participating in religious rituals, etc.), without undue interference.[6] Put

[2] CCPR/C/21/Rev.1/Add.4, 30th July 1993, para. 2.

[3] No. 7050/75, 12 October 1978.

[4] No. 18187/91, 10 February 1993.

[5] *Campbell and Cosans v. UK*, Nos. 7511/76 and 7743/76, 25th February 1982, para. 36; see also Donald and Howard (2015) and Attorney-General's Department, Australian Government (n.d.).

[6] CCPR/C/21/Rev.1/Add.4, 30th July 1993, para. 4.

simply, this provision requires the state to recognise that it cannot stop individuals from practising their religion or belief without a very good reason.

The principle of religious freedom, as enshrined in the Universal Declaration, also underlines the freedom to change one's religion. This means the freedom to convert to another religion of one's choice, even if the act or the new religion itself might be unpopular or disturbing to most people in society. It also includes the right of a person to leave a religion and to choose not to adhere to any religion or worldview (cf. New World Encyclopedia, 2017). This aspect is captured in article 18 subsection 2 of the ICCPR, which states that no person shall be subjected to any coercion which would impair his or her freedom to hold or adopt a religious or other belief. Here the authorities may be obliged to take any necessary and proportionate measures to protect the right, and this of course includes refraining from making policies having such intention or effect.[7] Article 18(4) of the ICCPR further expands the right to incorporate the right of parents and legal guardians to ensure the religious and moral education of their children in accordance with their own convictions. The Human Rights Committee noted that school-based religious education must be conducted in a neutral and objective manner and must be subject to exceptions that meet the wishes of parents and guardians.[8]

The right to freedom of thought, conscience and religion is one of the rights from which derogation is not permitted for any reason or under any circumstances, including in times of public emergency. This is premised on its fundamental character.[9] Apparently, human rights law does not mention any restrictions on this right under article 18 of the ICCPR. All the same, it recognises in the same place that reasonable restrictions may be imposed on the right to manifest religious or other beliefs, and this only in situations where such restrictive measures are lawful and "necessary to protect public safety, order, health, or morals or the fundamental rights and freedoms of others" [article 18(3)]. A good example of this is the observance of the customary practice of female genital mutilation (FGN). It is a very contentious issue between religious and human rights groups. The practice poses a real threat to public health and can be stopped by the state regardless of the opinion of those who engage in it (New World Encyclopedia, 2017). Likewise, the state may take measures to restrict other similar forms of religious practices that conflict with its legitimate interests or obligations, as prescribed by law. The Human Rights Committee, however, cautions that such measures must be consistent with the twin principles of necessity and proportionality.[10]

Article 18 of the ICCPR is widely considered to be the most important religious freedom provision in international law. Its importance is underscored by the fact that it recasts the primary definition of the right as contained in the Universal Declaration in strictly legal terms, thereby making it enforceable. In this way, it

---

[7] Ibid., para. 5.

[8] Ibid., para. 6.

[9] Ibid., para. 1.

[10] Ibid., para. 8.

became the reference point for other important documents of international law as far as the right is concerned (New World Encyclopedia, 2017). The provision has been adopted by a number of regional and specialised human rights instruments. For example, article 12 of the American Convention on Human Rights (1969), article 8 of the African Charter (1981) and article 30 of the Arab Charter on Human Rights (1994) all guarantee freedom of thought, conscience and religion in somewhat similar terms. The American Convention on Human Rights reproduces the provision almost verbatim. The provision of the Arab Charter on Human Rights is also similar to this guarantee but suggests in article 30(1) that the right to freedom of thought, conscience and religion is subject to limitations prescribed by law. The limitations are no longer stipulated in article 20 of the revised edition of the Cairo Declaration on Human Rights in Islam adopted in 2020. The African Charter contains a very condensed definition of the right, which reads as follows: "[f]reedom of conscience, the profession and free practice of religion shall be guaranteed. No one may, subject to law and order, be submitted to measures restricting the exercise of these freedoms."

Freedom of religion or belief is also enshrined in numerous other international treaties, declarations and conventions such as the 1950 European Convention on Human Rights (article 9), the 1951 Convention Relating to the Status of Refugees and the 1954 Convention Relating to the Status of Stateless Persons (article 4), the International Convention on the Elimination of All Forms of Racial Discrimination (ICERD) 1965 (article 5), the Convention on the Rights of the Child (CRC) 1989 (article 14), the 1994 Draft Declaration on the Rights of Indigenous Peoples (article 12) and the 1981 Declaration on the Elimination of All Forms of Intolerance and Discrimination Based on Religion or Belief (hereinafter 1981 Declaration on Religion or Belief), inter alia. Freedom of religion does not stand alone but is strengthened by a variety of rights such as freedom of discrimination, freedom of speech, freedom of the press, freedom of movement, freedom of peaceful assembly, and the right to education.

It has been widely recognised as a fundamental right since the second half of the twentieth century (Ziebertz, 2016). In spite of difficulties, there has been a steady upward movement towards acceptance as such worldwide, as shown by the ratification rate of relevant human rights instruments. Besides, many nation-states around the world, including Nigeria, have even codified it in their constitutions and statutory laws.

3.1.1 *The Context of Freedom of Religion in Nigeria*

Before exploring the legal status of the universal fundamental right to freedom of religion as enshrined in the Nigerian Constitution and other laws, it is first pertinent to situate the principle of religious freedom in the Nigerian context.

Religious freedom presupposes an atmosphere of diversity of beliefs and worldviews. Nigeria is a religiously diverse society with volatile religious terrain. The recurrence of religious unrest in the country therefore calls for a closer look at the status quo of the practice of this right in the Nigerian context.

Nigeria's Religious Landscape

The 2017 statistics released in 2018 by the National Bureau of Statistics (hereinafter NBS) indicate that Nigeria is by easily the most populous country in Africa, with a population estimate of 199 million people, and is home to about 17 percent[11] of the continent's total population. The country also houses a wide variety of world religious systems. African Traditional Religion (hereinafter ATR) is the oldest of them all. It was the religion of the native population of what is now known as Nigeria and is as old as the hills. The ATR is characterised by belief in a Supreme Being, in divinities and spirits, the veneration of ancestors, the use of magic and traditional medicine (Beyers, 2010; Uzoma, 2004). Its original founder is not known. It has no standard sacred text and is not mission-oriented. Partly for these reasons it has sometimes been misconstrued as heathenish, animistic, totemistic, etc. (Vontress, 2005; see also Mbiti, 1990). Be that as it may, the ATR was the dominant religion of the people before the advent of Islam and Christianity.

Islam was effectively established in Nigeria in the nineteenth century through the jihad of Usman dan Fodio, an ethnic Fulani Muslim scholar.[12] Before then, Muslim merchants from North Africa had first tried to introduce the religion to the local population of Kanem-Bornu Empire in Nigeria's north during the trans-Saharan trade in the eleventh century. Reportedly, similar attempts were also made in Kano in the fourteenth century by Muslim traders from Mali. But these efforts were unsuccessful. It only took Dan Fodio's jihad of 1804 to 1808 to firmly implant the Islamic religion in the northern parts of Nigeria, beginning from the city-state of Gobir. From there it rapidly spread to other parts of Hausaland and to Yoruba-speaking areas in the southwest, as well as to Cameroon. History has it that Dan Fodio's jihad was primarily motivated by a desire to spread a purer form of Islam in the region (Onwubiko, 1967).

As with Islam, Christian missionaries made initial contacts with Nigeria sometime earlier than the nineteenth century. It is the general belief that the first wave of missionaries from Portugal landed on Nigerian shores in the fifteenth century, followed by another wave from Italy and Belgium between the 17th and 18th centuries. These were all Roman Catholics. The Portuguese settled in the coastal areas of the south such as Benin, Brass and Warri where they carried out their missionary activities, whereas the Italians and Belgians operated in the northern areas, for instance, Kano, Katsina, and Borno. Again, these initial attempts failed. Christianity began effectively in Nigeria in 1841 with members of the Church Missionary Society

---

[11] The 17 percent ratio of the Nigerian population in relation to the continent's total population was the estimate in 2017. The figure was obtained from an anecdotal source, since the last time Nigeria had a detailed census was in 2006 (UNDESA, 2019; Population Pyramid, 2019). Therefore, this figure lacks statistical integrity, though it may not be outrightly false.

[12] The Fulani is an ethnic group that has resided in Hausaland in northern Nigeria since the early 1400s.

(hereinafter CMS) who came to the country in the company of freed Nigerian slaves of Yoruba origin who had converted to the religion in Sierra Leone. These settled in Lagos, Badagry and Abeokuta, all in the southwestern part of the country from where they operated going further southwards. Other Christian groups followed suit, such as the Methodist Church, the Baptist Church, and the Roman Catholic Church (Onwubiko, 1973).

Beside the ATR, Islam and Christianity, the country harbours other religious systems, such as Judaism, Hinduism, Buddhism and Bahaism, as well as religious bodies like Eckankar, the Church of Scientology, the International Society for Krishna Consciousness (ISKCON), and the Grail Movement. Alongside these are numerous quasi-religious organisations like the Rosicrucian Order, the Reformed Ogboni Fraternity, and Freemasonry. There are, of course, individuals who do not belong to any religion. This diversity notwithstanding, Islam and Christianity are two religions that have a large followership among Nigerians. Official census figures stating religious distribution of the Nigerian population are difficult to get. An opportunity to obtain these was lost when religious affiliation was left out as one of the parameters in the 2006 national census. As a result, most claims about the proportion of religious groups in the country are mere estimates. Some popular sources like the Democracy Web put the relative percentage at 50 for Muslims, 40 for Christians, and circa 10 for traditionalists. Conversely, others such as the Pew Research Center (2012) set the ratio at 49.3 percent for Christians, 48.8 percent for Muslims, with the remaining 2 percent belonging to no or other religions. While these figures are largely anecdotal, they appear to confirm the assertion that Islam and Christianity are the dominant religions in the country, with the ATR as a significant minority religion. That said, it is safer to conclude that the country has a near equal proportion of Muslims and Christians (Fumbo et al., 2020; Sampson, 2012). Nigeria's Muslims are mainly Sunnites, though a minority of them are affiliated to the Shi'a community. Among Christians, the denominations include the different Protestant categories—such as the Anglican Communion, the Baptist Convention, the Methodist Church, the Lutheran Church, the Presbyterian Church—as well as the Roman Catholic Church, the Seventh Day Adventists, the Jehovah's Witnesses, the Evangelical and Pentecostal churches (Osaghae & Suberu, 2005; Nwauche, 2008). Underneath these major subdivisions, both religions have witnessed the mushrooming of newer branches in the country since the 1970s. These include, on the one hand, the Izala movement, the Maitatsine, the Muslim Brothers and Boko Haram for Islam, and on the other hand, the country's many Pentecostal sanctuaries for Christianity. These new groups exhibit similar characteristics, namely they have a greater number of followers among the youth and appear more zealous than the main traditional subdivisions of their religions. They tend to use a confrontational proselytising approach and are more intolerant to nonbelievers. Because of this, their activities often constitute the immediate cause of religious conflicts in the country, as is particularly evident in the ongoing Boko haram crisis (Osaghae & Suberu, 2005; Uzoma, 2004).

There are other notable facts about these two dominant religious identities in Nigeria. In the first place, both religions are arguably the most potent source of identity in the country. Not long ago, Lewis and Bratton (2000) reported the outcome of a survey on Attitudes to Democracy and Markets in Nigeria, in which they identified ethnicity as the most salient source of identity in the country. This position was later challenged in 2006 by the findings of the Pew survey on Religion and Public Life, which instead showed that Nigerians tend to feel their religious identity more strongly than any other identity (Pew Report, 2020). Be that as it may, recent studies demonstrate the high level of religiosity among Nigerians. In the 2008 Religions Monitor, of the 99 percent of Nigerians sampled who described themselves as believers, about 92 percent identified as highly religious and considered participation in religious services and activities to be important (Huber, 2008). This high level of religiosity has remained relatively stable over time, as can be seen in the 2014 survey on Religion and Human Rights (see Chap. 5 of this study). But then, underneath this high level of religiosity, there is an ambience of mutual distrust and suspicion between the adherents of the dominant religions (Pew Report, 2020)—another finding that has also recently been corroborated (cf. Adimekwe & Ziebertz, 2018). That being the case, these dominant religious identities can easily be mobilised in the politics of identity and exploited in the quest for political power or in conflict over scarce resources. Although there are occasionally intra-religious conflicts among the diverse subcleavages of these two religions in the country, these denominations can still forge a common front for joint missionary and civil actions. For this purpose, they have their respective umbrella associations, namely the *Jama'atu Nasril Islam* (JNI: meaning in English the Society for the Support of Islam), which is usually the rallying point for Muslims, while Christians for their part have the Christian Association of Nigeria (hereinafter CAN).

Lastly, Islam and Christianity are aware of the existence of other religions in Nigeria and have largely responded to them in exclusivist terms, partly because of their logic of monotheism, which posits the existence of one God with only one correct way of relating to Him. Based on how their adherents seem to have witnessed to this belief, these religions are regarded as the mainstay of religious differentiation and conflicts in the country. To put it differently, their exclusivist tendencies have been attributed to their religious cosmologies, which appear to derive from their respective theological frameworks, teachings, and sacred writings. These are also due to their historical contexts, i.e., the way the two religions came into the country and the missionary strategy they adopted on arrival. In the case of Islam, the preferred approach to conversions in Nigeria was to first enlist conformity, often by brute force, and then to impose the superior Islamic culture on the conquered people. This is epitomised by the nineteenth-century jihad of Usman dan Fodio (Sampson, 2012). Nadel (1954: 255, 253) provides some support for this claim by describing the social impact of Islam on the Nupe kingdom of northern Nigeria as follows: "[c]oming as it did as a religion of conquerors and ruling class …", "[w]hat counts is, first and foremost, the assimilation to upper-class culture, and only secondarily the deliverance from unbelief." In other words, the emphasis was more on induction into a superior Islamic culture, and thus the conversion process tended more to inculcate a sense of pride and superiority in the convert than transform the inner person. Similarly, it should be recalled that Christianity finally came to Nigeria after the great wave of Reformation that swept across Europe in the sixteenth century and the country, like many other African countries, became 'a battleground for converts' for the various Christian denominations. In his book *History of West Africa*, Onwubiko (1967) wrote about the "Scramble for and Partition of West Africa" in which he portrayed the aggressive manner African borders were negotiated by European powers until an official model of annexation was endorsed at the Berlin conference of 1884–1885. This aggressive approach permeated the evangelisation strategies of the competing missionary groups, for whom christianising and civilising were one and the same mission, as Africa was considered 'a dark continent.' Here too, Mutua (1999: 102) summarises the foregoing analysis very critically: "'Christianity and Islam forcibly entered Africa … as masters.' The two traditions came either as conquerors or on the backs of conquerors. As they had done elsewhere, they were driven by the belief and conviction of their own innate superiority – and conversely what they saw as barbaric African religions and cultures." Given this background, it is not surprising that the proselytising methods of these two religions have been construed as elitist and competitive, which in turn seems to justify the follow-up negative assessment by some that their conversions were more social than religious (Mbiti, 1999; Nadel, 1954). Granted, both religions have come a long way in Nigeria, but the elitist and parochial tendencies have somehow remained with their adherents as enduring legacies of their missionary past and today often manifest themselves in the form of rivalry between these identities.

Religion in the Struggle to Define the Nigerian Identity

Nigeria always had official religions. The indigenous socio-political entities that make up Nigeria all had community-imposed belief systems. In the traditional setting, religion was "an integral part of life itself" (Thorpe, 1992: 3), or as Mbiti (1990: 256) aptly puts it, "[t]o be is to be religious in a religious universe." But life was also a communal affair, meaning that membership of a social group equally meant being part of the life and religion of that group, and one cannot separate oneself from these without grave consequences. Hence, clans, ethnic groups and kingdoms had their deities which held them together, and religion was a social cohesive force as such. There was no separation of the sacred and the profane. For instance, after the jihad of 1804, in which he overran greater part of the north, Usman dan Fodio set up an administrative system with its seat of authority at Sokoto in the northwest of Nigeria. Sokoto Caliphate, as it was officially known, was ruled with the Sharia to the effect that Islam became the official religion of the area with time. These systems remained intact until the British colonial government took over Northern and Southern Nigeria at the turn of the twentieth century.

To effectively accomplish the annexation, the colonial government introduced the British legal system in the Colony of Nigeria. This new legal system modified Islam and practically supplanted the traditional belief systems. In the south, the colonial government supported the Christian missionaries who provided social services in the area, and with time the region became increasingly Christian. In the north, the Sharia was incorporated into the administrative system together with other local customs and institutions. The colonial government initially did not meddle with the existing Islamic Maliki law[13] in accordance with the concept of indirect rule but had to gradually curtail the application of that law for the sake of administrative exigencies. As the Colony steadily marched towards nationhood, one of the concerns that came up in the north at the time was the issue of discrimination, as alleged by ethnic and religious minorities in the region. Based on what Paden (2007) described as "the all-consuming nature of Islamic identity", the minority groups expressed their displeasure at the marginalisation they suffered at the hand of the Muslim majority and agitated for better living conditions in the region. That way, the struggle for independence became in this context an opportunity to define Nigerianness not only in contrast to the colonial powers, but also in contrast to the dominant ethnic and religious identities with the tendency to impose their traditions as the basis of the Nigerian identity. The British responded to the agitations by setting up the Willink Commission, a move seen as the first attempt to address the problem of pluralism in the country. The commission's report led to the establishment of a Sharia Court of Appeal in Kaduna in the northwest and the promulgation of the English Common Law Penal Code (1959) for the region, as well as the incorporation of the Bill of Rights into the Independence Constitution. Meanwhile, the Maliki law remained in force until independence in 1960, when it was replaced by the Code, and from then on the application of the Sharia law was limited to the law of personal status and family relations (Peters & Barends, 2001). This is known in the country as the "Settlement of 1960" (Ostien, 2007: 178). While this new arrangement brought some flexibility in the application of the law, it drew the ire of many Nigerian Muslims who saw it as a subjugation of Sharia and Islam as a whole and regarded it as merely a temporary compromise.

After independence, the country witnessed intense pressures for the restoration of the Islamic legal system at the return to civil rule in 1979. At the 1978 Constituent Assembly set up to draft a new constitution for the country's Second Republic, Muslim leaders in the Assembly advocated a greater role for Sharia by establishing the Federal Sharia Court of Appeal (hereinafter FSCA). They argued that the existing secular law cannot satisfy the legal needs of Muslims because it originated from a Judaeo-Christian tradition. Therefore, they asked that the Sharia be accorded a federal status through the inclusion of the FSCA. Their Christian counterparts, especially those from the north, saw this move by Muslim elites as a clever ploy to re-establish their traditional hegemony and rejected it, insisting that such a provision would detract from the secularity of the Nigerian State. Consequently, the proposal polarised the Assembly along rigid religious lines. At a point in the debate, the Muslims shunned the activities of the Assembly in protest. To resolve the deadlock, a compromise was reached that included the introduction of Sharia Courts and State

[13] Of the four main Sunni schools of law, the Maliki legal doctrine is the one that operates in northern Nigeria. The other three are the Hanafi, Shafi'i and Hanbali Sunni schools of law (see Peters & Barends, 2001).

Sharia Courts of Appeal,[14] as well as a secular clause[15] in the Constitution. Subsequent Sharia debates followed the pattern of the 1978 Constituent Assembly, but the outcomes were not always the same. For instance, still not satisfied with the 1979 arrangement, the Muslim who were members of the Committee on State Judicature in the 1988 Constituent Assembly pressed for the extension of Sharia to the federal level through the establishment of the FSCA. Perhaps still angered by the country's controversial enlistment into the International Organisation of the Islamic Conference (OIC) in 1986 by the then military government led by a northern Muslim, the Christian members in the Assembly vehemently rejected the idea and accused their Muslim colleagues of a hidden islamisation agenda. Unlike 1977, the 1988 Constituent Assembly was unable to reach a compromise on the issue due to the extreme positions taken by Muslims and Christians. After a careful study of the deliberations and proposed modifications to the draft constitution, the status quo was maintained (Ajayi, 2001). In other words, in the 1989 draft constitution there was no change from the 1979 constitutional provisions on Sharia.[16]

The debate was raised again in the 1994 Constitutional Conference Commission and took on a more controversial form in the country at the dawn of the millennium. The 1999 Constitution was adopted only after much ado about Sharia and the issue of religion. In the end, the status quo remained intact. But in a federal system, which Nigeria practices, the Constitution allows the states to establish their own courts for matters not covered by federal law and to institute their own Sharia courts of appeal for civil matters. Hence, following the return to democratic rule in 1999, advocates of Sharia resorted to the state level, starting in Zamfara State in the northwest. In 2000, the Zamfara State government passed a law extending Sharia to criminal matters. Other northern States—about 12 of them—followed suit. This development is largely a reaction to the 1960 Settlement, which some Muslims never accepted and were determined to reverse with time (Okpanachi, 2012). Extreme versions of this reversal attempt have been experienced in the activities of Islamic sects such as the Maitatsine in the 1980s and Boko Harām today, which have cost the nation very

---

[14]The 1979 Constitution states in section 240(1) that: "[t]here shall be, for any State that requires it, a Sharia Court of Appeal for that State." Then, under section 242(1), it further states that: "[t]he Sharia Court of Appeal of a State shall, in addition to such other jurisdiction as may be conferred upon it by the law of the State, exercise such appellate and supervisory jurisdiction in civil proceedings in questions of Islamic personal law which the Court is competent to decide in accordance with the provision of sub-section (2) of this Section".

[15]In section 10, the same 1979 Constitution states: "[t]he Government of the Federation or of a State shall not adopt any religion as a State Religion." This clause found its way to the Nigerian constitutions in 1979. Up until then it was applied only informally in the country (Adegbite, 2012).

[16]The 1989 Draft Constitution was not promulgated in the end because the transition to civil rule, which would have inaugurated the Third Republic, was thwarted with the annulment of the Presidential Election of 12th June 1993. The same goes for the 1995 Draft Constitution. After the demise of the then Head of State, General Sanni Abacha, the idea of adopting a constitution he initiated was not welcomed by most Nigerians owing to the reservations about his personality. Hence, the succeeding military government decided to review and promulgate the 1979 Constitution as the new 1999 Constitution of Nigeria (**see** Amah, 2017).

dearly in terms of human lives and properties. In the aftermath of the reintroduction of Sharia law by the northern States, the northern minority population demonstrated against what they perceived as violations of their fundamental human rights. However, Sharia advocates claim that the move was not unconstitutional (Uzoma, 2004). Whether it is constitutional or not, Muslims are not alone in the tendency to infiltrate the public arena with religion. Christians have also been accused of a similar encroachment using ‘the second technique’, which involves invading public institutions such as academic establishments, hospitals, mass media, etc. and turning them into avenues of proselytisation (Eze, 2005). A close perusal of the foregoing thesis on the surface reveals a rivalry between the country’s dominant religions. But underneath, one tends to see a resolute effort by these religions to impose their mores as the basis for defining Nigerianness.

To conclude this subheading, we would like to reiterate that Nigeria is a multi-religious society and many Nigerians do not find this situation easy. Given this diversity, the challenge is to design the country’s socio-political life in such a way that adherents of different religions can live together peacefully. As Ziebertz (2016) puts it, the crucial question of religious pluralism is how people with different and sometimes hostile beliefs and worldviews can live together. To answer this question, Nigeria has, among other things, enshrined the principle of religious freedom in her laws.

3.1.2 Freedom of Religion in Nigerian Law

Section 38(1) of the 1999 Constitution states: “[e]very person shall be entitled to freedom of thought, conscience and religion, including freedom to change his religion or belief, and freedom (either alone or in community with others, and in public or in private) to manifest and propagate his religion or belief in worship, teaching, practice and observance.” This constitutional provision gives legal expression to the principle of religious freedom contained in the Universal Declaration. First, it guarantees freedom of thought, conscience and religion to every Nigerian and resident of the country. This includes the freedom to choose or change their religion or belief at will, without arbitrary restrictions or interference by state or non-state actors. Secondly, the same subsection generally also provides for outward demonstration of religious adherence. This may include, but is not limited to, the freedom to attend religious services, perform their religious duties, propagate their religion, and observe their religious customs. Thirdly, the provision obviously covers the right not to believe. To support this position, the Constitution provides for an anti-discrimination clause in article 42, which guarantees the protection of all persons from unfair treatment based on social characteristics, including religion or the lack thereof. It should be noted that this provision recognises the equality of all religions and faiths, as it is based on the constitutional principle of equality of all people within the Federation. In addition, it is intended to ensure that the State does not interfere in religious affairs beyond the threshold of protecting society (Nwauche, 2008).

This is the most important law protecting religious freedom in Nigeria. It is reinforced by other constitutionally guaranteed rights such as the right to privacy, freedom of expression, freedom of assembly and association, and freedom of movement. Apart from these, religious freedom is guaranteed in several international human rights instruments to which Nigeria has agreed. For example, the ICCPR (article 18), the CRC (article 30), the African Charter (article 8) and the African Charter on the Rights and Welfare of the Child (article 9). A corollary to the right to freedom of religion and outward manifestations of religious adherence is the freedom of parents and/or legal guardians regarding the religious education of their wards. This follows from the provisions of subsection 2 of the same section 38. The latter states that no person attending an educational institution "shall be required to receive religious instruction or to take part in or attend any religious ceremony or observance if such instruction ceremony or observance relates to a religion other than his own, or religion not approved by his parent or guardian." Subsection 3 contains more detailed provisions on the establishment of religious educational institutions.

Freedom of religion is a fundamental human right in Nigeria. However, unbridled freedom is both destructive and self-defeating, as it can lead to a brazen display of immoderation and acts detrimental to freedom itself. Thus, like other human rights, the constitutional provision on freedom of religion is not cast in absolute terms. It is not entirely clear whether the right to hold or to change religious or other beliefs is excluded from rights to which Nigerian law allows exceptions. The constitution is silent on this. That said, section 38(4) excludes so-called "secret societies" from enjoyment of the right but does not define which societies fall under that designation. Then section 45 lists some situations in which the exercise of the right to freedom of thought, conscience, and religion may be restricted based on individual and group considerations. The provision states that section 38 may be restricted where required by law and reasonably justified in a democratic society in the interests of defence, public safety, public order, public morality or public health, or to protect the rights and freedoms of other persons. It follows from the tenor of this provision that these limitations mainly concern the right to manifest or show one's faith and are intended to ensure that the exercise of this right does not violate the fundamental rights of others. Nigerian courts have also clarified that citizens' right to freedom of religion can sometimes be disregarded for reasons of public interest,[17] as was the case at the height of the Boko haram insurgency in the northwest of the country or in the recent outbreak of the coronavirus pandemic where the right was held in abeyance in the interest of public safety or public health. In any case, any permissible limitations of the right must be fair so as not to vitiate its enjoyment.

Furthermore, the freedom of religion is meant to be enjoyed in a context of no ties to a particular religion. For this reason, section 10 of the Constitution states that "[t]he Government of the Federation or of a State shall not adopt any religion as

[17] See *Medical and Dental Practitioners Disciplinary Tribunal v. Okonkwo* (2001) 6 NWLR (pt.710).

State Religion." At the margin note to the section, it reads "Prohibition of State Religion" (Adegbite, 2012). This constitutional language has led to differing conclusions about Nigeria's secular status, with some holding that the country is a *de jure* secular state (Odeku & Animashaun, 2012; Ojo, 2006), despite the term not appearing anywhere in the statute books. Others claim that the country is a *de facto* religious state in which religion plays a role in public policy, regardless of what is specified in section 10 (Nwauche, 2008). For others still, Nigeria is a quasi-secular state or simply a multi-religious State in which Islam and Christianity play a dominant role (Adegbite, 2012; Okeke & Eze, 2013). Unfortunately, this constitutional provision has yet to be interpreted by Nigeria's Supreme Court, although the country's secular status has been challenged on numerous occasions and the matter is still hotly debated among the people. The re-introduction of Sharia criminal law by the northern States is one of the recent developments that could have been used to define the country's model of secularism, but the federal government shied away from challenging this move by the States concerned in court.

Secularity is all about a state's neutrality in matters of religion, especially in a society with several competing religions. It does not mean atheism but rather a state of being separate from religion, of not being supportive of religion or irreligion. A secular state is, therefore, a state or country that is religiously neutral and not exclusively allied with or against any religion. The separation principle safeguards religions from the arbitrary intrusions of governments and guarantees a level playing ground for all in a nation. There are many ways of being secular depending on the national culture. For example, the US, whose political culture Nigeria imitates, combines the separation principle with a pro-religious stance towards the protection of religious freedom. Countries, such as France, and the Soviet Union, by contrast, have practised secularity in ways ranging from sharp separation to being strongly or totally anti-religion (Eller, 2017). The secular clause entered Nigeria's Constitution in 1979 as part of the compromise reached by the Constituent Assembly to resolve the deadlock in the Sharia debate. The aim of this provision was neither to exclude nor get rid of religion from the country—not when majority of the citizens are Muslims or Christians—but rather to ensure that religion does not stray into the public arena given the peculiar ethno-religious configurations of the country. Therefore, in the light of this historical context and in view of the combined constitutional provisions on 'no state religion', 'freedom of religious practice' and 'anti-discrimination clause', which are essential features of a secular state, it can be said that the draftsmen of the Constitution intended Nigeria to be a secular State. In practice, however, the country can at best be described as a self-styled secular State.

The Sharia Law Question

Sharia is not a new thing in the Nigerian political space. Its implementation has been a lingering issue in the contemporary history of Nigeria. Sharia was the standing legal order in Usman dan Fodio's Sokoto Caliphate prior to the British occupation of Northern Nigeria in 1903. Its application was gradually curtailed by the colonial government, especially in criminal law. This curtailment was informed by administrative exigencies which include, among other things, accommodating the diverse identities in the region. Sharia was thus limited to personal and family matters and was classified under Native Law and Custom in the statute books. A good number of Muslims in the country strongly oppose this arrangement and have repeatedly called for its complete reversal, the last time being at the Constitutional Conference in 1994. Therefore, some commentators believe that the reintroduction of Sharia law in the area of criminal justice in 2000 should be seen against this historical background, but also from the perspective of the Islamic revivalism that began in the country in the 1970s. In any case, this development had an enduring negative implication for the country's political economy. If anything, it exacerbated the deep divisions in the country across ethno-religious fault lines and reinforced their mobilisation in identity politics like never before. The following subsection explores the provisions of Sharia law vis-à-vis the fundamental right to freedom of religion.

The Sharia Penal Code

Sharia refers to canonical rules derived from the Quran, the Sunna or the actual practice of Prophet Muhammad as documented by hadith, and the Ijtihād (i.e., informed opinions of scholars based on these two sources). According to Sharia, criminal offences are classified into three. The first category is the hudûd offences. This domain gets the most attention from non-Muslims because the offences are regarded as specified by God (Allah) with fixed penalties and, as such, are unalterable by human agency. Hudûd offences include extra-marital sex (zinâ), theft (sariqa), robbery (hirâba), consumption of alcohol (shurb al-khamr) and false accusation of extra-marital sex (qadhf). Penalties range from flagellation, amputation, banishment, imprisonment to death sentence, including death by stoning. The second category of offences is made up of provisions on homicide and hurt. They sometimes carry direct retributive penalties (qisâs), or monetary compensations (diya). Lastly, the third category consists of offences with a wide range of punishments, mostly corporal punishments. This category allows a judge the discretion in choosing punishment (ta'zîr, siyâsa) (see Nwauche, 2008; Okpanachi, 2012; Peters & Barends, 2001).

In addition to these offences, the Zamfara Penal Code[18] proscribes the worship and invocation of juju,[19] which is defined to include "the worship and invocation of any subject or being other than Allah."[20] Such is made a capital offence. Other practices that involve magic and witchcrafts are also covered under the same sections.[21] The Code further provides that acts and omissions that are punishable offences under Sharia shall be punished even if they are not specifically mentioned in the

[18] Zamfara State, in the northwestern part of Nigeria, is the State where the Sharia reintroduction project all started. On 27th January 2000, the State enacted the first Sharia Penal Code—a Nigerian-adapted version of the Sharia criminal code—which is largely used in this study as a sample of Nigerian Sharia Law.

[19] Section 406(d) of the Zamfara Penal Code.

[20] Ibid., section 405.

[21] Ibid., sections 405–409.

Code.[22] Since the reintroduction of the Sharia Penal Code, a lot of sentences of different magnitudes have been passed by Sharia courts across the country, for instance, the 'famous' hadd sentence by the Upper Sharia Court in Sokoto State in 2001.[23] There have also been other recent rulings, although some have been appealed and overturned (Human Rights Report, 2013). Accurate reports on the status of execution of Sharia sentences are difficult to come by due to the apparent foot-dragging of convicted individuals to work with human rights defenders, among other things.

The reintroduction of the Sharia Penal Code in Nigeria remains the subject of unending controversy. At the heart of this controversy is the question of the constitutionality of the Sharia reintroduction vis-à-vis the secular status of the country. On the one hand, advocates of Sharia base their argument on the perceived status of Islam as one of the de facto State religions, on the principle of federalism that the country practises, and on the constitutional provision of section 275, which empowers every State Assembly to create a State Sharia Court of Appeal, to claim that the reintroduction of Sharia law in the northern States was constitutional (Nwauche, 2008). Opponents, on the other hand, contend that the practice of a state-mandated religion, as demonstrated by the reintroduction project, is inconsistent with the existing secular federal arrangement and therefore unconstitutional (Okeke & Eze, 2013; Zarifis, 2002). However, a cursory look at the relevant constitutional provisions on the Sharia issue, particularly sections 10 and 275, seems to allow both interpretations and even more. It should be recalled that these two provisions are the product of the 1978 Constituent Assembly Compromise adopted in the current Constitution and both provisions have been described at various times as equivocal and mutually contradictory (Eze, 2005; Okpanachi, 2012). Whichever way one looks at it, the controversy over the re-introduction of Sharia law appears to partly border on the question of the country's secularity model, which has not yet been formally defined. The government's apparent unwillingness to address this issue decisively suggests that it faces some form of dilemma regarding the place of religion in national life. This dilemma can be explained inter alia by the crisis of leadership.

The Reintroduction of Sharia in Public Spaces and Freedom of Religion

One unease many still have with the reintroduction of Sharia criminal law in the north concerns its relationship to human rights, especially freedom of religion. The reintroduction project was justified primarily on religious grounds. For many Muslims, it is important to live in an Islamic order in order to function properly. They consider this to be consistent with their constitutional right to religious freedom. But they also think that the said Islamic order must be enforced by the state

---

[22] Ibid., section 92.

[23] On 9th October 2001, Safiya Husseini Tungar-Tudu was sentenced to death by stoning for zinā by the Upper Sharia Court in Gwadabawa, Sokoto State. The conviction was one of the incidents that brought the whole Sharia saga of Nigeria to the attention of the world. There was also the one of Amina Lawal Kurami, who was equally given a *hadd* sentence for the same offence in March 2002. It drew a lot of international attention too (Zarifis, 2002).

(Peters & Barends, 2001). Whereas a nation-state is not prohibited from adopting an official religion in virtue of the right to freedom of religion, a state-imposed religion may not impair the rights of the minorities to live and practise their faith or irreligion freely and without discrimination in the politico-religious system. These rights are protected by the ICCPR and the Minorities Declaration under the right to freedom of religion.

The application of state-declared Sharia law infringes on the right of non-Muslims and residents of the states concerned to practise their own religions in several ways (Zarifis, 2002). For example, the provision in Section 405 of the Zamfara Penal Code, which prohibits the worship and invocation of any subject or being other than Allah, is contrary to Nigeria's international human rights obligations. This provision impairs the right of non-Muslims in this State to freely choose and profess their own faith. It also violates the rights of religious minorities. It contradicts article 18 of the ICCPR and article 2(1) of the Minorities Declaration and has no connection with the recognised permissible derogations to freedom of religion in both national and international planes. Hence, a state-declared Sharia law may not be used as an excuse for non-compliance with these obligations.[24] Alternatively, the Code addresses only Muslims and, if considered from this angle, then the precise intent of section 405 becomes uncertain. In that case, it has been suggested that the provision is likely to be addressed to persons who regard themselves as Muslims and yet indulge in the practices mentioned in the section (Peters & Barends, 2001). However rational that may be, the provision may affect the religious practices of non-Muslims, especially traditionalists.

Some Sharia provisions also impair the full exercise of freedom of religion by Muslims. It is certain that not all Nigerian Muslims support the Sharia Penal Code. There are some who would prefer to be tried in a regular criminal court rather than a Sharia court. These individuals have the right to choose between the options, but unfortunately are prevented from doing so in Sharia-declared States (Zarifis, 2002). Freedom of religion also includes the right to replace, renounce or retain a religion. A problem arises here with the right of renunciation, as Muslims cannot change their religion because apostasy (ridda) is a hadd offence. Granted, ridda is not included in any of the Sharia Penal Codes in Nigeria as a punishable offence, but it is believed that the provision of section 92 of the Zamfara Penal Code, which stipulates that acts and omissions that are punishable offences under the Sharia may be punished without being provided for in the Code, is targeted at apostates (Peters & Barends, 2001). So far, there have been some indictments for ridda in the country. For instance, Human Rights Watch (2005) reports on a case in Zamfara State, where two Muslims were arraigned before a Sharia Court in April 2002 on accusation of apostasy. But the case was dismissed.

The Sharia Penal Codes in Nigeria has further areas of conflict with the internationally protected right to religious freedom. These include regulations on the ban on the sale of alcohol, gender segregation in schools and public transport, dress

[24] See article 26 of the 1969 Vienna Convention on the Law of Treaties.

codes of women and their freedom of movement, etc. (Nwauche, 2008; Zarifis, 2002). However, some of these provisions do not strictly apply in Nigeria today.

3.1.3 Recurrent Issues in the Practice of Freedom of Religion in Nigeria

As already stated, the right to freedom of thought, conscience and religion guarantees everyone in Nigeria the freedom to observe, practice and propagate their religion without arbitrary restrictions or interference. The various ways in which this can happen have been highlighted in the analysis so far. The question of which religious practices are protected by this law and which ones are not concerns almost every society (Ziebertz, 2016), including Nigeria. Examples of such practices include the ritual slaughter of animals, the religious ritual of circumcision, wearing of headscarves or veils, the public presence of religious symbols, praying in public spaces, establishment of religious schools, construction of minarets or church towers, and reintroduction of Sharia in public spaces. The list is endless. Which of these individual practices belong to the respective religious practice is not only difficult to determine, but also controversial. In Nigeria, some of these practices are not only controversial, but they sometimes also trigger violent conflicts. The country has enshrined religious freedom in her Constitution and ratified several human rights instruments that protect this right. Nevertheless, the legal regulations do not seem to offer any direct or sustainable solutions to the conflicts, as many people are still denied equal rights or discriminated against because of their (ir)religion or worldview, or simply because they belong to minorities.

In the following subheading, we explore some of the religious practices in Nigeria that are highly controversial. These include the use of religious symbols in public spaces, the practice of religion in educational institutions, religious instruction in schools and the establishment of religious educational institutions. We chose them because they are recurring issues.

Religious Symbols in Educational Institutions

The use of religious symbols in public spaces is a topic that has generated intense controversies worldwide in recent decades (cf. Diehl et al., 2009; McGoldrick, 2006; Shadid & van Koningsveld, 1991). In Europe, for instance, the controversies centred around the place of religion in society and the role of women. In this way, the Islamic veil, hijab, and other head coverings worn by Muslim women easily became the most visible religious symbol and the subject of public debate in several European countries as well as many other countries of the West. The controversies are not limited to non-Islamic countries. The use of headscarves is also a highly contentious issue in Turkey and some other Islamic countries (Strabac et al., 2016). In Nigeria, too, the use of sacred symbols in secular settings has increasingly become a source of conflict. Several religious symbols are often mentioned in this connection, such as the Arabic inscriptions on Nigerian currency denominations, the cross sign on public hospital signposts, and the wearing of beads or crucifixes, etc., but none of these has generated much disagreement and tension in the country than the use of hijab in public spaces. Lately, most Muslim women insist on using headscarves in official settings irrespective of public sensibilities, and this does not easily go down well with others. This 'sudden new interest' by Muslim women in donning the hijab is regarded in some quarters as the most common expression of Islamic revivalism in the post-1999 Nigeria (Oba, 2009; Tolulope, 2019).

The hijab controversy has found its way into institutions of learning, especially in the north and southwest of the country. This issue mostly concerns public schools, as private schools normally have their internal dress codes, which intending students and their parents can either accept before enrollment or move to other schools. Based on this, only public schools are examined here on the issue of dressing. All schools in the country have school uniforms, including kindergartens, primary and secondary schools. This is the standard practice in the land and is old as the school system itself. In some schools in the north, students could wear hijab of certain colours as part of the school uniform, while in schools in the south students always strictly adhered to school uniforms prescribed by State governments. But lately, Muslim students have preferred to wear the hijab instead of the prescribed school uniform (Oba, 2009; Tolulope, 2019), and this has repeatedly led to reactions that disrupt the safe and orderly learning environments in schools. For example, in 2003, Muslim-Christian students' clashes over hijab were reported in some secondary schools in Oyo State, leading to the temporary closure of the schools by the government. In the same State, learning activities were also suspended at the University of Ibadan International School, Ibadan in 2018 and the Ladoke Akintola University of Technology International School, Ogbomosho in 2019 for the same reason. In the neighbouring Osun State as well as in Ogun State, all in the southwest, there were also reports of students' unrest over the use of hijab (cf. Guardian Newspaper, 2019). The crisis has assumed a more serious dimension in tertiary institutions, where female Muslim students are increasingly adopting the use of the full spectrum of hijab (Oba, 2009). Tertiary institutions across the country have responded to the trend with measures ranging from introduction of dress codes to outright prohibition of the use of hijab. Although these measures were implemented to preserve the secularity of public institutions of learning, they ended up causing more frictions in the institutions because Muslim students felt that the measures violated their right to freedom of religion. For instance, in 2005, the Muslim Students Society (hereinafter MSS) at the Ahmadu Bello University, Zaria (Kaduna State in northwestern Nigeria) issued a death sentence (fatwa) on a lecturer for refusing a female student on hijab entry into his lectures, following a ban on the use of headscarves in the institution (Sampson, 2012). The list is endless.

The use of hijab in public educational institutions in Nigeria was considered for the first time by the Ilorin High Court in *Bashirat Saliu and 2 Ors v. the Provost Kwara State College of Education, Ilorin and Ors*. In 2005, the college issued a dress code that inter alia prohibited the wearing of dresses or apparels that cover the entire face, for security purposes. Following this order, the college prevented three students from attending lectures and writing exams due to non-compliance. The students approached the court to contend that the veil was part of their religion and fell within the ambit of their fundamental right to religion. The Court upheld the contention that the dress code indeed violated the students' freedom of religion and judgment was entered in their favour. Dissatisfied with the judgement, the college appealed to the Appellate Court, insisting that the college is a secular educational institution where students are treated equally. In resolving the issue, the Appeal Court upheld the judgment of the High Court, namely that wearing the hijab is a tenet of Islamic faith and a constitutional right to expression of religious worship, the prohibition of which is discriminatory and a violation of the individual's human right.[25] Some other cases have endorsed *the Provost v. Basirat Saliu* on the point that the use of hijab in public schools constitutes an exercise of the inalienable fundamental right to freedom of religious practice.[26] However, in the case of *Ayisat Abdulkareem and Ors. v. Lagos State Government and Ors*, an Ikeja High Court in 2014 dismissed a suit instituted by two schoolgirls against the Lagos State government contesting the ban on the use of hijab in public schools in the State. The Court struck it out on the grounds that the ban was neither discriminatory nor a breach of the constitutional right to freedom of religion, as alleged by the students, and also in view of the country's secular status. Two years later, a panel of the Court of Appeal sitting in Lagos overruled the judgment of the High Court[27] and reaffirmed the decision delivered in *the Provost v. Basirat Saliu,* thus striking down the ban on the use of hijab in State schools in Lagos. The Lagos State government has since appealed the ruling and the matter is still pending in the Supreme Court. In other words, the last is yet to be heard on the matter, even as the crisis attends new heights in the country.[28] In the meantime, the status quo is that every Muslim female has the unfettered right to wear the hijab anywhere and that a ban of any sort is discriminatory.

From the foregoing, the following observations can be made: first, it is important to note that litigations and the accompanying judicial decisions on the issue of hijab are based primarily on socio-cultural grounds, unlike in some countries such as the US, where hijab disputes are not contested directly on religious or cultural grounds, but on other grounds such as the freedom of speech or expression. This observation is particularly relevant given the fact that Nigeria's democracy is modelled after the American template. Hence, the American approach to the hijab issue, which often demands less restrictive options from schools in response to the issue as against

---

[25] See *the Provost, Kwara State College of Education, Ilorin & 2 Ors v. Bashirat Saliu & 2 Ors*, Appeal no. CA/IL/49/2006. The judgment was delivered on 18th June 2009. See also Oba (2009), Tolulope (2019).

[26] See, for example, *Sheikh Oyinwola & Ors v. the Governor of Osun State & Ors* Suit No HOS/M17/2013.

[27] See *Ayisat Abdulkareem & Ors. v. Lagos State Government & Ors* (2016) 15 NWLR (Pt 1535) 177. See also Chukkol (2017).

[28] On 12th December 2017, Nigeria's Council of Legal Education refused to admit Amasa Firdaus, a University of Ilorin law graduate, to the Nigerian Bar on hijab for reasons that her hijab broke the dress codes. However, she was called to bar (in her hijab) seven months later, after the episode had stirred intense controversies nationwide (Guardian Newspaper 2019).

outright ban on the wearing of religious garb, might not fit the Nigerian situation owing to contextual differences (De Waal et al., 2011). Second, one of the major grievances against the Muslim headscarf in western societies concerns the fact that it is seen as a symbol of female oppression (Diehl et al., 2009). While this may not be wrong, the hijab appears to be seen differently in Nigeria. Most Muslim women in Nigeria seem to see the use of hijab as part of an expression of their cultural or religious identity (Oba, 2009). The point being made here is that identity and individual choice are closely linked. It would be recalled that many French Muslim women strongly opposed the ban on the hijab, even if they do not wear it themselves, arguing that women should have the opportunity to choose. Moreover, identity is protected by a combination of human rights, including freedom of religion, expression, and privacy (McGoldrick, 2006). That being the case, it may appear simplistic to conclude that the Nigerian Supreme Court should allow Muslim women and female students to function freely here and have the opportunity to define themselves. However, in deciding what direction society, especially public educational institutions, should take on this issue, the Supreme Court will not forget that schools perform a social function and that they remain important agents for the socialisation of the next generation into responsible citizens (Statham, 2016). As such, it may not be in the interest of the public for the long-awaited court decision to undermine the social service that school authorities perform or the enjoyment of the right to freedom of religion. Instead, there is need to weigh the balance between the two in order to enact an appropriate law (De Waal et al., 2011). In fact, respect for both secularism and freedom of religion is the balancing act if this issue is to be resolved permanently.

Prayer in Public Schools

Like wearing the hijab, prayer is also a source of frictions in Nigerian educational institutions. The frictions are felt more in institutions in those sections of the country with a mixed religious population. Prayer at school is an age-long practice traceable to the time of the European missionaries as pioneers of Nigeria's educational system. Originally, schools were set up by the missionaries to aid their work of getting people to embrace Christianity. Based on that, there was practically no demarcation between church and school. Schoolteachers took active part in church activities as agents and interpreters, and over time church practices were extended to schools, including saying prayers. In the north, quranic schools also had a strong religious character, as children were made to recite the Quran at school and gradually prayers became part of the school routine (Oladunjoye & Nanighe, 2015). In this way, prayer became an important part of the school programme. Today, every State of the federation has a mixed religious population thanks to urban and semi-urban migrations that took place at various points in the country's history, and this diversity is reflected in the population of most schools.

Across the nation, it is customary to start each school day with a prayer that is recited by schoolchildren and their teachers during a school programme generally known in Nigeria as 'Assembly'. The latter takes place twice daily, namely at the beginning and at the end of school, hence the tag 'Morning Assembly' and

'Afternoon Assembly.' Among other things, the morning assembly provides an opportunity for teachers to check the cleanliness of the students and provide them with vital information (Oladunjoye & Nanighe, 2015). But it is also a period for morning devotion. Taking part in this exercise is part of everyday school life and is mandatory for every child. Sometimes religious personnel from outside the school are invited to conduct this for students, though this move is usually fraught with controversies. In the first place, there could be a conflict of interest concerning the form or pattern of prayer to be recited. Besides, there could be issues with the content of the spiritual talk by the religious personnel, as well as the relevant question about whether a student is free to participate or not. The imposition of a particular form of prayer or religion on children at school is inconsistent with the constitutional principle of non-interference with one's religious belief. Entrusting religious personnel or organisations with the conduct of morning devotions in schools is usually a complicated matter. Experience has shown such to be a potential trigger of tension in the school and the wider society. This could lead to unnecessary conflicts with stakeholders, especially parents and guardians, who are wary of the indoctrination of their wards. Most Nigerian parents and guardians tend to object to prayers outside their faith for this reason because they fear that doing so would expose their wards to indoctrination that could ultimately affect their mode of worship at home (Oladunjoye & Nanighe, 2015). Furthermore, such an arrangement could lead to reactions from the government, which may act in several ways to show its neutrality towards all religions. On 12th January 2020, for instance, the government of the north-central State of Kwara banned religious activities in public schools across the State in response to an incident that reportedly took place in one government school in the State where a religious body conducted the morning devotion. Reacting to the incident earlier, the Secretary of Ilorin West Local Government Area, where the school is located, had directed that schools in the area offer separate devotions for Muslim and Christian students before the State government finally announced the ban. The stance of the government did not go down well with other stakeholders in the State, particularly the Kwara State Chapter of the Christian Association of Nigeria (CAN), which reacted to what it perceived as a 'blanket prohibition' that contradicted the status quo on morning devotion in public schools in the State (Oyekola, 2020). A similar incident also happened in 2015 in south-southern State of Cross River, where morning and afternoon devotions in all schools in the State were suspended indefinitely for putative security concerns, and the government was later constrained by interest groups to lift the suspension (see Oladunjoye & Nanighe, 2015).

There is evidence of a rise in conflicts related to religious activities in public schools in some States of the federation. The records show that most of the cases have been resolved by way of mediation. In all these cases, the consensus on this issue seems to be that domestic law does not prohibit prayer in schools, provided that the student is free to join or not to join. To put it differently, prayer in public schools in Nigeria is considered almost entirely within the purview of the constitutional provision of the right to freedom of religious practice. This remains the status quo till date.

Teaching of Religious Education

The teaching of religion in the Nigerian school programme is not a new phenomenon. Religious education (hereinafter RE) was introduced through the activities of missionaries (Falade, 2016). Under the missionaries, the Nigerian school system had a profound religious cast. The curricula were faith-oriented, given the specific educational objective, which was proselytisation rather than a formation for religious tolerance and dialogue (Sampson, 2012). In 1970, the Nigerian government took over public schools and educational institutions in the country with the aim of introducing secular values into education, among other things. This secularisation project failed because the education system still reflected the religious character of the nation—Islamic in the north and Christian in the south. One area where this came out more clearly was in the teaching of religious education in schools. In the north, Islamic Religious Knowledge was mostly taught and patronised, as was Bible Knowledge in the south, while the teaching of other religions was marginalised. One issue that needed to be addressed under this dispensation is whether State governments are obliged to promote the teaching of all RE in public schools. The issue was raised in the case of *Adamu v. Attorney-General of Borno State and Ors,*[29] in which the appellants alleged that the practice of requiring Christian parents or guardians to pay for Christian religious education of their wards in the same primary school while the Local Government Council (LGC) paid teachers of Islamic RE was unlawful and unconstitutional. Among other things, the appellants sought an order directing the Local Government Council in question (the Gwoza LGC) to also pay the salaries of teachers of Christian RE and a declaration stating that it was illegal to indoctrinate pupils against their will and the will of parents. The defendants wanted the case dismissed as lacking merit on the grounds that the main point of contention in the suit (i.e., the right to a particular form of education) is not justiciable under the Constitution. However, the Court held inter alia that wherever a local authority adopts a system which infringes on the fundamental right of a citizen in the implementation of the fundamental objectives of State policy, that breach of the citizen's right is justiciable. Consequently, the Court granted the remedies sought by the appellants on the grounds that they relate to their rights to freedom of religion and non-discrimination based on religion. *Adamu v. AG-Borno State* can be used as a benchmark to canvass for the equal treatment of religions, at least in terms of the teaching of RE, though the fundamental question was unfortunately skirted.

Be that as it may, the teaching of religion in schools is expected to inculcate in learners such values as love, respect for one another, justice and fair play, altruism, dedication to duty, etc. Overwhelmed by indoctrination, the country's dominant RE model—a confessional model as it appears in the national curriculum—did not guarantee these values as it left little room for reflective thinking. Individuals who were trained within this context tended to blindly accept the faith and were unwilling 'to think outside the box'. With the Nigerian society being increasingly bedevilled by a range of social ills such as religious extremism, fundamentalism and

[29] (1996) 8 NWLR (pt. 465) p. 203. See also Nwauche (2008).

bigotry even among schoolchildren, there was a clamour for reform of the system to instill the right values and skills in learners. Hence, in a recent review in 2008, the government introduced a 9-Year Basic Education Curriculum (hereinafter 9-Year BEC) and new subjects were injected into the school programme for the said purpose, but also as part of the objectives of the National Economic Empowerment Development Strategies (NEEDS) (Falade, 2016). The 9-Year BEC list of subjects for 2008 included both Islamic and Christian RE. This curriculum was well received by a cross section of the population, especially adherents of the dominant religious traditions. But it failed like the previous one to guarantee the desired link between RE and the acquisition of the relevant national values (Asue & Kajo, 2018). Following this, and in view of the need to reduce the number of subjects in line with global best practices, the government ordered the revision of the 9-Year BEC in 2012, with its implementation planned to begin in 2014. Part of the revision process included merging related disciplines to have fewer subjects in the school programme. Consequently, Islamic Studies (IS), Christian Religious Studies (CRS), Social Studies, Civic Education and Security Education were combined to be taught as themes in a new subject called Religion and National Values. According to the Nigerian Educational Research and Development Council (hereinafter NERDC), the reason for the amalgam is primarily to inculcate national values in learners, while the choice of the new subject title was informed by "the need to emphasize the importance of values across the educational spectrum" (Falade, 2016: 45). As expected, the outcome of the curriculum review exercise had supporters and critics across the nation. While supporters see many prospects for both the learners and the country in the new arrangement (Falade, 2016), the latter did not go down well with Christians, especially the Christian Association of Nigeria (CAN), which accused "NERDC of a grand design to Islamize the country with the new curriculum" (Asue & Kajo, 2018: 37). This reaction is particularly so because Arabic Studies / French Language was also introduced in the revised curriculum as a separate subject at the lower, middle, and upper basic levels. In a swift reaction, NERDC retracted its decision following the intervention of the National Assembly in 2017 and returned the schools to the 2008 arrangement that allowed Islamic Studies (IS) and Christian Religious Studies (CRS) to be taught as discrete subjects (Asue & Kajo, 2018).

Presently, RE is taught in Nigerian schools as a constitutionally protected right.[30] As stated in the current curriculum, no child is to be compelled to learn or be taught any RE subject other than that which is related to his or her belief system and that of his or her parents. Nigeria is signatory to all the international human rights laws that recognise this tenet. It is common knowledge that teachers in schools try to enforce compliance with some things such as class attendance, homework, school uniform, and even certain behaviours. But religious coercion is out of the question; it is specifically prohibited (Evans, 2008). This is one of the criticisms that have been levelled against the revised 9-Year BEC, namely that it tended to create room for the abuse of the right of religious non-compulsion. In this regard, Onwubiko

[30] See section 38(2) of the CFRN. See also article 18(1), (2) & (4) of the ICCPR, etc.

(2017) reports a case in Kwara State where a student was punished by the Arabic teacher for refusing to join the class when the French teacher was not available and Hebrew or Greek were not provided as alternatives in the said curriculum. Teachers need to be cautious about this right in religiously plural classrooms. At the same time, respect for the same right needs to be constantly balanced with another relevant right of every child—the right to education.[31] This right aims inter alia at preparing the child for responsible citizenship in a free and diverse society.[32] Sometimes it may be necessary for the school to encourage the child to attend some classes so as not to deny it an education appropriate to this goal. The school and indeed all the stakeholders in the education of the child need to recognise this tension between the two rights and, against this background, act in the child's best interest.

Nigeria has been struggling for many years to find a needs-based teaching method for religious education in schools. The existing model places great emphasis on intellectual growth of knowledge with little or no practical application (Asue & Kajo, 2018; Sampson, 2012). According to observations, this has not significantly improved on the legacy of the missionaries in school development. Given recent reforms in the education system, it may be necessary to evolve a more praxis-oriented and country-specific model of religious instruction.

The Establishment of (Faith-Based) Private Schools

Formal education was introduced in Nigeria in 1842 when the first primary school was opened in Badagry in the southwestern region. It was initiated by private agencies or religious organisations. Soon after arriving the country, the Christian missions established primary schools for the training of their converts. This was followed by the establishment of secondary schools a few years later, with the Church Missionary Society (CMS) Grammar School in Lagos, founded in 1859, considered the first of its kind. This school, and a few others like it, constitute the first-generation secondary schools in Nigeria. From 1842 the schools were managed by the missions. The colonial government did not show much interest in education until it felt the shortage of skilled labour to run its administration. Then came the Education Ordinance for British West African territories in 1882. Among other things, this first ordinance provided for the establishment of General and Local Boards of Education, and the general guidelines for school administration. Under this system, Lagos (a State in Nigeria) and Gold Coast (now Ghana) were administered as one. However, upon detachment in 1886, an Education Ordinance for Nigeria became necessary, and this was enacted in 1887. Between 1908 and 1952, about six education ordinances were enacted and each was an improvement on the one preceding it. These ordinances made it possible for the government to have partial control over education. It needs to be pointed out that in spite of its involvement, the colonial government did not discourage private initiatives in education (Abolade & Oyelade, 2018; Fabunmi, 2005; Odeleye et al., 2012).

[31] See article 13(1) of the ICESCR.

[32] See article 29(1)(d) of the CRC. See also Evans (2008).

As Nigeria tended towards self-government, she became a federation of three regions—East, West and North—and the then Federal Territory of Lagos under the 1954 Constitution. This Constitution embodied three legislative lists[33] that vested the regions with the power to make laws for their territories. The 1952 Education Ordinance had already granted them the power to further develop their education systems. Capitalising on these provisions, the regions enacted laws[34] to manage their respective education systems. This model of regional management remained largely in vogue during the First Republic and continued until the federal government took over the management of schools entirely from individuals and voluntary agencies in 1970. When the presidential system of government came on board with the Second Republic in 1979, the Constitution became the legal basis of education at that time (Fabunmi, 2005; Fafunwa, 2004). Thus, the 1979 Constitution put the management of education concurrently in the hands of the country's three tiers of government, namely the federal, state and local governments.[35] The experience over the years of poor education management by the State led to the reappearance of the private education sector to complement the efforts of the government (Abolade & Oyelade, 2018; Odeleye et al., 2012).

The 1999 Constitution grants citizens the right to establish religious schools in the country. In virtue of section 38(3), one can claim that religious organisations are free to establish faith-based private schools, be they regular academic institutions or the doctrinal establishments for the training of religious leaders such as clergy, imams, etc. Today, there is no level of education in Nigeria that is left without the involvement of religious organisations or voluntary agencies (Abolade & Oyelade, 2018). There is presently no law restricting religious bodies from establishing primary and secondary schools. The same is also true for the tertiary level of education. However, although the management of education is concurrently shared between State and Federal governments, the Constitution vests the latter with the power to control university and technological education[36] and it exercises this power through the National Universities Commission (hereinafter NUC). As it is, private or voluntary agencies are expected to obtain licences from the NUC to establish and operate universities. The Supreme Court of Nigeria recognised this right in the case of *Ukaegbu v. Attorney-General Imo State*[37] where it held that individuals or private agencies have the right to establish a university, a secondary school or a post-primary institution as a fundamental right to freedom of expression within the legal framework that regulates such establishment. Here, too, there is no law barring religious bodies from establishing universities and tertiary institutions in the country. Since the last two decades when the first four private universities obtained their

[33] These are the exclusive, concurrent and residual legislative lists. This three-list arrangement is maintained by the 1999 Constitution.

[34] For instance, there were the Education Laws of 1955 in the Western Region, 1956 in the Eastern and Northern Regions and then the Lagos Education Ordinance of 1957 (see Fabunmi, 2005).

[35] See items 25–28 of the Second Schedule to the 1979 Constitution.

[36] See item 27 of the Second Schedule to the CFRN.

[37] (1984) 5 NCLR 78.

licences, the number of mission-owned tertiary institutions in the country has increased. According to the 2019 NUC list of private universities, there are 79 approved private universities in the country, of which about 45 are affiliated with religious bodies. Having said that, one controversial aspect of religious-owned academic establishments in Nigeria concerns the student's right to freedom of religion. At issue is whether a student at such an institution has the right to object to any form of imposition of religious instruction or practice, given that some of these institutions consider certain moral rules to be attached to their identity and claim that they are entitled to some form of autonomy. In other words, it is a question of which one among the two things takes precedence—the moral rules of the institution or the freedom of religion of the student. A lot of religious-owned institutions in the country have gained some notoriety for being very uncompromising with their moral rules and do not seem to bother about the religious rights of their students (Nwauche, 2008). Whereas general opinion on the issue continues to differ based on individual perspectives and group affiliations, it is not clear to us whether any religious institution has been prosecuted for it to date.

3.1.4 Religion and Freedom of Religion

Religious freedom is an important part of human rights that is universally recognised by all religions. Here we review the theological perspectives of the country's dominant religions—ATR, Islam and Christianity—on this topic.

Freedom of Religion in ATR[38]

African Traditional Religion is the umbrella term for the African ancestral experience of the divine-human encounter (Opoku, 1993). Africa is not an island. Its historical development allowed for a variety of influences. As a result, the continent is made up of "multiple identities" (Maluleke, 2001: 37). Africa does not pretend to present itself as a united front of ideas and religion (Beyers, 2010). In fact, it houses a huge diversity of cultural and religious systems, so much so that it is difficult to talk of one type of religion as being uniquely African (Maluleke, 2001; see also Magesa, 2002). Despite the diversity, it is still assumed that the religious expressions in question have enough in common and that they are based on a coherent philosophy (cf. Mbiti, 1990; Mbiti, 1989).

Against this backdrop, religious pluralism in Africa—understood here as respect for the otherness of the other—is not an artefact of Arab and European civilisation. This claim is premised on the fact that prior to expansion of the oriental and occidental systems into Africa, there was a multiplicity of cults that co-existed in relative peace and tranquility in the traditional set-up. ATR's tolerance of pluralism can

[38] To treat this subheading, we relied extensively on Beyers, J. (2010). What is Religion? An African Understanding. *HTS Theological Studies*, 66(1), Article #341, 8 pages. Doi: 10.4102/hts.v66i1.341.

be explained, among other things, by its nature, basic philosophy and understanding of reality. Firstly, the ATR itself is inherently diverse in outward appearance and is as such no stranger to diversity. Religion was never seen as an invention of a particular race. According to scholars of African religion, the appeal of the transcendence of the human spirit was deemed universal. A uniform response to this appeal does not exist, rather there was a variety of responses to it in the traditional set-up (cf. Beyers, 2010). Second, the ATR thrived on the philosophy of 'live and let live.' Based on this, it readily embraced the principle of plurality. Thirdly, the African understanding of reality does not accept a clear-cut separation between the physical and spiritual spheres. Reality is one. It is beyond the exclusive reach of any individual. All humans can expand their knowledge of reality through social interaction. Likewise, divine reality is unfathomable and cannot be grasped by any single religious system, as no religion has the monopoly on the entire divine truth because the truth has its origin in the supernatural and not in humans (Opoku, 1993). The entire religious heritage of humanity is therefore welcome in the collective search for the knowledge of transcendence. From what has been said so far, it can be assumed that this attitude towards the plurality of religions also implies an acceptance of the equality of religions (cf. Turaki, 1999).

Of the three main religious traditions in Nigeria, the religion of the African forbearers is regarded as the least politically active and intolerant (Osaghae & Suberu, 2005). This is largely due to the African understanding of reality. It may be too simplistic to imagine that the ATR warmly embraced Islam or Christianity when they newly arrived in the country. Far from it, the ATR and/or the natives resisted the religions because they felt threatened by the disruptive influence, they believed the new religions would have on the established social order. Nevertheless, the ATR somehow accommodated them. For this reason, it is regarded by some as the most accommodating and tolerant "of all the religions practiced in Africa" (Etuk, 2002: 35). The same may not be said to the same extent about Islam and Christianity. Religious pluralism is a slightly more complicated issue when it comes to these religions.

Freedom of Religion in Islamic Theology

The two primary sources of Islam, the Quran and the Hadith, provide insight into the Islamic understanding of religious freedom (Ismail & Mat, 2016; Sumbulah, 2018). The latter covers a wide range of topics, such as the principle of non-coercion in religion, personal freedom of choice in matters of belief, the prohibition of forced conversions and tolerance of diversity.

The Quran recognises freedom of religion and belief. This is spread over several verses. The first is verse 2:256, where the Quran clearly states: "[l]et there be no compulsion in religion, for the truth stands out clearly from falsehood." This injunction excludes coercion from all spheres of religion—be it in relation to the decision to believe in God or not, or in relation to the choice of a religion This implies that everyone can freely choose their belief, and no one can be forced to accept Islam or abandon their original religion (cf. Ismail & Mat, 2016; Khan, 2019). Muslim leaders were committed to this principle, especially in antiquity and the Middle Ages.

In verse 99 of Chap. 10, the principle of religious freedom is further affirmed, and a new aspect is highlighted when the Quran states that if God had willed, everyone would have believed. Then it goes on to say: "The truth is from your Lord; so let him who please believe and let him who please disbelieve" (18:29). Islamic scholars consider this verse to be a general affirmation of the right (Ismail & Mat, 2016; Khan, 2019). Sequel to this, in verse 6:104, the Quran emphasises the individual's responsibility to believe or disbelieve with the following words: "[n]ow clear proof has come to you from your Lord: if anyone sees it, that will be to his advantage; if anyone is blind to it, that will be to his loss" (cf. Saeed et al., 2014). It immediately becomes clear that belief in Islam is essentially a matter of individual choice. This claim is firmly rooted in quranic anthropology, which emphasises the inherent worth and dignity of the human person (Quran 17:70). The Quran regards every human being as a creature of God, endowed with intellect and free will (Quran 95:4) and as such capable of distinguishing between right and wrong (Quran 6:104). Freedom is therefore part of human nature (Saeed, 2018; Ardelean, 2010). Building on this, Islam teaches that the issues of belief or non-belief is one of those issues that depends on one's will and inner conviction (El Sergani, 2019). It is a person's own decision and choice to belong to one religion or the other (Ismail & Mat, 2016). The use of force instead of persuasion in matters of faith, therefore, contradicts the anthropological perspectives of the Quran (Saeed, 2018).

In all this the work of Prophet Muhammad was clearly defined for him, namely to "warn" people or show them the true path (27:92; 13:40; 50:45), not "to compel them to believe" (cf. Quran 88:21–22; See also: 5:99; 10:108; 22:56–58; 39:41). He was constantly reminded never to resort to coercion when it came to conversion (cf. Moe et al., 2021). Islam has no need to compel belief in its divine truth "for the truth stands out clearly from falsehood." More importantly, Allah only accepts faith that comes from conscious decision of conscience, and not from coercion and threat (Sumbulah, 2018: 64). Religious decisions should be matters of personal choice, not a reason for state intervention (cf. Quran 24:54) because faith imposed by force is not true belief, but coercion. In many other places the Quran reiterates this idea of freedom of religion as non-compulsion in matters of faith (cf. Quran 5:99; 10:108; 11:28; 22:56–58; 39:41). Historical evidence suggests that this view was held not only by the Prophet but also by his political successors (Saeed, 2018; El Sergani, 2019). For example, it has been reported that he did not force the Quraish people, whom he defeated in the conquest of Mecca, to accept Islam.

That was not all, the Prophet is said to have practised inclusivism as a leader in Medina (Sumbulah, 2018). For instance, he recognised religious freedom in Medina's first constitution, which allowed Muslims to live together with Jews (El Sergani, 2019). He granted equal protection and equal rights to other religious adherents; they were allowed a certain degree of religious tolerance as long as they were not against Islam. This practice was observed in various Muslim empires from his time to the Umayyads, the Abbasids and the Ottomans (Saeed, 2018). This is also consistent with the Quran, which points out in 5:48 that religious diversity is a product of the divine plan (see also Quran 109:2–6). On this basis, some Muslim scholars strongly agree that the Quran advocates religious pluralism (Khan, 2019;

Saeed et al., 2014). However, in relation to 'the significant other', a differentiated treatment can be observed. Monotheist non-Muslims, particularly Jews and Christians (sometimes referred to as "People of the Book") are generally granted a high degree of freedom to practice their religion in Muslim lands (cf. Quran 3:113–114; 5:69; 5:85), while non-believers and polytheists are less tolerated and could be enslaved or even killed if they did not accept Islam (cf. Quran 9:5). Again, history shows that non-believers (identified as Kafirun) were more persecuted and punished by the leaders and believers (New World Encyclopedia, 2017; Saeed, 2018; Ardelean, 2010).

Although the Quran and hadith largely support freedom of religion, many parts of these texts have been perceived as denying it as well. An example is verse 9:29, which deals with the issue of jizyah, a tax on non-Muslims (cf. Saeed, 2018). In this verse, an intolerant attitude toward people of other faiths is evident, as the holy book proposes war against people of other religions, especially Arab pagans. An alternative reading of this and related quranic material (see 2:244; 4:89; 9:12–14) attempts to place these verses in a political context in which Muslims were not necessarily urged to wage war against opponents because they belonged to a different religious tradition per se, but because they allegedly threatened to destroy the Muslim community (cf. Saeed et al., 2014). Furthermore, the Prophet reportedly sometimes calls for the death penalty for renunciation of Islam (Saeed, 2018). Apostasy or 'ridda' remains controversial in Islam. The controversy arises from the fact that the Quran does not specify any temporal punishment for apostasy and that the Prophet appears to have allowed some converts to Islam to abandon the faith. But at the same time, proponents of the death penalty for apostasy often quoted this hadith of the Prophet: "[w]hoever changes his religion, kill him" (Sahih Al-Bukhari 9, 84, Hadith no. 57). Based on this and similar traditions, classical Islamic legal schools developed a law prescribing the death penalty for apostates, and this law is now viewed by many Muslims as divine law (cf. Saeed et al., 2014). Thus, in this age of the global movement of rights, the Muslim world guarantees religious freedom with qualification. For example, in articles 24–25 of the 1990 Cairo Declaration on Human Rights in Islam, the Organisation of Islamic Cooperation (OIC) made the validity and enjoyment of human rights dependent on the principles of Sharia and denied individuals the right to convert to another religion (Federal Foreign Office, 2021; Ziebertz, 2016). Many Muslim-majority countries guarantee religious freedom in their national laws with the understanding that Sharia law should be the supreme authority (Saeed et al., 2014: 65). As a result, Muslims and non-Muslims are punished in these states for apostasy, blasphemy and heresy. The cases of Mahmud Muhammad

Taha,[39] Nasr Abu Zayd,[40] and Nigeria's Deborah Samuel Yakubu[41] are some good examples. Individuals in such states generally experience various forms of arbitrary restrictions to their freedoms as well as religious persecutions by state and non-state actors, especially Islamic extremists. Besides, there have been repeated calls by some Islamic bodies to make freedom of religion a collective rather than an individual right because they believe that article 18 of the ICCPR is incompatible with the fundamental principles of Islam. That said, it is also important to note that most Islamic states have fully endorsed the provision and are legally committed to the ideal of religious freedom (Saeed et al., 2014; New World Encyclopedia, 2017).

Freedom of Religion in Christian Theology

The subject of religious freedom is dealt with extensively in the Bible. We find references to this in the Old and New Testaments. The first relates to the concept of human dignity. This derives equally from the biblical anthropology, in which humans are seen as created in the "image of God" and endowed with intelligence (Genesis 1:27; 5:1), and from the idea that Christ was wrapped with humanity via his incarnation. In other words, human dignity is of divine origin. This understanding of dignity is considered the basis of freedom, especially religious freedom (Little & Taliaferro, 2014; Ardelean, 2010). The second concerns the idea of conscience and its possible connection to belief in natural rights. Paul addressed the role of conscience in matters of faith in several of his letters. An example of this is his first letter to the Corinthians 10:29, where he asked rhetorically, "[w]hy should my liberty be determined by someone else's conscience?" (See also Romans 14:5). Hence, his teachings on the subject have been used to defend the concept of religious freedom as freedom of conscience (Little & Taliaferro, 2014). Another important concept is that of a good citizen. One of the biblical references in this regard is Romans 13:1–10, where Paul exhorts members of the new Christian church to respect conventional forms of socio-political control, "not only because of possible punishment but also as a matter of conscience" (see also 1 Timothy 2:1–8; 1 Peter 2:9–17). Last but not the least, Jesus' example and teachings represent a tremendous resource for religious freedom. His preference for persuasion rather than coercion, his acceptance of death over retaliation inter alia established a specific model of Christian communication that could be described as non-coercive. His instruction in Matthew 22:21—"[g]ive to Caesar what is Caesar's, and to God what is God's"—could be interpreted in terms of the principle of separation, a matter of religious liberty (Ardelean, 2010). Other teachings, such as the parable that recommends that

[39] In 1985, Sudan's President Jaafar Numeiri enforced rulings by instructing the execution of a political reformer Mahmud Muhammad Taha who was convicted of apostasy. Taha actively promoted Islamic revival throughout his life but was seen as a threat to the established social order (O'Sullivan, 2001).

[40] In 1995, Nasr Abu Zayd was found guilty of apostasy by an Egyptian Sharia Court. His marriage was annulled, and he later went on exile in The Netherlands (Zainol et al., 2014).

[41] On 12th May 2022, a female student, Deborah Samuel Yakubu, was accused of blasphemy against Islam and subsequently lynched by a mob of Muslim students in Nigeria's northwestern Sokoto State (cf. Ewang, 2022).

"wheat and weeds" can "both grow together until the harvest" (Matthew 13:30) simply legitimise tolerance, including religious tolerance (Little & Taliaferro, 2014).

The first generation of Christians brought these biblical resources together to develop their own understanding of freedom of religion as an individual natural right of all human beings. Some of the early church fathers were strong advocates of religious freedom, an issue that resonated with all Christians given the empire's attitude towards Christianity as an illegal religion. For example, the early Christian apologist Justin (ca. 100–165 AD) called on the emperor to show tolerance towards Christians (cf. Richardson, 1953). Tertullian (ca. 155–240 AD) is reportedly the first to use the term '*libertas religionis*' (Wilken, 2019). He defended the right of every person to worship according to their own convictions. With the theologian Lucius Lactantius (ca. 250–325 AD) he shared the same opinion as the young Augustine (354–430 AD) that authentic faith cannot be forced (cf. Lucius Lactantius, n.d.). Constantine's Edict of Milan (313 AD) gave Christianity legal status and respite from persecution while bringing it into close relationship with civil authority (Little & Taliaferro, 2014). The state then became the final arbiter of the distinction between correct doctrine and heresy, between true and false religion (cf. New World Encyclopedia, 2017). The church gradually "transformed from a voluntary association into a public institution" (Wilken, 2019: 26). By the time it became the official religion of the empire through the Edict of Thessalonica (380 AD), orthodox (Catholic) Christianity had evolved from a victim to a perpetrator of persecution and intolerance towards 'others' (Ardelean, 2010). In fact, it began using state power to persecute other Christians and pressure pagans to convert to Christianity. Evidence of its intolerant and assimilationist tendencies can be found in the wording of the Church's official documents from that period, for example the Athanasian Creed,[42] adopted at the Council of Nicaea (325 AD) in response to the Arian controversy.

One reason for the church's intolerant behaviour is attributed to the apparent ambivalence of Christian sacred sources, particularly the Bible, regarding religious freedom. The Old Testament contains narratives that express a commitment to the need for orthodoxy of belief. In ancient Israel, for example, a strict religious uniformity around a national religion was considered essential to the normal temporal order. Deviation from the established religious order was a civil crime punishable by death (cf. Exodus 22:20; Deuteronomy 6:14–15; 17:2–7). There are instances where righteous Old Testament people persecuted others, such as Elijah's killing of false prophets (1 Kings 18:16–46; see also Genesis 16:6; 2 Kings 18:4; 23:6–9;

[42] "Whosoever will be saved, before all things it is necessary that he hold the catholic faith. Which faith except everyone do keep whole and undefiled, without doubt he shall perish everlastingly.... This is the catholic faith, which except a man believe firmly and faithfully, he cannot be saved." This is the scholarly English rendition of the following original Latin text: "Quicunque vult salvus esse: ante omnia opus est, ut teneat catholicam fidem. Quam nisi quisque integram inviolatamque servaverit: absque dubio in æternum peribit. ... Hæc est fides catholicæ: quam nisi quisque fideliter firmiterque crediderit, salvus esse non poterit."Cf. Symbolum Quicunque: The Athanasian Creed. Creeds of Christendom, Vol. II. Available at: https://www.ccel.org/ccel/schaff/creeds2.iv.i.iv.html. Accessed on 08.08.2014.

Proverbs 23:14; 29:19). There are also many New Testament narratives that tend to legitimise the use of coercion against others. The parable of a great banquet where the host orders his servants to 'compel' all unwilling guests to attend is a typical example (Luke 14:16–23; see also Luke 4:35; Mark 1:34; 5:13; 11:15; Acts 9:1–18). The banquet was understood here as a symbol of the unity of the church and the unwilling guests as "heathen and schismatics" (cf. Little & Taliaferro, 2014: 9). The church's general understanding of these and other related texts largely determined how it dealt with those outside of the ecclesiastical institution (Ardelean, 2010). Thus, an older Augustine (in Augustin, n.d.: 637), citing the above account of the parable of the great banquet, called for "just persecution" of the Donatists in his letter to Boniface, a Roman general. Like him, another church father, Ambrose of Milan (ca. 340–397 AD), defended state intolerance towards Judaism and non-Christians. Even the theologian Thomas Aquinas (ca. 1225–1274) established a limited doctrine of freedom of conscience in which he called for civil punishment of Christian defectors (Summa Theologica II-II, Q. 11, a. 3). Such a mindset led to the Crusades (ca. 1095–1291), which can be described as a series of religious wars aimed primarily at wresting the Holy Land from Muslim control, but with hidden assimilationist motives. The same is even truer of the Inquisition.[43]

The Protestant reformers contributed significantly to the spread of the idea of religious freedom. Radical reformers, especially the Anabaptists, rejected any coercion in religious matters and the idea of the Corpus Christianum,[44] this implied a sharp separation of church and state. Mainstream reformers like Luther (1483–1546) and Calvin (1509–1564) did not go as far as the Anabaptists. Unlike the latter and other radical Christian groups (e.g., the Swiss Brethren, the Mennonites, etc.) who advocated a more expansive interpretation of freedom of conscience, Luther and Calvin held a similarly restrictive view of religious freedom as Thomas Aquinas. They were 'sacral' in their thinking in the sense that they believed that religious uniformity helped secure civil order. Basically, the sacral or 'cuius-regio-eius-religio' principle means that all persons in an area should have the same faith. They believed that a weakening of this unity would lead to disorder and disintegration. On that basis, they supported severe restrictions on freedom of conscience (Calvin, 1536; see also Ardelean, 2010; Clemen, 1967; Little & Taliaferro, 2014). This principle prevailed as a valid church-state model in the sixteenth century. Anyone who thought differently was brutally persecuted (James, 2020).

The long years of brutal religious wars in Europe led thinkers such as John Locke (1632–1704) to 'reinvent' the biblical principle of tolerance. He argued that tolerance was the key characteristic of the true church and defended the primacy of

[43] This term refers to a special ecclesiastical institution designed to combat or suppress heresy. Originally established by a papal bull in 1184, it targeted those considered to be heretics or defectors, such as the Cathars of southern France, the Waldensians, the Hussites, the Knights Templar, Spiritual Franciscans, witches (the most famous being Joan of Arc), Jews, Muslims, freethinkers, and Protestants (cf. New World Encyclopedia, 2017).

[44] This construct defined the organic unity between church and society, in which the church and state were coterminous.

conscience over church and state (Wilken, 2019). Locke's ideas played a major role in the emergence of a modern culture of religious freedom since the second half of the eighteenth century. During this period and throughout much of the twentieth century, the Roman Catholic Church disagreed with the emerging concept of religious liberty for those who practised a 'false religion,' as evidenced by papal encyclicals such as Pius VI's Quod Aliquantum (1791), Gregory XVI's Mirari Vos (1832, paras. 14–15), Pius IX's Quanta Cura (1864, para. 3) and Syllabus Errorum (1864, propositions 15, 55, 77 and 78), and Pius X's Vehementer Nos (1906, para. 3), among others. It was not until 1965 that it adopted the Second Vatican Council's Declaration on Religious Liberty, Dignitatis Humanae (hereinafter DH), which officially affirmed religious freedom as a universal right (DH no. 2). For the Catholic Church, the transition from 'the Church' to 'one of the churches' and from 'the true religion' to 'one of the religions' may not have been easy. Be that as it may, the Church still insists: "[w]e believe that this one true religion subsists in the Catholic and Apostolic Church …" (DH no. 1).

3.2 Right to Freedom from Discrimination Based on Sexual Orientation

Attitudes towards sexual diversity vary in different societies. Societies differ in their perceptions of proper and improper sexual conduct. Most modern societies are shaped by heterosexuality. For this reason, heterosexual practices tend to be seen as the natural order and homosexual activities as unnatural. For example, homosexuality is considered unacceptable in many countries in Africa, Asia and Latin America, while attitudes towards homosexuality are somewhat more tolerant in the West. But in all, most people tend to view homosexuality as abnormal. As a sexual orientation, it is outlawed in many cultures and homosexuals face all sorts of discrimination. Given this widespread unfriendly social context, they remained closeted for centuries. The last few decades have witnessed a phenomenal change in attitudes towards homosexuality around the world. This development has been attributed to various factors, such as a perceived increase in the visibility of homosexuals and their political activism since the later part of the twentieth century. The term 'homosexuals' or 'gays' ordinarily refers to lesbigay individuals, but it is used here as an umbrella term for other sexual minorities.

Although the origin of homophile movements can be traced back to the 1950s or an earlier date, most scholars believe that the modern gay rights movement began with the Stonewall confrontations between the New York city police and some homosexuals in 1969 (Ghaziani et al., 2016). Shortly after this incident, the Gay Liberation Front (GLF) was formed in New York, followed by other similar movements in different cities and educational institutions across the US. These movements held a series of protests demanding an end to discrimination against homosexuals. As a front, they adopted an anti-capitalist stance and attacked traditional ideas about family and gender roles, which they perceived as basic heteronormative structures. In 1970, they held the first-ever Gay Freedom Day parades at the one-year anniversary of the Stonewall riots, and homosexuals stepped out of their closets and into the streets to identify themselves as such and challenge the existing heteronormative space. By this time, as D'Emilio (2002, in Ghaziani et al., 2016: 173) aptly puts it, "[t]he world finally did turn and notice the gay folks in its midst." Emboldened by the Stonewall feat, gay rights movements gradually sprang up around the world, especially in much of North America and Western Europe, and homosexuals began to demand for societal acceptance and cultural assimilation.

Over the past three decades, the size of homosexuals worldwide has increased exponentially and a wealth of quantitative data on sexuality has been generated. However, the exact proportion of people in same-sex romantic relationships worldwide is difficult to estimate because intolerance towards homosexuals persists in many countries. Nevertheless, in the US, for instance, it is on record that 3.5 percent or approximately 9 million of the adult population identified themselves as lesbigay individuals in 2011 (Gates, 2011). A 2016 study by the Dalia Research, which involved 11,754 people across nine EU countries, puts the proportion of persons who identify as homosexual at 5.9 percent, the range being 7.4 percent in Germany up to 1.5 percent in Hungary (cf. Lam, 2016). Similar data are also available from countries such as South Africa, Australia, Bangladesh, India, and New Zealand, all of which suggest that the population of homosexuals worldwide is on the increase and is expected to increase even more with time given estimates of more young people. Thus, there have been some advancements in the rights of homosexuals in recent decades due to their increasing visibility and activism, as well as pressure from the UN Human Rights Committee and international human rights NGOs. Their right to exist is now generally recognised. Some countries have enacted anti-discrimination laws and homosexuals are entitled to equal treatment in employment practices, housing, and public policy. In addition, same-sex union has been legalised in several countries since the turn of the twenty-first century. As of March 2020, same-sex union is lawful in about 30 countries, including for instance the Netherlands (2001), South Africa (2006), England, Wales and Scotland (2014), Ireland (2015), the US (2015), Germany (2017), and Northern Ireland (2020). In spite of these improvements, human rights violations on account of the sexual orientation and gender identity persist in some corners of the globe, including Nigeria.

As in other societies, homosexual behaviour has always existed in Nigeria, despite claims to the contrary. Reliable evidence for the existence of such conducts in pre-colonial traditional cultures of Nigeria is well documented (Igwe, 2008; Nwoko, 2012). Unfortunately, the prevalence of gender identities such as 'female husbands' among the Yoruba and Igbo tribes in the south and transvestites (yan daudu) among the Hausa ethnic group in the north, etc. are often cited to support this view. Granted, to an outsider these relationships or behaviours may seem more like homosexuality, but in these cultures or even to the people who engage in them, they mean something different. Among the Igbos, for example, the practice essentially served to ensure the perpetuation of the paternal lineage in such a case where a girl was the only child. Nevertheless, there is enough evidence to show that same-sex sexual relations have always existed and still exist in the country, albeit closeted due to the social aversion to such unconventional forms of intimacy. The International Centre for Reproductive Sexual Rights (hereinafter Increse) study, which surveyed 5626 Nigerians in 2009, found that 4.3 percent (or about 240 respondents) indicated having had same-sex sexual advances. The study further reveals that most respondents (97.1%) consider homosexuality to be abnormal and homosexual practices to be unacceptable (91.8%). In 2013, the estimate of those who believe homosexuality should not be accepted by society rose to around 98 percent, according to a report from the Pew Survey on the Global Divide on Homosexuality. These findings do not represent the official national estimates but provide vital information about the existence of homosexuality and general attitudes towards it in the country. Homosexuality is an unpopular sexual orientation in Nigeria. Most Nigerians tend to be heterosexuals and as such homosexuals are considered deviant and sometimes even obsessed. As Izugbara (2004: 6) notes, "[h]omosexuals dwell at the very margins of respectability in the larger Nigerian public imaginary" in consequence and are subjected to all forms of ill-treatments, including sometimes the death penalty. This intolerant attitude, it has been argued, is largely based on socio-cultural considerations (Igwe, 2008; Increse Report, 2009; Pew Report, 2013).

But then, Nigeria is a secular state, at least in principle. So, before we get down to the basic facts of the situation, let us first examine the legal status of homosexuality in the country because we imagine that the position of the Nigerian law on this issue would provide more reliable information about the national culture on sexualities.

3.2.1 The Legal Status of Homosexuality in Nigeria

Since the 7th January 2014 when the Same Sex Marriage (Prohibition) Act 2013 (hereinafter SSMPA) was signed into law, the legal status of homosexuality in the country is no longer a secret. However, the issue of same-sex relations had been addressed under the Nigerian law before the Act came into being, precisely in the Nigerian Penal and Criminal Codes.[45] Under section 214 of Chapter 21, the Criminal Code bans carnal knowledge against the order of nature and prescribes a fourteen-year prison term for the offence. The Code also considers any attempt to commit

[45] The Penal and Criminal Codes are some of the abiding legacies of Nigeria's colonial past. The Criminal Code of 1916 was made applicable to the whole of Nigeria by the British government after the amalgamation of the Northern and Southern Protectorates in 1914. But the application of the Criminal Code was soon restricted to the south, following intense advocacy by the northern Muslims who claimed that it was suitable only for a Christian society based on its British Christian origins. Therefore, the Penal Code was enacted for Northern Nigeria in 1959, but it came into force in 1960. Both Codes have undergone several amendments and are still part of Nigeria's penal system, as Criminal Code Act Cap. C38 LFN 2004 (hereinafter CCA) and Penal Code (Northern States) Federal Provisions Act Cap. P3 LFN 2004 (hereinafter PC).

such an act to be a felony punishable on conviction with a seven-year prison term.[46] Likewise, procuring another male person for same-sex activities or attempting to do so personally in public or private is also a crime. The Code calls it "gross indecency" and attaches a three-year prison sentence to it in the event of violation.[47] The Penal Code has similar provisions but with heavier sanctions. In section 284, the offence of having "carnal intercourse against the order of nature with a man, woman or an animal" attracts a jail term of up to fourteen years as a penalty. The term "order of nature" is understood in the above provisions to refer to penile penetration of a vagina. This implies that any sexual intimacy outside this form of heterosexual sex, including the use of sex toys, oral and anal penetration would qualify in this context as unnatural. Lastly, there is also a provision relating to cross-dressing under section 405(2)(e). The Penal Code considers a male cross-dresser to be a vagabond and stipulates a jail term of up to 2 years, a fine, or both for such (section 407). In addition to these, same-sex conduct and activities are criminalised by the Sharia codes applicable in several northern States. Therefore, consensual homosexual acts between adults are illegal under previously existing laws in Nigeria.

Building on these legislations, the country enacted the SSMPA in 2014 with far-reaching provisions. The SSMPA prohibits marriage contracts or civil unions between persons of the same sex in Nigeria, regardless of where these were contracted (see section 1). It further prohibits any cohabitation between same-sex sexual partners in the country and emphasises instead that only the union between a man and a woman would be regarded as valid in Nigeria (sections 3 and 7). By virtue of these provisions, all such unions contracted elsewhere by Nigerian citizens or other persons residing in the country are effectively nullified [section 1(2)]. A defiance of this ban is an offence punishable with a fourteen-year prison term [section 5(1)]. Furthermore, the Act forbids any public show of same-sex amorous relationship [section 4(2)]. Persons who officiate, or witness to same-sex marriages are deemed to have committed a crime. The formation of gay clubs, associations or organisations under any pretext is outlawed [section 4(1)]. A ten-year jail term is extended to all these offences [section 5(2) and (3)]. Advocacy for gay rights is equally illegal in Nigeria under Section 5(2) of the Act. This provision effectively bans all forms of activity supporting or promoting the human rights of sexual minorities and prescribes a ten-year prison sentence for offenders.

Given that consensual same-sex relationships between adults were already prohibited under previously existing laws, one wonders why the introduction of the SSMPA was necessary. In this context, it was noted that the Codes were limited to same-sex activities and did not address the issue of gay marriage or union. The purpose of the SSMPA is therefore to prohibit same-sex marriages or civil unions and to impose criminal penalties for violations. Unconventional sexualities are also comprehensively criminalised, gay associations banned and punishments imposed for gay rights' advocacy (Adebanjo, 2015; Human Rights Watch, 2016).

---

[46] See section 215 of the Criminal Code Act Cap. C38 LFN 2004.

[47] Ibid., section 217.

Incompatibility of Nigeria's Anti-homosexuality Laws with Human Rights Principles

The provisions of the SSMPA and other anti-homosexuality laws contravene the basic principles of the Nigerian Constitution as the nation's supreme law. The Constitution protects a set of fundamental human rights such as the rights to dignity, personal liberty, due process, private and family life, expression, and the rights to freely assemble and associate with other persons for the protection of one's interest. Section 42 provides that no citizen of Nigeria may be unfairly treated based on his or her social attributes. The above anti-homosexuality laws not only contravene these constitutional provisions but are also inconsistent with the terms of several regional and international human rights treaties that Nigeria has ratified, which obligate her to protect all persons within her territory, including homosexuals, from all forms of violence.

Indeed, the primary obligation of the State is the security of all individuals within its territory and subject to its jurisdiction. As the country's foremost human rights instrument, the Constitution provides in section 33 for the fundamental human right to life and the possible exceptions to the State's duty to protect life. The right to life is also protected under article 6 of the ICCPR and article 4 of the African Charter. Therefore, by imposing a capital punishment on sodomy (liwāṭ) in section 131, for instance, the Zamfara Penal Code directly contradicts the country's human rights obligation in this regard at the national, regional, and international levels. The right to life is not just about taking life. Rather, it includes "the protection of both life and limb" (Increse Report, 2009: 126). The media is awash with stories of threats to the lives and bodily integrity of homosexuals. Research has shown that sexual minorities in the country are often subjected to ill-treatments despite the provisions of the Constitution (section 34), the ICCPR (article 7) and the African Charter (article 5) that guarantee the right to dignity of the human person and prohibit torture or inhuman and degrading treatment. To achieve this right to dignity, therefore, there is need to understand homosexuality as a sexual orientation and to prohibit acts that dehumanise individuals because of their orientations. The UN Human Rights Committee sees the ban on torture as a way to protect the right to dignity.[48] For this reason, in May 2014, the African Commission adopted a resolution, in which it reaffirmed the right to dignity of the sexual out-group and condemned all forms of violence against them.[49] The Violence against Persons (Prohibition) Act 2015 (hereinafter VAPP Act) recently passed by the Nigerian National Assembly also broadly captures this point.[50]

The right to private and family life is another fundamental right violated by anti-homosexuality laws. It is guaranteed under section 37 of the Constitution and article 17 of the ICCPR. The SSMPA violates this right by criminalising same-sex

[48] See CCPR/C/GC/20, 10th March 1992, para. 2.

[49] See ACHPR/Res.275 (LV) 2014.

[50] See VAPP Act, 25th May 2015. Available at: https://www.refworld.org/docid/556d5eb14.html. Accessed 30.04.2020.

marriage and the public show of same-sex amorous relationships under sections 1(1) and 4(2), respectively. The same applies to sections 215 and 217 of the Criminal Code. The right to privacy is not an absolute right. The Constitution in section 45 outlines some of the conditions under which the enjoyment of this right can be circumscribed to include, inter alia, concerns for public morality and public health. These terms do not lend themselves to easy interpretation, not even in the country's human rights enforcement law. In order to interpret public morality as a permissible limitation on human rights, for instance, the Sub-Commission on Prevention of Discrimination and Protection of Minorities of the UN Economic and Social Council (hereinafter ECOSOC) referred to the Siracusa Principles on the Limitation and Derogation of Provisions in the ICCPR (hereinafter Siracusa Principles), which defines it in terms of what is "essential to the maintenance of respect for fundamental values of the community."[51] Based on this, it could be argued that the ban on the open display of same-sex romantic relationships is appropriate in the Nigerian context, where open discussion about sex is a taboo. But then, what goes on in the privacy of a home between two consenting adults is a private affair, and for anyone to interfere in that matter would constitute an arbitrary invasion of the right to privacy.[52] Marriage, by contrast, is a matter of public morality because it is a social institution, especially in Nigeria, where it affects not only the two consenting adults but also their families and extended families, as well as the community at large. Notwithstanding this social aspect, declaring null and void same-sex unions contracted elsewhere by all persons in Nigeria, including gay foreigners, is tantamount to overstretching the principle of public morality beyond bounds. Little wonder the passage of the Act was immediately followed by massive reactions on the international scene (Adebanjo, 2015). Then, from a public health perspective, existing data show that homosexuals have a higher risk of HIV infection. In fact, according to the Nigeria National Agency for the Control of AIDS (hereinafter NACA), 32 percent of new infections in the country are attributable to men who have sex with men (MSM) and their partners (NACA, 2015, in Human Rights Watch, 2016). NACA maintains, in spite of this, that heterosexual relationships remain the main route of HIV transmission in the country, meaning that the public health principles do not seem to justify the introduction of anti-homosexuality laws.

The Constitution has provisions on discrimination, though it does not define the term. In section 42, it provides for the non-discrimination against persons based on sex. It has to be noted from the onset that sex here refers strictly to biological characteristics, and not to sexual orientation. In fact, the latter is not enumerated as a prohibited ground for discrimination, neither does the Constitution include the usual all-encompassing phrase 'other status' anywhere in its provisions (Adebanjo, 2015; Adejugbe & Adejugbe, 2018). This phrase embraces effectively sexual orientation, or HIV status, etc. However, the African Charter as domesticated

[51] See UN. Doc. E/CN.4/1985/4, 28th Sept. 1984, para. 27.

[52] See UN. Doc CCPR/C/50/D/488/1992, 31st March 1994, section 8.2.

incorporates the said phrase 'other status'[53] in its anti-discrimination clause (article 2) and the ICCPR (articles 2 and 26), as well as some other instruments to which Nigeria is a state party. The phrase embraces effectively sexual orientation or HIV status. Apart from these, in the case *Toonen vs. Australia*, the Human Rights Committee held that the references to sex in articles 2(1) and 26 of the ICCPR have to be taken to include sexual orientation.[54] The courts in Nigeria are yet to adhere to this resolution. Instead, homosexuals are still being unfairly treated in many areas of public life via, for instance, expulsion from academic institutions, labour market and public policy discriminations. The country's legislations, especially the SSMPA, authorise this contrary to her human rights obligations.

Furthermore, there is a clear conflict between the domestic anti-homosexuality laws and the fundamental rights to freedom of expression, assembly and association for all without discrimination. The Constitution provides for these rights in sections 39 and 40, respectively. They are also guaranteed by the African Charter (articles 9, 10 and 11) and the ICCPR (articles 19, 21 and 22). By endorsing these instruments, Nigeria commits to ensuring that all its citizens and residents enjoy these rights and that permissible restrictions are not imposed in a discriminatory manner. That said, sections 1(1)(a) and 5(1) of the SSMPA, sections 215 and 217 of the Criminal Code and section 284 of the Penal Code, all of which prohibit and prescribe penalties for same-sex practices, violate the right of some persons to express their sexual orientation. This right is also breached by the ban on the formation of gay clubs under section 5(2) of the SSMPA. By prohibiting and criminalising the registration of gay clubs under sections 4(1) and 5(2) and (3), the SSMPA also contravenes the right of persons to form an association to protect their interests. And to bar homosexuals from coming together for advocacy purposes on account of their sexual orientation or gender identity constitutes simultaneous breaches of the non-discrimination, expression, assembly, and association principles. Of course, these rights are not absolute rights, but their restrictions must comply with the general principles of necessity and proportionality.

Lastly, the right to health is an internationally recognised socio-economic human right. It is protected under international law by article 16 of the African Charter and article 12 of the ICESCR. State parties are obliged to protect the health of their citizens and provide them with adequate medical attention in the event of sickness. The Committee on Economic, Social and Cultural Rights (CESCR) stipulates in its General Comment no. 14 on the right to the highest attainable standard of health[55] that quality health services should be accessible to everyone[56] and proscribes discrimination in access to healthcare on any grounds at all, including sexual

---

[53] This phrase can be seen in other instruments, such as article 2 of the African Charter, articles 2(1) and 3 of the ICCPR, and article 2 of the Universal Declaration.

[54] See UN. Doc CCPR/C/50/D/488/1992, 31st March 1994, section 8.7.

[55] See UN Doc. E/C.12/2000/4, 11th August 2000.

[56] Ibid., para. 12(b).

orientation and other status.[57] By imposing a prison sentence in section 5(3) on persons who might aid or support same-sex union and romantic relationships, the SSMPA compromised the right to health of homosexuals, especially those living with HIV/AIDs. This is because individual health workers or organisations providing necessary healthcare services to the key affected population, among whom are homosexuals, may be unwilling to help them for fear of prosecution by the State. That way, the access to the best attainable healthcare services of these persons is curtailed. Access to health for all HIV/AID patients including homosexuals is particularly relevant in Nigeria, where a relationship between the high prevalence of HIV/AIDs among homosexuals and criminalisation of homosexuality has been suggested (Human Rights Watch, 2016). Criminalising sexuality makes it difficult for the sexual out-group members to assess relevant HIV-healthcare services. It also leads to abuses that result in these people being pushed further into the closet, with serious consequences for the victims themselves and for the country in its efforts to contain the spread of the epidemic (Adebanjo, 2015). For reasons such as these, the African Commission on Human and Peoples' Rights in 2015 urged the Nigerian government to review the SSMPA to stem the ever-rising tide of discriminations against the sexual out-group in the country and ensure access to relevant HIV-healthcare services for all (Human Rights Watch, 2016).

For all its contributions, the question of whether the introduction of the SSMPA was necessary or not can be answered by considering its societal import.

3.2.2 Social Implications of Nigeria's Anti-homosexuality Laws

Homosexuals or persons suspected of being homosexuals have always faced all manners of discrimination in Nigeria, such as social stigmatisation, ritual purification, intimidation, lashing, destruction of homes and property, and exclusions. In some parts of the country, they could be put to death, although there is limited evidence that this ever took place. There is no comprehensive record of the experiences of homosexuals in the pre-SSMPA era, but there is sufficient evidence of the prevalence of intolerance towards this sexual out-group. Intolerance drove them into the closets, compelling them to some form of self-censorship. Although there were laws prohibiting same-sex practices at the time, members of the public were largely intolerant due to their religious beliefs and their perceptions of African culture and sexual mores (Adebanjo, 2015; Human Rights Watch, 2016).

Then came the SSMPA in 2014 and its impact was both severe and instant. In many ways, the Act appeared to have officially authorised abuses against homosexuals, thereby exacerbating their plight. First, the debates and media interests that greeted this legislation made homosexuals more visible and vulnerable than usual.

[57] Ibid., para. 18.

The law itself has been used as a tool by some police officers and members of the public to abuse the rights of the sexual out-group. Homosexuals and human rights groups have since reported a surge in the crackdown by the state and non-state actors on them and suspected homosexuals in the wake of this legislation. For instance, Human Rights Watch (2016) reported an attack on about 14 men in Gishiri village in Abuja in 2014, barely one month after the passage of the Act. These were dragged from their homes and severely beaten by a group of about 50 well-armed people on the mere suspicion of being gay. In July of the same year, the police in Lagos arrested about 70 persons, including 13 minors at a hotel party where the police alleged that homosexual activities took place, and in August the hotel owner and two staff members were arraigned for aiding and abetting homosexual activities in violation of section 5(2) of the SSMPA. Notably, this was the first time a formal accusation had been made by the government under the SSMPA (Human Rights Report, 2013). Similar incidents reoccurred in Lagos, sometime in November, but also in other places such as Bauchi and Ibadan in May 2015, where individuals were reportedly apprehended, detained and released on bail by the police only after money had been extorted from them (Human Rights Watch, 2016).

Discrimination against homosexuals under the SSMPA has not yet abated in Nigeria. This usually manifests itself in physical, psychological or sexual violence and the denial of rights. No known SSMPA-based convictions have been made by the courts to date. But the Act has created a general climate of fear and self-censorship for sexual minorities, increased their isolation and, in some cases, eventually compelled them to conform to conventional lifestyles (Human Rights Watch, 2016). Furthermore, it foreclosed the possibility of supporting or promoting the rights of sexual minorities. Gay rights activists and human rights defenders in Nigeria have reported that since the passage of the 2013 SSMPA, they have been subjected to hostilities by members of the public who accuse them of bringing 'western ideas' to Nigeria. To buttress this point, Human Rights Watch (2016) reports a 2014 incident in which the police raided an HIV awareness event in Abuja and arrested 12 participants in the programme for allegedly promoting homosexuality. They were detained in police custody for about three weeks and had to pay heavily for their release. In a word, the SSMPA made a bad situation worse for homosexuals in Nigeria. It emboldened the state security operatives and the public to act out their homophobia without any fear of legal consequences (Human Rights Watch, 2016). Because of this single legislation, Nigeria has been described as a homophobic nation.

3.2.3 Religion and Homosexuality

Religion is of course a source of moral discourse. In Nigeria, it plays a vital role in private and public morality, including the issue of sexual orientation. The three main religious traditions in the country represent a potent sexual-moral discourse. In the following part, we explore their positions in the discourse on homosexuality.

Homosexuality in ATR

In Africa, sex is a complex topic that is rarely discussed. Sexuality was defined in terms of reproduction. A person's sexual identity was constructed according to their sexual role. Those who performed the act of penetration were considered 'real men' and the recipients 'women' (Msibi, 2011). In other words, sexual identity was categorised along classic binary gender roles. However, this assertion is in no way intended to support the so-called "myth of heterosexual Africa," as ethnographic and historical studies provide evidence of same-sex relationships in pre-colonial African societies. In their opinion, the evidence can be found in paintings, customs, healing methods and punishments (cf. Baum, 1995; Epprecht, 2004; Igwe, 2008; Murray, 2019; Murray & Will, 1998; Nwoko, 2012). Homosexual acts reportedly occurred in pre-colonial Africa but were kept secret due to public perception. Homosexuality was seen as a perversion of morally acceptable patterns of marriage. Marriage was usually "a union between a man and a woman, purposely designed as a framework for procreation and perpetuation of the human race" (Amusan et al., 2019:46f). Same-sex activities are then perceived as a cultural distortion because they lack the basic intent of sexual union, namely procreation. Furthermore, such unconventional forms of intimacy are believed to have the potential to destroy local traditions and heterosexual family values. As such, they are relatively unacceptable, and their supporters are treated with contempt.

This is exactly the situation in Nigeria (Adejuwon, 2020). Heterosexuality is the only acceptable sexual practice across the local cultures, and the purpose of sexual union is procreation. Although the perception of sex in the country has evolved over time, Nigerian cultures still place great emphasis on childbearing, which can only be ensured through heterosexual relationships as a fruitful sexual behaviour. Heterosexuality is also considered a 'cultural artifice' in Nigeria. The reason for this is that it encompasses a set of values and gender relations that fit well with the dominant social system of patriarchy (Izugbara, 2004). Viewed from this cultural perspective, it is very unlikely that homosexuality would be seen as an alternative sexual orientation, essentially equivalent to heterosexuality. Instead, it is perceived as unnatural and unproductive and a threat to the survival of the community. There is currently a general aversion to the practice in Nigeria, and persons caught engaging in the act may be punished in a variety of ways, such as payment of fines, performance of ritual cleansing, and banishment from the community. These may vary slightly in different parts or regions of the country (Increse Report, 2009).

Homosexuality in Islamic Tradition

The beliefs of Muslims on issues of homosexuality cannot be easily summed up because Islam is not a homogeneous faith. Although the basic tenets are the same everywhere, different cultures and regions have influenced different manifestations and perceptions of the Islamic religion (Hendricks, 2010). Besides, Islam has no central governing body. This allows communities and individuals to make their own decisions on issues. The traditional Abrahamic religions of this world are less tolerant of homosexuality. Their sacred texts contain passages that have been interpreted as a rejection of homosexual relationships (Ananyev & Poyker, 2020). Islam belongs to this group. Admittedly the word 'homosexuality' does not appear in the Quran, but there are terms that have been construed as homosexual practices (Rehman & Polymenopoulou, 2013). For instance, homosexuals are reportedly referred to as "qaum Lut", meaning Lot's people (Kligerman, 2007:53). The term relates to the story of Lot and Sodom in the Quran. Based on this, same-sex relationships were defined as sodomy in Islam. Apart from verse 4:15, where it is referred to outside the context of Sodom, homosexuality is mentioned throughout the Quran solely in the context of this story. A traditional reading of the story along with other relevant verses (Quran 7:80–84; 26:166; 29:28–29) shows that the Quran is clearly against homosexual practices. The Quran presents Islam as a religion of nature. It advocates heterosexuality as the natural order of things and disapproves of all unconventional sexual inclinations. Islam supports heteronormative sexual behaviour with the effect of procreation. Conversely, sexual relations between people of the same sex are viewed as a deviation from Allah's will, threatening Muslims with extinction (Kligerman, 2007). It is therefore proscribed, and punishment prescribed for such a conduct (cf. Quran 4:16; 7:80–84; 26:162–68). However, the Quran does not specify what form of punishment should be meted out for consensual homosexual or lesbian activities (Rehman & Polymenopoulou, 2013). While the Quran vaguely describes the punishments associated with homosexuality, the Ulama (Islamic scholars) and the community resort to the hadith, which quotes the Prophet as saying: "[w]hoever you find doing as the people of Lot did, kill the one who does it and the one to whom it is done." (Sunan Ibn Majah Volume 3, Book 20, Hadith 2561). Here homosexuality is clearly no longer just viewed as a sin, but also as a crime and, moreover, as a crime under Hadd punishment (cf. Martin, 1997).

Given the vagueness of the Quran regarding homosexuality and the ambiguity of Sharia law in its interpretation of the authoritative sources on the subject, the details of punishments for homosexual acts were worked out by Islamic jurists based on resources from the sacred texts. All major Islamic schools of thought criminalise homosexuality as sodomy or carnal intercourse against the order of nature and as the equivalent of an adulterous act. All, except the Hanafi school in Sunni Islam, agree that it is punishable by death provided the evidentiary requirements are met. But they differ in terms of method or style of execution (Hendricks, 2010; Ahmadi, 2012; Rehman & Polymenopoulou, 2013; Kligerman, 2007). For the Hanafi school, homosexual behaviour is considered a slightly less serious offense and is punished with corporal punishment at the discretion of the ruling authorities. But even at this school the death penalty can be imposed on a persistent offender. In Nigeria in particular, Sharia categorized same-sex desires and acts between men as sodomy (liwāṭ),[58] and that between women as lesbianism (siḥāq).[59] For the former, rajm (death by stoning, a symbol of the brimstones used to destroy Sodom and Gomorrah) was imposed if the offence was committed by married men,[60] whereas the same

[58] See chapter 8 section 130 of the Zamfara Penal Code.

[59] Ibid., section 134.

[60] Ibid., section 131.

offence by women was punished with flogging or imprisonment.[61] Due to the different criminal laws of different states, lesbianism could also be punished with the death penalty depending on the marital status of the perpetrator and the state[62] in which the crime is committed (see Increse Report, 2009).

Over the past two decades, revisionist Muslim scholars have attempted to propose a tolerant Islamic approach to the issue of homosexual sexual orientation based on essentialist epistemology (see, for example, Alipour, 2017), and the process is still ongoing. In the meantime, Islamic theology fundamentally denounces same-sex desires and acts portraying them as an unnatural desire and a perversion of the natural aim of sexual activity, respectively.

Homosexuality in Christian Tradition

The Christian discourse on sexuality is basically similar to that of Islam. To begin with, the word 'homosexuality' does not appear in the original Bible, either. As in Islam, it is defined as 'sodomy' in reference to the biblical account of Sodom and Gomorrah (cf. Genesis 19: 5), but this link is still being debated (cf. Nkosi & Masson, 2017; Adejuwon, 2020). The Bible is the decisive text on which Christians base their understanding of sexuality. At the heart of the Christian narrative about sexuality is the belief that heterosexuality is divine, natural, and essentially procreative (cf. Genesis 1:28; 2:18; Matthew 19:4). As Izugbara (2004:15) aptly puts it," [t]he belief that God created them Adam and Eve, and not Adam and Steve, is used as narrative basis to inscribe heterosexuality with normality." At the same time, homosexuality is framed in categorical terms as an aberrant sexual orientation. The Bible outrightly condemns both male and female same-sex practices in Romans chapter 1, verses 26 and 27. The condemnation is reinforced in other letters of the Apostle Paul (1 Corinthians 6:9–10; 1 Timothy 1:9–11). The Code of Holiness (Leviticus 17–26) not only condemns homosexuality as an unnatural relationship but also identifies it as "an abomination" deserving capital punishment (Leviticus 20:13; 18:22).

Based on these scriptural texts and their attendant early Christian teachings, much of Christianity condemns same-sex sexual relations and teaches that such behaviour is immoral. Certain Roman Christian emperors over the centuries brutally persecuted those who indulged in homosexual relations,[63] and this led to 'a culture of intolerance' towards homosexuals among many Christian denominations (Ananyev & Poyker, 2020). The Roman Catholic Church, for example, views homosexual acts as "intrinsically disordered [and] … contrary to the natural law" (CCC no. 2357). It does not recognise such unions and even refuses to bless them, considering the practice illicit (cf. Congregation for the Doctrine of the Faith, 1965). According to the Catechism of the Catholic Church (hereinafter CCC), the Catholic

[61] Ibid., section 135.

[62] For instance, section 132 of the Kebbi Penal Code (2000) makes no such distinction, as all offenders in this regard are to be stoned to death. Maybe, in Bauchi State too (see section 134 of the Bauchi Penal Code 2001).

[63] See, for example, the Codex Theodosianus, which inter alia called for homosexuals to be subjected to "avenging flames".

Church bases its disapproval on the principles of complementarity and openness to fecundity of the sexual act, which it does not do justice to. Nevertheless, the Church urges respect for homosexuals and condemns "[e]very sign of unjust discrimination" against them (CCC no. 2358). Martin Luther also believed that homosexuality is was inconsistent with God's plan for humanity. He termed it a "monstrous depravity" (Pelikan, 1958, in Ananyev & Poyker, 2020: 6). With him, some Protestant churches oppose same-sex relations. In contrast to him, many Protestant denominations accept homosexuality. They do not consider it theological sinfully, as long as the practices do not dehumanise or demean the people involved (cf. Cooper & Kit Dorey, 2016). In a recent development, some Protestant denominations allow gay clergy, and offer blessings for same-sex marriage. For example, the Anglican Communion in New Hampshire appointed an openly gay bishop in 2003.[64] That same year, a gay man, Gene Robinson, was elected bishop of the Episcopal Church in the US. However, both incidents were met with mixed reactions within the two churches (Adejuwon, 2020; Ananyev & Poyker, 2020). Thus, the Protestant community, and indeed the various Christian denominations, are divided on the issue of same-sex practices, with some supporting it and others opposing it, depending on how they interpret the Bible. For their part, an overwhelming majority of Nigerian Christians denounce same-sex intimacy as sinful and un-Christian and do not advocate the acceptance of homosexuality (Adejuwon, 2020; Dickson, 2014; Izugbara, 2004).

3.3 The Right to Life

3.3.1 Right to Life in the Global Context

Although it had been in the US Declaration of Independence since 1776, the right to life was only enshrined in a global instrument for the first time in 1948 through its inclusion in the Universal Declaration. In article 3 of this document, the UN General Assembly states in precise and unequivocal terms that "[e]veryone has the right to life, liberty and security of person." The right to life is a fundamental human right. Life is a precondition for the enjoyment of all human rights. As such the right to life is elaborated in a vast array of human rights treaties. For instance, the European Convention for the Protection of Human Rights and Fundamental Freedoms (1950) specifies this right in article 2 with a solemnly promise, as follows: "[e]veryone's right to life shall be protected by law. No one shall be deprived of his life intentionally save in the execution of a sentence of a court following his conviction of a crime for which this penalty is provided by law." The American Convention on Human Rights (1969) makes a similar provision when it states in article 4, thus: "[e]very person has the right to have his life respected. This right

[64] See The Guardian, 14th September 2003. *Anglicans Face Schism Over Gay Row*. Available at: https://www.theguardian.com/uk/2003/sep/14/religion.world. Retrieved on 01.08.2018.

shall be protected by law and, in general, from the moment of conception. No one shall be arbitrarily deprived of his life." The provision here is nuanced by the introduction of an additional detail 'from the moment of conception' to its formulation. This feature, however, does not detract from the main idea of the right, but rather it serves to emphasise this aspect of the right based on contextual considerations. The African Charter (1981) also guarantees the right to life for all persons in article 4 using relatively similar terms: "[h]uman beings are inviolable. Every human being shall be entitled to respect for his life and the integrity of his person. No one may be arbitrarily deprived of this right." Again, although conceptually similar to others, this guarantee chooses to highlight another equally important dimension of the right, namely the "integrity of the person," which is likely based on certain historical experiences such as slavery and colonialism. Lastly, the Arab Charter on Human Rights (ACHR), adopted by the Council of the League of Arab States in 2004, also affirmatively refers to the same right in article 5, in the exact words of the ICCPR, which states that every human being has the inherent right to life, that this right shall be protected by law and that no one shall be arbitrarily deprived of his [or her] life. It follows, therefore, from the foregoing that the right to life is universally recognised as a precious right and that it is foundational to the practice of human rights.

The commitment to the protection of the right to life needs to be understood comprehensively, and not restrictively as is often the case. UN HRC (2018) underscores this point in paragraph 3 of its General Comment no. 36 on the right to life as recognised in Article 6 of the ICCPR.[65] Then the Committee goes on to clarify the nature of the right to life to include the entitlement of individuals to be free from acts and omissions that may lead to arbitrary loss of life and to enjoy a life with dignity. The African Commission on Human and Peoples' Rights (hereinafter African Commission) also did not miss the point in paragraph 3 of its General Comment no.3 on the right to life as recognised in Article 4 of the African Charter when it interpreted the right to include "the protection not only of life in a narrow sense, but of dignified life." As with human rights in general, the concept of human dignity and the respect for human life are inherently connected. This relationship is recognised in several human rights declarations, including for instance, the Universal Declaration (in articles 1 and 3), the ICCPR (in its Preamble and article 6), and the African Charter (in articles 4 and 5). When properly understood, therefore, the right to life means not only the adoption of adequate preventive measures to protect the life of the individual from arbitrary deprivation and life-threatening situations, but also the positive obligation to promote the enjoyment of a life with dignity. This imposes certain obligations on all and sundry, most especially the state. The sentence following the provision of the right to life in article 6(1) of the ICCPR provides that the right to life "shall be protected by law." This implies, among other things, that the protection of life is primarily a state obligation. On the one hand, this

[65] See CCPR/C/GC/36, 30th October 2018.

obligation requires the state to prevent arbitrary deprivation of life by both state[66] and non-state actors.[67] It extends to individuals in particularly vulnerable situations, including detainees. The state must protect them from violence and self-harm and provide them with the necessary medical care.[68] In the event of attempted or unlawful deprivations of life, the state must investigate and bring perpetrators of such incidents to book and provide effective remedy to victims, including, where appropriate, their relatives.[69] The use of lethal force is permitted to protect life from an imminent danger. But the application of force by the state must adhere to the principles of necessity and proportionality.[70] On the other hand, the state is required to design measures to ensure access to food and other essentials for well-being.[71] The state should also develop plans to address issues of natural and man-made disasters.[72] It should establish a functional health system, improve access to medical care, and eliminate discriminatory practices which debar individuals from seeking healthcare.[73] In a nutshell, the state should not only ward off threats to life, but it is also obliged to take positive action, so that people can live a good life (Ziebertz & Zaccaria, 2019).

Indeed, the right to life relates to a wide variety of issues, as we can see. However, in the context of human rights, it is not "the question of what a good life should be" that is the primary concern, but rather the question of whether the strict obligation to protect life could be restricted or even suspended under any circumstance (Ziebertz & Zaccaria, 2019: 1). Having said that, it has to be noted that the fundamental right to life is a non-absolute right.[74] The international community allows some exceptions to the obligation to protect life. By saying that deprivations of life must not be arbitrary in the third sentence of article 6(1), the ICCPR indirectly recognises that some deprivations of life could be non-arbitrary.[75] Practically all the regional human rights documents cited above somehow included this clause in their right to life provisions, meaning that this right may be limited under the due process of law. The ICCPR does not enumerate the permissible grounds for deprivation of life, but a comprehensive reading of the relevant articles of the respective human rights treaties reveals some of the situations under which an arbitrary deprivation of life can be excused to include, for example, the cases of self-defence, arresting a fleeing suspect, and quelling riots and insurrections. There are also some ethical

[66] Ibid., para. 13.

[67] Ibid., para. 7.

[68] Ibid., para. 25.

[69] Ibid., para. 27.

[70] Ibid., paras. 10 and 12.

[71] Ibid., para. 26.

[72] Ibid.

[73] Ibid. See also General Comment No. 3 of the African Charter on The Right to Life (Article 4), 4th to 18th November 2015, para. 42.

[74] See CCPR/C/GC/36, 30th October 2018, para. 10.

[75] Ibid.

dilemma situations under which a non-arbitrary limitation of the protection of life can be contemplated, such as abortion, euthanasia, etc. The dilemmas arise due to divergences between values and worldviews, as well as tensions between the right to life and other human rights. Apart from these legal exceptions, all societies across the globe detest deliberate killing, and the right not to be arbitrarily deprived of one's life is recognised today as part of international law. The African Commission (2015) described it as "a *jus cogens* norm", which means that it is a universal law from which no exception is allowed.[76] In Nigeria too, the right to life is recognised as a fundamental right.

3.3.2 Right to Life in Nigeria

The Nigerian Constitution guarantees the right to life in section 33(1) in the following terms: "[e]very person has a right to life, and no one shall be deprived intentionally of his life save in execution of the sentence of a court in respect of a criminal offence of which he has been found guilty in Nigeria." This provision grants the right to respect for and protection of their lives to every citizen and all individuals within the territorial confines of Nigeria. As a matter of fact, the idea of the right to life long existed in the pre-colonial era because the local belief system held life, including that of animals, to be sacred (Ojo, 2006; see also Ilo, 2005). Lack of respect for human life was not tolerated and deliberate killing abhorred. Threats to life were also restricted as much as possible. Although customary practices such as killing of twins and various types of human sacrifice also ironically existed, it was forbidden to take another's life "except in cases of need" (Ojo, 2006: 19). Most Nigerians are either Muslims or Christians. These religious traditions too subscribe to the notion of the sacredness of human life, as affirmed by the judicial pronouncement in the case of *Kaza v. The State*[77] where, for example, the Court held inter alia that the sanctity of human life under the Sharia is sacrosanct and can only be overturned in accordance with due process of law. Thus, the sanctity of the human life is generally recognised by Nigerians.

The Constitution further recognises the right to life in qualified terms (cf. Dada, 2012). In the same article cited above, some exceptions to the rule relating to protection of life are provided. To begin with, the Constitution permits the State to kill its citizens pursuant to the sentence of a court of law in Nigeria in a criminal offence. In the subsequent subsection, more conditions and circumstances under which life may be justifiably deprived are added thus: first, in exercise of one's right to self-defence or in defence of another person from unlawful violence, or in defence of

[76] Ibid., para. 5.

[77] (2008) 7 NWLR (pt. 1085) p.125. Cf. Nigeria's 6th Periodic Country Report 2015–2016 on the Implementation of the African Charter in Nigeria, p. 48. The same can be said of the Christian religion too.

one's property [section 33(2)(a)]; second, in order to effect a lawful arrest[78] or to prevent the escape of a suspect from lawful custody [section 33(2)(b)]; and/or third, to quell a riot, insurrection or mutiny [section 33(2)(c)]. The last exception refers to the loss of life which could result from the use of force for the purpose of dealing with situations of emergency or of lawful acts of war [section 45(2)]. Apart from these, any other form of killing is illegal in Nigeria. It is clear by virtue of the permissible exceptions that the Constitution allows the use of excessive and sometimes lethal force to the extent that it is 'reasonably necessary' to deal with these specific situations [section 33(2)]. This means that under these circumstances, one can rightly deprive another of his or her life, for instance, in order to prevent his or her property from vandalisation. The amount of property that could warrant such attack on life, however, is not specified by the Constitution nor any other domestic law. For this lacuna and more, it has been suggested that the Constitution tends to place value of property over that of human life (Dada, 2012). Again, state security operatives are granted an unrestricted use of force in handling civil unrests, inter-ethnic violence or preventing a suspect from absconding, and a loss of life in the process will not be seen as a violation of the right to life. The implication is that a suspect—no matter the nature of the offence—may be summarily but lawfully killed in the bid to prevent his or her escape from detention. Based on these considerations, the Constitution has been criticised for the scope of the limits it sets on the right to life, which are thought to be so vague to give room for the abuse of the right (Dada, 2012). Be that as it may, it can be concluded that the right to life is sacrosanct in Nigerian law, but that its sacrosanctity may be tampered with under due process of law (Mendie, 2014).

The constitutional provision on the right to life is complemented by other relevant international human rights instruments that the country recognises. These include the Universal Declaration, the ICCPR, the CRC (article 6), the AU Charter on the Rights and Welfare of the Child (article 5), and particularly the African Charter Act, as well as many other domestic legislations relating to this right. The African Charter Act guarantees the right to life in article 4. This provision does not envisage the right to life as an absolute right. It is still guaranteed in qualified terms, like in the Nigerian Constitution. The qualification here being that the right is not considered violated when life is not deprived arbitrarily. The practice of the death penalty is arguably contemplated under this provision.

As in some other countries, the exercise of the right to life in Nigeria is fraught with controversy, particularly regarding the death penalty. This applies not only to

[78] The discretionary powers given by the law to state security operatives in matters of arrest have been fine-tuned in more recent domestic legislations. The Administration of Criminal Justice Act (hereinafter ACJA), 2015 provides for humane treatment of a suspect with regard to the right to the dignity of the human person as contained in section 34 of the Constitution, though it does not prescribe penalties for violation [see section 8(1)(a)]. This lacuna has been made up for by the Anti-Torture Act which the country signed recently, in December 2017. In section 9, the latter criminalises acts of torture and other cruel, inhuman, and degrading treatment and prescribes punishment of up to 25 years' imprisonment for torture offenders.

the death penalty, but also to the moral issues of abortion and euthanasia. Together these are the three classic instances of the right to life that are explored in this study. At a time when the global trend in right to life is tending towards the abolition of the death penalty, Nigeria appears to be drifting deeper into this practice. This claim is supported by recent executions in the country, as well as the government's alleged plan some years ago to mass execute death row inmates to decongest prisons nationwide (Death Penalty Database, 2014). Killings take place at various levels of Nigerian society by both state and non-state actors. It is worrisome and therefore important to understand the factors underlying the perceived preference for this practice among Nigerians. When it comes to abortion, bioethical issues are often the subject of endless controversy and tension in societies around the world, including Nigeria. In fact, in Nigeria it is rarely a topic of public discussion—almost taboo. The country has a very restrictive abortion law that is supported by most of the citizens. Yet, current research results indicate a steadily increasing abortion rate in the country with the concomitant of maternal morbidity and mortality (cf. Atere et al., 2012; Ayanleye, 2013; Okonofua, 2015). Although attitudes towards bioethical issues are usually attributed to societal values and worldviews, it needs to be examined what specifically are the driving forces of attitudes towards abortion in the Nigerian context. This is applicable to euthanasia; it is worth clarifying the factors on which the public perception of euthanasia in Nigeria depends. This is one bioethical issue where tensions between the right to life and other human rights are sporadically extremely high in the country. It has long been considered illegal and is viewed by Nigerians as a closed chapter. But a recent Supreme Court ruling recognising a patient's constitutional right to self-determination appears to have brought the matter into public debate. The ensuing lack of clarity on the issue has exacerbated the dilemma surrounding its permissibility in the country.

It is against this backdrop that we decided to examine these right-to-life cases in Nigeria. We start with the death penalty.

3.3.2.1 Death Penalty

(1) The Death Penalty in Nigerian Law

The death penalty refers to "the deliberate taking of a life by the legitimate government as punishment for a certain crime" (Webb & Asa'd, 2019: 162). It is allowed in Nigeria under several federal and state laws.[79] The legality of this practice is primarily based on section 33(1) of the Constitution which authorises the deprivation

[79] Laws and statutes relating to capital punishment in Nigeria include the 1999 Constitution (as amended), the ACJA 2015, the Criminal Code Act (CCA), and its Criminal Procedure Act (hereinafter CPA) Cap. C41 LFN 2004 [for southern States], the Penal Code Act (PC), and its Criminal Procedure Code (hereinafter CPC) Cap. C42 LFN 2004 [for northern States, including the Federal Capital Territory]. Others are the Robbery and Firearms (Special Provisions) Act Cap. R11 LFN 2004, the Armed Forces Act Cap. A20 LFN 2004, the Evidence Act 2011, the Terrorism (Prevention) (Amendment) Act 2013, and the various Sharia Penal Codes of the 12 Sharia States.

of life as long as it is imposed for a criminal offence by a court of law. The Supreme Court of Nigeria upheld it as a lawful process in the case of *Kalu v. The State,*[80] where it held that the practice of the death penalty in Nigeria is constitutional, and so far the practice has not been successfully challenged in court as a breach of the right to life clause of the Constitution (Ojo, 2006).

The Nigerian law stipulates a mandatory capital punishment for various offences. The import of the term 'mandatory' to the practice is to show that once the suspect is found guilty of a capital offence, the judges' discretion to impose penalty based on his or her culpability is excluded (Nzeribe & Abangwu, 2013). Some of the capital offences can be distinguished: murder,[81] armed robbery,[82] treason,[83] and treachery.[84] Others are perjury leading to execution of an innocent person,[85] assisting the suicide of a minor or lunatic,[86] presiding over a trial by ordeal that results in the death of a person,[87] as well as military offences such as aiding the enemy[88] or communicating intelligence with the enemy,[89] cowardly behaviour,[90] mutiny,[91] and dereliction of duty.[92]

More capital offenses have recently been introduced. Some states, particularly in the south of the country, have added kidnapping to the long list of crimes requiring the death penalty in response to the rising rate of abduction and kidnap-related offences in their territories (Badejogbin, 2018). In some northern States that use Sharia law, offences such as adultery (zina),[93] sodomy (liwat),[94] lesbianism (sihaq),[95] incest,[96] rape,[97] and the practice of witchcraft and juju[98] are also death-eligible offences depending on the marital status and the state of origin of the offender. However, the convictions thereto require tough evidentiary examinations as may be

[80] (1998) 13 NWLR (pt.583) p. 531; see also section 402(2) of the ACJA 2015.

[81] Sections 316 and 319 of the CCA; sections 221 of the PC; section 106 of the Armed Forces Act.

[82] Section 402(2a) of the CCA; section 1(2)(a) of the Robbery and Firearms (Special Provisions) Act; section 107(2) of the Armed Forces Act.

[83] Sections 37 and 38 of the CCA; section 411 of the PC.

[84] Section 49 (a)(1) of the CCA.

[85] Ibid., section 310; section 159(2) of the PC.

[86] Section 227 of the PC.

[87] Section 208 of the CCA; section 214(b) of the PC.

[88] Section 45 of the Armed Forces Act.

[89] Ibid., section 46.

[90] Ibid., section 47.

[91] Ibid., section 52.

[92] Ibid., section 63.

[93] Section 127(b) of the Zamfara State Penal Code 2000.

[94] Ibid., section 131(b).

[95] Section 132 of the Kebbi State Penal Code, 2000.

[96] Sections 133(b) of the Zamfara State Penal Code 2000.

[97] Ibid., section 129(b).

[98] Ibid., sections 406(f).

decided by the Sharia courts of various states. These additions to the catalogue of capital offences by the States were possible because most criminal offences fall under state jurisdiction in line with the federal political culture. Under the existing law, certain categories of offenders cannot be sentenced to death in Nigeria. These include minors or juveniles under 18 years of age,[99] provided that such persons have not reached puberty or the age of responsibility. This was the basis of the Supreme Court decision in *Modupe v. The State,*[100] where it held that the Court of First Instance made a mistake by failing to determine the age of a juvenile offender before imposing the death penalty on him. Apart from child offenders, pregnant women are exempt from capital sentence[101] as well as insane offenders.[102] In the case of pregnant women, the concession is given in view of the rights of the unborn child and based on this the execution of the capital sentence is to be suspended until a later date.

There are more modes of execution in Nigeria than most Nigerians know. The most popular methods are hanging,[103] and shooting or firing squad.[104] Executions can also be carried out via lethal injection,[105] stoning (rajm)[106] and crucifixion (salb),[107] though the Sharia States tend to differ on what is meant by crucifixion. The propriety of these modes of execution has often been questioned at one time or another. For instance, a Lagos State High Court in the case of *James Ajulu and Ors v. Attorney General of Lagos State*[108] held inter alia that execution of the death sentence by hanging or firing squad is unconstitutional, in other words, that it violates the convict's constitutional guarantees of freedom from torture and human dignity. However, Nigerian courts have held otherwise in a number of cases. In the case of *Okoro v. The State*, for instance, the court upheld the constitutionality of the said modes of execution.[109]

There are no accurate records of executions in the country. Reports have it that ca. 2629 people had been executed between 1970 and 2019. The last known executions took place in 2016 and involved three inmates convicted by military tribunals of armed robbery. There is currently no official moratorium on executions in the country. The rate of executions has dropped considerably, even though with an

---

[99] Section 368(3) of the CPA; section 319(2) of the CCA; section 405 of the ACJA 2015.

[100] (1988) 4 NWLR (pt. 87) p. 130.

[101] Section 368(2) of the CPA; section 270 of the CPC; section 404 of the ACJA 2015.

[102] Section 28 of the CCA.

[103] Section 402(1) of the ACJA 2015; sections 367(1) & (2) of the CPA; section 1(3) of the Robbery and Firearms (Special Provisions) Act; see also Death Penalty Database, 2014.

[104] Section 1(3) of the Robbery and Firearms (Special Provisions) Act.

[105] Section 402(1) of the ACJA 2015. Note that this method has so far not been used in the country.

[106] Section 131(b) of the Zamfara State Penal Code 2000.

[107] Ibid., section 153(d).

[108] (Unreported) Suit No. ID/76 M/2008; see also Death Penalty Database (2014).

[109] See *Okoro v. The State* (2000) 49 NWLR 356; *Kalu v. The State* (1998) 13 NWLR (pt.583) p. 531.

alarming increase in the number of death sentences of late. In 2017, for instance, the country imposed 621 death sentences, making her the country with the highest death penalty globally. She also had the largest number of people on death row in the region (Amnesty International, 2018; Death Penalty Database, 2014). In fact, Amnesty International (2020) estimates that the number of death row inmates nationwide was about 2700 by the end of 2019. Human rights groups have continued to call for the complete abolition of the death penalty or the form used in Nigeria, or better still for a halt to the practice in the country until the relevant laws are reviewed. So far, the government has not responded positively to their demands, although the country reported to the UN Human Rights Council during the third cycle of the Universal Periodic Review in November 2018 that efforts were still being made between federal and state governments to formalise a moratorium.[110]

From the records, the death penalty serves the country two principal purposes, namely retribution and deterrence. But whether the practice has proved particularly effective in reducing crime and whether it satisfies the essence of punishment is a question that is often asked by pro-abolition groups.

(2) Public Attitude Towards the Death Penalty in Nigeria

Public attitudes towards the death penalty in Nigeria vary depending on geographical location. Some parts of the country tend to be more supportive of maintaining this practice than others. This can be explained socio-culturally. The existing differences in attitudes towards this practice can be traced to the differences in penal laws of pre-colonial local cultures. Take for example the three major ethnic blocs in the country. In the southeast there was the death penalty, which could be imposed for crimes such as murder, slave trade, witchcraft, profanation of the gods of the land, etc. Alternatively, banishment was often imposed to show utmost disproval of such conduct. In the north the death penalty was practiced; it was applied to similar crimes. The practice also took place in the southwestern part of the country and included other crimes such as crimes against human life and disrespect for the traditional ruler. The minority tribes are not left out of this issue as they all had similar penal practices. Therefore, despite pretensions to the contrary, the death penalty was common in virtually all traditional Nigerian societies. However, it was rarely applied, and this only in cases of injustice and where the perpetrator was thought to be a threat to public safety (Ilo, 2005).

With the introduction of British rule and the subsequent abolition of the customary criminal law, capital crimes were trimmed, but the practice remained enshrined in the law. The list of capital crimes was enlarged once again during the long years of military rule (Anwo & Arowolo, 2011). So, the death penalty has been part of the Nigerian penal system. Today it is a widely accepted practice in the country (OHCHR, 2006), and this claim is well documented. According to Ilo (2005), more than sixty percent of Nigerians support the retention of the death penalty. Proof of this is the way they support the public execution of criminals (e.g. armed robbers,

---

[110] UN Doc. A/HRC/40/7, 26th December 2018, para. 20.

coup plotters, etc.) as well as the activities of ethnic militias, such as the Bakassi Boys and several other vigilante groups, known for their use of lethal force when dealing with criminals. Another reason is the widespread use of the so-called "jungle justice" (i.e. summary execution) on apprehended criminals by the public themselves. Their support for the death penalty is predicated mainly on the belief that this practice is an effective deterrent against the rising crime rate in the country, but also on the natural tendency towards revenge. The support could also be attributed to other factors, such as ignorance of the inadequacies of the Nigerian criminal justice system, a misunderstanding of the concept of punishment, etc. Such considerations do not seem to play a role for most Nigerians when it comes to capital crimes. However, despite the enormous support that the practice appears to enjoy from a large section of the Nigerian population, there is still a relevant minority who view it negatively in the context of the contemporary global culture of human rights.

Recent Developments in the Application of the Death Penalty in Nigeria

There is a global trend towards the abolition of the death penalty. Since the 1980s and 1990s, the perception of punishment has changed tremendously. The idea of rehabilitation and resocialisation of a felon found greater acceptance in punishment research and practice than the classic models of deterrence and retribution. As a result, a lot of serious questions are being asked about the propriety of the death penalty. In Nigeria, its application has been the subject of a long-standing political debate, especially since the return to democratic governance. The debate became more intense in 2013 after the execution of four death row inmates (APPGN Report, 2013). The fact is that of the total estimate of executions given above, about 29 took place under civilian rule. The rest was carried out by military governments. Since the return to civilian rule in 1999, the civil society organisations and human right bodies in the country have constantly engaged the government on the need to abolish the practice in line with global trends. In 2003, the Presidency responded by establishing a National Study Group on the Death Penalty (hereinafter Study Group), tasked with conducting research on the issue and then advising the government based on the results of its study. Accordingly, the Study Group recommended a moratorium on the death penalty in its final report in 2004. In another development, a certain Presidential Commission on Reform of the Administration of Justice (PCRAJ) reiterated the position of the Study Group in 2007. But these recommendations were not heeded. The government instead voted against the first resolution calling for a global moratorium on executions at the UN General Assembly, in November of the same year.[111] Likewise, a bill to abolish the mandatory death penalty under the Robbery and Firearms Act of 1984 that was presented to the National Assembly in 2008 was also defeated. When all these happened, the pro-abolition groups seemed not to worry so much because there were coincidentally no executions going on in the country for a period of seven years between 2006 and 2013, until the execution of the said four prisoners. It was this incident that rekindled the

[111] See UN Doc. A/RES/62/149, 18th December 2007.

debate over the application of the death penalty. In all of this, however, the general views of ordinary citizens seem to be that the practice should be retained.

The most common reasons for supporting this practice in Nigeria are retribution and deterrence. Many people think it fits with their inherent sense of justice that convicts deserve to be punished in proportion to the gravity of their offence. They also perceive the punishment to serve as a deterrent to certain classes of crimes and to prevent recidivism (Anwo & Arowolo, 2011; Nzeribe & Abangwu, 2013). A lot of judicial decisions literarily endorse this line of reasoning. For instance, in *Akinyemi v. The State* the court held thus: "[t]he sentence was well pronounced for the capital offence. It has the semblance of the Law of Moses: 'an eye to an eye', it is good law to serve as deterrence in a mundane society where heartless and dangerous citizens abound in plenty."[112] Secondly, proponents of the death penalty contend that capital punishment is a legal practice in the country and that its legality is founded on the Nigerian law.[113] In other words, they do not see it as constituting a violation of the fundamental right not be subjected to inhuman and degrading treatment. The Supreme Court affirms this position in *Okoro v. The State*,[114] where it held the death penalty to be consistent with sections 33(1) and 34(1)(a) of the 1999 Constitution. Several judicial pronouncements have upheld this position too.[115] On the contrary, opponents of the death penalty base their arguments on human rights. They reject the practice as being unfriendly to human rights. First, they argue that it violates the right to life. For them, the existing practice of the mandatory death penalty is inconsistent with regional and international guidelines that reserve the penalty for the most serious crimes. They contend that capital offences do not qualify as such.[116] They also insist that capital punishment violates the convict's constitutional right to protection from inhuman and degrading treatment, both in context and method of execution. This has been contested several times in Nigerian courts.[117] Furthermore, opponents contend that the practice of the death penalty violates the accused person's right to a fair trial, including the right to appeal. A typical example of this is always cited in the case of *Nasiru Bello v. Attorney-General of Oyo State,*[118] where the convicted felon was prematurely executed by the respondent while his appeal was pending in a higher court. Many Nigerian States have at one time or the other been indicted for this abuse. Reports even have it that all seven persons involved in the last two sets of executions in the country still had appeals pending against their sentences when they were executed, in utter violation of both Nigerian

---

[112] (1999) 6 NWLR (pt. 465) p. 607. See also *Obidike v. The State* (2014) 10 NWLR (pt. 1414) 53.

[113] See section 33(1) of 1999 CFRN.

[114] (2000) 49 NWLR 356; see also *Okoro v. The State* (1998) 14 NWLR 584.

[115] See *Kalu v. The State* (1998) 13 NWLR (pt. 583) p. 531; *Adeniji v. The State* (2000) 645 NWLR 356; *Akinyemi v. The State* (1999) 6 NWLR 465.

[116] CCPR/C/GC/36, 30th October 2018, para. 35.

[117] *Peter Nemi v. Attorney General of Lagos State & Anor* (1996) 6 NWLR (pt. 452) p. 42. See also CCPR/C/GC/36, 30th October 2018, para. 40.

[118] (1986) 5 NWLR (pt.45) p.828.

and international law.[119] Most importantly, opponents also argue that the death penalty almost exclusively affects a certain class of Nigerian citizens, namely the poor and people who are not connected to government officials and, as such, represents a form of discrimination based on social origin. This fact was highlighted by the NGO HURILAWS in its 2004 Country Report and later reiterated by both the Study Group and the Presidential Commission mentioned above (Amnesty International, 2008).

Other reasons given by supporters of the abolition of the death penalty relate to the irrevocable character of punishment, which, in their opinion, on the one hand, does not correspond to the logic of the inherent imperfection of the justice system, as exemplified in cases of judicial errors across the world. In the Nigerian context, for instance, innocent persons have been executed and the court awarded damages as in the case of Nasiru, but the truth remains that the life lost cannot be restored. On the other hand, they also contend that the irreversibility of the death penalty defeats the essence of punishment, which necessarily includes the rehabilitation and social reintegration of the felon, since in practice (s)he is instead denied that possibility of reformation. They therefore assume that the country is going against the tide when it comes to the death penalty, as the evolution of international law tends towards its abolition.[120] They challenge the unfounded claim that the punishment is a real deterrent, point out that despite its long history it has failed to curb the escalating number of heinous crimes in Nigeria, and recommend life imprisonment as a humane alternative to the death penalty (Anwo & Arowolo, 2011; Babalola, 2016).

Now, the debates and activities of human rights bodies may not have yielded the desired results, but some major strides have been made in the struggle for the abolition of the death penalty in the country. Through media advocacy and public sensitisation, a great deal of awareness has been created in the public perception of crime and punishment, as well as the practice of the mandatory death penalty, and some

[119] Sections 233(2)(d) & 241(1)(e) of the CFRN. See also African Commission, 29th May 2003, section N10(2)(b); and CCPR/C/GC/36, 30th October 2018, para. 41.

[120] On 17th December 2018, the UN General Assembly adopted its seventh resolution (A/RES/73/175, 2018) calling on retentionist states to impose a moratorium on executions, with a view to abolishing the death penalty. Many countries supported the resolution. Of the 193 UN member states, 121 voted in support of the resolution while 35 voted against, 32 abstained and 5 did not vote at all (see also Amnesty International, 2019). This represents an improvement from the outcome in December 2016, where about 117 States voted in favour. Apart from these, the UN has since drafted its second Optional Protocol to the ICCPR, which aims to abolition the death penalty. As of September 2020, Nigeria has not yet signed this instrument. At the regional level, Protocol no. 6 of the European Convention for the Protection of Human Rights and Fundamental Freedoms partially abolished the death penalty in 1983, allowing exceptions only in time of war or national emergency. But Protocol no. 13 has outlawed capital punishment in all circumstances since 2002 and this has been implemented in most member countries of the Council. Similarly, the African Commission has also passed a series of resolutions calling on states in the region to abolish the death penalty or establish a moratorium in line with continental and global trends [Cf. General Comment no. 3, 2015, para. 22). It follows that most countries in the world are working towards eliminating this practice.

Nigerians now appear ready to take a second look at the country's penal policy. Human rights groups have also revived the Nigeria Anti-Death Penalty Group. This group continues to push for the passage of The Death Penalty Moratorium Bill.

(3) Religion and the Death Penalty

The role of religious beliefs in the attitudes of Nigerians towards the death penalty cannot be overemphasised. Usually, the death penalty is discussed from a secular perspective, but sometimes religious people also refer to religious principles.[121] The three main religious traditions in Nigeria recognise the inviolability of human life, but their principles can also be used to support the death penalty.

Theological Perspectives of ATR

The ATR conscientiously respects life, including the life of animals. Human life was considered sacred and the sanctity of human blood inviolable. The waste of life was detested "even in certain wars" (Ojo, 2006: 19). No blood was allowed to be shed except in emergencies. Despite this fact, studies on African law have postulated that the death penalty existed in pre-colonial African societies (cf. Elias, 1956; ACHPR, 2012; Mbiti, 1969). It was usually applied to crimes such as unlawful homicide, desecration of local shrines, slave trade and witchcraft. Societies like the Nuer in Sudan, the Barotse in Zambia, the Ashanti in Ghana, the Bantu in southern Africa, and the Zulu in South Africa all permitted the death penalty for murder. Among Nigeria's ethnic groups or nationalities, the Yoruba in the south-west, the Nupe, Tiv and Jukun in the north-central, the Benin in the south-south, and the Igbo in the south-east, for example, murder was recognised as a crime punishable by death. It was perceived as a crime against society and a violation of divine law since all life comes from the 'supreme being' (Ojo, 2006).

Other crimes such as cannibalism, theft, killing sacred animals, unmasking the masquerade,[122] sacrilegious acts and speaking ill of elders also attracted the death penalty (Olasunkanmi, 2016; Nhlapo, 2017). These are viewed as serious crimes because its commission is believed to have serious consequences for the entire community. Execution methods in pre-colonial Africa varied. These included hanging, suicide, decapitation, impaling, poisoning, and burying alive (Dalgleish, 2005; ACHPR, 2012). In many cases, capital punishment may be substituted with banishment, for example, among the Igbos. In pre-colonial Africa, the philosophy behind the death penalty, for instance, for deliberate killing was restoration of a life for a life (literal retribution) or the complete removal of the offender from the ranks of the tribe (permanent incapacitation). Both aims were intended to serve deterrent purposes. The death penalty as an intentional infliction of pain or deprivation is considered the worst on the penal scale (Olasunkanmi, 2016).

---

[121] See Christianity: Capital Punishment (2009). Available at http://www.bbc.co.uk/religion/religions/christianity/christianethics/capitalpunishment_1.shtml. Accessed 08.08.2020.

[122] That, according to Achebe (1958), is tantamount to killing an ancestral spirit.

Islamic Theological Perspectives
In Islam, the death penalty is accepted in principle to punish severe crimes. It is allowed by all the authoritative texts and sources of the Islamic religion. However, the implementation of this penalty cannot take place without express authorisation from God because all life issues belong to His exclusive territory of moral jurisdiction (hudûd Allah). Furthermore, killing has to be commanded by a court, otherwise it would be a crime. This is clearly stated in the Quran (6:151), thus: "[t]ake not life, which God has made sacred, except by way of justice and law." Therefore, death penalty can be implemented by the State in the name of God. In Islamic law, it is considered appropriate for two groups of crime, namely "for murder and for spreading mischief in the land" (Quran 5:32). The crime of 'spreading mischief in the land' [fasad fil-ardh] is an open-ended term but usually includes offences, such as treason or apostasy, terrorism, rape, adultery, and homosexual conduct. These are regarded as crimes that threaten to undermine authority or destabilise the state and deserve the maximum penalty as such. Even in such cases, the punishment is usually meted out for the purpose of deterrence, as a means of retributive justice and for saving life (Webb & Asa'd, 2019). Thus, it is prescribed by Sharia law, and Muslim jurists accept it in principle but make its implementation procedurally arduous. In the case of murder, for instance, the deceased's relatives are given the option to exact a revenge or not. This possibility is given because forgiveness is preferable to vengeance and retaliation according to the higher moral vision of Islam (Ziebertz & Zaccaria, 2019). Nevertheless, the Islamic religion is largely retentionist in orientation,[123] and according to Greenberg and West (2008), countries that practise Islamic law strictly tend often to be more retentionists than others.

Christian Theological Perspectives
The idea of the death penalty is not foreign to the Christian religion either. Christian theologians accepted the practice as something in consonance with Scripture, tradition, and the natural law. In the biblical tradition, the Old Testament (hereinafter OT) specifies a long list of capital offences which includes idolatry, magic, blasphemy, incest, adultery, and kidnaping, as well as murder. The punishment is imposed mainly as a means of retributive justice (Leviticus 24:20; Numbers 35:16–21), expiation (Numbers 35:33), and for the sake of preserving life itself (Genesis 9:6). It was also believed that the penalty can serve as a deterrent in view of the commandment 'not to kill' (Exodus 20:13), and as a help to bring orderliness in the society. However, although the Mosaic Law permitted the practice in such cases as mentioned here, the rabbinic traditions tended to use it restrictively (Anthony & Sterkens, 2019). In the New Testament (hereinafter NT), the state's authority to exact capital punishment seems to be taken for granted (cf. John 19:11). Besides, patent references to it are scattered throughout the NT writings (Matthew 15:4; Luke 23:41; Acts 5:1–11; Romans 13:4; etc.), and these even though the tenor of the NT is that of forgiveness and compassion. For much of history, this practice was accepted in Christendom as an essential mechanism of society, and the Church

[123] See Islam and Capital Punishment (2009). Available at https://www.bbc.co.uk/religion/religions/islam/islamethics/capitalpunishment.shtml. Accessed 08.08.2020.

recognised the state as a legitimate authority to administer it (CCC, 1992, no. 2266). A cursory glance at the teachings of the Church over the centuries shows that the Church not only supported it, but also at some point empowered the Inquisition to turn heretics over to the state for execution. The Church's support for the death penalty over time was premised on common good, protection of society, deterrence, retribution, expiation, and repentance (Anthony & Sterkens, 2019; Dulles, 2001). Up until the second half of the twentieth century, the consensus among Christian theologians tilted in the favour of this practice.

In recent times, opinions have changed significantly among Christian Churches, and many Christians now argue against the death penalty on the grounds that Christianity should support life. In the Catholic Church, for example, the magisterium has become increasingly critical of the practice. In his encyclical letter, Evangelium Vitae (hereinafter EV 1995, no. 56), Pope John Paul II referred to it as "cruel and unnecessary" and backed the move towards its abolition. Sequel to this, the Vatican later updated the Catechism (cf. CCC, 1997, no. 2267) to reflect the teaching of the Church on the death penalty, in line with the position enunciated by the Pope. In 2018, Pope Francis further revised the same paragraph, so that the Catholic Church now teaches that the "death penalty is inadmissible because it is an attack on the inviolability and dignity of the person" (CDF, 2018). Likewise, the contemporary Catholic theology rejects the practice as incompatible with the biblical teachings on forgiveness, hope and redemption (Anthony & Sterkens, 2019). The same applies to most Christian denominations, even as recent studies indicate that those who interpret the Bible literally tend to be more disposed to its application.[124]

Conclusively, it has been claimed that most Nigerians are more in support of the death penalty, and the doctrinal perspectives of the Islamic and Christian faiths have also been pinpointed as an important determinant of this public attitude, given their status as the dominant religions in the country. However, such claims have often not been supported empirically.

3.3.2.2 Abortion

(1) The Moral Question of Abortion

Abortion refers to "a process in which [pregnancy or] life in the womb is terminated" (Webb & Asa'd, 2019: 162). This may occur spontaneously or intentionally. Abortion is deemed spontaneous if the pregnancy terminates on its own and intentional if it happens on purpose; in this case it is described as induced. The term abortion in the context of this study refers to induced abortion because it is the type that is of interest to human right discourse.

Induced abortion is seen as a major social affliction in most societies around the world. The World Health Organisation (hereinafter WHO) once described it as a

[124] Christianity: Capital Punishment (2009), above at no. 121.

silent pandemic. Based on data from 2010 to 2014, an estimated 227 million women become pregnant each year worldwide. About 44 percent, or 99 million, of these pregnancies are unintended, and around 56 million (i.e., about 56% of unintended pregnancies) end in induced abortion. In other words, an estimated 25 percent of all pregnancies end in induced abortion each year. The data also provides insights into the global spread of this scourge. According to the Guttmacher Institute (Singh et al., 2018), between 2010 and 2014, about 49.3 million of the estimated 56 million induced abortions worldwide occurred in developing regions, while the rest of 6.6 million took place in developed regions. This corresponds to 36 and 27 induced abortions per 1000 women of reproductive age in developing and developed regions, respectively, meaning that abortions occurred more frequently in developing regions than in developed regions. Furthermore, an estimated 45 percent of induced abortions worldwide each year—representing approximately 25 million abortions—are considered unsafe, resulting in the deaths of approximately 23,000 women and tens of thousands of significant health complications. As a matter of fact, it is reported that 8–11 percent of global maternal deaths are related to abortion. Again, the burden of these (about 97%) lies largely in the developing world, with the highest rates in Africa. The WHO (2012) estimates that the continent accounted for 29 percent of all unsafe abortions and 62 percent of all abortion-related deaths in 2008, despite having just 14 percent of the world's total share of women of childbearing age at that time. More than half of these deaths are believed to have occurred in sub-Saharan Africa and was highest among low-income women and adolescent girls.

Thus, it can be said that induced abortion is a global phenomenon, though the rate is higher in developing countries. Women procure abortion for several reasons, but accumulated evidence shows that most abortions result from unwanted, unintended pregnancies. While unintended pregnancies typically result from rape, incest, incidents of teenage pregnancies, failure of contraceptives, etc., some pregnancies may become unwanted for reasons, such as economic, cultural, and medical reasons. Be that as it may, these reproductive health outcomes occur irrespective of socio-economic status, country or region of origin, or the legal status of abortion. And once they occur, women, including adolescents, often resort to abortion. Abortion is a complex reality; it has legal, moral, religious, cultural, public health and human rights implications. All these factors come into play when considering the matter (Ubajaka et al., 2014). For instance, induced abortion may be legal or illegal depending on the country. According to the 2019 World Map of Abortion Laws, abortion is prohibited altogether in 26 countries of the 201 nation-states and sovereign entities around the globe, while it is either authorised restrictively or simply on request in the rest.[125] The simple implication, then, is that whereas unwanted

[125] In the World Abortion Laws Map, countries across the globe are sorted into a five-category continuum from severe restrictions to relative liberality based on their legal stand on abortion. Category I is for countries that prohibit abortion altogether. As of 2019, there are 26 countries in this category. The countries in Category II (39 of them) authorise abortion to preserve the woman's life, while those in Category III (56 countries in all) do so on health or therapeutic grounds. In Category IV, there are 14 countries. The laws of these countries permit abortion for a broad range

pregnancy may be the major motivating reason for induced abortion, both the decision to abort and the procurement itself are guided, among other things, by a country's abortion policy.

The Facts About Abortion in Nigeria

Abortion is generally not considered a typical Nigerian problem (Atere et al., 2012). But it is a major challenge in developing regions of the world, especially in sub-Saharan Africa, where Nigeria holds sway. There are incidents of induced abortions in Nigeria. Available statistics indicate that an estimated 1.25 million induced abortion occurred in Nigeria in 2012, which corresponds to the rate of 33 abortions per 1000 women of reproductive age. Although this is a conservative estimate, as the Federal Republic of Nigeria (2018) reports that over 80 percent of such abortions take place in private settings, recent research confirms that there is a high and steadily rising incidence of abortion in Nigeria (Okonofua, 2015; see also Atere et al., 2012; Ayanleye, 2013). Pregnant Nigerian women procure abortion for reasons similar to those mentioned above and the commonest of these is also unwanted, unintended pregnancy (Ubajaka et al., 2014). The estimated rate of unintended pregnancy in the country for 2012 is put at 59 per 1000 women of reproductive age, and the Federal Ministry of Health (hereinafter FMH) further noted that 56 percent of these pregnancies ended in abortion.

Another important feature of unintended pregnancy and induced abortion in Nigeria is that they affect a considerable number of adolescents. A lot of factors expose them to these reproductive health challenges. The first is the sexual vitality of most adolescent girls, which makes them vulnerable to unwanted pregnancies. It has been observed that attitudes towards sexuality have considerably changed over the last decades due to globalisation and the influence of social media. Young people have become increasingly tolerant of premarital sex and the average age of first intercourse has declined. It is not uncommon to find girls of 15 years or less who are sexually active (Atere et al., 2012). In some settings even, girls as young as 9 to 12 years old are exposed to sex by older men who seek them as sexual partners or in line with some socio-cultural practices. While these changes are taking place, the Nigerian society has not provided adolescents with the relevant sexual health information, partly because sexuality and sexual-related issues are viewed as very private issues. In fact, these are rarely discussed in public and facts about them are usually misrepresented to young people, so that they often have to discover them on their own and often at their peril. Another issue here concerns the parental influence on girl child morality. The parental influence has waned manifestly due to lack of care and monitoring. Some parents leave their children to the care of the maid or even

---

of socio-economic reasons. Lastly, the Category V is made up of countries whose laws allow abortion on request. In the meantime, there are 66 countries in this category. According to the Map, countries with liberal abortion laws are those in Categories IV and V. Though some countries in Categories II-III recognise additional grounds under which abortion is permitted, such as cases of rape, incest, or fetal impairment, etc., they do not belong to the group of countries that allow abortion broadly (Center for Reproductive Rights, 2019).

sometimes unattended to in the quest for material wealth. As such, they do not know who their children really are and how to deal with their sexuality. Lastly, the high level of poverty in the land also contributes to the problem. That is because poverty has forced many young girls to embrace hawking as a way of helping to augment family income. In doing so, they are often exposed to the risks of sexual exploitation. Moreover, this same unfavourable social condition accounts largely for the increased rate of disruptive conduct (e.g., substance abuse, drugs, etc.) and violent crimes (e.g., armed robbery, rape, etc.). All these contribute by some means to making adolescent girls increasingly vulnerable to accidental pregnancy (Ayanleye, 2013).

If it happens incidentally that adolescents experience such pregnancies that are unplanned, they are usually confronted with the dilemma arising from the tough choice between keeping the pregnancy and losing their girlhood or being expelled from school or the stigma of being tagged as accidental mothers due to pregnancies arising from rape, incest, etc., or sometimes being socially rejected because society frowns at pregnancy outside wedlock, or all of the above. Such considerations, and especially the public's hostile attitude towards teenage pregnancy, tend to predispose most pregnant girls to seek an abortion. They often patronise all sorts of abortion inducing devices in private settings, and this with dire consequences. But why and what other options does the Nigerian society have for adolescents in such a predicament?

(2) The Position of the Nigerian Law on Abortion

Abortion is not legally defined under Nigerian law. Instead, the term 'procuring miscarriage' is used. Procuring miscarriage is generally illegal under the Nigerian criminal law system irrespective of the duration of pregnancy. The relevant statutes are strict about procuring miscarriage[126] and attempting to secure a miscarriage or terminate a pregnancy[127] by any means whatsoever. The foetus is regarded as a human life from the moment of conception. As such, the Criminal and Penal Codes disallow abortion to be performed at all stages of foetal development, no matter the justification. As punishment, the codes prescribe up to 14 years in jail and/or payment of a fine for all offenders, including healthcare professionals who mastermind an abortion, even if it turns out that the woman was never pregnant, and the woman herself who commits or attempts to commit abortion. The only overriding interest that allows a pregnancy to be interfered with is when the mother's life is at risk.[128] This exception has been noted since *Rex v. Edgal*[129] where the West African Court of Appeal held that it is lawful to procure a miscarriage for the purpose of preserving the life of the mother. It follows, therefore, that in practice Nigeria largely allows therapeutic abortion where it is performed in good faith and strictly for the purpose

[126] Section 228 of CCA; section 232 of the PC; see also section 328 of the CCA, and section 236 of the PC.

[127] Section 229 of the CCA.

[128] Ibid., section 297, and sections 232 and 235 of the PC.

[129] (1938) 4 WACA 133 (Nigeria).

of saving a woman's life. In this singular circumstance, spousal consent or a third-party authorisation is not required for the medical intervention to save the life of a pregnant woman, and the abortion services are reportedly not subsidised by the State either. Apart from that, abortion is illegal in all other circumstances.

The Criminal and Penal Codes also covered some other abortion-related offences. For instance, the Criminal Code criminalises the provision of materials (e.g., drugs, concoctions, poison, and ampoules) or other instruments which one knows are meant to be unlawfully used to procure miscarriage, irrespective of whether the woman is pregnant or not. It stipulates a prison term of 3 years for such a person upon conviction.[130] The Penal Code for its part makes it an offence to cause the death of a woman with the intention of making her to miscarry. This offence is punishable on conviction by a 14-year prison term and a fine. The sentence could be heavier depending on the circumstances of the case. Consent is not a valid defence here but could serve as a mitigating factor.[131] Lastly, it is an offence to cause a woman to miscarry by using force on her,[132] even if it is not intentional.[133] The respective statutes prescribe various forms of punishment ranging from payment of fine to different jail terms.

Abortion in Nigeria is also regulated by the Sharia legal systems of the various Sharia States. In Zamfara State, for example, the provisions against miscarriage are found in the Zamfara Sharia Penal Code Law chapter IX sections 207–211. These provisions are virtually like those in the Penal Code except that there are additional provisions of punishments like payment of compensation, and caning.

Criticisms of the Abortion Law

Nigerian law has been described differently by different people, particularly in relation to abortion policy. Some find it more or less life-sensitive because of the nature of its provisions on abortion. Others consider it to be rather conservative for the same reasons (cf. Izunwa & Ifemeje, 2011). Be that as it may, the country's existing abortion law has been criticised for some of the following limitations. First, it has been pointed out that the abortion law is grossly inadequate to meet the reproductive health needs of women and adolescent girls in the country (Ilobinso, 2007). Some consider the statutory exception, which only allows abortion to be performed when the woman's life is at stake, to be too narrow and insensitive to the already mentioned social realities that confront women and girls in the present-day Nigeria. They see these as genuine concerns that any meaningful law should address, and for failing to recognise them they feel that the abortion law is inefficient (Ayanleye, 2013). Second, the national statutes on abortion are merely restrictive,

[130] Section 230 of the CCA. This provision was applied in *The State v. Njoku* [1973] ECSLR 638 (Nigeria).

[131] Section 233 of the PC. This provision was applied in *Attorney-General of the Federation v. Ogunro*, (2001) 10 NWLR (pt.720) p. 175.

[132] Section 228 of the CCA.

[133] Section 234 of the PC.

not prescriptive. They only criminalise the practice but do not design any specific legislation to regulate it. Regarding the legal exception, for instance, there is no formal instrument detailing how the exercise should be done within this legal framework (CEDAW Shadow Report, 1998). The Federal Ministry of Health (hereinafter FMH) has tried over time to make up for this by providing national standard guidelines, but these hardly ever find the necessary political support. So, the codes do not specify the minimum medical standards necessary to perform a safe abortion. Among other things, they are silent on who should perform an abortion and for once such matters have never arisen for consideration by the courts. The implication is that anybody can perform an abortion anywhere and have the protection of the law once it can be technically certified that (s)he acted in good faith to save the life of the mother. This is easily a lacuna in the existing abortion law that seriously endangers the reproductive health and well-being of women and girls (see Ilobinso, 2007).

Lastly, the Nigerian abortion law is also viewed from a human rights perspective. In recent times, the issue of abortion is considered to affect a range of human rights, namely the right to life, the right to freedom and personal dignity, the right to privacy and family life, freedom of thought and religion, and particularly the right to health, including sexual and reproductive health. Over the last few decades, we notice some adjustments in the nuances, as abortion is no longer seen as just a legal exception to the right to the integrity of life, but rather as more of women's right to sexual and reproductive health. We find insinuations of this in the UN Convention on the Elimination of All Forms of Discrimination against Women (CEDAW).[134] The Maputo Protocol is believed to be the first treaty to clearly recognise abortion as a human right of women under certain conditions. Article 14(2)(c) states that "state parties shall protect the reproductive rights of women by authorising medical abortion in cases of sexual assault, rape, incest and where the continued pregnancy endangers the mental and physical health of the mother or the life of the mother or the foetus." The African Commission's General Comment no. 2, which provides interpretive guidance on the obligations of states parties towards the application of the same Article 14 of the Protocol, expands on this by providing guarantees of access to therapeutic abortion for women (para. 35) and calls on all ratifying countries to prevent undue interference with the exercise of women's sexual and reproductive rights (para. 43). It also obliges them to ensure the full realisation of these rights, to create an enabling environment for the exercise of the rights, including, where appropriate, the revision of restrictive laws, policies and administrative procedures related to safe abortion in the cases provided for in the Protocol and the domestication of its provisions (para. 45f). Due to these considerations, abortion is now seen by some as a human right (see Okorie & Abayomi, 2019), and the existing Nigerian abortion law is viewed as overly criminalising and incompatible with human rights standards as such.[135] It is also considered a violation of the human

[134] UN. Doc. A/RES/34/180, 18th December 1979, article 16(1)(e); see WHO (2012).

[135] See CCPR/C/GC/36, 30th October 2018, para. 8; UN. Doc. E/C.12/GC/22, 2nd May 2016, paras. 38 and 40.

rights of Nigerian women and girls and therefore requires to be amended since it "is observed more in breach than compliance" (Okorie & Abayomi, 2019: 187).

(3) The Social Impact of the Abortion Law

Obviously, Nigeria falls under Category II of the World Abortion Laws Map which contains countries that allow abortion only for the purpose of preserving the life of the mother, and this makes Nigeria one of the countries with the most restrictive laws on abortion. Despite this restriction, Nigerian women and girls have always had and continue to procure abortion for unwanted pregnancies and other reasons. The records even indicate that the practice is steadily on the rise. The FMH (2018) reported the country's estimated induced abortion rate to be 1.25 million as of 2012 and then went on to indicate that this represents the double of the figure in 1996 which is 610,000. It is well documented that legal restrictions on, and even criminalisation of, abortion do not result in fewer abortions.[136] Instead, women are compelled to resort to clandestine facilities and/or unskilled abortion providers, thereby putting their health and life at risk (WHO, 2019). This appears to be case in the Nigerian context. The FMH further reports in the same place that majority of the abortions (ca. 80%) are done by medical practitioners in private settings, while the rest of about 20 percent are either self-induced or provided by other health personnel and quacks. In this latter case, the abortions are performed in a number of different settings by unskilled individuals including for example traditional medical practitioners, herbalists, and chemists, who sometimes carried out these interventions under unhygienic, unsterile conditions. That said, all abortions in the country can be classified as clandestine abortions because they usually take place in private settings, except they belong to the category of the legal exception. The consequences of clandestine and unsafe abortion are enormous and can lead to maternal death, among other things. Ayanleye (2013: 136) describes it as "one of the greatest dangers to women's reproductive health and cause of the high rate of mortality in the female adolescent population." Nigeria is currently ranked as the country with the second largest burden of maternal mortality in the world. Records show that of the global estimate of 287,000 maternal deaths per year in 2012, the country alone accounts for a whopping 14 percent. Abortion is reportedly the second leading cause of maternal death in the country, accounting for about 20 to 40 percent of the fatalities, of which approximately 10 to 14 percent are due to unsafe abortion alone (FMH, 2018).

---

[136] It has been suggested that legal restrictions on abortion do not necessarily lead to fewer abortions (WHO, 2019). The WHO (2012) reports in its guidelines on safe abortion that the rate of abortions due to unwanted pregnancies is about the same in countries with less restrictive abortion laws as in others with highly restrictive abortion laws. The Guttmacher Institute supports this with the evidence of a data from 2010–2014 which reports that the estimated abortion rate is 37 and 34 per 1000 women in countries with the most restrictive abortion laws and countries with less restrictive laws or that broadly allow for abortion, restrictively. More still, empirical evidence has shown consistently that complications and deaths from unsafe abortion tend to be higher in countries with highly restrictive abortion policies (Singh et al., 2018).

Regarding the latter, existing research further highlights two points that are of interest to this study. First, it indicates that over 50 percent of deaths arising from the patronage of all sorts of unsafe abortions involve young women, particularly adolescents (Okorie & Abayomi, 2019). Second, it suggests that such deaths affect poor citizens more. The fact is that pregnant women who urgently want an abortion for reasons other than legal exemption will do absolutely anything to get it, including paying, because they cannot access safe abortion services due to legal restrictions. While clients from wealthy backgrounds pay exorbitant fees for abortions at private hospitals or clinics, young women and girls from low-income backgrounds have to resort to unsafe procedures from unskilled abortion providers and often lose their lives due to complications. The country's abortion policy has been heavily criticised for exposing women to reproductive health risks and for its other perceived deficiencies.

Debate About the Reform of the National Law on Abortion

Access to abortion is one of the most hotly contested issues in societies across the globe, with arguments usually based on legal, moral, religious, cultural, human rights, feminist, medical and even practical perspectives. For a long time, there was no robust public debate on this issue in Nigeria. This can be attributed to African attitudes towards discussions about sex (Ayanleye, 2013). But in the last few decades, the issue has gradually come into the public discourse due to the rising reproductive health challenges in the country and, as usual, has divided Nigerians into two recognisable groups, namely the anti-reform and pro-reform groups. On the one hand, the anti-reform group is made up of a large army of citizens who want the country's abortion policy to remain as it is. They reject any idea of elective abortion and centre their arguments on the personhood of the foetus. For most people in this group, "there is no differential value between the life of the foetus and that of the mother" (Izunwa & Ifemeje, 2011: 123). In other words, the foetus is regarded as a human being or potentially human from the moment of conception and as such has the right to life, which must be respected just like other human beings. The dominant religious groups in the country belong to this group. Furthermore, they contend that elective abortion or the legalisation of abortion will engender a promiscuous lifestyle, especially among young people, and that this situation could wreck the moral and social fabric of the Nigerian society. Finally, this group assumes that amending the abortion law will result in a "slippery slope," which simply means that once the law is amended, there is always the possibility that it will be expanded further and arbitrarily (cf. Izunwa & Ifemeje, 2011). This position expresses a deep-seated fear that appears to be buoyed by an attitude of mistrust towards the Nigerian government. Based on these, any plan to reform of the existing abortion law is dead on arrival for the anti-reform group.

The pro-reform group, on the other hand, is a small group of Nigerians who advocate a more liberal abortion law. Although few, the group is made up of medical professionals, women's rights activists, journalists, researchers, and lawyers. They are of the opinion that the current state of the abortion law in the country is defective, which is why abortions still go on in the hands of unskilled individuals in private hospitals, clinics, and other secret places. More importantly, they largely anchor their arguments in health and human rights perspectives. First, they consider the law to be too restrictive to allow abortion only for therapeutic reasons and that it is imprecise in its idea of what constitutes a therapeutic maternal indication. They insist that the preservation of a mother's life is not the only maternal indication that should warrant abortion in the country. They usually demonstrate this with recourse to the relevant data and try to show how the current law has failed to meet the overwhelming reproductive health needs of women in the country and indirectly encouraged unsafe abortions. For this reason, they call for reform of the law in line with the provisions of the Maputo Protocol (Ayanleye, 2013).

To summarise, the abortion discourse in Nigeria is also fraught with controversies. The controversies arise more due to ideological differences between Nigerian citizens. Upon closer observation, two main underlying ideological strands can be identified, namely the classic pro-life and pro-choice categories.

The Attempted Reform of the Abortion Law: Patterns and Outcome

Several attempts have been made to reform Nigeria's abortion law. The first of these was made by the Nigerian Medical Association (hereinafter NMA) in 1972. The initiative was taken during its yearly convention that year, but the move was quickly abandoned due to lack of support. Three years later, the National Population Council advocated women's access to elective abortion for health and welfare reasons. This recommendation was supported by NMA and Society of Gynaecologists and Obstetricians of Nigeria (hereinafter SOGON), alongside other professional bodies. Again, the recommendation was shelved the following year after a furore arose because the address of the then Honourable Minister of Health at the 9th yearly convention of SOGON, which hinted at the possibility of a reform of the national abortion law, was misconstrued by many to mean that the government in effect was legalising abortion (Ilobinso, 2007). In 1981, a bill was presented to the House of Representatives of the National Assembly calling for the termination of pregnancy in specific circumstances, such as rape, incest, etc. The bill was sponsored by SOGON. Pressure groups, namely religious groups, the National Council of Women's Societies and the Nigerian press lobbied against it and the bill was not approved. The bill was largely unsuccessful at the floor of the house because it was feared that its passage would promote moral laxity, or as Izunwa and Ifemeje (2011: 122) technically put it, "[t]he proposed law derogated from the moral credit of the existing law." This bill resurfaced later in 1992 under a new title "The Termination of Unsafe Pregnancy and Other Related Matters." This time, it was sponsored by a team of professionals and officials of the Ministries of Health and Justice known as the Campaign Against Unwanted Pregnancy (hereinafter CAUP), who advocated a reform of the extant abortion law. The proposed new law was presented to the Presidency for approval, and the latter was alleged to be favourably disposed towards it because of the high rate of maternal morbidity and mortality due to unsafe abortion in the country. However, opponents of abortion learnt about the development and raised objections to it. Again, like its forbears, the bill failed. Still not deterred by this, the CAUP has reportedly been working on the bill since 2002 hoping to return it to the National Assembly in the future. The bill was said to be in its eighth stage of revision as of 2004 (Oye-Adeniran et al., 2004).

In another development, the Violence Against Persons (Prohibition) (VAPP) Act was eventually signed into law in 2015 after many years of legislative intervention. The Act intends to eliminate violence, particularly sexual violence, from the Nigerian system and protect the rights of survivors to receive comprehensive medical services including abortion care, etc. (see section 38). However, the Act applies only to the Federal Capital Territory (FCT) and all federal institutions nationwide in line with the federal system that the country practises (cf. section 47). This means that it has to be enacted by the different state governments for their respective federal states, and that is exactly what is being done. As of 2015, thirteen states have enacted the law as expected. For example, in 2013, the Imo State government enacted the Violence Against Persons Law in Imo State, a southeastern State. The law guarantees therapeutic abortion in certain circumstances such as rape, incest, and sexual assault, or when continuing the pregnancy endangers the life or health of the mother. In other words, the aim is to promote the reproductive health and rights of Imo women in accordance with international and regional human rights laws. But the law, particularly the sections addressing these concerns, was not accepted by a large section of the Imo public as the provisions were viewed as immoral. Hence, the government was forced to repeal the said sections later that year following a protest from traditional and religious leaders (Okorie & Abayomi, 2019; Onyemelukwe, 2018).

Overall, it can be said that some efforts have been made to reform the extant abortion law in Nigeria, but the efforts have not yielded the expected result. To this effect, the national abortion law has remained what it was under colonial system, despite the country's endorsement of most of the international human rights instruments which relate to this subject matter. Recently, the FMH published a document titled "National Guidelines on Safe Termination of Pregnancy for Legal Indications (2018)."[137] This development is thought to be important because the document represents a fresh attempt to interpret and operationalise the circumstances in which abortion can be performed within the legal framework, since the domestication of the VAPP. First, the guideline recognises that abortion can be performed to promote health or well-being of the mother (cf. introduction). Then, more importantly, it provides a compendium of medical conditions that fit into this category (cf. Chap. 4), as well as a description of the step-by-step options for proper management of all the cases (cf. Chaps. 5 and 6).

[137] See Center for Reproductive Rights, 2019: Law and Policy Guide: Life Exceptions. Available at https://reproductiverights.org/law-and-policy-guide-life-exceptions. Accessed on 01.08.2020.

(4) Religion and Abortion

Globally, abortion is a subject of wide-ranging discourses. The aspect of the abortion discourse that tends to engage the Nigerian public the most is the moral cum religious dimension. In the Nigerian context, it is difficult to think about morality without reference to the role of religion. Public morality relies heavily on the interpretations of religious principles. Particularly in matters of sexuality, religions shape the values and conduct of their adherents. That way, they influence the culture of a society and help to determine state policies. This assertion is often made in connection with Nigeria's policy on abortion (Ayanleye, 2013). Based on this assumption, it may be important to briefly consider the teachings of the dominant religious traditions in Nigeria on abortion to see if a relationship could be established at last.

Theological Perspectives of ATR

In the traditional setting, nuanced discussions about abortion most likely did not take place because such a topic was treated as a family secret and as such not discussed in public. However, human life was considered sacred and worthy of protection, including that of a foetus. Abortion was unacceptable because any such act was interpreted as killing, albeit of an unborn human life. Such was abhorred. Nevertheless, as a potential life, the life of a foetus was not deemed to have more value than that of its mother. For that reason, should a woman's life be in danger because of the continuation of a pregnancy, abortion can be allowed by invoking the common proverbial maxims of optimism such as "it is better for the water to pour away than for the calabash to be broken" (Olaide & Aderibigbe, 2014: 187). This maxim simply expresses the hopefulness that a woman would always have other pregnancies, if she is alive and healthy. Regarding the procedure, local herbs and/or other traditional practices were usually employed to cause a miscarriage. This is the only permissible exception to induced abortion in the traditional society. Extramarital pregnancies were not tolerated, nonetheless such was never considered to be a sufficient reason for inducing abortion.

Islamic Theological Perspectives

The question of abortion is also important to Islamic and Christian faiths both of which most Nigerians adhere to. To begin with, the Quran may not have made explicit reference to abortion, but it regards all life as sacred (6:151). Islamic ethics is firmly rooted in the belief in the sacredness of life and this belief shapes its teachings on life issues, including abortion (Francis et al., 2019). Islamic theology on abortion is differentiated according to the different legal schools of thought and different streams within each school. Some schools reject abortion outrightly. Others teach that it can be allowed under certain circumstances within a time frame. There are also others who think that pregnancy can still be terminated after the said time frame for health reasons (Ziebertz & Zaccaria, 2019). The fact is that Islam is generally opposed to abortion (Ok & Eren, 2013). But some Muslim scholars recognise that it is permitted (halal) in certain cases, such as where continuing the pregnancy would put the lives of both the mother and foetus in real danger. They believe that abortion may be performed in such a situation to preserve the life of the mother, though this is expected to take place before the time of ensoulment.

The Quran and Sunna describe the formation of the foetus as a stepwise development leading up to the point that it is infused with life (Quran 23:12–14; 22:5). Muslim scholars disagree about the exact moment when this happens. Various estimates have been suggested, such as the first 40, 90 or 120 days of pregnancy. However, the majority assumes that the foetus becomes human after the 120th day by virtue of ensoulment and as such has a right to survival. From this point onwards, abortion is equal to killing and therefore forbidden. It is important to note here that there is also a minority scholarly position that opposes abortion at any stage based on their belief that a human being is formed from the moment of fertilisation (Webb & Asa'd, 2019). Apart from them, others recognise that abortion is not permitted in Islam after 120 days of pregnancy unless it is necessary to save the life of a pregnant woman. Having said that, it is not allowed to kill a foetus for health, eugenic, extramarital pregnancies, or any other reasons. To do so is not only immoral but also criminal.[138]

Christian Theological Perspectives

The Christian religion has even stricter restrictions on abortion. The Bible also does not explicitly address abortion, but it does view human life as a sacred gift from God (Genesis 1:26; Psalm 139: 13), and Christian moral teachings about abortion over time have appealed to this belief. Early Christianity condemned abortion. The earliest teaching on abortion is found in the Didache, a 2nd century document, which clearly condemns the practice (Didache 2:2 in Francis et al., 2019). Early and medieval Christian thinkers and Church Councils all viewed abortion as the killing of an innocent person, though there was no consensus among them as to when the foetus becomes a person (Anthony & Sterkens, 2019). So, building on this long history of opposition to abortion, the different Christian denominations today also view it as killing and as such a grave sin. The Catholic Church, for instance, teaches that life must be protected from the moment of conception until death (CCC no. 2270). This teaching is echoed in many other instructional documents (cf. EV no. 61; Donum Vitae, hereinafter DV chaps. 4 and 5). The Church regards the embryo and subsequently the foetus as a human being based on the principles of continuity and potentiality and demands that it be recognised by virtue of this status as a subject of rights, especially the inalienable right to life. It also requests that the foetus' right to life be safeguarded "as far as possible, like any other human being" (CCC no. 2274). For the Church, therefore, abortion signifies the killing of an innocent human being and is intrinsically evil (Veritatis Splendor, hereinafter VS no. 80). The Church's teaching office constantly reaffirms its moral condemnation of any kind of abortion, thus: "[t]his teaching has not been changed and is unchangeable" (DV chap. 1; CCC no. 2271). This position is rooted in the belief in the sanctity of human life,[139] which

---

[138] See chapter IX, sections 207–211 of the Zamfara State Sharia Penal Code, 2000. The penalty for abortion includes payment of compensation, lashes, and retaliation.

[139] Pius XI in Casti Connubii (1930, no. 64, hereinafter CC) referred to abortion as a violation of the sacredness of an innocent life. Reportedly, this was the first time the human life was explicitly described as sacred by the Catholic teaching authority (cf. Anthony & Sterkens, 2019); see also EV nos. 57 & 62.

gives rise to its inviolability and integrity at every stage and in every situation, as the Church teaches.[140] Nevertheless, there is one exception to the strict Catholic prohibition of abortion. This concerns extreme cases of pregnancy that put the life of the mother and child at risk, for example, cases of uterine cancer, ectopic pregnancy, etc. Only such conditions would warrant medical interventions that may lead to saving the life of the mother or that of the unborn baby. This is referred to as unintentional abortion in the sense that the intended outcome of the medical procedures here is to save the woman's life and not to terminate the pregnancy. So, the death of the foetus is tolerated as an unintended result. Interpretation of this doctrine varies and sometimes clashes among theologians, but unintentional abortion is a possibility within the Catholic tradition.[141] Apart from this singular instance, abortion is not permitted in all other circumstances.[142] It is a grave sin[143] punishable with excommunication for all the concerned persons (CCC no. 2272; Can. 1398).

The Protestant and Pentecostal churches in Nigeria are also opposed to abortion. Despite their slightly different theological perspectives and doctrinal nuances on life issues, they too affirm the protection of unborn human life based on the principle of the sanctity of life.

3.3.2.3 Euthanasia

(1) The Bioethical Issue of Euthanasia

Euthanasia, also known as mercy killing, is a multidimensional concept. It refers to the practice of intentionally ending a life by painless means in order to relieve persistent suffering. It is often performed on people with a terminal illness who are in real pain. It can occur with or without the consent of the patient or victim and as such is classified as voluntary, non-voluntary or involuntary. Euthanasia is said to be voluntary when it is performed at the request of the person who dies, and non-voluntary if it involves a second party or an appropriate person, for example, a close family member, a healthcare professional, or even a court making the decision to end a person's life on his or her behalf. A typical situation here would be where a patient lacks the capacity to make a choice (e.g., a child) or is unable to consent due to his or her current health condition (e.g., a person in coma). Otherwise, it is involuntary euthanasia to kill a person who can give consent and whose consent has not been sought, or against his or her expressed wishes, even though it is done for compassionate reasons. This would pass for murder in many climes. It is a complex process as such and therefore requires a lot of considerations. Euthanasia exists in

[140] EV nos. 40 & 53; see also Gaudium et Spes (hereinafter GS) 1965, no. 51.

[141] Unintentional abortion is recognised within the Catholic Church through what in technically theological terms is known as the principle of double effect (cf. CCC 1752).

[142] See Congregation for the Doctrine of the Faith (hereinafter CDF) 1980. Declaration on Euthanasia, chap. 2.

[143] See CDF (1974). Declaration on Procured Abortion, no. 13.

several different forms.[144] Basically it can be active or passive. It is active when a person directly and deliberately intervenes to end someone's life, for instance, by administering a lethal dose of a sedative to treat a severe pain. This contrast significantly with the situation where a person causes death of a patient by passively doing nothing to prolong life or withdrawing life-support measures such as a ventilator or a feeding tube, etc., knowing that death will follow. In this case, euthanasia is said to be passive, and this is the less controversial of the two.

Euthanasia is unquestionably an emotive subject and perhaps one of today's most contested bioethical issues. The controversy here arises from the question of what choices a terminally ill patient, a physician, and the patient's family have in the face of persistent suffering, and what the moral implications of their choices are. Like other issues, this controversy extends across societies and time periods. The Graeco-Roman philosophers carried out serious discussions about the issue. For instance, the Pythagoreans were opposed to the practice of euthanasia, whereas Socrates, Plato, and particularly the Stoics considered it morally permissible in cases of terminal illness (Anderson, 1998). But these early contributions could not go far because of Judeo-Christian principles as well as the widespread acceptance of the tenets of the Hippocratic Oath.[145] The traditional Christian belief regarded euthanasia as a breach of the ban on prohibition of murder in the Decalogue. Thus, with the increasing dominance of Christianity which practically reinforced the position of the Hippocratic school, euthanasia came to be seen as a form of homicide and was outlawed in the medical field. This position represents the prevalent public attitude towards euthanasia from the first few centuries A.D. through the Middle Ages to the Renaissance and Reformation. It was not until the Age of Enlightenment, when the Church's authoritative teaching on all matters was challenged, that serious discussions about the permissibility of euthanasia were possible, and people soon began to advocate for the practice. However, the advocacy for the legalisation of euthanasia reached its climax in the twentieth century thanks to the twin advancements in human rights and medical technology (Oniha, n.d.). The potential of modern medicine to prolong and sustain life through technological means even in a persistent vegetative state (PVS) provoked such questions as what courses of action should be available to a physician and a patient's family in cases of extreme suffering, especially when the patient is incapable of choice (Augustyn et al., 2019).

---

[144] Assisted suicide is sometimes mentioned as a kind of euthanasia, but these are two different concepts. Assisted suicide differs from euthanasia in that in assisted suicide it is the patient who kills himself or herself with the aid of another person, usually a physician or other healthcare provider. Hence the name 'physician-assisted suicide' (PAS). However, both concepts are also closely related because they refer to death, which results out of the desire to ease the persistent suffering of a terminally ill patient (see Nwafor, 2010a).

[145] Although it is not specifically known when this oath was written, it is widely attributed to the physician Hippocrates and dated from around 5th to 3rd century B.C. In the oath, doctors are prohibited from giving a deadly drug to anybody, not even if asked for, or from suggesting such a course of action (Augustyn et al., 2019; Anderson, 1998). It is likely that it has undergone significant modifications over time.

In Europe and America, where human rights had gained more acceptances, such concerns gave rise to organised movements for the recognition and legalisation of a right to die or to die with dignity, such as the Voluntary Euthanasia Legalisation Society founded in England in 1935, and the Euthanasia Society of America (ESA) founded in New York in 1938, to mention just a few. Their advocacy has since induced inter alia the acceptance and legalisation of euthanasia in several countries. As of August 2020, active euthanasia is legal in the Netherlands, Belgium, Colombia, Luxembourg, Canada, and a few Australian States, while physician-assisted suicide is permitted in Switzerland, Finland, Germany, Japan, and some US States. Although these countries have legalised these practices, euthanasia remains a crime in many other countries, including Nigeria.

(2) The Law on Euthanasia in Nigeria

There is no specific law on euthanasia in Nigeria. The legal provisions relating to the practice are embedded in the country's bifurcated penal laws, namely the Criminal Code Act and the Penal Code Act. The Criminal Code does not use the term "euthanasia" but contains several provisions that many believe relate to the practice of euthanasia. First and foremost, the Code considers any form of killing of another person to be unlawful unless such is sanctioned by law.[146] Then, under section 308 it talks about the causing of another's death "directly or indirectly, by any means whatever" as equal to killing that other person. Here, the use of the words, directly or indirectly, is interpreted by some to include, for example, any act or omission by a healthcare professional to hasten death in any way, whether by giving an overdose of a lethal injection or by withdrawal of ventilators, and respirators, etc. (see Sani et al., 2017). That said, any person who unlawfully kills another is likely to be convicted for murder or manslaughter, depending on the facts and circumstances of the case.[147] Even if the killing was done at the request of the victim or even out of compassion, it is immaterial as the perpetrator will still be liable for either murder or manslaughter. According to the Code, free will or consent, or good motive "does not affect the criminal responsibility of any person by whom such death is caused."[148] For the punishment in this instance, it prescribes a mandatory death sentence on conviction for murder[149] and life imprisonment for manslaughter.[150]

Secondly, in section 311 the Code addresses more specifically the offence of killing by conduct or omission. It provides that "[a] person who … hastens the death of another person who, when the act is done or the omission is made, is labouring under some disorder or disease arising from another cause, is deemed to have killed that other person." Again, no mention is made of euthanasia in this provision, but it

[146] Section 306 of the CCA.

[147] Ibid., section 315. Murder is defined more elaborately under section 316.

[148] Ibid., section 299.

[149] Ibid., section 319(1).

[150] Ibid., section 325.

is implied in the references to the words 'conduct' and "omission" both of which have strong association with the active and passive forms of euthanasia (Oniha, n.d.). The same can be said of assisted suicide as well.[151] The Code made additional provisions in section 316(5) and (6) where it talks about causing death "by administering any stupefying or overpowering things" or "by wilfully stopping the breath of any person", respectively. These too are thought to be referring to euthanasia. According to the Code, a person who kills another in any of these circumstances is guilty of murder, irrespective of whether the conduct or omission was with the patient's consent, in his or her best interest, or for compassionate reasons. A combined reading of these provisions therefore shows that euthanasia is a crime under the Criminal Code.

The Penal Code also has similar provisions regarding killing in general and suicide. It addresses the offence of murder and manslaughter much like the Criminal Code but uses the terms 'culpable homicide punishable with death'[152] and 'culpable homicide not punishable with death'[153] for them, respectively. It also criminalises abetting a suicide.[154] But it has little or nothing to say about euthanasia. The Penal Code does not make any provision for killing that is carried out with the assistance of a medical practitioner, irrespective of the condition of the patient. The closest it came to considering this topic can be found in section 249 where it criminalises any person who "administers to or causes to be taken by a person a poison or any stupefying, intoxicating or unwholesome drug or thing with intent to cause hurt to that person." It prescribes a prison term of up to ten years and a fine for persons who commit such an offence. From the foregoing analysis, it can be concluded that euthanasia is equal to murder or homicide under the Nigerian penal system and as such is illegal, like in most common law countries. However, the tenability of this position has been challenged lately by some scholars within the broader frame of the Nigerian legislation.

(3) Trends in the Debate over the (Il)legality of Euthanasia in Nigeria

As with most bioethical issues, euthanasia is not a hotly debated issue in Nigeria, not because Nigerians do not face the dilemma of choosing between quality and sanctity of life in normal life situations, but because it is regarded as a family issue and is often discussed in the familial setting (cf. Sakali, 2013). Another reason could be that this is not a prime concern of Nigerians. Above all, they seem to assume that the practice is illegal, as most local cultures do not tolerate any assistance to terminate life for any reasons.

---

[151] Under section 326, the practice of assisted suicide is a felony punishable upon conviction with life jail.

[152] Section 221 of the PC.

[153] Ibid., section 222.

[154] Ibid., sections 227, and 228.

However, a recent decision of the Nigeria Supreme Court in the case of *Medical and Dental Practitioners Disciplinary Tribunal v. Okonkwo* (hereinafter *MDPDT v. Okonkwo*),[155] which recognised a patient's constitutional right of self-determination, appears to have moved the subject of euthanasia from the familial circles into the public arena and since then the legal status of the practice in Nigeria is being publicly discussed, at least, in academic circles. As a matter of fact, the Supreme Court decision in the above case is one judicial pronouncement that is deemed to have directly challenged the blanket criminalisation of euthanasia in the country's penal system. In this case, a 29-year-old woman, Mrs. Martha Okorie, had post-delivery complications and needed life-saving blood transfusion which she declined on account of her religious beliefs. She was discharged by the first hospital she consulted with a note that she refused transfusion and might die as a result. She was taken to another hospital where the respondent, Dr. Okonkwo, re-admitted her. Her husband presented the doctor with a card signed by her and two witnesses instructing that no blood transfusion should be administered to her in compliance with her rights as a patient and her religious belief. She also left a note absolving the hospital from liability in case of any undesirable outcome. The doctor accepted and managed her with alternative treatment until she passed on. In the wake of her death, the respondent was charged by the MDPDT with negligence and professional misconduct contrary to section 16 of the Medical and Dental Practitioners Act.[156] He was convicted and then suspended from practice for six months. But the Supreme Court cleared him of any wrongdoing arising from the patient's treatment and interpreted his conduct as a recognition of the latter's fundamental right to consent to medical intervention expressed within the context of the constitutionally guaranteed rights to privacy and freedom of religion, which can only be limited "where they impinge on the rights of others or where they put the welfare of society or public health in jeopardy." Explaining this a little further the Court said: "[t]he sum total of the [said] rights ... which an individual has, ... is that an individual should be left alone to choose a course for his life, unless a clear and compelling overriding state interest justifies the contrary."[157]

Although this judicial pronouncement was acclaimed as a landmark decision in that it introduced a shift from medical paternalism (i.e., a practice where medical professionals impose their decisions on their patients) to a patient's autonomy (i.e., a system where the medical decision is dominated by the patient), it also attracted critical comments from by a cross-section of Nigerians, especially the opponents and proponents of euthanasia. Opponents argue that some other outside considerations should have overridden the subjective decision of the patient in this specific instance, such as the interests of the dependants of the patient who may be adversely

[155] (2001) 6 NWLR (pt. 710).

[156] Medical and Dental Practitioners Act Cap. M8 LFN 2004.

[157] (2001) 6 NWLR (pt. 710), p. 244. Note: parenthesis and emphasis are mine.

affected by the latter's decision (see Nwafor, 2010a). Based on this, they claim that the Court was not circumspect enough in reaching its decision with apparent disregard of the Nigerian social context, where the consideration of the self is not possible outside the concept of a community. Opponents also strongly criticised the Court's decision because of their opposition to all types of euthanasia. They contend that the decision would create a platform for the emergence of pro-euthanasia and assisted-suicide attitudes and/or agitations. According to them, in upholding the patient's autonomy or right to self-determination without restriction, a downhill movement towards the practice of euthanasia and the right to die has been initiated. Thus, they call on the Court to revisit its decision with a view to setting the 'necessary limitations' to a patient's right (Salihu, 2017).

For their part, the proponents assert that a patient's right to consent to medical intervention flows from the fundamental right to self-determination which is guaranteed by the Constitution. The concept of self-determination as an individual right is intended to give individuals full control over their lives, including their health. In this context, medical intervention without a patient's permission would constitute some form of invasion of the bodily integrity and private sphere of the patient. For this reason, proponents insist on the paramountcy of the informed consent of a patient in all medical dealings with a physician. For them, any medical treatment of a radical nature requires valid consent, which must be obtained before the treatment begins. To proceed with treatment without this or against the wish of a patient amounts to a trespass that would expose the physician to the pain of criminal sanction.[158] On the flip side, however, they insist that a physician cannot be held responsible for the consequences of an informed consent of a patient. With this consideration, they conclude that it constitutes a breach of the rights to personal liberty (self-determination) and the dignity of the person to deny any terminally ill adult with his or her full mental capacity the right to choose or reject a mode of treatment which may result in his or her death. Thus, for them, the concept of passive voluntary euthanasia is well-accommodated in the Supreme Court decision in *MDPDT v. Okonkwo* (Oniha, n.d.; Nwafor, 2010a).

They further claim that voluntary euthanasia is not inconsistent with the constitutional provision on the right to life, if the latter is properly interpreted in line with the 'principle of community reading' as envisaged by the draftsmen of the Constitution and which the Nigerian judiciary adopts in relation to fundamental human rights provisions.[159] With this as a guide, it means that the principle of sanctity of life as enshrined in section 33(1) of the Constitution is to be read together with a concomitant provision in section 34(1), namely that of the right to dignity of every human person. Other relevant provisions include the right to be free of a permanent state of torture and inhuman or degrading treatment as guaranteed in section 34(1)(a), also the right to personal liberty in section 35(1), and the right to freedom

---

[158] See *Okekearu v. Tanko* (2002) 15 NWLR (pt.791) p. 657.

[159] See *Nafiu Rabiu v. The State* (1981) 2 NCLR 293.

from discrimination in section 42, to mention just a few. This implies that for the constitutionally guaranteed right to life to be enjoyed meaningfully, it has to be enjoyed alongside these rights. According to them, if this is applied in equal measure to all Nigerians irrespective of a state of health or circumstances, including the terminally ill patient, then it follows that the right to euthanasia is recognised under the Constitution as an integral part of the right to life (Oniha & Oniha, 2015).

Lastly, regarding the position held by opponents in *MDPDT v. Okonkwo* that the interests of the patient's dependants should have overridden the decision of the latter, proponents responded that the issue of this case concerned the patient's right to self-determination expressed within the context of the right to freedom of thought, conscience, and religion, a right whose legal exceptions are expressly stated in the Constitution. And according to the Constitution, the interest of another individual is not one of the statutory exceptions. Any other interest that overrides this freedom must be of benefit to the public, as is clearly highlighted in the Supreme Court's decision.

So far, there may not have been any direct case of euthanasia in any Nigerian court since the determination of this case. But if anything, the judicial pronouncement therein has put a question mark on the legal status of euthanasia in Nigeria and provided the impetus for public discussion on the topic.

(4) Religion and Euthanasia

According to Nigerian criminal law, euthanasia is murder or homicide, and most Nigerians tend to perceive it as such. However, it is believed that the public attitude to equate euthanasia with murder or homicide is based mainly on socio-cultural grounds.

Theological Perspectives of ATR

The religion of African forebears viewed life as a divine gift and most traditional societies had taboos and rituals designed to protect life (Nwafor, 2010a). The customary laws of these societies strictly prohibited any form of assistance to end life, even if for good motives.[160] That was murder simpliciter and persons convicted of such were usually banished from the land. The request for an assistance to die was also understood as suicide when it leads to the death of the one who makes the request. Suicide was generally regarded as a taboo. Persons who died by this means were normally denied a befitting burial rite; their corpses were thrown away in the 'evil forest'[161] after which the community or land would be cleansed of defilement.

[160] Here, scholars often allude to a certain practice that obtained among some Yoruba communities in southwestern Nigeria, where an Alafin (i.e., a king) that had fallen out of favour with the generality of his subjects was presented with a calabash representing a call to suicide (Obi, 2014; Oniha, n.d.). Although it is usually mentioned as one ancient practice with a semblance of euthanasia, but the practice is more like suicide than anything else.

[161] Evil forests were thought to be the abode of the malign spirits and forces. In the ancient times, people who died untimely, mysteriously or shamefully could not be buried at home. Instead, their corpses were thrown into the evil forest (Ikeke, 2013).

In the traditional system, sickness was not considered to be of any salutary value. In fact, it was often viewed as an attack by bad spirits or punishment from ancestors and was therefore abhorred. All the same, people suffered from painful, incurable illnesses that aroused the desire for euthanasia. Sometimes a patient is in such a state that people think (s)he would be better off dead. If such a patient is a relative or friend, people usually heave a sigh of relief when (s)he eventually dies and could be heard muttering such sad words about the deceased as: "at least let him [or her] go and rest" (Oniha & Oniha, 2015). However, many Nigerians would not consider mercy-killing or mercy-dying as the best choice in such a situation, citing the popular maxim: "the worst health is better than death."[162] That being the case, great care is given to the sick and sickly members of society, and they are supported until death (Nwafor, 2010a).

Islamic Theological Perspectives

Similarly, Islam discourages euthanasia. In fact, it regards it as a crime. Islamic teaching on euthanasia is rooted in the same principle of the sanctity of life. Muslims generally believe that life is a divine gift and as such euthanasia is not allowed because the Quran expressly forbids 'taking a human life that Allah has made sacred' (6:151). This position is accepted by most of the theological and legal schools of thought in Islam. Moreover, the Quran teaches that the length of human life is determined by God (3:145; 16:61). He is the sovereign of life and as such the time, manner and circumstances of death are fixed by Him and no one else. Humans are stewards, not the owners, of life. It was given to them to protect. Therefore, to kill an innocent person or to actively influence death under any guise at all is strictly forbidden.

It follows then that this is specifically about the active form of euthanasia, though Islam does not legally differentiate between active and passive euthanasia (cf. Ilkilic, 2008). Islamic theological opinions on euthanasia may differ slightly among Muslim scholars, but active euthanasia is outrightly rejected by all. Any assistance to terminate life in any way is not allowed, no matter how good the motive might be. Even the use of pain-therapy is forbidden if this would influence the time of death. Mercy killing, whether at the patient's or the family's request, is morally wrong in the same way as complying with such a request (Ok & Eren, 2013). The principle of individual autonomy does not apply here because life belongs to God and the rights of the individual ought to be weighed against it along with other factors such as community values and family considerations (Webb & Asa'd, 2019). Otherwise, both the patient and the assistants are deemed to have committed sin and will suffer for it at the Judgment Day.

Passive euthanasia presents a more complicated challenge in Islam due to modern developments in medicine. This is largely so because the main concern here is not to assist dying but to allow death. Modern Islamic jurists agree, for instance, that

[162] The maxim literarily translates as follows among the Igbo tribe in the southeast of Nigeria: "*mkpomkpo ndu ka onwu mma*" (Obi, 2014: 81). Similar versions of it can be found among other ethnic nationalities in Nigeria.

life-support may be withdrawn to allow for natural death in a terminal situation where a patient's life is only maintained on the device. Although removing the device contributed to the patient's death, death in this case is construed as the natural consequence of the patient's illness. That way, they perceive this form of euthanasia as allowing God's plan to occur (Ibrahim, 2008; Ziebertz & Reindl, 2013). Lastly, Sharia law has a list of statutory exceptions for killing, and euthanasia is not one of such exceptions (Francis et al., 2019). It is therefore not allowed in Islam to take life under any guise without the due process of law.

Christian Theological Perspectives

The Christian teaching on euthanasia is also anchored in the belief in the sanctity of life, which is based on biblical tradition. According to the Bible, human life is a divine gift that should evoke respect and gratitude (Genesis 1:26; Psalm 139: 13). Thus, voluntary euthanasia constitutes a wilful refusal of this precious gift. Furthermore, God gave human beings rationality, but this does grant them absolute control over their lives. They are custodians rather than owners of this gift. Life belongs to God. It should also be protected in view of the commandment not to kill (Exodus 20:13), as well as Jesus' command to love one's neighbour (Ziebertz & Zaccaria, 2019). Christians believe that there are situations in which it may be permitted to take life, such as self-defence, just war, etc., but that euthanasia is certainly not one of the established biblical categories. Again, life should not be terminated simply because it is difficult or inconvenient. Christianity ascribes a redemptive value to suffering whereby it is viewed as a way of sharing in Jesus' suffering on the cross in the hope of rising to new and eternal life (Van der Ven, 2016). In addition, there is belief in miracles through which God can intervene positively in human affairs even in hopeless situations. Finally, another principle on which Christian perspectives on euthanasia have been articulated is the biblical view of death. The Bible teaches that death is inevitable (Ecclesiastes 3:2) and that life should be protected until death. However, Christians do not accept the notion that everything must be done to save life at all costs, since, for them, 'to be home is to be with the Lord' (2 Corinthians 5:8). Therefore, as death approaches some treatments have to be offered but certainly not all, especially the ones that will extend life only transiently. The administering of drugs to ease pain is morally allowed (Proverbs 31:6), though these may have a side effect of shortening life (Anderson, 1998). Based on the foregoing considerations, Christians generally regard euthanasia as immoral and even criminal.

Official teachings of the Catholic Church, for example, strongly reject euthanasia as an "intrinsic evil" (VS no. 80) that should be avoided in all circumstances. The CCC, however, makes a distinction between direct and indirect euthanasia. Direct euthanasia is considered murder and is therefore morally unacceptable, regardless of the motive or means (cf. CCC no. 2277). As far as indirect euthanasia is concerned, the CCC (no. 2278) sums it up in this way: "[h]ere one does not will to cause death; one's inability to impede it is merely accepted." The Church, therefore, acknowledges the inability of modern medicine to prevent death and cautions against medical treatments which are disproportionate to the expected outcome or particularly burdensome for the patients. Within this context, palliative care is acceptable in line with the doctrine of double effect, whereby wanting to alleviate the pain of a patient may result in death as an indirect effect (CCC no. 2279). In a word, the concern of Christians, as clarified by the Catholic Church, is that there should be no direct attack on human life from conception till the end and that sick people should be able to lead their lives as normal as possible (CCC no. 2276).

Based on these perspectives, it has been repeatedly suggested that public attitudes towards euthanasia in Nigeria are driven by religious beliefs. Be that as it may, some other reasons have also been advanced that may contribute to how Nigerians react to the permissibility of euthanasia, such as fear of a slippery slope. In relation to euthanasia, the term describes a downward movement from voluntary to involuntary euthanasia that is likely to occur if the practice is legalised. Given the examples of such occurrences that are now readily cited in some civilised countries such as the Netherlands, Belgium, etc., proponents of this idea believe that some Nigerians are already thinking about the likelihood of such abuses in the country if the practice is legalised (see Sani et al., 2017). Another factor that may also determine public attitudes towards euthanasia in Nigeria is the level of illiteracy. Since a high percentage of Nigerians are still illiterate or semi-literate, some argue that Nigerian society is not yet ready for euthanasia because majority of the citizens do not understand the processes and how the practice works (Salihu, 2017).

3.4 Political Rights[163]

Political rights refer to those rights that enable individuals to associate freely and to participate in the political life of their society without discrimination or repression. These can take various forms, such as the right to vote or stand for public office, the right to join or form a political party, the right to hold meetings, peaceful processions, rallies or demonstrations, the freedom to express political ideas, the right to strike and participate in trade unions or other interest groups, and refugee rights. They are granted to citizens by the constitution of their country and are important because they enable citizens to influence their government. The principles of procedural justice such as the right to a fair trial, the right to due process of law, and the right to a judicial remedy, etc. are sometimes viewed as part of political rights. Strictly speaking, however, political rights are rights of participation in civil society and politics of one's country, the most notable form being the right to vote. These rights are closely tied to citizenship status.

As a concept, citizenship is a form of nationality. It is used in international law to identify nationals with full political rights and, as such, is the most privileged form of nationality. Over the centuries, full political rights were not enjoyed by all nationals; in most cases they were granted on the basis of citizenship status.

[163] In this subheading, Carvajal, E.T. (2013)'s paper, "The Political Rights of Mexican Migrants: Nationality and Citizenship in Mexico", was extensively consulted for the international context of political rights.

In ancient Rome, for example, only full Roman citizens were afforded the said rights. Other nationals such as women, slaves and semi-citizens were excluded, as were non-nationals and foreigners. Likewise, in ancient Greece, to which the origin of the concept of citizenship is often attributed, only adult male landowners were entitled to vote. The French Revolution is considered a major landmark in the history of political rights in Europe and beyond because it played an important role in the evolution of political rights and in the enhancement of the concept of citizenship, among other things. The Revolution's most famous document, the Declaration of the Rights of Man and of the Citizen of 1789, was the first to distinguish between fundamental rights and political rights. Although it guaranteed a range of rights to a larger segment of the population, political rights were not granted to all citizens (Carvajal, 2013). The holders of the latter rights were officially designated as active citizens and included only men aged at least 25 who paid poll tax, i.e., property owners (Censer & Hunt, 2001). This arrangement was premised on the assumption that only those who have a stake in the nation could make "informed political decisions" (Popkin, 2006: 46). Others who did not belong to this group, such as women, slaves, children, and foreigners, were referred to as passive citizens.

The situation of political inequality among citizens, especially the exclusion of women from political rights, was not limited to France. It was the global situation until around the middle of the nineteenth century when it was decisively questioned by women's suffrage movements and women's rights activists. As a result, the barriers, including the property requirements for exercising the right to vote, were gradually reduced and finally dismantled, so that all citizens had equal access to political participation. In 1948, political equality, along with other political rights, was recognised as a universal human right in the Universal Declaration and has been part of customary international law ever since. The model of political rights enunciated in the Universal Declaration[164] has been further elaborated in other UN conventions like the ICCPR, and the African Charter.[165] In article 25, for instance, the ICCPR stipulates that "[e]very citizen" shall have the right to take part in the conduct of public affairs, vote and be elected at genuine periodic elections, and have equal access to public service positions in his country. Although the ICCPR does not specify the meaning of the term citizenship here, it simply guarantees every citizen equal access to political rights without discrimination,[166] and this includes citizens residing abroad.[167] The African Charter also follows this line of thought by

[164] The Universal Declaration states in article 21(1) that "[e]veryone has the right to take part in the government of his country". Here, it refers to "everyone" instead of citizens or nationals.

[165] See also the Convention on the Elimination of All Forms of Discrimination Against Women (CEDAW), and the International Convention on the Protection of All Migrant Workers and Members of Their Families (ICRMW).

[166] Cf. UN Doc. A/RES/34/180, 18th December 1979, article 7.

[167] The ICRMW states in article 41(1) that "[m]igrant workers and members of their families shall have the right to participate in public affairs of their state of origin and to vote and to be elected at elections of that state, in accordance with its legislation" (UN Doc. A/RES/45/158, 18th December 1990).

recognising the political rights of every citizen in article 13(1–3). The question of the political rights of citizens living abroad and the participation of foreigners in the public life of their place of residence is complex, but relevant in the context of international migration. Political rights are now protected in the laws of many countries around the world. Nigeria is no exception.

3.4.1 Political Rights Provisions in Nigerian Law

The Nigerian Constitution provides for the fundamental rights to freedom of assembly and association. Under Section 40, it states that "[e]very person shall be entitled to assemble freely and associate with other persons, and in particular he may form or belong to any political party, trade union or any other association for the protection of his interests". Although both rights—freedom of assembly and association—are lumped together in this single provision, they have different but related meanings.[168] On the one hand, the freedom of assembly entails the ability of individuals to come together to pursue a common goal or to express and defend their shared ideas. The UN Special Rapporteur on the rights to freedom of peaceful assembly and association, Maina Kiai defines assembly as "an intentional and temporary gathering in a private or public space for a specific purpose."[169] This right therefore primarily concerns the freedom of individuals to assemble in public places and is often used in connection with the right to protest. But also, indoor meetings, rallies, or even sit-in strikes are part of it. It is important to note that the term 'assembly' as used herein refers to peaceful assemblies and not those with violent intent. This point is clearly made in a number of international and regional human rights instruments that guarantee this right.[170] The constitutional provision on the right of assembly is supplemented by domestic statutes, such as the Public Order Act 2004[171] and the African Charter Act, as well as court judgments.[172]

---

[168] The Inter-American Court of Human Rights in the Case of *Escher* et al. *v. Brazil* held, among other things, that freedom of association "establishes the right of assembly". Or differently put, assembly is part and parcel of the activities of associations (see para. 169 of the Preliminary Objections, Merits, Reparations, and Costs. Judgment of 6th July 2009, in Lanza, 2019).

[169] UN Doc. A/HRC/20/27, 21st May 2012, para. 24.

[170] Article 20 of the Universal Declaration; article 21 of the ICCPR, article 5(d)(ix) of the ICERD, article 15 of the CRC, article 11 of the African Charter and article 8 of the ACRWC.

[171] The Public Order Act, Cap. P42 LFN 2004 is particularly a relevant piece of legislation here, as the primary legislation regulating assemblies in the country. The Act was promulgated as a decree under the military regime in 1979 (International Federation for Human Rights, 2010). But it was deemed superfluous in a democratic dispensation and unconstitutional, and thus has been judicially voided since 2007 by the Nigerian Court of Appeal (hereinafter C.A.) in the case of *Inspector General of Police v. All Nigeria Peoples Party & Ors.* [(2007) 18 NWLR (pt. 1066) 457 C.A.].

[172] For example, in this same case of *Inspector General of Police v. All Nigeria Peoples Party & Ors.* (2007), the Court held inter alia that the freedom of assembly is part of the foundation on which government itself rests.

Freedom of association, on the other hand, protects the right of individuals to form and join associations to protect their collective interests without being compelled to do so.[173] Examples of such associations are trade unions, political parties, professional associations, civil society organisations (CSOs), cooperatives, religious bodies, foundations, sports or online clubs.[174] It is more commonly used in labour relations and means that workers can unionise and engage in all union activities including, for example, strikes to demand better and safer working conditions, etc. (Okene & Okpara, 2007). Thus, this provision bars employers, including the government itself as an employer, from interfering with the individual's right to freedom of choice in matters of trade union formation and membership. This was the point of contention in the *Anigboro v. Sea Trucks Limited* case,[175] in which the Court of Appeal held inter alia that the summary dismissal of workers who persisted in choosing a union constituted an abuse of their right to freedom of association. Like the freedom of assembly, the exercise of the right to freedom of association in Nigeria is supported by several domestic laws, such as the Trade Union Act 2004 as amended, and the Electoral Act 2010.[176] These local efforts are further strengthened by all the relevant regional and international human rights treaties to which the country is signatory.

The rights of assembly and association are an integral part of participatory democracy. They are also a means of realising or ensuring respect for other human rights (Okene & Okpara, 2007). For instance, the freedom of religion may only be exercised jointly with others if these freedoms exist. Besides, freedom of expression is regarded as a corollary of people's rights to assemble and associate.[177] A combination of this and the two freedoms can strengthen a responsive democratic system and ensure the meaningful exercise of the right to participate in public affairs. Furthermore, the rights of assembly and association are recognised as an extension of the right to personal liberty. Through the exercise of these civil liberties, individuals and groups have advocated justice and advanced the human rights agenda throughout history.

Apart from these twin rights, the basic human right to freedom of movement is another political right that is also perceived as civil liberty in Nigeria. The Constitution recognises it as a fundamental right in section 41(1) and provides for it

---

[173] UN Doc. A/HRC/20/27, 21st May 2012, para. 53.

[174] Ibid., para. 52.

[175] (1995) 6 NWLR (pt. 399) p. 35.

[176] Some other important legislations here include the Electoral (Amendment) Act (no.2) 2011–2015, States Electoral Laws, States Independent Electoral Commission Laws, the African Charter as amended, and perhaps the Companies and Allied Matters Act (CAMA) 2020, as well as the Independent National Electoral Commission (INEC) Regulations and Guidelines for the Conduct of Elections 2019.

[177] For example, in its General Comment no. 34 interpreting Article 19 of the ICCPR (on Freedoms of Opinion and Expression), the UN Human Rights Committee stated that freedom of expression is "integral to the enjoyment of the rights to freedom of assembly and association, and the exercise of the right to vote" (CCPR/C/GC/34, 12th September 2011, para. 4).

in following terms: "[e]very citizen of Nigeria is entitled to move freely throughout Nigeria and to reside in any part thereof, and no citizen of Nigeria shall be expelled from Nigeria or refused entry thereby or exit therefrom." It should be noted from the outset that the right to freedom of movement, in contrast to the twin rights that apply to every person, is accorded only to Nigerians. In fact, the Constitution here grants it only to Nigerian citizens. According to legal commentators, however, this does not necessarily imply that foreigners and non-citizens are excluded from exercising this right in Nigeria. Instead, it simply means that their right of unrestricted movement is not a constitutional right (Chijioke, 2020). The legal status of foreigners and non-citizens in Nigeria, as well as their rights, including the right to free movement, are elaborated in other laws, such as the Immigration Act 2015, the Criminal and Penal Code Acts, in accordance with their purpose of residence. Their freedom of movement is also guaranteed in relevant human rights treaties endorsed by the country.[178] Therefore, in principle, all persons in Nigeria are granted freedom of movement. The purview of this right is further strengthened by section 15(3) of the Constitution, which obligates the country to "(a) provide adequate facilities for and encourage free mobility of people, goods and services throughout the Federation, [and]; (b) secure full residence rights for every citizen in all parts of the Federation."

The concept of freedom of movement in the constitutional context embraces a wide range of topics like the right of unrestricted internal mobility and residence. This entails that a citizen of Nigeria can move freely in and/or to any of part of the country and reside there without unlawful restrictions. This right cannot be taken away, even under the guise of some executive regulations, or state security policies, etc. This was the subject of the judicial decision in *Attorney-General and Commissioner for Justice, Kebbi State v. Jokolo and Ors,*[179] where the Court held inter alia that the banishment of the deposed Emir of Gwandu (in Kebbi State, in north-western Nigeria) to Lafia and later to Obi (both in Nasarawa State in the north-central zone) amounted to an abuse of his right of freedom of movement. The constitutional provision on freedom of movement also covers the rights of egress and ingress. In other words, every Nigerian has the right to leave the country at will, without hindrances. This includes as a matter of necessity the right to hold a Nigerian passport to facilitate the exercise of the right.[180] An indispensable concomitant of the right to leave is the right to return, which implies that no citizen of Nigeria should be refused entry into the country. A Nigerian living abroad cannot be prevented from returning to Nigeria, not even for reason of public health, as specified in section 19(6) of the Immigration Act. Likewise, freedom of movement includes the right of every Nigerian not to be expelled from Nigeria. Every Nigerian citizen

[178] For instance, the Universal Declaration (article 13), the ICCPR (articles 12 and 13), the ICERD [article 5(d)(i)], the African Charter (article 12), and the Treaty of the Economic Commission of West African States. All these documents describe various forms of freedom of movement.

[179] (2013) LPELR—22349 (C.A).

[180] The Nigeria Court of Appeal affirmed the right to hold a passport as the inevitable corollary of the right of egress in the case of *The Director of State Security Service & Anor v. Agbakoba* (1999) 3 NWLR (pt. 595) 314.

is at home in Nigeria and as such cannot possibly be rendered stateless by being forced out of the country. Or better put, every citizen has by virtue of this constitutional provision immunity from expulsion from Nigeria. The High Court decision in *Shugaba v. Minister of Internal Affairs*[181] is the locus classicus on this subject in Nigeria. In this case, the court held that the deportation of the applicant was an abuse of his fundamental right to free movement as a Nigerian citizen. Thus, the power of the federal government regarding deportation and, by extension, that of the state government in residency issues was delineated (cf. Chijioke, 2020).

Freedom of movement is an important right. It is important for the exercise of the rights of assembly and association, the right to personal liberty, as well as several other rights. The country's obligations to protect this right are set out in the above-mentioned relevant human rights instruments she has signed. The Nigerian Constitution does not regard political rights of freedom of movement, assembly and association as absolute rights. Under section 45, it provides that the exercise of these rights may be curtailed in the interest of defence, public safety, order, morality or health, or in order to protect the rights of other persons. The Boko Haram insurgence in the north-eastern part of the country is a typical example of how freedom of movement can be limited out of concerns for safety. The insurgence has not only displaced some persons from their chosen areas of residence, it has also hampered the free movement of others within the country. This right can also be restricted by extradition [section 41(2)]. Then, in the case of the twin rights of assembly and association, the preventive measures of social distancing, and partial and/or total lockdowns introduced by the government during the coronavirus pandemic can be viewed as necessary legal restrictions on the right of assembly in the interests of public health and safety. However, these restrictions only apply in exceptional cases, but not as a rule, and must be based on the principles of necessity and proportionality.

3.4.2 Contentious Issues in the Exercise of Political Rights in Nigeria

So far, we have dealt with the constitutional provisions of political rights in a general sense. In the following part, we focus on three aspects of rights that, in our opinion, deserve more attention than others due to the extent of their violations in the Nigerian context. These are the right to vote, the right to protest and the rights of refugees, who are considered a special group of foreigners.

Right to Participate in Elections and Governance

In his Study Guide, Ferguson (2003) defines voting as "a formal expression of preference for a candidate for office or for a proposed resolution of an issue." It is used in the first sense in this study and is regarded as the most notable form of political

[181] (1981) 2 NCLR 459.

participation. It usually takes place within the framework of an election or a referendum and provides individuals the opportunity to participate in choosing political leaders or in the decision-making process of their society. Voting is an essential part of democracy. It is also widely recognised as a basic human right (NHRC, 2007).

Nigeria operates a democratic system of government.[182] Nigeria's democracy operates on the principle of popular sovereignty as the source of all political power or authority.[183] To ensure that the people exercise their sovereignty, elections are held every four, in which the citizens can elect their representatives to government. Regular elections and the right of citizens to vote are therefore the keystones of Nigeria's democracy. Voting rights entered the country's legal system for the first time during the colonial period, with the introduction of the electoral principle by the Clifford Constitution of 1922. Although it gave Nigerians limited franchise, the elective principle granted access to the formation of political parties in the country, which eventually gave room for more local participants in government. Since then, periodic elections and elective representation have become permanent features of later Nigerian constitutions.

Given this background, the 1999 Constitution in section 40 provides the right of individuals to form or belong to political parties or associations in order to encourage greater participation by Nigerians in civil society and politics. In fact, in Nigeria (as of March 2020) around 18 political parties are registered with the Independent National Electoral Commission (hereinafter INEC).[184] This is a significant decrease from the previous figure of 91. However, the Constitution does not provide for voting rights in unequivocal terms. In several places it somehow recognises the people's right to vote[185] but does not guarantee it in a specific provision as a fundamental political right. This lacuna has been strongly criticised by some commentators as constituting a clog in the legal enforcement of the voting right of citizens (Ibirogba, 2018). For others, it represents a deliberate attempt to place the Nigerian voter on the sidelines, and not at the centre, of the electoral process (Ugochukwu, 2012). Be that as it may, the constitutional provisions on the electoral process in general are supplemented by various domestic electoral laws. Prominent among these are the

---

[182] Ibid., section 14(1) of the CFRN.

[183] Ibid., section 14(2)(a).

[184] INEC is the regulatory body for elections in Nigeria. It was established by virtue of section 153 of the Constitution (CFRN) and its power is well defined in Part 1 of the Third Schedule of the same CFRN and in Part 1 of the 2010 Electoral Act. As the Election Management Body (EMB) in the country, the Commission is empowered to prepare and maintain a national register of voters, to fix dates for elections and supervise the conduct of same. In principle, it is an independent electoral body. The CFRN (in section 158) confers on the Commission its independence. This means, among other things, that it is vested with the power to appoint and exercise disciplinary control over its staff (Jegede & Idiaru, 2020; Idayat & Shamsudeen, 2015).

[185] There are provisions which touch on the right to vote, such as section 7(4) of the CFRN which states that "[t]he Government of a State shall ensure that every person who is entitled to vote or be voted for at an election to House of Assembly shall have the right to vote or be voted for at an election to a local government council." And other provisions like sections 65, 77, inter alia, which concern more the right to register to vote in an election (see also Ugochukwu, 2012).

Electoral Act 2010, the Companies and Allied Matters Act (CAMA) 2020, the INEC Regulations and Guidelines for the Conduct of Elections 2019, plus numerous case laws and judicial decisions[186] as well as the relevant sub-regional, regional and international human rights instruments that the country has ratified or acceded to.[187] It can be said from a combined reading of these legal instruments that the right to vote is the fundamental right of every qualified Nigerian citizen.

One key issue in elections is the question of voter eligibility. Although the right to vote is recognised as a universal human right, it is not granted to millions of people around the world. Basically, it is granted to individuals in countries based on citizenship status. However, in some countries there may be more restrictions apart from citizenship. Under Nigerian law,[188] only citizens over the age of 18 who are properly registered as voters in the national voters' register are eligible to vote. In order to be registered as a voter, one must not be affected by certain criminal offences that constitute the so-called legal incapacity to vote such as the declaration of allegiance to a foreign state, conviction for capital crimes, etc.[189] In addition, foreigners are excluded from the electoral process; they cannot vote nor be voted for. Also, a Nigerian citizen residing abroad cannot legally exercise the right to vote. The law does not extend political franchise to citizens or members of the diaspora. It does not provide them the opportunity to register or to vote, though the matter is still being discussed.[190] Apart from these statutory limitations, a bona fide citizen's voting rights cannot be denied for any other reason. As of February 2019, Nigeria boasts about 84 million registered voters.

Voting rights are not just about the right to vote; they also include the right to run for public office. It may be important to point out here that every potential voter in Nigeria does not necessarily qualifies as a candidate or political aspirant. To qualify

---

[186] Other legal instruments guiding the conduct of elections in Nigeria include, for example, the Civil Procedure Code, the Nigerian Code of Advertising Practice and Sales Promotion (APCON), Guidelines and Regulations for Political Parties, Political Parties' Code of Conduct, the Nigeria Broadcasting Code, the Police Act, and Guidelines for the Conduct of Police Officers on Electoral Duty (cf. Idayat & Shamsudeen, 2015).

[187] For instance, the ICCPR (article 25), the Universal Declaration (article 21), the ICERD [article 5(c)], the CEDAW [art. 7(a)], the Convention on the Rights of Persons with Disabilities [art. 29(a)(ii)], the ICRMW [art. 41(1)], and the African Charter [art. 13(1)], the African Charter on Democracy, Elections and Governance (ACDEG) and the ECOWAS Supplementary Protocol on Democracy and Good Governance.

[188] Section 12 of the Electoral Act 2010, and Rule 2 of the INEC Regulations and Guidelines for the Conduct of Elections 2019.

[189] The term *legal incapacity* in this context is defined in Part 1 section 1(3) of the 1982 Electoral Acts as: "(a) the acknowledgement of allegiance, obedience, or adherence … to any foreign power or State; (b) the imposition of sentence of death or, in respect of an offence involving dishonesty, of imprisonment … for a term exceeding six months or such other punishment as may lawfully be substituted therefore, and the voter has not at the date of the election suffered the punishment or received a free pardon; (c) disqualification under this Act in respect of corrupt practices and other electoral offenses at elections."

[190] Reportedly, diaspora voting passed the second reading at the House of Representatives on 15th December 2020. Cf. Idayat and Shamsudeen (2015).

for election into elective positions, a prospective candidate must be a citizen of Nigeria by birth and have attained at least the age of 25 years, depending on the office one is vying for.[191] (S)he must have been educated up to at least School Certificate level or its equivalent. A potential public office holder must belong to a political party on whose platform (s)he can run for elected office, as the country's electoral law does not allow independent candidature.[192] However, a candidate could be disqualified for various reasons, including criminal indictments, criminal convictions, bankruptcy, and document forgery cases. Likewise disqualified is a person who is deemed insane, a lunatic, or a member of a secret society, as well as an official who remains in his or her service at least 30 days before the election date.[193] Nigerian law does not restrict access to the various electoral offices in the country based on social characteristics such as gender, income level, etc. Under the Clifford Constitution, only resident adult men exercised voting rights, while women were excluded. But nothing in the existing laws prevents women from assuming positions of power or authority; they can vote and run for an elected office at any level in the country without any legal restrictions. According to the report by the Stakeholder Democracy Network 2019 (hereinafter SDN), 2970 women (that is, 11% of all candidates) ran for political offices in the last federal elections in 2019, though only 57 of them (or 4%) were elected. Women currently hold around 6 percent of all political offices at the federal level. Lastly, under the elective principle of 1922, participation in the public service was predicated on income level. As such, only candidates with a gross annual income of one hundred pounds sterling (£100) in the year before the election could run (Idayat & Shamsudeen, 2015). This restriction has also been lifted over time. In its place, the electoral law contains some provisions that are intended to guide the use of money in the electoral process, so as not to weaken the effective participation of all citizens.[194] Today, at least in principle, it can be said that the citizens' right to stand is no longer restricted due to their socio-economic background.

Elections are important events in Nigeria (Idayat & Shamsudeen, 2015). Since the country's independence, several efforts have been made to design a credible electoral system (NHRC, 2007). That being the case, all elections held in the country since then, including especially the most recent ones, can be used to gauge the

[191] On 31st May 2018, Nigeria passed the Age Reduction Bill (popularly) known as "#Not Too Young To Run Bill". This new law reduced the age of running for elective positions from 30 to 25 years old for the House of Representatives and State House of Assembly, from 35 to 30 years for the Senate and Governorship, and from 40 to 35 years for the office of the President. This move—a successful bid to amend the constitutional provisions of sections 65, 106, 131, 177—is aimed at ensuring a greater representation of young people in the country's political systems, since about 65% (or nearly 70%) of the population and circa 53% of registered voters are below the age of 35 years.

[192] For the eligibility of candidates for elections, see sections 65, 106, 131, and 177 of the CFRN.

[193] Sections 66, 107, 137, and 182 of the CFRN highlight the criteria for the disqualification of a candidate.

[194] For instance, section 91(2–7) of the Electoral Act limits the amount that could be spent on electioneering campaign for various political positions.

credibility of her electoral process. To be fair, some elections were better than others, and some even enabled the transfer of power from one civilian government to another. However, the general assessment of these elections shows that the process is plagued by myriad challenges that not only undermine its integrity but also limit the space for effective citizen participation. Challenges include election malpractices, electoral violence, the use of power of incumbency, non-compliance with financial regulations, and the deliberate attempt to incapacitate some qualified citizens. Experience has shown that misconduct such as rigging, multiple voting, underage voting, impersonation, delays in delivering ballot papers to polling stations, illegal possession of ballot papers and result sheets characterise the elections in Nigeria (Idayat & Shamsudeen, 2015). Thuggery is also commonplace. Politicians use young people as thugs to intimidate voters, snatch ballot boxes and results sheets, set election materials ablaze and attack election officials in desperate moves to win elections. There were reports of widespread violence by thugs during the 2019 general election. In some States there have been reports of violent clashes between military personnel deployed by the government to safeguard the electoral process and political thugs, resulting in multiple deaths. According to a 2019 report by the Situation Room of the Nigeria Civil Society (hereinafter the Situation Room), at least 626 people were killed between October 2018 and March 2019 during the pre-election campaign and the election itself. As expected, the resulting scary atmosphere rubbed off significantly on the voter turnout. While voter registration rose from 68,833,476 to 84,004,084 between 2015 and 2019 and the collection rates for permanent voter cards (PVC) rose from 82.03 percent to 86.63 percent, voter turnout fell from 43.7 percent in 2015 to just 35.6 percent in 2019 (Situation Room 2019). This created the loopholes desired by many politicians to skillfully use unused votes to their advantage (Idayat & Shamsudeen, 2015).

The Situation Room also elaborates on the use of state security agencies by the ruling party to prevent political opponents from effectively exercising their political rights and the failure to comply with the established rules of financial fair play by politicians and their parties. For instance, it claimed that the country's leading political parties, namely the People's Democratic Party (PDP) and the All-Progressives Congress (APC), not only used public funds to campaign for the 2015 general election, but also failed to comply with the relevant financial regulations (cf. Idayat & Shamsudeen, 2015). Vote buying[195] and selling were also reported, and INEC did not seem to care. This gave the privileged few the opportunity to use their financial resources to influence the election results and thus limit the political participation of other citizens, especially those with lesser financial stability such as women and other minority groups including people with disabilities (PWDs), and the internally displaced persons (IDPs). This explains in part why women make up a scant 4 percent of all elected candidates in the 2019 general elections, which is far too low a

[195] Situation Room (2019: 34) describes it as "the act of paying a voter to cast his vote for a particular candidate or to abstain from voting." This practice takes place particularly in rural areas where poverty is high and voter education is low.

proportion than Nigeria's pledge to have 35 percent of women's participation in parliament (SDN 2020: 3; see also World Bank Report, 2021).

Similarly, the Nigerian electoral system unjustifiably restricts the political participation of absentee voters[196] and prison inmates. Many countries already extend the right to vote by absentee ballot to their citizens living abroad. A lot of Nigerians living overseas or in the country but living outside their home state are eligible to vote and should be able to vote from where they live. They should not be deprived of their democratic right to vote for the government of their country because decisions taken in Nigeria affect her citizens around the world. Nigeria has an incredible voter population. The aim of the right to political participation is to involve as many qualified citizens as possible in the decision-making process of their society. Their massive participation would facilitate the choice of the right calibre of persons to hold public offices.[197] It would also contribute to the legitimacy of the government (Fierro et al., 2007). On the contrary, the current practice in Nigeria where many qualified citizens are deprived of the right to vote certainly raises questions about the integrity of the process. In fact, it has rubbed off negatively on the confidence of many in the electoral system (NHRC, 2007). It is for such reasons that the country is classified as a hybrid regime[198] on the global Democracy Index.

Right of Protest

The right to protest is another political right that is under attack in Nigeria. In the first place, the right to protest is not recognised in Nigeria's Constitution as a separate right (Unini, 2020). It is derived from the fundamental rights to freedom of assembly and expression. This is in line with the Human Rights Council's report on effective measures and best practices to promote and protect human rights in the context of peaceful protests, which describes protest as a "form of exercise of the rights to freedom of peaceful assembly and freedom of expression."[199] The Council recognised it further as a manifestation of the right to freedom of association.[200] Thus, the right to protest is protected by the Constitution in sections 39 and 40 as well as by the various human rights treaties on this right that the country has ratified.

---

[196] It is used specifically in this case to refer to citizens of the country who live far from their constituency and cannot travel back to their constituency on election day.

[197] Nigeria: Voter Education Handbook (VEH n.d.). ACE Project 1998–2020. Available at: http://aceproject.org/ero-en/regions/africa/NG/voter-education-handbook.pdf/view. Accessed 01.12.2020.

[198] The Economist Intelligence Unit (EIU)'s Democracy Index provides an overview of the state of democracy worldwide for 165 independent states and two territories. The index is based on five sets of criteria: electoral process and pluralism, civil liberties, the functioning of government, political participation, and political culture. These criteria classify countries according to four types of regimes, namely "full democracy", "flawed democracy", "hybrid regime" and "authoritarian regime." In its 2019 edition of the Democracy Index (DI), Nigeria is ranked the 109th place in the world (22nd in Africa) as hybrid democracy, which means "halfway between authoritarian rule and democracy" (Ecofin Agency, 2020).

[199] UN Doc. A/HRC/22/28, 21st January 2013, para. 3.

[200] Ibid., para. 4.

Protest in general is a public display of opinions (Abū Zahrā, 2011). It is the practice of publicly expressing dissent and disapproval through words or actions. As a political right, it describes a series of actions adopted by individuals or groups to pursue or prevent changes in a political system "without overturning the system itself".[201] The actions in question can assume several forms, ranging from individual statements to mass demonstrations. Petition signings, sit-in strikes, boycotts, summits and counter-summits, strikes, street marches, blockades, occupying a specific space and internet protests are some concrete examples of a protest. If not managed in a timely manner, protests can gradually grow and snowball into riots, insurgencies or even revolutions. Della Porta and Diani (2006: 165) described these actions as "non-routinized ways of affecting political, social, and cultural processes." In their opinion, these are non-routinised actions in the sense that they differ from the conventional forms of political participation, such as voting, joining political party or interest group, organising election campaign events, or writing letters, etc., through which individuals can influence the decision-making process in their society. Moreover, they are newer compared to these traditional forms, but have found more acceptance in advanced democracies because they are viewed as non-anti-system techniques of activism (Della Porta & Diani, 2006). They can also be used by individuals or groups to help them achieve their goals.

As we can see, protests are not an end in themselves, but a means to an end. They are some of the strategies people use to draw attention to a topic of concern like a perceived injustice in established norms etc. Protests can be used for other purposes, depending on the need or circumstances. But they are usually driven by a desire to disrupt the status quo. The desired change is not only aimed at the political system, but can also target the values, norms, principles or the functioning of a society. Protests are therefore channels through which citizens can interrogate the law, policies or decisions of their government and press home their demands for change. Understood in this way, the right to protest is an essential component of a functioning democracy and a central form of political participation. Like its foundational rights, the right to protest is not an unconditional right. Governments around the world have an obligation to uphold peace and public order in their countries and can therefore restrict protest activities. In Nigeria, the law also recognises protests and allows them as long as they are peaceful and do not destroy the sovereign status of the nation (Unini, 2020).

Protests are not new in Nigeria. In fact, the country has a long history of civil unrest. In this context, there are incidents such as the Aba Women's riot of 1929 and the Egba Women's revolt of 1947, in which Nigerian women demonstrated against what was perceived as intolerable taxation of women by the colonial government, and the Iva Valley miners' strike of 1949. Others include more recent protests like the "Ali Must Go" protest of 1978, the Structural Adjustment Programme (SAP)

---

[201] See Political Protest. Governments of the World: A Global Guide to Citizens' Rights and Responsibilities. Available at: https://www.encyclopedia.com/international/legal-and-political-magazines/political-protest. Accessed 19.12.2020.

riots of 1989, the June 12 protests of 1993 (against the annulment of presidential elections that year), the Nigeria Labour Congress (NLC) and Trade Union Congress (TUC) protests of 2012, and—last but not the least—the 2020 Youth Protest against police brutality tagged #EndSARS protest,[202] to mention just a few. All these agitations have something in common: they were all driven by the desire for change in the system. They were also used by protesters as channels for exerting pressure on the government. Sometimes the protests brought about a definite change or changes in the system. For example, the NLC and TUC protests were organised against the supposed arbitrary rise in the price of petroleum products (from 65 to 141 Naira per litre), which led to an immediate rise in the prices of goods and services. The unrest led to a reduction in the price of petrol from 141 to 97 Naira per liter (Aborisade, 2012). At other times they triggered a larger chain of reactions (International Federation for Human Rights, 2010). The Nigerian State consistently relied on two control strategies to manage these mass movements, namely the physical and the non-physical control strategies (Aborisade, 2012).

The non-physical strategy involves the use of stringent statutes, rules and regulations to forestall the free exercise of the right to protest. Examples of this strategy are the Public Order Act 2004, the proposed NGOs Regulatory Commission of Nigeria (Establishment) Bill 2016 (hereinafter NGO Bill) and the use of curfews and ex parte orders by the State at different times to thwart civil unrests. According to section 1(2) of the Public Order Act, before rallies, assemblies, or processions are held on public roads or in places of public resort, approvals must be obtained. This requirement is not specific to Nigeria. In fact, there is a similar requirement in many advanced democracies around the world. In contrast to the latter, however, Nigerian law does not provide for judicial control or review mechanisms in the event of a refusal of a permit (International Federation for Human Rights, 2010). There is no denying that this law also served some useful purposes. In this way, for example, the government was able to curtail the activities of ethnic champions from rallying their ethnic groups for some irrelevant ethnic-oriented goals. It also enabled the government to regulate open-air religious services at hotspots of religious tension in the country. At the same time, this legal provision restricted the political space by subjecting the exercise of the citizens' basic right to protest to the whims of the government. As usual, the latter made maximum use of this to stifle protests perceived as anti-government (International Federation for Human Rights, 2010). Furthermore, the Act gave the police a margin of discretion to disrupt public gatherings that have not been approved,[203] and even those that they have approved if they deem it necessary to maintain public order.[204] Again, the police and other State security operatives often took advantage of this provision to temporarily disrupt or outrightly ban several public gatherings and to suppress and harass demonstrators. The security operatives' peremptoriness sometimes led to peaceful, anti-government mass movements

[202] SARS is the acronym for the Special Anti-Robbery Squad of the Nigerian police force.

[203] Section 2 of the Public Order Act.

[204] Ibid., section 4(1), (2) and (3).

becoming violent (International Federation for Human Rights, 2010). Because of the contradiction between its provisions and the fundamental rights of citizens to freedom of assembly and association, civil society organisations (CSOs) in Nigeria, in particular the Civil Liberty Organisation (CLO), sued for the Act to be repealed (Aborisade, 2012). Accordingly, the Act or provisions in question were voided in 2007 by the Nigerian Court of Appeal in the *Inspector General of Police v All Nigeria Peoples Party and Ors* case,[205] which means that citizens no longer need police clearance before they can organise protest actions—a move applauded by the African Commission on Human and Peoples' Rights in its 2015 Concluding Observations on Nigeria.[206] However, this court decision has not yet resulted in any changes in the system, as the provisions of the Act are apparently still being applied (International Federation for Human Rights, 2010). Another attempt by the government to apply the non-physical strategy can be seen in the proposed 2016 NGO Bill. The law aims to establish a federal agency that will regulate the activities of NGOs and CSOs in the country. If passed, the draft law would bring these human rights bodies under the firm grip of the government and thus restrict their activities or even stifle them in the "national interest".[207] The bill was not passed after being strongly criticized by a cross section of Nigerians but is still pending in the National Assembly. In a similar development, the government implemented curfews to stop the #EndSARS protest by the determined Nigerian youth in October 2020. It also obtained an injunction from the National Industrial Court (NIC) to prevent the NLC and TUC from commencing a planned nationwide strike (Aborisade, 2012).

The physical strategy, by contrast, involves the use of brute force to crack down on demonstrators and suppress their actions (Aborisade, 2012). Nigerian law criminalises torture and inhuman treatment of citizens. Having said that, the same law also provides for the use of force by law enforcement agencies, and even specifies the circumstances in which it is permitted, including the dispersal of gatherings, rallies, and marches.[208] Section 73 of the Criminal Code Act (CCA) empowers law enforcement agents to use as much force as is "reasonably necessary" to disrupt illegal gatherings.[209] This provision falls short of the required international standard, but it is even better than the provision of section 102 of the Criminal Procedure Code (CPC) which simply grants the law enforcement agent the power "to disperse such assembly by force." Both provisions clearly give security personnel extensive discretion in questions of protest that are not clearly defined. Among other things, they did not specify the extent of force that is required for such a dispersal. In particular, the CCA demonstrated that it was not primarily concerned about the prin-

[205] (2007) 18 NWLR (pt. 1066) 457 C.A.

[206] Para 31. See also Casey-Maslen (2020).

[207] Clause 2 of the draft NGO bill. See also Amnesty International 2017.

[208] To explore the legal framework on the use of force during assemblies in Nigeria, we referred to the short but interesting write-up by S. Casey-Maslen (ed.) (2020) with the title "Laws on the Right of Peaceful Assembly Worldwide: Nigeria." Available at: https://www.rightofassembly.info/country/nigeria. Accessed 01.12.2020.

[209] See also section 9(a) of the ACJA 2015.

ciple of proportionality when it concluded the same provision by stating that security personnel "shall not be liable in any criminal or civil proceeding for having, by the use of such force, caused harm or death to any person." Elsewhere, the law empowers the police to use firearms when it is "necessary to disperse rioters or to prevent them from committing serious offences against life and property."[210] In such situations, however, it is not allowed to fire indiscriminately into a mob, only ringleaders at the forefront may be fired, and warning shots shall not be fired over the head of rioters.[211] These provisions relate specifically to riots. Nevertheless, the use of force and firearms at gatherings by law enforcement agencies under Nigerian law does not comply with international regulations. According to the UN Basic Principles on the Use of Force and Firearms by Law Enforcement Officials, the dispersal of a non-violent gathering, which is illegal under some domestic laws, does not require the use of force. However, if the state chooses to use force, that decision must be based on the twin principles of proportionality and necessity.[212] Firearms can only be used as a last resort to save lives during violent assemblies.[213]

Executive violence against assemblies is endemic in Nigeria (Okene & Okpara, 2007). Nigerian governments are known to have used excessive and sometimes lethal force at various times in policing mass movements. This is not limited to violent, riotous assemblies; it also extends to harmless, peaceful protests. The Human Rights Committee highlighted this fact in its Concluding Observations on Nigeria 2019 when it expressed concern about the widespread use of lethal force against protesters.[214] Despite the government's commitment to an impressive array of human rights treaties protecting the fundamental right to protest, it used heavily armed security forces to suppress largely peaceful protests in 2012, during the NLC and TUC nationwide protest actions, killing about 20 protesters and injuring hundreds of others (Aborisade, 2012). Similarly, Amnesty International (2019) reports on the government's use of military personnel to crack down on the separatist group, the Indigenous People of Biafra (hereinafter IPOB), during their non-violent gatherings between 2015 and 2017. The incident is said to have resulted in the deaths of over 150 IPOB members and supporters. Soldiers also killed about 350 supporters of the Islamic Movement of Nigeria (hereinafter IMN) in 2015 in Zaria, Kaduna state, because they had blocked a section of the road in front of the IMN headquarters and refused a military convoy passage. Investigations into these incidents were initiated, but no further government action has been taken. The government's high-handed attitude towards demonstrators reared its head once again during the #EndSARS protests. The State used heavily armed police and soldiers to quell a series of protests by unarmed students and youth, and the former's high-handedness resulted turned a peaceful protest violent. The exact report of the casualties is still

[210] Police Force Order 237, para. 3(c).

[211] Ibid., para.6.

[212] Basic Principle no.13; see also UN Doc. A/RES/34/169, 17th December 1979, article 3.

[213] Basic Principle no.14. This principle should be read conjointly with Basic Principle no. 9.

[214] CCPR/C/NGA/CO/2, 29th August 2019, para. 26.

pending (Casey-Maslen, 2020). The Nigerian government and its security agencies are not alone in the aversion to protest behaviour and actions. The attitude has also a horizontal dimension as was witnessed in 2019, when members of the CSO were attacked by a pro-Buhari mob[215] during their peaceful protest outside the office of the National Human Rights Commission (NHRC) in Abuja. In summary, it is clear from the foregoing that the respect for the dignity and the safety of protesters are not really guaranteed in Nigeria despite the many human rights instruments the country has ratified (Okene & Okpara, 2007). But rather than suppress this right, it is the positive obligation of the State and its agencies to protect citizens during peaceful assemblies.[216] And not just the State alone, it is also the duty of everyone to ensure the full enjoyment of the right to protest by all.

Rights of Political Refugees

Forced displacement is "not specific to modernity" (Oltmer, 2016: 26). It is an unfortunate but enduring feature of the chequered human history. Refugee movements as part of it always existed as an immediate human impulse in the face of violent threats and socio-political disintegration; in fact, refugee movements are coeval with persecutions and warfare. For much of antiquity, these movements were more or less individual flights. The emigrations, however, took on a remarkable pattern in size and spread in the twentieth century. For the most part, they became not only a mass phenomenon on a grand scale, but also a global reality. The gory events of World Wars I and II resulted in the displacement of an unprecedented number of people. According to reports, after World War I (1914–1918) at least 10 million people were displaced within and across the borders in search of refuge (Gatrell, 2014). Today this is considered the first mass refugee movement or first wave of refugees of the twentieth century (Guterres, 2011). During and after World War II (1939–1945) this number increased almost sixfold within just 20 years (Oltmer, 2016). The mass movement of people was also a defining characteristic of post-Cold War Europe. That resulted chiefly from the disintegration of states and the associated socio-political restructurings. The decolonisation of Africa and Asia as well as civil conflicts in the Middle East and South Asia, East and West Africa, and Latin America also contributed immensely to massive displacement of people either internally, i.e., within their respective states, or as refugees due to the flight across an international border. Two categories of displaced persons emerge therefore under international law, namely internally displaced persons (hereinafter IDPs) and refugees (Oduwole & Fadeyi, 2013). These mass movements of people around the world are among the most delicate problems the international community has ever had to deal with.

One of the notable accomplishments of the twentieth century in the humanitarian field is the introduction of a universal standard for refugee protection. Throughout history, societies have protected and supported threatened strangers and victims of persecution and violence. Before the twentieth century, these efforts were spontaneous and context-specific in principle. In the twentieth century, however, an

[215] Supporters of the then President of Nigeria, namely Mr. Muhammadu Buhari.

[216] UN Doc. A/HRC/RES/31/37, 24th March 2016, preamble.

international model for dealing with the refugee problem was established and adopted—a model of international cooperation and burden-sharing. This model recognised the problem as a concern of the international community and emphasised the need for a collective approach anchored in the general principles of human rights (Guterres, 2011). The real handling of the matter began under the League of Nations in 1921 with the appointment of successive High Commissioners for Refugees and culminated under the UN in 1951 with the establishment of the Office of the United Nations High Commissioner for Refugees (hereinafter UNHCR) and the drafting of the Convention relating to the Status of Refugees (hereinafter Refugee Convention). The UNHCR office was immediately given the task of dealing with the waves of refugees that resulted from the two world wars. It served as the custodian of the Refugee Convention and, as such, had the duties to oversee the international scheme for the protection of refugees in State parties to the Convention (Guterres, 2011).

This Convention, which was adopted at a diplomatic conference in Geneva on 28th July 1951 and entered into force on 22nd April 1954, is considered a particularly important document for dealing with the refugee issue for several reasons. It delineates, among other things, the refugee status, the kind of legal protection to which this group of persons is entitled, their obligations to host societies and certain categories of persons who do not qualify for refugee status. According to article 1a, paragraph 2, a refugee is defined "as a person who is outside his or her country of nationality or habitual residence; has a well-founded fear of being persecuted because of his or her race, religion, nationality, membership of a particular social group or political opinion; and is unable or unwilling to avail him- or herself of the protection of that country, or to return there, for fear of persecution."[217] In this definition, the Convention emphasises the "push" factor of persecution or fear of persecution as one of the main criteria for refugee status and a sufficient humanitarian reason for which this group of persons needs special protection. Refugees are therefore primarily victims of persecution based on certain social attributes. But other groups of persons, such as persons fleeing armed conflicts, generalised violence, war and human rights abuses, also fit into this category,[218] regardless of whether they have a well-founded fear of persecution or not, and as such are entitled to claim refugee status in the contracting states of the Convention (Guterres, 2011). Again, it is believed that these persons need special protection because they have lost the protection of their own governments by being outside their country under the given circumstances and therefore need "a substitute or a surrogate protection" for their rights as human beings and as refugees (Oduwole & Fadeyi, 2013: 6).

Refugees are granted an impressive array of rights under the Convention. The most basic of these is the right not to be refused entry into a country or to be returned to the country from which one is fleeing [art. 33(1)]. This right also obliges a state

[217] This definition is adopted from Guterres (2011: 3). It perfectly summarises the original definition of the term in the Refugee Convention.

[218] Cf. Article 1a(2) of the Refugee Convention. They are referred to as categories of persons who have fled their country of origin "[a]s a result of events occurring before 1 January 1951".

not to send a refugee or an asylum seeker back into a situation of possible persecution by repatriation to the place from which (s)he has fled or by returning him or her to a place where his or her life or freedom would be seriously threatened. The principle of non-refoulement is an all-binding norm of customary international law and naturally accompanies the humanitarian rights enshrined in article 14 of the Universal Declaration. The Convention also grants refugees the right not to be penalised for illegally entering or staying in a country of asylum provided that they apparently did so in good faith and report to the authorities as soon as possible [art.33(1)]. This right—an integral part of the right not to be subjected to torture and inhuman treatment—is granted against the background of the widespread practice of compulsory detention for illegal entry or residence that countries typically use to deal with the influx of persons claiming refugee status. Other rights that the Refugee Convention considers to be extremely important for the well-being of refugees in countries of asylum are labour rights (articles 17, 18, and 19) and social rights (articles 20, 21, 23, and 24)—especially education (article 22)—freedom of movement (article 26), the right to be issued identity cum travel documents (articles 27 and 28), freedom from discrimination (article 3), access to justice (article 16), freedom of religion (article 4) and the right not to be expelled, except for certain categories of persons who do not deserve refugee protection, such as persons suspected of being against the UN principles or of having committed a crime against peace, a war crime, a crime against humanity or a serious non-political crime [articles 32(1) and 33(2)]. Overall, the convention grants refugees the right to assistance, but also defines their obligations towards their host countries.

Despite these internationally recognised standards, the Refugee Convention was not considered to be comprehensive enough because it dealt specifically with the European refugee problem of the world wars. Consequently, the Protocol Relating to the Status of Refugees was introduced in 1967 to broaden the scope of the Convention and make it universally applicable as the problem of displacement became increasingly globalised. Together, the two instruments are still the most important sources for dealing with the global refugee crisis within the framework of the UN. Their principles have been redefined in several contemporary international and regional instruments.[219] The same principles have found their way into the national law of several countries, thus leading to the development of a globally uniform asylum system (Guterres, 2011). Obviously there have been successes in the handling of the global refugee crisis over the years since the adoption of these instruments. Nevertheless, refugee situations persist. Many people are still being displaced from their place of habitual residence due to violent conflicts and human rights violations. In the past decade, the international community has once again had to contend with mass emigrations. According to the UNHCR Annual Report (2019), an estimated 79.5 million persons were displaced worldwide at the end of 2019. Of these, about 26 million persons were classified as refugees and about 4.2

[219] The 1969 OAU Convention Governing the Specific Aspects of Refugee Problems in Africa (hereinafter the OAU Refugee Convention) and the 1984 Cartagena Declaration on Refugees in Latin America (hereinafter the Cartagena Declaration) are some examples.

million as asylum seekers, the majority of whom were fleeing diverse life-threatening situations in Syria, Venezuela, Afghanistan and South Sudan. The remaining 49.3 million persons are estimated to be internally displaced—almost twice as many as refugees and asylum seekers. UNHCR's 2018 report shows that most of these internally displaced persons came from Africa, with countries such as Ethiopia, Nigeria and the Democratic Republic of Congo making up the majority of this group of persons. In fact, the push factors or causes of today's mass displacements have changed significantly and include variables such as extreme poverty, famine, floods, earthquakes, bad weather and other natural or environmental disasters. Therefore, many of today's refugees do not fall within the definition of a refugee under the Refugee Convention. For this reason, among others, the Convention has been supported with a protocol and other regionally sensitive human rights instruments.

Nigeria is one of the countries severely affected by the widespread refugee crisis. The country has experienced a number of mass displacements in the past since the Nigeria-Biafran War (1967–1970) (Adeejat-Kubra, 2013). During and after the 30-month conflict, millions of Biafrans and other minorities from the eastern region were internally displaced, while many others moved across borders in the thousands into neighbouring countries such as Cameroon, Ivory Coast, Gabon, and Equatorial Guinea (Goetz, 2001; Orji & N-Ue, 2013). Today, the country is struggling with recurring mass emigration due to ethno-religious conflicts, conflicts between farmers and herders over grazing rights, inter-communal border disputes, electoral violence, natural disasters such as floods, famine and, above all, the ongoing Boko Haram insurgency in the northeast of the country. At least in the last decade, these have led to mass refugee movements and a dramatic increase in the number of persons in refugee-like situations in the country (Adeejat-Kubra, 2013; Oduwole & Fadeyi, 2013). There is no locally generated official data on the number of displaced citizens, but UNHCR records (2019) show that Nigeria had a total population of about 2.5 million persons at the end of 2018, including those displaced either internally or as refugees or asylum-seekers. Many of these Nigerian refugees live in Cameroon, Chad and Niger.

For her part, Nigeria hosts a significant proportion of displaced persons from other countries who are either seeking or taking refuge there. According to UNHCR (2020), there were about 66,057 refugees and 2794 asylum seekers in Nigeria at the end of 2020. These people are mainly from Cameroon (63,634 people), the Central African Republic (711), the Democratic Republic of Congo (646), Syria (308), Mali (145), Ivory Coast (136), Chad (86), Sudan (47) and others (344). The profiles of these persons show that they have been granted refugee status not only on the basis of international standards but also in accordance with the regional instrument that extends refugee status to a broader category of persons of concern (PoCs), namely persons who were compelled to leave their country because of "external aggression, occupation, foreign domination or events seriously disturbing public order."[220] These displaced non-citizens have therefore fled or are fleeing various life-threatening situations in their countries. Nigeria welcomes all such persons. Nigerian law provides a refugee protection system that is overseen by the National Commission for Refugees (hereinafter NCFR).[221] The latter is thus the official national body responsible for the welfare of refugees and asylum seekers in the country. The NCFR Act 2004—as the Commission's enabling law is called—incorporates the provisions of the Refugee Convention, its Protocol and the OAU Refugee Convention to create the necessary legal and administrative framework for the protection and management of refugees and other PoCs in the country. The Act provides recommendations for applicants seeking for refugee status in Nigeria[222] and the procedures for appeals if one's application is refused.[223] It makes extensive provisions geared towards protecting the internationally recognised human and humanitarian rights of refugees,[224] including material aid. Overall, refugees enjoy an impressive number of their basic rights, such as non-refoulement, non-penalisation for irregular entry or stay, the rights to liberty, non-discrimination and freedom of movement, especially for refugees whose status is regularised (cf. Chijioke, 2020). Regarding social security, they are given skill acquisition programmes to aid their integration and economic independence. They could work, though employment opportunities are few in the country (Human Rights Report, 2013). They have a healthcare package that is supplemented by the UNHCR. It is instructive to note here that refugees are accorded these rights because of Nigeria's status as a signatory state, but above all because of the socio-cultural value of the hospitality of the Nigerian population, which tends to predispose them to welcome foreigners and strangers, especially the displaced and marginalised category.

It can be concluded that while Nigeria has accounted for a significant proportion of the world's forcibly displaced population over the past decade, she has also actively participated in collaborative international efforts to find sustainable solutions to the global refugee crisis. Besides, a closer look at the country's past commitment to this cause shows that the protection of refugees and asylum seekers tends to receive more attention than that of internally displaced persons, even though the latter represent a more serious national crisis (cf. Adeejat-Kubra, 2013; Oduwole & Fadeyi, 2013).

---

[220] See article 1(2) of the 1969 OAU Refugee Convention; see also section 1(1)(b) of the NCFR Act 2004.

[221] The Commission was established by Decree 52 of 1989, now the National Commission for Refugees Act Cap. N21 Laws of the Federation of Nigeria, 2004 (hereinafter NCFR Act) which incorporated the provisions of the relevant international and regional instruments for the protection of refugees. The Commission was given the additional responsibilities in 2002 by the Federal Government to manage Internally Displaced Persons (IDPs) in Nigeria (Periodic Country Report 2015–2016). It does this in collaboration with the Nigeria National Emergency Management Agency (NEMA), its states' equivalent SEMA, NCFR, Red Cross, etc. (Adeejat-Kubra, 2013).

[222] Section 8 of the NCFR Act.

[223] Ibid., section 8(7).

[224] Ibid., section 15; see also articles 3–4, 7–35 of the 1st Schedule, and 3rd Schedule of the Act.

3.4.3 *Religion and Political Rights*

Public attitudes towards political rights, like attitudes to human rights in general, can be determined by worldviews and orientations, including religious beliefs. It is therefore necessary to briefly outline the teachings of Nigeria's three main religious traditions on the political rights under study.

Political Rights in ATR

In traditional Nigerian societies, the idea of a person's right to participate in the affairs of the community was not foreign. Somehow, these societies can be described as democratic, though not in the sense of majority rule as there was little or no documented evidence that elections ever took place. Even if they did, the system was more or less a patriarchal system that viewed politics as a male domain and thus restricted the active participation of women in politics (Adejugbe & Adejugbe, 2018). Democracy in this traditional milieu operated the African way "in the form of discussions geared towards consensus" and decisions were made through this process (Gathogo, 2013: 284). Times have changed, but this pattern of political engagement can still be observed today. Furthermore, traditional societies also experienced political participation through protests and the public display of dissent, as demonstrated by the mass movements of the colonial era. Forms of protest such as boycotts, chanting marches, and confrontations were often used by people to express their discontent over perceived injustice or violations of their customs or policies that they deemed unfavorable to their community life. Lastly, displaced persons were welcomed with open arms in cases of persecution and war. The practice of giving refuge to persecuted people was seen as an ethical duty. Hospitality is a way of life in Africa; It is a core value in the African socio-cultural worldview. Another relevant feature of this hospitality is that it presupposes a readiness to share with guests or strangers (Olikenyi, 2001). The things to share here include both material and non-material things such as food, shelter, clothing, property and essential services etc., and no sacrifice in this regard is considered too much to make for a visitor. In this way, a stranger or displaced person is helped to adjust to the new environment and to integrate into the life of the host community. (S)he can stay indefinitely, provided (s)he does not disturb the peace of the community.[225]

Political Rights in Islamic Tradition

Muslims perceive their religion as a comprehensive value system that encompasses practically all areas of life, including modern politics (Issa, 2016). Whether Muslims can be loyal democrats has long been debated in view of the "authoritarian vision" of Islamic principles that Muslim scholars have presented over time (Voll, 2007:

[225] The clearest expression of a stranger and, by extension, a displaced person's obligation to his or her host community is found in a popular maxim of the Igbo tribe of Nigeria, thus: *'obiara nga onye abiagbule ya, mgbe oga alawa, mkpumkpu apukwala ya n'azu'*, meaning literarily "come in peace, go in peace." But it expresses a subtle caution to visitors or strangers to stay in such a manner so as not to overstretch the goodwill of the host.

173). This question has been asked anew since the terrorist attack of 11th September 2001. Democracy here includes—but not exclusively—concepts such as sovereignty of the people, representative government, the secularity of the state and the secular basis of state laws, as well as procedures like membership in a political party or an advocacy group, voting in elections and running for office. According to Muslih and Browers (2009), Muslim scholars can be sorted into three broad ideological leanings based on their attitudes towards secular democracy, namely rejectionist, moderate, and liberal perspectives. The rejectionists view democracy as a foreign political tradition. They consider it as incompatible with Islam because democracy vests authority in the people and legislative powers in the parliament and, as such, violates the basic Islamic principle of hākimīyah (belief in the absolute sovereignty of God), the divine basis for civil codes (i.e., Sharia) and its immutability (cf. Miller et al., 2012; Voll, 2007). This rejectionist tendency is said to be common among the Salafists, the Taliban, and the Wahhabi clerics (Roy, 2021). An impressive number of Nigerian Muslims tend to share this view, though there is no empirical support for this claim. The moderate Islamic view, on the contrary, does not see Islam as incompatible with democracy. However, it completely rejects the notion of popular sovereignty as a synonym for shirk (the sin of associating partners with Allah). The moderate Islamic thinkers instead refer to some basic principles of Islamic political culture such as ‘adl (justice) and shūrā (consultation) “as evidence for Islam’s democratic credentials” (Khan, 2015: 3). Shūrā, for example, is a discussion forum with an advisory function (cf. Quran 3:159; 42:38) and is also vested with powers to elect the leader (amir) (see Roy, 2021). Proponents of this view therefore are of the opinion that shūrā is a typical Islamic institution that can be likened to a secular democracy.[226] Based on this premise, they conclude that democracy, as Khan (2015: 3) puts it, “is inherent to Islamic values and Islamic historical experience”. The liberal Islamic view agrees with the latter’s compatibility thesis, but stresses on the role of ijtihād (independent reasoning) in understanding religion. Liberal Islamic thinkers argue that religion and democracy can coexist but insist that a constant rational confrontation between the two is required (Muslih & Browers, 2009). They support pluralism and religious freedom based on relevant Islamic texts (cf. Quran 2:256) and advocate a non-literal interpretation of the scriptures. The liberal orientation is mostly associated with lay Muslim intellectuals and educational institutions (Roy, 2021).

These perspectives are distinct but not mutually exclusive and only roughly represent the notable trends among modern Muslims on the subject. Lately, some scholars opine that the incompatibility debate is no longer sustainable since the so-called Arab Spring uprisings (2010–2012), in which political Islam and democracy seemed to coincide (cf. Roy, 2021; Leininger, 2011). To support this thesis, they refer to the wave of political democratisation that swept across Tunisia, Egypt, Libya, Syria and Yemen afterwards and even to similar processes that took place

---

[226] Cf. article 11(b) of Universal Islamic Declaration of Human Rights (hereinafter UIDHR) (1981); also, Muslih and Browers (2009).

twenty years earlier in the Arab world. Be that as it may, the new compatibility narrative seems to focus on practical rather than theological issues because Islamist ideology was initially not concerned with democracy (Roy, 2021). If anything, it shows that Islam can adapt to new situations (Leininger, 2011). Perhaps it also indicates the emergence of new forms of religiosity that accord more with democratic values (Roy, 2021).

Like the perception of democracy, Islamic teachings on protests are also differentiated. One side of the teachings considers protests as permissible (cf. Abū Zahrā, 2011). Proponents of this view see protests basically as a public expression of opinion and argue based on this perception that such an exercise is permissible in Islam depending on the aims and purpose. According to them, if Muslims, for instance, come out to demonstrate in support of ribā (usury) or against the ban on the sale or intake of alcoholic beverages, such a protest would not be halāl (permissible) because it calls for something that is harām. But if it is aimed at bringing an oppressive ruler to account for neglecting the people's rights from the Islamic point of view, then such a protest is obliged by Sharia and therefore permitted.[227] A widely cited hadīth to that effect is: "[a] word of truth in front of a tyrant ruler or leader, that is the best form of jihad." This hadīth encourages believers to speak out against a despot, though it does not specify the manner. Relying on the Islamic legal maxim that anything that has not been forbidden by another text is permitted, advocates of this view conclude that protests are permissible provided no other Sharia rules are violated (Abū Zahrā, 2011). The other side of Islamic teachings proposes an anti-protest or a somewhat quietist stance. This view holds that protests and civil disobedience are outlawed in Islam (cf. Abdul-Wahid, 2019). Protagonists of this stance argue that there is no evidence in the Quran and Sunnah to validate such activities. They often cite the following hadīth to support their point: "If one of you sees something from the ruler that he hates, let him not publicise it." According to them, the hadīth specifies how to behave towards an oppressive Muslim ruler in an Islamic context, such as meeting in person or by proxy through a government minister or scholar of Sunnah, or via letter writing. In the latter case, writing should be done in private and devoid of foul language. Then the hadīth further adds: "If he accepts the advice, then that is good. If he refuses, then you have fulfilled your duty." This also applies between employees and employers in the context of a workplace. Thus, anti-protest advocates totally condemn open protests or even publicly speaking against a ruler, especially if he identifies himself as a Muslim. Instead, they preach uncritical submission to authority (Quran 4:59), except in the event of shirk. Some Muslim scholars justify this quietist approach as a wise measure against fitna (civil disorder) (Abdul-Wahid, 2019). Although this approach has been traced to the period in the early ninth century during which Muslims were apprehensive of civil war and foreign conquest, it is today a dominant Islamic perspective on protests and civil disobedience (Miller et al., 2012). There was evidence of these two perspectives in the #EndSARS protests in Nigeria, where most Muslim youth from the southern

---

[227] Ibid., article 12(c).

part of the country joined in the protests, whereas those from the north withdrew. However, the said protests were a much more complex reality.

Unlike participation in democracy and protests, the Islamic religion has a unified doctrine on the issue of refugees. Islam enjoins Muslim believers to provide sanctuary to displaced persons. It sees this as an obligation and offers a set of mechanisms for this in its sacred sources and tradition. First, the Quran formally addresses the issue of asylum seekers and refugees in the ninth surah, where it commands Muslims to protect refugees and praises those who assist people in distress (9:100, 117). In the eighth surah (8:72–75, 16:41) displaced persons are generally entitled to certain rights, and in the fifth (5:1) the believers are required to obey all agreements and treaties they have signed regarding the rights of refugees. Other verses of the Quran show that migration is not only necessary when one's life and/or beliefs are threatened, but that Muslims are even encouraged to migrate to the dar-al-Islam (abode of Islam), if need be, to enjoy a full Islamic life or to seek refuge from injustice and abuse (4:97–99). Islam obliges the host societies to receive asylum seekers generously and assures that the hosts will be rewarded for this. The Prophet Muhammad himself (peace be upon him) fled the persecution in Mecca and sought refuge in Medina in 662 AD. While his migration (hijrah) became a symbol of the flight from oppression, the hospitable treatment by the inhabitants of Medina exemplifies the Islamic model of refugee protection (cf. UNHCR, 2012; RfP and UNHCR, 2018). The Islamic responsibility to protect the asylum seeker and refugee (al-mustamin) is then formalised in the Sharia following these. According to the Islamic Migration Law (hereinafter Hijrah law), all individuals, including non-Muslims, have the right to seek and to be granted asylum in any Islamic community or state to which they have fled.[228] Overall, the granting of refugee aid is obligatory and guaranteed under the 'aman' institution (refuge and protection for non-Muslims). This arrangement is non-discriminatory and remains inviolate even if the beneficiary is in a conflict with Muslims (cf. Quran 9:6; UNHCR, 2012; RfP and UNHCR, 2018). Compared to modern refugee law, Hijrah law offers displaced persons more protection by also supporting forced displacement due to illness, or financial insecurity (Kirmani et al., 2008). In a word, Islam promotes humane treatment of displaced persons. But the Hijrah law is rarely mentioned by Muslim states today (Munir, 2011).

Political Rights in Christian Tradition

Christianity, like Islam, initially did not support democracy as a system of government. In fact, it had a vague or even hostile relationship with democracy, despite claims that "certain fundamental impulses within democracy may be traced to the ancient Hebrew prophets, and Western Christendom historically provided the womb within which modern democracy gestated" (De Gruchy, 1997: 324). Today most, if not all, Christian traditions tend to conform to the ethos of democracy. The Roman Catholic Church, for example, has strongly advocated democracy and human

[228] See also article 12 of the 1990 Cairo Declaration on Human Rights in Islam (hereinafter Cairo Declaration); and article 23 of the Arab Charter on Human Rights 1994 (hereinafter Arab Charter).

rights[229] in its social doctrine, particularly since the Second Vatican Council (hereinafter Vatican II 1962–1965). In his encyclical Centesimus Annus (hereinafter CA no. 46), Pope John Paul II clearly stated: "[t]he Church values the democratic system inasmuch as it ensures the participation of citizens in making political choices, guarantees to the governed the possibility both of electing and holding accountable those who govern them, and of replacing them through peaceful means when appropriate."[230] It has been pointed out, however, that this new appreciation does not mean an unreserved endorsement of democracy as the ideal Christian political system, since Christianity does not have an "ideal political model written into its foundation charter" (Hastings, 1991: 4). After all, Christian acceptance of democracy only came after the historical experiences of the Reformation, the Enlightenment and the French Revolution (cf. Roy, 2021).

From the onset, Christians have not supported the same forms of democracy. De Gruchy (1997) attributes this attitude to four historical trajectories within Christianity that influenced the evolution of modern democracy, namely the personalist, covenantal, liberal and socialist trajectories. According to him, the first path that represents the trajectory of Christian personalism arose within medieval Catholicism. During this time, Christian perspectives on the common good and the principle of subsidiarity were formulated based on a critical reflection on the political philosophy of Aristotle. These led to the rejection of the idea of a human society consisting of narcissistic, self-seeking individuals and the acceptance of solidarity and participation in the life of an organic society. The covenantal trajectory grew out of the Reformed or Calvinist tradition. The focus here was on creating a just social order that exemplifies God's righteousness. Hence, the emphasis was on accountability to God and fellow citizens under the authority of God. Somehow, this trajectory sounds a lot like the social contract theory, but here the commitment to the electorate is the binding force. This tradition is said to have influenced the US democracy ab initio. For De Gruchy, the liberal path is encapsulated in the triad of Radical Reformation, English Nonconformity and the Liberal Protestantism that arose in North America. Here, the intrinsic worth of the individual was strongly emphasised. In this way, liberal Christians uphold the value of human dignity, human rights and individual freedoms, as well as the separation of church and state. Last but not the least, the fourth trajectory represents the broad Christian socialist tradition. The socialist path was a major paradigm in the World Council of Churches as well as in all of ecumenical Christianity. It manifests itself today in liberation theology, and its key concepts include inter alia solidarity, civic participation, and economic justice. These are the basic principles of democracy for socialist Christians. These trajectories developed in specific historical contexts as Christians of different traditions tried to practice their faith in public spaces guided by the prevailing theological views of the time. The trajectories are complementary but differ in their internal

[229] See Gaudium et Spes (hereinafter GS 1965, no. 26); DH (no.1ff); CA (no. 47); and Redemptor Hominis (hereinafter RH 1979, no.17); Pacem in Terris (hereinafter PT 1963, nos. 11–27).

[230] See also PT no. 52. However, some perceive the Roman Catholic Church as an oligarchy. They argue that its support for democracy does not reflect its own practices (cf. Roy, 2021).

logic. This in turn led to the support for different types of democracy among the diverse Christian adherents and perhaps to observable differences in the democratic cultures among some nations (cf. De Gruchy, 1997).

The right to protest is a contentious issue in Christianity. The Bible does not give a clear answer about its permissibility but did say a lot about the relationship of the Christian believer to civil authorities. In the letter to the Romans (Romans 13:1–7) written during the reign of the despotic Roman emperor Nero (37–68 AD), Paul urged Christians in Rome to be submissive to civil authorities because, according to him, all authorities are established by God and rulers are serving Him in their political office. The apostle Peter also gave a similar instruction in his writings (cf. 1 Peter 2:13–17). Christians understand these biblical provisions as a call to obedience to civil authorities and thus as a ban on all forms of protest. This injunction was, however, delimited in the Acts of Apostles where the imperative of obedience to civil authority conflicts with obedience to God (Acts 4:19–20). In such situations, the Bible allows or even recommends to a Christian to act in civil disobedience to the government if it commands evil—and that is, if it requires him or her to act against the teachings and requirements of God's Word (Acts 5:29; see also Exodus 1:15–22; Daniel 3; Mark. 2:23–28; John 5:1–16).[231] St Augustine of Hippo (354–430 AD) later summarised these provisions in his political philosophy and calls on citizens to relentlessly obey the authorities. But he also advises citizens, in the event of a conflict between human and divine laws, to choose the latter and then willingly accept the punishment of disobedience rather than submit to an unjust law. In his words, "a law that is not just does not seem to me to be a law".[232] Thomas Aquinas (1225–1274) defines in his legal theory the so-called unjust law (lex iniqua) as one that "departs from reason".[233] The Catholic Catechism (CCC no. 2242) further elaborates the term to include official directives that are "contrary to the demands of the moral order, to the fundamental rights of persons or the teachings of the Gospel." Therefore, relying on scriptures and tradition, Christian traditions largely subscribe to peaceful protests and civil disobedience and see the imposition of an unjust law as their sufficient justification.

The Roman Catholic position is evident in its social teachings, for example, in the encyclical Pacem in Terris (no. 51) by Pope John XXIII, in which he declares that an unjust law has no binding force in conscience. The Catholic Church also recognises the right of the faithful to a peaceful manifestation of dissent in the defence of the dignity of persons and the common good (CCC no. 2238). The Catholic Church is not alone in this. Protestant theologians and clergymen like Dietrich Bonhoeffer (1906–1945) and Martin Luther King Junior (1929–1968) not only supported civil disobedience but also took active part in the struggle against injustice. Their methods of political resistance have continued to inspire resistance

---

[231] See When is civil disobedience allowed for a Christian? https://www.gotquestions.org/civil-disobedience.html. Accessed 01.02.2021.

[232] On Free Choice of the Will, Book 1.5.11.33.

[233] Summa Theologiae Ia-IIae, q. 93., art.3, ad 2 m.

movements worldwide, within and outside the Christian church. We recently witnessed this in Nigeria in the period between January and March 2020, when Christians across the country took to the streets with their prayer items and placards to protest the increasing insecurity and incessant killings in the land. All the same, it must be pointed out that there are some Christian denominations that interpret the Pauline injunction in his Letter to the Romans chapter 13, literally and therefore do not support protests of any kind. Examples of these abound in Pentecostal Churches.[234]

Finally, the Christian response to the global refugee issue tilts more in favour of hospitality towards refugees and advocacy of their rights. The roots of this attitude can be traced to the biblical tradition of hospitality towards strangers. The Old Testament makes a lot of references in favour of the stranger. For example, in the Torah (i.e., the Five Books of Moses), it says in the book of Leviticus (19: 33–34): "If you have resident aliens in your country, you will not molest them. You will treat resident aliens as though they were native-born and love them as yourself, for you yourselves were once aliens in Egypt" (see also Exodus 22:21; 23:9; Deuteronomy 10:19; 24:14, 17; 27:19). In the New Testament, Jesus enjoins Christians to welcome strangers (Matthew 25: 35). Jesus himself lived as a refugee child in Egypt earlier in his life (Matthew 2:13–18). In the Letter to the Hebrews (13:1–2), Christians are also strongly advised to imbibe a culture of welcoming strangers, "for by doing this, some people have entertained angels without knowing it" or even the risen Christ (Luke 24: 13–15). Based on these premises, early Christian communities saw themselves as witnesses of non-discriminatory love for all people (Colossians 3:10–11) (Zaccaria et al., 2018). Following this tradition, the moral teachings of various Christian traditions therefore recognise the imperative of compassion for and hospitality to strangers, immigrants and refugees as part of the core Christian virtues. For the Roman Catholic Church, it is not only a distinguishing feature of the Church of God but also a sign of its "fidelity to the gospel" (Pontifical Council for the Pastoral Care of Migrants and Itinerant People, 2004, no.22).

In its social teachings and official statements, the Roman Catholic Church further explains its position on the issue of forced displacement and migration in general. In the first place, it does not encourage migration. But it upholds the right of persons to emigrate in danger of conflict, persecution, and violence (CCC 2241; GS no. 65; PT nos. 25 and 106; LE no. 23), as well as in the face of hunger, and poverty owing to environmental degradation (LS no. 25). At the same time, the Church recognises the right of governments to regulate migration flows (GS no. 87; Caritas in Veritate, hereinafter CV no. 62). It defends the dignity of migrants (GS no. 66; PT no. 105) and invokes the principles of human solidarity (Sollicitudo Rei Socialis no. 38) and subsidiarity, meaning the need for stronger international cooperation as ways to tackle this social phenomenon (CV no. 62). In his recent address to the participants in the Sixth International Forum on Migration and Peace (2017: 2f), Pope Francis sums up the position of the Catholic Church as follows: "[o]ur shared

[234] Ibid.

response may be articulated by four verbs: to welcome, to protect, to promote and to integrate… I believe that conjugating these four verbs, in the first person singular and in the first person plural, is today a responsibility, a duty we have towards our brothers and sisters who, for various reasons, have been forced to leave their homeland: a duty of justice, of civility and of solidarity" (see also RfP and UNHCR, 2018).

3.5 Judicial Rights

Judicial rights are another interesting set of rights examined here as some of the rights that are commonly violated in Nigeria and, more importantly, because of their overarching importance in a democratic society. In addition to freedom of religion, freedom from discrimination, the right to life and political rights, they belong to the first generation of human rights. Judicial rights refer more or less to the right to a fair trial (Sterkens & Ziebertz, 2018: v).

In this study, a fair trial is understood to mean a just and transparent hearing by a knowledgeable, independent and impartial judge or a legally appointed jury. This is internationally recognised as a basic human right. The principle of fair trial is not novel; several elements associated with it already existed in the legal systems of ancient societies. Something similar can be found in the Magna Carta Act of 1215[235] and the Sixth Amendment to the US Constitution of 1791. Despite its long history, the principle of fair trial did not become a universal human right until 1948, when it was enshrined in the Universal Declaration. Article 10 of the Universal Declaration states: "[e]veryone is entitled in full equality to a fair and public hearing by an independent and impartial tribunal, in the determination of his rights and obligations and of any criminal charge against him." This provision has been further elaborated and codified in article 14 of the ICCPR and article 7 of the African Charter, as well as many other regional and international human rights conventions.[236] The right to a fair trial is an extremely important human right. The Human Rights Committee identifies it in General Comment no. 32 on Article 14 concerning the Right to Equality before Courts and Tribunals and to a Fair Trial as a key element of human rights protection and as a procedural means to maintain the rule of law.[237] It has a broad scope and embraces a set of ground rules, minimum guarantees and other

[235] Clause 39 of the Magna Carta, for example, speaks about issues like preservation of individual liberty and property, trial by a jury, and due process of law, whereas clause 40 sets the standard for a speedy trial.

[236] The right is also guaranteed by article 6 of the European Convention on Human Rights (and articles 2–4 of its 7th Protocol), article 8 of the American Convention on Human Rights and article 13 of the Revised Arab Charter. See also the UN Convention against Torture and Other Cruel, Inhuman or Degrading Treatment or Punishment (CAT), and the CRC [articles 37, 39 & 40(2)], as well as all other relevant UN standards and norms.

[237] CCPR/C/GC/32, 23rd August 2007, para. 2. The Human Rights Commission too describes it as "[a] fundamental guarantee of human rights and the rule of law" (OHCHR (2014b: 7).

specific provisions that apply in criminal proceedings or in situations, in which the rights and obligations of a person are determined in a suit at law (Zhang, 2009). These include the following: the equality before the law,[238] the respect for the right to liberty,[239] the right to independent and impartial judgement,[240] the presumption of innocence,[241] the right to legal aid or counsel,[242] the right to a public hearing,[243] the right not to be forced to incriminate oneself,[244] the right to a fair chance to present a defence,[245] the right to interpretation,[246] and the right to be heard within a reasonable time.[247] The right to a fair and open trial, like most rights, can be lawfully restricted. For example, article 14(1) of the ICCPR recognises that the right to a public hearing by a court may be restricted for reasons of morals, public order or national security, or to protect the private lives of those involved in the trial. In certain cases, the media and the public can be excluded from the hearing.[248] Even in such circumstances, the ICCPR requires that the judgment, including the essential findings, evidence and legal grounds of the court's decision, be made public, unless the interests of juveniles necessitate otherwise, or if the issues under trial concern matrimonial disputes or the guardianship of children. In these situations, then the restriction on the publicity of a process must be both necessary and proportionate.

The right to a fair trial is intended to ensure the proper administration of justice.[249] It is considered the legal bastion of a functioning democracy as such. To that end, it is protected in the constitutions, case laws and other legislations of several, if not all, nations around the world. Nigeria is no exception. The right to a fair trial is entrenched in Nigerian law. Apart from the constitutional guarantees, the judicial rights of an accused person are extensively covered in a host of domestic laws and statutes.[250]

---

[238] Article 7 of the Universal Declaration, and article 3 of the African Charter.

[239] Article 3 of the Universal Declaration, article 9(1) of the ICCPR, article 6 of the African Charter, and article 17(2)(a) of the African Charter on the Rights and Welfare of the Child (hereinafter ACRWC).

[240] Article 10 of the Universal Declaration, and article 14(1) of the ICCPR.

[241] Article 11 of the Universal Declaration, article 14(2) of the ICCPR, article 7(1)(2) of the African Charter and article 17(2)(c)(i) of the ACRWC.

[242] Article 14(3)(d) of the ICCPR, article 7(1)(3) of the African Charter, and article 17(2)(c)(iii) of the ACRWC.

[243] Article 10 of the Universal Declaration, and article 14(1) of the ICCPR.

[244] Article 14(3)(g) of the ICCPR.

[245] Ibid., article 14(3)(b); see also article 17(2)(c)(iii) of the ACRWC.

[246] Article 14(3)(f) of the ICCPR, and article 17(2)(c)(ii) of the ACRWC.

[247] Article 14(3)(c) of the ICCPR, article 7(1)(4) of the African Charter, and article 17(2)(c)(iv) of the ACRWC.

[248] See also CCPR/C/GC/32, 23rd August 2007, para. 3.

[249] Ibid., para. 2.

[250] The following are some of the enactments that guide the delivery of justice in Nigeria: the Administration of Criminal Justice Act (ACJA 2015); Violence Against Persons (Prohibition) Act 2015; Trafficking in Persons (Prohibition) Law Enforcement and Administration Acts 2015; Terrorism (Prevention)(Amendment) Act 2013; Nigerian Legal Aid Act 2011; Evidence Act 2011;

3.5.1 *Right to a Fair Trial in Nigerian Law*

The Nigerian Constitution grants the right to a fair trial to anyone standing trial for an alleged crime under the national criminal justice system. The basic provision is contained in section 36(1), which reads as follows: "[i]n the determination of his civil rights and obligations, including any question or determination by or against any government or authority, a person shall be entitled to a fair hearing within a reasonable time by a court or other tribunal established by law and constituted in such manner as to secure its independence and impartiality." From this provision, three basic components of the right to a fair trial in Nigeria can be identified, namely a fair hearing, a timely hearing and a hearing by a legally established independent and impartial court or tribunal. It is important to briefly examine each of these core principles here.

Right to a Fair Hearing

The Constitution makes no specific mention of fair trial in the above-cited substantive provision, instead it uses its core component of fair hearing to define the right. As a term, fair hearing means giving a party that needs to be heard an opportunity to be heard before a decision is made. This is the elementary understanding of this principle. The Constitution recognises this as a basic requirement for a fair trial and incorporates it as a fundamental right. As a judicial right, fair hearing is therefore the right of everyone to present his or her case or to be heard in civil and criminal proceedings before a judicial decision can be arrived at. It presupposes that not only one party, in particular the accused person(s), is heard in a case. Rather, as Bamgbose (2014: 237) aptly formulates it, it is "a two-way operation" and involves hearing both sides in a lawsuit, and affording them equal opportunity of hearing in all material issues in a case before a decision which may affect any of them is reached.[251] For this reason, it is also referred to in legal circles as "the whole hearing."[252] But even then, there is much more to a fair trial than just hearing all the concerned parties in a dispute; this also includes fairness,[253] which means that the hearing has to follow the rules of natural justice.[254] The Constitution enshrines the common law concept of natural justice with the twin traditional pillars of hearing the other party

---

Fundamental Rights (Enforcement Procedure) Rules 2009; Criminal Procedure Code (CPC 2004); and Criminal Procedure Act (CPA 2004)]. Others are African Charter Act, Robbery and Firearms Act, Public Complaints Commission Act 2004, Nigerian Law Reform Commission Act, Cap. N118 LFN 2004, Arbitration and Conciliation Act Cap. A18 LFN 2004, Prisons Act Cap. P29 LFN 2004, National Drug Law Enforcement Agency Act (hereinafter NDLEA) Cap. N40 LFN 2004, Customs and Exercise Management Act (CEMA) Cap. C45 LFN 2004, the Child Rights Act, among others. All these enactments complement the relevant constitutional provisions.

[251] See also *Njideka Ezeigwe & 2 Ors v. Chief Sir Benson Chuks* (2010) 2–3 SC (pt.1) 2.

[252] *Oged Ovunwo & Anor v. Iheanyichukwu Woko & 2 Ors* (2011) 6–7 SC (pt. 1) 1. See also Akpambang (2016).

[253] *Ezechukwu v. Onwuka* [2005] All FWLR (pt. 280) 1514 at pp. 1542, 1553.

[254] *Sumanya Issah Torri v. The National Park Service of Nigeria* (2011) 6–7 Sc (pt. III) 171.

(audi alteram partem) and that no one is allowed to be a judge in his or her own case (nemo iudex in causa sua).[255] In other words, by ensuring compliance with the right of a person not to be condemned unheard and the principle of non-bias. Judicial officers must strictly adhere to these principles before hearing would be adjudged fair.[256] Fairness here lies in the method by which a case is determined, and not necessarily in the correctness of the decision.[257] The test or measure of fairness of any trial in Nigerian courts is whether a reasonable observer at the trial can conclude that justice has been served to the parties in the case.[258] In the event of any actual or alleged irregularity in the conduct of the litigation, the aggrieved party is expected to make it an issue by complaining.[259] A remote implication of the former is that it presupposes that hearing can be observed by the public in the context of a fair trial. This is supported by section 36(4) of the Constitution, which guarantees a public hearing in all criminal matters. However, this can also be done privately under certain circumstances.[260] From the foregoing, it can be said that the right to a fair hearing is very important to the administration of justice in Nigeria.[261] In *Torri v. National Park Service of Nigeria*,[262] the court described it inter alia as an inalienable right of the accused and indispensable in any trial.[263] It cannot be waived or legally withdrawn; it is not such a rule that parties can apply at their convenience. A breach of it will vitiate or nullify the entire proceedings.[264] Regarding the scope of application, the principle of fair hearing applies sensu stricto to criminal proceedings. However, it extends to any situation in which a person or an authority is involved in enforcing the rights of another (Bamgbose, 2014).

Right to a Timely Hearing

The right to a timely hearing signifies in plain language that a suspect is entitled to be tried without unnecessary delays; (s)he ought to be brought before a court of law and that the trial process must finish within the shortest possible time. Delays in a trial process could lead to the abuse of certain constitutionally guaranteed rights of a suspect, such as the right not to be unlawfully deprived of one's liberty [section

[255] *Kennon v. Tekam* (2001) 10 SCM 138. See also Bamgbose (2014).

[256] *Deduwa & Ors v. Okorodudu* (1976) 9–10 SC 207.

[257] *Tim Orugbo & Anor v. Bulara UNA & Ors* (2002) 13 SCM 153. See also *State v. Onagoruwa* (1992) 2 NWLR (pt. 221) p. 33, and *Kim v. State* (1992) 4 NWLR (pt. 233) p. 17.

[258] *Ndukuba v. Kolomo & Ors* (2005) 1 SCM 114]. No. 422.

[259] *Segun Ogunsanya v. The State* (2011) 6–7 SC (pt. II) 56; *Nwaekweghinya v. State* (2005) 9 NWLR (pt. 930) p. 227; *Udo v. State* (2005) 8 NWLR (pt. 228) 2. 521; and *Adeniyi v. State* (2001) 13 NWLR (pt. 730) p. 375.

[260] See ACJA 2015, sections 259, 232, 260 and 262; also, Akpambang (2016). Besides, a comprehensive list of the legal limitations of the right to a public hearing in criminal matters can be found in subsection 36(4)(a-b). Here, the Constitution repeats practically the legal exceptions to public hearing as contained in article 14(1) of the ICCPR.

[261] See *Oged Ovunwo & Anor v. Iheanyichukwu Woko & 2 Ors* (2011), above at no. 252.

[262] See *Sumanya Issah Torri v. The National Park Service of Nigeria* (2011), above at no. 254.

[263] Ibid.

[264] *Tim Orugbo & Anor v. Bulara UNA & Ors* (2002) 13 SCM 153.

35(1)], the right to be arraigned within a reasonable time, or to release [section 35(4)(b)]. Conversely, delays could reduce unlawful pre-trial detention and trim down the human impact of criminal proceedings (OHCHR, 2014b). This right is therefore specifically designed to prevent such delays in judicial proceedings. This constitutional guarantee covers the time between the suspect's arrest or arraignment and the delivery of the judgment, including any appeals or reviews that may arise therefrom. This right exists at all stages of the proceedings, and what counts as "a reasonable time" for the Constitution depends on the facts of a case. For instance, in the case of arrest or detention in execution of court order or upon a well-founded suspicion of the commission of an offence or to prevent the commission of a criminal offence [section 35(1)(c)], the reasonable time means a period of one day within which the suspect must be charged, if a competent court can be found in a vicinity within forty kilometers of the place of arrest or detention [section 35(5)(a)]. Otherwise, the court may consider a period of two days or a longer period appropriate to the circumstances [section 35(5)(b)]. If still untried within two months of detention in the case of a suspect denied bail [section 35(4)(a)], or three months from the date of arrest for a suspect granted bail, then the suspect shall be released either unconditionally or upon such conditions as are reasonably necessary to ensure that (s)he appears for trial at a later date [section 35(4)(b)]. In the context of criminal proceedings, however, the phrase has to be assessed based on a number of criteria, such as the nature and gravity of the offence, and relevant procedural guidelines for each case (cf. Zhang, 2009). Cases where the suspect is denied bail by the court must be tried in a speedy manner. The right to a timely hearing also embraces the entitlement to a timely judgment, meaning that a court's decision must be pronounced without undue delay (OHCHR, 2014b).

Right to a Hearing by an Independent and Impartial Court of Law

In countries governed by the rule of law, independence and impartiality are essential requirements for the judiciary as "a central pillar of the right to a fair trial" (OHCHR, 2014b: 14). These requirements are absolute and non-derogable.[265] The Nigerian Constitution recognises them as such and includes them in its provisions. On the one hand, the concept of an independent judiciary means the absence of any influence, for example by the government, litigants or third parties such as the media.[266] This requirement is a function of the system of appointment of judicial officers, the security of their term of office, as well as the existence of adequate safeguards to shield them from external pressures.[267] To ensure this, the status of judges must therefore be comprehensively secured by law. This requirement is important because it concerns the "credibility, legitimacy and effectiveness" of the judiciary as a guarantor of fair trials.[268] On the other hand, the constitutional requirement of impartiality serves to underscore the need for the court to treat all parties in a lawsuit equally

[265] CCPR/C/GC/32, 23rd August 2007, para. 19. See also OHCHR (2014b).

[266] Ibid., para. 25. See also OHCHR (2014b).

[267] Ibid., para. 19.

[268] UN Doc. A/HRC/22/26), 17th December 2012, para. 40. See also OHCHR (2014b).

because, as the Supreme Court held in *Kim Chungwon v. The State*, "a trial studded with partiality for one side is not fair hearing."[269] This imperative of impartiality is double-barrelled, that is, it has both subjective and objective aspects. Subjective impartiality means that judicial officers should be disinterested and free from personal bias, prejudice or preconceptions about a case before them, while objective impartiality means that they should also appear impartial to every reasonable observer present at a trial.[270] Impartiality in judicial proceedings is a sine qua non to fair hearing (Bamgbose, 2014).

The constitutional guarantees to protect the right to a fair trial of a suspect in Nigeria are not limited to these three basic requirements or imperatives. Additional guarantees are set out in sections 34, 35 and 36 of the Constitution.

Additional Constitutional Safeguards to Protect the Right to a Fair Trial
The Constitution also provides other safeguards to ensure a fair trial against a suspect. These include:

The Right to Personal Liberty
Criminal proceedings in Nigeria usually begin with arrests. Incarceration, also a form of the deprivation of liberty, is the ultimate penalty for crimes in the country alongside capital punishment. That being the case, any such deprivations of liberty need to be justified through a fair legal process.[271] The Constitution in section 35(1) guarantees every individual the right to respect for his or her liberty. This protects the individual from arbitrary arrests and detentions. In the event of a violation, the victim is entitled to redress in the form of financial or other compensation[272] and, if necessary, to a public apology from the authority or person specified by law.[273] But in situations where the loss of liberty is legal, this right safeguards the suspect's non-derogable entitlements to a prompt trial and humane treatment.[274]

The Right to Be Presumed Innocent
The right to be presumed innocent is guaranteed under section 36(5) of the Constitution, and it means that anyone accused of committing a crime is presumed innocent unless and until his or her guilt is proved.[275] According to this principle, the onus probandi lies on the prosecution, as expressed by the Latin maxim of common law "ei incumbit probatio, qui dicit, non qui negat"—which literarily means that the burden of proof lies upon the one who declares, not on the one who denies. The

[269] (1991–92) All NLR 371; See also Bamgbose (2014).

[270] CCPR/C/GC/32, 23rd August 2007, para. 21. See also OHCHR (2014b).

[271] See the Justice Programme of the European Union: Legal Experts Advisory Panel, Defence Rights Map, Case Law Database, Advice Guides and Latest News. Available at: https://www.fairtrials.org/right-fair-trial#the-right-to-a-fair-trial. Accessed 01.02.2021.

[272] See *Jim-Jaja v. COP* (2013) 6 NWLR (pt. 1350), 225.

[273] See section 35(6) of 1999 CFRN. This provision formed the basis of the Court's decision in *Nemi v. Attorney General of Lagos & Anor* (1996) 6 NWLR (pt. 452), 42 at 55.

[274] Section 34(1)(a) of 1999 CFRN.

[275] See *Ani v. The State* (2002) 1 NWLR (Pt 747) 217 at 230.

accused is therefore not obliged to prove his or her innocence but can be asked to state certain facts, for example, in the case of intoxication, or insanity.[276] Apart from these, it is up to the prosecution to prove that the accused has actually committed an alleged crime and the required standard of proof is 'beyond reasonable doubt'.[277] It is only when this is done that the burden of proof can be shifted to the accused.[278]

The Right to Be Informed Promptly of the Offence

In section 36(6)(a), the Constitution also grants every person charged with a criminal offence the right to be promptly informed in the language (s)he understands and in detail of the nature of the crime committed.[279] In the *Francis Durwode v. The State* case[280] the Supreme Court of Nigeria maintained, inter alia, that the charge or information has to be read out and explained to the accused to the satisfaction of the court, before the plea is taken. This information must therefore be given to the accused within 24 hours of being arrested,[281] unless (s)he is arrested while committing the crime. Under the Nigerian criminal justice system, a good charge must provide the accused with enough information about the offence (s)he is being accused of to enable him or her prepare for trial.

The Right to Adequate Time and Facilities to Prepare One's Defence

This constitutional right means that every accused person is entitled to adequate time and facilities to prepare a defence.[282] The opportunity to defend an allegation is said to be of central importance to a fair trial.[283] The facilities referred to here include variables, such as granting the accused person in custody access to his or her lawyer, or access to all relevant materials to enable them to prepare a defence. The meaning of adequate time is relative; it depends on the individual case. In any case, a lawyer may request an adjournment of proceedings if there is not enough time to prepare a defence (cf. Akpambang, 2016).

The Right to Examine Witnesses

By virtue of the constitutional provision of section 36(6)(d), an accused person has the right to cross-examine witnesses against him or her called by the prosecution. The essence of this exercise is to give one the opportunity to dismantle the case of the opposing party. It can be done by the suspect personally and through his or her counsel. The Nigerian Supreme Court affirms in *Tolu v. Bauchi Native Authority*[284]

---

[276] Section 139 (3)(c) of the Evidence Act 2011; see also *Air Force v. James* (2003) FWLR (Pt. 143) 257, p. 282.

[277] *Igabele v State* (2006) 6 NWLR (pt.975) p.100.

[278] Section 135 of the Evidence Act; see also *Babalola .v. The State* (1989) 4 NWLR (pt.115) 264; and Akpambang (2016).

[279] See also sections 6(1) of the ACJA 2015.

[280] (2000) 12 SCNJ 1 at 9.

[281] Section 35(3) of 1999 CFRN.

[282] Ibid., section 36(6)(b).

[283] See *Ugwu v. The State* (1998) NWLR (pt. 558) p.397, 408.

[284] (1965) NMLR 343. See also Akpambang (2016).

that a denial of this opportunity constitutes an abuse of the suspect's right to a fair trial. The right to examination of witnesses also includes the right of the suspect to call witnesses on his or her behalf under the same conditions as the prosecution witnesses.[285] Then ultimately only witnesses deemed relevant by the court can be admitted for the defence.

The Right to the Free Assistance of an Interpreter
The right to an interpreter guaranteed under section 36(6)(e) of the Constitution provides that every suspect is entitled to have the free assistance of an interpreter if (s)he does not understand the language used in court.[286] This right is necessary to ensure the effective participation of a suspect in legal proceedings regardless of language difficulties and to ensure a fair trial. However, to exercise this right, a suspect or his (or her) counsel must inform the court of the need (cf. Akpambang, 2016). This provision is important and applies to non-citizens and citizens alike, as many Nigerians are illiterate or semi-literate, while criminal proceedings in the country are conducted in English (cf. Salihu, 2017; Onoja, 2013).

The Right to a Copy of (the) Judgment
Pursuant to Section 36(7), the Constitution directs trial courts to keep records of their criminal proceedings, and all parties are entitled to have official copies of them sent to them directly or by proxy within seven days of the conclusion of the case.[287] This is a directive that the courts or tribunals must comply with. Although failure to comply with it cannot be considered a miscarriage of justice,[288] compliance with same will enable the parties to exercise their right of appeal.

The Right Not to Be Held Guilty on Account of Retroactive Law
Retroactive criminal legislations, otherwise known as *ex post facto* criminal laws, are expressly prohibited by the Constitution under section 36 subsection 8.[289] By virtue of this provision, one cannot be held guilty of a criminal offence because of an act or omission which was not a crime at the time it took place. The same applies to penalties. Without an existing law there can be no punishment. Furthermore, no one shall be given a heavier penalty than that applied at the time the offence was committed. However, if the law provides for a lighter sentence after the crime is committed, the offender could benefit from it.

---

[285] In the case of *Idirisu v. The State* (1967) 1 All NLR 32, the Supreme Court of Nigeria contended inter alia that the suspect's application for adjournment to that effect ought to have been granted. See also Akpambang (2016); Zhang (2009).

[286] See also section 17(3) of the ACJA 2015; and *Umaru v. Federal Republic of Nigeria* (2013) LPELR-20192 (C.A).

[287] See also section 294(1) of 1999 CFRN; and Akpambang (2016).

[288] See *Adekeye & Ors v. Akin-Olugbade* (1987) NWLR (pt. 60).

[289] See also section 4(9). In addition, the basic constitutional provision has been given judicial interpretation in the case of *Hope Democratic Party v. Peter Obi & 5 Ors* (2011) 18 NWLR (pt. 1278) 80 at 100.

The Right Not to Be Tried Twice for the Same Offence

The Constitution guarantees every suspect the right to a trial for just one crime. This is also known as the right against double jeopardy and is contained in section 36 subsection 9. It provides that no person shall be subject to a retrial for an offence of which (s)he has already been finally convicted or acquitted in accordance with the law.[290] To enjoy this right, an accused has to convince the court that (s)he has been factually and legally acquitted or convicted of the same crime by a competent court or tribunal (Kana et al., 2017). According to this provision, however, it is only a superior court, that is, a court superior to the trial court that can overturn a conviction or acquittal of the accused and order a retrial.[291]

The Right to the Enjoyment of Pardon

The Constitution empowers the President [in section 175(1)(a)] and the Governor of a State [in section 212(1)(a)] to grant pardon to certain persons convicted of a crime under the provisions of the law. Once a convicted criminal is granted this pardon by the competent authority, his or her previous conviction would appear as if (s)he had never been convicted of a crime.[292] Therefore, the right to enjoyment of pardon guaranteed under section 36(10) of the same Constitution protects any person who shows that (s)he has been granted pardon for a criminal offence from a retrial for that offence.

The Right to Be Tried for Only an Offence Known to Law

This right is guaranteed by section 36 subsection 12 of the Constitution, which provides that a suspect can only be convicted of a criminal offence defined in a written law with its clear-cut punishment. The overall import of this provision is that no one can be brought to justice and convicted or punished for acts that do not constitute a criminal offence under Nigerian law. This was the basis of the decision in the case of *Faith Okafor v. Lagos State Government and Anor,*[293] where the Court of Appeal held, inter alia, that the directive of a state governor is not a law and a violation of it cannot attract criminal punishments.

There are also other guarantees, such as the right to remain silent and the right to legal assistance, which complete the long list of constitutional safeguards for protecting the right to a fair trial of accused persons in Nigeria. The grand design of all these guarantees is to protect a suspect, particularly in criminal proceedings, in such a way that justice is not only served but is also clearly seen to be done.

---

[290] See also sections 226, 238(1) and 277(1)(a) of the ACJA 2015; sections 181(1)(a) and 221(1) of the Criminal Procedure Act (CPA); section 223(1) of the Criminal Procedure Code (CPC). Besides, this right was invoked by the Supreme Court of Nigeria in the case of *Nigerian Army v Aminu Kano* (2010) 5 NWLR (pt. 1188) 429 at pp. 461–462 (cf. Kana et al., 2017).

[291] See also sections 238(2) of the ACJA 2015.

[292] See *Falae v. Obasanjo* (1999) 4 NWLR (pt. 599) 476 at 495; see also Akpambang (2016), and Kana et al. (2017).

[293] (2016) LPELR 41066 (C.A.).

3.5.2 Topical Issues in the Right to a Fair Trial in Nigeria

In this part, the right to silence and the right to legal assistance are further examined and are used in this study as indicators to measure the attitudes of Nigerians towards the right to a fair trial and ultimately judicial rights. They have been chosen because they are perceived by many Nigerian scholars as the most frequently violated safeguards of fair trial in the country (Onoja, 2013; Ogunnoiki, 2020; Mustapha, 2010).

Right to Silence in Criminal Proceedings

The legal principle of silence is a basic common law right (Eruaga, n.d.). It means that a suspect is not legally obliged to respond to interrogations by investigating officials and that (s)he is also entitled to choose whether or not to give evidence in court. The first part of this definition pertains to the pre-trial right of a suspect to silence and the second to the at-trial right to same. The pre-trial silence is so called because barring unnecessary details the right usually begins once a suspect is in police custody, that is, from the moment of arrest up until his or her arraignment before the court for prosecution, and it is to the effect that (s)he can decide whether or not to speak to law enforcement officers or to answer their questions without any legal consequences. There are enough reasons why a suspect may need not speak to law enforcement officers or any person in authority. Among other things, (s)he may not understand the nature of the offence for which (s)he has been apprehended and its legal implications and would need to do so. As such, the essence of this provision is to protect him or her from self-incrimination. It was originally given as a privilege to "the poor, weak and ill-educated" to protect them against the abuse of the criminal justice system by the state or its agencies (Hocking & Manville, 2001: 91). But today it is considered a human right. The right against self-incrimination protects every suspect from being forced to incriminate him- or herself by providing information during interrogation. It also serves to prevent mistreatment of a suspect, often with the aim of forcing him or her to make dubious confessions during investigation. This has been the purpose of the privilege from the onset. By contrast, the application of the at-trial silence takes place during criminal proceedings in court. Here an accused cannot be compelled to testify against him- or herself or to confess guilt. (S)he has a right to not testify at his or her trial, and prosecutors are not allowed to call him or her as a witness. In other words, (s)he has a choice whether to testify or not and thus has a right to remain silent when questioned at trial.

The right to silence has an additional angle which concerns the right not to have silence used against one in deciding a case,[294] since silence is often perceived as "a behaviour consistent with guilt".[295] This implies that a suspect is not to be adjudged

[294] See also article 55(2)(b) of the Rome Statute of the International Criminal Court; and N(6)(d)(2) of the Principles and Guidelines on the Right to a Fair Trial and Legal Assistance in Africa.

[295] In his seminal work 'A Treatise on Judicial Evidence', Jeremy Bentham (1825: 241) argued about at-trial silence that "[i]nnocence never takes advantage of it. Innocence claims the right of speaking, as guilt invokes the privilege of silence." See also Scrutiny of Acts and Regulations Committee (1998). The Right to Silence: An Examination of the Issues. Available at: https://www.

guilty merely because of the conscious exercise of this right whether at investigation or during trial. For this reason, the law in more civilised jurisdictions requires that a suspect in custody be cautioned, that is, be informed of his or her right to silence before being questioned.[296] In this way, silence can then be attributed to a conscious exercise of the right and thus no adverse inference can be drawn. The right to silence is closely related to the procedural guarantee of the presumption of innocence, in which, as already mentioned, the burden of dislodging the presumed innocence of a suspect via establishment of guilt beyond reasonable doubt is thrust entirely upon the prosecution. Even though a suspect is a competent witness for the defence in criminal trials, (s)he is exempt from any obligation to answer questions or provide information that may expose him or her to criminal charges. By virtue of this right and the privilege against self-incrimination, (s)he cannot be compelled to respond to interrogations before or during the trial. More importantly, the silence cannot be commented on by the prosecution and cannot be used as evidence of guilt. However, the records show that a suspect's failure to testify may, in certain circumstances, be used by the court to assess the strength of the evidence brought against him or her by the prosecution.[297] The current practice of this common law principle therefore does not guarantee absolute immunity to inferences. Having said that, the right to remain silent basically means that a suspect facing a criminal charge has the right to choose whether or not to answer official questions at all stages of the criminal proceedings and that (s)he does not have to suffer any disadvantages at trial for that choice (Eruaga, n.d.). Despite much controversy surrounding this practice today, this right is recognised across legal systems as one of the fundamental guarantees of the universal human right to a fair trial, as it is enshrined in relevant international and regional human rights documents,[298] as well as in the constitutions and domestic laws of numerous nations.

---

parliament.vic.gov.au/archive/sarc/Right_to_Silence/Issues_Paper/tablecontents.htm. Accessed 01.02.2021.

[296] The caution—or Miranda rights as it is also called because of its close connection to the US landmark case of *Ernesto Miranda v. Arizona*, 384 U.S. 436 (1966)—which posits that suspects must be informed prior to questionings that they have a right to remain silent and have an attorney present during interrogation, has since become part of the standard practice of the right to silence. Clear references are made to it in several international documents, e.g., the respective Rules of Procedure and Evidence of the International Criminal Tribunal for Rwanda and for the former Yugoslavia, under Rule 42(A)(iii), inter alia.

[297] See *Weissensteiner v. R* (1993) 178 CLR 217228 per Mason CJ, Deane and Dawson JJ; also Hocking and Manville (2001), Ogunnoiki (2020), and Scrutiny of Acts and Regulations Committee (1998), above at no. 295.

[298] The ICCPR provides in article 14(3)(g) that, in the determination of any criminal charge against him, every person is entitled not to be compelled to testify against himself or herself or to confess guilt. Although there is no explicit reference to it in the ICCPR, the right to remain silent issues from the foregoing provision. However, both rights are clearly guaranteed in articles 55(1)(a) and 55(2)(b) of the Rome Statute of the International Criminal Court, article 20(4)(g) of the Statute of the International Criminal Tribunals for Rwanda (hereinafter ICTR Statute) and Rule 42(A)(iii) of its Rules of Procedure and Evidence, as well as article 21(4)(g) of the Statute of the International Criminal Tribunals for the former Yugoslavia (hereinafter ICTY Statute) and Rule 42(A)(iii) of its

The right to remain silent is also entrenched in the Nigerian Constitution. Under section 35(2), a suspect has the right to remain silent or avoid answering questions until after consultation with a legal practitioner or any other person of his or her choice. The Constitution further provides in section 36(11) that an accused person standing trial must not be compelled to give evidence at his or her trial. On the one hand, these provisions imply that any person under arrest is entitled to remain silent while in police custody. In addition, (s)he has the right not only to consult a legal practitioner before responding to police interrogations but also to have one present during custodial interrogations. In the absence of a legal practitioner, the list of persons who could be present in the same capacity as a legal practitioner is enlarged to include the following: an officer of the Legal Aid council of Nigeria (hereinafter LACON), an official of a civil society organisation (CSO), a Justice of the peace (JP), or still any other person as may be wished by the suspect. The presence of a legal practitioner or any of these designated persons during custodial interrogation of a suspect is to ensure the integrity of the process. This right may be waived. This is well documented in Nigerian law.[299] Furthermore, the Administration of Criminal Justice Act (ACJA) 2015 provides that a suspect should be informed of his or her Miranda rights during arrest by the police officer or another person making the arrest.[300] This particular inclusion is believed to be consistent with the original intent of the Constitution, although it did not exist in any federal law prior to 2015.[301] On the other hand, the constitutional right to remain silent also implies that the accused must not be forced to confess guilt or to testify against him- or herself during the judicial process. It also means that despite being the competent witness, the accused may elect not to give evidence on his or her own behalf as (s)he is entitled so to do.[302] Here too, this exercise is envisaged to protect the suspect from making self-incriminating avowals. The allegation of the commission of a criminal offence is for the prosecution alone to prove, who should explore several other legitimate methods to arrive at this end rather than rely on the assistance of the accused. The prosecutor may not comment on the accused person's refusal to testify in his or her defence or use it as admission of guilt. But then, the exercise of this right does not prevent a trial court from drawing inferences "as it thinks fit" from the evidence available to

---

Rules of Procedure and Evidence. Similarly, a suspect's right to pre-trial silence and the right not to be compelled to testify against him- or herself or to confess guilt are also guaranteed in M(2)(f) and N(6)(d) of the Principles and Guidelines on the Right to a Fair Trial and Legal Assistance in Africa, respectively.

[299] See section 17(2) of ACJA 2015; section 9(3) of Administration of Criminal Justice Law (hereinafter ACJL), No. 32, 2011 of Lagos State, Nigeria.

[300] Section 6(2)(a), (b) and (c) ACJA 2015.

[301] A somewhat similar provision can be found in the British Judges' Rules adopted by Nigeria in 1912, but which came into effect in 1914 and were last amended in 1964. For instance, Rule 2 is *in pari materia* with the Miranda rights. However, the rules do not have the force of law, they are rather rules of practice to guide the police (Idem, 2018; see also Onoja, 2013). Before 2015, the provision can only be found in section 3(2) of the ACJL 2011 of Lagos State, Nigeria.

[302] Section 180(a) of the Evidence Act; see also section 287(1)(iii) of the CPA.

it.[303] This implies in simpler terms that an accused person standing trial in Nigeria is expected to speak up when wrongly accused or incriminating evidence is presented against him or her by the prosecution, otherwise it can be assumed that (s)he has admitted the accusation (cf. Mustapha, 2010). This is one of the findings in the case of *Babalola v. The State*,[304] where the Supreme Court of Nigeria reasoned thus: "it is a reckless hazard to insist on the exercise of that right when the prosecution has made out a prima-facie case which calls for the accused person's explanation."

One of the main purposes of the right to silence is to protect the citizen from possible incidents of torture and coerced confessions (Onoja, 2013). The fact is that one of the statutory duties of the Nigerian police force under the Police Act is to prosecute criminal cases as an agency of the State.[305] Since the standard proof required in the prosecution process is 'beyond reasonable doubt', the police tend to rely heavily on confessions or statements to establish the guilt of a suspect (Mustapha, 2010). The reason for this attitude is that a confessional statement is seen as the best proof of guilt under Nigerian law, because it is assumed to have issued voluntarily from the mind of an accused person (Onoja, 2013). Therefore, circumstances that portray anything to the contrary, namely that the confession was not made voluntarily, will vitiate it.[306] The admissibility of confessions in Nigeria is largely regulated by the Evidence Act 2011, and the common law Judges Rules.[307] According to section 29 of the Evidence Act, a confession or statement is considered reliable if it is not subject to oppression, defined in subsection 5 as torture, inhuman treatment, and the use of violence. If a suspect alleges that a statement or confession was obtained from him or her through torture, coercion, threat or any form of inducement, the court must go through a trial-within-trial to decide whether to admit or reject the evidence. In such circumstances, it is up to the prosecution to prove that the statement is voluntary.[308] Otherwise, such a confession is inadmissible and would ordinarily be excluded from the evidence in court, although the judges' discretion is required.[309]

---

[303] Section 236(1)(c) of the CPC; see also *Sugh v The State* (1988) 2 NWLR (pt. 77) p.475; and Ogunnoiki (2020).

[304] (1989) 4 NWLR (pt.115) 264; *Nwede v. The State* (1985) 12 SC 32; see also Mustapha (2010).

[305] Section 23 of the Police Act Cap P19 LFN 2004.

[306] In the following cases, the courts held inter alia that a confessional statement is admissible only if voluntarily given: *Ebot v. State* (1993) 4 NWLR (pt.240) 644; and *Nwosu v. State* (1986) 4 NWLR (pt.186) 428.

[307] In the case of *Usman v. The State* (1981) 2 Nigerian Criminal Report 335, the court held among other things that the Judges Rules are functional in the country. But they are mere rules of administrative procedure, and not laws.

[308] However, the onus of objecting to the propriety of the circumstances surrounding the taking of a confession is on the accused and his or her counsel. In *Arogundare v. The State* (2009) 6 NWLR (part 1136) 165, the Supreme Court of Nigeria held that an oral confession made to a senior police officer at 2 am while the accuser was in custody was admitted for the main reason that the accused and his counsel did not challenge it for reasons best known to them. See also Onoja (2013).

[309] Section 14 of the Evidence Act provides that a court may exclude an improperly obtained evidence where it is convinced that the desirability of admitting the evidence is outweighed by the

The Evidence Act does not provide for Miranda rights, or even the right to silence itself. It does not consider the caution before interrogation as part of the necessary requirements for the admissibility of a confessional statement. The absence of these provisions in the Act has been interpreted in various ways by Nigerian courts, with the dominant perspective being that failure to invoke the caution does not necessarily make a confession inadmissible, notwithstanding section 35(2) of the Constitution.[310] In this way, Nigeria's confessions law differs significantly from the system in many other countries, particularly the US, whose constitutional model she has adopted (Onoja, 2013; Ogunnoiki, 2020). This disregard of the Miranda caution in the context of the provisions on the admissibility of confessions under applicable law and its inconsistent interpretation by Nigerian courts has impacted adversely on the exercise of the right to remain silent in the country. To begin with, Nigeria has a high percentage of semi-literate and illiterate people, most of whom do not even know about the right to silence. It has also been reported repeatedly that criminals in the country tend to belong to this group of people with little or no education (cf. Onoja, 2013). It then remains to be seen how they would exercise this right in such a situation if they are not made aware of this by law enforcement officers. The latter, for their part, may wish to take advantage of the situation to obtain useful confessions for the prosecution from the unsuspecting suspects. As a result, the abuse of the Miranda rights of suspects in criminal proceedings is widespread in the country, despite the constitutional right to silence. Over the years, it has been difficult to determine whether a suspect must be informed of Miranda rights before interrogation. The controversy seemed to have subsided somewhat with the recent inclusion of the provision in Lagos State ACJL 2011 and ACJA 2015. As part of this development, the Court of Appeal has in its rulings in recent cases urged the law enforcement officials to notify suspects of their Miranda rights in such situations.[311] But the Supreme Court is yet to make a binding decision on this.[312]

There are also overwhelming reports of torture and ill-treatment of suspects by law enforcement officers in the country, the most common reason being to obtain incriminating avowals for prosecution (cf. Mustapha, 2010; Onoja, 2013; Human Rights Report, 2013). In any case, this attitude or predilection for undue pressure as a main instrument of criminal investigations is also attributed to the weak investigative capacity of the concerned agencies and a lack of respect for human rights

undesirability of the way the evidence was obtained, and then section 15 enumerates the considerations upon which the desirability decision, or otherwise, would be based.

[310] Cf. *Akinmogu v. The State,* (2000) 6 NWLR (pt. 662) 608 at 617.

[311] Cf. *Nnajiofor v. The* Federal Republic of Nigeria (2018) LPELR-43925(CA).

[312] In the case of *Fatai Olayinka v. State* [(2007) 9 NWLR (pt. 1040) 561], which some consider as a lost opportunity to have an interpretation of the constitutional provision of the right to remain silent from the apex court of the land, the appellant contended that his confession to the police during custodial interrogation was contrary to the provisions of section 35(2) of the CFRN (cf. Ogunnoiki, 2020). The lead judgment did not react to the argument requesting the court to invoke the decision of the US Supreme Court in *Miranda v Arizona*, whereas the supporting judgment did but quickly added that the issue had been overtaken by events. This happened prior to the introduction of the ACJA 2015.

(NHRC, 2007). The law forbids the introduction of involuntary confessional statements into trials. But somehow, they get admitted as evidence using avenues such as the discretionary powers granted to judges in sections 14 and 15 of the Evidence Act. It is on record that most cases in court are prosecuted by the police based on confessions obtained under such circumstances.[313] Since these provisions are understood to mean that an improperly obtained confession may ultimately find its way to court, the consequence is, among other things, the increasing use of undue pressure as a method of interrogation. This abuse was endemic during the military era, but it is still not uncommon in this democratic era, which is why the ACJL 2011 of Lagos State provides in section 9(3) for mandatory electronic recording of confessions to forestall for such abuse. Granted that such a provision is gradually gaining traction in and around Lagos State as a method of corroborating confessions and could help minimise cases of forced confessions during custodial interrogation, it is the effective application of the right to silence, which would ensure more fairness in the judicial process.

Right to Defence in Criminal Proceedings

It is axiomatic that every accused person ought to be afforded the opportunity to defend an allegation. This fundamental principle of justice is not just a legal axiom; it is today recognised worldwide as a universal human right. The right to defend oneself is one of the minimum guarantees of the right to a fair trial.[314] It is enshrined in the constitutions and laws of numerous nations around the world. It is also entrenched in the Nigerian criminal justice system.

Nigeria's Constitution stipulates in section 36(6)(c) that every person who is accused of a criminal offence shall be entitled to defend himself [or herself] in person or by legal practitioners of his [or her] own choice.[315] Here the constitution clearly identifies two types of defence that are consistent with international law, namely a defence to be conducted in person and another to be with the assistance of a legally trained person of one's own choice. Both are not mutually exclusive in the sense that persons who engage the services of a learned counsel to defend their interests in legal proceedings still have the right to testify on their own behalf (cf. Zhang, 2009). The right to defend oneself in person means that every individual, as a suspect, is entitled to defend himself or herself at all stages of criminal proceedings. It also implies that one is fundamentally entitled to refuse any imposition of legal assistance by the state and to use all one's rights to defend oneself (cf. OHCHR, 2014b). However, this right is not absolute; it can be restricted in certain situations. For example, cases of the death penalty or life imprisonment under the ACJA 2015 require mandatory legal representation.[316] The same goes for cases involving minors

[313] See *Effiong Edet George v. State* (2009) 1 NWLR (Part 1122) 325; also, Human Rights Report, 2013.

[314] See article 14(3)(d) of the ICCPR; CCPR/C/GC/32, 23rd August 2007, para. 37.

[315] This formed part of the Supreme Court's decision in *Nigeria Custom Prison Service v. Adekeye* (2002) 7 SC (pt. 111) p.188, 195.

[316] Section 349(6)(b) of the ACJA 2015.

or suspects with health impairments that hinder the exercise of their procedural rights. In short, in cases where accused persons are generally viewed as incapable of acting in their own interest, self-representation is not allowed, and this means that the court may be required to appoint a lawyer to defend them. The rationale for mandatory assistance in legal proceedings is set out by the Supreme Court of Nigeria in the case of *Godwin Josiah v. The State*, where it stated thus: "[t]he right to counsel is thus at the very root of and is the necessary foundation for a fair hearing. The ordinary layman, even the intelligent and educated layman is not skilled in the science of law and he therefore needs the aid and advice of counsel."[317] The limitation to the right to defend oneself in person is therefore imposed in the interest of a fair judgment.

That said, an accused person still retains the right to decline the assistance of a lawyer. In situations where (s)he elects to represent himself or herself, the court is obliged to inform him or her of the right to be assisted by a legal practitioner of choice, while at the same time alerting him or her of the risks of the choice, as a way to facilitate the full exercise of the rights.[318] Failure to comply with this rule may mean that the accused was not given a fair hearing. But if the accused decides to defend him- or herself in person after being informed, it will be assumed that (s)he has waived the right to a learned counsel of choice, and this shall not be a ground to void the trial.[319] Apart from that, a trial will be nullified if an accused person is arraigned before a court without legal representation in any case where the interest of justice requires him or her to be legally assisted. This is another import of the court decision in the above case of *Godwin Josiah v. The State*, where the Nigerian Supreme Court held that the appellant's conviction for armed robbery and murder despite not being represented by a lawyer, amounted to a denial of fair hearing. Generally, the right to legal counsel is seen as an important safeguard for the right to a fair trial in Nigeria. It is so important that it is granted not only to the accused alone, but also to all parties to a lawsuit.[320]

Still in the context of legal representation, the Constitution makes a specific mention of a legal counsel of choice as the ideal for the full exercise of the right. However, choosing a counsel is subject to certain limitations in Nigeria. It may be limited in situations where a legal aid counsel would normally be assigned, such as in all cases where, as noted above, the interests of justice require that an accused person be defended by an assigned counsel, regardless of his or her consent or wishes, and when free legal assistance is required.[321] The limitation of the right in the former case does not deviate from the main objective of the constitutional right

[317] (1985) 1 NWLR (pt.2) p.125 at 140, per Oputa JSC.

[318] Sections 267(3), 349(1)(a) and 349(6)(a) of the ACJA 2015.

[319] Ibid., section 267(4); see also Akpambang (2016).

[320] Ibid., section 267(1).

[321] See article 14(3)(d) of the ICCPR; CCPR/C/GC/32, 23rd August 2007, para. 38; article 20(4)(d) of the ICTR Statute; article 21(4)(d) of the ICTY Statute; Principles and Guidelines on the Right to a Fair Trial and Legal Assistance in Africa (2003), article H(a); Rule 42(A)(i) of the Rules of Procedure and Evidence of the Rwanda and Yugoslavia Tribunals; and OHCHR (2014b).

to a counsel of choice, which is to ensure that an accused person standing trial for a criminal charge is effectively assisted by a learned counsel in appropriate cases to exercise his or her fair trial rights and have easier access to justice. This applies even more to the latter case of restricting the right by hiring a free legal aid counsel to assist the accused.

The pertinence of legal aid, in particular free legal assistance by counsel, as an instrument of access to justice in the Nigerian society cannot be overemphasised. Alongside little or no education, poverty has been identified as one of the major obstacles to the realisation of access to justice in the country (Adeyemi, 2007; Dada, 2012). According to reports, most suspects in Nigeria are people of low socio-economic status, who for this reason are in most cases unable to hire the services of a private lawyer. Aware of this fact and the persistent high levels of poverty in the country, the drafters of the Constitution included a clause in the legal instrument obliging the National Assembly to pass a law that grants financial assistance to indigent citizens whose rights have been violated, so that they can hire the services of a lawyer to prosecute their claims.[322] Pursuant to this provision, the Nigerian government set up a legal aid scheme in 1976, represented by the Legal Aid Council of Nigeria (LACON). LACON was established as a corporate body under the supervision of the Federal Ministry of Justice to provide free legal services to indigent citizens defined in the Legal Aid Act 2011 as persons "whose income does not exceed the national minimum wage."[323] As the official service provider, LACON contracts and coordinates the activities of lawyers who render pro bono services, that is, free legal services ranging from advice to legal representation in court. LACON also takes on the conduct of cases such as murder, manslaughter, rape, affray, assaults, stealing and robbery. Besides, it handles certain civil matters, including alleged breaches of human rights, as well as mediation services.[324] Granted, the services are provided on a pro bono basis, the Nigerian Supreme Court insists in *Udofia v. The State* case[325] that legal aid counsel must have the required skill and experience to effectively assist indigent citizens. LACON is not alone in this, as there are several other NGOs in the country that provide Nigerians with free legal aid, especially in the area of human rights (Adeyemi, 2007; Latham and Watkins, 2015). These include, for example, the Human Rights Law Service (HURILAWS), the Women's Rights Advancement and Protection Alternative (WRAPA), the Prisoners Rehabilitation and Welfare Action (PRAWA), and the Inter-African Network for Human Rights and Development (AFRONET). The functioning of the legal aid scheme in the country may be hampered by a number of setbacks, such as the paucity of legal aid lawyers in the country vis-à-vis the demand

---

[322] Section 46(4)(b)(i) of 1999 CFRN.

[323] Section 10 of the Legal Aid Act 2011. The original Act, the Legal Aid Decree no.56 of 1976, has since been repealed under democratic dispensation and replaced with the Legal Aid Act 2011, which is still in force.

[324] Cf. Second Schedule to the Legal Aid Act 2011; also, Periodic Country Report (2015–2016), and Latham and Watkins (2015).

[325] (1988) 3 NWLR. (pt. 4) p. 533; see also Adeyemi (2007).

for their services, inadequate funding, lack of publicity, inaccessibility of the scheme in some parts of the country due to insecurity, and delays in the criminal justice system. Nevertheless, the scheme itself is a means of improving access to justice.

It is clear from the foregoing that the right to counsel is enshrined in the Constitution and other relevant national statutes. Despite the enshrinements, worrisome abuses of the right persist in the country. A key concern is the right to free legal aid, which is not taken seriously in the country. The consequence is, among other things, the violation of the fundamental guarantee against the illegal detention of accused persons, especially indigent or ignorant crime suspects (Dada, 2012). Over the years, it has been consistently reported that Nigerian prisons are not only in appalling conditions but are also severely congested. A recent March 2021 report by the Nigerian Correctional Service (NCS) shows that a total of 67,631 prisoners are housed in the country's 240 prisons originally designed to house 50,153 inmates, somehow confirming the claims. It goes on to say that around 72.7 percent or 49,180 inmates are pre-trial detainees and remand prisoners who are still awaiting trial[326] and often have to wait for years. It is not uncommon for people accused of capital crimes to spend tens of years in pre-trial detention. These reports have also been corroborated by other studies (Fact Sheet, 2013). This state of affairs is significant in the context of prisons congestion in the country. More importantly, the congestion is partly due to the shortage of lawyers to represent the detainees. For example, at some point in 2014 it was suggested that LACON only had 280 legal aid lawyers for the entire federation. This resulted in most prison inmates having to wait indefinitely for legal assistance, which made the proportion of pre-trial inmates extremely high (69.3% of all inmates at the time) (Latham and Watkins, 2015).

Added to this is the issue of inmates awaiting execution after being convicted of a capital crime. These usually spend much longer periods of time, sometimes two decades or more, on death row to exhaust the opportunity to appeal before their sentence is served. Studies suggest that many of the convictions would be overturned if appealed with effective legal representation. In this context, the results of the free legal services sponsored by the Department for International Development (DfID) on behalf of fifteen death row inmates in 2012–2013 are instructive. According to the report of the All-Party Parliamentary Group on Nigeria (APPGN, 2013), eight of the fifteen convictions were overturned, while six were completely quashed. As laudable as these efforts may be, they show that overcrowding in Nigeria's prisons is due in part to the lack of effective legal assistance for accused and convicted persons. Therefore, the right to counsel and free legal assistance can help ease pressure on prisons and ensure that suspects and convicts exercise their right to a fair trial, thereby improving access to justice (cf. Okoronkwo, 2015).

---

[326] See Nigeria: World Prison Brief data. Institute for Crime and Justice Policy Research (ICPR) Birkbeck, University of London. Available at: https://www.prisonstudies.org/country/nigeria. Accessed 01.04.2021. See also Human Rights Reports, 2013.

3.5.3 *Religion and the Right to a Fair Trial*

Justice is a human attribute that is rooted in the innate sense of humans for fairness. Here, we refer to justice as realised in judicial administration, which is one aspect of the concept. The principle of fairness requires an arbiter to be fair to a suspect standing trial. Although this is an age-old rule, it is still recognised today as a principle of justice (Ekundayo, 2013). The concern for justice is common to all people; it is not the reserve of any particular race. But the delivery of the same differs according to contexts (Issa, 2016).

Right to a Fair Trial in ATR
In traditional Nigerian societies one can say that justice was not perceived as fairness in its strict legal sense, but as "fairness to parties with a view to a stronger society" (Okafọ, 2006: 42). Based on this, the justice systems in the traditional Igbo and many African societies were largely dispute resolution mechanisms, the main aim of which was to resolve conflicts, settle disputes, eliminate injustices, uphold social norms and thus preserve the harmony of the community (Nzimiro, 1972). Even so, they were not limited to just minor community-level issues. They also handled more serious criminal cases such as murder, homicide, etc., as the distinction between civil and criminal issues never really arose. Another notable feature of traditional judicial mechanisms is their procedures. Unlike the modern judicial institutions, whose procedures are impersonal, the traditional systems had case management organs that were close to the people. Nonetheless, these enjoyed credibility in the eyes of the locals due, in part, to the integrity of case managers. Community leaders and/or elders usually played the role of judges and advocates, while decisions were often implemented by groups and institutions, such as the youth age grades, and the masquerade institution (Okafọ, 2006). Despite the peculiar form of these traditional systems, trial procedures were mainly based on the principle of hearing from all sides to a litigation (see Achebe, 1958). Other protections specific to parties in a criminal context, such as the right to be informed about the crime committed, the possibility to defend oneself, the right to a public and swift hearing, the right to be liable only for an offence known to customary laws of respective societies, the right to call witnesses and the right to compensation for mistakes in trial, also existed in the traditional judicial systems which were not dominated by either the judges or the parties. However, none of these guarantees were provided in the way prescribed in human rights instruments today. These old systems somehow subsist today in customary courts and have been preserved in some communities as an alternative forum for out-of-court dispute settlement (OHCHR, 2016).

Right to a Fair Trial in Islamic Tradition
Islam regards itself as a religion of justice. In fact, the Islamic religion perceives justice (`adl) as a basic objective and ideal that should be pursued regardless of the circumstances (Issa, 2016). In the Quran (5:8), believers are solemnly instructed as follows: "[b]e just: this is closest to piety". Other authoritative Islamic sources too are awash with similar references (cf. Quran 4:58; 4:135; 42:15; 49:9; 60:8; etc.).

Muslim scholars teach that the goal of the Islamic law is the establishment of a just society (Haneef et al., 2019; Al 'Alwani, 1994). They also believe that judicial justice must be sought with fairness (ihsan) in proceedings, and this for them is why the two concepts are often found together in several quranic injunctions.[327] For the realisation of justice, Islamic law incorporates a lot of principles and procedures that are drawn from the Quran, Sunna and ijtihad, as well as legal maxims. These have been compiled by Muslim jurists to serve as a yardstick for a fair trial and just adjudication. Some of the principles deserve a brief mention here. The first is the principle of equality before the law, which is firmly established in Islamic law.[328] This principle is based on the Islamic belief that all humans are born equal and guarantees everybody standing trial under Islamic justice system equal protection of the law.[329] Second, every person is presumed innocent under Islamic law until proven otherwise.[330] This is comparable to the legal principle of the presumption of innocence in secular law. But in the Islamic context it is based on the saying of the Prophet that everyone is born pure by nature. Elsewhere he is also reported to have said that "the burden of proof is on the claimant, and the oath is incumbent on him who denies."[331] Thus, Muslims regard this principle as a valid rule of evidence and apply it to all categories of crime, so that 'doubts' in trials are generally resolved in favour of the accused. Third, Islam teaches that every person has dignity conferred to him by Allah (cf. Quran 17:70). Even the accused retains his or her right to human dignity which must be respected as specified by the Sharia. Hence, arbitrary arrests, detention, use of force, or torture are forbidden and, if proven, will vitiate any criminal trial.[332] Fourth, Islam insists that an accused person must be given a fair trial. This entails that (s)he must not be punished until (s)he has had a fair chance to be heard publicly and promptly by a neutral judge. This also means that the accused must be informed in good time of the allegation made against him or her and that (s) he is given the opportunity to refute it personally or, under certain circumstances, through a legal representative.[333] Furthermore, the accused must have the right to a free interpreter where necessary,[334] the right to call witnesses and cross-examine

[327] For example, God declares in the Quran: "God commands justice and fair dealing" (16:90). In another place, believers are ordered to judge justly, as follows: "O you who believe, stand up as witnesses for God in all fairness, and do not let the hatred of a people deviate you from justice. Be just: This is closest to piety; and beware of God. Surely God is aware of all you do." (Quran 5:8).

[328] See article 11 of the Arab Charter, article 19(a) of Cairo Declaration, and article 3(a) of the UIDHR.

[329] See article 3(a) of the UIDHR.

[330] Ibid., article 5(a); and article 19(e) of Cairo Declaration.

[331] Al Baihagi, in: An-Nawawi (1999, no. 33).

[332] See article 7 of the UIDHR.

[333] For instance, Islamic jurists are divided on the admissibility of representation by a lawyer in cases involving the violation of the right of God, such as adultery (Haneef et al., 2019).

[334] For example, in the event of language difficulty. The Quran recognises that human beings are to be spoken to in the language they understand (see Quran 14:4). This is particularly important in the context of trial to enable the accused to defend him- or herself.

prosecution witnesses, and the right to appeal. The accused also has additional rights of defence, such as the right to remain silent if (s)he so wishes and the right not to be forced to witness against oneself.[335] Muslim jurists agree that a confession obtained under duress or deception is inadmissible (Al 'Alwani, 1994; Sambo, 2018; Haneef et al., 2019). Likewise, a person can only be charged or punished for a crime specified by law,[336] and lastly the accused is entitled to compensation for procedural errors. It is clear from the foregoing that most of the relevant principles of a fair trial within the framework of universal human rights already existed in Islamic judicial system—albeit with a different philosophy. For this reason, some consider Islamic law to be a useful basis for protecting the right to a fair trial (Sambo, 2018). Be that as it may, this exposition shows that educated Muslims are likely to be familiar with the principles of a fair trial.

Right to a Fair Trial in Christian Tradition

The same can be said of Christians. Educated Christians may not be unaware of the principles of a fair trial in Christian ethics. Like Islam, the Christian religion views justice as a cardinal virtue. It regulates interpersonal relationships and means essentially treating people fairly.[337] The definite goal of the virtue of justice for Christians is the rights of the other—that is, to give other people their rights. Judicial justice is part and parcel of the biblical notion of justice. In the biblical context too, justice is considered in terms of fairness. In the Old Testament, for instance, Israel's judicial system was ordered not to act unjustly, no matter who is on trial, but to be fair (Leviticus 19:15; see also Deuteronomy 1:17; 16:19). Jesus did not repudiate the law (Matthew 5:17–19), though he put a premium more on restorative justice. In keeping with Jesus' teachings, early Christians recognised the necessity of the law to the society (cf. Romans 3:31). They were, at the same time, radically averse to unjust laws. The question of the law, including criminal law, did not escape the attention of influential Christian thinkers of earlier centuries, particularly St. Augustine and St. Thomas Aquinas. Like St. Augustine before him, Thomas Aquinas posited that laws are binding when they are just (Regan, 2003). The reformers—Martin Luther, John Calvin, and many others—"were not antinomians"; they also recognised the usefulness of the law, including "its criminal side" (Hill, 2020: 5). It has been strongly suggested in modern legal scholarship that some aspects of the modern criminal law have their origins and/or initial support in Christian law and thought. Prominent examples here include, first, the right to silence and its corollary provision of the privilege against self-incrimination. These are often traced to a specific church practice in medieval canon law, popularly expressed by the Latin maxim "nemo tenetur accusare se ipsum nisi coram Deo", meaning that no one is obliged to accuse himself except before God (cf. Wigmore, 1891; Hill, 2020). The

[335] See article 7 of the UIDHR.

[336] See Quran 17:15, article 5(d) of the UIDHR, and article 19(d) of Cairo Declaration.

[337] The CCC (no. 1807) succinctly captures this biblical perspective on the concept of justice when it declares that a just person "is distinguished by habitual right thinking and the uprightness of his [or her] conduct toward his neighbour." Parenthesis mine.

second is the hearing rule, which is regarded as a principle of natural justice. Although its origin is still highly debated, this found early support in the biblical account of the events in the Garden of Eden (Genesis 3: 1–24), where God gave Adam and Eve the opportunity to defend themselves before sentencing them (cf. Akpambang, 2016; Issa, 2016). Third, the traditional teaching of Church emphasises the principle of the dignity of the human person, based on the belief that everyone is created "in the image of God" (Genesis 1:27). In the context of criminal proceedings, this principle draws attention to the human dignity of the crime victim and the perpetrator as well as to the various actors involved in the judicial process (Kammer, 2010). It may be instructive to point out that at some point in history the church de-emphasised the dignity of the individual criminal in the interests of 'common good'.[338] However, as a result of a far-reaching re-evaluation of the morality of the death penalty that is ongoing since the second half of the twentieth century, the Roman Catholic Church recently reaffirmed the original Christian doctrine that no one, not even a murderer, loses his or her personal dignity (EV no. 9) and that this must be protected in judicial process. Besides, the Christian religion draws ideas from the biblical narrative of the trial against Jesus to work for a fair criminal justice system worldwide.

For its part, the Roman Catholic Church in its social teachings perceives the promotion of justice and peace as an integral part of its missionary mandate (CA nos. 53–59). This is also reflected in its commitment to the advancement of human rights (Iustitia et Pax 1975, no. 54). The Justice, Development and Peace/Caritas Advocates (hereinafter JDPCA) is one of structural mechanisms through which it works to advance peace with justice. The activities of this Commission in Nigeria include, among other things, legal assistance. It provides this service in cooperation with other CSOs and NGOs (cf. Okoronkwo, 2015). To sum up, this analysis tries to demonstrate that the dominant religious traditions in Nigeria are aware of the constitutive principles of the right to a fair trial.

3.6 Socio-economic Rights

All along we have dealt with the human rights of the first generation. We turn now to the so-called second-generation rights, which are the domain of socio-economic human rights. The latter describes "those rights that protect the necessities of life or that provide for the foundations of an adequate quality of life" (Kutigi, 2017: 129). The necessities in question comprise those material resources such as food and nutrition, shelter and housing, basic healthcare and education, and a wide range of

[338] For instance, Thomas Aquinas in his Summa Theologiae (II-II, q 64, a 2) declared that a grave sinner loses his human dignity and falls into the state of beasts and could be treated as such. It was a common-good-over-individual-good argument with which he sought to support the moral right to kill in the case of capital punishment (cf. Anthony & Sterkens, 2019).

socio-economic factors that promote conditions for people to thrive.[339] Examples of socio-economic rights are thus the right to an adequate standard of living, including food and housing, the right to healthcare, the right to work, the right to social security, the right to a healthy environment, the right to education, the rights of vulnerable groups and the right to science and culture. These rights are officially known as Economic, Social and Cultural Rights (ESCR). Sometimes they are also traditionally referred to as positive rights because they are "defined in terms of positive entitlements" (Ahmed & Bulmer, 2017: 8). Socio-economic human rights are considered controversial in human rights discourses, as scholars tend to argue that they are not deeply connected to the general idea of human rights, which is to limit undue political interference in the private domain of the citizen, as is the case with the first-generation rights (cf. Davis, 2012; Ziebertz & Ziebertz, 2016).

The emergence of socio-economic rights is usually attributed to the social movements of the early twentieth century. But there are indications that the concept has a deeper historical pedigree. Of particular note in this connection are the English Poor Laws of 1601, also known as the Elizabethan Poor Law, which provided some form of social protection scheme for the elderly and poor (Hansan, 2011). Davis (2012: 1021) too suggests that concerns about the social question also existed in eighteenth-century Prussia and Bavaria, where the state was perceived as an "agent of social happiness". More concrete evidence of the existence of socio-economic rights in the pre-twentieth century era can be found in the French Constitution of 1793, which contained provisions on the right to public education, the right to work and public assistance. Be that as it may, the broader recognition of these rights is linked to the idea of welfare (Ziebertz & Ziebertz, 2016). The labour and social movements of the nineteenth century played a decisive role and contributed significantly to the emergence of the concept of welfare. After the revolutions of 1848, in which these groups actively participated, the social question took the centre stage. According to King (2003), most social welfare laws in Europe were introduced during this period and, in fact, by 1916 nearly all European countries had adopted basic welfare legislation. The International Labour Organisation (hereinafter ILO) was therefore founded in 1919 under the aegis of the League of Nations, primarily to establish international labour standards from these social policy legislations. This event officially marked the international recognition of socio-economic rights, or one could call it the internationalisation of socio-economic rights. More importantly, it entrenched the latter in the legal discourse as a positive obligation of the state (Ahmed & Bulmer, 2017). As a result, by the first half of the twentieth century, socio-economic rights had found their way into the constitutions and laws of several nations, mostly in European countries as well as some other Western nations. For example, the 1936 Soviet Constitution contained a comprehensive list of these rights in Part VII (see Davis, 2012).

Having said that, the articulation of the social demands in their current form as universal human rights was only achieved through their incorporation into the 1948

[339] Cf. UN Doc E/C.12/2000/4, 11th August 2000, para. 4.

Universal Declaration and its codified version, the International Covenant on Economic, Social and Cultural Rights (hereinafter ICESCR), later in 1966. The ICESCR requires states parties to respect, protect and fulfil socio-economic rights.[340] Article 2(1) states that every state party, regardless of its scarce resources, is bound to guarantee a basic level of socio-economic rights.[341] During the Cold War, the generations of human rights were ideologised, with the Soviet Union prioritising the second generation and the USA the first (Vincent, 2010). In some circles, for example within trickle-down economics, this led to the conscious attempt to de-emphasise socio-economic rights by misbranding them as 'benefits' (King, 2003). However, with the entry into force of the ICESCR in 1976 and the establishment of the UN Committee on Economic, Social and Cultural Rights (CESCR) in 1985, this trend was reversed.[342] With its general comments and country-specific reports, this body continues to stimulate the further development and strengthening of socio-economic rights at all levels.[343]

The importance of socio-economic rights for human development has been adequately studied (Ahmed & Bulmer, 2017; King, 2003; Van der Ven, 2013). They are essential for the well-being of the human person and for human prosperity. Moreover, they promote the conditions that enable individuals to effectively enjoy their civil liberties. For example, an individual needs education to be able to exercise his or her freedom of the press, the right to silence or even the right to political participation. Likewise, employees need a reasonable limitation of working hours to be able to exercise their freedom of association effectively. With similar examples, scholars have consistently shown that the relationship between civil liberties and a fair access to socio-economic resources is a persistent historical fact (Ahmed & Bulmer, 2017). In fact, they go hand in hand. It is against this backdrop that we chose to include a range of socio-economic rights in this study. In other words, their inclusion here is a tacit recognition of the salience of socio-economic determinants in the practice of human rights.

[340] In paragraph 15 of the General Comment no.12 on Article 11 of the ICESCR, the Committee indicates that socio-economic rights, like other human rights, impose "three types or levels of obligations on States parties: the obligations to respect, to protect and to fulfil" (UN Doc. E/C.12/1999/5, 12th May 1999). According to the Maastricht Guidelines (no. 6), "[f]ailure to perform any one of these three obligations constitutes a violation of such rights."

[341] See UN Doc. E/1991/23, 14th December 1990, para. 10; UN Doc. E/C.12/1999/5, 12th May 1999, para. 17.

[342] See UN Doc. E/RES/1985/17, 28th May 1985.

[343] Socio-economic rights are enshrined in international instruments, such as the Optional Protocol to the ICESCR (2008), the ICERD, the CEDAW, the CRC, the ILO Declaration on Fundamental Principles and Right at Work, and the Convention on Rights of Persons with Disability. The Maastricht Guidelines on Violations of Economic, Social and Cultural Rights (1998) also comprise far-reaching provisions relating to the rights. Regional human rights instruments such as the African Charter, the African Charter on the Rights and Welfare of the Child, and the Protocol to the African Charter on the Rights of Women, as well as the Principles and Guidelines on the Implementation of Economic, Social and Cultural Rights in the African Charter on Human and Peoples' Rights are all important within the socio-economic rights discourse. Cf. Davis (2012); King (2003).

3.6.1 Socio-economic Rights in Nigerian Law

An impressive collection of socio-economic rights issues can be found in the Nigerian Constitution. The list includes the right to shelter [section 16(2)(d)], the right to food [section 16(2)(d)], the right to work [section 17(3)(a-c, e)], the right to social security [sections 14(2)(b), 16(2)(d)], the right to healthcare [section 17(3)(d)], and the right to education (section 18). These provisions are assigned to Chapter II, sections 13 to 24 (under the fundamental objectives and directive principles of state policy) and not to Chapter IV of the Constitution, which specifically deals with fundamental rights. This arrangement is deliberate, as the Constitution does not recognise socio-economic rights sensu stricto as fundamental human rights entitlements such as the civil, political and judicial rights guaranteed in Chapter IV, but as "mere aspirational goals" (Anifalaje, 2017: 418). Accordingly, it requires the State to steer its policies towards ensuring the progressive realisation of these basic national socio-economic goals. However, if this obligation is not met, the State cannot be held liable because the Constitution qualifies the said human rights issues as non-justiciable provisions in accordance with section 6(6)(c).[344] This implies in rather oversimplified terms that these provisions cannot be enforced through a legal process. The matter has received substantial interpretation in Nigerian courts.[345] By the way, it has also been suggested that these rights are viewed as unenforceable in Nigeria due to resource constraints (cf. Anifalaje, 2017).

Nonetheless, the lack of juridical enforceability does not exonerate the State from non-compliance with its immediate and progressive obligations in relation to these provisions,[346] since the constitutionally guaranteed fundamental objectives are goals whose realisation ought to guide the exercise of public power in the country. Besides, their status as non-justiciable provisions does not deprive them of their legal value since, contrary to popular opinion, their non-justiciability is not total. Rather, according to jurisprudence, they are only unclaimable to the extent that the constitution prescribes this.[347] In this case, legal scholars propose some legal channels through which these so-called non-justiciable provisions can be enforced in the

[344] According to section (6)(6)(c) of 1999 CFRN, "[t]he judicial powers vested in accordance with the foregoing provisions of this section—shall not except as otherwise provided by this Constitution, extend to any issue or question as to whether any act of omission by any authority or person or as to whether any law or any judicial decision is in conformity with the Fundamental Objectives and Directive Principles of State Policy set out in Chapter II of this Constitution."

[345] Prominent examples are the cases of *Archbishop Anthony Okogie & Ors. v. Attorney-General of Lagos State* (1981) 1 NCLR 218; *Adewole v. Jakande, Governor of Lagos State* (1981) 1 NCLR 152; and *Uzuokwu v Ezeonu II* (1991) 6 NWLR (pt. 200).

[346] See sections 13 and 224 of 1999 CFRN. In *Attorney-General of Ondo State v Attorney-General of the Federation & Ors.* [(2002) 9 NWLR (pt. 772) 222], the Supreme Court restated that it would be tantamount to a failure of duty and responsibility of state organs if they acted in clear disregard of the provisions of Chapter II of the Constitution, just because they are non-justiciable.

[347] Interpreting section 6(6)(c) of 1999 CFRN in *Federal Republic of Nigeria v Alhaji Mika Anache & Ors.* [(2004) 14 WRN 1–90 61], the Supreme Court reiterated inter alia that the non-justiciability of the section is "neither total nor sacrosanct" (see also Kutigi (2017).

country, as follows: first, through an Act of the National Assembly (Anifalaje, 2017; Ibe, 2010; Kutigi, 2017). In the performance of its statutory duties under section 4 of the Constitution,[348] the National Assembly may, with respect to item 60(a) of the Exclusive Legislative List,[349] convert any of the provisions of Chapter II into law, if need be, thereby making it enforceable. An example of this is section 15(5) of the Constitution which provides that "the State shall abolish all corrupt practices and abuse of power." This provision is embedded in Chapter II and as such could not be enforced. Then, to implement it for the country's anti-corruption campaign, the National Assembly enacted the Corrupt Practices and Other Related Offences Act 2000.[350] Second, provisions on socio-economic rights can be enforced in the country via competent national organs, including the courts. This position is in consonance with article 7(1)(a) of the African Charter, which gives everyone the right to appeal to such bodies against abuses of their rights guaranteed by the applicable human rights instruments. In this respect, courts can decide to enforce the socio-economic rights issues indirectly through their corollary provisions in the constitutionally guaranteed fundamental rights. This means, for instance, that the right to food and shelter can be sought through the fundamental right to life, since both are elements of the quality of life (NAP 2009–2013). Third, the country has ratified and/or acceded to several human rights treaties that recognise socio-economic rights.[351] Therefore, some scholars suggest that the courts could rely directly on these instruments to enforce the rights. However, given the dualist model that the country practises in relation to treaties, these instruments need to be domesticated before they can be applied locally. Against this background, the African Charter has been ratified and domesticated, but the domestic implementation of its socio-economic rights guarantees may still be stalled due to the principle of primacy of the Constitution.[352] Then lately, there have also been strong suggestions that socio-economic rights can be enforced in the country through regional and/or sub-regional organs and mechanisms such as the African Commission for Human and Peoples' Rights,[353] the African Court of Human Rights, and the Court of Justice of the Economic Community of West African States (Ibe, 2010; NAP 2009–2013). Whichever way one looks at it, one thing is clear: socio-economic rights issues are

[348] Under section 4 of the CFRN, the legislative powers are vested in the legislature at both federal and state levels.

[349] Item 60(a) of Part I of the Second Schedule to 1999 CFRN empowers the National Assembly to establish and regulate authorities to "promote and enforce the observance of the Fundamental Objectives and Directive Principles contained in this Constitution."

[350] Hereinafter the ICPC Act. See no. 5 of the Act 2000 (but now, Cap. C31, LFN, 2004). Similar enactments include the Federal Environmental Protection Agency (Amendment) Act 1992, the Universal Basic Education Act 2004, National Housing Fund Act, Cap. N45 LFN, 2004.

[351] Some of the relevant human rights instruments are the ICESCR, the ICERD, the CEDAW and its Optional Protocol, and the CRC.

[352] Cf. section 1(3) of 1999 CFRN; and *Abacha v. Fawehinmi* (2000) 6 NWLR (pt. 660) 228.

[353] Article 45 of the African Charter.

recognised by the Constitution, but their implementation in the country is contentious and difficult.

3.6.2 *Topical Issues in Socio-economic Rights in Nigeria*

In the following subheadings we present workers' rights in more detail, as well as a cluster of rights related to work. We believe that labour rights, alongside the right to education, which has been addressed elsewhere (see Fumbo et al., 2020), are currently the most debated, contentious and violated socio-economic rights issues in Nigeria. In the selection process, we also considered the importance of work to the immediate and future needs of our study population.

Labour Rights

Labour rights cover a broad spectrum of rights such as the right to freedom of association, the right to collective bargaining, the right to protection from forced and child labour, and the right to protection from discrimination in the workplace (cf. Scherrer & Greven, 2001). These rights are intended to protect workers and their organisations in the course of their work life (Adewumi & Adenugba, 2010). Of all labour rights, the right to work is the focus of this study, in particular the right to fair working conditions in terms of working hours and wages, freedom from discrimination at work, the prohibition of child labour, and the right to social security of labour. The importance of work to the welfare and sustenance of individuals is well documented in the literature. In addition, these labour principles are examined due to the recurrent labour crises in Nigeria, especially since the return to civilian rule. Among other things, the crises have deteriorated due to poor management and have a negative impact on the country's unemployment rate. The human right to an appropriate working time limit is also highlighted here because of its effects on the health of the employee and on maintaining a healthy work-life balance. Unfortunately, it is perceived as a grossly violated labour right in Nigeria. The same applies to the principle of non-discrimination in the workplace, and the right to social security.

As already mentioned, the international labour standards are provided by the ILO. Based on our research interest, the relevant ILO conventions include: the Freedom of Association and Protection of the Right to Organise Convention, 1948 (no. 87) and the Right to Organise and Collective Bargaining Convention, 1949 (no. 98); the Discrimination (in Employment and Occupation) Convention, 1958 (no. 111) and the Equal Remuneration Convention, 1951 (no. 100); the Minimum Age Convention, 1973 (no. 138) and the Worst Forms of Child Labour Convention, 1999 (no. 182); and the Forced Labour Convention, 1930 (no. 29) and its supplementing Protocol of 2014, together with the Abolition of Forced Labour Convention, 1957 (no. 105). These are the fundamental conventions that must be adhered to by all member states of the ILO, regardless of their signatory status. Others important instruments are Convention no. 103, which addresses maternity protection, and Convention no. 102 dealing with social security—both of 1952—as well as the

1998 ILO Declaration on Fundamental Principles and Right at Work and its Follow-up. Several components of the above-mentioned labour rights are scattered across these instruments. Together they form the basis on which other rights in the world of work are built (Adewumi & Adenugba, 2010). Labour rights are strengthened by their inclusion in the Universal Declaration (arts. 22, 23 and 24) and the ICESCR (arts. 6, 7, 8 and 9). These provisions cover all major issues in the field of work, from the right to work to more complex issues such as occupational health and safety (cf. Ziebertz & Ziebertz, 2016). For example, article 6 of the ICESCR guarantees the right to work, the right to form and join trade unions and to strike, the right to social security and insurance, and the right to a decent standard of living. Article 7 deals with the right to work under fair conditions and is based, inter alia, on the minimum conditions of fair wages and equal pay for work of equal value without discrimination, health and safety standards, and reasonable limitation of working hours. Alongside the guarantees of the ILO conventions and recommendations, these are the key elements of workers' rights.

However, these instruments only prescribe minimum standards that workers can invoke to protect their rights. The standards need to be complemented by local laws that grant workers specific rights as citizens of their country and "as producers of national wealth" (Adewumi & Adenugba, 2010: 11). Accordingly, the rights in Nigeria are enshrined in the Constitution. Section 17(3) states:

> The State shall direct its policy towards ensuring that- (a) all citizens, without discrimination on any group whatsoever, have the opportunity for securing adequate means of livelihood as well as adequate opportunity to secure suitable employment; (b) conditions of work are just and humane ...; (c) the health, safety and welfare of all persons in employment are safeguarded and not endangered or abused; ... (e) there is equal pay for equal work without discrimination on account of sex, or on any other ground whatsoever; (f) children, young persons and the age are protected against any exploitation whatsoever, and against moral and material neglect; (g) provision is made for public assistance in deserving cases or other conditions of need.

By virtue of this provision, the country recognises the importance of employment as a means of improving the quality of life of individuals and commits herself to work towards the realisation of the labour rights of her citizens (Oginni & Adesanya, 2013). Nevertheless, the concerned rights cannot be enforced in the country based on these provisions alone, as they are not enforceable. To this end, additional laws protecting workers' rights are provided for in Nigerian law. The following can be distinguished: Labour Act,[354] National Minimum Wage Act,[355] Trade Union Act,[356] Workmen's Compensation Act,[357] Factories Act,[358] Pensions Reform Act,[359] National

[354] Cap. L1 LFN 2004.

[355] Cap. N61 LFN 2004, as amended in 2011.

[356] Cap. T14 LFN 2004. It has since been amended in 2005.

[357] Cap. W6 LFN 2004. It has been repealed by the Employee's Compensation Act 2010.

[358] Cap. F1 LFN 2004.

[359] No. 2, 2004 has been replaced by Pensions Reform Act 2014.

Health Insurance Scheme Act,[360] and Trade Disputes Act.[361] These statutes are supported by the relevant ILO and UN treaties to which the country is a signatory,[362] and all these legal frameworks govern labour relations in the country.

Nigerian law does not obligate the State to provide work to all citizens who are willing to work, but it does oblige the State to ensure the safety and job security of workers. In the first place, the Factories Act makes a specification for a factory and demands that a factory be registered (sections 2 and 3). It imposes extensive obligations on employers regarding the health, safety and welfare of workers within the factory (Adewumi & Adenugba, 2010). Among other things, the employer is obliged to ensure that the regulations on occupational safety such as cleanliness, overcrowding, ventilation, drainage and sanitary conveniences, etc. are complied with. The Act also mandates that factory workers be provided with protective clothing and appliances (sections 47 and 48) as well as other appropriate protective devices such as gloves, footwear, goggles and head coverings, when necessary. The law then goes a step further by placing the responsibility on employers not only to provide them but also to ensure that workers use them. This was one of the points of contention in the case of *Western Nigeria Trading Company Limited v. Busari Ajao*,[363] where the respondent suffered an injury (i.e., loss of an eye) due to an accident that occurred while working as an employee of the appellant. The court held inter alia that the employer's obligation under common law is not only to provide safety equipment (i.e., protective goggles), but also to ensure that it is used.[364] The Labour Act also contains similar provisions relating to the health and safety of workers (sections 66 and 67). The Employee Compensation Act, for its part, spells out conditions for indemnification for temporary or permanent injuries that occur during job performance (Adewumi & Adenugba, 2010).

Issues of wage and salary are covered by the National Minimum Wage Act. The latter specifies the normal working time as 40 hours per week, that is, an average working time of 8 hours a day and 5 days a week (section 9). Nevertheless, according to the Labour Act, working hours in any undertaking have to be mutually agreed or determined through collective bargaining or by an industrial wages board if there is no platform to bargain collectively (section 13). The Labour Act further specifies that an employee who works six hours or more per day is entitled to one or more reasonably spaced rest breaks totaling at least one hour. If the work is stressful, the worker must be granted an appropriate number of suitably adapted breaks [section

---

360 Cap. N42 LFN 2004, though it was at first enacted as National Health Insurance Scheme Decree (no. 35) 1999. A bill to amend the 2004 version has been proposed in 2018.

361 Cap. T8 LFN 2004

362 As of December 2018, Nigeria has ratified 40 Conventions of the ILO, including the eight core conventions. However, out of these 40 Conventions, 26 are in force, nine have been denounced, while the five are abrogated.

363 (1965) NMLR 178; see also *Green Pack Rubber Industry Limited v. Ossai* (2004) 2 FWLR (pt. 194) 668.

364 Industrial Law, Hasawa and Labour Law (n.d.). Available at: https://prog.lmu.edu.ng/colleges_CMS/document/books/GEC524. Accessed 28.05.2021.

13(3)]. An employee who works seven days a week is entitled to a day of rest which cannot be less than 24 consecutive hours. In exceptional cases, employees can be required to work on weekly rest days or on public holidays. In such cases, appropriate vacation is to be granted as soon as possible within fourteen days or overtime wages are to be paid for the work done [section 13(7)]. Section 18 of the Act also provides that every employee with an uninterrupted period of employment of 12 months is entitled to a minimum paid holiday of six working days per year or twelve working days for persons under the age of 16, including apprentices. The vacation time can be postponed to a later date by mutual agreement of the parties, but not beyond 24 months of continuous service and cannot be exchanged for monetary compensation. Employees are also entitled to paid time-off in the case of illness or injury (sections 16 and 19) and pregnancy (section 54).

The employer's obligation to pay an employee's wages is usually the primary basis on which the latter provides services to the former. The payment of wages is therefore mandatory for employers under Nigerian law and may not be made at intervals of more than one month.[365] The new national minimum wage in Nigeria will be 30,000 naira[366] per month (about 80 US Dollars) as of 1st April 2019. Under the National Minimum Wage Act, the minimum wage does not apply to all businesses. For example, employers with fewer than 50 employees are exempt from paying the minimum wage. Some other categories of workers are also excluded from the package.[367]

In Nigeria, formalised labour relations are guided by statute. This means that issues such as dismissal or termination of contracts must also comply with the relevant statutes. Otherwise, it would be illegal and cannot prevail. While there are reasons for which one can be dismissed from employment,[368] union membership or non-membership is definitely not such a reason. An employee cannot be victimised for this.[369] The Labour Act in section 9(6)(a) adds that this should not be a requirement for employment either. The Trade Union Act reinforces this provision in Section 24, where it obliges employers to recognise all registered trade unions within the industry.

Apart from the legal framework, labour relations are run by means of numerous structures and institutions that make up the national labour administration system. The most important among them is the Federal Ministry of Labour and Employment

---

[365] Sections 1 and 9 of National Minimum Wage Act.

[366] Nigeria's legal tender.

[367] Under section 2 of the National Minimum Wage Act, these include employees on a part-time working arrangement (defined as work of a duration of less than 40 hours per week); employees that are paid on commission or on piece rate basis; those in seasonal employment; or persons employed in a vessel or aircraft. See also Nigeria Human Rights Report 2017.

[368] One such ground for a possible dismissal of an employee from service is redundancy. But there are laid down rules for this, according to section 20 of the Labour Act. Other reasons for dismissal are allegation of crime, gross misconduct, breach of conduct, and inability to work or negligence in carrying out responsibilities.

[369] Section 12(4) of the Trade Unions Act.

with its various departments and agencies as well as the National Industrial Court, which is a specialised court set up to deal with cases arising in the world of work.[370] Others are the National Labour Advisory Council (NLAC), the Nigeria Labour Congress (NLC), and a host of social partners at all levels. While the national labour administration is tasked with enforcing labour law in the country, the labour movements exist as a necessary institutional framework to monitor compliance with labour standards and to ensure that workers' rights are protected (cf. Adewumi & Adenugba, 2010).

From the foregoing, it can be said that Nigeria has enough legal and institutional depth to ensure compliance with international labour standards and respect for workers' rights. However, reports from human rights organisations and other relevant bodies indicate that the said standards are rather observed in breach in the country and that workers' rights are abused with impunity by employers in the private and public sectors, including the government. For example, the Factories Act stipulates that a site inspection must be carried out to determine the safety of the environment before a company is set up. It also provides for routine supervision of factory premises in the country as part of the work-related health and safety management strategy. According to reports, however, this provision is constantly being neglected by the relevant national agencies to the effect that many factories in the country are in a despicable condition, thereby exposing workers to occupational hazards that result in high rate of injuries and deaths. When this happens, only very few of these injured workers are duly compensated, especially those connected to very important personalities (VIPs) in the country (cf. Oginni & Adesanya, 2013). Furthermore, the average Nigerian worker has no job security. For example, during the 1999–2007 Public Service Reforms that the government initiated shortly after the country's return to civil rule in 1999, many workers were arbitrarily dismissed. Although part of the goals of the reform was to rightsize the public service, and the government, through the Bureau for Public Service Reform (BPSR), even issued guidelines for conducting this exercise, the National Human Rights Commission (2007) reports that the exercise was marred by irregularities with many workers alleging that their jobs were terminated because of their union activities. In addition to their loss, the government promised to pay affected workers their pension benefits upon their official disengagement from service. But two years later, over 70 percent of them said they had not received their benefits. Such incidents of arbitrary layoffs are widespread in the country (cf. Adewumi & Adenugba, 2010). Similarly, at the time of writing this paper, the Kaduna State government laid off some workers from the State's civil service and casualised many others without recourse to any known law, all in its bid to downsize the State's workforce as part of the ongoing Public Service Revitalisation and Renewal Programme (Soji-Eze, 2021). Resident doctors in state hospitals are also currently on a nationwide strike over poor welfare.

The private sector is not a safe haven for Nigerian workers either. Serious violations of labour rights are also taking place there, as the country most recently

[370] Industrial Law, Hasawa and Labour Law (n.d.), above at no. 364.

suffered from recessions in 2016 and 2020, which led to massive layoffs of workers. As for the new minimum wage, this is another area where employers in the public and private sectors brazenly refuse to comply with national labour laws. Enforcement is yet to be settled, though the amount is absolutely not a fair living wage even by Nigerian standards (Human Rights Report, 2013). Under the old salary scale, workers were sometimes owed up to three to four months of their wages and were still expected to perform at their best on an empty stomach. Several reasons have been proffered for the lack of protection or abuse of workers' rights in Nigeria. These include weak institutions, inadequate resources, lack of political will by the government, lack of commitment from trade union officials and, above all, what Adewumi and Adenugba (2010: 65) aptly describe as "the conspiratorial indifference of a consuming public that is quick to condemn any collective action of workers because of possible inconveniences without being commensurately bothered about the plight of the workers." The government is aware of this poor public attitude and always takes advantage of it to clampdown on industrial actions. It is widely believed that the scale of violation of workers' rights in the country is enormous. Some of the examples relate to vulnerable groups in society, particularly women and children.

Non-discrimination Against Women in Employment

Discrimination against women in employment is a form of gender discrimination. In general, gender discrimination refers to an unfair treatment of an individual based on sex or gender. Sex or gender discrimination in employment is considered unfair because it can have varied effects on labour relations, such as hiring, salary, job placements, promotions, transfers, training or other benefits, as well as layoffs (cf. Adejugbe & Adejugbe, 2018). It is a common practice in the world of work and cannot be avoided entirely. It can occur at any stage of employment but is often associated with employers' hiring behaviour, as employers have a lot to do when confronted with a hiring decision. They have the legitimate duty to determine the qualities of the applicants in the job queue that match the available jobs. Although this might be referred to as differentiation in official parlance, it does involve some form of discrimination and, within reasonable legal limits, employers are allowed to do so in hiring decisions. In other words, discrimination is not always negative per se. It is unlawful if such decisions are based on irrelevant factors or personal characteristics such as sex or gender rather than on merit and a person's ability to do a job (Odeku & Animashaun, 2012). This is the type of discrimination that is at issue here. It can be targeted at men at times, but it is mostly a problem for women. In this subtopic, therefore, sex and gender discrimination in employment are used almost interchangeably to mean the same thing and simply to denote a prejudicial treatment of a person in the labour market precisely because she is a woman, regardless of whether she applies for a job or is already an employee. Discrimination against women in the workplace persists around the world. It keeps popping up in new and more subtle forms, although giant strides have been made in recent times in tackling inequalities.[371] Gender equality and non-discrimination against women are

[371] UN Doc. HR/PUB/14/2, 2014, introduction.

recognised today as fundamental human rights, and the UN targets the global implementation of these values by its member states.[372]

Nigerian law provides for the equality of all citizens before the law and prohibits all form of discrimination. As noted in section 17, the Constitution guarantees every Nigerian, man or woman, equal employment opportunities and prohibits discrimination based on sex "or on any other ground whatsoever". Of particular importance in this provision are paragraphs A and E of subsection 3, which address employment rights such as equal access to jobs and equal pay respectively, though these are all non-justiciable provisions. Section 42 also guarantees the right to be free from discrimination based on sex, gender or other social attributes. This provision covers discriminatory practices in all forms and as such can be used to claim protection from gender-based discrimination in the workplace. It should be noted, however, that this provision does not directly target employment-related discrimination. Rather, it is a mere "blanket constitutional declaration" whose application in the employment context could at best ensure the minimum enjoyment of the protection that the right to freedom from discrimination is intended to provide (Odeku & Animashaun, 2012: 4691). To strengthen this provision, the Constitution, in its Third Alteration in 2010, enlarged the jurisdiction of the National Industrial Court (NIC) to include inter alia matters regarding labour relations and conditions of service [section 254(C)(1)(a)], unfair labour practices or international best practices in labour [section 254(C)(1)(f)] and disputes relating to discrimination or sexual harassment at workplace [section 254(C)(1)(g)]. In this way, all the specificities of the world of work, including gender equality, non-discrimination and equal opportunities for workers irrespective of their gender, are covered and thus made enforceable (Adejugbe & Adejugbe, 2018). Besides, Nigeria has domestic statutes that also prohibit gender-based discrimination. Prominent among these are the African Charter Act of 2004 and the Fundamental Rights Enforcement Procedure Rules of 2009. The country is also party to many other international treaties that deal with discrimination against women, such as the Discrimination (in Employment and Occupation) Convention 1958 (no. 111), the Equal Remuneration Convention 1951 (no. 100), the CEDAW and the Beijing Platform of Action 1995. These instruments provide the necessary tools to ensure the protection of women's right to non-discrimination. In a recent case of *Mrs Folarin Oreka Maiya v. The Incorporated Trustees of Clinton Health Access initiative, Nigeria and 2 Ors*[373] where the applicant was dismissed from job for being pregnant, the National Industrial Court declared the dismissal to be wrong and illegal under these instruments and granted the applicant the necessary compensation.

Despite this legal and institutional framework, the plight of Nigerian women in the labour market has not improved significantly. Gender discrimination is not only widespread in the country, it can also be described as systemic in the sense that some discriminatory practices are enshrined in the law (Odeku & Animashaun,

---

[372] Ibid.

[373] (2012) 27 NLLR (pt. 76) 110 NIC. See also Adejugbe and Adejugbe (2018).

2012). Take, for instance, it has been argued that none of the country's main labour laws, namely the Constitution and the Labour Act, contain a specific provision aimed at redressing gender inequality. Although the Constitution recognises the disadvantaged position of women in the country to a certain extent and provides for non-discrimination based on sex, it does not have any specific provision on gender equality or for redressing gender-specific inequalities (Anyalebechi, 2016). Neither does the Labour Act contain any such provisions on equal employment opportunities for everyone regardless of gender and on protection against gender-specific discrimination in employment (Adejugbe & Adejugbe, 2018). Instead, the Act itself contains some discriminatory provisions. For example, section 56(1) prohibits the employment of women in underground work in mines. According to section 55(1), women are also prohibited from doing nightwork, except nurses and women in managerial positions.[374] The law criminalises any violation of these two provisions, and convicted employers are liable to a fine or a jail term, or both.[375] Similar discriminatory provisions regarding conditions of recruitment and service based on issues such as marriage, pregnancy and childbirth can be found in many other statutes.[376] Attempts to remove these discriminatory provisions and to accord women equal rights in various spheres of life have been very slow. A bill to amend the Labour Act was proposed in 2015 and has only gone through the second reading at the Senate as of March 2021. Previously, in March 2016, the same House rejected a Gender and Equal Opportunities (GEO) bill, which is a draft law to domesticate international law on gender equality in Nigeria as stipulated in the CEDAW (Goitom, 2016).

The apparent lack of commitment to gender equality is not peculiar to state actors; it tends to permeate all levels of Nigerian society. This is believed to contribute to the mistreatment of women in the country, particularly in the workplace, which in turn is partly responsible for the low proportion of women in the workforce (Adejugbe & Adejugbe, 2018). A World Bank Report (2021) shows evidence of the gender gap in labour force participation in Nigeria over the past decade. According to the report, women's labour force participation rate was 56.9 percent in 2011, 7.32 percentage points lower than men's. The gap becomes wider with 11.61 percentage

---

[374] Section 55(2) of the Labour Act. See also section 57 for another such provision empowering the minister of labour to make regulations that can prohibit or restrict the employment of women in certain fields of work.

[375] Ibid., section 58(2).

[376] For example, under Regulation 127 made pursuant to the Police Act Cap. P19 LFN 2004, an unmarried pregnant policewoman would be discharged from the police force and can only be re-enlisted with the approval of the Inspector General of Police. Regulation 124 requires female officers desirous of marrying to apply requesting for permission and to have their would-be spouses investigated before marriage. However, a Federal High Court in Ikeja, Lagos State, Nigeria recently declared this provision to be illegal and unconstitutional in the case of *Women Empowerment and Legal Aid Initiative (WELA) v. Attorney General of the Federation* [(Unreported) Suit No. FHC/IKJ/CS/M128/2010]. All the same, this alteration is yet to be enforced by the government. For more examples, see section 118(a), (c) & (g) of the same Act. Cf. Adejugbe and Adejugbe (2018), and Ekhator (2019).

points in 2019, even as the participation rate declines for both men (60.89%) and women (49.28%). The report of the National Bureau of Statistics (2021) shows that the differences become more pronounced in the fourth quarter of 2020, as women's participation rate dropped further to 43.28 percent and men's to 56.72 percent. The civil service is reportedly the largest single employer in Nigeria (cf. Ejumudo, 2013). The distribution of employment in both the state and the federal civil service shows further evidence of gender-specific participation gaps over time. From 2010 to 2015, the proportion of men employed in the state civil service in both higher and lower positions was 68.84 percent, while that of women was 38.16 percent. At the federal level, 42 percent of women were represented in the civil service between 2014 and 2016, with men, as usual, dominating the sector in all categories. We have no official records of employment in the corporate sector. It appears that more and more women are entering this sector, although they tend to be overrepresented in the informal economy. Yet their low representation in top managerial positions and decision-making cadres in the corporate sector is well documented. For instance, the outcome of a 2016 survey by Deloitte Corporate Services Limited (DCSL) in the period between 2013 and 2015 shows that women accounted for only 14 percent of the 915 board members of 132 companies (World Bank, 2019). Men also dominate in other areas such as medicine and politics. It is on record that no woman has ever served as President of Nigeria or governor of any state in the country. These are some of the glass ceilings for Nigerian women. From 1999 to 2015, the proportion of women in the National Parliament was 5.76 percent and the proportion of men 94.71 percent. In the same period, the proportion of women in State Assemblies was 5.29 percent and that of men was 94.71 percent. The same pattern runs through local government, with minor differences. The picture is no different in the judiciary, as the proportion of federal court judges between 2011 and 2016 was 29.38 percent for women and 70.62 percent for men (NBS, 2021). The status quo did not change in the 2019 general elections. Men held 94 percent of all national political leadership positions, compared to 6 percent of women, despite the 30 percent target for women's participation in government set by the Beijing Platform for Action.[377] This unequal representation in national leadership positions can therefore not only be seen as the result of a normal democratic process, but also reflects the country's status quo in terms of gender equality (cf. Benisheikh et al., 2016). In any case, restricting access to decent job opportunities prevents women from fully integrating into the labour market and impairs their ability to contribute meaningfully to the economy (Ejumudo, 2013). Above all, it is an abuse of their basic human rights.

Another form of discrimination women experience in Nigeria is the wage gap, which refers to the relative average difference between the wages of male and female workers within the Nigerian economy. As part of its social policy, the Nigerian Constitution provides in section 17(3)(e) that it is the duty of the state to ensure that equal pay for equal work is guaranteed without discrimination based on

---

[377] The proportion has been increased to 35 percent in the National Gender Policy 2006 and implemented in 2008 (SDN, 2020).

sex. However, the country has not yet enacted a law to implement this provision as she has done with some other non-justiciable provisions. The last time this issue came up in any legislation was in 2016 in the draft law on Gender and Equal Opportunities (GEO). The right to equal pay and equal treatment for work of equal value was included in the bill, but the bill was unsuccessful. Thus, the constitutional provision on gender pay parity has no specific legislation that currently enables its implementation in the country. In other words, it is as good as not being enforced. It has been observed that gender discrimination due to wage disparities is a notable feature of the Nigerian labour market (Fapohunda, 2013; Nweke, 2014). The World Economic Forum in its 2020 report noted that Nigeria's gender gap in the Global Gender Gap Index increased from 0.610 in 2006 to 0.635 in 2020. Despite this improvement, the country is still considered one of the countries with high gender inequality in the world and ranks 128th out of 153 countries in the index (2020). The pay disparity between the sexes has been amply studied in the context of labour economics. It has been shown that many factors explain a significant part of the gap, and these include differences in education, training and working hours, work experience, job performance and competence, job flexibility, career breaks, and occupational segregation (cf. Becker, 1994; Altonji & Blank, 1999). Occupational segregation, for instance, refers to the distribution of female and male workers in and across different occupations. According to Soetan (2002, in Fapohunda, 2013; see also Nweke, 2014), Nigerian women tend to be more active in services and office jobs, that is, in fewer and lowly paying jobs compared to men. Part of the reasons for this is that women are more likely to self-select into professions that offer more flexibility for their domestic roles as mothers. However, apart from these largely observable individual and professional characteristics, the gender pay gap in the Nigerian context can also be explained by a number of unobservable factors, such as direct discrimination by employers, gender stereotypes and biases, as well as traditional and religious beliefs (Nweke, 2014; Fapohunda, 2013).

There is yet another problem that female employees encounter at work in Nigeria. It is sexual harassment, a form of sex-based discrimination in employment.[378] Sexual harassment is not defined in Nigerian (labour) law. It refers to sexual and gender-specific behaviours that are undesirable for the recipient (McCann, 2005). These can take many forms such as symbolic, verbal, physical or visual form and can occur as 'a one-off thing' or persist over time (Fapohunda, 2014). They are considered discriminatory when the recipient has enough reasons to believe that objection would disadvantage her in connection with her employment, including hiring or promotion, or when such creates a hostile working environment.[379] Although sexual harassment can happen to anyone, including men, most of the victims are women, especially those "in a less-powerful labour market position" (McCann, 2005: 7). Sexual harassment also happens in Nigeria. Recent studies show that the issue is relatively pervasive in various areas of Nigerian society, for

---

[378] UN Doc. A/47/38, 1992, para.18; see also article 1(a) of the ILO Convention no. C111.

[379] UN Doc. A/47/38, 1992, para.18.

example in the industrial, medical and educational sectors. Seductive advances, fondling, unnecessary touches, sexual remarks, sensuous gestures, display of sexually suggestive images, incessant local trips, financial inducement, requests for sexual favours and intimidation have all been identified as the most common forms available (Aina-Pelemo et al., 2018; Fapohunda, 2014; Human Rights Report, 2013). Sexual harassment has very serious implications for the ILO's agenda of decent work for women.[380] It hinders the smooth assimilation of women into the world of work and reduces their productivity. Its putative high prevalence in the workplace in Nigeria is attributed to several factors, including the patriarchal nature of Nigerian society, which enables men to dominate women, low reporting rates, and the tolerance of victims for fear of job loss, social stigma or self-esteem (Aina-Pelemo et al., 2018; Adejugbe & Adejugbe, 2018). There is also a legal angle to this. In Nigeria, sexual harassment in the workplace is perceived as an affront to the dignity of a worker[381] and thus as an unfair labour practice. Yet it has been reported that there is no specific national legislation criminalising the act, although it is widespread in the country.[382] In the absence of this, the National Industrial Court of Nigeria (NICN) relies on the broad constitutional provisions and the largely undomesticated international human rights treaties for their decisions in legal disputes. This lacuna, some have argued, makes the duty to eradicate sexual harassment a herculean task in Nigerian society (cf. Aina-Pelemo et al., 2018; Fapohunda, 2014). Be that as it may, sexual harassment is a form of violence against women[383] and a violation of their basic human right.[384] Eliminating this and other forms of discrimination against women is one of the means to achieve gender equality and women empowerment as one of the 17 Sustainable Development Goals (hereinafter SDGs) that UN member states aim to achieve by 2030.

Child's Socio-economic Rights

A child is generally defined as any person who has not yet reached the age of 18.[385] Along with women, children are one of the vulnerable groups in society. They are

---

[380] The idea of a decent work for women is an essential part of the SDGs no. 8 (on promoting "decent work for all"), which all UN member states target to achieve by the year 2030 (cf. ILO, 2000).

[381] In the landmark case of *Ejieke Maduka v. Microsoft Nigeria Limited & 2 Ors,* (2013) [NICN/LA/492/2012 (National Industrial Court, Lagos Division, 19th December 2013), in which the applicant was dismissed from employment for refusing to succumb to the persistent sexual harassment by the third respondent, the National Industrial Court of Nigeria held, inter alia, that the dismissal violated the applicant's fundamental right to human dignity and awarded the necessary compensation. See also *Pastor (Mrs.) Abimbola Patricia Yakubu v. Financial Reporting Council of Nigeria & Anor,* unreported Suit No NICN/LA/673/2013; and Adejugbe and Adejugbe (2018).

[382] The recently enacted Violence Against Persons (Prohibition) Act 2015 (VAPP) criminalises assaults, stalking, abuse and acts of intimidation, inter alia. But it does not expressly criminalise sexual harassment (cf. Human Rights Report, 2013).

[383] UN Doc. A/44/38, 1989, para. 1.

[384] UN Doc. A/RES/48/104, 20th December 1993, preamble.

[385] Article 1 of the CRC; see also section 277 of Nigeria's Child Rights Act 2003 (hereinafter CRA). The latter regulates all issues concerning the rights and welfare of the Nigerian child.

even considered to be the most vulnerable members of this group due to their immaturity in terms of overall human development. Based on this, it is believed that they require special care and protection to blossom. Another reason children need to be protected is that they are "the assurance of the continuity of the human society" (Tajudeen, 2015: 46). That being so, their effective contribution to society as adults depends largely on the treatment they received in childhood (cf. Okpukpara et al., 2006). Throughout history, children have never been totally deprived of care and protection as bona-fide members of their society. Nevertheless, the concept of child protection or special protection for children—defined here as the systematic preservation of children from violence, abuse and exploitation—is relatively new. According to reports, prior to the era of organised child protection in the nineteenth century, abuse of children by adults was common and there was no idea or mechanism for special protection of children. In the nineteenth century, the child was gradually perceived as more in need of protection than it had received all along, and the idea made significant progress in the early twentieth century, leading to the introduction of international protection standards for children (Myers, 2008). The first of its kind was the Geneva Declaration of the Rights of the Child, adopted by the League of Nations in 1924, although the 1919 ILO Convention contains some provisions on child labour. The Geneva Declaration dealt with child-specific rights and social responsibility for the protection of children. It thus became the forerunner of later UN child rights measures. Its basic principles were included in the universal code of human rights[386] in 1948, and between 1946 and 1953 the UN International Children's Emergency Fund (hereinafter UNICEF)[387] was established as a worldwide specialised agency for vulnerable children. In addition, 1959, the UN adopted the expanded version of the Geneva Declaration, which not only recognised the child as a legal subject, but also paved the way for the adoption of the first international treaty on the rights of the child, the Convention on the Rights of the Child (CRC), thirty years later (Myers, 2008). This convention was unanimously approved by the UN General Assembly[388] and, together with its three Optional Protocols,[389] remains the overarching global mechanism for the protection of children.

The care and protection of children have always been of interest to the Nigerian people. But the concept of special protection for children apparently did not exist in

[386] Article 25(2) of the Universal Declaration states that "[m]otherhood and childhood are entitled to special care and assistance."

[387] The agency is now officially known as United Nations Children's Fund.

[388] As of 18th June 2021, this treaty has been ratified by 196 States, making it perhaps the most widely ratified human rights treaty in the world. See Convention on the Rights of the Child: Status of Ratification Interactive Dashboard. Available at: https://indicators.ohchr.org/. Accessed 26.06.2021.

[389] These include the Optional Protocols on child involvement in armed conflicts and on the sale of children, child prostitution and child pornography, both of 2000, and a third Optional Protocol on a communications procedure of 2011, introducing a mechanism by which children may submit complaints to the Committee on the Rights of the Child.

the country until 1943 with the enactment of the Children and Young Persons Ordinance by the British colonial government. This ordinance formed the legal framework for the protection of children and young persons, but its provisions mainly concerned issues of juvenile justice (cf. Abdulraheem-Mustapha, 2016; Iguh & Nosike, 2011). The ordinance subsists currently in the Children and Young Persons Laws (hereinafter CYPL) of various States in Nigeria.[390] The main national legislation protecting the Nigerian child today is the Child Rights Act 2003, which is seen as a fair attempt to domesticate the CRC and the African Charter on the Rights and Welfare of the Child in one document (cf. Nigeria, 2004). According to the CRA, every child is entitled to respect for its own dignity. It provides a system and special measures to protect the rights of children in Nigeria. It also updates and incorporates the provisions of the CYPL and other previously existing statutes dealing with child protection issues (Nigeria, 2004). The provisions of the CRA are complemented and/or reinforced by other laws such as the Constitution,[391] the African Charter Act, the Labour Act, the Criminal and Penal Code Acts and some recent enactments, e.g., the Trafficking in Persons (Prohibition) Enforcement and Administration Act 2015, the Violence Against Persons (Prohibition) Act 2015, as well as the relevant UN and ILO conventions endorsed by the country.[392] Child rights cover a wide range of topics. We focus on the welfare of the child as an indicator of socio-economic development of a society. According to Okpukpara et al. (2006): 3), the indices of child welfare include "child labour, child schooling, street children and child health." Of these items, we do not focus here on child health, as access to health is not currently a child-specific challenge in our context; it is more of a general problem. This may not apply to child education which is a major challenge in Nigeria. Regardless, we also refrain from examining child education here because we have done this extensively elsewhere (cf. Fumbo et al., 2020). So, we are left with child labour, which includes child forced labour and street children, who are basically child labourers.[393] Although these three concepts are technically different, for the purposes of this study they have been grouped under the heading of "child labour" and we focus on them as some of the most common forms of child exploitation in our context.

[390] Originally enacted as Ordinance no. 41 of 1943 for the colony of Lagos, the Ordinance was modified in 1948 as Children and Young Persons Act (hereinafter CYPA) for the whole country. It was later reproduced with more modifications in 1958 as CYPA Cap. 32 Laws of the Federation of Nigeria and Lagos. The last amendment of same was probably in 2004 (cf. NHRC, 2007).

[391] Section 17(3) states that the State shall direct its policy towards ensuring that- (f) children, young persons and the age are protected against any exploitation whatsoever, and against moral and material neglect.

[392] Examples of these are besides the CRC, the Optional Protocols on the involvement of children in armed conflicts and on the sale of children, child prostitution and child pornography, the Palermo Protocol on Trafficking in Persons, the ILO Convention on Minimum Age for Admission to Employment Convention (no. C182), and ILO Convention on Elimination of the Worse Forms of Child Labour (no. C138), to mention just a few.

[393] The street children refer broadly to children who work and sleep on the streets. They are usually not distinguished in the analysis of child labour (cf. Okpukpara et al., 2006).

It is not all work done by children that can be branded as child labour and as such is unacceptable for them (ILC Report, 2012, no. 59). Activities such as routine household chores or supporting parents in the family business, or an activity outside of school and during the holidays to earn pocket money, provided this is done within the framework of the legal regulations, are beneficial to both children and their families (ILO, 2004). Such activities are not considered child labour as they are compatible with the concept of legitimate light work for children within a certain age bracket, which is guaranteed in ILO Convention no. C138 on Minimum Age (article 7). Instead, child labour refers to work performed by children who are under the minimum legal age for that kind of work, or work that is considered unacceptable and prohibited for children because of its harmful nature or conditions (ILC Report, 2012, no. 59). From this definition, three categories of child labour have been identified by analysts based on the relevant international treaties, as follows: first, the underage work; second, the hazardous work and; third, the unconditional worst forms of child labour (cf. Rai, 2011). The first category of child labour comprises work that children are too young for (ILO and UNICEF Report, 2021). It is usually defined locally in line with international standards, but it often includes activities that affect school attendance and performance. The hazardous work refers to activities which, in themselves or due to the conditions in which they are carried out, are so dangerous or too strenuous for children that their participation in them may harm their health and personal development or expose them to abuse.[394] Typical examples are underground mining, deep sea diving, working at heights on construction sites, operating power-operated machinery, the use of dangerous chemicals, night or isolation work, rock crushing, scavenging or rag-picking, or carrying heavy loads.[395] These activities are viewed as some of the worst forms of child labour 'by condition', which means that their worst-form status can be changed through improved working conditions. As with the first category, the activities that qualify as prohibited hazardous work are determined by each country. In contrast, the unconditional worst forms of child labour consist of extreme activities that are considered unacceptable for children and are forbidden no matter how attempts are made to improve working conditions. The scope is defined at the international level to include activities such as slavery, trafficking, debt bondage and other forms of forced labour, the conscription of children for use in armed conflict, child prostitution and pornography, and other illicit activities.[396] These activities are prohibited because they rob children of their dignity and hinder their development and thus deprive them of the opportunity to lead a productive adult life in their society (ILO, 2004). Therefore, underage school age children and other minors need to be protected from child labour, and this generally entails both a withdrawing and rescuing job (ILO, 2018b).

---

[394] Ibid., article 3(1); article 3(d) of ILO Convention no. C182; see also ILO (2004).

[395] Cf. ILO Recommendation no. R190; ILO (2004).

[396] Article 3(a), (b) and (c) of ILO Convention no. C182; ILO (2004).

Like in most countries, child labour is prohibited in Nigeria. Under section 59(1) of the Labour Act, the general minimum age for employment in Nigeria is 12 years. Before reaching this minimum age, a child may therefore not do any work[397] other than light agricultural, horticultural, or household tasks for family members.[398] From the age of 12, a young person[399] may do an apprenticeship in skilled trades or as a domestic servant with the consent of his or her parent or legal guardian. A young person under the age of 14 may only be employed on a daily basis for a daily wage but should be able to return to his or her parents or to the guardian's place of residence at the end of work every day. In other words, night work is not foreseen for them and is illegal as such. However, this provision does not apply to persons who are employed in a household service.[400] Regarding work in the larger formal sector, the Act sets the minimum age for employment at 15 years for work in industries[401] and on ships, where no family member is employed.[402] This corresponds to the age for the completion of compulsory basic education.[403] Nigerian labour law has several provisions on hazardous work by children and young persons. For instance, the Labour Act prohibits exploitative and hazardous domestic tasks by children. Section 59(1)(b) prohibits a child from doing any work that involves lifting or carrying loads that could impair its physical development.[404] Young persons under the age of 16 are not allowed to do underground or machine work, or to work during public holidays.[405] Likewise, they are not permitted to work for a longer period than four consecutive hours or for more than eight hours per day,[406] as well as night work.[407] In sections 60, the Act allows young persons between 16 and 18 years of age to be employed in tedious industrial activities such as iron and steel production, glass work, gold mining, etc. Apart from these activities, child labour is generally outlawed in Nigeria, especially its worst forms. In section 59(6) of the Labour Act, it is prohibited to engage a young person in an employment that may be considered "injurious to his [or her] health, dangerous, or immoral".[408] The CRA also criminalises forced and exploitative labour by children and provides fines and/

[397] Underage labour is criminal and punishable on conviction in Nigeria [cf. section 23(1)(a) of the Trafficking in Persons (Prohibition) Enforcement and Administration Act 2015 (hereinafter NAPTIP Act)].

[398] Section 59(1)(a) of the Labour Act; section 28(1)(b) of the CRA.

[399] The Labour Act in section 91(1) defines a child as "a young person under the age of 12 years" and a young person as "a person under the age of 18 years.

[400] Ibid., section 59(3).

[401] Ibid., section 59(2).

[402] Ibid., section 61.

[403] Sections 2 and 15 of the Compulsory, Free Universal Basic Education Act, 2004 (hereinafter Education Act); see also section 15 of the CRA; and Human Rights Report 2017.

[404] See also section 28(1)(c) of the CRA.

[405] Section 59(5) of the Labour Act.

[406] Ibid., section 59(8).

[407] Ibid., section 60(1).

[408] See also section 23(1)(b) of the NAPTIP Act. The bracket in the quotation is mine.

or prison sentence for convicted persons.[409] More unconditional worst forms of child labour are absolutely criminalised in several labour laws. These include the use of children for the purpose of hawking, street begging, child prostitution,[410] armed conflicts,[411] slavery-like practices such as trafficking and serfdom,[412] as well as other illicit activities.[413] At the state level, there are several statutes that prohibit various forms of exploitative labour practices.[414]

Despite the above legal framework and other policy initiatives, many Nigerian children still suffer from abuse of their socio-economic rights by adults, sometimes by their parents, guardians and other caregivers (NHRC, 2007). Of the 160 million children aged 5 to 17–63 million girls and 97 million boys—who were estimated to be engaged in child labour in early 2020 prior to the outbreak of the COVID-19 pandemic, nearly 87 million (or 24%) live in Sub-Saharan Africa (ILO-UNICEF 2021). Nigeria is believed to have the highest number of such children and one of the highest proportions of child labour in both the sub-region and Africa. Current national estimates are largely unavailable. Having said that, Nigeria Living Standards (NLS) Survey 2018–2019 reports that 13 percent of Nigerian boys and 10 percent of girls aged 5–14 years indicated to be working only (NBS, 2020). The 2017 Multiple Indicator Cluster (MIC) Survey also estimates that 50.8 per cent of all working Nigerian children aged 5–17 years were involved in some form of child labour, as defined in the survey (NBS and UNICEF, 2017). This figure corresponds in absolute terms to circa 15 million child labourers in the country (cf. Ejekwonyilo, 2021). More male children (54.3%) compared to females (47.2%) were subjected to the practice and, geographically speaking, a higher percentage (59.1%) is concentrated in rural areas than in urban centres (33.4%). The survey further showed significant differences in the distribution of child workers across the six geopolitical zones, with North-Central having the highest percentage (56.8%) and South-West the lowest (38%). The most common forms of child labour in the country are intensive farm work such as production of manioc, rice and cocoa, tedious domestic work, fishing, pastoral and herding activities. Others are street begging, highway hawking, scavenging, works in cottage industries such as iron and metal works, mining and quarrying of gravel, granite, and gold, sand harvesting, textile manufacturing, works in hazardous mechanical workshops, in construction sites including brickworks or carrying of building materials, and in transportation as commercial bus conductors or car wash. Others still are bonded labour on farms, in restaurants

[409] Section 28(3)(c) of the CRA; sections 22(b) and 23(1)(b) of the NAPTIP Act; Nigeria, 2004; and Human Rights Report 2017.

[410] Section 30 of the CRA; sections 14–17 of the NAPTIP Act.

[411] Section 19 of the NAPTIP Act. The minimum age for voluntary military recruitment is 18 years (section 34 of the CRA; section 28 of the Armed Forces Act.

[412] Sections 30 of the CRA; sections 24 and 25 of NAPTIP Act.

[413] Sections 25, 26 and 30 of the CRA.

[414] Examples of such statutes by States are Anambra State Street Trading Restriction Law (2004), Bauchi State Hawking by Children (Prohibition) Edict (1985), Edo State Trafficking in Persons Prohibition Law 2018, and Kaduna State Child Welfare and Protection Law 2018.

as commercial sex workers, or for small businesses, and recruitment of children by armed groups for use in armed conflicts as child soldiers, or involvement of children in drug peddling and human trafficking for various purposes (cf. USDOL Report, 2019[415]; Human Rights Report, 2013).

In line with current global estimates,[416] it has been suggested that the agricultural sector has the largest share of child labour in Nigeria (Okpukpara et al., 2006). Due to poverty, many children are forced into various agricultural activities to supplement the meagre family income (cf. USDOL Report, 2019). The activities are usually strenuous and sometimes take longer than normal each week, making it difficult for a child to perform at its best in school. According to the 2017 MIC survey, the same applies to the service sector. Millions of Nigerian children are reportedly engaged in the service sector, including child domestic work (APPGN Report, 2013). The fact is that most children from poor backgrounds would voluntarily accept work as domestic help in families to which they are not biologically related as part of foster parenthood (Onwe, 2014). But they would end up being used for exploitative labour practices like domestic bondage and sexual abuse. The phenomenon of child begging is also notorious in Nigeria, in part due to the 'Almajiri' practice or a system of quranic education in the north. In this system, pupils of a quranic school are taught and made to beg for a living or to finance their education. Although the practice has been criticised, street begging is still an issue in Nigeria (cf. Imam 1998, in NCLS Report 2001). The Universal Basic Education Commission estimates that there were 9.5 million Almajiri children in the country in 2010. However, the 'Almajiri' practice does not exclusively explain the phenomenon of child begging in Nigeria. Street begging is also commonplace in the major cities such as Kano, Abuja, Lagos, etc. and exposes children to harmful facets of street life, including for example being recruited as child soldiers by local vigilante groups or being used as "human bombs" by terrorist groups such as Boko Haram (Human Rights Report, 2013: 21). The same report confirms that over 563 children had been abused in this way by Boko Haram in 2016. Lastly, it has been reported that Nigerian children are also victims of human trafficking. The report of the All-Party Parliamentary Group on Nigeria (2013: 11) describes the country as "one of the top source, destination and transit countries for human trafficking", with states in the south of the country being mentioned more frequently. This practice is not limited to Nigeria. In fact, it occurs throughout Africa and beyond, but is considered one of the largest forms of organised crime in West Africa due to its high prevalence in the sub-region. Human trafficking in Nigeria is often viewed as a cross-border phenomenon. On the contrary, it is well known that it occurs at the domestic level and affects individuals across ages and sex. However, women and girls tend to be more at risk of being trafficked. This assertion largely corresponds to NAPTIP's recent data showing the profiles of rescued Nigerian human trafficking victims in

[415] Acronym for United States Department of Labor (USDOL).

[416] The agricultural sector accounts for the largest share (70%) of child labour among children aged 5 to 17 years worldwide (ILO and UNICEF, 2021).

2019. Of the 1152 rescued persons, 573 (or 49.8%) were children between the ages of 0 and 17, while around 75 percent were girls—that is 423 persons in absolute numbers (NAPTIP 2019 Data Analysis). Whereas the total figure does not represent the annual percentage of human trafficking in Nigeria, it confirms the prevalence of the practice in the country. It is hardly reported (APPGN report, 2013; EASO report, 2021). But it goes on and happens for different purposes.

A host of factors contribute to and/or exacerbate the incidence of child labour in Nigeria. These include poverty, ignorance, high demand for cheap labour, absence of relevant legislations with national force,[417] ineffective enforcement of available child labour laws and, of course, socio-cultural reasons.[418] The consequences of child labour and forced child labour are enormous. First and foremost, it endangers the well-being, health and development of a child (OHCHR, 2006). Perhaps the most noticeable adverse consequence of the practice in our study context is the denial of access to educational opportunities or the unwarranted interruption of the education of child labourers. Some of them do not go to school or are withdrawn from school and forced into economic activities to support their poor parents (NHRC, 2007). Many drop out of school by themselves because the long hours of work leave them no room for meaningful academic exercise (Onwe, 2014). According to estimates from the Multiple Indicator Cluster (MIC) Survey 2017, the net attendance rate for primary school in Nigeria is 60.9 percent and 46.9 percent for secondary school. Both also show remarkable differences in the urban-rural divide and in the geopolitical zones. This simply means that millions of children and adolescents are out of school, and this situation is likely to get worse given the COVID-19 pandemic and the rapidly increasing prevalence of banditry and the accompanying kidnapping of school children in the country. This deficit will certainly affect the chances of upward social mobility of the concerned children. For all these reasons, the country is ranked 174th out of 180 countries in the 2020 End of Childhood Index.[419]

[417] Take for instance the case of the CRA. Although it was enacted to domesticate the CRC since 2003, the CRA only applies in the Federal Capital Territory, Abuja, and must be adopted and implemented by every state in the country in order to become law on its territory. As of 2019, and perhaps to date, only 25 of the 36 States have done so, meaning the law has no national application (cf. USDOL Report, 2019).

[418] A typical socio-cultural argument is the disagreement on minimum age among Nigerians based on which one finds varieties in the minimum age limit in several legal texts and customary laws all over the country. Among other things, the lack of a consensus on this issue poses a lot of problem in the application of child labour laws. For instance, 11 states are yet to adopt the CRA, and incidentally all 11 states are northern states with a predominant Muslim population. It is generally believed that part of their reasons for the non-adoption of the CRA is their disagreement with the document as to when childhood begins, based on their religious belief (Abdulraheem-Mustapha, 2016; Akinwumi, 2009; Egede, 2007; Iguh & Nosike, 2011).

[419] In the End of Childhood Index piloted by Save the Children Federation Incorporated, countries are scored and ranked according to performance across a set of variables known as 'enders', which indicate where childhood is most and least threatened (Global Childhood Report, 2020).

In recognition of the peculiar circumstances of the Nigerian child, the Nigerian State has taken some anti-child labour measures over the years as part of its efforts to meet the Target 8.7 of the SDGs, which calls for an end to the practice by 2025. Some of the measures are the establishment of Nomadic and Continuing Education Centres, the Universal Basic Education, the National Policy on Child Labour, the 2021 National Action Plan (NAP) for the Elimination of Child Labour, the NAPTIP 2019 Plan of Action, the National Action Plan for Preventing and Countering Violent Extremism, the Accelerating Action for the Elimination of Child Labour in Supply Chains in Africa (hereinafter ACCEL Africa) 2018–2022, and an impressive number of programmes funded by the World Bank (cf. EASO Report, 2021; NHRC, 2007). Child labour issues in the country are managed through a synergy of institutional mechanisms such as the Federal Ministry of Labour and Employment, the National Agency for the Prohibition of Trafficking in Persons and Other Related Matters (NAPTIP), the Nigeria Police Force, the Nigeria Immigration Service, the National Steering Committee on Child Labour (NSCCL), the Ministry for Women Affairs, and the NGO bodies (cf. USDOL Report, 2019). However, the role of the government and its agencies in protecting individuals from exploitative labour practices cannot be overemphasised. As the authority responsible for protecting the rights of citizens and persons within its territory, especially of young and vulnerable persons, the State has the primary responsibility for enforcing child labour laws. The Nigerian government often claims to have some of the best child protection policies in place but has also been repeatedly criticised for failing to effectively protect the Nigerian child. In the broadest sense, child protection as a right encompasses protection against abuse, exploitation, discrimination and neglect. It also includes a positive commitment to empowering the child (cf. Rai, 2011). In the Nigerian context, this can therefore mean, among other things, withdrawing school-age underage children from work and sending them back to school, as well as rescuing young persons or minors from all kinds of exploitation, in particular human trafficking and sexual abuse. This also includes offering them an adequate standard of living, healthcare and the opportunity to play and relax. This is so because, as Onwe (2014: 285) puts it, a child is psychologically and socially balanced if "[s]he is loved, adored, cared for and given the opportunity of play and leisure, exploring the world, interacting fully with peers and bonding with the family." Only a well-balanced child can meaningfully participate in the Nigerian project later in adult life.

Right to Social Security

The popular belief is that Nigeria is an odd paradox because the country is rich in human and natural resources and yet many of her citizens live in abject poverty. A 2017 statistical report published by NBS (2018a) shows that the country has a population of circa 199 million people with a growth rate of 3.2 percent. In the same period, the country generated a gross domestic product (GDP) of 375.75 billion US dollars, making her the largest economy in Africa. This grew by 2.2 percent in 2019 (equivalent to 448.12 billion US dollars in real terms).[420] The 2020 Human Development report of the UN Development Programme (hereinafter UNDP) shows more specifically how these national achievements affect the life of the man in the street. According to the report, the country posted a Human Development Index (HDI) score of 0.539 in 2019, an increase of 15.9 percent from the 2005 value of 0.465. A disaggregation of this value according to the HDI indicators also shows that life expectancy (at birth) in the country was 54.7 years, the expected years of schooling 10, the mean years of schooling 6.7, and the gross national income (GNI) per capita—which measures standard of living—4910 US dollars (based on 2017 purchasing power parity conversion rates). This report shows a steady increase in each of the indicators over the past three decades. Nevertheless, the country performs poorly in human development with a score of 0.539 and is therefore placed in the low human development category in the index. According to the report, the value is even lower than the average of 0.547 for countries in sub-Saharan Africa. For this reason, the country ranked 161st out of 189 countries and UN-recognised territories studied. As if to confirm this report, recent World Bank 2020 data for 2018 shows that over 79 million Nigerians live in extreme poverty—defined as those living on less than 1.90 US dollars per day. They supposedly make up 20 percent of the total poor population in sub-Saharan Africa, the highest proportion in the region and the second highest proportion in the world. It is also estimated that around 20 million people (or 23.13 percent of the national workforce) were unemployed in the country during the period under review.[421] Given these "miserable statistics" and the logical social implications, many strongly believe that the country needs a well-articulated national social security policy to protect the countless vulnerable Nigerians from the harsh effects of the above-mentioned socio-economic profile and enable them to maintain a living standard in line with socially recognised standards (Nwafor, 2010b: 11; see also Anifalaje, 2017; Usman, 2015). The same concern is the reason for choosing this topic here.

The right to social security is one of the most important socio-economic rights. It is an aspect of social welfare that concerns itself mainly with the economic and social well-being of individuals and families. Social security refers to a set of organised collective measures aimed at reducing and/or preventing poverty by providing protection against contingencies throughout the life cycle (ILO, 2017b; Nwafor, 2010b). In simpler terms, it is about guaranteeing people and their dependants effective access to healthcare and income security, especially in the event of accidents, illness, maternity, disability, old age, death and unemployment. For the most part, it is an income maintenance programme that is often deployed as a palliative measure

[420] See World Data Atlas (n.d.). Nigeria: Gross Domestic Product in Current Prices. Available at: https://knoema.com/atlas/Nigeria/GDP. Accessed 01.06.2021.

[421] In Nigeria, the unemployed are defined as persons who either do nothing or work for less than 20 hours a week (NBS, 2021). It is reported that the unemployment rate in Nigeria has arisen to 33.3 percent of the labour force—and that is about 23 million persons—in the Fourth Quarter of 2020. A similar increase could be expected in the poverty rate due to a number of intervening variables including, for example, the COVID-19 pandemic (cf. World Bank, 2019).

to cushion the effects of life changes on the individual and can be carried out in both governmental and non-governmental form (Altmeyer, n.d.). In the narrower sense, which is predominantly used here, this refers to state social protection policies and programmes, since effective social security without the involvement of the state would be a mirage (Davis, 2012). Social security in this study is therefore understood to mean policies and programmes developed by government and society to protect individuals from various shocks throughout their life cycle, improve their standard of living and promote a life of dignity via a mix of contribution-based schemes and tax-financed benefits.

As already mentioned, the practice of social security goes back a long way in history, and Germany is mentioned as the first country to introduce a national social security system in 1883. This was basically a social health insurance system (Busse et al., 2017; Davis, 2012). Other countries in western and non-western societies followed suit over the next couple of decades with context-specific schemes. Social security experts claim that the Great Depression (1929–1939) played a key role in the development and diffusion of institutionalised social security schemes in societies around the world (Altmeyer, n.d.; Badru, 2017). They suggest that the Depression stimulated great thinking about the role of the state in social welfare in countries such as the US and Great Britain, to mention just a few. Then the concept was strengthened by inclusion in the 1941 Atlantic Charter. Three years later, it was first enshrined as a basic human right in the Philadelphia Declaration, in which the International Labour Conference recognised the extension of social protection to all persons worldwide as one of the ILO's primary objectives.[422] Since then, social security protection has been defined in subsequent ILO and UN instruments as such[423] and comprises nine policy areas. These include medical care, illness, unemployment, old age, work accidents, family and child, maternity, disability, and survivorship (ILO, 1952). Several nations have it anchored in their laws, either as a fundamental right or as a fundamental objective (Anifalaje, 2017). For countries like Nigeria, social security protection has many advantages. When it works properly, its effects can be felt at all levels of society. A viable social protection system

[422] Article 3(f) of the Philadelphia Declaration 1944.

[423] The Philadelphia Declaration inspired the draft of other ILO documents which contain important provisions for the practice of the right to social security, such as Income Security Recommendation 1944 (no. R067), Social Security (Minimum Standards) Convention 1952 (no. C102), and Social Protection Floor Recommendation 2012 (no. R202). Social security protection is also recognised as a basic human right in articles 22, 23(1) & 25 of the Universal Declaration, articles 6, 9(1) & 10(2) of the ICESCR, article 5 of the ICERD, articles 11(1)(e) & 14(2)(c) of the CEDAW, and articles 18(2), 20, 26 & 27 of the CRC. Others are the African Charter, the 2004 Ouagadougou Declaration and Plan of Action on Employment Promotion and Poverty Alleviation, the 2008 Social Policy Framework for Africa, and the 2010 Yaounde Tripartite Declaration on the Implementation of the Social Protection Floors, together with a host of regional-level guidelines, recommendations, and policy activities (cf. Anifalaje, 2017). See also ILO (n.d.). Facts on Social Security in Africa. Available at: https://www.ilo.org/public/english/protection/socsec/pol/campagne/files/africafactsheet.pdf. Accessed 01.06.2021.

can contribute to overall national development by promoting inclusive socio-economic growth and is thus a key enabler of the SDGs.[424]

The history of social security in Nigeria can be traced back to the kinship systems in pre-colonial times, in which the extended family provided members with services that are now offered by social agencies (Ekpe, 1983; Usman, 2015). The first formal social security system was introduced in the country by the colonial administration with the 1951 Pension Ordinance. This was a state pension system that has been modified several times since then (Nwafor, 2010b; Onyeonoru et al., 2013). Today, Nigeria can be seen as a country that offers her citizens social security because the Constitution creates the basis for a sustainable social security system in the country.[425] In section 16(2)(d), the Constitution stipulates that the State shall ensure the provision of suitable shelter and food, old-age care and pensions, unemployment and sickness benefits, and the care of people with disabilities. Likewise in section 17(3)(d), it refers to the State's obligation to provide all persons with adequate medical and health facilities. All these are concrete elements of a social security scheme. These provisions are underpinned by a number of statutes, as the Constitution sees them as fundamental objectives rather than rights. The statutes include the Pension Reform Act (PRA), the National Health Insurance Scheme (NHIS) Act, the Employee's Compensation Act (ECA) and the Labour Act. The Pension Reform Act (hereinafter PRA) regulates the provision of retirement benefits as applicable to all employees in the public service of the Federal Government, the Federal Capital Territory, the States, Local Government Councils and somehow also the organised private sector (section 2). It also regulates the payment of disability benefits [section 5(5)] and survivors' benefits to the registered relatives of a deceased or missing employee (sections 8 and 9, respectively). These are dealt with more comprehensively in the Employee's Compensation Act (hereinafter ECA), which provides compensation for employees or their relatives in the event of injury, illness, disability or death as a result of an industrial accident. For its part, the National Health Insurance Scheme Act (hereinafter NHIS Act) regulates a contribution-based health insurance scheme that provides insured persons and their dependents with the benefits of specified qualitative and affordable healthcare services.[426] In addition, maternity and sickness benefits are covered in the Labour Act.

At this point it is important to highlight some of the notable features of the Nigerian social security system. First, the foregoing analysis shows that so far only five of the nine recommended policy areas have been directly legislated in Nigeria, namely old age, work injury, disability, survivors, and medical care. Others such as maternity and sickness benefits are mentioned, but are only sparsely provided for in the Labour Act, while unemployment support, and child and family benefits have not yet been considered (Anifalaje, 2017). Second, all the available social security

---

[424] Cf. ILO (n.d.). Facts On Social Security in Africa, ibid.; see also ILO (2017b).

[425] To treat the Nigerian social security system, we made extensive use of papers by Anifalaje (2017) and Nwafor (2010b).

[426] Section 1(1) of the NHIS Act.

schemes in the country are contribution-based. Apart from work injuries, where the cost of benefits is borne solely by employers, the remaining schemes are funded by contributions from employers and employees. For example, the pension system requires both employers and employees to pay a certain percentage of the employee's emoluments to finance the latter's retirement benefits.[427] The NHIS Act contains a similar provision, but the exact amount of the contribution is at the discretion of the scheme's board of directors.[428] Sickness and maternity benefits are clearly subject to employers' liability provisions under the Labour Act. Overall, the State is exempt from financial contributions to the above schemes, except in situations where it is directly involved as an employer. This contradicts standard ILO practice, which recommends a fair distribution of benefit costs between insured persons, employers and taxpayers.[429] In some cases, it even requires the State to bear the cost of benefits that cannot be adequately covered by contributions.[430] This regulation has the advantage, among other things, that insured persons with limited resources or employers are protected from avoidable hardship. Third, another feature of the contributory social security system is that it is largely employment-related, as coverage is limited to workers in the public and organised private sectors. Again, private sector participation in some existing schemes is further restricted in certain circumstances. For example, the pension scheme limits it to employees of organisations with at least fifteen employees[431] and the health insurance scheme to at least ten,[432] while others not covered by these schemes, including the self-employed, can only participate as voluntary contributors.[433] Scholars suggest that the main flaw in this arrangement is that it does not cover the myriad of vulnerable Nigerians working in the informal sector or unemployed, as well as people with disabilities and children in need of special protection, leaving them without a safety net (Anifalaje, 2017; Nwafor, 2010b). The government has consistently tried to fill this void by introducing policies and practices with poverty reduction goals, such as the Family Support Programme, the Better Life Programme for Rural Women (BLP), the National Poverty Eradication Programme (NAPEP), especially for the unemployed youth and recently the Government Enterprise and Empowerment Programme (GEEP) with a special focus on small businesses and craftsmen. However, like the existing insurance schemes, these initiatives are often undermined by poor budgetary discipline, poor management and institutional weaknesses (Anifalaje, 2017; Nwafor, 2010b). Fourth, Nigeria has not yet ratified any of the relevant ILO conven-

[427] Under section 4(1), the PRA stipulates a minimum of 10 percent of each employee's monthly wage from employers a minimum of 8 percent from employees themselves, for their retirement benefits. An employee is, however, free to contribute more if (s)he so wishes [see section 4(3)].

[428] Section 16(1) of the NHIS Act.

[429] ILO Recommendation no. R067, para. 26; ILO Recommendation no. R069, para. 6(c); and article 71(1) of ILO Convention no. C102.

[430] ILO Recommendation no. R067, para. 26(8).

[431] Section 2(2) of the PRA.

[432] Section 16(1) of the NHIS.

[433] Ibid., section 17(3); see also section 2(3) of the PRA.

tions on social security. This is sometimes interpreted as a sign of a lack of commitment to the welfare of the citizens and other persons in the country. Be that as it may, it can be concluded from the foregoing that the existing social security framework is not policy-driven and does not adequately protect the social security rights of individuals in the country.

3.6.3 Religion and Socio-economic Rights

As with the first-generation rights, religions in Nigeria are not unconcerned about socio-economic rights. To conclude this chapter, we briefly examine the theological perspectives of our three religious traditions of interest on the socio-economic rights issues discussed so far.

Socio-economic Rights in ATR

The concept of social justice existed in traditional Nigerian society. It referred to the process of ensuring that individuals receive their due within the limits of their expectations, which were more or less dictated by their social roles. It served to maintain social stability and cohesion (Shorter, n.d.). In the pre-industrial setting, the economy was predominantly agrarian. Nonetheless, certain socio-economic rights were guaranteed, such as the right to work, the right to property, the right to protection and education for children and, above all, the right to some form of social protection for vulnerable members of society. Land was the most important means of production. It was owned by groups such as the family or clan and belonged to individuals as such based on their membership in their social group. Everyone was guaranteed enough land to meet his own needs (Ekpe, 1983). In addition, traditional society was based on kinship and family ties. A family consisted of a nuclear family and relatives; it was referred to as an extended family whose members traced their identity back to a common ancestry and who lived in a network of interdependence. Attention was paid to child protection. Raising children was seen as a shared responsibility of the extended family and even the community, but the natural obligation to feed, shelter, raise and protect their children still rested with the parents. Children also had their own responsibilities. They not only represented additional hands for their parents in farm work but were also supposed to look after the parents in old age (Ekpe, 1983). Here, too, the family takes care of its members, not just the children, but every needy family member, including the elderly, the sick, the disabled, orphans and the poor; the well-being of each family member was a common concern of all. The extended family provided most of the social protection services to its members. This traditional arrangement is now being weakened by urban migration and economic hardship (Ekpe, 1983).

Socio-economic Rights in Islamic Theology

Islam is not neutral on socio-economic issues either. As stated earlier, justice, including social justice, is a fundamental objective of Islam. Islamic scholars agree that ensuring social justice is one of the main tasks of an Islamic state and that this can only be achieved through the way in which the state manages socio-economic affairs. According to them, social justice does not entail equal income or equal redistribution of wealth. Instead, it is about "the provision of education, training, employment and access to economic opportunities" (Zaman, 2008: 52). Of course, Muslims have different opinions on many employment issues, but they are certainly not indifferent to workers' rights (Ziebertz & Ziebertz, 2016). Islam's general position on socio-economic rights can be gleaned from documents like the Universal Islamic Declaration of Human Rights (1981), the Cairo Declaration of Human Rights in Islam (1990) and the Arab Charter of Human Rights (1994), which in some ways can be regarded as authoritative texts in Islam. For example, article 13 of the Cairo Declaration states that work is primarily a right for everyone who is able to work.[434] Then the free choice of occupation of the individual is emphasised, whereby forced labour is excluded.[435] The declaration also recognises workers' right to a decent life in accordance with Sharia law and insists that workers should be treated with respect, since they are engaged in a cooperative enterprise with employers, albeit doing a different kind of work (Zaman, 2008). Several labour principles are also mentioned and confirmed in these instruments. These include the right to fair treatment, fair and punctual wages, the right to paid vacation, and the right to safe and healthy working conditions.[436] Others are the right to strike,[437] the right to equal employment opportunities and equal pay for work of equal value,[438] and the right to promotion without discrimination based on sex.[439] As in all areas of interpersonal relationships, Islam does not confer only rights; it also prescribes corresponding duties. Therefore, workers have the duty to be loyal and thorough in their work. The state, for its part, is obliged to resolve possible labour disputes.[440] Other relevant socio-economic issues such as the right to child protection,[441] the right to education,[442] the right to medical care[443] and the right to a comprehensive social security[444] are not lost to Islamic social theory. Islam recognises them as

---

[434] See also article 30 of the Arab Charter.

[435] Ibid., article 31. Here the document makes it clear that "[f]orced labour does not include compelling a person to carry out work in execution a judicial decision."

[436] Article 13 of Cairo Declaration; and article 17 of the UIDHR.

[437] Article 29 of the Arab Charter.

[438] Ibid, article 32.

[439] Article 13 of Cairo Declaration.

[440] Ibid., article 13.

[441] Article 38 of the Arab Charter; article 19(d), (e) & (f) of UIDHR. This provision is consistent with the teachings of the Quran 17:24; 65:7; 30: 21; inter alia.

[442] Article 34 of the Arab Charter. Interestingly, this provision further states that "[e]lementary education is compulsory and free", and that "[s]econdary and university education shall be accessible to all." See also Article 21 of the UIDHR.

[443] Article 17(b) of Cairo Declaration; article 18 of the UIDHR.

[444] Articles 30 and 38 of the Arab Charter; see also article 17(b) & (c) of Cairo Declaration and article 18 of the UIDHR.

rights and, like the guarantees in the ILO and UN conventions, the state is obliged to ensure that these rights are realised within the limits of its resources.[445]

Socio-economic Rights in Christian Theology

The Christian religion, too, is concerned with social issues. Social justice—understood as promoting a just society and guaranteeing access to equal opportunities and rights for all—is also "a major topic and goal of Christian faith and theology" (Bobbert, 2017: 2). If one looks at the biblical narratives, traditions and teachings of Christian churches in the past centuries, various concepts of justice emerge in the Christian context. For example, the Old Testament is primarily concerned with righteousness, retribution and social justice, while the New Testament focuses on preferential care for the poor and distributive justice. The Church's commitment to justice in early Christianity prioritised the support for vulnerable members of society. Then, the late antiquity and the Middle Ages witnessed the erection of social institutions such as poorhouses, hospices and hospitals to compensate for injustice (Bobbert, 2017; Van der Ven, 2013). Despite the different theological trajectories of the Reformation, the Christian religion always viewed the pursuit of social justice as an essential part of its message and missionary mandate. Today, Christian churches across the denominational spectrum tend to support the fight against social injustice.

The Catholic Church takes a more detailed position on social questions in its social doctrine. The teachings of the encyclicals and other papal letters as well as the Vatican documents are not only instructive here, but also authoritative. In relation to the socio-economic issues addressed in this study, the following sources deserve special mention: Rerum Novarum,[446] Quadragesimo Anno,[447] Mater et Magistra[448] and Pacem in Terris,[449] Laborem Exercens[450] and Centesimus Annus,[451] and Caritas in Veritate.[452] Rerum Novarum (hereinafter RN) is the first of the social encyclicals. It was written in response to the Industrial Revolution and as such dealt with the situation of the emergent urban workforce. It recognises the dignity of human work from the outset and affirms the right to work.[453] It also supports a

[445] Article 17(b) of Cairo Declaration; article 18 of the UIDHR.

[446] Pope Leo XIII (1891). Encyclical Letter "on Capital and Labour".

[447] Pope Pius XI (1931). Encyclical Letter "on Reconstruction of the Social Order" (hereinafter QA).

[448] Pope John XXIII (1961). Encyclical Letter "on Christianity and Social Progress" (hereinafter MM)

[449] Pope John XXIII (1963). Encyclical Letter "on Establishing Universal Peace".

[450] Pope John Paul II (1981). Encyclical Letter "on Human Work".

[451] Pope John Paul II (1991). Encyclical Letter "on the Hundredth Anniversary of Rerum Novarum" (hereinafter CA).

[452] Pope Benedict XVI (2009). Encyclical Letter "on Integral Human Development in Charity and Truth" (hereinafter CV).

[453] RN no. 2. See also MM no. 44.

number of other socio-economic rights, such as the right to private property,[454] the right to a just wage,[455] the right to private association,[456] the entitlement to leisure and rest, the protection of the family, including children.[457] Other documents, notably Pacem in Terris, add the rights to education[458] and social security[459] to the recognised list of rights. In Laborem Exercens (hereinafter LE), the Catholic Church speaks about what it calls the right to "a family wage", that is, a fair and adequate wage (no. 19), as well as the right to a safe and healthy working environment, the right to strike (no. 20), and the rights of immigrant workers (no. 23). As in Islam, Catholic social teaching usually grants rights with concomitant duties.[460] For this reason, and in the interests of harmony in the workplace, Leo XIII recommends that workers diligently perform their agreed duties and refrain from violence and riot in pressing their demands, while employers must respect the dignity of workers and treat them fairly,[461] among other things. The Catholic Church also recognises the social obligation of the state towards its citizens, in particular those in need of protection,[462] but emphasises that the principle of subsidiarity must be observed.[463] Virtually all social encyclicals defend and promote the dignity of the worker and view unemployment, underemployment, insufficient wages and forced labour as abuse of that dignity.[464] On the basis of this doctrine, the Catholic Church sees itself, in Ziebertz and Ziebertz (2016: 52) own words, "as a promoter of social rights in the whole tradition of human rights."

At this point, however, it is important to highlight some common features of these religions that have gross implications for the public discourse on socio-economic rights. First, these three religious traditions can be described as hierarchically structured systems. Like most African societies, traditional Nigerian society was communitarian, but not necessarily egalitarian (Shorter, n.d.). The idea of equality of the sexes never really existed. Decision-making and administrative powers were concentrated in the hands of men, while women played a subordinate role (Dada & Ibanga, 2011; Benisheikh et al., 2016). Women's subordinate status appears to be theologically legitimised by certain references in Christian and Islamic scriptures, which are often interpreted as allusions to the inequality of the sexes.[465]

[454] RN nos. 6 and 13. See also PT no. 21; CA no. 6.

[455] RN nos. 44 and 45. See also CA no. 8.

[456] RN no. 51. See also PT no. 23; CA no. 3; MM no. 22.

[457] RN no. 42. See also MM no. 20; and the Compendium of the Social Doctrine of the Church no. 244.

[458] PT no. 13; Gravissimum Educationis no. 1.

[459] PT no. 11. See also LE nos. 18–19.

[460] PT no.44.

[461] RN no. 20.

[462] MM no. 20; QA no.25.

[463] CA no 48; Caritas in Veritate, para. 57.

[464] LE nos. 8–9.

[465] The Hebrew Scriptures which both the Christian and Islamic religions recognise narrate in Genesis (2:7,21–22; see also Surah An-Nisa 4:1) that God created man from the dust of the ground, but woman God created from man. Furthermore, the citations from the Christian New Testament

However, the myth of gender inequality or even misogyny has been conscientiously challenged in the social doctrines of Christian and Islamic religions,[466] while in the case of the traditional belief system, the practice has been strongly confronted with modernity. Second, all three religious systems adhere to a gender role ideology.[467] The occupations of individuals are mostly tied to their family roles, which are determined by sex, and there is a gendered division of labour that is accepted as normal (Adejugbe & Adejugbe, 2018; Shorter, n.d.). Men are breadwinners and women are basically mothers and wives whose main duties are home-keeping and caregiving.[468] The current context of occupational segregation and the legacy of gender gap in all indicators of socio-economic development worldwide are sometimes attributed to this arrangement (Makama, 2013). Finally, these three religious traditions seem to tolerate the use of physical discipline in raising children.[469] In addition, they define childhood based on various criteria. For Islam, this is largely based on biological criteria, especially puberty, though Islamic jurists tend to differ on the issue (Peters & Barends, 2001; Sambo, 2018). The same could be said of the ATR. But most Christian churches have other measures for this, such as age.[470] Religious adherents sometimes use this as a pretext to abuse the socio-economic rights of the child.

Summary

So far, this chapter attempts to show that Nigerians, like people in other parts of the world, care about the right to freedom of religion, the right to freedom from discrimination based on sexual orientation and gender identity, the right to life, especially issues of the death penalty, abortion and euthanasia, as well as political rights, the right to a fair trial and socio-economic rights. For each of these human rights

(cf. 1 Corinthians 11:8–9)—which hold that a woman was made from and for man, much like the Surah An-Nisa (QS 4:34) which see men as the leaders of women—appear to uphold not only men's headship of the family but also the subordinate position of women (cf. Van der Tuin & Fumbo, 2012; Francis et al., 2016).

[466] For instance, in his Apostolic Letter Mulieris Dignitatem (1988) which focuses "on the Dignity and Vocation of Women", Pope John Paul II speaks of an essential equality of both sexes "created in the image and likeness of God" (MD no.16). This teaching runs through all the social encyclicals and is shared by all Christian Churches across the denominational spectrum (cf. Ziebertz & Ziebertz, 2016; Francis et al., 2016). The Cairo Declaration takes a clear position on the equality of sexes in article 6(a) where it states that a "[w]oman is equal to man in human dignity". To mention just a few.

[467] Cf. RN no. 42; QA no.71; and article 19(h) of UIDHR.

[468] Cf. article 19(c) of the UIDHR; article 6(b) of Cairo Declaration; RN nos. 42 and 46; LE no. 19; Ejumudo (2013); and Fapohunda (2014).

[469] For example, the Book of Proverbs (13:24) says: "[h]e who spares the rod hates his son, but he who loves him is diligent to discipline him." See also Prov. 22:15; 23:13–14. Section 2166 of the Zamfara State Sharia Penal Code recognises that parents, guardians, and schoolteachers may chastise their children, wards, pupils and servants reasonably (see also Peters & Barends, 2001). In traditional society, members of the extended family are allowed to discipline a child (Egede, 2007).

[470] For instance, the 1983 Catholic Code of Canon Law (Canon 97 para. 1) regards every person under the age of 18 as a child.

issues, we examined the legal, social and religious dimensions. We believe that these three aspects are important to fully understand human rights practices in the Nigerian context. We typically start by identifying the extent to which these human rights issues have been codified in the relevant national legal instruments. Each time we try to comment on the degree of conformity of the provisions of certain national legal instruments with generally accepted human rights standards. Next, we try to show what is going on in everyday interactions between Nigerians regarding these rights. We then conclude the exposé on each topic by presenting the fundamental teachings of various religious traditions, particularly the leading religions in Nigeria. With this three-pronged approach, we wanted to see the status of the selected rights in Nigeria, the level of compliance with these rights by Nigerians, including the government, and the positions of the ATR, Islam and Christianity on these rights. Regarding the positions of religions, we wanted to know whether there are notable similarities between their teachings on human rights and the exercise of those same rights among the Nigerian population.

We did this for each of the above rights and saw that, for instance, freedom of religion is guaranteed in the Nigerian Constitution. The latter also prohibits the adoption of state religion. From a practical point of view, however, we observed that there tends to be a rivalry between the country's leading religions, Islam and the Christian religion, which bears on issues of national importance such as politics, education, national culture, etc. We postulated that this is due, among other things, to their historical context in the country and often resulted in multiple cases of violations of this right. Regarding freedom from discrimination against homosexuals, we observed that this right is barely respected in the country and that the violation is systemic. Nigerian law criminalises all forms of same-sex behaviour and relationships. The country's position has strong support from both the Nigerian public and the religious groups under study. The same applies to the right to life issues of the death penalty, abortion and euthanasia. The right to life is guaranteed in Nigerian law. It is not an absolute right, as in many other countries. But unlike most countries, Nigeria has a mandatory principle of the death penalty and very restrictive abortion and euthanasia laws. While the former has varying degrees of support among the country's public and religious groups, the country's position on the latter two issues enjoys the vociferous support of most Nigerians and religious adherents in Nigeria. Political rights feature prominently in the Constitution and other laws of the federation. Here, too, the popular stance on thematic issues such as voting, protest and refugee law and the theological perspectives of the Islamic and Christian religions on the same topics tend to coincide. This is even truer for the judicial right to a fair trial, which is also one of the constitutionally recognised fundamental human rights in Nigeria. Socio-economic rights, in contrast, are not recognised as rights in Nigeria; they are non-justiciable provisions of the Constitution. However, some aspects of socio-economic rights, such as labour rights, gender discrimination in employment, child protection and social security are somehow protected by means of supplementary enactments in the country. The concerned statutes are in most cases consistent with universal standards, but again the public attitude towards these socio-economic human rights issues tends to align more with the teachings of the leading religious traditions in the country. These observations are all mere assumptions that require further explanation—and in our case empirical explanation.

In the next chapter, we present some of the theoretical frameworks on which our assumptions are based.

References

A. Books and Journals

Abdulraheem-Mustapha, M. A. (2016). Child justice administration in the Nigerian Child Rights Act: Lessons from South Africa. *African Human Rights Law Journal, 16*, 435–457.

Abolade, S. B., & Oyelade, A. F. (2018). Historical development of private secondary school education in Nigeria: 1859-present. *E-Journal of Education Policy*, 1–8.

Aborisade, F. (2012). *May day: Why the right to protest should be sacred*. Commonwealth Advisory Bureau.

Achebe, C. (1958). *Things Fall Apart*. Heinemann.

Adebanjo, A. T. (2015). Culture, morality and the Law: Nigeria's anti-gay law in perspective. *International Journal of Discrimination and the Law, 15*(4), 256–270.

Adeejat-Kubra, A. K. (2013). Towards the evolution of legal and institutional framework for the protection of internally displaced persons (IDPs) in Nigeria. *OIDA International Journal of Sustainable Development, 6*(5), 141–154.

Adejuwon, E. A. (2020). Homosexuality: An African Christian ethical perspective. *International Journal of Innovative Social Sciences and Humanities Research, 8*(1), 159–168.

Adewumi, F., & Adenugba, A. (2010). *The state of workers' rights in Nigeria: An examination of the banking, oil and gas and telecommunication sectors*. Friedrich-Ebert-Stiftung.

Adeyemi, A. A. (2007). A demand-side perspective on legal aid: What services do people need? The Nigerian situation. In K. Shaw & E. Walter (Eds.), *Access to Justice in Africa and beyond: Making the Rule of Law a reality* (pp. 117–127). Northwestern University School of Law.

Adimekwe, M., & Ziebertz, H.-G. (2018). Attitudes towards Freedom of Religion among Nigerian Students. In H.-G. Ziebertz & C. Sterkens (Eds.), *Religion and Civil human rights in empirical perspectives* (pp. 177–214). Springer.

Ahmadi, S. (2012). Islam and homosexuality: Religious Dogma, Colonial Rule, and the Quest for Belonging. *Journal of Civil Rights and Economic Development, 26*(3/2), 537–563.

Ahmed, D., & Bulmer, E. (2017). *Social and economic rights* (2nd ed.). International Institute for Democracy and Electoral Assistance.

Aina-Pelemo, A. D., Mehanathan, M. C., & Kulshrestha, P. (2018). Sexual harassment at workplace: Judicial impact in Nigeria and India. *Indian Journal of Law and Human Behavior, 4*(2), 208–221.

Akinwumi, O. S. (2009). Legal impediments on the practical implementation of the Child Right Act 2003. *International Journal of Legal Information, 37*(3), 385–396.

Akpambang, E. M. (2016). Fair hearing: Sine Qua Non under Nigerian Criminal justice jurisprudence. *Journal of Law, Policy and Globalization, 52*, 34–44.

Al 'Alwani, T. J. (1994). The rights of the accused in Islam. *American Journal of Islam and Society, 11*(3), 348–364.

Alipour, M. (2017). Essentialism and Islamic theology of homosexuality: A critical reflection on an essentialist epistemology toward same-sex desires and acts in Islam. *Journal of Homosexuality, 64*(14), 1930–1942.

Altonji, J. G., & Blank, R. M. (1999). Race and gender in the labor market. In O. Ashenfelter & D. Card (Eds.), *The handbook of labor economics* (Vol. 3, pp. 3143–3259). Elsevier Science Press.

Amah, E. I. (2017). Nigeria – The search for Autochthonous constitution. *Beijing Law Review, 8*, 141–158.

Amusan, L., Saka, L., & Adekeye, M. O. (2019). Gay rights and the politics of anti-homosexual legislation in Africa: Insights from Uganda and Nigeria. *Journal of African Union Studies, 8*(2), 45–66.

Ananyev, M., & Poyker, M. (2020). *Christian missions and anti-gay attitudes in Africa*. University of Nottingham.

Anifalaje, K. (2017). Implementation of the right to social security in Nigeria. *African Human Rights Law Journal, 17*, 413–435.

An-Nawawi, Y. b. S. (1999). *The Forty Ḥadīth of Al-Imām An-Nawawi: Text with explanatory notes*. Abul-Qasim Publishing House.

Anthony, F. V., & Sterkens, C. (2019). Religion and the right to (dispose of) life: A study of the attitude of Christian, Muslim and Hindu students in India concerning death penalty, Euthanasia and Abortion. In H.-G. Ziebertz & F. Zaccaria (Eds.), *Euthanasia, abortion, death penalty and religion – The right to life and its limitations* (pp. 13–64). Springer.

Anwo, J. O., & Arowolo, G. A. (2011). Critical analysis of abolition of death penalty in international law: An analysis of death penalty under the United States and Nigerian Laws. *Journal of International Law and Jurisprudence, 2*, 247–256.

Anyalebechi, L. (2016). The issue of gender inequality in Nigeria. *Journal of Policy and Development Studies, 10*(2), 63–71.

Ardelean, B.-O. (2010). The Bible and religious freedom. *Evangelical Journal of Theology, 4*(2), 181–194.

Asue, D. U., & Kajo, D. (2018). Pedagogy of Christian religious education in Nigerian Schools. *Journal of Education and Practice, 9*(8), 37–49.

Atere, A. A., Ayodele, J. O., & Omololu, O. (2012). Abortion and challenges of teenage pregnancy in Lagos, Nigeria. *International Journal of Scientific and Engineering Research, 3*(4), 1–10.

Augustin. (n.d.). Epistle CLXXXV. Translated by J. R. King. In P. Schaff (Ed.) (1887). *Nicene and Post-Nicene Fathers*. (Vol. 4, pp. 633–651). Christian Literature Co.

Ayanleye, O. A. (2013). Women and reproductive health rights in Nigeria. *OIDA International Journal of Sustainable Development, 6*(5), 127–140.

Badejogbin, O. (2018). Onuoha Kalu v. The State and Flaws in Nigeria's Death Penalty Jurisprudence. *African Human Rights Law Journal, 18*, 551–578.

Badru, F. A. (2017). *Social Welfare Administration in Nigeria*. National Open University of Nigeria.

Bamgbose, O. J. (2014). *Digest of Judgments of the Supreme Court of Nigeria* (Vol. 3 & 4). Safari Books Ltd.

Baum, R. M. (1995). *Homosexuality in the traditional religions of the Americas and Africa*. Trinity Press.

Becker, G. S. (1994). *Human capital: A theoretical and empirical analysis with special reference to education* (3rd ed.). University of Chicago Press.

Benisheikh, B.I.S, Ghide, H. B., & Dunoma, Y. A. (2016). Gender discrimination in employment: An analysis of issues of violation of women's rights. *Uni-Maid Journal of Private and Property Law, 1*(1), 21–37.

Beyers, J. (2010). What is religion? An African Understanding. *HTS Theological Studies, 66*(1), 1–8. https://doi.org/10.4102/hts.v66i1.341

Bobbert, M. (2017). Religious education towards justice: What kind of justice is to be taught in a Christian context? *Educational Sciences, 7*(30), 1–16.

Busse, R., Blümel, M., Knieps, F., & Bärnighausen, T. (2017). Statutory health insurance in Germany: A health system shaped by 135 years of solidarity, self-governance, and competition. *Lancet, 390*, 882–897.

Calvin, J. (1536). *Institutes of the Christian Religion* (H. Beveridge (1845), Trans.). Christian Classics Ethereal Library.
Carvajal, E. T. (2013). The political rights of Mexican migrants: Nationality and citizenship in Mexico. *Mexican Law Review, 6*(1), 177–198.
Censer, J. R., & Hunt, L. (2001). *Liberty, equality, fraternity: Exploring the French Revolution*. Pennsylvania State University Press.
Chijioke, E. (2020). The right to freedom of movement in Nigeria. *Auxano Law Journal, 1*(5), 80–108.
Clemen, O. (Ed.). (1967). *Luthers Werke in Auswahl, II*. de Gruyter.
Cooper, R., & Kit Dorey, K. (2016). *Christian role models for LGBT equality*. Stonewall.
Dada, J. A. (2012). Human rights under the Nigerian constitution: Issues and problems. *International Journal of Humanities and Social Science, 2*(12), 33–43.
Dada, J. A., & Ibanga, M. E. (2011). Human rights protection in Nigeria: From Rhetoric to Pragmatic Agenda. *African Journal of Law and Criminology, 1*(2), 70–81.
Dalgleish, D. (2005). Pre-colonial criminal justice in West Africa: Eurocentric thought versus africentric evidence. *African Journal of Criminology and Justice Studies, 1*(1), 55–69.
Davis, D. M. (2012). Socio-economic rights. In M. Rosenfeld & A. Sajó (Eds.), *The Oxford Handbook of Comparative Constitutional Law* (pp. 1020–1035). University Press.
De Gruchy, J. W. (1997). Christianity and democracy: Understanding their relationship. *Scriptura, 62*, 323–333.
De Waal, E., Mestry, R., & Russo, C. J. (2011). Religious and cultural dress at School: A comparative perspective. *Potchefstroom Electronic Law Journal, 14*(6), 62–95.
Della Porta, D., & Diani, M. (2006). *Social movements: An introduction*. Blackwell.
Diehl, C., Koenig, M., & Ruckdeschel, K. (2009). Religiosity and gender equality: Comparing natives and Muslim migrants in Germany. *Ethnic and Racial Studies, 32*(2), 278–301.
Donald, A., & Howard, E. (2015). *The right to freedom of religion or belief and its intersection with other rights* (A research paper for ILGA-Europe). Middlesex University.
Dulles, A. (2001). Catholicism and capital punishment. *A Monthly Journal of Religion and Public Life, 121*, 30–35.
Egede, E. (2007). Bringing human rights home: An examination of the domestication of human rights treaties in Nigeria. *Journal of African Law, 51*(2), 249–284.
Ejumudo, K. B. O. (2013). Gender equality and women empowerment in Nigeria: The desirability and inevitability of a pragmatic approach. *Developing Country Studies, 3*(4), 59–66.
Ekhator, E. O. (2019). Protection and promotion of women's rights in Nigeria: Constraints and prospects. In M. Addaney (Ed.), *Women and Minority Rights Law* (pp. 17–36). Eleven International Publishing.
Ekpe, C. P. (1983). Social welfare and family support: The Nigerian experience. *Journal of Sociology and Social Welfare, 10*(3/11), 484–496.
Ekundayo, L. O. (2013). Jurist-biblical perspective of Jesus' and Saro-Wiwa's trials: The challenges of human rights violations in Niger Delta, Nigeria. In D. J. Plevak (Ed.), *Human rights: Theory, developments and ethical issues* (pp. 47–57). Nova Science Publishers.
Elias, T. O. (1956). *The nature of African Customary Law*. Manchester University Press.
Eller, J. D. (2017). Varieties of secular experience. In P. Zuckerman & J. R. Shook (Eds.), *The Oxford handbook of secularism* (pp. 499–514). Oxford University Press.
Epprecht, M. (2004). *Hungochani: The history of a dissident sexuality in Southern Africa*. McGill-Queen's University Press.
Etuk, U. (2002). *Religion and cultural identity*. Hope Publications.
Evans, C. (2008). Religious education in Public Schools: An international human rights perspective. *Human Rights Law Review, 8*(3), 449–473.
Eze, E. O. (2005). *Religion and state in Nigeria*. Available at: http://iheu.org/ReligionandStatein Nigeria_InternationalHumanistandEthicalUnion.htm. Accessed 2 Nov 2015.
Fabunmi, M. (2005). Historical analysis of educational policy formulation in Nigeria: Implications for educational planning and policy. *International Journal of African and African American Studies, 4*(2), 1–7.

Fafunwa, A. B. (2004). *History of education in Nigeria*. NPC Educational Publishers Ltd.

Falade, D. A. (2016). Problems and prospects of teaching religion and national values in the Nigeria Upper Basic School. *Nigerian Journal of Social Studies, 29*(2), 41–49.

Fapohunda, T. M. (2013). The gender pay gap in Nigeria: causes and remedies. *Mediterranean Journal of Social Sciences, 4*(2), 211–220.

Fapohunda, T. M. (2014). Gender differences in perceptions and experiences of sexual harassment in the workplace. *Global Journal of Management and Business, 1*(2), 35–44.

Fierro, C. N., Morales, I., & Gratschew, M. (2007). *External voting: A comparative overview* (pp. 11–34). Trydells Tryckeri AB.

Francis, L. J., Robbins, M., & McKenna, U. (2016). Women's socio-economic rights and religion among Christian, Islamic and non-religiously affiliated students in England and Wales. In H.-G. Ziebertz & E. H. Ballin (Eds.), *Freedom of religion in the 21st century. A Human rights perspective on the relation between politics and religion* (pp. 239–256). Brill.

Francis, L. J., McKenna, U., & Sahin, A. (2019). Religion, human rights and matters of life and death: Exploring attitude toward abortion and Euthanasia among adolescents in England and Wales. In H.-G. Ziebertz & F. Zaccaria (Eds.), *Euthanasia, abortion, death penalty and religion – The right to life and its limitations* (pp. 139–160). Springer.

Fumbo, C., Adimekwe, M. C., & Ziebertz, H.-G. (2020). Right to education in Tanzania and Nigeria: A comparative study. In H.-G. Ziebertz (Ed.), *International empirical studies on religion and socio-economic human rights* (pp. 193–233). Springer.

Gates, G. (2011). *How many people are lesbian, gay, bisexual, and transgender?* The Williams Institute of the University of California.

Gathogo, J. M. (2013). Some expressions of African hospitality today. *Scriptura, 99*, 275–287.

Gatrell, P. (2014). Refugees. In U. Daniel, P. Gatrell, O. Janz, H. Jones, J. Keene, A. Kramer, & B. Nasson (Eds.), *Online Encyclopedia of the First World War 1914–1918*. Freie Universität Berlin.

Ghaziani, A., Taylor, V., & Stone, A. (2016). Cycles of sameness and difference in LGBT social movements. *The Annual Review of Sociology, 42*, 165–183.

Goetz, N. H. (2001). *Humanitarian issues in the Biafra conflict* (New Issues in Refugee Research, Working Paper No. 36). Pepperdine University School of Public Policy.

Greenberg, D. F., & West, V. (2008). Siting the death penalty internationally. *Law and Social Inquiry, 33*(2), 295–343.

Haneef, S. S. S., Razak, M. A. A., & Laluddin, H. (2019). Shariah criminal mode of adjudication: Distinctive features vis-à-vis modern systems. *Journal of Education and Social Sciences, 13*(1), 129–137.

Hastings, A. (1991). *Church and State: The English experience*. University of Exeter Press.

Hendricks, M. (2010). Islamic texts: A source for acceptance of Queer individuals into mainstream Muslim society. *The Equal Rights Review, 5*, 31–51.

Hill, M. (2020). An introduction. In M. Hill, N. Doe, R. H. Helmholz, & J. Witte Jr. (Eds.), *Christianity and criminal law*. Routledge.

Hocking, B. A., & Manville, L. L. (2001). What of the right to silence: Still supporting the presumption of innocence, or a growing legal fiction? *Macquarie Law Journal, 1*(1), 63–92.

Huber, S. (2008). Aufbau und strukturierende Prinzipien des Religionsmonitors. In: Bertelsmann-Stiftung (Hrsg.), *Religionsmonitor 2008* (pp. 21–31). Gütersloher Verlagshaus.

Ibe, S. (2010). Implementing economic, social and cultural rights in Nigeria: Challenges and opportunities. *African Human Rights Law Journal, 10*, 197–211.

Ibrahim, A. R. (2008). Euthanasia in the light of Islamic Law and ethics. *Journal of the Nigeria Association of Teachers of Arabic and Islamic Studies, 11*, 1–12.

Idem, U. J. (2018). Administration of criminal justice and the relevancy of judges' rules and police interrogation in Nigeria. *International Journal of Recent Research in Social Sciences and Humanities, 5*(1), 49–58.

Iguh, N. A., & Nosike, O. (2011). An examination of the child rights protection and corporal punishment in Nigeria. *Nnamdi Azikiwe University Journal of International Law and Jurisprudence, 2*, 97–111.

Igwe, L. (2008). Africa and gay rights. In A. Moreau et al. (Eds.), *Theorizing (Homo)Eroticism in Africa. outliers: A collection of essays and creative works on sexuality in Africa* (Vol. 1(1), pp. 46–49). IRN-Africa.

Ikeke, M. O. (2013). The Forest in African traditional thought and practice: An ecophilosophical discourse. *Open Journal of Philosophy, 3*(2), 345–350.

Ilkilic, I. (2008). Medizinethische Entscheidungen am Lebensende in einer wertpluralen Gesellschaft am Beispiel muslimischer Patienten. *Zeitschrift für Evangelische Ethik, 52*(1), Seiten 34–49.

Ilobinso, L.-K. O. (2007). *Policy on abortion in the Nigerian Society: Ethical Considerations.* M.A. thesis, Linkopings Universitet, Sweden.

Ismail, S. Z., & Mat, M. Z. A. (2016). Faith and freedom: The Qur'anic notion of freedom of religion vs. the act of changing religion and thoughts on the implications for Malaysia. *Religions, 7*(88), 1–18.

Issa, M. R. (2016). Natural justice in Islam and Humans Law. *Journal of Philosophy, Culture and Religion, 15*, 5–10.

Izugbara, C. O. (2004). *Patriarchal ideology and discourses of sexuality in Nigeria* (Understanding Human Sexuality Seminar Series, 2). Africa Regional Sexuality Resource Centre.

Izunwa, M. O., & Ifemeje, S. (2011). Right to life and abortion debate in Nigeria: A case for the legislation of the principle of double-effect. *Journal of International Law and Jurisprudence, 2*, 111–128.

James, S. (2020). Biblical Christianity promotes religious freedom. *Affinity Social Issues Bulletin,* 1–5.

Kana, A. A., Rilwanu, S. M., & Yusuf, A. M. (2017). The principle of Double Jeopardy versus the principle of condonation: Revisiting the Supreme Court's decision in Nigerian Army v. Aminun Kano. *Nnamdi Azikiwe University Journal of International Law and Jurisprudence, 8*(1), 118–127.

Khan, M. A. M. (2019). *Islam and good governance: A political philosophy of Ihsan* (1st ed.). Palgrave Macmillan. https://doi.org/10.1057/978-1-137-54832-0

King, J. (2003). *An activist's manual on the international covenant on economic, social and cultural rights.* Law and Society Trust.

Kirmani, N., Khan, A. A., & Palmer, V. (2008). Does faith matter: An examination of Islamic relief's work with refugees and internally displaced persons. *Refugee Survey Quarterly, 27*(2), 41–50.

Kligerman, N. (2007). Homosexuality in Islam: A difficult paradox. *Macalester Islam Journal, 2*(3/8), 52–64.

Kutigi, H. D. (2017). Towards justiciability of economic, social, and cultural rights in Nigeria: A role for Canadian-Nigerian cooperation? *The Transnational Human Rights Review, 4*, 125–145.

Lewis, P., & Bratton, M. (2000). *Attitudes towards democracy and markets in Nigeria: Report of a national opinion survey 2000.* International Foundation for Election Systems and Management Systems International.

Little, D., & Taliaferro, K. (2014). *Christianity and religious freedom: A sourcebook of scriptural, theological, and legal texts.* Religious Freedom Project.

Lucius Lactantius. (n.d.). Divine Institutes (W. Fletcher, Trans.). In A. Roberts, J. Donaldson, & A. C. Coxe (Eds.) (1886). *Ante-Nicene Fathers* (Vol. 7, pp. 9–328). Christian Literature Co.

Magesa, L. (2002). *African religion: The moral traditions of abundant life*. Orbis Books.

Makama, G. A. (2013). Patriarchy and gender inequality in Nigeria: The way forward. *European Scientific Journal, 9*(17), 115–144.

Maluleke, T. S. (2001). Identity and integrity in African theology: A critical analysis. *Religion and Theology, 8*(1), 26–39.

Martin, S. L. (1997). The role of homosexuality in classical Islam. *Chancellor's Honors Program Projects*, 1–32.
Mbiti, J. S. (1969). *African religions and philosophy*. Heinemann Educational Publishers.
Mbiti, J. S. (1989). *African religions and philosophy*. Heinemann Educational Publishers.
Mbiti, J. S. (1990). *African religions and philosophy*. Heinemann Educational Publishers.
Mbiti, J. S. (1999). *African religions and philosophy*. Heinemann Educational Publishers.
McGoldrick, D. (2006). *Human rights and religion: The Islamic Headscarf debate in Europe*. Hart Publishing.
Mendie, A. (2014). Status and limit of human rights: Right to life under Nigerian Constitution, 1999 with focus on rural women in Akwa Ibom State. *Mediterranean Journal of Social Sciences, 5*(26), 154–160.
Miller, L. E., Martini, J., Larrabee, F. S., Rabasa, A., Pezard, S., Taylor, J. E., & Mengistu, T. (2012). *Democratization in the Arab World: Prospects and lessons from around the globe*. National Defense Research Institute.
Moe, C., Masud, M. K., Vogt, K., & Larsen, L. (Eds.). (2021). *Religion without compulsion: Knowledge to challenge Blasphemy and Apostasy Laws*. 07 Media AS.
Msibi, T. (2011). The lies we have been told: On (Homo) sexuality in Africa. *Africa Today, 58*(1), 55–77.
Muehlhof, I. (2000). Freedom of religion in public schools in Germany and in the United States. *Journal of International and Comparative Law, 28*(405), 405–492.
Munir, M. (2011). Refugee Law in Islam. *Journal of Social Sciences, 4*(2), 1–18.
Murray, R. (2019). *The African Charter on human and peoples' rights: A commentary*. Oxford University Press.
Murray, S., & Will, R. (Eds.). (1998). *Boy-wives and female husbands: Studies of African homosexualities*. Macmillan.
Muslih, M., & Browers, M. (2009). Democracy. In J. L. Esposito (Ed.), *The Oxford Encyclopedia of the Islamic World*. Oxford University Press.
Mustapha, I. A. (2010). Right of accused person to remain silent: A critical analysis. *Confluence Journal of Jurisprudence and International Law, 3*(1), 1–24.
wa Mutua, M. (1999). Limitations on religious rights: Problematizing religious freedom in the African context. *Buffalo Human Rights Law Review, 5*(2), 75–105.
Myers, J. E. B. (2008). A short history of child protection in America. *Family Law Quarterly, 42*(3), 449–463.
Nadel, S. F. (1954). *Nupe Religion*. The Free Press.
Nhlapo, T. (2017). Homicide in traditional African societies: Customary Law and the question of accountability. *African Human Rights Law Journal, 17*(1), 1–34.
Nigeria. (2004). *UN Convention on the Rights of the Child (CRC): Second country periodic report*. Federal Ministry of Women Affairs.
Nkosi, S., & Masson, F. (2017). Christianity and homosexuality: Contradictory or complementary? A qualitative study of the experiences of Christian Homosexual University students. *South African Journal of Higher Education, 31*(4), 72–93.
Nwafor, A. O. (2010a). Comparative perspectives on Euthanasia in Nigeria and Ethiopia. *African Journal of International and Comparative Law, 18*(2), 170–191.
Nwafor, F. C. (2010b). The viability of the social security system in Nigeria: An economic perspective. In E. C. Eboh & S. Oluwadare (Eds.), *Towards a sustainable social security in Nigeria* (pp. 10–19). Institute for Applied Economics.
Nwauche, E. S. (2008). Law, religion and human rights in Nigeria. *African Human Rights Law Journal, 8*, 568–595.
Nweke, N. N. (2014). *Gender wage differences: The case of Nigeria*. M.Sc. thesis, Swansea University, Swansea.
Nwoko, K. C. (2012). Female husbands in Igbo Land: Southeast Nigeria. *The Journal of Pan African Studies, 5*(1), 69–82.

Nzeribe, E., & Abangwu, A. (2013). Death penalty in Nigeria: To be or not to be: The controversy continues. *Arabian Journal of Business and Management Review, 3*(3), 23–33.
Nzimiro, I. (1972). *Studies in Ibo political systems: Chieftaincy and politics in four Niger States*. University of California Press.
O'Sullivan, D. (2001). The death sentence for Mahmoud Muhammad Taha: Misuse of the Sudanese Legal System and Islamic Shari'a law? *International Journal of Human Rights, 5*(3), 45–70.
Oba, A. A. (2009). The Hijab in educational institutions and human rights: Perspectives from Nigeria and Beyond. *Identity, Culture and Politics: An Afro-Asian Dialogue, 10*, 51–74.
Obi, M. C. (2014). A critical appraisal of Euthanasia under Nigerian Laws. *Nnamdi Azikiwe University Journal of International Law and Jurisprudence*, 75–88.
Odeku, K., & Animashaun, S. (2012). Ensuring equality at the workplace by strengthening the law on prohibition against discrimination. *African Journal of Business Management, 6*(12), 4689–4699.
Odeleye, D. A., Oyelami, O., & Abike, O. O. (2012). Private ownership and educational management in Nigeria: Issues and challenges. *Journal of Research in National Development, 10*(2), 223–229.
Oduwole, T. A., & Fadeyi, A. O. (2013). Issues of refugees and displaced persons in Nigeria. *Journal of Sociological Research, 4*(1), 1–18.
Oginni, B. Y., & Adesanya, A. S. (2013). The workers' rights in Nigeria: Myth or reality? *International Journal of Business and Management Invention, 2*(1), 100–104.
Ogunnoiki, K. (2020). Right to silence: The perception of Nigeria Courts. *International Journal of Comparative Law and Legal Philosophy, 2*(3), 117–183.
Ojo, E. O. (2006). Human rights and sustainable democracy in Nigeria (1999–2003). *Journal of Social Science, 13*(1), 15–29.
Ok, Ü., & Eren, S. (2013). Attitudes towards human rights and religiosity: A case of Turkish Adolescents. In J. A. van der Ven & H.-G. Ziebertz (Eds.), *Human rights and the impact of religion* (pp. 145–162). Brill.
Okafọ, N. (2006). Relevance of African traditional jurisprudence on control, justice, and law: A critique of the Igbo experience. *African Journal of Criminology and Justice Studies, 2*(1), 36–62.
Okeke, G. N., & Eze, G. E. (2013). The Ambivalence of the 1999 Nigerian constitution in matters relating to Secularism: A case for a constitutional review. *International Journal of Humanities and Social Science Invention, 2*(3), 65–69.
Okene, O. V. C., & Okpara, G. A. (2007). Freedom of association and the protection of trade union rights in Africa – Nigeria as a case study. *Recht in Afrika*, 175–197.
Okonofua, F. (2015). Is abortion incidence rising in Nigeria? *African Journal of Reproductive Health, 19*(4), 9–13.
Okorie, P. C., & Abayomi, O. A. (2019). Abortion Laws in Nigeria: A case for reform. *Annual Survey of International and Comparative Law, 23*(1/7), 165–192.
Okpanachi, E. (2012). *Ethno-religious identity and conflict in Northern Nigeria: Understanding the dynamics of Sharia in Kaduna and Kebbi States*. French Institute for Research in Africa.
Oladunjoye, P., & Nanighe, B. M. (2015). Prayer in Schools: Legal and administrative perspectives in Nigeria. *British Journal of Education, 3*(12), 1–8.
Olaide, G., & Aderibigbe, T. O. (2014). Justification of women's right of access to safe and legal abortion in Nigeria. *African Journal of Legal Studies, 7*, 177–202.
Olasunkanmi, A. (2016). Interrogating capital punishment and indigenous Yoruba African culture. *International Journal of History and Philosophical Research, 4*(2), 23–29.
Olikenyi, G. (2001). *African hospitality: A model for the communication of the Gospel in the African cultural context*. Steyler Verlag.
Oltmer, J. (2016). Germany and global refugees: A history of the present. *CESifo DICE Report, 14*(4), 26–31.
Onoja, E. O. (2013). The relationship between the constitutional right to silence and confessions in Nigeria. *African Journal of Legal Studies, 6*(2-3), 189–211.

Onwe, S. O. (2014). Championing the campaign against child abuse in Nigeria: A call to save the needy. *International Journal of Humanities and Social Science, 4*(10/1), 279–286.
Onwubiko, K. B. C. (1967). *History of West Africa A.D. 1000–1800*. Africana-FEP Publishers.
Onwubiko, K. B. C. (1973). *History of West Africa (Book Two), 1800 – Present Day*. Africana Educational Publishers.
Onyemelukwe, C. (2018). Medico-legal abortion law in Nigeria. *The Bey Health Quarterly, 2*, 34–38.
Onyeonoru, I. P., Eghareuba, M. E., & Imhonopi, D. (2013). Social policy and the retrenchment of the welfare state in Nigeria: The old and new pension schemes and lessons from the Nordic Model. *Journal of Developing Country Studies, 3*(10), 31–39.
Opoku, K. A. (1993). African traditional religion: An enduring heritage. In J. K. Olupona & S. S. Nyang (Eds.), *Religious plurality in Africa: Essays in Honour of John S. Mbiti* (pp. 67–82). Mouton de Gruyter.
Orji, K. E., & N-Ue, U. S. (2013). Nigerian Civil War and Refugee Crisis: The fate of the minorities in the former Eastern Region. *IOSR Journal of Humanities and Social Science, 16*(2), 45–57.
Osaghae, E., & Suberu, T. (2005). *A history of identities, violence, and stability in Nigeria*. University of Oxford.
Ostien, P. (Ed.). (2007). *Sharia Implementation in Northern Nigeria 1999–2006: A sourcebook* (Vol. 4(5),, pp. 171–203). Spectrum Books Ltd.
Oye-Adeniran, B. A., Long, C. M., & Adewole, I. F. (2004). Advocacy for Reform of the Abortion Law in Nigeria. *Reproductive Health Matters, 12*(24), 209–217.
Paden, J. (2007). *Comments at the symposium on religious conflict religious conflict in Nigeria: Contemporary religious dynamics in Nigeria* (Vol. 2). Council on Foreign Relations.
Pelikan, J. (1958). *Luther's works*. Concordia Publishing House.
Peters, R., & Barends, M. (2001). *The reintroduction of Islamic Criminal Law in Northern Nigeria*. European Commission.
Popkin, J. (2006). *A history of modern France*. Pearson Education.
Rai, R. K. (2011). *History of Child Rights and Child Labour*. National Coalition for Education.
Regan, R. J. (Ed.). (2003). *Aquinas, a summary of philosophy*. Hackett Publishing Company.
Rehman, J., & Polymenopoulou, E. (2013). Is Green a Part of the Rainbow? Sharia, homosexuality and LGBT rights in the Muslim world. *Fordham International Law Journal, 37*(1/7), 1–52.
Richardson, C. C. (1953). *Early Christian Father*. Westminster Press.
Saeed, A., Anderson, M., & Taliaferro, K. (2014). *Islam and religious freedom: A sourcebook of scriptural, theological, and legal texts*. Religious Freedom Project.
Sakali, F. (2013). The contemporary Euthanasia debate in the light of African worldview and ethics. *SEGi Review, 6*, 5–15.
Salihu, S. I. (2017). Right to refuse medical treatment: A Case Review of Medical and Dental Practitioners Disciplinary Tribunal v. Okonkwo. *Uni-Maid Journal of Private and Property Law, 2*.
Sambo, A. O. (2018). Right of politically exposed persons to Fair Trial in Nigerian Courts: Piecing through the constitutional and Islamic perspectives. *Uni-Maid Journal of Public Law, 5*(2), 292–314.
Sampson, I. T. (2012). Religious violence in Nigeria: Causal diagnoses and strategic recommendations to the state and religious communities. *African Journal on Conflict Resolution, 12*(1), 103–134.
Sani, I. S., Yuhanif, Y., & Rohizan, H. (2017). Legal application of the offence of murder and Euthanasia in Nigeria. *Universiti Utara Malaysia Journal of Legal Studies, 8*, 113–132.
Scherrer, C., & Greven, T. (2001). *Global rules for trade. Codes of conduct, social labeling, workers' rights clauses*. Westfalisches Dampfboot.
Shadid, W. A. R., & van Koningsveld, P. S. (1991). Institutionalization and integration of Islam in The Netherlands. In W. A. R. Shadid & P. S. van Koningsveld (Eds.), *The integration of Islam and Hinduism in Western Europe*. Kok Pharos Publishing House.

Singh, S., Remez, L., Sedgh, G., Kwok, L., & Onda, T. (2018). *Abortion worldwide 2017: Uneven progress and unequal access*. Guttmacher Institute.
Statham, P. (2016). How ordinary people view Muslim group rights in Britain, The Netherlands, France and Germany: Significant 'Gaps' between majorities and Muslims? *Journal of Ethnic and Migration Studies, 42*(2), 217–236.
Sterkens, C., & Ziebertz, H.-G. (2018). Introduction. In C. Sterkens & H.-G. Ziebertz (Eds.), *Political and judicial rights through the prism of religious beliefs* (pp. v–xi). Springer.
Strabac, Z., Aalberg, T., Jenssen, T. A., & Valenta, M. (2016). Wearing the Veil: Hijab, Islam and job qualifications as determinants of social attitudes towards immigrant women in Norway. *Journal of Ethnic and Racial Studies, 39*(15), 2665–2682.
Sumbulah, U. (2018). Freedom of religion in Qur'anic perspectives: The inclusive interpretations of contemporary Muslim scholars. *Advances in Social Science, Education and Humanities Research, 137*, 60–70.
Tajudeen, O. I. (2015). Legal framework for the protection of child rights in Nigeria. *AGORA International Journal of Juridical Sciences, 3*, 46–52.
Thorpe, S. A. (1992). *Primal religions worldwide: An introductory descriptive review*. University of South Africa.
Tolulope, A. A. (2019). The wearing of Hijab in public educational institutions in Nigeria: A call for alternative dispute resolution. In M. C. Green (Ed.), *Law, religion and human flourishing in Africa* (pp. 63–76). Conference-RAP.
Turaki, Y. (1999). *Christianity and African Gods: A method in theology*. Potchefstroom University for Christian Higher Education.
Ubajaka, C. F., Adogu, P. O. U., Ilika, C., & Ilika, A. L. (2014). Perception of abortion and abortion laws by Lawyers in Anambra State Nigeria. *International Journal of Clinical Medicine, 5*, 695–703.
Ugochukwu, B. (2012). Ballot or bullet: Protecting the right to vote in Nigeria. *African Human Rights Law Journal, 12*, 539–563.
UN Department of Economic and Social Affairs (UNDESA) Population Division. (2019). *World population prospects 2019 – Special aggregates*. Available at: https://population.un.org/wpp/Download/SpecialAggregates/EconomicTrading/. Accessed 2 Mar 2020.
Usman, A. Y. (2015). Social security as a veritable tool for achieving millennium development goals. *Research on Humanities and Social Sciences, 5*(3), 50–53.
Uzoma, R. C. (2004). Religious pluralism, cultural differences, and social stability in Nigeria. *Brigham Young University Law Review, 7*(3), 651–664.
Van der Tuin, L. W. J. M., & Fumbo, C. D. (2012). Women rights and religion among Christian and Islamic students in Tanzania. In J. A. van der Ven & H.-G. Ziebertz (Eds.), *Tensions within and between religions and human rights* (pp. 203–222). Brill.
Van der Ven, J. A. (2010). *Human rights or religious rules?* Brill.
Van der Ven, J. A. (2013). Towards a legitimate role of religion in the domain of socio-economic rights. An empirical study among adolescents in North-West European countries. In J. A. van der Ven & H.-G. Ziebertz (Eds.), *Human rights and the impact of religion* (pp. 165–202). Brill.
Van der Ven, J. A. (2016). On the brink of death: Euthanasia from the angle of law, morality and religion: A cross-cultural perspective. In H.-G. Ziebertz & E. H. Ballin (Eds.), *Freedom of religion in the 21st century. A human rights perspective on the relation between politics and religion* (pp. 257–299). Brill.
Vincent, A. (2010). *The politics of human rights*. Oxford University Press.
Voll, J. O. (2007). Islam and democracy: Is modernization a barrier? *Religion Compass, 1*(1), 170–178.
Vontress, C. E. (2005). Animism: Foundation of traditional healing in Sub-Saharan Africa. In R. Moodley & W. West (Eds.), *Integrating traditional healing practices into counseling and psychotherapy* (pp. 124–137). Sage Publications.

Webb, R. J., & Asa'd, F. J. (2019). The right to life: A perspective of young Palestinian Muslims. In H.-G. Ziebertz & F. Zaccaria (Eds.), *Euthanasia, abortion, death penalty and religion – The right to life and its limitations* (pp. 161–186). Springer.

Weissbrodt, D., & Hutchinson, A. (Eds.). (2016). *Study guide: Freedom of religion or belief.* University of Minnesota Human Rights Center.

Wigmore, J. H. (1891). Nemo Tenetur Seipsum Prodere. *Harvard Law Review, 5*(2), 71–88.

Wilken, R. L. (2019). *Liberty in the things of God: The Christian origins of religious freedom.* Yale University Press.

Zaccaria, F., Anthony, F. V., & Sterkens, C. (2018). Religion and civil rights in Italy. An empirical exploration among secondary school students. In H.-G. Ziebertz & C. Sterkens (Eds.), *Religion and civil human rights in empirical perspective* (pp. 91–119). Springer.

Zainol, N. Z. N., Majid, L. A., & Kadir, M. N. A. (2014). Nasr Hamid Abu Zayd as a Modern Muslim thinker. *International Journal of Islamic Thought, 5*, 61–70.

Zaman, A. (2008). *Islamic economics: A survey of the literature* (Working Paper no. 22). University of Birmingham.

Zarifis, I. (2002). Rights of religious minorities in Nigeria. *Human Rights Brief, 10*(1), 22–25.

Zhang, J. (2009). Fair Trial rights in international covenant on civil and political rights. *Journal of Politics and Law, 2*(4), 39–43.

Ziebertz, H.-G. (2016). Freedom of religion as challenge for religion and society. In T.-M. Courau, M. Babić, & J. J. Vila-Chã (Eds.), *Religious freedom* (pp. 87–96). SCM Press.

Ziebertz, H.-G., & Reindl, M. (2013). Religion and attitudes towards Euthanasia and abortion. An empirical study among young Christians and Muslims in Germany. In J. A. van der Ven & H.-G. Ziebertz (Eds.), *Human rights and the impact of religion* (pp. 119–144). Brill.

Ziebertz, H.-G., & Zaccaria, F. (2019). The right to life questioned: Introductory remarks. In H.-G. Ziebertz & F. Zaccaria (Eds.), *Euthanasia, abortion, death penalty and religion – The right to life and its limitations* (pp. 1–12). Springer.

Ziebertz, H.-G., & Ziebertz, C. M. (2016). Labour rights and the impact of human dignity, Religious belief and perception of society. An empirical study among youth in Germany. *Journal of Empirical Theology, 29*(1), 45–77. https://doi.org/10.1163/15709256-12341337

Dailies

Adegbite, K. (2012). Is Nigeria a Secular or Non-Secular State? *The Newjurist*, 28th May 2012. Available at: http://www. newjurist.com/. Accessed 01 Oct 2014.

Ajayi, F. (2001). Religious intolerance: Where is Nigeria heading? A look at the 1988 Constituent Assembly Debate – (Conclusion). *Nigeria World*, 4th October 2001. Available at: https://nigeriaworld.com/columnist/ajayi/100401.html. Accessed 01 Mar 2016.

"Anglicans Face Schism Over Gay Row". *The Guardian Newspaper*, 14th September 2003. Available at: https://www.theguardian.com/uk/2003/sep/14/religion.world. Accessed 1 August 2018.

Chukkol, O. G. (2017). What the Law Says About Use of Hijab in Public Institutions. *News Express*, 23rd December 2017. Available at: https://www.newsexpressngr.com/news/47852-What-the-law-says-about-use-of-Hijab-in-public-institutions. Accessed 12 Feb 2020.

Ejekwonyilo, A. (2021). Group Bemoans Nigeria's 15 million Child Labourers. *Premium Times*, 12th June 2021. Available at: https://www.premiumtimesng.com/news/more-news/467420-group-bemoans-nigerias-15-million-child-labourers.html. Accessed 01 July 2021.

Goitom, H. (2016). Nigeria: Gender Equality Bill Fails in the Senate. *Global Legal Monitor*, 28th March 2016. Available at: https://www.loc.gov/item/global-legal-monitor/2016-03-28/nigeria-gender-equality-bill-fails-in-the-senate/. Accessed 01 Jan 2021.

Oyekola, T. (2020). Public Schools: Kwara, C.A.N. Differ on Conduct of Prayers. *Punch Newspaper*, 19th January 2020. Available at: https://punchng.com/public-schools-kwara-can-differ-on-conduct-of-prayers/. Accessed 12 Feb 2020.

Soji-Eze, F. (2021). Kaduna crisis: FG directs state government to follow principle of redundancy. *Tribune Newspaper*, 21st May 2021. Available at: https://tribuneonlineng.com/labour-crisis-fg-directs-kaduna-state-government-to-follow-principle-of-redundancy/. Accessed 28 May 2021.

Still on Hijab-for-School Controversy. *The Guardian Newspaper*, 7th February 2019. Available at: https://guardian.ng/opinion/still-on-hijab-for-school-controversy/. Accessed 12 Feb 2020.

Policy Documents (Ecclesiastical Documents)

Benedict XVI. (2009). *Caritas in Veritate. Encyclical letter on Integral human development in charity and truth.* Available at: https://www.vatican.va/content/benedict-xvi/en/encyclicals/documents/hf_ben-xvi_enc_20090629_caritas-in-veritate.html. Accessed 01 Feb 2019.

Catechism of the Catholic Church (CCC). (1992). I & II Editions. Libreria Editrice Vaticana.

Catechism of the Catholic Church (CCC). (1997). I & II Editions. Libreria Editrice Vaticana.

CDF. (1974). *Declaration on procured abortion.* Vatican Publishing House.

CDF. (1980). *Declaration on Euthanasia.* Available at. https://www.vatican.va/roman_curia/congregations/cfaith/documents/rc_con_cfaith_doc_19800505_euthanasia_en.html. Accessed 3 May 2018.

CDF. (1987). *Donum Vitae: Instruction on respect for human life in its origin and on the dignity of procreation.* Libreria Editrice Vaticana.

CDF. (2018). *Rescriptum "ex Audentia SS.mi": New Revision of No. 2267 of the CCC on the Death Penalty.* Available at https://press.vatican.va/content/salastampa/en/bollettino/pubblico/2018/08/02/180802a.html. Accessed 01 July 2019.

CDF. (2021). *Responsum to a Dubium regarding the Blessing of the unions of persons of the same sex* (Bollettino No. 210315b). Holy See Press Office.

Francis. (2015). *Laudato Si': Encyclical letter on care for our common home.* Available at: https://www.vatican.va/content/francesco/en/encyclicals/documents/papa-francesco_20150524_enciclica-laudato-si.html. Accessed 01 Feb 2019.

Francis. (2017). *Address to participants in the International Forum on "Migration and Peace", 21st February 2017.* Available at: https://www.vatican.va/content/francesco/en/speeches/2017/february/documents/papa-francesco_20170221_forum-migrazioni-pace.html. Accessed 01 Apr 2017.

Gregory XVI. (1832). *Mirari Vos: Encyclical Letter on Liberalism and Religious Indifferentism.* Available at: https://www.papalencyclicals.net/greg16/g16mirar.htm. Accessed 08 Jan 2019.

John Paul II. (1981). *Laborem Exercens: Encyclical Letter on Human Work.* Available at: https://www.vatican.va/content/john-paul-ii/en/encyclicals/documents/hf_jp-ii_enc_14091981_laborem-exercens.html. Accessed 01 Feb 2019.

John Paul II. (1987). *Sollicitudo Rei Socialis (SRS): Papal Encyclical on Social Concern.* Available at: https://www.vatican.va/content/john-paul-ii/en/encyclicals/documents/hf_jp-ii_enc_30121987_sollicitudo-rei-socialis.html. Accessed 01 July 2015.

John Paul II. (1988). *Mulieris Dignitatem: Apostolic Letter on the Dignity and Vocation of Women.* Available at: https://www.vatican.va/content/john-paul-ii/en/apost_letters/1988/documents/hf_jp-ii_apl_19880815_mulieris-dignitatem.html. Accessed 01 Feb 2021.

John Paul II. (1991). *Centesimus Annus: Encyclical letter on the hundreth anniversary of Rerum Novarum.* Available at: https://www.vatican.va/content/john-paul-ii/en/encyclicals/documents/hf_jp-ii_enc_01051991_centesimus-annus.html. Accessed 1 July 2015.

John Paul II. (1993). *Veritatis Splendor: Papal Encyclical on the Splendor of the Truth.* Available at: https://www.vatican.va/content/john-paul-ii/en/encyclicals/documents/hf_jp-ii_enc_06081993_veritatis-splendor.html. Accessed 01 July 2015.

John Paul II (1995). *Evangelium Vitae: Encyclical Letter on the Value and Inviolability of Human Life*. Available at: https://www.vatican.va/content/john-paul-ii/en/encyclicals/documents/hf_jp-ii_enc_25031995_evangelium-vitae.html. Accessed 17 August 2019.

John XXIII. (1961). *Mater et Magistra: Encyclical Letter on Christianity and Social Progress.* Available at: https://www.vatican.va/content/john-xxiii/en/encyclicals/documents/hf_j-xxiii_enc_15051961_mater.html. Accessed 01 Feb 2019.

John XXIII. (1963). *Pacem in Terris: Encyclical Letter on Establishing Universal Peace.* Available at: https://www.vatican.va/content/john-xxiii/en/encyclicals/documents/hf_j-xxiii_enc_11041963_pacem.html. Accessed 01 Feb 2019.

Leo XIII. (1891). *Rerum Novarum: Encyclical letter on Capital and Labour.* Available at: https://www.vatican.va/content/leo-xiii/en/encyclicals/documents/hf_l-xiii_enc_15051891_rerum-novarum.html. Accessed 01 Feb 2019.

Pius IX. (1864a). *Quanta Cura: Encyclical Letter Condemning Current Errors.* Available at: https://www.papalencyclicals.net/pius09/p9quanta.htm. Accessed 08 Jan 2019.

Pius IX. (1864b). *Syllabus of Errors: Issued as an Annex to the Encyclical Quantum Cura.* Available at: https://www.papalencyclicals.net/pius09/p9syll.htm. Accessed 08 Jan 2019.

Pius VI. (1791). *Quod Aliquantum: Encyclical Letter issued in Condemnation of the Civil Constitution of the Clergy.* Available: https://www.vatican.va/content/pius-vi/it/documents/breve-quod-aliquantum-10-marzo-1791.html. Accessed 08 Jan 2019.

Pius X. (1906). *Vehementer Nos*: *Encyclical Letter on the French Law of Separation.* Available at: https://www.vatican.va/content/pius-x/en/encyclicals/documents/hf_p-x_enc_11021906_vehementer-nos.html. Accessed 08 Jan 2019.

Pius XI. (1930). *Casti Connubii: Encyclical Letter on Christian Marriage.* Available at https://www.vatican.va/content/pius-xi/en/encyclicals/documents/hf_p-xi_enc_19301231_casti-connubii.html. Accessed 01 July 2015.

Pius XI. (1931). *Quadragesimo Anno: Encyclical letter on Reconstruction of the Social Order.* Available at: https://www.vatican.va/content/pius-xi/en/encyclicals/documents/hf_p-xi_enc_19310515_quadragesimo-anno.html. Accessed 01 Feb 2019.

Pontifical Council for Justice and Peace. (2006). *Compendium of the Social Doctrine of the Church.* Libreria Editrice Vaticana.

Pontifical Council for the Pastoral Care of Migrants and Itinerant People. (2004). *Erga Migrantes Caritas Christi (EMCC): Instruction on people on the move.* Available at: http://www.vatican.va/roman_curia/pontifical_councils/migrants/documents/rc_pc_migrants_doc_20040514_erga-migrantescaritas-christi_en.html. Accessed 1 Jan 2021.

Pontificia Commissio Justitia et Pax. (1975). *The Church and human rights.* Vatican Publishing House.

The Holy Bible. (2011). New International Version. Zondervan.

Vatican II Council. (1965a). *Gaudium et Spes: Pastoral Constitution on the Church in the Modern World.* Available at: https://www.vatican.va/archive/hist_councils/ii_vatican_council/index.htm. Accessed 7 July 2018.

Vatican II Council. (1965b). *Ad gentes: Decree on the Church's Missionary Activity.* Available at: https://www.vatican.va/archive/hist_councils/ii_vatican_council/index.htm. Accessed 07 July 2018.

Vatican II Council. (1965c). *Gravissimum Educationis: Declaration on Christian Education.* Available at: https://www.vatican.va/archive/hist_councils/ii_vatican_council/index.htm. Accessed 7 July 2018.

Vatican II Council. (1965d). *Dignitatis Humanae: Declaration on religious freedom.* Available at: https://www.vatican.va/archive/hist_councils/ii_vatican_council/index.htm. 7 July 2018.

Policy Documents (Islamic Documents)

Islamic Council of Europe. (1981). *Universal Islamic Declaration of Human Rights (UIDHR)*. Available at: http://www.alhewar.com/ISLAMDECL.html. Accessed 01 Feb 2017.

League of Arab States. (1994). *Arab Charter on Human Rights, 15th September 1994*. Available at: https://www.refworld.org/legal/agreements/las/1994/en/10672. Accessed 04 Mar 2017.

League of Arab States. (2004). *Arab Charter on Human Rights, 22nd May 2004*. Available at: https://www.refworld.org/legal/constinstr/las/2004/en/123762. Accessed 04 May 2017.

Organization of the Islamic Conference (OIC). (1990). *Cairo Declaration on Human Rights in Islam*. Available at: https://www.refworld.org/docid/3ae6b3822c.html. Accessed 03 Feb 2021.

Sharia Penal Code Law Zamfara State of Nigeria. (2000). Available at: https://www.f-law.net/law/threads/37487-Shari-ah-Penal-Code-Law-Zamfara-State-Of-Nigeria-January-2000. Accessed 01 July 2019.

The Quran, with Surah Introductions and Appendices. (2013). Saheeh International Translation. Edited by A.B. al-Mehri. Maktabah Booksellers and Publishers.

International Human Rights Instruments

Council of Europe. (1950). *European convention for the protection of Human Rights and fundamental freedoms, as amended by protocols Nos. 11 and 14*, ETS 5, 4th November 1950. Available at: https://www.refworld.org/legal/agreements/coe/1950/en/18688. Accessed 04 Feb 2014.

Global Childhood Report. (2020). *The hardest places to be a Child*. Save the Children Federation Incorporated.

Guterres, A. (2011). *The 1951 Convention relating to the Status of Refugees and its 1967 Protocol*. UNHCR.

Human Rights Council. (2016). *The promotion and protection of human rights in the context of peaceful protests, UN Doc. A/HRC/RES/31/37, 24th March 2016*. Available at: https://www.right-docs.org/doc/a-hrc-res-31-37/. Accessed 01 Dec 2020.

ILO. (1944a). *Declaration of Philadelphia*. Available at: http://blue.lim.ilo.org/cariblex/pdfs/ILO_dec_philadelphia.pdf. Accessed 10 Oct 2017.

ILO. (1944b). *Income Security Recommendation (No. R067)*. Available at: https://www.ilo.org/dyn/normlex/en/f?p=NORMLEXPUB:12100:0::NO::P12100_ILO_CODE:R067. Accessed 01 Feb 2017.

ILO. (1944c). *Medical Care Recommendation (No. R069)*. Available at: https://www.ilo.org/dyn/normlex/en/f?p=NORMLEXPUB:12100:0::NO:12100:P12100_INSTRUMENT_ID:312407:NO. Accessed 01 Feb 2017.

ILO. (1952). *Convention Concerning Minimum Standards of Social Security* (No. C102). Available at: https://www.refworld.org/docid/5c77a1bc7.html. Accessed 02 Aug 2021.

ILO. (1958). *Discrimination (Employment and Occupation) Convention (No. C111)*. Available at: https://www.refworld.org/docid/3ddb680f4.html. Accessed 15 June 2021.

ILO. (1973). *Minimum Age Convention (No. C138)*. Available at: https://www.refworld.org/docid/421216a34.html. Accessed 02 Aug 2021.

ILO. (1998). *Declaration on Fundamental Principles and Rights at Work and its Follow-up*. International Labour Office.

ILO. (1999a). Worst Forms of Child Labour Convention (No. C182). Available at: https://www.refworld.org/docid/3ddb6e0c4.html. Accessed 02 Aug 2021.

ILO. (1999b). *Worst Forms of Child Labour Recommendation (No. R190)*. Available at: https://www.ilo.org/dyn/normlex/en/f?p=NORMLEXPUB:12100:0::NO:12100:P12100_INSTRUMENT_ID:312528:NO. Accessed 01 Feb 2017.

ILO. (2000). *Decent work for women: An ILO proposal to accelerate the implementation of the Beijng Platform for Action*. International Labour Office.

ILO. (2004). *Child labour – A textbook for university students*. International Labour Office.

ILO (2012). *Recommendation Concerning National Floors of Social Protection (No. R202)*. Available at: https://www.refworld.org/docid/5c77a49f7.html. Accessed 02 Aug 2021.

ILO. (2017b). *World Social Protection Report 2017–19: Universal Social Protection to Achieve the Sustainable Development Goals*. International Labour Office.

ILO. (2018b). *An introduction to legally prohibiting hazardous work for children*. Available at: https://www.ilo.org/ipecinfo/product/download.do?type=document&id=30296. Accessed 01 June 2021.

ILO. (n.d.). *Facts on social security in Africa*. Available at: https://www.ilo.org/public/english/protection/socsec/pol/campagne/files/africafactsheet.pdf. Accessed 01 June 2021.

ILO and NBS. (2001). *Nigeria National Child Labour Survey (NCLS) report 2000/2001. International Programme on the Elimination of Child Labour (IPEC)*. Available at: https://www.ilo.org/ipecinfo/product/download.do?type=document&id=8671. Accessed 1 Jan 2014.

ILO and UNICEF. (2021). *Child labour: Global estimates 2020, trends and the road forward*. ILO and UNICEF.

International Commission of Jurists (ICJ). (1997). *Maastricht guidelines on violations of economic, social and cultural rights.*. Available at: https://www.refworld.org/docid/48abd5730.html. Accessed 03 May 2021.

International Criminal Tribunal for Rwanda. (1994). *Rules of Procedure and Evidence, UN. Doc. ITR/3/REV.1, 8th November 1994*. Available at: https://unictr.irmct.org/sites/unictr.org/files/legal-library/950629-rpe-en.pdf. Accessed 01 March 2021.

International Criminal Tribunal for the former Yugoslavia. (1993). *Rules of Procedure and Evidence, UN Doc. IT/32/Rev.50, 25th May 1993*. Available at: https://www.icty.org/en/documents/rules-procedure-evidence. Accessed 01 March 2021.

International Federation for Human Rights. (2010, April). *Defending human rights – Not everywhere not every right: International fact-finding mission report on Nigeria, April 2010*. Available at: https://www.refworld.org/docid/4bed03412.html. Accessed 16 July 2014.

International Labour Conference (ILC) Report. (2012). *Fundamental principles and rights at work: From commitment to action (Recurrent discussion under the ILO declaration on social justice for a fair globalization and the follow-up to the ILO declaration on fundamental principles and rights at work)*. International Labour Office.

Lanza, E. (2019). *Protest and human rights: Standards on the rights involved in social protest and the obligations to guide the response of the state*. Office of the Special Rapporteur for Freedom of Expression of the Inter-American Commission on Human Rights. OAS. Available at: http://www.oas.org/en/iachr/expression/publications/Protesta/ProtestHumanRights.pdf. Accessed 01 Dec 2020.

McCann, D. (2005). *Sexual harassment at work: National and international responses* (Conditions of Work and Employment Series, 2). International Labour Office.

OHCHR. (1992). *CCPR General Comment No. 20: Article 7 (Prohibition of Torture, or Other Cruel, Inhuman or Degrading Treatment or Punishment), CCPR/C/GC/20, 10th March 1992*. Available at: https://www.refworld.org/docid/453883fb0.html. Accessed 30 April 2020.

OHCHR. (2014a). *Women's rights are human rights, UN Doc. HR/PUB/14/2, 2014*. Available at: https://www.refworld.org/docid/5566cfd14.html. Accessed 07 June 2021.

OHCHR. (2014b). *Basic human rights reference guide: Right to a fair trial and due process in the context of countering terrorism*. UN CTITF Publication Series. Available at: https://www.ohchr.org/EN/newyork/Documents/FairTrial.pdf. Accessed 01 Feb 2021.

OHCHR. (n.d.). *Status of Ratification of 18 International Human Rights Treaties*. Available at: http://indicators.ohchr.org/. Accessed 01 June 2019.

Organization of American States (OAS). (1969). *American Convention on Human Rights, 22nd November 1969*. Available at: https://www.refworld.org/legal/agreements/oas/1969/en/20081. Accessed 04 April 2017.

Religions for Peace (RfP) and UN High Commissioner for Refugees (UNHCR). (2018). *Guide to action on mobilizing faith communities to welcome migrants and refugees*. Available at: https://www.rfp.org/wp-content/uploads/2020/10/RfP-Refugees-and-Migrants-Resource-Guide.pdf. Accessed 01 Feb 2021.
UN CEDAW. (1989). *General Recommendation No. 12: Violence against Women, UN Doc. A/44/38, 1989*. Available at: https://www.refworld.org/docid/52d927444.html. Accessed 16 June 2021.
UN CEDAW. (1992). *General Recommendation No. 19: Violence against Women, UN Doc. A/47/38, 1992*. Available at: https://www.refworld.org/docid/52d920c54.html. Accessed 15 June 2021.
UN Commission on Human Rights. (1984). *The Siracusa Principles on the Limitation and Derogation Provisions in the ICCPR, UN Doc. E/CN.4/1985/4, 28th September 1984*. Available at: https://www.refworld.org/legal/resolution/unchr/1984/en/57200. Accessed 29 Feb 2017.
UN ECOSOC. (1985). *Implementation of the International Covenant on Economic, Social and Cultural Rights, UN Doc. E/Res/1985/17, 28th May 1985*. Available at: https://ap.ohchr.org/documents/alldocs.aspx?doc_id=8704. Accessed 01 Feb 2017.
UN ECOSOC. (1990). *CESCR General Comment No. 3: The Nature of States Parties' Obligations (Art. 2, Para. 1, of the Covenant), UN Doc. E/1991/23, 14th December 1990*. Available at: https://www.refworld.org/legal/general/cescr/1990/en/5613. Accessed 27 Sept 2021.
UN ECOSOC. (1999). *CESCR General Comment No. 12: The Right to Adequate Food (Art. 11 of the Covenant), UN Doc. E/C.12/1999/5, 12th May 1999*. Available at: https://www.refworld.org/docid/4538838c11.html. Accessed 03 May 2021.
UN ECOSOC. (2000). *CESCR General Comment No. 14: The Right to the Highest Attainable Standard of Health (Art. 12 of the Covenant), UN Doc. E/C.12/2000/4, 11th August 2000*. Available at: https://www.refworld.org/docid/4538838d0.html. Accessed 03 May 2020.
UN ECOSOC. (2016). *CESCR General Comment No. 22: The Right to Sexual and Reproductive Health (Article 12 of the International Covenant), UN. Doc. E/C.12/GC/22, 2nd May 2016*. Available at: https://digitallibrary.un.org/record/832961?ln=zh_CN. Accessed 01 July 2020.
UN General Assembly. (1965). *International Convention on the Elimination of All Forms of Racial Discrimination (ICERD), 21st December 1965*. United Nations Treaty Series (UNTS), 660, p. 195. Available at: http://www.refworld.org/docid/3ae6b3940.html. Accessed 10 Oct 2017.
UN General Assembly. (1979a). *Code of Conduct for Law Enforcement Officials, UN Doc. A/RES/34/169, 17th December 1979*. Available at: https://www.refworld.org/docid/48abd572e.html. Accessed 31 Dec 2020.
UN General Assembly. (1979b). *Convention on the Elimination of All Forms of Discrimination against Women (CEDAW), UN Doc. A/RES/34/180, 18th December 1979*. UNTS, 1249, p. 13. Available at: https://www.refworld.org/docid/3b00f2244.html. Accessed 11 Sept 2017.
UN General Assembly. (1981). *Declaration on the elimination of all forms of intolerance and of discrimination based on religion or belief, UN Doc. A/RES/36/55, 25th November 1981*. Available at: https://www.refworld.org/legal/resolution/unga/1981/en/5952. Accessed 04 March 2017.
UN General Assembly. (1989). *Convention on the Rights of the Child (CRC), 20th November 1989*. UNTS, vol. 1577, p. 3. Available at: http://www.refworld.org/docid/3ae6b38f0.html. Accessed 10 Oct 2017.
UN General Assembly. (1990). *International Convention on the Protection of the Rights of All Migrant Workers and Members of their Families, UN Doc. A/RES/45/158, 18th December 1990*. Available at: https://www.refworld.org/legal/agreements/unga/1990/en/27627. Accessed 08 Feb 2016.
UN General Assembly. (1993a). *Declaration on the Elimination of Violence against Women, UN Doc. A/RES/48/104, 20th December 1993*. Available at: https://www.refworld.org/docid/3b00f25d2c.html. Accessed 16 June 2021.
UN General Assembly. (1998). *Rome Statute of the International Criminal Court (Last Amended 2010), UN Doc. A/CONF.183/9, 17th July 1998*. Available at: https://www.refworld.org/docid/3ae6b3a84.html. Accessed 24 March 2021.

UN General Assembly. (2019). *Moratorium on the Use of the Death Penalty, UN Doc. A/RES/73/175, 17th December 2018*. Available at https://undocs.org/pdf?symbol=en/A/RES/73/175. Accessed 02 Feb 2020.

UN HRC. (1992). *CCPR General Comment No. 20 on Article 7 (Prohibition of Torture, or Other Cruel, Inhuman or Degrading Treatment or Punishment), CCPR/C/GC/20, 10th March 1992*. Available at: https://www.refworld.org/docid/453883fb0.html. Accessed 30 April 2015.

UN HRC. (1993). *CCPR General Comment No. 22: Article 18 (Freedom of Thought, Conscience or Religion), CCPR/C/21/Rev.1/Add.4, 30th July 1993*. Available at: https://www.refworld.org/docid/453883fb22.html. Accessed 18 Dec 2015.

UN HRC. (1994). *Toonen v. Australia, Communication No. 488/1992, UN. Doc CCPR/C/50/D/488/1992, 31st March 1994*. Available at: http://hrlibrary.umn.edu/undocs/html/vws488.htm. Accessed 01 March 2016.

UN HRC. (2007). *General Comment No. 32: Article 14 (Right to Equality Before Courts and Tribunals and to Fair Trial), CCPR/C/GC/32, 23rd August 2007*. Available at: https://www.refworld.org/docid/478b2b2f2.html. Accessed 27 Feb 2021.

UN HRC. (2011). *CCPR General Comment No. 34 on Article 19 (Freedoms of Opinion and Expression), CCPR/C/GC/34, 12th September 2011*. Available at: https://www.refworld.org/docid/4ed34b562.html. Accessed 01 Dec 2020.

UN HRC. (2018). *CCPR General Comment No. 36 on Article 6 (Right to Life), CCPR/C/GC/36, 30th October 2018*. Available at: https://www.ohchr.org/EN/HRBodies/CCPR/Pages/GC36-Article6Righttolife.aspx. Accessed 23 June 2020.

UN Human Rights Council. (2007). *A resolution on Moratorium on the Use of the Death Penalty, UN Doc. A/RES/62/149, 18th December 2007*. Available at: https://documents.un.org/doc/undoc/gen/n07/472/71/pdf/n0747271.pdf?token=j2TD1excZ4BWQo3cgF&fe=true. Accessed 02 Dec 2019.

UN Human Rights Council. (2012a). *Report of the special Rapporteur on the Rights to Freedom of Peaceful Assembly and of Association, UN Doc. A/HRC/20/27, 21st May 2012*. Available at: https://www.refworld.org/docid/525fad894.html. Accessed 21 Dec 2020.

UN Human Rights Council. (2012b). *The protection of human rights and fundamental freedoms while countering terrorism, UN Doc. A/HRC/22/26, 17th December 2012*. Available at: https://www.refworld.org/docid/5118eb762.html. Accessed 27 Feb 2021.

UN Human Rights Council. (2013). *Report on effective measures and best practices to ensure the promotion and protection of human rights in the context of peaceful protests, UN Doc. A/HRC/22/28, 21st January 2013*. Available at: https://www.refworld.org/docid/5118f0612.html. Accessed 21 Dec 2020.

UNHCR. (2012). *High commissioner's dialogue on protection challenges*. UNHCR. Available at: https://www.refworld.org/pdfid/510a6c662.pdf. Accessed 01 July 2019.

UNHCR. (2020). *Global trends: Forced displacement in 2019*. Available at: https://www.unhcr.org/statistics/unhcrstats/5ee200e37/unhcr-global-trends-2019.html. Accessed 01 Feb 2021.

UN Security Council. (1993). *Statute of the International Criminal Tribunal for the Former Yugoslavia (ICTY), 25th May 1993 (Last Amended on 17th May 2002)*. Available at: https://www.refworld.org/docid/3dda28414.html. Accessed 24 March 2021.

UN Security Council. (1994). *Statute of the International Criminal Tribunal for Rwanda (ICTR), 8th November 1994 (Last Amended on 13th October 2006)*. Available at: https://www.refworld.org/docid/3ae6b3952c.html. Accessed 24 March 2021.

UNHCR. (2010). *Convention and protocol relating to the status of refugees*: UNHCR Communications and Public Information Service. Available at: https://www.unhcr.org/protect/PROTECTION/3b66c2aa10.pdf. Accessed 01 Feb 2021.

United States Department of Labor's (USDOL) Report. (2019). *Findings on the worst forms of child labor* (pp. 907–914). Bureau of International Labor Affairs. Available at: https://www.dol.gov/sites/dolgov/files/ILAB/child_labor_reports/tda2019/2019_TDA_Report_Online_Final.pdf. Accessed 01 June 2021.

WEF Global Gender Gap Report. (2020). Available at: https://www.weforum.org/reports/gender-gap-2020-report-100-years-pay-equality. Accessed 01 May 2021.

WHO. (2012). *Safe abortion: Technical and policy guidance for health systems* (2nd ed.). WHO Press.

WHO. (2019). *World health statistics 2019: Monitoring health for the sustainable development goals*. World Health Office.

Regional Human Rights Instruments

African Commission on Human and Peoples' Rights (African Commission). (2003). *Principles and Guidelines on the Right to a Fair Trial and Legal Assistance in Africa, 29th May 2003*. Available at https://www.achpr.org/legalinstruments/detail?id=38. Accessed 01 July 2014.

African Commission on Human and Peoples' Rights (ACHPR). (2012). *Study on the Question of the Death Penalty in Africa*. Baobab Printers. Available at: https://www.achpr.org/news/viewdetail?id=165. Accessed 01 Aug 2018.

African Commission (2014a). *General Comment No. 2 on Article 14.1(a), (b), (c) and (f) and Article 14. 2(a) and (c) of the Protocol to the ACHPR on the Rights of Women in Africa, 28th November 2014*. Available at: https://www.achpr.org/legalinstruments/detail?id=13. Accessed 11 Sept 2020.

African Commission (2014b). *Resolution on Protection against Violence and Other Human Rights Violations against Persons on the Basis of their Real or Imputed Sexual Orientation or Gender Identity, ACHPR/Res.275 (LV), 28th April – 12th May 2014*. Available at: https://www.achpr.org/adoptedresolution. Accessed 01 July 2014.

African Commission (2015). *General Comment No. 3 of the African Charter on Human and Peoples' Rights: The Right to Life (Article 4), 4th to 18th November 2015*. Available at: https://www.achpr.org/legalinstruments/. Accessed 01 July 2014.

OAU (1982). *African Charter on human and peoples' rights ("Banjul Charter"), CAB/LEG/67/3 rev. 5, 21 I.L.M. 58, 27th June 1981*. Available at: https://www.refworld.org/docid/3ae6b3630.html. Accessed 24 March 2021.

OAU (1990). *African Charter on the Rights and Welfare of the Child, CAB/LEG/24.9/49 (1990), 11th July 1990*. Available at: https://www.refworld.org/legal/agreements/oau/1990/en/13798. Accessed 05 Nov 2018.

Organization of African Unity (OAU) (1969). *Convention governing the specific aspects of refugee problems in Africa ("OAU Convention"), 10th September 1969. 1001* UNTS, 45. Available at: https://www.refworld.org/docid/3ae6b36018.html. Accessed 16 Jan 2021.

OHCHR. (2006). *National Action Plan (NAP) for the promotion and protection of human rights in Nigeria 2006*. Federal Republic of Nigeria. Available at: https://www.ohchr.org/sites/default/files/Documents/Issues/NHRA/nigeria.pdf. Accessed 2 July 2015.

OHCHR. (2016). *Human rights and traditional justice systems in Africa*. UN Publication.

National Human Rights Instruments

Abuja: *Penal Code Act, Cap. 53 Laws of Federation of Nigeria (LFN) 1960*. Available at: http://oceansbeyondpiracy.org/sites/default/files/Nigeria_Penal_Code_Act_1960.pdf. Accessed 01 Jan 2020.

All-Party Parliamentary Group on Nigeria (APPGN) Report. (2013). *Too many to count? Human rights, justice and accountability in Nigeria*. Chatham House.

Amnesty International Nigeria. (2008). *Waiting for the Hangman* (Index No.: AFR 44/020/2008). Amnesty International Publications.

Amnesty International Nigeria. (2018). *Nigeria: Still no Accountability for Human Rights Violations* (Index No.: AFR 44/8529/2018). Amnesty International Publications.

Amnesty International Nigeria. (2017). *NGO Bill Threatens Freedoms in Nigeria*. Index No.: AFR 44/7590/2017. Amnesty International Publications.

Amnesty International Nigeria. (2019). *Human Rights Agenda* (Index No.: AFR 44/0431/2019). Amnesty International Publications.

Amnesty International Nigeria. (2020). *One year since #Endsars protests, no justice for victims of police brutality.* Available at: https://www.amnesty.org.uk/press-releases/nigeria-one-year-endsars-protests-no-justice-victims-police-brutality. Accessed 01 Dec 2021.

CEDAW Shadow Report. (1998). *Women's reproductive rights in Nigeria* (pp. 1–25). Center for Reproductive Law and Policy (CRLP).

European Asylum Support Office (EASO). (2021). *Country of origin information report – Nigeria: Trafficking in human beings*. Ministry of Foreign Affairs.

Fact Sheet. (2013). *Improving Pretrial Justice in Nigeria*. Open Society Justice Initiative. Available at: https://www.justiceinitiative.org/publications/fact-sheet-improving-pretrial-justice-nigeria. Accessed 01 Mar 2021.

Federal Republic of Nigeria. (2018). *National guidelines on safe termination of pregnancy for legal indications*. Federal Ministry of Health.

Human Rights Council. (2018b). *Report of the Working Group on the Universal Periodic Review – Nigeria, UN Doc. A/HRC/40/7, 26th December 2018.* Available at: https://www.ecoi.net/en/file/local/1457455/1930_1549370422_g1844665.pdf. Accessed 01 June 2019.

Human Rights Report. (2013). *Nigeria: Country reports on human rights practices*. US Department of State. Bureau of Democracy, Human Rights and Labor.

Human Rights Watch. (2005). *Nigeria events of 2004.* Available at: https://www.hrw.org/world-report/2005/country-chapters/nigeria. Accessed 03 May 2015.

Human Rights Watch. (2016). *Tell me where i can be safe: The impact of Nigeria's same sex marriage (prohibition) act.* Available at. https://www.hrw.org/report/2016/10/20/tell-me-where-i-can-be-safe/impact-nigerias-same-sex-marriageprohibition-act. Accessed 1 Jan 2020.

Ilo, J. U. (2005). *Nigeria country report on death penalty application*. Available at: https://www.biicl.org/files/2300_country_report_nigeria__ilo.pdf. Accessed 07 July 2014.

ILO & NBS. (2001). *Nigeria National Child Labour Survey (NCLS) Report 2000/2001.* International Programme on the Elimination of Child Labour (IPEC). Available at: https://www.ilo.org/ipecinfo/product/download.do?type=document&id=8671. Accessed 01 Jan 2014.

Increse Report. (2009). *The survey on sexual diversity and human rights in Nigeria*. The Ford Foundation. Available at: https://www.sxpolitics.org/wp-content/uploads/2009/10/report-on-sexual-diversity-and-human-rights-in-nigeria-1.pdf. Accessed 02 Feb 2017.

Industrial Law, Hasawa and Labour Law. (n.d.). Available at: https://prog.lmu.edu.ng/colleges_CMS/document/books/GEC524. Accessed 28 May 2021.

International Federation for Human Rights. (2010, April). *Defending Human Rights – Not Everywhere Not Every Right: International Fact-Finding Mission Report on Nigeria, April 2010.* Available at: https://www.refworld.org/docid/4bed03412.html. Accessed 16 July 2014.

National Bureau of Statistics (NBS). (2018a). *Statistical Report on women and men in Nigeria 2017.* Proshare.

National Bureau of Statistics (NBS). (2020). *Nigeria Living Standards (NLS) Survey 2018/2019.* Proshare.

National Bureau of Statistics (NBS). (2021). *Labor force statistics: Unemployment and underemployment report (Q4 2020).* Proshare.

National Human Rights Commission (NHRC). (2007). *A report on the state of human rights in Nigeria*. Bluesland Communications Ltd.

NBS and UNICEF. (2017). *Multiple indicator cluster survey 2016–17, Survey Findings Report.* Abuja, Nigeria.

Nigeria. (2004a). *The Compulsory, Free Universal Basic Education Act 2004. Compendium of Education Sector Laws in Nigeria* (Vol. 1, 3rd ed.). Federal Ministry of Education.

Nigeria (2004b). *UN convention on the rights of the child: Second country periodic report*. Federal Ministry of Women Affairs.

Nigeria (2006). *National Gender Policy*. Federal Ministry of Women Affairs and Social Development.

Nigeria. (2017). *6th Periodic country report 2015–2016 on the implementation of the African Charter on human and peoples' rights in Nigeria*. Federal Ministry of Justice.

Nigeria Civil Society Situation Room (2019). *Report of Nigeria's 2019 general elections*. Available at: https://www.placng.org/situation_room/sr/wp-content/uploads/2019/09/Report-on-Nigerias-2019-General-Elections.pdf. Accessed 01 Dec 2020.

Nigeria: *Administration of Criminal Justice Act (ACJA), Cap C40 LFN 2015*. Available at: http://lawsofnigeria.placng.org/laws/C23.pdf. Accessed 01 Jan 2016.

Nigeria: *Armed Forces Act, Cap. A20 LFN 2004*. Available at: https://laws.lawnigeria.com/2018/04/19/lfn-armed-forcesact/. Accessed 01 Feb 2020.

Nigeria: *Children and Young Persons Act, Cap 32 LFN 1958*. Available at: https://laws.lawnigeria.com/2020/06/19/indexlfn-laws-of-the-federation-of-nigeria-3/. Accessed 01 Jan 2020.

Nigeria: *Child's Rights Act (CRA), 31st July 2003*. Available at: https://www.refworld.org/docid/5568201f4.html. Accessed 01 June 2016.

Nigeria: *Constitution of the Federal Republic of Nigeria (CFRN)*. (1999). *Updated with the First, Second and Third Alterations (2010) and the Fourth Alteration (2017)*. Federal Ministry of Justice.

Nigeria: *Criminal Code Act, Cap C38 LFN 2004*. Available at: https://www.refworld.org/docid/49997ade1a.html. Accessed 10 June 2020.

Nigeria: *Employee's Compensation Act 2010*. Available at: https://laws.lawnigeria.com/2020/06/19/index-lfn-laws-of-thefederation-of-nigeria-3/. Accessed 01 Jan 2020.

Nigeria: *Evidence Act, 2011*. Available at: https://www.refworld.org/legal/legislation/natlegbod/2011/en/104226. Accessed 01 Aug 2018.

Nigeria: *Factories Act 2004*. Available at: https://laws.lawnigeria.com/2020/06/19/index-lfn-laws-of-the-federation-ofnigeria-3/. Accessed 01 Jan 2020.

Nigeria: *Labour Act, Cap. L1 LFN 2004*. Available at: https://laws.lawnigeria.com/2020/06/19/index-lfn-laws-of-thefederation-of-nigeria-3/. Accessed 01 Jan 2020.

Nigeria: *National Commission for Refugees Act, Cap N21 LFN 2004*. Available at: https://www.refworld.org/docid/3ae6b522e.html. Accessed 16 Jan 2021.

Nigeria: *National Health Insurance Scheme Act, Cap. N42 LFN 2004*. Available at: https://www.placng.org/lawsofnigeria/view2.php?sn=304. Accessed 01 Aug 2018.

Nigeria: *National Minimum Wage Act 2011*. Available at: https://laws.lawnigeria.com/2020/06/19/index-lfn-laws-of-thefederation-of-nigeria-3/. Accessed 01 Jan 2020.

Nigeria: *Penal Code Act Cap 53 LFN (Abuja)*. Available at: http://oceansbeyondpiracy.org/sites/default/files/Nigeria_Penal_Code_Act_1960.pdf. Accessed 01 Jan 2015.

Nigeria: *Pensions Reform Act 2014*. Available at: https://laws.lawnigeria.com/2020/06/19/index-lfn-laws-of-thefederation-of-nigeria-3/. Accessed 01 Jan 2020.

Nigeria: *Same Sex Marriage (Prohibition) Act, 17th December 2013*. Available at: https://www.refworld.org/docid/52f4d9cc4.html. Accessed 23 April 2015.

Nigeria: Shari'ah Penal Code Law 2000, Zamfara State of Nigeria. Available at: https://www.f-law.net/law/threads/37487-Shari-ah-Penal-Code-Law-Zamfara-State-Of-Nigeria-January-2000. Accessed 01 Feb 2015.

Nigeria: *Trade Union Act, Cap. T14 LFN 2004*. Available at: https://laws.lawnigeria.com/2020/06/19/index-lfn-laws-ofthe-federation-of-nigeria-3/. Accessed 01 Jan 2020.

Nigeria: *Trafficking in Persons (Prohibition) Enforcement and Administration (NAPTIP) Act 2015*. Available at: https://laws.lawnigeria.com/2020/06/19/index-lfn-laws-of-the-federation-of-nigeria-3/. Accessed 01 Jan 2020.

Nigeria: *Violence Against Persons (Prohibition) Act, 2015 (VAPP), 25th May 2015*. Available at: https://www.refworld.org/docid/556d5eb14.html. Accessed 30 April 2016.

OHCHR (2006). *National Action Plan (NAP) for the Promotion and Protection of Human Rights in Nigeria 2006*. Federal Republic of Nigeria. Available at: https://www.ohchr.org/sites/default/files/Documents/Issues/NHRA/nigeria.pdf. Accessed 02 July 2015.

Onwubiko, E. (2017). *A minister's bigoted agenda*. Available at: http://huriwa.blogspot.com/2017/06/a-ministers-bigotedagenda-by-emmanuel.html. Accessed 12 Feb 2020.

PEW Report. (2020). *The global god divide*. Available at: https://www.pewresearch.org/global/2020/07/20/the-global-god-divide/. Accessed 01 July 2021.

Pew Research Center. (2007). *Nigeria's Presidential Election: The Christian-Muslim Divide*. Available at: https://www.pewresearch.org/religion/2007/03/21/nigerias-presidential-election-the-christian-muslim-divide/. Accessed 02 July 2015.

Pew Research Center. (2012). *The global religious landscape: A report on the size and distribution of the world's major religious groups*. Available at: https://www.pewresearch.org/religion/2012/12/18/global-religious-landscape-exec/. Accessed 02 July 2015.

Pew Research Center. (2013). *The global divide on homosexuality*. Available at: https://www.pewresearch.org/global/2013/06/04/the-global-divide-on-homosexuality/. Accessed 02 July 2015.

Stakeholder Democracy Network (SDN). (2020). *Women's political participation and representation in the Niger Delta*. Available at: http://www.stakeholderdemocracy.org/wp-content/uploads/2020/02/More-women-in-governance.-Report.-2019.-DIGITAL.pdf. Accessed 01 Dec 2020.

The World Factbook. (2021). *Nigeria: People and Society*. Available at: https://www.cia.gov/the-worldfactbook/countries/nigeria/#people-and-society. Accessed 23 Jan 2022.

UBEC Annual Report. (2010). *National Framework for the Development and Integration of Almajiri Education into UBE Programme*. Universal Basic Education Commission.

US Department of States. (2014). *Nigeria: Human Rights Reports 2013*. Available at: https://2009-2017.state.gov/documents/organization/220358.pdf. Accessed 3 May 2015.

UN HRC. (2019). *Concluding Observations on Nigeria in the Absence of its 2nd Periodic Report, CCPR/C/NGA/CO/2, 29th August 2019*. Available at: https://undocs.org/CCPR/C/NGA/CO/2. Accessed 14 Nov 2019.

UN Human Rights Committee (HRC). (2019). *Concluding Observations: Nigeria, UN Doc. CCPR/C/NGA/CO/2, 29th August 2019*. Available at: https://www.ohchr.org/en/documents/concluding-observations/ccprcngaco2-human-rights-committee-concluding-observations. Accessed 14 Dec 2019.

US Department of State. (2014). *Nigeria: Human Rights Report 2013*. Available at: https://2009-2017.state.gov/documents/organization/220358.pdf. Accessed 03 May 2015.

World Bank. (2019). *Women on boards in Nigeria*. Available at: https://documents.worldbank.org/curated/en/775651567754681552/Women-on-Boards-in-Nigeria. Accessed 01 June 2021.

World Bank Report. (2021). *Nigeria: Labor force participation rate*. Available at: https://data.worldbank.org/indicator/SL.TLF.CACT.NE.ZS?end=2020&locations=NG&name_desc=false&start=2010&view=chart. Accessed 01 Dec 2021.

Other Internet Sources

Abdul-Wahid, A. K. (2019). *Protests, demonstrations and civil disobedience in the light of Islam*. Available at: https://www.abukhadeejah.com/protests-demonstrations-and-civil-disobedience-in-the-light-of-islam-ethics-3-8/. Accessed 01 Feb 2021.

Abū Zahrā, K. (2011). The Islamic ruling on protests and demonstrations. *The Khilafah*. Available at: http://www.khilafah.com/the-islamic-ruling-on-protests-and-demonstrations/. Accessed 01 Feb 2020.

Adejugbe, A., & Adejugbe, A. (2018). *Women and discrimination in the workplace: A Nigerian perspective*. Available at: https://ssrn.com/abstract=3244971 or https://doi.org/10.2139/ssrn.3244971. Accessed 01 July 2019.

Altmeyer, A. J. (n.d.). *Social welfare in the United States*. Available at: https://www.ssa.gov/history/aja964.html. Accessed 01 July 2021.

Anderson, K. (1998). Euthanasia: A Christian perspective. *Probe Materials*. Available at: https://probe.org/euthanasia/. Accessed 02 Feb 2018.

Attorney-General's Department, Australian Government. (n.d.). *Right to freedom of thought, conscience and religion or belief*. Available at: https://www.ag.gov.au/rights-and-protections/human-rights-and-anti-discrimination/human-rights-scrutiny/public-sector-guidance-sheets/right-freedom-thought-conscience-and-religion-or-belief#topofpage. Accessed 01 Feb 2018.

Augustyn, A., Lotha, G., Lewis, R., Chauhan, Y., Murray, L., & Duignan, B. (Eds.). (2019). *Euthanasia. Encyclopaedia Britannica*. Available at: https://www.britannica.com/topic/euthanasia. Accessed 01 Oct 2020.

Aquinas, T. (n.d.). *On The Law: Summa Theologiae* (A. J. Fredosso, Trans.). St. Thomas Education Project (STEP). Available at: http://www.thomasinternational.org/projects/step/treatiseonlaw/delege000.htm. Accessed 01 Feb 2021.

Babalola, A. A. (2016). *The constitutionality of death penalty: Need to amend the law*. Available at: http://www.abuad.edu.ng/the-constitutionality-of-death-penalty-need-to-amend-the-law/. Accessed 01 June 2017.

Casey-Maslen, S. (Ed.). (2020). *Laws on the right of peaceful assembly worldwide: Nigeria*. University of Pretoria Centre for Human Rights. Available at: https://www.rightofassembly.info/country/nigeria. Accessed 01 Dec 2020.

Center for Reproductive Rights. (2019). *The World's Abortion Laws*. Available at https://reproductiverights.org/worldabortionlaws. Accessed 01 Aug 2020.

Christianity and Capital Punishment. (2009). Available at http://www.bbc.co.uk/religion/religions/christianity/christianethics/capitalpunishment_1.shtml. Accessed 08 Aug 2020.

Death Penalty Worldwide Database. (2014, 2019). *The death penalty*. Available at: https://iachr.lls.edu/sites/default/files/iachr/Court_and_Commission_Documents/wing_025_cornell_center_on_the_death_penalty_worldwide.pdf. Accessed 02 Oct 2020.

Dickson, P. C. (2014). Homophobia unites Muslims and Christians in Nigeria. *GlobalPost*, 13th February 2014. Available at: https://www.pri.org/stories/2014-02-13/homophobia-unites-muslims-and-christians-nigeria. Accessed 01 Jan 2020.

Ecofin Agency. (2020). *2019 ranking of democracies in Africa according to the economist intelligence unit (EIU)*. Available at: https://www.ecofinagency.com/public-management/2301-40885-2019-ranking-of-democracies-in-africa-according-to-the-eiu. Accessed 01 Dec 2020.

El Sergani, R. (Ed.). (2019). Freedom of belief in Islam. *Islamstory*. Available at: https://islamstory.com/en/artical/3408704/Freedom-of-belief-in-Islam. Accessed 03 Aug 2020.

Eruaga, A. (n.d.). *The Right of silence of crime suspects is an unnecessary clog in the wheels of justice*. Available at: https://theunfamousseries.com/nials-laws-of-nigeria-evidence-act-2011.html. Accessed 01 Feb 2021.

European Union. (n.d.). *The Justice Programme: Legal Experts Advisory Panel, Defence Rights Map, Case Law Database, Advice Guides and Latest News*. Available at: https://www.fairtrials.org/right-fair-trial#the-right-to-a-fair-trial. Accessed 11 Aug 2021.

Ewang, A. (2022). *Student in Nigeria murdered over Blasphemy allegation*. Available at: https://www.hrw.org/news/2022/05/16/student-nigeria-murdered-over-blasphemy-allegation. Accessed 01 Aug 2022.

Federal Foreign Office. (2021). *Freedom of religion and belief*. Available at: https://www.auswaertiges-amt.de/en/aussenpolitik/themen/menschenrechte/-/227624. Accessed 02 Jan 2022.

Ferguson, S. (2003). *The Right to Vote*. University of Minnesota Human Rights Center. Available at: http://hrlibrary.umn.edu/edumat/studyguides/votingrights.html. Accessed 01 Dec 2020.

Hansan, J. E. (2011). *English poor laws: Historical precedents of tax-supported relief for the poor*. Social Welfare History Project. Available at: http://socialwelfare.library.vcu.edu/programs/poor-laws/. Accessed 01 Jan 2020.

Ibirogba, E. (2018). Nigeria Should Amend its Constitution to Guarantee Voting Rights. *Good Governance Africa – Nigeria, 4*(13). Available at: https://gga.org/nigeria-should-amend-its-constitution-to-guarantee-voting-rights/. Accessed 01 Dec 2020.

Idayat, H., & Shamsudeen, Y. (2015). *Addressing electoral integrity in Africa: Nigeria case study*. Available at: https://www.africaportal.org/publications/addressing-electoral-integrity-africa-nigeria-case-study/. Accessed 01 Dec 2020.

Islam and Capital Punishment. (2009). Available at https://www.bbc.co.uk/religion/religions/islam/islamethics/capitalpunishment.shtml. Accessed 08 Aug 2020.

Jegede, O., & Idiaru, W. (2020). *Nigeria: Overview of electoral Laws in Nigeria*. Available in: https://www.mondaq.com/nigeria/constitutional-administrative-law/987696/overview-of-electoral-laws-in-nigeria. Accessed 01 Dec 2020.

Kammer, F. (2010). *Catholic social teaching and criminal justice*. Jesuit Social Research Institute. Available at: http://www.loyno.edu/jsri/catholic-social-teaching-and-criminal-justice. Accessed 01 Apr 2021.

Khan, M. A. M. (2015). *What is Islamic democracy? The three Cs of Islamic Governance*. Available at: https://www.e-ir.info/2015/01/07/what-is-islamic-democracy-the-three-cs-of-islamic-governance/. Accessed 01 Feb 2021.

Lam, A. (2016). *Counting the LGBT population: 6% of Europeans identify as LGBT*. Available at: https://daliaresearch.com/blog/counting-the-lgbt-population-6-of-europeans-identify-as-lgbt/. Accessed 16 Apr 2020.

Latham and Watkins LLP. (2015). *Pro Bono practices and opportunities in Nigeria*. Available at: https://www.lw.com/admin/upload/SiteAttachments/pro-bono-in-nigeria.pdf. Accessed 05 Feb 2017.

Leininger, J. (2011). *Awakening in the Spring, democracy in the Autumn? Why Islam and democracy are compatible*. German Development Institute. Available at: https://www.die-gdi.de/en/the-current-column/article/awakening-in-the-spring-democracy-in-the-autumn-why-islam-and-democracy-are-compatible/. Accessed 01 Feb 2021.

Miranda Rights in Nigerian Criminal Jurisprudence. (n.d.). Available at: https://www.lawyard.ng/wp-content/uploads/2020/07/Miranda-in-Nigerian-Criminal-Jurisprudence.pdf. Accessed 01 Feb 2021.

New World Encyclopedia. (2017). *Freedom of religion*. Retrieved August 02, 2020. Available at: https://www.newworldencyclopedia.org/p/index.php?title=Freedom_of_religion&oldid=1004879

Nigeria: *Voter Education Handbook (VEH)*. (n.d.). ACE Project 1998–2020. Available at: http://aceproject.org/ero-en/regions/africa/NG/voter-education-handbook.pdf/view. Accessed 01 Dec 2020.

Nigeria: *World Prison Brief Data*. University of London. Available at: https://www.prisonstudies.org/country/nigeria. Accessed 01 Apr 2021.

Okoronkwo, I. (2015). *Legal aid in Nigeria*. Available at: http://www.legalaidcouncil.gov.ng/. Accessed 08 Aug 2020.

Okpukpara, C. B., Chine, P. U., Uguru, F. N. O., & Chukwuone, N. (2006). *Child welfare and poverty in Nigeria*. A Paper Presented at Poverty Phase II Dissemination Workshop in Addis Ababa, Ethiopia on 12th to 13th October 2006. Available at: http://sarpn.org/documents/d0002269/Child-welfare_Nigeria_Okpukpara_Oct2006.pdf. Accessed 02 Feb 2017.

Oniha, B.E. (n.d.). *Legality of Euthanasia and the right to Die in Nigeria*. Available at: http://edojudiciary.gov.ng/legal-articles/legality-of-euthanasia-and-the-right-to-die-in-nigeria-by-bright-e-oniha/. Accessed 02 Feb 2020.

Oniha, B. E., & Oniha, O. M. (2015). *Euthanasia and assisted suicide as basic constitutional rights under the 1999 constitution of Nigeria*. Available at: https://www.nigerianlawguru.com/articles/humanrightslaw/EuthanasiaandAssistedSuicide.Pdf. Accessed 01 Oct 2020.

Population Pyramid. (2019). *Nigeria population*. Available at: https://www.populationpyramid.net/nigeria/2019/. Accessed 02 Mar 2020.

Political Protest. (n.d.). *Governments of the world: A global guide to citizens' rights and responsibilities*. Available at: https://www.encyclopedia.com/international/legal-and-political-magazines/political-protest. Accessed 19 Dec 2020.

Roy, O. (2021). *Islam: The Democracy Dilemma*. The Wilson Center. Available at: https://www.wilsoncenter.org/islam-the-democracy-dilemma-0. Accessed 01 Feb 2021.

Saeed, A. (2018). Religious freedom in Islam: The witness of the Qur'an and the Prophet. *ABC Religion & Ethics*. Available at: https://www.abc.net.au/religion/religious-freedom-in-islam/10419798. Accessed 08 Mar 2019.

Scrutiny of Acts and Regulations Committee. (1998). *The right to silence: An examination of the issues*. Available at: https://www.parliament.vic.gov.au/archive/sarc/Right_to_Silence/Issues_Paper/tablecontents.htm. Accessed 01 Feb 2021.

Shorter, A. (n.d.). *Concepts of social justice in traditional Africa*. Available at: https://traditions-afripedia.fandom.com/wiki/Concepts_of_Social_Justice_in_Traditional_Africa. Accessed 01 May 2021.

Symbolum Quicunque: The Athanasian Creed. Creeds of Christendom, II. (n.d.). Available at: https://www.ccel.org/ccel/schaff/creeds2.iv.i.iv.html. Accessed 08 Aug 2014.

Unini, C. (2020). *Protest right and limitations under the Nigerian Human Rights Law amidst the #EndSars Protest in Nigeria*. Available at: https://thenigerialawyer.com/protest-right-and-limitations-under-the-nigerian-human-rights-law-amidst-the-endsars-protest-in-nigeria/. Accessed 01 Dec 2020.

When is Civil Disobedience Allowed for a Christian? (n.d.). Available at: https://www.gotquestions.org/civil-disobedience.html. Accessed 01 Feb 2021.

World Data Atlas. (n.d.). *Nigeria: Gross Domestic Product in current prices*. Available at: https://knoema.com/atlas/Nigeria/GDP. Accessed 01 June 2021.

Chapter 4
Explaining Human Rights Attitudes

Contents

4.1 Human Rights Attitudes Defined 236
4.2 Social Significance of Religion 238
4.3 Theories of Empathy 241
4.4 Theory of Basic Human Values 243
4.5 Theory of Human Dignity 246
4.6 The Integrative Theory of the Quality of Life 249
4.7 Social Identity Theory 252
4.8 Socialisation Theory 254
4.9 State of Research 255
References 257

Introduction

Having described the status quo of human rights in Nigeria, particularly in relation to the human rights issues examined here, what is next? We intend to further investigate the human rights attitudes of Nigerians. The reason is simple. Upon closer inspection of the above reports, there tends to be a certain pattern of observance of human rights among Nigerians. Some rights are generally recognised and respected, while others are explicitly rejected and abused, and in some cases the abuse even appears to be 'state sponsored', that is, they are sanctioned or supported by the State through the instrumentality of its laws, for example, discrimination based on sexual orientation and the right to life issue of the death penalty, among others. For this reason, we feel it is necessary to investigate the human rights attitudes of the Nigerian people, especially from below, to see the emerging tendencies in relation to the selected rights and to try to identify the determinants of the possible tendencies.

At the onset, we introduce the concept of human rights attitudes in precise terms as it is a central concept of the study. We then present theories that can be used to explain the said attitudes. These include the theory of social significance of religion,

M. C. Adimekwe, *The Impact of Religion, Personality, Values and Worldviews on Attitudes Towards Human Rights*, Religion and Human Rights 11,
https://doi.org/10.1007/978-3-031-65749-8_4

also known as the theory of secularisation based on existential security. Others are the theories of empathy, basic human values, human dignity, perceived quality of life, and social identity. Originally used in social psychology, they are now considered interdisciplinary mechanisms and are used as such in research in all fields, including human rights. We find them useful for this study. The theory of the social relevance of religion and socialisation theory stress a socio-cultural explanation of human rights attitudes, while the others more or less focus on a cognitive-affective explanation. Of this latter group, the integrative theory of the quality of life and the social identity theory refer to the social-political context. The socialisation theory, for its part, is only employed as an alternative explanation in the study. All these theoretical frameworks are briefly presented here and then used to derive testable hypotheses. After all these considerations, the chapter closes with an overview of the current state of research.

4.1 Human Rights Attitudes Defined

Following Haddock and Maio's (2012) definition of attitude,[1] we define human rights attitudes as evaluative tendencies towards human rights that are based on a set of cognitive, affective and behavioural factors. In relation to a person, attitude towards human rights simply refers to the way a person perceives human rights issues, his or her own predisposition towards them, which can be positive, negative or neutral. In contemporary social psychology, the study of attitudes is considered very important because attitudes are believed to have a tremendous impact on the perception and behaviour of individuals (Haddock & Maio, 2012; Allport, 1935). Despite this awareness and the increasing global importance of human rights, limited attention has been paid to human rights attitudes in scholarship (Diaz-Veizades et al., 1995). Of course, studies of social interactions have focused on group attitudes such as ethnocentrism (Campbell, 1965; LeVine & Campbell, 1972), in-group favouritism (Tajfel & Turner 1986; Wagner et al., 2010), nationalism and patriotism (Adorno et al., 1950; Blank & Schmidt, 2003; Herrmann, 2001) or attitudes towards out-groups such as prejudice, xenophobia, intolerance and racism (cf. Hjerm, 2007) as well as exclusionism (Scheepers et al., 2002; Gorodzeisky & Semyonov, 2009) and preference for expulsion (McLaren, 2003) all in connection with human rights attitudes. However, the human rights domain is more expansive and embraces other policy areas such as social security, healthcare, child upbringing, education, labour relations, religious practice, participation in democracy, environmental protection and self-determination (see Diaz-Veizades et al., 1995). Against the background of persistent human rights violations worldwide in the areas of racism, discrimination, inequality, intolerance, terrorism, poverty, corruption, exploitation, etc., it is high

[1] Haddock and Maio (2012: 173) defined attitude as "an overall evaluation of an object that is based on cognitive, affective and behavioural information." So, we derived our definition of human rights attitudes from their definition of the concept of attitude.

time appropriate attention is paid to other aspects of human rights as a way to promote a holistic practice. More recently, efforts have been made in the field of psychology by professional organisations such as the American Psychological Association (APA) and the International Society for Political Psychology, and in the field of theology by the International Programme Religion and Human Rights (RHR) to fill this void in scholarship.

Theological research on human rights attitudes focuses on the legitimacy of human rights. Drawing on the seminal work of Jürgen Habermas, *Between Facts and Norms: Contributions to a Discourse Theory of Law and Democracy* (1996), Ziebertz and Ziebertz (2016: 46) differentiate between legitimacy and the concept of legality in this way: "[l]egality refers to the fact that human rights are 'positivised' by being juridical inscribed in human rights law. The legitimacy of human rights refers to the extent to which the people at large agree with these positivised rights" (see also van der Ven et al., 2004). The legality of human rights therefore relates to the codification of human rights issues in the relevant national legal instruments, while legitimacy has to do with their acceptance by the population. Empirical research on human rights attitudes in theology examines the degree of acceptance of universal human rights norms by people and the factors that influence the whole process, especially religion. That is precisely the purpose of this research, which uses a select group of Nigerians as a case study. The results of the studies by the International Programme Religion and Human Rights (RHR) so far show a complex empirical connection between religion and attitudes towards human rights. For this reason, more attention is paid to the role of religion in this study. As with attitudes in general, human rights attitudes can also be shaped by an array of factors such as the psychological trait of empathy, the value preferences of the individual, the principle of human dignity, the perception of threats and the perceived quality of life. The supporting theories have been adopted from the social sciences, especially social psychology.

The use of social science paradigms in theological research is sometimes contested by scholars. However, theology is not an isolated discipline. Rather it has dialogical links with science, especially the social sciences, and is fundamentally open to infiltrations by them. Theology advocates an interdisciplinary approach which entails incorporating the method and useful social science insights into an overall theological perspective (Ziebertz, 2002; Wronka, 1992). This is exactly what is going on in practical theology. Similarly, religious education is interdisciplinary and recognises contributions from relevant disciplines in the field of education (Heywood, 1989). Likewise, theological research on human rights attitudes cannot ignore useful findings from social sciences when dealing with human rights attitudes because, as Haddock and Maio (2012: 172) have put it, "[t]he study of attitudes is at the core of social psychology." With that said, we shall now briefly introduce the theories.

4.2 Social Significance of Religion

The inevitable decline of religion was the dominant model in Western sociology of religion during the 19th and most of the 20th centuries. Already in the time of the Enlightenment, standard theories of secularisation predicted that the emergence of industrial society would lead to a decline in religiosity and a decrease in the practical relevance of religion (Diehl et al., 2009; Pickel, 2017). Among other things, the Enlightenment had introduced a new worldview with an emphasis on science and intelligence. Based on this, scholars, including the founding fathers of the sociological system—Auguste Comte (1798–1857), Karl Marx (1818–1883), Émile Durkheim (1857–1917), and Max Weber (1864–1920)—believed that industrial modernity would come to finally supplant religion in its historical role in meeting human needs, especially in education and social services. This narrative of secularisation was recently challenged by the counter-narrative of a return of religion (Pickel, 2017) and critics alluded inter alia to the continued vitality of religion in the US, the growth in Islamic fundamentalism and the upsurge of ethno-religious conflicts in international affairs. In their book *Sacred and Secular: Religion and Politics Worldwide*, Norris and Inglehart (2004) responded to the criticism of the classic secularisation theories of the permanent decline of religion. They partly agree with the critics and call the theories inadequate, relying on massive evidence of cross-national data from the World Values Survey. They then revised the theories to develop their own version of the secularisation model based on the core idea of human security and the historical legacy of the respective religious traditions. First, they argue that the varying influence of religion on societies around the world is closely related to different levels of existential security. In other words, the level of religiosity in any society is determined by the level of perceived security. And so, the practical relevance of religion in poorer countries, among population groups that are particularly vulnerable to inequality, poverty and inadequate state social services, would not diminish or disappear entirely, but would remain. Second, they assume that religious traditions have had a lasting influence on the cultures of every nation and that their values are now transmitted to citizens primarily through national institutions (see Norris & Inglehart, 2012). In this case, the nature of religiosity in a particular society would therefore reflect the historically dominant religions in that society. Likewise, differences in values in today's societies, for example in the areas of gender roles, gender equality, sanctity of life, importance of marriage and family, sexual liberalisation, etc., can be traced back to the different religious traditions. And to the extent that these religions are still able to influence social and moral issues in societies today, Norris and Inglehart predict that they will continue to be socially relevant (cf. Breskaya et al., 2019).

Norris and Inglehart may not have been alone in their views on the continuing social relevance of religion. José Casanova (1994) had already recognised this in his de-privatisation thesis, in which he alluded to the new visibility of religion in the public arena of political discourse in Western societies (cf. Botvar et al., 2019). However, while Casanova was more interested in the role of religion on a societal level, Norris and Inglehart stressed the influence of religion on the moral and ethical values of populations. Their theories are deemed appropriate for this study as they assert the continued societal relevance of religion. Here we examine the influence of religion and religiosity on human rights attitudes. Recent studies of the International Program Religion and Human Rights show that there is indeed an empirical connection between religion and attitudes towards human rights. For example, Zaccaria, Anthony and Sterkens (2019) found in their study that religion—defined in terms of religious beliefs and practices—shaped the bioethical attitudes of young Italians. Similar research by Francis et al. (2018) also showed that their measures of religious attitudes proved to be strong predictors of attitudes of young people in England and Wales towards political rights. Ziebertz and Ziebertz (2016) also affirm that dimensions of religiosity such as religious-intellectual interest and belief in the social function of religion can help explain the attitudes of young Germans towards labour rights.

Now Norris and Inglehart formulated their theory based on the Western context. Hence, the application of secularisation theory as part of our theoretical framework can lead to questions of its plausibility for our study context or even to questions of its universal validity, as Pickel (2017) did. However, the theory is applied here based on its basic tenet of the enduring social relevance of religion and its accompanying double logic of human security and the historical heritage of religious traditions. The importance of religion in social issues has also been observed by African scholars with reference to the African context (Egede, 2007; Mbiti, 1989). The narrative of a return of religion is not an issue because religion never left the public space in the first place. It has always been an integral part of life of the African (Thorpe, 1992) and shapes the entire life of individuals and groups, including their attitudes towards the fundamental values of peace, human security and rights (cf. Bolatito, 2013). Van der Ven et al. (2004) showed that the religious attitudes of young South Africans have a significant influence on their assessment of human rights issues. Van der Tuin and Fumbo (2012) later confirmed in their research that religious factors such as beliefs and practices have a significant general influence on attitudes of Tanzanian youth towards the socio-economic rights of women.

Current studies and index reports indicate a high level of religiosity among Nigerians (Huber, 2008; Odoeme, 2011; PEW Report, 2020), with an equally high religious participation (approximately 88%)—measured in terms of mosque or church attendance or as ritual participation in our dataset. Coincidentally, the country also has a high level of existential insecurity (UNDP Report, 2020; Nwafor, 2010; World Bank, 2020). The Nigerian context therefore seems to be a suitable test case for the theory of the social relevance of religion. We view religion as a relevant social actor in Nigeria and an important cultural factor shaping the opinions and decisions of Nigerians regarding human rights. Nigerians are mainly Muslims, Christians and adherents of a variety of indigenous beliefs (ATR). These three religious traditions constitute the main religious identity marker in Nigeria and define the country's religiosity, as Norris and Inglehart suggest. Hence, we expect that public attitudes towards human rights in the country will be strongly influenced by the teachings of these religions. For example, freedom of religion is anchored in the sacred texts and teachings of these religious traditions. Regardless of the narrative of a rivalry between these religions in Nigeria, which can be explained by a variety of contextual factors, we expect Nigerians to fundamentally support the right to religious freedom. With regard to the right to freedom from discrimination based on sexual orientation, the three religious identities are heterosexually oriented. Hence, we expect Nigerians to be less receptive to gay rights. As the dominant religious identities in the country, it is undeniable that they largely determine what becomes government policy. They may have in some way contributed to the government's signing of the 2013 Same Sex Marriage (Prohibition) Act (SSMPA), a law that supports discrimination against homosexuals in the country. So, we do not expect Nigerians to support gay rights. The same applies to the right to life issues of the death penalty, abortion and euthanasia, which are part of a political and religious discourse. All three religions in our context have always supported the death penalty from the start. So, we expect Nigerians to oppose the prohibition of the death penalty, despite the recent reorientation of the Christian religion on this issue. Even more so if other contextual factors, such as the high crime rate in the country, etc. are considered. We do not expect them to endorse the legality of abortion either, as all three religions claim to be pro-life, albeit with slight doctrinal differences. The religions have contributed in some way to the failure to sustain any reforms of the national abortion law, as they did in connection with the Violence Against Persons (Prohibition) (VAPP) Law. Abortion is an issue on which the religious traditions in the country are very active. Another is the bioethical question of euthanasia. Hence, we expect any notion of the permissibility of abortion and euthanasia to be rejected by Nigerians, mainly because it is fundamentally unacceptable on religious grounds.

In contrast, we expect their attitudes towards political rights to be generally positive but follow the same religious logic. Religious top organisations in Nigeria, such as the Jama'atu Nasril Islam (JNI) and the Christian Association of Nigeria (CAN), are continuously committed to good governance and politics. These religious bodies also organise seminars, workshops and crusades to educate and sensitise the population about the peaceful conduct of national elections. They speak out loudly against a national policy that creates a feeling of disenfranchisement among the Nigerian people, and they are committed to caring for refugees and displaced persons. Granted, Muslims may be divided on some aspects of political rights such as participation in democracy and protests, but overall we do not expect Nigerians to oppose political rights. Instead, most of them are likely to support the rights. We are more optimistic about the right to a fair trial than about political rights. We expect Nigerians to stand up for the right to a fair trial, since dominant religious traditions all have strong support for justice. Here, too, religious bodies such as Justice, Development and Peace/Caritas Advocates (JDPCA) and many others are actively involved in the fight against corruption and injustice in the country. Based on these, massive support for the right to a fair trial can be expected from the Nigerian people.

As far as socio-economic rights are concerned, religious traditions in Nigeria, especially Islam and Christianity, are not neutral towards workers' rights (cf. Ziebertz & Ziebertz, 2016). They preach against government policies that are unjust to Nigerian workers and are somehow employers of labour themselves. For example, many vocational schools in the country are founded by religious organisations, and these institutions have teachers who they maintain without subventions from the government. In addition, the religious traditions in Nigeria advocate the empowerment of women and the appropriate representation of women in the necessary decision-making bodies of society. They are also actively involved in child education, especially the girl child, through establishment of schools, and in caring for vulnerable members of society, including orphans, the physically disabled and the mentally ill. Even so, religious beliefs and practices are sometimes used to legitimise the subordination of women and gender inequality (Van der Tuin & Fumbo, 2012; Francis et al., 2016). In addition, certain local customs that run counter to women's rights, such as marriage, property and inheritance, persist in the country. Children's rights are also faced with religious and cultural challenges. Religious adherents use their beliefs as a pretext to abuse the socio-economic rights of the child, especially in child marriage and corporal punishment (see APPGN Report, 2013). Nonetheless, we expect Nigerians to support socio-economic rights in relation to selected socio-economic issues, although there can be significant differences due to the theological perspectives of different religious traditions. Indeed, it would be interesting to see how religion as a whole affects human rights attitudes in the Nigerian context.

While we assume that socio-cultural factors are the key factor influencing the decisions and opinions of Nigerians regarding human rights, it is erroneous to think that human rights attitudes in Nigeria have only a cultural explanation. Empirical evidence has shown that orientations to social processes like human rights can have multiple explanations. For this reason, we have also included other theoretical mechanisms here, such as the psychological trait of empathy.

4.3 Theories of Empathy

When examining social issues such as attitudes towards human rights, there are compelling reasons to include the individual's ability to feel empathy as one of the explanatory factors. Among other things, social psychological research has consistently found close associations between empathy and prosociality, including altruism (McDonald & Messinger, 2011). Empathy theorists have so far provided several definitions of empathy, enough definitions to give us a comprehensive overview of the term (cf. Cacioppo & Patrick, 2008; Davis, 1983; Eisenberg & Miller, 1987; Hodges & Myers, 2007; Hoffmann, 2000; McDonald & Messinger, 2011). When a person sees someone in pain, distress or suffering, is discriminated against or exploited, (s)he may put him- or herself in that other person's position and experience his or her feelings as if they were his or her own (Hodges & Myers, 2007). This ability to perceive and share another person's emotional experiences is empathy, and that is how the term is used in this study. It is defined as "the reactions of one individual to the observed experiences of another" (Davis, 1983: 113).

As one's reaction to the perceived situation of another person, empathy can be cognitive or affective, and these two components are distinct from one another (Hodges & Myers, 2007; McDonald & Messinger, 2011; Preston & de Waal, 2002). Cognitive empathy, on the one hand, refers to the ability to understand another's perspective or feelings. It can be decomposed into a number of scales, including for instance perspective-taking, that is, the ability to see another person's situation from his or her viewpoint, rather than one's own. Cognitive empathy is also closely related to the theory of mind. It is believed that this side of empathy does not necessarily involve caring about the other person (Hodges & Myers, 2007; Cherry, 2020). Affective or emotional empathy, on the other hand, refers to the ability to respond appropriately to another's emotions. According to Hodges and Myers (2007), it has three subcomponents namely emotional contagion, personal distress and empathic concern. In short, emotional contagion is called feeling the same emotions as the other person. Personal distress is described as an egocentric feeling of discomfort in response to being aware of someone else's predicament, while empathic concern means feeling sympathy and compassion for him or her in response to the predicament (see also Cherry, 2020). It is important to note that empathic concern is the most common understanding of empathy in psychology. Researchers consider it a key ingredient of an other-oriented moral reaction (Hodges & Myers, 2007; Knafo et al., 2008).

Empathy is usually directed towards the other, and this can be individuals or social groups (Hoffmann, 2000). The ability to empathise develops early in humans. Research has demonstrated that infants begin to show signs of empathy as early as 18 h after birth, with the affective components emerging first. Then, the trait develops steadily through childhood and adolescence. In the end, the empathy skill still turns out differently in people, and this is due to the nature-nurture factors of biology and socialisation, including the question of context (McDonald & Messinger, 2011). Furthermore, individuals tend to empathise more with people of their social groups (e.g., family, ethnic or religious group members, etc.) and less with out-groups.

Empathy is conceptualised in social psychological literature as a prosocial personality trait, a potential psychological motivator for prosociality. Prosociality here refers more generally to any behaviour that is positive, helpful, and intended to promote the interest of another person (Lexicon Dictionary, 2021). Empathy plays an important role in social interactions; it helps individuals connect with others and improve the quality of their interactions (McDonald & Messinger, 2011). It also helps them make moral choices. This important link between empathy and morality was underpinned by Hoffmann (2000). Having empathy can inspire people to act in a prosocial manner when they see others in need. They can do this for them even if they are not directly observing the target's emotion or situation, provided there is an "imaginative identification" (van der Ven, 2013: 178). This assumption of a close link between empathy, in particular affective empathy, and prosocial behaviour has been confirmed by several studies (cf. Davis, 2015; Eisenberg & Miller, 1987; Hodges & Myers, 2007; McDonald & Messinger, 2011; Knafo et al., 2008). The same is true of human rights. Empathy has been shown multiple times to predict support for human rights. McFarland and Mathews (2005) found empathy as a predictor for advocating human rights ideals in their study. In a separate study, McFarland (2015) consistently found a positive correlation between dispositional empathy and support for human rights. Ziebertz et al. (2018) also came to a similar result in their research, namely that empathy in young Germans triggered strong support for the right to the inherent dignity of all persons. The same applies to Ok et al. (2020) in their study on attitudes towards socio-economic rights among Turks. They also found that empathy positively predicted these rights. Case et al. (2008), however, came to a different conclusion; their study showed another possible character of empathy. Not only was their construct of empathic concern unable to predict prejudice or discrimination against women, but it also had positive effects on discrimination against homosexuals.

Even so, we still believe that empathy helps people understand the perspectives, needs, and intentions of others, increasing the likelihood that they will intervene for the benefit of others. Building on this, the standard hypothesis is that empathy leads to advocacy of other people's rights (cf. Hunt, 2007). As far as Nigeria is concerned, we expect all empathic Nigerians to support the rights of others, especially the rights under study. All the same, it would not really surprise us to find similar results to Case and colleagues when it comes to, for instance, the right to freedom from discrimination against homosexuals and the possibility of the right-to-life issues of abortion and euthanasia, based largely on socio-cultural factors.

4.4 Theory of Basic Human Values[2]

Attitude is a multi-dimensional entity. The human rights attitudes of the Nigerian population cannot therefore be explained solely by their psychological profile in relation to empathy. Values are also a possible explanatory element (Sousa & Bradley, 2006). To understand the human rights attitudes of individuals and groups of people in Nigeria, their value systems must therefore be taken into account.

The term 'value' has no overarching definition. In everyday language, values refer to the things or objects that we value, desire or need. They can be social, moral, religious, economic, political, aesthetic, organisational and so on. In the social sciences, values refer to ideals, standards and guiding principles for the decisions and actions of people in society. The study of human values is not new. Social psychological research on this topic over the past century has been well developed in the writings of contemporary value theorists such as Clyde Kluckhohn (1951), Milton Rokeach (1968, 1973), and Shalom H. Schwartz (1992, 1994, 2012), to mention just a few. Schwartz and associates focus on the content and structure of values. Their theory of basic human values is considered one of the most influential and

[2] In this study, we followed largely Sousa and Bradley's (2006) and Ziebertz's (2019) ways of presenting Schwartz's Theory of Basic Human Values because they suit our research method very well. This is explained in detail in the Research Design.

comprehensive value theories in the field, as it offers an understanding of values that integrates the views of earlier value theories (cf. Miloš & Novak, 2018).

Drawing on Rokeach's value research, Schwartz (1994: 21) defines values "as desirable transsituational goals, varying in importance, that serve as guiding principles in the life of a person or other social entity." From this definition the following three points can be highlighted. First, values are not attitudes towards particular situations or actions. For Schwartz, they are broad motivational goals (cf. Potts, 2015). Hence, he refers to them as transsituational. Second, Schwartz sees values as guiding principles of conduct, and life orientations that serve the interests of individuals and social groups. At the individual level, values represent internalised guides for personal action (Schwartz, 2012). Rokeach (1973) also describes them in this context as a central part of a person's identity, which function as cognitive standards for personal action. Usually, individuals differ in the way they perceive situations. Values influence how a person interprets a situation so that potential outcomes are assessed as desirable or undesirable, for example (Feather, 1995, in Sousa & Bradley, 2006). They are a sustainable basis for subjective evaluations and actions and shape the individual's perception of the world (cf. Kluckhohn, 1951; Rokeach, 1973). At the societal level, values represent common goals that motivate and regulate the attitudes and behaviour of group members in order to promote the survival of the group and the smooth functioning of society (Schwartz, 1992, 2012). They are shared ideals that guide social interactions and stable standards that determine people's choices between alternative courses of action. They are acquired through the process of socialisation in particular contexts and can therefore differ depending on the society due to differences in context (cf. Gulati & Pant, 2005). Notwithstanding this fact, Schwartz (2012) still believes that they are likely to be universal because they help humans cope with one or more of the three universal human needs, namely biological needs of the individual, social needs and societal needs of group survival and of welfare. Values can also be experienced, taught and learnt; they can be cultivated at home, or in school, etc. Third, although they are universal, values have a hierarchy, meaning that they vary in importance as guiding principles in life; some are thought to be more important than others (Schwartz, 2012; cf. Gennerich & Ziebertz, 2016; Potts, 2015).

The importance of human values has long been recognised in research. The difficulty all along was the question of how to assess individual values and that is Schwartz's main contribution. Schwartz's work (1992) addresses this question by shifting the level of analysis from the cultural to the individual level (cf. Sousa & Bradley, 2006). Since then, individual human values have been successfully used in research to assess religious attitudes (Gennerich & Huber, 2006), psychic distance (Sousa & Bradley, 2006), consumer behaviour (Strack et al., 2008), and human rights attitudes (Gennerich & Ziebertz, 2016; McFarland, 2015; Miloš & Novak, 2018; Ziebertz, 2019). The plausibility of the model has further been confirmed based on results from 82 countries in which it was tested, including Nigeria. It is important to note that Schwartz's theory was originally based on a value survey conducted on student and teacher samples (Schwartz, 2012). We therefore assume that the model is likely to match our sample.

The value theory (Schwartz, 1992) identifies ten comprehensive core values based on universal human needs. The values are arranged in four higher-order value domains, namely self-transcendence (universalism and benevolence), self-enhancement (achievement and power), openness to change (self-direction and stimulation), and conservation (conformity, tradition, and security). The basic values are given in parentheses after each of the four master values. The remainder of these basic values—hedonism—sits somewhere between self-enhancement and openness to change. The basic values differ from one another in their defining goal or motivation. The defining goal of universalism is understanding, appreciation, tolerance, and protection for the welfare of all people and for nature. The single value types that represent universalism include, inter alia, broadmindedness, social justice, equality, peace, wisdom, and the protecting of the environment. Benevolence relates to prosocial values like concern for the welfare of one's in-group, especially family members, and the more specific values that express benevolence are honesty, tolerance, helpfulness, and loyalty. Achievement values stress demonstrating successful performance according to prevailing social standards. The specific values that epitomise achievement are ambition, personal success, competence and being influential. Power represents the goal to attain or preserve social status and prestige, control or dominance over people and resources. Power is exemplified by single value types such as authority, wealth, social power, social recognition, and preservation of public self-image. Self-direction is defined by independent thought and action in choosing, creating, and exploring. The specific values that characterise self-direction are creativity, mastery, freedom and independence. The defining goal of stimulation is excitement, novelty, and being positive to face challenges in life, while the single value types are a varied life, an exciting life, and boldness. Conformity emphasises restraint of actions, inclinations, and impulses that are likely to upset or harm others and violate social expectations or norms. The specific values that typify conformity are obedience, self-discipline, politeness, and filial piety. Tradition depicts values such as respect, commitment, and acceptance of the customs and ideas that one's culture or religion provides. The single value types that exemplify tradition are respect for tradition, humility, devotion, moderation, and acceptance of one's own fate in life. Security values embody safety, harmony, and stability of society, of relationships, and of self. The single value types that represent security include keeping social order and harmony. Last—but not the least—hedonism is defined by the goal to enjoy pleasure or sensuous gratification for oneself. The specific values of hedonism are pleasure, enjoying life, and self-indulgence (Schwartz, 1992, 2012; Schwartz & Sagiv, 1995; see also Gennerich & Ziebertz, 2016; Potts, 2015; Sousa & Bradley, 2006). When considered collectively as domains, it can be observed that the values that constitute the self-transcendence domain represent the motivation to transcend selfish concerns and promote the welfare of others, whereas the values of self-enhancement symbolise the motivation to enhance self-interests, even at the expense of others. The values of openness to change, for their part, emphasise independent action, thought and feeling as well as readiness for new experience, while conservation values emphasise self-restriction, order, and resistance to change. These three features represent the motivation to preserve established arrangements to maximise certainty. Hedonism shares elements of both openness and self-enhancement (Schwartz, 1992; Sousa & Bradley, 2006).

In the second part of the value theory, these four value domains are further classified into two opposing dimensions, namely self-enhancement versus self-transcendence, and openness to change versus conservation. Based on this arrangement, values on opposite sides of the divide are portrayed as competing for priority. In his work, Schwartz addresses extensively the dynamic relationship between values. However, we were not particularly interested in this aspect of the theory as it does not fall within the scope of this study. The focus here is on the relationship between individual values and human rights attitudes, and we are looking at the value priorities that can help explain this relationship. We consider the roles of self-transcendence and openness to change in Schwartz's work to be particularly important because they are more or less prosocial values (Potts, 2015). More recent studies suggest an empirical connection between prosocial values and attitudes towards human rights. In their study, Miloš and Novak (2018) hypothesised that people with prosocial value ideals are likely to support human rights, and rightly found, among other things, a significantly positive relationship between support for human rights and the value domains of self-transcendence and openness to change, both of which are defined in their paper as prosocial value orientations. The only exception was the single value type of stimulation which showed a significant negative link with judicial rights. Gennerich and Ziebertz (2016) also came to interesting results. In their opinion, the human rights attitudes of their study population were largely located in the values of universalism and benevolence. There is consistent evidence for the relationship between the two value domains (self-transcendence and openness to change) and attitudes towards human rights at various levels of analysis (cf. Doise et al., 1999; McFarland, 2015). We therefore postulate that the values that make up the self-transcendence and openness-to-change domains will induce support for the selected human rights of this study. In any case, it would also be interesting to see what other value orientations predict human rights attitudes in the Nigerian context and how Schwartz's value theory fares in this study.

4.5 Theory of Human Dignity

The term 'human dignity' does not lend itself to easy definition. Despite its definitional difficulties, the concept is a topical theme in the field of human rights and has played a significant role in shaping the concept of human rights. For this study, we adopt Lebech's (2003: 12) definition of the term as "the fundamental value of the human being" as our working definition. Human dignity describes the intrinsic value which every individual has for the sake of being human. This concept did not emerge in a vacuum. Although ideas about the meaning of dignity in human life were already present in the thinking of the Socratic philosophers in ancient Greece[3] and it is attributed to the Stoics, especially Cicero (106–43 BC),[4] that they were the first to use the term 'human dignity' in Western philosophical thinking, there is a broad consensus the modern understanding of dignity is an intellectual invention of the humanists scholars of the Renaissance, notably Giovanni Pico della Mirandola (1463–94) (cf. Bayertz, 1996; Lebech, 2003; McCrudden, 2008; Nordenfelt, 2021; van der Ven et al., 2004; Ziebertz et al., 2018). In his influential treatise *De Hominis Dignitas* (Oration on the Dignity of Man 1486, in Nordenfelt, 2021) Pico is said to have argued that the human being is special and has a special dignity. Pico premised this dignity on the human ability to choose freely. He also viewed it as a gift from God (see also McCrudden, 2008; Ziebertz et al., 2018). However, the universalisation of this understanding of dignity, a dignity that covers all human beings irrespective of their individual characteristics, only occurred through the relatively recent inclusion of this provision in the Universal Declaration[5] of 1948 and its legal versions, the ICESCR[6] and the ICCPR[7] in 1966.

Based on existing historical discourses on the concept, Nordenfelt (2004, 2009, 2021) formulates four interrelated forms of dignity. The first is the dignity of merit, which he recently renamed 'attributed dignity' because it is entirely based on human attribution (cf. Nordenfelt, 2021). This dignity describes the type of dignity that is usually given to a person of rank, for example, a respected leader or a high-ranking person on social standing, etc. It is very unevenly distributed among people, can vary greatly in degree and can be gained or lost. The second, the dignity of moral stature, has also been given a more expansive label, namely the dignity of inflorescence. According to Nordenfelt (2021), it represents the kind of dignity that is due to a person who has a certain excellence. This can be intellectual, athletic, aesthetic, or moral excellence. Hence, the dignity of moral standing is now a subcategory of this. Although the line between these two revised concepts of dignity now seems to have blurred somewhat, there is evidence that inflorescent dignity is still tied to character, virtue, elegance, and the like. As such, it can be affected by social expectations. It can also vary in degree and can be gained or lost through one's conduct. The third kind of dignity is the dignity of identity. This relates to the integrity of the

[3] In this connection, for instance, Lebech (2003: 3) suggests that the Greek word αξια (axia), which is a rough translation of the Latin phrase 'dignitas' (dignity), occurs in Aristotle's Nichomachean Ethics. Axia means "the worth whereby someone or something counts for more or less." In addition, she points out that Aristotle also emphasised the possession of rationality as the reason for the supereminence of humans.

[4] The idea of human dignity is traced to the ancient stoic philosophers. Cicero's seminal work, *De Officiis (On Duties)*, is mentioned in this connection as first of the classical sources on the subject. As Palenčár (2016: 467) summarily and aptly puts it "[i]n the work of Cicero, the ontological (ontic) thinking on human nature is mixed-up with axiological thinking …". Similarly, Rosen (2012, in Ziebertz et al., 2018) opines that Cicero prepared the ground for an inherent concept of human dignity.

[5] Cf. Preamble and arts. 1, 22, & 23(3).

[6] Cf. preamble.

[7] Cf. preamble.

body and mind of individuals and in many cases, but not always, to people's perception of who they are. It can be affected by how others treat a person, as well as age, physical disfigurement, or disability. Then there is a fourth type of dignity, which is a universal type of dignity (Menschenwürde). This is common to all persons because of their humanity. Unlike the other types, it is neither socially constructed nor dependent on any situation or condition other than their humanity (cf. Dwyer, 2008). So, while the other types are more of a temporary nature, 'Menschenwürde' can never be lost as long as the persons exist; it is the universal high value of all human beings and remains throughout their lives (Nordenfelt, 2021). This is the kind of dignity Lebech tries to define above. It is referred to as inherent dignity in human rights literature.

The concept of inherent dignity is surrounded by much controversy, with modern thinkers such as Arthur Schopenhauer, Karl Marx and Friedrich Nietzsche largely dismissing it as a meaningless term (cf. McCrudden, 2008; Ziebertz et al., 2018). However, Meehan (2014) points out that said controversy is due to the explanations given for the source of the concept. The Stoics in the Hellenistic-Roman period of philosophy located this, for example, in social status and human rationality (van der Ven et al., 2004; see also Palenčár, 2016). Christian theology ascribed it to the special position that humans occupy in creation as *'imago Dei'* (the image of God). Based on this narrative, human dignity is understood as a share in the dignity of God. But then this dignity can be lost if human beings deviate from God's plan in their life through sin (cf. Bayertz, 1996; Lebech, 2003; Ziebertz et al., 2018). The Judeo-Christian perspectives were championed by scholastic thinkers, particularly Thomas Aquinas (1225–1274). Lastly, there is another explanation, a secular one. This is represented by the modern philosopher Immanuel Kant (1724–1804). In his work *Groundwork of the Metaphysics of Morals*, Kant based the concept of dignity on humanity alone, that is, on the ability of human beings to make free moral choice. For Kant (1785) the concept of autonomy is the most central element of dignity. His understanding of dignity can best be understood with the idea of dignity as autonomy, according to which to treat people with dignity means to treat them as autonomous individuals who can choose their destiny (cf. McCrudden, 2008; Meehan, 2014; Nordenfelt, 2021). To arrive at this position, modern philosophy relied on the model of self-reflective, creative freedom of human nature that it had adopted from the humanist thinkers of the Renaissance, while leaving out the religious elements (van der Ven et al., 2004).

In these explanations, the idea of dignity remained fundamentally dependent on behaviour and status and, as such, was only associated with duties, but not with rights. The connection was only specified in the ICCPR in 1966, where it was finally defined as the basis of human rights,[8] as it was only loosely linked to it in other founding documents of the UN (cf. Ziebertz et al., 2018; McCrudden, 2008). This connection was not well received by critics, who then questioned the direct line

[8]The preamble to the ICCPR reads that the "rights derive from the inherent dignity of the human person." The rights in question are the human rights provisions contained in it. It goes on to elaborate on the rights in subsequent articles and paragraphs.

from dignity to rights and thus the eligibility of the former as a justification for the latter (Rosen, 2012). Be that as it may, the concept of inherent dignity justifies the association, and in recognition of this contemporary conception, the UN agrees that universal human dignity establishes universal human rights, at least from a practical political perspective. The concept is also entrenched in the African Charter as an essential goal for the realisation of the legitimate aspirations of the African peoples.[9] Overall, dignity is now recognised as the principle that legitimises all rights.

An empirical investigation with the concept of dignity is not easy because of the controversies and conceptual difficulties mentioned above. Nevertheless, in this study we use a threefold operationalisation of the term that has been used in a number of studies to date (cf. Anthony & Sterkens, 2019; Webb & Asa'd, 2019; Ziebertz & Ziebertz, 2016; Ziebertz et al., 2018). Hence, we distinguish between the dignity of merit, the dignity of moral stature, and the inherent dignity. The three summarise the two prevailing trends of contingent and non-contingent interpretations in the historical development of the concept of dignity. According to Ziebertz and Ziebertz (2016), the contingent interpretation of dignity refers to the forms of dignity that are believed to accrue to individuals based on their social status, personal achievements, or moral behaviour, etc., while the non-contingent interpretation understands dignity as inherent to all human beings. Human rights within the framework of the UN are anchored in the concept of inherent dignity, that is, dignity as something that people have because they are humans, and research has shown that this concept predicts attitudes towards human rights. Ziebertz and Ziebertz (2016), for example, consider it to be a strong predictor of labour rights. Similarly, we expect it to induce support for our selected human rights.

4.6 The Integrative Theory of the Quality of Life

Perception of quality of life is the other contextual variable we included in the study. Although it may seem straightforward, quality of life (hereinafter QoL) is a multifaceted construct that covers a wide range of domains and topics. Research in this area began not so long ago and is the result of numerous attempts in many disciplines to measure and generate social progress. The research effort has produced impressive literature within and across disciplines. Due to its multidisciplinary character, there is no uniform definition of quality of life, no definitive theoretical framework and no standardised form of measurement. It has actually been studied using a variety of approaches and indicators (Brown et al., 2004; Çakiroğlu, 2007; Veenhoven, 2000). We consider the integrative quality of life theory of Ventegodt et al. (2003) to be one of the most comprehensive models of the term quality of life. There are four reasons to want to apply the integrative quality of life theory

[9] African Charter, Preamble, and para. 5; see also Protocol to the African Charter on the Rights of Women in Africa 2003, art. 3, inter alia.

(hereinafter IQoL) in this study. First, we believe that we still have the free hand to do so. Although the subject may have been treated under other headings since ancient times, such as good life, well-being, etc., as some suggest (see Bowling & Windsor, 2001), quality of life is still an evolving area of research that has yet to stabilise. It has so far no generally accepted theory. Second, one of the goals of the IQoL model is to be able to measure the quality of life on a global level. For this reason, it is not out of place to apply it to this study on the assumption that it would fit into our context. Third, this study measures quality of life at the micro level (individual, subjective) and some of the concepts that Ventegodt and colleagues highlighted as proxy indicators of quality of life in their theory such as well-being, life satisfaction and happiness, correspond to how we understand and measure the concept in this study. We define it with Dalkey and Rourke (1973, in Kerce, 1992: 3) as "a person's sense of well-being, his satisfaction or dissatisfaction with life, or his happiness or unhappiness". We chose this as our working definition because it aligns with our approach to the subject. Above all, however, we assume that subjective assessments of life and society are an important source of information about people's well-being and an essential part of their overall perceived quality of life (cf. Campbell, 1981 in Brown et al., 2004; Kerce, 1992). Fourth, and this in continuation of the last point, we presented objective indicators of quality of life in detail earlier in the study (e.g., data on life expectancy, GDP per capita, literacy rate, etc.) as well as some relevant indices (e.g., UN Human Development Index, Global Democracy Index, End of Childhood Index, etc.). Perhaps the subjective approach could help us to get a bigger picture of the quality of life in Nigeria. But that is not the aim of this study; instead, we intend to examine the link between the perception of QoL and the human rights attitudes of Nigerians.

The IQoL defines quality of life in terms of "a good life" or "living a life with a high quality" (Ventegodt et al., 2003: 1030). According to Ventegodt et al. (2003), the concept of a good life cannot be traced to any person or group of people. All major religions and philosophies have an idea of the good life and how they feel it can be achieved. Societies, too, have ideas of a good life that are closely related to their cultures. These notions can, according to IQoL, be arranged into three groups, each dealing with one aspect of a good life, namely the subjective, existential and objective aspect. The subjective quality of life refers to how good a life each individual feels (s)he has and how (s)he perceives things. Life satisfaction and *joie de vivre* (happiness) are common features of this aspect. The existential quality of life refers to the level of being that goes beyond the biological level, that is, the deeper level and how good life is on this level. It is believed that this level represents the depth of the essence of humanity. The objective quality of life concerns non-subjective facts. It is about how one's life is perceived by the outside world. This perception is shaped by the culture in which one lives and is expressed in the ability of a person to adapt to the values of a culture. For Ventegodt et al. (2003) these three aspects of quality of life have no clear boundaries. They tend to overlap and can be further divided into a subjective-existential-objective spectrum comprising eight domains that make up the IQoL theory. The domains are well-being, satisfaction with life, happiness, the meaning in life, the biological information system, realising life potential, fulfillment of needs, and objective factors. In this study we only focus on one of the them, namely satisfaction with life because it is relatively easy to measure (cf. Ventegodt et al., 2003).

Satisfaction with life is a cognitive activity that is about evaluating one's life. It is a feeling that life is as it should be (Ventegodt et al., 2003). When one's aspirations in life are met by the environment, one is satisfied. Quality of life researchers believe this is the result of a comparison that reflects a perceived discrepancy between aspirations and accomplishments. If the discrepancy between these hardly deviates from the benchmarks, a higher level of life satisfaction is achieved. For this reason, Diener et al. (1985, in Brown et al., 2004:23) defined it "as a cognitive judgmental process dependent upon a comparison of one's circumstances with what is thought to be an appropriate standard." It has to be noted that for IQoL theorists, satisfaction is not so much about realising all one's aspirations objectively, but rather about finding harmony in what one wants life to be and how one thinks it is. Satisfaction is also not to be confused with happiness, as it is very common to be satisfied but not happy. It is not the same as experiencing meaning in life because again one can be content with life but feel bad inside. Life satisfaction alone is not to be equated with quality of life, as some believe; rather, it is only a superficial aspect of the quality of life (Brown et al., 2004). Therein lies the problem of using it as the only measure of quality of life, namely that a good life means more than just being satisfied. Most quality-of-life theories, however, focus on satisfaction because researchers prefer it to other more emotionally and intuitively achieved concepts (Ventegodt et al., 2003). Like them, this study uses the term to measure the perceived quality of life.

Furthermore, most quality-of-life studies often used life satisfaction as a predicted variable (e.g., Harrison et al., 2016). There are some that use it as a predictor variable (cf. Religion and Human Rights' questionnaire). We used it in this study like the latter group and would like to know the connection between it and the human rights attitudes of the Nigerian people. While people do not necessarily have to lead dissatisfied lives to support human rights, advocating for human rights is stronger in an atmosphere of dissatisfaction. This is reflected in the Nigerian context. It was the dissatisfaction of the population with their political rights situation that led the Nigerian elites to demand independence from colonial rule under the banner of human rights. In a more recent development, the nationwide #ENDSARS protest, in which the rights to life and protest are now being discussed in Nigeria, emerged from the young people's dissatisfaction with the functioning of the police or the state's security agencies. In such cases, the character of human rights as a political solution to the fight against experiences of injustice and oppression becomes clearer. Therefore, based on this precedent and theoretical reasons, it is expected that perceived quality of life will influence the attitude of the Nigerian population towards human rights.

4.7 Social Identity Theory

Recently, the need to consider social context when examining social issues such as human rights has been highlighted. It is suggested that the factors that drive the human rights attitudes of a population can be embedded in their socio-political context (Sommer & Stellmacher, 2009; McFarland, 2015; Webb et al., 2012). For this reason, we have included two contextual variables in this study. One of them is threat perception. It makes sense to include "a threat perception factor" here as social media is flooded with reports of all sorts of tension and conflict between social groups in Nigeria. It is also assumed that identity politics is widespread in the country (Osaghae & Suberu, 2005; Okpanachi, 2012). It would be interesting to know whether the perception or awareness of threats in their milieu triggers Nigerians' attitudes towards human rights, as the development of moral thinking is expected to be linked to specific thematic experiences (Ziebertz et al., 2018). There are several theoretical mechanisms used in research to explain intergroup relations. But the theory of social identity (hereinafter SIT) formulated by the social psychologists Henri Tajfel and John Turner (1979) interests us here for two reasons: first, because it uses the concept of a social identity to explain attitudes towards one's own social group (i.e., the in-group) as well as those towards another group (the out-group). Hence, given the context of the perceived identity politics in the country, it could theoretically be plausible. Second, the model has been widely used in research to explain intergroup dynamics.

The SIT states that individuals strive to achieve a positive social identity, partly by making positive comparisons between the in-group and relevant out-groups. The theory is anchored on the concept of social identity—define here as "those aspects of an individual's self-image that derive from the social categories to which he perceives himself as belonging" (Tajfel & Turner, 1979: 40). The theory has two components, namely the motivational and cognitive components (Zárate, 2009). The desire for positive self-esteem is the motivational component. Tajfel and Turner (1979) suggest that people desire a positive self-esteem and that the groups which they belong to are an important source for it. In order to increase their self-image, people therefore make their group appear more positive by derogating relevant out-groups. Then, for the cognitive component, Tajfel and Turner identified three complex mental processes that drive the perception of group memberships, namely social categorisation, social identification and social comparison. It is assumed that these processes follow a certain sequence (McLeod, 2019). Just as the physical world (e.g., objects, events, etc.) is systematically made understandable through categorisation, people are assigned to social groups through social categorisation, with categories such as "them" and "us", white/black, stranger/son of the soil,[10] females/males, Muslims/Christians, northerners/southerners, rich/poor, and nomads/farmers, etc. Although this process is based on the normal cognitive

[10] This expression means 'a native', in contrast to a stranger. In fact, it is the most effective Nigerian way of communicating the 'native' mentality.

tendency to sum things up, this process is often done with a bit of an exaggeration, where i:) the in-group is perceived to be different from the out-group, and ii:) the out-group members to be more similar than they are. Social categorisation as the process by which the distinction between in-group and out-group arises is a possible trigger for negative perceptions that underlie some intergroup attitudes (Coenders, 2001).

After assigning themselves to one or more groups, people assume the identity of the group(s) (i.e., social identification). They become emotionally attached to the group and their self-esteem is bound up with group membership. Social identities thrive on comparison. As Tajfel (1981: 258) puts it, "the definition of a group … makes no sense if there are no other groups around." Hence after categorisation and identification have taken place, people try to compare their groups with others. Given the urge for a positive self-esteem, they are motivated to evaluate their groups positively (in-group favouritism) and tend to evaluate other groups negatively (out-group derogation). Studies have shown that these two processes correlate (Coenders, 2001), and both can help explain how negative perceptions are driven between groups under competitive conditions. In summary, SIT suggests that in-group members look for negative aspects of an out-group to improve their self-image (McLeod, 2019). However, social identity theorists also claim that out-group actions are often responsible for the perception of in-group threats. The interaction of these processes can generate certain negative attitudes between groups, such as prejudice, stereotypes and discrimination, etc. Empirical research has demonstrated a great deal that threat perceptions can motivate individuals to express out-group derogation (cf. Schlueter & Scheepers, 2010; Stephan & Renfro, 2002; Stephan & Stephan, 2000). SIT has been criticised for failing to fully account for the essential differences in intergroup conflict (Coenders, 2001). Notwithstanding this fact, the theory offers a true glimpse into intergroup relations.

Some elements of the SIT can be seen in the Nigerian situation. A typical example is the ongoing herder/farmer crisis. The perception of the threat posed by the Fulani cattle herders, often associated with land grabbing and other grueling activities by the majority of the Nigerian population who are farmers, has sometimes resulted in the violation of the right of movement of an average Fulani person. While the arbitration process often results in human rights standards being invoked as part of the solution, the perception of threats in Nigeria is, intuitively, always likely to meet the negative reaction of in-group members—and this corresponds to the central principle of SIT. In terms of human rights, however, the whole situation is seen a little differently. The perception of conflictual relationships between social groups, in particular the categories that are named in article 2 of the Universal Declaration, such as race, sex, language, religion, political opinion, social status etc., is likely to induce support for human rights (Doise et al., 1999; Spini & Doise, 1998), since human rights by their nature are products of such socio-political processes and experiences (Wronka, 1992; Santuraki, 2016; van der Ven, 2013). It is based on this fact that the perception of threats is expected to induce the readiness to support human rights not only for one's own group, but also for marginalised groups as well. This assumption seems to be confirmed by the findings of Doise and colleagues in their study, but it has to be pointed out that they included both perceived threats and personal experiences of tensions and injustices in their measurements. What is more, their findings do not seem generalisable. Nevertheless, there are certain events in the Nigerian context that tend to make this human rights hypothesis credible. For example, it was the minority's fear of marginalisation by the country's ethnic majorities—a form of threat perception—that eventually led to the bill of rights being included in the Nigerian Independence Constitution as recommended by the Willink Minority Commission of 1957. In addition, perception of the threat posed by the ruling All Progressives Congress (APC) party, accused of desperation to remain in power in the country, has led to more calls from other political parties and a cross-section of Nigerians for electoral reform and for policies that would ensure that their votes count at the end of the day, or rather that the votes reflect the will of the people. From the above two perspectives, the perceived threat hypothesis can go either way. However, if one considers that only perceived threats are measured in this study, we assume based on the SIT that threatened individuals or groups react negatively to the source of the threat and are therefore less favourable to human rights. All the same, it would be interesting to see how the perceived threat hypothesis relates to the human rights attitudes of Nigerians and which of the two models better captures the Nigerian situation, the SIT or the human rights hypothesis.

4.8 Socialisation Theory

One other factor that can lead to improvements in interpersonal and intergroup relations is education. The socialisation theory offers one possible explanation for the effect of education on social interactions. Usually, educational attainment is a determinant of a person's placement in the job market and relative position in the job queue. But it also has a social value (Schneider, 2008; Statham, 2016). According to the socialisation theory, educational institutions transmit norms, values and models of behaviour that are considered relevant in a given society (Coenders & Scheepers, 2003). Studies of the relationship between education and interactions between persons and groups have stressed the cognitive component of attitudes towards in- or out-group members, etc. In the cognitive approach, attitudes such as discrimination, stereotypes, etc. are seen as intellectually unenlightened ideas because such attitudes thrive largely on simplified views of social reality and sweeping generalisations applied to a person or group of persons. As crude and simple as these attitudes may be, they are inevitable social realities and usually come about as simple-minded approaches to complex social realities. In other words, people with such a cognitive mindset tend to do so because they fail to understand abstract causes (Selznick & Steinberg, 1969). In contrast, educated people tend to reject such attitudes, and the more educated they are, the more so. Empirical evidence has shown that there is a negative relationship between education and, for example, ethnic intolerance (Coenders & Scheepers, 2003), exclusionism (Selznick & Steinberg, 1969), to name just a few. According to the cognitive approach, the ability to reject these negative attitudes can be interpreted in terms of certain processes that can be traced back to the educational system, namely "the transfer of knowledge and information, the development of cognitive capacities and the transfer of norms, values and modes of behaviour" (Coenders & Scheepers, 2003: 317). This can be termed the 'educational effect', that is, a part of the cultural capital that education furnishes the learner with.

It is not limited to the antisocial attitudes mentioned above. Education essentially opens the minds of learners to the vastness of the world in which they live. It familiarises them with the complexities of their societies and empowers them to deal with them by instilling in them the right attitudes and values (Falade, 2016). In addition, it increases their cognitive abilities, which are necessary for developing critical and balanced problem-solving skills. In this way, educational institutions transmit democratic value orientations that can reduce or prevent social disharmony and foster social cohesion (Schneider, 2008). However, the impact of education on intergroup and interpersonal relationships varies from context to context, as educational institutions around the world have a social function. This means that they transmit the values and norms of their country's political culture. This implies that they are likely to only instill in their younger generation liberal values and attitudes that are appropriate for their society. Depending on the society, this could have negative consequences for human rights. Apart from that, in various societies, school is essentially an institution that helps young people deal effectively with life's critical problems (Tyler, 1971). Based on this, we can also expect some educational effects on the human rights attitudes of our study population as they are students. Meanwhile, this study uses socialisation theory as an alternative explanation, that is, it is regarded as a possible surrogate cause for an observed outcome or the observed relationship between the explanatory factors and the human rights attitudes of Nigerian students.

Having outlined the theoretical framework for this study, it is important to highlight the state of research on this topic in the Nigerian context and why it is necessary to conduct this study.

4.9 State of Research

Whereas the overarching impact of religion and religiosity on socio-political issues like human rights in Nigeria has been suggested in an array of studies (e.g., Abara, 2012; APPGN Report, 2013; OHCHR, 2018; Izugbara, 2004), only very few published works have tried to assess this assertion empirically, and most of them focus on specific issues such as the moral question of abortion. One such study was conducted by Ubajaka et al. (2014) on the perception of abortion and abortion laws among lawyers in Anambra State, southeastern Nigeria. It identifies the religiosity of the participants as one of main reasons for their largely negative attitudes to abortion. A similar but comparative study conducted in 2019 by Adisah-Atta and Dim with the World Values Survey (2010–2014) on attitudes of Ghanaians and Nigerians towards abortion found a statistically positive association between religion and the justification of abortion in both countries. Datasets for empirical research are not that easy to come by in Nigeria. Hence, it is possible that most of these studies focus on a topic or area of research for which data are available.

Regarding the UN spectrum of human rights, there are several well-written empirical papers that focus on Nigerians' attitudes towards various specific rights such as workers' rights (Adewumi & Adenugba, 2010), sexual harassment in the workplace (Noah, 2008), wage discrimination against women (Nweke, 2014), and child welfare (Okpukpara et al., 2006). Most of these studies used different sets of variables that did not include religion-related variables, while others had different study populations. Their decisions about this were understandably guided by their research interests. Our study has more in common with an earlier study conducted by Atolagbe and Otubanjo in 1984, in which they examined college students' attitudes towards fundamental human rights in Nigeria and in which they found that more than half of the respondents (circa 60%) believe that fundamental human rights exist in Nigeria. In addition to the research topic of human rights attitudes and a study population very similar to ours, the paper also covers a whole range of fundamental human rights.

However, the study that is very close to our research interests was conducted by Odoeme (2011) who examined the human rights attitudes of adolescents in Nigeria. The study found that young people's religious and human rights attitudes were strongly correlated, but it did not specify whether this relationship was causal or not. This is exactly what this study aims to do, namely to examine the influence of religion and religiosity of young people in Nigeria on their human rights attitudes.

Summary

In this chapter, the aim of this study, namely to examine attitudes towards human rights, was presented in more detail. First, the term 'human rights attitudes' was delineated; it refers to evaluations people make about human rights, which can be positive, negative or ambivalent. So, in relation to Nigeria, it means the way the Nigerian people evaluate human rights. The second facet of the study, which concerns the predictors of human rights attitudes, was then highlighted. Attempts were made to select suitable theories from theological and related disciplines that would enable the research objective to be achieved. A total of seven widely used theoretical models were found and selected from related social sciences. These include the social significance of religion, empathy, basic human values, human dignity, social identity, perceived quality of life and socialisation theories.

Contrary to the prevailing model of the inevitable demise of religion championed by existing theories of secularisation, the social significance of religion predicts that religion will continue to play a vital role in contemporary society. The theory is deemed relevant to this study for its position on religion as an enduring social actor. The study assumes that religion-related variables are possible predictors of the human rights attitudes of the Nigerians based on reports of high religiosity in Nigeria. The central hypothesis of the social significance of religion has been substantiated by a number of quantitative studies. Some of the studies were cited accordingly to justify both the inclusion and suitability of the theory. Empathy theories conceptualise empathy, especially affective empathy, as a prosocial personality trait. Its prosocial character implies that, among other things, it helps people make moral choices. Empathy should therefore be a predictor of human rights attitudes. The same applies to value orientations because apart from values being guiding principles of conduct for individuals and groups, the theory of basic human values also presents the value domains of self-transcendence and openness to change as prosocial value preferences. This means that basic values as well as empathy can be viewed as possible predictors of human rights attitudes. This is even truer for the value of human dignity. The theory of human dignity defines inherent dignity as a type of dignity that accrues to all human beings based on their humanity. Inherent dignity is recognised by the UN as a founding value of human rights and therefore its inclusion in the list of possible predictors is a must. The theories of social identity and integrative quality of life are equally important because they are theoretical frameworks that are used to introduce contextual variables into the study. On the one hand, the social identity theory clarifies the influence of threat perception on social interactions. It states that perceived threats by an in-group can lead to negative reactions against an out-group. It is believed that given the alleged prevalence of identity politics in Nigeria, this theory will help us to derive a relevant hypothesis. On the other hand, the integrative theory of quality of life focuses on one's own assessment of one's life and society. It is believed that people's satisfaction with their life and society may in some ways affect their human rights attitudes. Finally, socialisation theory describes the effect of education as a cultural capital on interpersonal and intergroup relationships. Besides, the theory is provided in the study as an alternative explanation and functions only in that capacity.

All these are well-known theories in social sciences. The expectation is that they would enable us to find answers to the second part of the research question on predictors of human rights attitudes of young Nigerians, since the question, as indicated in the review of previous research, remains largely unanswered, at least quantitatively.

References

A. Books and Journals

Abara, C. J. (2012). *Inequality and discrimination in Nigeria tradition and religion as negative factors affecting gender*. A paper presented at the Federation of International Human Rights Museums, 8th–10th October 2012. Liverpool, UK.

Adewumi, F., & Adenugba, A. (2010). *The state of workers' rights in Nigeria: An examination of the banking, oil and gas and telecommunication sectors*. Friedrich-Ebert-Stiftung.

Adisah-Atta, I., & Dim, E. E. (2019). Justification of abortion in West Africa and interplay of sociodemographic predictors: A comparative study of Ghana and Nigeria. *Sage Open, 9*(1), 1–9. https://doi.org/10.1177/2158244019834368

Adorno, T. W., Frenkel-Brunswik, E., Levinson, D. J., & Sanford, R. N. (1950). *The authoritarian personality*. Harper and Row.

Allport, G. (1935). Attitudes. In C. Murchison (Ed.), *A handbook of social psychology* (pp. 789–844). Clark University Press.

Anthony, F. V., & Sterkens, C. (2019). Religion and the right to (dispose of) life: A study of the attitude of Christian, Muslim and Hindu students in India concerning death penalty, Euthanasia and Abortion. In H.-G. Ziebertz & F. Zaccaria (Eds.), *Euthanasia, abortion, death penalty and religion – The right to life and its limitations* (pp. 13–64). Springer.

Atolagbe, E. O., & Otubanjo, F. (1984). Attitudes of Nigerian College students towards fundamental human rights. *Social Behavior and Personality: An International Journal, 12*(1), 91–96.

Bayertz, K. (1996). Human dignity: Philosophical origin and scientific erosion of an idea. In K. Bayertz (Ed.), *Sanctity of life and human dignity* (Vol. 52, pp. 73–90). Springer. https://doi.org/10.1007/978-94-009-1590-9_5

Blank, T., & Schmidt, P. (2003). National identity in a United Germany: Nationalism or patriotism? An empirical test with representative data. *Political Psychology, 24*(2), 289–312.

Bolatito, L. A. (2013). Modernism and secularization: Towards a reconciliation of religious freedom and national security in the realization of peace in Nigeria. *Canadian Social Science, 9*(1), 135–146.

Botvar, P. K., Sarti, C., Zielińska, K., & Zwierżdżyński, M. K. (2019). Religion and attitudes towards abortion and Euthanasia among young people in Poland and Norway. In H.-G. Ziebertz & F. Zaccaria (Eds.), *Euthanasia, abortion, death penalty and religion – The right to life and its limitations* (pp. 243–270). Springer.

Bowling, A., & Windsor, J. (2001). Towards the good life: A population survey of dimensions of quality of life. *Journal of Happiness Studies, 2*, 55–81.

Breskaya, O., Botvar, P. K., Sjöborg, A., & Rogobete, S. (2019). Religion, trust in institutions and attitudes towards abortion: A comparison of Lutheran and Orthodox countries. In H.-G. Ziebertz & F. Zaccaria (Eds.), *Euthanasia, abortion, death penalty and religion – The right to life and its limitations* (pp. 271–299). Springer.

Brown, J., Bowling, A., & Flynn, T. (2004). *Models of quality of life: A taxonomy, overview and systematic review of the literature*. University of Sheffield.

Cacioppo, J., & Patrick, W. (2008). *Loneliness: Human nature and the need for social connection*. Nortion and Company.

Çakiroğlu, A. (2007). *Relationship between quality of life and happiness in Turkey*. M.Sc. thesis, Middle East Technical University, Turkey.

Campbell, D. T. (1965). Ethnocentric and other Altruistic motives. In D. Levine (Ed.), *Nebraska symposium on motivation* (pp. 283–311). University of Nebraska Press.

Casanova, J. (1994). *Public religions in the modern world*. University of Chicago Press.

Case, K. A., Fishbein, H. D., & Ritchey, P. N. (2008). Personality, prejudice, and discrimination against women and homosexuals. *Current Research in Social Psychology, 14*(2), 23–38.

Coenders, M. (2001). *Naturalistic attitudes and ethnic exclusionism in a comparative perspective: An empirical study of attitudes toward the country and ethnic immigrants in 22 countries*. KUN.

Coenders, M., & Scheepers, P. (2003). The effect of education on nationalism and ethnic exclusionism: An international comparison. *Political Psychology, 24*(2), 313–343.

Davis, M. H. (1983). Measuring individual differences in Empathy. Evidence for a multidimensional approach. *Journal of Personality and Social Psychology, 44*, 113–126.

Davis, M. H. (2015). Empathy and prosocial behavior. In D. A. Schroeder & W. G. Graziano (Eds.), *The Oxford handbook of prosocial behavior* (pp. 282–306). Oxford University Press.

Diaz-Veizades, J., Widaman, K. F., Little, T. D., & Gibbs, K. W. (1995). The measurement and structure of human rights attitudes. *The Journal of Social Psychology, 135*(3), 313–328.

Diehl, C., Koenig, M., & Ruckdeschel, K. (2009). Religiosity and gender equality: Comparing natives and Muslim migrants in Germany. *Ethnic and Racial Studies, 32*(2), 278–301.

Doise, W., Spini, D., & Clémence, A. (1999). Human rights studied as social representations in a cross-national context. *European Journal of Social Psychology, 29*, 1–29.

Dwyer, L. L. (2008). *Dignity in the end of life care – What does it mean to older people and staff in nursing homes?* Örebro University.

Egede, E. (2007). Bringing human rights home: An examination of the domestication of human rights treaties in Nigeria. *Journal of African Law, 51*(2), 249–284.

Eisenberg, N., & Miller, P. A. (1987). The relation of empathy to prosocial and related behaviors. *Psychological Bulletin, 101*, 91–119.

Falade, D. A. (2016). Problems and prospects of teaching religion and national values in the Nigeria Upper Basic School. *Nigerian Journal of Social Studies, 29*(2), 41–49.

Francis, L. J., Robbins, M., & McKenna, U. (2016). Women's socio-economic rights and religion among Christian, Islamic and non-religiously affiliated students in England and Wales. In H.-G. Ziebertz & E. H. Ballin (Eds.), *Freedom of religion in the 21st century. A Human rights perspective on the relation between politics and religion* (pp. 239–256). Brill.

Francis, L. J., McKenna, U., & Robbins, M. (2018). Attitude toward political rights and religious affiliation, experience, saliency and openness: An empirical enquiry among students in England and Wales. In C. Sterkens & H.-G. Ziebertz (Eds.), *Political and Judicial rights through the prism of religious belief* (pp. 1–21). Springer.

Gennerich, C., & Huber, S. (2006). Value priorities and content of religiosity – New research perspectives. *Archive for the Psychology of Religion, 28*, 253–267.

Gennerich, C., & Ziebertz, H.-G. (2016). Human rights and value priorities. In H.-G. Ziebertz & E. H. Ballin (Eds.), *Freedom of religion in the 21st century. A human rights perspective on the relation between politics and religion* (pp. 207–238). Brill.

Gorodzeisky, A., & Semyonov, M. (2009). Terms of exclusion: Public views towards admission and allocation of rights to immigrants in European Countries. *Ethnic and Racial Studies, 32*(3), 401–423.

Gulati, S., & Pant, D. (2005). *Education for values in schools – A framework.* National Council of Educational Research and Training.

Haddock, G., & Maio, G. R. (2012). Attitudes. In M. Hewstone, W. Stroebe, & K. Jonas (Eds.), *An introduction to social psychology* (5th ed., pp. 171–200). BPS Blackwell.

Harrison, E., Saini, R., & Zwiener, N. (2016). Perceived quality of society. In E. Harrison, A. Quick, & S. Abdallah (Eds.), *Looking through the wellbeing Kaleidoscope* (pp. 51–73). New Economics Foundation.

Herrmann, A. (2001). *Ursachen des Ethnozentrismus in Deutschland. zwischen Gesellschaft und Individuum.* VS Verlag für Sozialwissenschaften.

Heywood, D. S. (1989). *Revelation and Christian learning.* Ph.D dissertation, University of Durham, Durham.

Hjerm, M. (2007). Do numbers really count? Group threat theory revisited. *Journal of Ethnic and Migration Studies, 33*(8), 1253–1275.

Hodges, S. D., & Myers, M. W. (2007). Empathy. In R. F. Baumeister & K. D. Vohs (Eds.), *Encyclopedia of social psychology* (pp. 296–298). Sage Publications Ltd.

Hoffmann, M. L. (2000). *Empathy and moral development. Implications for caring and justice.* University Press.

Huber, S. (2008). Aufbau und strukturierende Prinzipien des Religionsmonitors. In: Bertelsmann-Stiftung (Hrsg.), *Religionsmonitor 2008* (pp. 21–31). Gütersloher Verlagshaus.

Hunt, L. (2007). *Inventing human rights.* Norton.

Izugbara, C. O. (2004). *Patriarchal ideology and discourses of sexuality in Nigeria* (Understanding Human Sexuality Seminar Series, 2). Africa Regional Sexuality Resource Centre.

Kant, I. (1785). *Groundwork of the metaphysics of morals* (Translated and edited by M. Gregor and J. Timmermann (1997)). Cambridge University Press.

Kerce, E. W. (1992). *Quality of life: Meaning, measurement, and models.* Navy Personnel Research arid Development Center.

Kluckhohn, C. (1951). Values and value-orientations in the theory of action: An exploration in definition and classification. In T. Parsons & E. Shils (Eds.), *Toward a general theory of action* (pp. 388–433). Harvard University Press.
Knafo, A., Zahn-Waxler, C., van Hulle, C., Robinson, J. L., & Rhee, S. H. (2008). The developmental origins of a disposition toward Empathy: Genetic and environmental contributions. *Emotion, 8*(6), 737–752.
Lebech, M. (2003). What is human dignity? In M. Lebech (Ed.), *Maynooth Philosophical Papers* (Vol. 2, pp. 1–13). National University of Ireland.
LeVine, R. A., & Campbell, D. (1972). *Ethnocentrism: Theories of conflict, ethnic attitudes, and group behavior*. Wiley.
Mbiti, J. S. (1989). *African religions and philosophy*. Heinemann Educational Publishers.
Mccrudden, C. (2008). Human dignity and judicial interpretation of human rights. *European Journal of International Law, 19*(4), 655–724.
McDonald, N. L., & Messinger, D. S. (2011). The development of Empathy: How, when, and why. In J. J. Sanguineti, A. Acerbi, & J. A. Lombo (Eds.), *Moral behavior and free will: A neurobiological and philosophical approach* (pp. 341–368). IF Press.
McFarland, S. (2015). Culture, individual differences, and support for human rights: A general review. *Peace and Conflict: Journal of Peace Psychology, 21*(1), 10–27.
McFarland, S., & Mathews, M. (2005). Who cares about human rights? *Political Psychology, 26*(3), 365–385.
McLaren, L. M. (2003). Anti-immigrant prejudice in Europe: Contact, threat perception, and preferences for the exclusion of migrants. *Social Forces, 81*(3), 909–936.
Meehan, T. C. (2014). Therapeutic Milieu: Inherent human dignity. *Journal of Clinical Nursing, 21*, 2905–2916.
Miloš, D., & Novak, K. (2018). The role of value orientations and political preference on political and judicial human rights among the Croatian Youth. In C. Sterkens & H.-G. Ziebertz (Eds.), *Political and judicial rights through the prism of religious belief* (pp. 71–94). Springer.
Noah, Y. (2008). Experience of sexual harassment at work by female employees in a Nigerian work environment. *International NGO Journal, 3*(7), 122–127.
Nordenfelt, L. (2004). The varieties of dignity. *Health Care Analysis, 12*(2), 69–81.
Nordenfelt, L. (2009). *Dignity in care for older people*. Blackwell.
Nordenfelt, L. (2021). *The concepts of dignity: An analysis*. Ersta Sköndal Bräcke Högskola.
Norris, P., & Inglehart, R. (2004). *Sacred and secular: Religion and politics worldwide*. Cambridge University Press.
Norris, P., & Inglehart, R. F. (2012). Muslim integration into western cultures: Between origins and destinations. *Political Studies, 60*, 228–251.
Nwafor, F. C. (2010). The viability of the social security system in Nigeria: An economic perspective. In E. C. Eboh & S. Oluwadare (Eds.), *Towards a sustainable social security in Nigeria* (pp. 10–19). Institute for Applied Economics.
Nweke, N. N. (2014). *Gender wage differences: The case of Nigeria*. M.Sc. thesis, Swansea University, Swansea.
Odoeme, P. C. (2011). *Human rights and the mission of the Church in Nigeria*. Lit Verlag.
Ok, Ü., Gören, A. B., Akbulut, S., & Getir, S. D. (2020). Religion and attitude to economic deprivation among Muslims: Checking the roles of value preference and empathy. In H.-G. Ziebertz (Ed.), *International empirical studies on religion and socio-economic human rights* (pp. 277–298). Springer.
Okpanachi, E. (2012). *Ethno-religious identity and conflict in Northern Nigeria: Understanding the dynamics of Sharia in Kaduna and Kebbi States*. French Institute for Research in Africa.
Osaghae, E., & Suberu, T. (2005). *A history of identities, violence, and stability in Nigeria*. University of Oxford.
Palenčár, M. (2016). Some remarks on the concept and intellectual history of human dignity. *Human Affairs, 26*, 462–477.

Pickel, G. (2017). Secularization – An empirically consolidated narrative in the face of an increasing influence of religion on politics. *Política and Sociedade – Florianópolis, 16*(36), 259–294.

Preston, S. D., & de Waal, F. B. M. (2002). Empathy: Its ultimate and proximate bases. *Behavioral and Brain Sciences, 25*, 1–72.

Rokeach, M. (1968). *Beliefs, attitudes and values: A theory of organization and change*. Jossey-Bass Inc.

Rokeach, M. (1973). *The nature of human values*. Free Press.

Rosen, M. E. (2012). *Dignity: Its history and meaning*. Harvard University Press.

Santuraki, S. U. (2016). Reflections on the concept and foundational convictions of human rights. *Uni-Maid Journal of Private and Property Law, 1*(1), 52–62.

Scheepers, P., Gijsberts, M., & Coenders, M. (2002). Ethnic Exclusionism in European Countries. Public opposition to civil rights for legal migrants as a response to perceived ethnic threat. *European Sociological Review, 18*(1), 17–34.

Schlueter, E., & Scheepers, P. (2010). The relationship between outgroup size and anti-outgroup attitudes: A theoretical synthesis and empirical test of group threat and intergroup contact theory. *Social Science Research, 39*(2), 285–295.

Schneider, S. L. (2008). Anti-immigrant attitudes in Europe: Outgroup size and perceived ethnic threat. *European Sociological Review, 24*, 53–67.

Schwartz, S. H. (1992). Universals in the content and structure of values: Theoretical advances and empirical tests in 20 countries. In M. P. Zanna (Ed.), *Advances in experimental social psychology* (Vol. 25, pp. 1–65). Academic.

Schwartz, S. H. (1994). Are there universal aspects in the structure and contents of human values? *Journal of Social Issues, 50*, 19–45.

Schwartz, S. H. (2012). An overview of the Schwartz Theory of basic values. *Online Readings in Psychology and Culture, 2*(1), 1–20.

Schwartz, S. H., & Sagiv, L. (1995). Identifying culture-specifics in the content and structure of values. *Journal of Cross-Cultural Psychology, 26*(1), 92–116.

Selznick, G. J., & Steinberg, S. (1969). *The tenacity of prejudice: Anti-semitism in contemporary America*. Harper and Row.

Sommer, G., & Stellmacher, J. (2009). *Menschenrechte und Menschenrechtsbildung*. Verlag für Sozialwissenschaften.

Sousa, C. M. P., & Bradley, F. (2006). Cultural distance and psychic distance: Two peas in a pod? *Journal of International Marketing, 14*(1), 49–70.

Spini, D., & Doise, W. (1998). Organising principles of involvement in human rights and their social anchoring in value priorities. *European Journal of Social Psychology, 28*, 603–622.

Statham, P. (2016). How ordinary people view Muslim group rights in Britain, The Netherlands, France and Germany: Significant 'Gaps' between majorities and Muslims? *Journal of Ethnic and Migration Studies, 42*(2), 217–236.

Stephan, W. G., & Renfro, C. L. (2002). The role of threats in intergroup relations. In D. M. Mackie & E. R. Smith (Eds.), *From Prejudice to intergroup emotions: Differentiated reactions to social groups* (pp. 191–207). Psychology Press.

Stephan, W. S., & Stephan, C. W. (2000). An integrated threat theory of prejudice. In S. Oskamp (Ed.), *Reducing prejudice and discrimination* (pp. 23–45). Lawrence Erlbaum Associates Publishers.

Strack, M., Gennerich, C., & Hopf, N. (2008). Warum Werte? In E. H. Witte (Ed.), *Sozialpsychologie und Werte* (pp. 90–130). Pabst Science Publisher.

Tajfel, H. (1981). *Human groups and social categories. Studies in the social psychology*. University Press.

Tajfel, H., & Turner, J. C. (1979). An integrative theory of intergroup conflict. *The Social Psychology of Intergroup Relations*, 33–47.

Tajfel, H., & Turner, J. C. (1986). The social identity theory of intergroup behavior. In S. Worchel & W. G. Austin (Eds.), *Psychology of intergroup relations* (pp. 7–24). Nelson-Hall.

Thorpe, S. A. (1992). *Primal religions worldwide: An introductory descriptive review*. University of South Africa.
Tyler, W. T. (1971). *Basic principles of curriculum and instruction*. University of Chicago Press.
Ubajaka, C. F., Adogu, P. O. U., Ilika, C., & Ilika, A. L. (2014). Perception of abortion and abortion laws by Lawyers in Anambra State Nigeria. *International Journal of Clinical Medicine, 5*, 695–703.
Van der Tuin, L. W. J. M., & Fumbo, C. D. (2012). Women rights and religion among Christian and Islamic students in Tanzania. In J. A. van der Ven & H.-G. Ziebertz (Eds.), *Tensions within and between religions and human rights* (pp. 203–222). Brill.
Van der Ven, J. A. (2013). Towards a legitimate role of religion in the domain of socio-economic rights. An empirical study among adolescents in North-West European countries. In J. A. van der Ven & H.-G. Ziebertz (Eds.), *Human rights and the impact of religion* (pp. 165–202). Brill.
Van der Ven, J. A., Dreyer, J. S., & Pieterse, H. J. C. (2004). *Is there a God of human rights? The complex relationship between human rights and religion: A South African case*. Brill.
Veenhoven, R. (2000). The four qualities of life. *Journal of Happiness Studies, 1*(1), 1–39.
Ventegodt, S., Merrick, J., & Andersen, N. J. (2003). Quality of life theory, I. The IQOL theory: An integrative theory of the global quality of life concept. *The Scientific World Journal, 3*, 1030–1040.
Wagner, U., Christ, O., & Heitmeyer, W. (2010). Anti-immigration bias. In J. F. Dovidio, M. Hewstone, P. Glick, & V. M. Esses (Eds.), *The Sage handbook of prejudice, stereotyping and discrimination* (pp. 361–376). Sage Publications.
Webb, R. J., & Asa'd, F. J. (2019). The right to life: A perspective of young Palestinian Muslims. In H.-G. Ziebertz & F. Zaccaria (Eds.), *Euthanasia, abortion, death penalty and religion – The right to life and its limitations* (pp. 161–186). Springer.
Webb, R. J., Ziebertz, H.-G., Curran, J., & Reindl, M. (2012). Human rights among Muslims and Christians in Palestine and Germany. In J. A. van der Ven & H.-G. Ziebertz (Eds.), *Tensions within and between religions and human rights* (pp. 177–201). Brill.
Wronka, J. (1992). *Human rights and social policy in the 21st century*. University Press of America.
Zárate, M. A. (2009). Racism in the 21st century. In D. N. Todd (Ed.), *Handbook of prejudice, stereotyping, and discrimination* (pp. 387–406). Psychology Press.
Ziebertz, H.-G. (2002). Normativity and empirical research in practical theology. *Journal of Empirical Theology, 15*(1), 5–18.
Ziebertz, H.-G. (2019). Human dignity, religious ethics or hedonism: what can predict young people's attitudes in Germany towards the right to life in the cases of euthanasia and abortion? In H.-G. Ziebertz & F. Zaccaria (Eds.), *Euthanasia, abortion, death penalty and religion – The right to life and its limitations* (pp. 83–104). Springer.
Ziebertz, H.-G., & Ziebertz, C. M. (2016). Labour rights and the impact of human dignity, Religious belief and perception of society. An empirical study among youth in Germany. *Journal of Empirical Theology, 29*(1), 45–77. https://doi.org/10.1163/15709256-12341337
Ziebertz, H.-G., Döhnert, S., & Unser, A. (2018). Predictors of attitudes towards human dignity. An Empirical Analysis among Youth in Germany. In H.-G. Ziebertz & C. Sterkens (Eds.), *Religion and Civil Human Rights in Empirical Perspective* (pp. 17–60). Springer.

International Human Rights Instruments

United Nations Development Programme (UNDP). (2020). *Human Development Report 2020. The Next Frontier: Human Development and the Anthropocene.*
World Bank Group. (2020). *Poverty and shared prosperity: Reversals of fortune*. World Bank Publications.

National Human Rights Instruments

All-Party Parliamentary Group on Nigeria (APPGN) Report. (2013). *Too many to count? Human rights, justice and accountability in Nigeria*. Chatham House.

OHCHR. (2018). *UN human rights report 2017*. Available at: https://www2.ohchr.org/english/OHCHRreport2017/allegati/Downloads/1_Whole_Report_2017.pdf. Accessed 1 July 2019.

PEW Report. (2020). *The global god divide*. Available at: https://www.pewresearch.org/global/2020/07/20/the-global-god-divide/. Accessed 01 July 2021.

Other Internet Sources

Cherry, K. (2020). *What is Empathy. Social psychology*. Available at: https://www.verywellmind.com/what-is-empathy-2795562. Accessed 02 Oct 2021.

Lexicon Dictionary. (2021). *The meaning of prosocial*. Available at: https://www.lexico.com/definition/prosocial. Accessed 29 Oct 2021.

McLeod, S.A. (2019). *Social Identity Theory*. Simply Psychology. Available at: https://www.simplypsychology.org/social-identity-theory.html. Accessed 01 Nov 2021.

Okpukpara, C. B., Chine, P. U., Uguru, F. N. O., & Chukwuone, N. (2006). *Child welfare and poverty in Nigeria*. A Paper Presented at Poverty Phase II Dissemination Workshop in Addis Ababa, Ethiopia on 12th to 13th October 2006. Available at: http://sarpn.org/documents/d0002269/Child-welfare_Nigeria_Okpukpara_Oct2006.pdf. Accessed 02 Feb 2017.

Potts, D. (2015). *The Schwartz theory of basic values and some implications for political philosophy*. Available at: https://irfankhawajaphilosopher.com/2015/08/12/the-schwartz-theory-of-basic-values-and-some-implications-for-political-philosophy/. Accessed 10 Nov 2021.

Part II
Empirical Study

Chapter 5
Research Design

Contents

5.1 Differentiated Research Questions and Hypotheses 268
5.2 Data Collection and Sample 270
5.3 Conceptual Model 271
5.4 Measuring Instruments 272
5.5 Method of Analysis 283
References 286

Introduction

With the conclusion of the theoretical perspectives, the context of discovery closes. The context of justification opens with the empirical part. Overall, the section consists of two chapters on research design and empirical results, namely this chapter and Chap. 6 respectively. They are dedicated to empirical analyses. This chapter, the fifth chapter, focuses on research design. The latter contains a detailed description of the study method. It begins with differentiated research questions and hypotheses. As a matter of fact, the research question and hypotheses have already been introduced in the general introduction and in the theoretical perspectives that have just been completed, but not specifically. Here they are turned into researchable questions. This is followed by a description of the data collection method and sample as well as the conceptual model of the study. In addition, the measuring instruments are presented and explained. This applies to all the concepts used in the empirical analyses. Then the chapter closes with a description of the method of analysis.

M. C. Adimekwe, *The Impact of Religion, Personality, Values and Worldviews on Attitudes Towards Human Rights*, Religion and Human Rights 11,
https://doi.org/10.1007/978-3-031-65749-8_5

5.1 Differentiated Research Questions and Hypotheses

The study explores the attitudes of a select group of Nigerian young people towards the set of human rights already presented in Chap. 3. For this reason, we ask: how do young people in Nigeria evaluate human rights and what factors emerge as predictors of their human rights attitudes? Once again, the concerned rights are the right to freedom of religion, the right to freedom from discrimination based on sexual orientation, the right to life under the three classical issues of the death penalty, abortion and euthanasia, the political rights, the right to a fair hearing, and socio-economic rights. The selection of these rights was guided by their relevance to the context. Some of them are frequently abused by most Nigerians while others are still very much debated in controversial circumstances. The choice of the young people—and in this case the young people—as the study population is no coincidence either; it was informed by the following six reasons. First, this study has a futuristic orientation because it looks at the future of human rights practice in the Nigerian context. In that case, the youth represent the future of their society, including Nigeria. They are also the future leaders of their society at all levels of society. Second, it has been indicated that Nigeria has one of the youngest populations in the world. According to reports, of the estimated population of over 200 million people in the country, about 49% were under 19 years old and over 62% were under 24 years old in 2020. In addition, the median age of the Nigerian population over the same period was estimated to be 18.6 years.[1] Thus, young people, especially adolescents, constitute a clear majority of the country's population and should as such be reckoned with when it comes to the future of human rights in the country. Third, the study aims to contribute to the formation of a human rights culture in Nigeria and therefore sees adolescence as the most realistic age for such a formation. Fourth, since the dataset was prepared under the auspices of the International Programme on Religion and Human Rights, it was necessary for comparable studies to collect data from a comparable group. Fifth, and on a more pragmatic note, the data collection for such a study in our context at the time was relatively more feasible for us with this group than with any other as it was possible to meet them in their schools. Lastly, young people are an integral part of their society because they live in it. They are aware of what is going on in terms of the practice of rights. They encounter these through the process of socialisation and their daily life experience and based on this can be described as the products of their society. Hence the question. Thus, the choice of youth was equally shaped by the same consideration of relevance to the context.

Based on the foregoing, we sharpen the general research question a little further to read thus:

---

[1] The World Factbook. (2021). Nigeria: People and Society. Available at: https://www.cia.gov/the-world-factbook/countries/nigeria/#people-and-society. Accessed 23.01.2022. See also UNDESA (2019). World Population Prospects: Special Aggregates. Available at: https://population.un.org/wpp/Download/SpecialAggregates/EconomicTrading/. Accessed 02.03.2020.

1. How do senior secondary school (hereinafter SSS) students in Nigeria evaluate the right to freedom of religion, the right to protection from discrimination against homosexuals, the right to life issues of prohibition of the death penalty and the possibility of abortion and euthanasia, as well as political rights, the right to a fair trial and socio-economic rights?
2. Are there significant differences in attitudes towards these human rights issues between student subgroups as defined by their religious affiliation?
3. How do the students' religious worldviews, the psychological trait of empathy, the value systems and the perception of Nigeria's socio-political context relate to their human rights attitudes?
4. Are their human rights attitudes predicted by these same factors?
5. What tentative relevant conclusions may be drawn from the results of this study for the development of an appropriate culture of human rights among the youth in Nigeria?

Regarding the first question, in line with the theory of the social relevance of religion and the implied religious logic, we expect the students to evaluate:

- freedom of religion and the right to a fair trial in strong positive terms (***hypothesis 1a***),
- the political and socio-economic rights with positive ambivalence (***hypothesis 1b***),
- but the protection of homosexuals from discrimination, the prohibition of the death penalty, and the possibility of abortion and euthanasia, negatively (***hypothesis 1c***).

With reference to the second question, it is assumed that the teachings of the Islamic and Christian faiths reflect the attitudes of students towards these human rights issues. We therefore expect that the students differ significantly in their attitudes towards the possibility of abortion and their willingness to support political rights based on the doctrinal orientations of their religions (***hypothesis 2***). That means in simpler terms, we expect:

- Christian students to have more unfavourable attitudes towards abortion than Muslims (***hypothesis 2a***), and
- Muslim students to have less favourable attitudes towards political rights than Christians (***hypothesis 2b***).

With reference to the fourth question, we expect:

- the religiosity of the students to strongly predict their support for freedom of religion, and the right to a fair trial (***hypothesis 3a***), and
- to predict weakly the support for political and socio-economic rights (***hypothesis 3b***),
- but to strongly predict their rejection of the protection of homosexuals from discrimination, the prohibition of the death penalty and the possibility of abortion and euthanasia (***hypothesis 3c***).

Furthermore, in line with the respective theoretical frameworks, we expect:

- the students' feeling of empathy to impact their human rights attitudes in strong positive terms (***hypothesis 3d***);
- positive effects from the values of self-transcendence (universalism and benevolence) and openness to change (self-direction, stimulation, and hedonism) on the adolescents' human rights attitudes (***hypothesis 3e***);
- the notion of inherent dignity to induce stronger support for human rights from the students (***hypothesis 3f***);
- that the more dissatisfied the students are with their lives and the way their society works is the stronger their advocacy of human rights will be (***hypothesis 3 g***); and
- perceived threats by the students to lead to negative human rights attitudes (***hypothesis 3 h***).

Overall, we expect that the students' religiosity is the main predictor of their human rights' attitudes (***hypothesis 4***).

5.2 Data Collection and Sample

The data collection for this study took place in 2014 in six states of Nigeria, namely Abia, Ebonyi, Imo, Kaduna, Lagos and Sokoto, as well as in the federal capital Abuja. The choice of these States was guided by convenience and purpose. During the search, we found helpers in these places with relative ease. But more importantly, we wanted to spread the exercise across the country to get a fuller picture of the views of Nigerian youth. Two of the states, Kaduna and Sokoto, and Abuja, are in the north of the country, while the rest are in the south. At least two schools in each of the states were sampled. A total of 18 secondary schools were visited, so more schools were examined in some states such as Lagos and Abuja. Seven of the schools are private and the rest public schools. Here, too, the selection of schools was based on whether the composition of the schools was considered relevant for the research project. This simply means that only schools where there are likely interactions between different social groups and identities in the country (e.g., men, women, Muslims, Christians, traditionalists, rich, poor, etc.) were considered. Public schools are more likely to guarantee this and are therefore more in the sample. Only SSS students (1–3) took part in the exercise. Most of the adolescents in the country can be found in this age group. In addition, collecting data from this group provided us with the comparable sample that we needed to be able to take part in the International Programme Religion and Human Rights (hereinafter RHR). But it also implies that the resulting data are not representative of the entire youth population of Nigeria and that the results of the study cannot be generalised as such.

The instrument we used for the same exercise was the English version of the questionnaire prepared by RHR. We only made small adjustments to it. In most cases, copies of the questionnaire were distributed through the teachers for the students to fill out. Participation was voluntary and the students were assured of the anonymity and confidentiality of their responses. Despite the adjustments in the questionnaire, some students said that the grammar and vocabulary were difficult and that they could not understand some of the questions. Others, citing the volume, complained that the instrument was too long for their attention span. Others were still suspicious of the exercise and seemed to have the impression that for whatever reason the exercise was targeted at their social groups. In some of these cases, however, many students stayed behind to complete the exercise under the guidance of the teacher and sometimes the researcher, who sometimes explained some items. Participants were sometimes given light refreshments in appreciation. Overall, 1800 questionnaires were either distributed directly to the students or sent via the schools. Of these, 1682 were filled in and returned, but only 1191 are usable after data cleaning. The sample includes participants within the age bracket of 14–22 years, which means their average age is 17.36 years. According to the data, 656 of the sampled students (ca. 55%) are females and 535 (ca. 45%) are males. Regarding religious affiliations, 774 persons (ca. 66%) identified themselves as Christians, 403 persons (ca. 34%) are Muslims. Another 14 persons who assigned themselves to other religious groups were excluded from the analysis from the outset, as their number did not achieve statistical significance. Christians are slightly overrepresented in this survey, while Muslims are underrepresented judging from the official estimates of religious affiliation in the country. For more information on population characteristics, see Table 5.2 below.

5.3 Conceptual Model

To be able to answer the differentiated research questions, a good number of concepts are required. The concept model (see Fig. 5.1) shows a collection of concepts selected for this purpose. They are grouped in three separate columns with the following names: dependent, independent, and control variables. The dependent variables represent the main objective of this study which is to explain attitudes of young Nigerian students towards these human rights issues: freedom of religion, freedom from discrimination based on sexual orientation, right to life, political rights, right to a fair trial, and socio-economic rights. It is believed that there are factors that could be used to explain the said attitudes. The factors include religious beliefs, beliefs and practices, the psychological trait of empathy, value orientations and the value of human dignity, the perceived quality of life and the threat perception of social groups. All these factors make up the independent variables. Some population characteristics such as age, gender, social class, religious affiliation, and influence of peers are included as control variables in the study. The use of the control variable is important, among other things, to meet the backdoor path criterion, which is necessary to avoid the problem of confounding bias. It is believed that these variables can obscure the relationship between human rights attitudes and the explanatory factors if their effects are not controlled or "held constant". Their

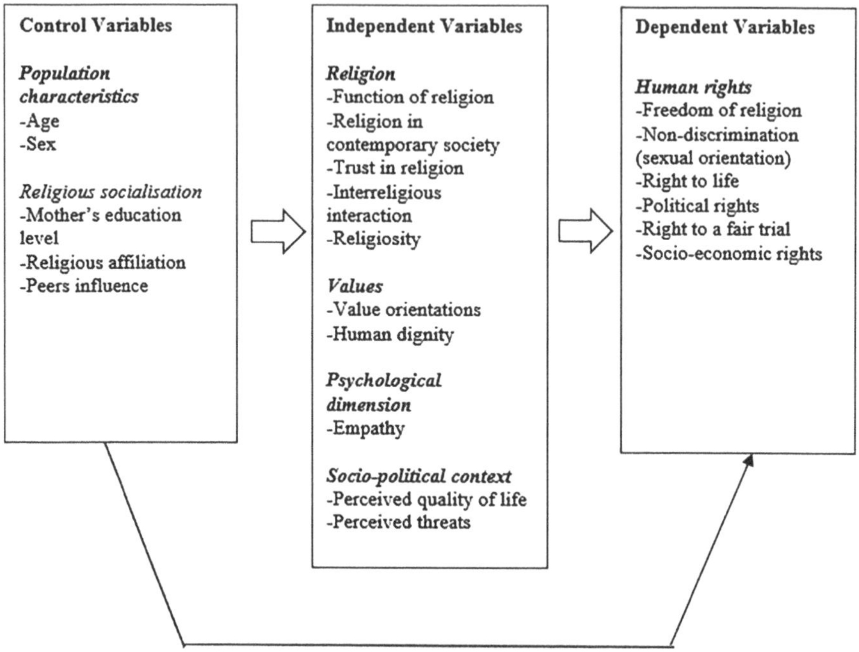

Fig. 5.1 Conceptual model: The impact of independent variables on dependent variables, controlling for population characteristics. The arrows show the path of the observed relationships

inclusion in the study is therefore to enable a better assessment of the net effects of the independent variables on the dependent variables. The observed relationships between these three sets of variables are demonstrated by the arrows.

5.4 Measuring Instruments

The psychometric instruments for all variables used in the study are presented here. These are presented in the anti-clockwise direction according to the arrangement order in the conceptual model.

Human Rights Attitudes

In this study, the term 'human rights attitudes of young people in Nigeria' is understood to mean the way in which a group of Nigerian youths evaluate human rights issues as positive, negative or ambivalent. Human rights attitudes are the dependent variables. They are measured with six (but in all eight) human rights provisions. These include the right to freedom of religion, non-discrimination against homosexuals, the three classic cases of restricting the right to life (i.e., the death penalty, abortion and euthanasia), political rights, the right to a fair trial and socio-economic rights.

The freedom of religion, historically a hard-won human right, describes the freedom to choose a religion or no religion without any interference. It is enshrined in the Universal Declaration as a safeguard of democratic society. Due to the character of Nigeria as a multi-religious society, it is entrenched in her Constitution and entitles every person living in the country to freedom of thought, conscience and religion, or irreligion. Various indicators for assessing religious freedom can be found in the literature, such as the use of religious symbols in public spaces or the state-controlled environment of the public school (e.g., cross signs, beads, crucifixes, veils or headscarves, etc.), religious practice in educational institutions, establishment of denominational private educational institutions, provision of religious education (hereinafter RE) in the curriculum, political non-interference in activities of religious groups, etc. We found enough psychometric tools in the RHR questionnaire and decided to use the following: 'students should be offered time, space and a room in schools to do their prayers'; 'the state should not prevent female teachers from wearing a head scarf for religious reasons'; 'the state should respect the right of religions to establish schools'; and 'the government should provide for enough space that religion could be taught in schools.' Students were asked to indicate to what extent they agree or disagree with these statements on religious freedom based on a five-point Likert scale, which ranges from "1 = totally disagree" to "5 = fully agree". Responses in the lower and higher categories are assumed to mean negative and positive attitudes towards human rights respectively, while the middle option "3 = I am not sure" represents ambivalence. However, to be sure whether the four items are compatible with each other, we conducted a reliability analysis, which resulted in a Cronbach's alpha (α) of .62. Although not an optimal score,[2] this figure still shows that the items had a good measure of internal consistency and can be used as a scale.

The right to freedom from discrimination on the basis of sexual orientation is one of the categories contained in the anti-discrimination clause of the Universal Declaration and guarantees the protection of all persons, especially homosexuals and other sexual minorities, from all forms of abuse and violence because of their sexual orientations. The following two items were used to measure attitudes towards this right: 'homosexuals should have the right to hold any public office'; and 'the state should prosecute behaviour which discriminates against homosexuals'. The Cronbach's alpha ($\alpha = .70$) looks good and as such the items are used as a scale in the study.

The right to life is widely recognised as the basis of all other rights. Correctly interpreted in the context of the UN, it includes the protection of both life and a dignified life. This further implies that it is not an absolute right. In this study, we examine the three classical cases in which the limitation of the duty to protect the life is being discussed, namely the death penalty, abortion and euthanasia. With regard to the death penalty, the current global trend is towards its abolition,

[2] The general rule of thumb is that a Cronbach's alpha of .70 and above is good, .80 and above is better, and .90 and above is best. See Statistics Solutions (2021). Cronbach's Alpha. Available at: https://www.statisticssolutions.com/cronbachs-alpha/. Accessed 01.11.2021.

particularly the mandatory death penalty, and the UN recommends commuting death sentences to life imprisonment instead. However, Nigerian law provides a mandatory death penalty for various offences. We wanted to know what the students think, so we picked up these two items, which address the main issues raised by the right: 'the death penalty should strictly be prohibited because of the right to life'; and 'a death sentence should always be commuted to a life sentence.' The two items generated a weak but manageable Cronbach's alpha (α) of 0.54, and so we decided to use them here as a scale. In the case of abortion, a combined reading of the right to life and the reproductive rights of women under the framework of the UN indicates that induced abortion could be allowed under certain conditions, such as threat to life of a mother, health risks for a mother or baby, cases of rape, incest, or fetal impairment, as well as a broad range of socio-economic reasons, etc. Nigeria has a very restrictive abortion law which allows abortion only for the purpose of preserving the life of a mother and which criminalises other forms of abortion. We want to know where the students stand on this topic and in order to assess this, the following seven items were used: 'abortion should be permitted (1) in case of rape'; (2) 'in case of incest'; (3) 'when there is a strong chance of serious defect in the baby'; (4) 'when the woman's own health is seriously endangered by the pregnancy'; (5) 'when the woman cannot afford any more children economically'; (6) 'when the woman cannot afford any more children psychologically'; and (8) 'abortion should be prohibited in all circumstances because it terminates beginning human life.' Obviously, these items cover several reasons why abortions are often requested. We wanted to use the eight items as a scale, but not without knowing whether they form a unit or differentiate themselves in the minds of the students as reasons for abortion. For this reason, we carried out a factor analysis (results not given here) and can use the factor loadings to confirm that all items except the last (i.e., item no. 8) have a single dimension. We therefore excluded it and then carried out a reliability test for the remaining items, which resulted in a Cronbach alpha of 0.75. Thus, they are used here as a scale. As with abortion, a community reading of the right to life and the associated individual human right to self-determination guarantees individuals full control over their lives, including their health. This includes the right to choose or reject a mode of treatment which may result in their deaths. Though not stated in clear worded terms, euthanasia is understood as murder or homicide in Nigerian law. In the questionnaire we found three items with which the attitude of the students to the bioethical topic of euthanasia could be assessed. These include: 'euthanasia should be prohibited in all circumstances'; 'euthanasia should be permitted in the case of unbearable and irreversible suffering'; and 'euthanasia should be permitted in the case of unbearable and irreversible suffering, if palliative care is exhausted.' We wanted to use the three items as a scale, but they did not seem to be compatible. Once again, we confirmed that the first item did not fit together well with the other two items and excluded it. We then computed scores for the remaining two items and found them reliable as a scale ($\alpha = .81$).

In human rights literature, the concept of political rights embraces an array of topics. Interestingly, the questionnaire provided six items which discuss thematic issues such as political participation, protests, and political asylum, etc. The items are: 'everybody, living here for some period prescribed by law, should have the right to vote for political leaders' and 'everybody, living here for some period prescribed by law, should have the right to run for public office' (on right of political participation); 'the police should not use force against political demonstrations that put public order at risk' and 'the government should not forbid public protests, however controversial they might be' (on right of protest); 'the government should guarantee political refugees' freedom to travel' and 'the government should provide a decent standard of living for political refugees' (on right of political refugees). With factor analysis, we found that all the items form a single concept in the mind of the respondents and decided to keep them together as an additive index of political rights. The ensuing reliability analysis, which produced a manageable Cronbach's Alpha ($\alpha = .60$), showed that they can be used as such to assess the political rights attitudes of the students.

In this study, the human right to a fair trial is simply understood to mean a fair trial by a knowledgeable judge or jury. It is an internationally recognised basic human right, the aim of which is to ensure the orderly administration of justice. This right is also enshrined in the Nigerian Constitution. There are many indicators that can be used to study the right, as demonstrated in the theoretical part of the study. Here it is measured with four items that relate to the specific aspects of the right under study, namely the right to remain silent and the right to defence. The items are as follows: 'a suspect taken into custody should not be obliged to speak'; 'a suspect taken to court should not be obliged to answer questions by the court'; 'mass murderers should be guaranteed access to a lawyer'; and 'someone suspected of repeated sexual abuse of children should be given legal aid.' The first two relate to the right to silence and the last two to the right to defence. The items have a clearly low Cronbach's alpha of 0.58, but we still considered them as a scale to be manageable.

Lastly, socio-economic rights are second generation rights. As a concept, it describes those rights that protect the necessities of life or create the basis for an appropriate quality of life. Socio-economic human rights are controversial in Nigeria insofar as most of the universal provisions of these rights are not viewed as rights, but as desirable goals of the Nigerian state. We want to know what the students' views are on a wide variety of socio-economic rights issues. Socio-economic rights have many branches, some of which were highlighted in the theoretical part. Examples are labour rights and the right to social security. Labour rights also include a cluster of rights such as workers' rights, non-discrimination against women in the workplace, protection from child labour, etc. For each of these rights there are indicators that are widely supported in research, and we found many of them in the questionnaire. For example, workers' rights are assessed using four items that discuss concepts such as the state's obligation regarding the right to work, living wages, equal pay for equal work, and reasonable limitation of working hours. The items read thus: 'the government should provide a job for everybody who wants one'; 'everyone should have the right to just and reasonable pay for work performed'; 'everyone should have the right to equal pay for equal work'; and 'everyone should have the right to reasonable limitation of working hours to get enough rest.' Women's rights are measured with the following three items: 'the state should protect women's right to adequate job opportunities'; 'women should have the right to be equally paid for equal work'; and 'women should have the right to be protected from sexual harassment in the workplace.' There are other psychometric instruments in the questionnaire, but we consider these ones to be appropriate because of the primacy of women's economic empowerment to the issue of gender equality. In contrast to women's rights, we did not find enough items that cover the spectrum of abuses of socio-economic rights of children in the Nigerian context, as was highlighted in the theoretical part. So, we had to be content with two items, which deal with the protection against child labour and the right to recreation. The items state: that 'the state should be obliged to protect children from (forced) child labour'; and that 'the state should be obliged to protect children's right to engage in play and recreation.' The right to social security is based on items relating to the state's obligation to care for the unemployed, the sick and the elderly. These items are operationalised as follows: 'the government should provide a decent standard of living for the unemployed'; 'the government should provide health care for the sick'; and 'the government should provide a decent standard of living for the old.' We wanted to use them as an index. We therefore carried out a factor analysis that confirmed their coherence in the minds of the adolescents. The reliability analysis that followed also attested to their internal consistency ($\alpha = .83$).

To sum up, all the items of the dependent variables are rated on a five-point scale of "1 = I totally disagree", "2 = I disagree", "3 = I am not sure", "4 = I agree" and "5 = I fully agree". Once more, the lower and higher values are interpreted to mean negative and positive human rights attitudes respectively, while the middle ground stands for a state of ambivalence.

Religion

The societal relevance of religion was rated using a cluster of variables related to religious beliefs, conviction, and practices. These include the function of religion, the perception of religion in contemporary society, trust in both religious in- and out-groups, perspectives on interreligious interactions, and religiosity. Religion is the main independent variable in the study. The function of religion was to be measured with 10 items that express all possible ideas about the expected role of religion in society such as spiritual service, public prophetic voice, cultural conformity, Influence on public opinion and national culture. Here, too, a confirmatory factor analysis was carried out to test their unidimensionality and the ten items were loaded onto three factors with the explained variance of 51.113%. We designated the first factor as 'social religion', the second factor as 'spiritual religion' and the third as 'cultural religion', the short forms of the social, spiritual and cultural roles of religion. The social role of religion comprises five items, which include: 'religions should take public responsibility for the societal development'; 'religions should consolidate nation against alien influences and deprivation of its originality'; 'religions should take a joint responsibility with the state for our national culture'; 'religions should use their authority to intervene in societal affairs'; and 'religions should try to influence public opinion on social problems.' The resultant scale yielded a manageable Cronbach's alpha of .57. The spiritual role of religion has three items with Cronbach's alpha of .60. These include: 'religions should take responsibility for their members' spiritual growth'; 'religions should publicly stand up for the underclass'; and 'religions should create places for deep spiritual experiences.' The remaining two items—namely, 'religions should go along with changing ideas in society', and 'religions should always keep up with current social trends'– go to the cultural role of religion. With a Cronbach's alpha of 0.65, the two items seem to form a more reliable scale. All the items of the function of religion were rated on a five-point scale ranging from "1 = I totally disagree" to "5 = I fully agree".

The perception of religion in contemporary society was gauged with a single item that expresses the view that religion is still relevant, as follows: 'for the morality of contemporary society, it is good that there is religion'. For the rating of this item the same answer scheme was used as above, which means that a response in the lower category will be assumed to mean that religion is perceived as irrelevant for today's society. The importance of trust in interpersonal and intergroup relations cannot be overemphasised. Two single items were used to measure the trust capital among religious adherents. The items are: 'if you are committed to a religion, to what degree (low or high) do you generally trust your religion?'; and 'to what degree (low or high) do you generally trust other religions in your country?' They were rated with a different response format ranging from "1 = low" to "10 = high". To make it easier to interpret the findings, the responses were later recoded to read: "1 = low trust", "2 = slightly low trust", "3 = I don't know", "4 = moderately high trust", and "5 = high trust". The concept of interreligious interaction is operationalised in this study with "religious pluralism", which is understood here in the theological sense and presupposes that there are also other religious paths (Rouméas, 2015). A two-item scale was used to evaluate the construct that expresses such pluralistic orientations towards religions. The items are: 'religions are all equal; they are just different paths to a flourishing life'; and 'there is no difference between religions, they all long for a flourishing life.' We consider them suitable. A Cronbach's alpha of .60 is good enough and seems to show that they are reliable. Here, too, the students were to indicate their agreement to these items by using the answer format "1 = I totally disagree" to "5 = I fully agree".

Religiosity is a multidimensional concept (Glock & Stark, 1965). In the study, it is conceptualised as the personal meaning of religion and its importance in one's daily life. It is regarded as a key component of the concept of religion. Religiosity was gauged with the Centrality of Religiosity Scale by Huber (2008), which includes the five dimensions of religiosity from Glock and Stark, such as: interest in religious thoughts, belief in God, religious experience, consequence of belief on daily life and religious participation. The items are: 'how often do you think about religious issues?'; 'to what extent do you believe that God or something divine exists?'; 'how often do you experience situations in which you have the feeling that God or something divine intervenes in your life?'; 'what is your position on the statement – my religion or worldview has great influence on my daily life?'; 'how often do you pray?' and 'how often do you take part in religious services at a church or mosque or another place?' The students responded to these questions with different answer formats as stated in the questionnaire, which were later recoded as "1 = never", "2 = rarely", "3 = occasionally", "4 = often", and "5 = very often", according to the Huber scale. The items appeared to be good enough to form a reliable scale ($\alpha = .67$).

Psychological Dimension

In the study, the psychological profile of the students was examined with the concept of empathy. Empathy is seen as a prosocial personality trait that can lead to support for human rights. It is a multidimensional construct. Here it was gauged with Davis' Empathic Concern Scale, which is part of his Interpersonal Reactivity Index (1980) but is included in the RHR questionnaire. We only used two items of the scale that express a tendency to feel compassion for others in unfortunate circumstances. The items are: 'I often have tender, concerned feelings for people less fortunate than me'; and 'when I see someone being taken advantage of, I feel kind of protective toward them'. They have a tolerable Cronbach's alpha of .51. Rating was done using the usual five-point scale of "1 = I totally disagree" to "5 = I fully agree".

Value Systems

Two concepts are used to explore the value system, namely basic human values and the concept of human dignity. According to Schwartz and colleagues, values are guiding principles in the lives of individuals and social groups. They are also possible predictors of human rights attitudes. There are two common ways to measure basic human values, namely the Schwartz Value Survey (hereinafter SVS) and Portrait Values Questionnaire (hereinafter PVQ) (Schwartz, 2012). We decided in favour of the PVQ, not only because it is provided for in the RHR instrument, but because it appears more specific, and we believed it would be easier for the students to respond to than the SVS. The PVQ measures values in an indirect manner, and its stimuli are people who are presented in relation to their goals, aspirations, and desires (Schwartz & Bardi, 2001; Schwartz & Sagiv, 1995). A respondent is only expected to use the options—"1 = not like me" to "6 = like me"—to show how similar the person in the description is to him or her. The items that reflect the ten basic value constructs highlighted in the previous chapter are: (1) 'he/she strongly believes that people should care for nature. Looking after the environment is important to him/her' (Universalism); (2) 'it's very important to him/her to help the people around him. He/she wants to care for their well-being' (Benevolence); (3) 'being very successful is important to him/her. He/she hopes people will recognise his achievements' (Achievement); (4) 'it is important to him/her to be rich. He/she wants to have a lot of money and expensive things' (Power); (5) 'thinking up new ideas and being creative is important to him/her. He/she likes to do things in his own original way' (Self-direction); (6) 'he/she looks for adventures and likes to take risks. He/she wants to have an exciting life' (Stimulation); (7) 'having a good time is important to him/her. He/she likes to 'spoil' himself/herself' (Hedonism); (8) 'it is important to him/her always to behave properly. He/she wants to avoid doing anything people would say is wrong' (Conformity); (9) 'tradition is important to him/her. He/she tries to follow the customs handed down by his religion or his/her family' (Tradition); and (10) 'it is important to him/her to live in secure surroundings. He/she avoids anything that might endanger his safety' (Security). We wanted to use the four value domains as scales but were constrained to use them as single items due to their very low reliability scores.

Inherent dignity is the founding value of human rights. This point is captured by the major international and regional human rights instruments. To measure the concept of dignity, we used the three-pronged operationalisation of Ziebertz and associates (2016, 2018) of 'dignity of merit', 'moral dignity' and 'inherent dignity'. This model originally came from Nordenfelt (2004). The dignity of merit refers to a dignity that is accorded to one based on one's social position. Moral dignity depends on one's behaviour, while inherent dignity is the dignity that accrues to all persons because of their humanity. One item each was used to assess these three types of dignity: 'the value of a person depends on the appreciation given to him or her by others' (dignity of merit); 'the honor to be given to a person depends on his moral behavior' (moral dignity); and 'each human being should be recognised just because he is a human being, irrespective of credit or moral behavior' (inherent dignity). The response options ranged from "1 = I totally disagree" to "5 = I fully agree".

Socio-political Context

The perception of the socio-political context was studied with two concepts that deal with the perceived quality of life and society as well as the perceived threat. There is ample evidence that these two concepts can trigger human rights attitudes. The perceived quality of life was operationalised with six items in which respondents were asked to indicate their (dis)satisfaction with their life and with the functioning of some social institutions such as the state, democracy, level of education and healthcare, etc. That means, the assessment of the perceived quality includes items from different domains of life and not just satisfaction with life alone. This is in line with the classic literature on the subject, in which life satisfaction is recognised as a social indicator of quality of life (Brown et al., 2004; Harrison et al., 2016). The measuring items of the perceived QoL are as follows: 'all things considered, how satisfied are you with your life as a whole nowadays?'; 'on the whole how satisfied are you with the present state of the economy in your country?'; 'now thinking about the government in your country, how satisfied are you with the way it is doing its job?'; 'And on the whole, how satisfied are you with the way democracy works in your country?'; 'Please say what you think overall about the state of education in your country nowadays?'; and 'Please say what you think overall about the state of health services in your country nowadays?' The measurement here used a slightly different five-point scale, namely "1 = extremely dissatisfied", "2 = dissatisfied", "3 = neither dissatisfied nor satisfied", "4 = satisfied", "5 = extremely satisfied". The Cronbach's alpha of these items ($\alpha = .71$) supports using them as a scale.

A scale of eight items ($\alpha = .59$) was used to gauge perceived threats or the awareness of tensions and conflicts in the context of study. The students were asked to state in their own views to what extent there are tensions or conflicts in Nigerian society: (1) 'between rich and poor'; (2) 'between languages'; (3) 'between sexes'; (4) 'between regions'; (5) 'between citizens and non-citizens'; (6) 'between religions'; (7) 'between political parties'; and (8) 'between ethnic groups.' The items were rated on a five-point scale of "1 = never", "2 = very seldom", "3 = occasionally", "4 = often", and "5 = very often".

In summary, despite the slight differences in the rating scales of the independent variables, it can be noted in each of the cases that a higher score indicates greater amounts of the measured concept. For an overview of what is going on among the students in relation to these independent variables, see Table 5.1.

Control Variables

In principle, control variables are also independent variables, but are usually not strictly recognised as such because they are not among the main variables of interest. However, it is believed that they can influence or distort research results if not taken into account. In our case, these are variables whose influence needs to be measured in order to determine the net effects of the explanatory factors on attitudes towards human rights. For example, for such variables we included some population characteristics such as age, gender, and religious socialisation. Despite conflicting results in this regard, there is still considerable evidence in research that age can sometimes influence attitudes towards human rights (cf. Botvar et al., 2019; Francis et al., 2019). To measure age, therefore, this item—'what is your age?'—was used. It was later recoded into a dummy variable of "0 = younger students" and "1 = older students", with the former as the reference category. The younger students are between the ages of 14 and 17 and the older students between 18 and 22 years of age. From a theoretical perspective, the division makes sense considering the widely accepted definition of a child as any person under the age of 18 years. In this way the students were divided into middle and late adolescents.

Just like age, sex is also likely to influence young people's attitudes towards human rights (cf. Botvar et al., 2019; Anthony & Sterkens, 2019; Lewis et al., 2009a). An added incentive to control for sex here was provided by the fact that societal gender roles remain an issue in Nigeria and most parts of Africa, despite modern advances in gender equality around the world. Here, too, the sex item was coded into a dummy variable, where "0 = male" was the reference category and "1 = female" the alternative category.

Religious socialisation is considered in the study through three concepts, namely mother's education level, religious affiliation and peer influence. As outlined in the theoretical perspectives, religiosity is a key component of the study's main independent variables. Individual religiosity has a context within religious socialisation

Table 5.1 (continued) Scale: 1 = I totally disagree; 2 = I disagree; 3 = I am not sure; 4 = I agree; and 5 = I fully agree. Except [a]Scale: from 1 = low trust; to 5 = high. [be]Scale: 1 = never; 2 = rarely; 3 = occasionally; 4 = often; and 5 = very often. [c]Scale: from 1 = is not like me; to 6 = is like me. [d]Scale: 1 = extremely dissatisfied; 2 = dissatisfied; 3 = neither dissatisfied nor satisfied; 4 = satisfied; 5 = extremely satisfied. NA = not applicable. Value domains are self-transcendence (universalism and benevolence), self-enhancement (power and achievement), openness to change (hedonism, self-direction, and stimulation), and conservation (conformity, security, and tradition)

Table 5.1 Descriptive summary of the independent variables

Variable	Observation	Mean	Sd.	Min.	Max.	CA = (α)	Items
Religion							
Function of religion:							
Social religion	1191	3.50	.72	1	5	.57	5
Spiritual religion	1191	4.31	.68	1	5	.60	3
Cultural religion	1191	3.04	1.04	1	5	.65	2
Rel. in contemp. society:							
Religion good for morality	1191	4.25	.98	1	5	NA	1
Trust in religion[a]**:**							
Trust religious in-group	1191	4.42	.81	1	5	NA	1
Trust religious out-group	1191	2.64	1.23	1	5	NA	1
Interreligious Interaction:							
Pluralism	1191	3.11	1.00	1	5	.60	2
Religiosity[b]	1191	4.35	.52	1	5	.67	6
Psychological dimension:							
Empathy	1191	4.04	.85	1	5	.51	2
Values							
Value orientations[c]**:**							
Universalism	1191	4.30	1.43	1	6	NA	1
Benevolence	1191	4.87	1.21	1	6	NA	1
Power	1191	3.69	1.63	1	6	NA	1
Achievement	1191	4.81	1.37	1	6	NA	1
Hedonism	1191	2.39	1.44	1	6	NA	1
Self-direction	1191	4.38	1.42	1	6	NA	1
Stimulation	1191	3.86	1.60	1	6	NA	1
Conformity	1191	4.62	1.40	1	6	NA	1
Security	1191	5.04	1.19	1	6	NA	1
Tradition	1191	4.17	1.50	1	6	NA	1
Human dignity:							
Dignity of merit	1191	3.80	1.16	1	5	NA	1
Moral dignity	1191	4.37	.90	1	5	NA	1
Inherent dignity	1191	3.57	1.25	1	5	NA	1
Socio-political context:							
Satisfaction[d]	1191	2.55	.68	1	5	.71	6
Perceived threats[e]	1191	3.56	.58	1	5	.59	8
Between rich and poor	1191	3.77	1.09	1	5	NA	1
Between languages	1191	3.45	1.15	1	5	NA	1
Between sexes	1191	3.23	1.26	1	5	NA	1
Between regions	1191	3.28	1.23	1	5	NA	1
B/w citizens & non-citizens	1191	3.20	1.28	1	5	NA	1
Between religions	1191	4.23	.94	1	5	NA	1
Between political parties	1191	3.80	1.10	1	5	NA	1
Between ethnic groups	1191	3.63	1.14	1	5	NA	1

processes that take place in the family (Ziebertz & Riegel, 2008). The construct 'mother's education level' is often used to assess social origin, but we included it here to observe the influence of the family as an agent of socialisation on the formation of human rights attitudes. One could argue that since Nigeria is supposedly a male-dominated society, we should have also included an item measuring the role of the father. However, relevant studies on the topic emphasise the priority of the mother's role in the child's (character) formation and socialisation processes (cf. Lewis et al., 2009b), including religious socialisation. This is no different in a patriarchal social system. The level of education of parents, particularly mothers, is believed to have some relationship with the quality of education and information available to a child, which could be important for social issues, such as human rights. The mother's level of education was therefore rated with the following individual item: 'what is the highest level of your mother's education?'; and the response scale of "1 = Primary School", "2 = Secondary School", "3 = College/other tertiary Institutions", "4 = University" to "5 = Other degree (higher degrees)".

The religious socialisation of a child takes place not only in the family, but also in extra-familial circumstances such as school, religious participation and through interactions with peers (Lewis et al., 2009b). Therefore, the indirect influence of students' religious affiliation on their human rights attitudes needs to be assessed, as students are expected to refer to their religious convictions when assessing human rights issues (Webb & Asa'd, 2019; Ziebertz & Ziebertz, 2016). To assess this, students were asked to assign themselves to their religious groups using the options provided in the questionnaire. There are seventeen of them, but during the amendment process an eighteenth option, African traditional religion, was added to the instrument used for the survey in Nigeria. We were interested in an ATR-Muslim-Christian comparison, which was the reason for including the ATR in the questionnaire. But we abandoned the idea and settled for a Muslim-Christian comparison because the students did not assign themselves to the ATR category. The responses of students in the two subgroups they used were recoded into a dummy variable, with "0 = Christians" as the reference category and "1 = Muslims". In addition, the statistical methods we chose for this study (see below) allowed us to assess the spread of the data, as an important prerequisite for a comparative study.

Finally, we assumed that the peer group represents a relevant source of influence on cognitive-affective orientations. To assess the role of the peer group, therefore, the best friend's religious belief was used, as in the item: 'how would you describe your best friend's belief and faith in God or a higher reality?' Responses were rated with a five-point scale of "1 = absolutely unbelieving", "2 = rather unbelieving", "3 = doubtful", "4 = believe", and "5 = believe absolutely". To get a clearer picture of the population characteristics, see Table 5.2.

Table 5.2 Characteristics of the study sample (N = 1191)

Variable		N	%	Valid %
Age	14	7	.6	.6
	15	71	6.0	6.0
	16	281	23.6	23.6
	17	367	30.8	30.8
	18	231	19.4	19.4
	19	122	10.2	10.2
	20	63	5.3	5.3
	21	36	3.0	3.0
	22	13	1.1	1.1
Sex	Male	535	44.9	44.9
	Female	656	55.1	55.1
Religious socialisation:				
Mother's education level	Primary school	195	16.4	16.4
	Secondary school	300	25.2	25.2
	College/other tertiary institutions	162	13.6	13.6
	University	263	22.1	22.1
	Other/higher degrees	271	22.8	22.8
Religious affiliation	Christians	774	65.0	65.8
	Muslims	403	33.8	34.2
	Missing	14	1.2	
Best friend's belief	Absolutely unbelieving	10	.8	.9
	Rather unbelieving	14	1.2	1.3
	Doubtful	181	15.2	16.6
	Believe	503	42.2	46.1
	Believe absolutely	384	32.2	35.2
	Missing	99	8.3	

5.5 Method of Analysis

The collected data from the students were subjected to a series of analyses using the Statistical Package for the Social Sciences (hereinafter SPSS). The relevant analyses include descriptive, variance, correlation and regression analyses. These were chosen in view of the research questions and hypotheses. In the descriptive analysis, the means and standard deviations for the responses to the items on human rights issues were calculated. The mean values obtained in the process gave us an overview of the respondents' evaluation of the human rights provisions. The usual five-point scale was used to interpret the mean values. It was slightly, but not substantially, adjusted in view of the first research question to read like this: "1.00–1.79 = total disagreement"; "1.80–2.59 = disagreement"; "2.60–2.99 = negative ambivalence"; "3.00–3.39 = positive ambivalence"; "3.40–4.19 = agreement"; and "4.20–5.00 = full agreement". In general, it can be said that disagreement indicates negative evaluation or rejection and agreement positive evaluation or legitimation, while the midpoints represent a state of ambivalence.

We then conducted variance analysis, in particular independent samples t-tests, to answer the second research question, which deals with differences in human rights attitudes between Muslim and Christian students in the sample. There are two reasons for using independent samples t-test. First, the latter is appropriate for comparing two subgroups. Second, the SPSS allows the homogeneity of the variances to be tested while a t-test is being performed. The independent samples t-test output in SPSS gives Levene's test for equality of variances by default. Besides, the output provides results for situations in which equal variances can be assumed (pooled t-test) and when these cannot be assumed (Welch t-test). Hence, we could run a homogeneity test to verify the assumption that our data show the same variance in the relevant subpopulations. It was important for the validity of our results that the analysis of variance captured the true structure of variance of the sample.

To clarify the relationships between the main variables of interest, as required by the third research question, we carried out a correlation analysis with the Pearson correlation coefficient. Although nothing in the main research question strictly suggests a correlation analysis, in view of the overall research results it is important to know the relationships between the set of variables in the study, especially the independent variables. It is believed that high linear relationships (perfect multicollinearity) between the independent variables can obscure their respective effects on the dependent variable. In empirical research, it is not uncommon to hear that certain variables are strongly interrelated. Examples include the concepts of affective empathy and religion, suggested by some researchers as closely related, as these tend to work towards similar goals, including helping and giving affection to those in need (cf. Ok et al., 2020; Ziebertz & Ziebertz, 2016). Instead of perfect collinearity, having variation in the independent variable is deemed necessary to identify their separate effects on the dependent variable. Because of this, we calculated the correlation coefficients for all our independent variables, including the control variables. In some cases, a correlation value of 0.4 is already rated as multicollinearity, but a coefficient of greater than 0.7 clearly indicates a multicollinearity problem. A review of the correlation Tables 1–8 in the appendix shows that the correlation values of our variables are generally at a good level or are not close to the threshold values (cf. De Vaus, 2001).

Finally, we ran a series of multiple linear regression (hereinafter MLR) models in order to answer the fourth question about (the extent of) the impact of the explanatory factors on the human rights attitudes of the students. The MLR is a predictive analysis used to explain the relationship between a dependent variable and several independent variables. It does this by creating a linear combination of all the independent variables to predict the dependent variable. A typical multiple linear regression model runs as follows: $y = \beta 0 + \beta 1x1 + \beta 2x2 + \ldots + \beta kxk + u$, where $\beta 0$, $\beta 1$, $\beta 2$ and βk are parameters; $\beta 0$ is the intercept term; $\beta 1$, $\beta 2$ and βk are partial regression coefficients; Y and the Xs represent the dependent and independent variables, respectively; and u is the error term. The parameter $\beta 1$ stands for the change in the mean response corresponding to a unit change in x1 when x2 through to xk are held constant. The same goes for all the partial regression coefficients. The error term stands for other relevant variables that have an independent influence on y, that are left out. In summary, the MLR assumes that the dependent variable (y) can be calculated as a linear function of a certain set of independent variables plus an error term. In statistics, MLR has many uses, including predicting impacts. It can also be used to analyse causal relationships and forecast trends. This implies that we can use it to simultaneously assess the predictive strength of the religious worldviews, the feeling of empathy, the value systems and the perception of Nigeria's socio-political context on the human rights attitudes of the students. The model is also efficient in testing the research hypotheses of this study, and in terms of measurement levels, it is also compatible with our choice of variables, which are mainly drawn from metric, ordinal and nominal data (cf. De Vaus, 2001). Hence, we consider it appropriate for this work. On the whole, there are eight models. These correspond to one for each of the eight human rights issues being examined. The models are presented in the following order: right to freedom of religion, non-discrimination against homosexuals, prohibition of the death penalty, permissibility of abortion, permissibility of euthanasia, political rights, right to a fair trial, and socio-economic rights.

Summary

This chapter introduced the research design, which is only a detailed description of the study method. The chapter began with a presentation of the central research question, which is to explore the human rights attitudes of young people in Nigeria and the predictors of those attitudes. This was followed by the differentiated research questions, in which the general research question was sharpened and made empirically researchable. The highlights of the sharpening exercise include the delimitation of the human rights provisions under study—mostly from civil, political and socio-economic rights—as well as the description of both the data collection method and the study population. In short, the study involved students of senior secondary schools in Nigeria aged 14–22.

Based on the differentiated research questions and the theoretical perspectives, three main hypotheses were derived. First, young people in Nigeria are expected to evaluate human rights positively, negatively and ambivalently. Second, it is expected that attitudes of Muslim and Christian students towards the permissibility of abortion and support for political rights will differ significantly, consistent with the broad principles of their respective religious traditions. Thirdly, it is postulated that students' religious worldviews, feeling of empathy, value systems and perception of the socio-political context of Nigeria predict their human rights attitudes. And this if age, gender, social class and religious socialisation—defined as religious affiliation and influence of peers—are held constant.

To test these hypotheses, four analytical methods were chosen, which practically represent four possible approaches to answering the four differentiated research questions. The methods include descriptive, variance, correlation and regression analyses. The mean values and standard deviations obtained by means of descriptive analysis provide an overview of the evaluation of the selected rights by the respondents. T-tests were used to measure whether the students differ significantly in their attitudes towards human rights based on their religious affiliation. A correlation analysis enabled us to know the relationships between the variables of interest and the extent of the relationships. Finally, we performed a series of regression analyses to obtain the necessary information about predictors of students' attitudes towards human rights.

All information about this study is presented in graphical form on the conceptual model, which serves as a compass for the study.

References

A. Books and Journals

Anthony, F. V., & Sterkens, C. (2019). Religion and the right to (dispose of) life: A study of the attitude of Christian, Muslim and Hindu students in India concerning death penalty, Euthanasia and Abortion. In H.-G. Ziebertz & F. Zaccaria (Eds.), *Euthanasia, abortion, death penalty and religion – The right to life and its limitations* (pp. 13–64). Springer.

Botvar, P. K., Sarti, C., Zielińska, K., & Zwierżdżyński, M. K. (2019). Religion and attitudes towards abortion and Euthanasia among young people in Poland and Norway. In H.-G. Ziebertz & F. Zaccaria (Eds.), *Euthanasia, abortion, death penalty and religion – The right to life and its limitations* (pp. 243–270). Springer.

Brown, J., Bowling, A., & Flynn, T. (2004). *Models of quality of life: A taxonomy, overview and systematic review of the literature*. University of Sheffield.

Davis, M. H. (1980). A multidimensional approach to individual differences in Empathy. *JSAS Catalog of Selected Documents in Psychology, 10*(85), 1–19.

De Vaus, D. (2001). *Research design in social research*. Sage.

Francis, L. J., McKenna, U., & Sahin, A. (2019). Religion, human rights and matters of life and death: Exploring attitude toward abortion and Euthanasia among adolescents in England and Wales. In H.-G. Ziebertz & F. Zaccaria (Eds.), *Euthanasia, abortion, death penalty and religion – The right to life and its limitations* (pp. 139–160). Springer.

Glock, C. Y., & Stark, R. (1965). *Religion and society in tension*. Rand McNally & Co.

Harrison, E., Saini, R., & Zwiener, N. (2016). Perceived quality of society. In E. Harrison, A. Quick, & S. Abdallah (Eds.), *Looking through the wellbeing Kaleidoscope* (pp. 51–73). New Economics Foundation.

Huber, S. (2008). Kerndimensionen, Zentralität und Inhalt – Ein interdisziplinäres Modell der Religiosität. *Journal für Psychologie, 16*(3), 1–17.

Lewis, C. A., Cruise, S. M., Fearn, M., & Guckin, C. M. (2009a). Religiosity of female and male adolescents. In H.-G. Ziebertz, W. K. Kay, & U. Riegel (Eds.), *Youth in Europe III: An international empirical study about the impact of religion on life orientation* (Vol. 10, pp. 59–86). Lit Verlag.

Lewis, C. A., Cruise, S. M., Fearn, M., & Guckin, C. M. (2009b). The influence of parents on the religious socialisation. In H.-G. Ziebertz, W. K. Kay, & U. Riegel (Eds.), *Youth in Europe III: An international empirical study about the impact of religion on life orientation* (Vol. 10, pp. 87–104). Lit Verlag.

Nordenfelt, L. (2004). The varieties of dignity. *Health Care Analysis, 12*(2), 69–81.

Ok, Ü., Gören, A. B., Akbulut, S., & Getir, S. D. (2020). Religion and attitude to economic deprivation among Muslims: Checking the roles of value preference and empathy. In H.-G. Ziebertz (Ed.), *International empirical studies on religion and socio-economic human rights* (pp. 277–298). Springer.

Rouméas, E. (2015). What is religious pluralism? In A. Bardon, M. Birnbaum, L. Lee, K. Stoeckl, & O. Roy (Eds.), *Religious Pluralism: A resource book* (pp. 11–17). European University Institute Press.
Schwartz, S. H. (2012). An overview of the Schwartz Theory of basic values. *Online Readings in Psychology and Culture, 2*(1), 1–20.
Schwartz, S. H., & Bardi, A. (2001). Value hierarchies across cultures: Taking a similarities perspective. *Journal of Cross-Cultural Psychology, 32*(3), 268–290.
Schwartz, S. H., & Sagiv, L. (1995). Identifying culture-specifics in the content and structure of values. *Journal of Cross-Cultural Psychology, 26*(1), 92–116.
Webb, R. J., & Asa'd, F. J. (2019). The right to life: A perspective of young Palestinian Muslims. In H.-G. Ziebertz & F. Zaccaria (Eds.), *Euthanasia, abortion, death penalty and religion – The right to life and its limitations* (pp. 161–186). Springer.
Ziebertz, H.-G., & Riegel, U. (2008). Post-secular Europe – A concept questioned. In H.-G. Ziebertz & U. Riegel (Eds.), *Europe: Secular or post-secular?* (pp. 9–41). Lit.-Verlag.
Ziebertz, H.-G., & Ziebertz, C. M. (2016). Labour rights and the impact of human dignity, Religious belief and perception of society. An empirical study among youth in Germany. *Journal of Empirical Theology, 29*(1), 45–77. https://doi.org/10.1163/15709256-12341337
Ziebertz, H.-G., Döhnert, S., & Unser, A. (2018). Predictors of attitudes towards human dignity. An Empirical Analysis among Youth in Germany. In H.-G. Ziebertz & C. Sterkens (Eds.), *Religion and Civil Human Rights in Empirical Perspective* (pp. 17–60). Springer.

Other Internet Sources

Statistics Solutions. (2021). *Cronbach's Alpha*. Available at: https://www.statisticssolutions.com/cronbachs-alpha/. Accessed 01 Nov 2021.
The World Factbook. (2021). *Nigeria: People and Society*. Available at: https://www.cia.gov/the-worldfactbook/countries/nigeria/#people-and-society. Accessed 23 Jan 2022.
UN Department of Economic and Social Affairs (UNDESA) Population Division. (2019). *World population prospects 2019 – Special aggregates*. Available at: https://population.un.org/wpp/Download/SpecialAggregates/EconomicTrading/. Accessed 02 Mar 2020.

Chapter 6
Empirical Findings

Contents

6.1 Evaluations of Human Rights by Students 290
6.2 Differences in Human Rights Evaluations by Religious Affiliation 297
6.3 Nexuses Between Human Rights Attitudes and Explanatory Factors 301
6.4 Predictors of Human Rights Attitudes of Students 307
6.5 Are the Findings as Expected? 314
References 317

Introduction

This chapter focuses on the research results and their interpretation. The outcomes of the analysis of Nigerian SSS students' responses to survey questions on human rights issues and the hypothesised relationship between the explanatory factors and students' human rights attitudes are presented. For this reason, there are a whole series of tables in this section. The first eight tables of the chapter contain the results of the descriptive analysis. These are results of the students' evaluation of the survey questions or statements on the selected human rights issues. The results are not only reported here, but also interpreted in the light of the theoretical perspectives. The first set of tables is followed by another set of eight tables with the results of the analysis of variance. This group of tables shows whether and to what extent there are significant differences in students' human rights attitudes based on their religious affiliation. The results of the correlation analysis then follow. The latter is contained in a table and simply shows the relationships between the explanatory factors and human rights attitudes. The tables with the results of the correlation analyses between the independent variables themselves and the correlations between the control and dependent variables can be found in the appendix. Finally, the eight regression models are also contained in a table. The models report on the predictors

M. C. Adimekwe, *The Impact of Religion, Personality, Values and Worldviews on Attitudes Towards Human Rights*, Religion and Human Rights 11,
https://doi.org/10.1007/978-3-031-65749-8_6

of students' human rights attitudes. At this point, after presenting these results, the chapter ends with the confirmation or rejection of the research hypotheses based on the general research results. In all cases, the order of presentation of the analyses corresponds to the order of the research questions.

6.1 Evaluations of Human Rights by Students

The first task of this study is to examine how a select group of Nigerian SSS students evaluate the right to freedom of religion, the protection of homosexuals from discrimination, the prohibition of the death penalty, the possibility of the bioethical issues of abortion and euthanasia, political rights, the right to a fair trial and socio-economic rights. For this reason, questions and/or statements about these rights were made available to them, with which their responses were obtained. It is assumed that the mean scores of the responses indicate their evaluation of the respective rights. The standard deviation is just as important here as it further describes the extent of students' consensus or divergence in relation to each individual human rights issue. In short, the lower the value of the standard deviation, the greater the consensus among students. Conversely, the higher the value of the standard deviation, the greater the dissent within the group (van der Ven, 2016; Ziebertz, 2019). Now, according to the outcomes of the responses in Table 6.1, the following human rights issues were rated positively: the right to freedom of religion (M = 4.24, Sd = .67), political rights (M = 3.64, Sd = .63) and socio-economic rights (M = 4.34, Sd = .54). However, the right to non-discrimination against homosexuals (M = 2.14, Sd = 1.06) and the possibility of abortion (M = 2.46, Sd = .89) were rated negatively, while the rest, namely the prohibition of the death penalty (M = 3.29, Sd = 1.01), the possibility of euthanasia (M = 2.79, Sd = 1.29) and the right to a fair trial (M = 3.00, Sd = .89) were rated ambivalently.

Table 6.1 Descriptive summary of the dependent variable

Variable	Observation	Mean	Sd.	Min.	Max.	CA = (α)	Items
Human Rights							
Freedom of religion	1191	4.24	.67	1	5	.62	4
Nondiscrim.- homosexuals	1191	2.14	1.06	1	5	.70	2
Prohibition- the death penalty	1191	3.29	1.01	1	5	.54	2
Possibility of abortion	1191	2.46	.89	1	5	.75	6
Possibility of euthanasia	1191	2.79	1.29	1	5	.81	2
Political rights index	1191	3.64	.63	1	5	.60	6
Right to a fair trial	1191	3.00	.89	1	5	.58	4
Socio-economic rights index	1191	4.34	.54	1	5	.83	12

Response scale: 1 = I totally disagree; 2 = I disagree; 3 = I am not sure; 4 = I agree; and 5 = I fully agree. Scale for interpretation of means: 1.00–1.79 = total disagreement; 1.80–2.59 = disagreement; 2.60–2.99 = negative ambivalence; 3.00–3.39 = positive ambivalence; 3.40–4.19 = agreement; and 4.20–5.00 = full agreement

A cursory look at Tables 6.2, 6.3, 6.4, 6.5, 6.6, 6.7, 6.8, and 6.9 could give us a better insight into what is going on among the respondents regarding each human rights issue.

Looking at Table 6.2, one can see, at least from the quality of the mean scores of their responses to the individual items, which are high, and from the standard deviations, that the students clearly support the right to freedom of religion. The possible exception is to be seen in connection with the use of religious symbols, in particular the wearing of religious garbs or headscarves etc., which we discussed in the theoretical part as controversial in Nigeria. We can see that the alleged controversy seems to rub off on students' responses based on the scores of the mean and standard deviations of the item. Even so, the difference is not much because, in the long run, the students still threw their support behind the use of the said religious symbols in the school (a public space). Their support can be better appreciated if one considers that the majority of students admitted that they did not trust members of other religious groups (M = 2.64), coupled with the fact that, in their opinion, there were conflicting relationships between religions in the country (M = 4.23), as can be seen in Table 5.1. We already hypothesised, based on the theory of social identity, that perceived threats lead to rejection or, rather, less support for rights in general. But that is not supported here. Nonetheless, their massive endorsement of the right tends to support our major expectation that the students' evaluation of human rights will be consistent with the teachings of their religions on this right, irrespective of

Table 6.2 Freedom of religion (frequencies (%), means and standard deviation)

Items	−−	−	−+	+	++	M	SD
Students should be offered time, space and a room in schools to do their prayers.	2.3	3.1	8.8	28.6	57.2	4.35	.93
The state should not prevent female teachers from wearing a head scarf for religious reasons.	5.2	6.6	17.3	28.1	42.7	3.97	1.16
The state should respect the right of religions to establish schools.	1.7	3.4	9.6	30.3	55.0	4.34	.91
The government should provide for enough space that religion could be taught in schools.	1.3	4.4	10.6	30.4	53.4	4.30	.92

Note: the right to freedom of religion is operationalised with a scale of four items. CA = .62, M = 4.24 and Sd = .67

Table 6.3 Non-discrimination against homosexuals (frequencies (%), means and standard deviation)

Items	−−	−	−+	+	++	M	SD
The state should prosecute behaviour which discriminates against homosexuals.	32.8	14.1	35.2	11.8	6.1	2.44	1.23
Homosexuals should have the right to hold any public office.	60.5	11.1	16.7	7.2	4.5	1.84	1.20

Note: the right of non-discrimination against homosexuals is operationalised with a scale of two items. CA = .70, M = 2.14 and Sd = 1.06

Table 6.4 Prohibition of the death penalty (frequencies (%), means and standard deviation)

Items	––	–	–+	+	++	M	SD
The death penalty should strictly be prohibited because of the right to life.	12.9	14.4	26.4	25.0	21.2	3.27	1.30
A death sentence should always be commuted to a life sentence.	8.1	12.5	35.4	27.4	16.5	3.32	1.14

Note: the prohibition of the death penalty is operationalised with a scale of two items. CA = .54, M = 3.29 and Sd = 1.01

Table 6.5 Possibility of abortion (frequencies (%), means and standard deviation)

Items	––	–	–+	+	++	M	SD
Abortion should be permitted in case of rape.	41.0	12.8	21.2	13.9	11.1	2.41	1.42
Abortion should be permitted in case of incest.	42.1	18.3	21.9	8.8	8.9	2.24	1.32
Abortion should be permitted when there is a strong chance of serious defect in the baby.	36.6	14.7	21.0	16.5	11.3	2.51	1.41
Abortion should be permitted when the woman's own health is seriously endangered by the pregnancy.	18.1	8.8	26.5	23.2	23.4	3.25	1.39
Abortion should be permitted when the woman cannot afford any more children economically.	49.0	20.3	16.8	8.8	5.1	2.01	1.21
Abortion should be permitted when the woman cannot afford any more children psychologically.	37.9	18.7	23.3	11.6	8.6	2.34	1.32

Note: the possibility of abortion is operationalised with a scale of six items. CA = .75, M = 2.46 and Sd = .89

Table 6.6 Possibility of euthanasia (frequencies (%), means and standard deviation)

Items	––	–	–+	+	++	M	SD
Euthanasia should be permitted in the case of unbearable and irreversible suffering.	30.1	16.7	23.8	17.4	12.0	2.64	1.38
Euthanasia should be permitted in the case of unbearable and irreversible suffering, if palliative care is exhausted.	24.6	13.5	23.2	20.3	18.4	2.94	1.43

Note: the possibility of euthanasia is operationalised with a scale of two items. CA = .81, M = 2.79 and Sd = 1.29

the perceived conflicts, rivalry, etc. Therefore, we assume that their support of this right could be explained by their religiosity, and the educational effects, among other things.

In Table 6.3, the students disapproved of any form of state protection for homosexuals. Even a two-thirds majority of them (71.6%) rejected the idea that homosexuals hold public office at all, in other words, they were against the political and economic empowerment of this minority group. This type of response largely confirms the claims about the hetero-normative sexual orientation of Nigerian society (cf. Izugbara, 2004). It also reflects the prevailing climate of discrimination against LGBTI people and/or the level of homophobia in the country, as presented in the theoretical part of the study. The responses also provide a better understanding of

Table 6.7 Political rights index (frequencies (%), means and standard deviation)

Items	––	–	–+	+	++	M	SD
Everybody, living here for some period prescribed by law, should have the right to vote for political leaders.	2.8	5.4	14.7	39.2	38.0	4.04	1.00
Everybody, living here for some period prescribed by law, should have the right to run for public office.	12.7	18.0	28.8	27.5	13.1	3.10	1.22
The police should not use force against political demonstrations that put public order at risk.	6.9	11.9	21.3	32.9	27.0	3.61	1.20
The government should not forbid public protests, however controversial they might be.	6.0	10.7	28.3	34.3	20.7	3.53	1.11
The government should guarantee political refugees' freedom to travel.	3.9	8.6	25.4	42.1	20.0	3.66	1.02
The government should provide a decent standard of living for political refugees.	2.9	5.3	22.0	41.1	28.8	3.88	.98

Note: the index of political rights is operationalised with six items. CA = .60, M = 3.64 and Sd = .63

Table 6.8 Right to a fair trial (frequencies (%), means and standard deviation)

Items	––	–	–+	+	++	M	SD
A suspect taken into custody should not be obliged to speak.	22.5	21.2	27.2	16.8	12.3	2.75	1.31
A suspect taken to court should not be obliged to answer questions by the court.	21.6	22.7	25.6	18.0	12.2	2.76	1.31
Mass murderers should be guaranteed access to a lawyer.	15.4	12.4	23.6	31.9	16.7	3.22	1.30
Someone suspected of repeated sexual abuse of children should be given legal aid.	18.3	10.7	20.1	27.7	23.2	3.27	1.41

Note: the right to a fair trial is operationalised with a scale of four items. CA = .58, M = 3.00 and Sd = .89

the claims made by various human rights organisations about the negative impact of the 2014 Same Sex Marriage Prohibition Act (SSMPA) on the plight of homosexuals in the country. But more importantly, the students' responses—and indeed their negative evaluation of the LGBTI's rights—will help to drive home the point we already made that our respondents are products of their society; they understand what is going on in their environment and come into contact with it during the process of religious socialisation, in school, and when dealing with their peers. And as such, they are aware of the socio-cultural and sociopolitical processes of their context. However, we need to find out whether their evaluation really depended on socio-cultural factors.

In Table 6.4 we see again the type of the responses that deepen the last point we made, responses that serve as an update of the current situation of the death penalty in Nigeria and the context of this practice in the country. The death penalty is generally permitted by the dominant religions and the cultures of the various ethnic nationalities in the country, as well as the laws of the Federation. There is, however,

Table 6.9 Socio-economic rights index (frequencies (%), means and standard deviation)

Items	−−	−	−+	+	++	M	SD
The government should provide a job for everybody who wants one.	3.1	8.8	12.1	26.0	50.0	4.11	1.11
Everyone should have the right to equal pay for equal work.	.8	5.2	11.3	26.8	55.9	4.32	.93
Everyone should have the right to just and reasonable pay for work performed.	.9	1.3	5.1	28.0	64.7	4.54	.73
Everyone should have the right to reasonable limitation of working hours to get enough rest.	1.2	4.9	14.0	28.5	51.5	4.24	.95
The state should protect women's right to adequate job opportunities.	1.0	2.4	6.0	37.5	53.1	4.39	.79
Women should have the right to be equally paid for equal work.	1.3	4.7	8.3	27.9	57.9	4.36	.91
Women should have the right to be protected from sexual harassment in the workplace.	1.8	2.3	2.6	20.2	73.2	4.61	.80
The state should be obliged to protect children from (forced) child labour.	1.5	3.1	7.1	21.2	67.1	4.49	.87
The state should be obliged to protect children's right to engage in play and recreation.	3.1	5.1	14.4	32.2	45.2	4.11	1.03
The government should provide a decent standard of living for the unemployed.	4.4	9.1	21.0	26.6	39.0	3.87	1.16
The government should provide health care for the sick.	.6	1.2	3.6	22.7	72.0	4.64	.67
The government should provide a decent standard of living for the old.	1.5	3.3	7.7	26.0	61.5	4.43	.88

Note: the index of socio-economic rights is operationalised with twelve items. CA = .83, M = 4.34 and SD = .54

a form of reorientation towards the abolition of the practice that is taking place in the teachings of these religions and in Nigerian society in line with the global trend to the extent that the question of the abolition of the practice is being discussed. As this is happening, crime and banditry in the country are steadily increasing. In fact, these are the main reasons the death penalty is even practiced in the country, and they are getting worse by the day. With these considerations perhaps going on in the minds of the students, one might expect that they answer questions or reply to statements about the practice of the death penalty in the country with a certain ambivalence as they have done, as shown in Table 6.4.

Table 6.5 gives us a picture of how students reacted to statements that suggested the legality or possibility of abortion for several reasons. As we can see, the students disapproved of all such suggestions, including situations where pregnancy resulted from rape, incest, or the like, regardless of the plight of the children born under such circumstances in Nigerian society. A closer look at the table reveals that the students' position on termination of pregnancy in relation to situations in which "a woman's own health is seriously endangered by the pregnancy" changed slightly but significantly. Almost half of the respondents (46.6%) indicated that an abortion could be carried out in such a situation. Again, this position essentially reflects the socio-cultural and acceptable legal standards of abortion in the country. Apart from this isolated case, the students evaluate the idea of abortion negatively and tend to disapprove of it as a legal or legitimate condition under which the right to the integrity of life can be limited. Against this background, it can be said that they have a positive attitude towards the right to life, even if their attitude towards abortion is restrictive according to the world map of abortion laws.

Although, as expected, students were generally negative about the possibility of euthanasia, Table 6.6 shows a certain tendency among students that can be described as "un-Nigerian" as it represents a marked departure from the typical Nigerian immediate response to the question of euthanasia. Particularly in the second item, one third of the students (38.7%) support euthanasia for a terminally ill person in situations in which palliative care has been exhausted. The element of surprise might disappear if one considers that their response may have been influenced by the subordinate clause "where palliative care is exhausted" in the wording of the psychometric instrument. As we suggested in the theoretical part, such situations sometimes lead Nigerians to desire passive euthanasia (cf. Oniha & Oniha, 2015), even though the practice of mercy-killing or mercy-dying is unacceptable (cf. Nwafor, 2010). According to the results, the standard deviation is relatively high, indicating greater disagreement among students on the issue. The clause in question could have been one of the reasons for this, as it was not entirely clear to the students what specific form of euthanasia is involved. We cannot tell exactly what was going on in their heads. Be that as it may, it is worth noting that despite the ambiguity, the students in this one situation tended to support euthanasia rather than oppose it. If anything, this is an indication that students can sometimes think outside the legal and socio-cultural parameters of their society. Further research may be needed to explain the cause of this new trend.

The students showed positive attitudes towards all rights in the index of political rights, namely the right to political participation, the right to protest and the right of refugees (see Table 6.7). Regarding the right to political participation, around a third (30.7%) seemed uncomfortable with the idea of granting this right to run for public office to everyone, almost as many people (28.8%) are also ambivalent about the same. Even so, a greater majority of them still agreed with the right. Most students also supported the right to protest, although around a third (28.3%) are not sure whether the government should allow controversial public protests or not. In any case, we previously highlighted some of the controversial aspects of these two rights, arising particularly from the theological perspectives of the dominant religions in Nigeria, and based on these aspects, we hypothesised that students' attitudes towards political rights will be ambivalent. It is interesting, however, that all three components of the index, in particular the rights of refugees, are supported by the students.

The results of the students' responses to statements about the right to a fair trial are shown in Table 6.8. Overall, their attitudes to the right to a fair trial are positively ambivalent. Of the two safeguards of this right examined in the study, Table 6.8 shows that the students reacted to the right to remain silent with negative ambivalence and the right to legal defence with positive ambivalence. Their responses come as a surprise to us as the right to a fair trial is about justice and justice, including procedural justice, is a central part of the teachings of Islam and Christianity. In addition, the right is also enshrined in Nigerian law. For this reason, we expected the students to have a very positive attitude towards the right. However, upon examining the responses to the items in the table, a number of considerations come to mind that we thought may have contributed to this type of result. The first concerns one of the components of the right to a fair trial in our study, namely the right to remain silent. The responses to the two items used to measure it all fall into the negative category, with about 43.7% and 44.3% of students showing outright disapproval of them, respectively. These negative responses may be traced to a misreading of these psychometric instruments and ultimately to a misunderstanding of the concept of the right to remain silent in criminal proceedings. Second, it is also possible that some of the terms used in the psychometric instruments to operationalise the right to a fair trial made it difficult for students to assess it dispassionately. For instance, in the remaining two items on the other component of the right to a fair trial, namely the right to defence in criminal proceedings, terms such as 'mass murderers', and 'a suspect of sexual abuse of children' were used. The most recent incidents in Nigeria that have resulted in the mass killings of citizens are ethno-religious crises and the activities of terrorists. Students may have associated the term 'mass murderer' with Boko Haram terrorists, among others, whose activities have led to the wanton destruction of lives and property in the country since last two decades. It is noteworthy that the data collection for this study coincided with the infamous kidnapping of school children at the Government Secondary School Chibok in Borno State by this terrorist group. In addition, the news media frequently report incessant incidents of child sexual abuse in Nigeria. It is therefore possible that all of this and more may have influenced the students' responses to the items and led to their low scores on the right to a fair trial. In any case, these are mere guesses that would require another study to clarify.

Finally, the students in the sample supported socio-economic rights the most (see Table 6.9). Obviously, the students advocate women's rights, measured in terms of economic indicators. They are also a strong advocate of children's rights, and this should not be taken for granted. The same applies to employee and social security rights. Apart from the high mean values of these rights, which mostly indicate full agreement, the standard deviations are consistently low in almost all cases, suggesting unanimous agreement among students with regard to the legitimacy of these rights. A significant minority of students (21%) did not appear to be sure whether the state was obliged to provide some form of social security for the unemployed. However, most students are clearly in favour of the right. The findings of the study on socio-economic rights are interesting for several reasons. First, Nigerian law does not provide for socio-economic rights in the strictest sense. Second, most of the rights in this category receive little or no attention in the country based on this and more. In fact, the government does not seem to feel it has a social contract with the Nigerian people to provide these rights. Third, students have enough socio-cultural pretexts to draw on to support the continued abuse of the socio-economic rights of women, children, workers, etc.—reasons for which we expected less support for the rights from them. However, they decided to give massive support to the right. We suspect that part of the reason for this is again due to the 'school effect'. The school system performs an enormous social function. Among other things, schools instill liberal attitudes in learners that could broaden their horizons about culture and religion and thus help them to be effective citizens. Even so, it would be interesting to know what the bastion of the students' massive support for socio-economic rights is.

In summary, with reference to the first research question the findings show evidence of high support for socio-economic rights and freedom of religion, as well as a decent support for political rights. A combined reading of the results of the three right-to-life issues shows that the right to life is rated rather positively by the students. First, the prohibition of the death penalty is rated with positive ambivalence. And then the idea of abortion is evaluated negatively, while euthanasia is viewed with negative ambivalence. These outcomes indicate that the students are likely to disapprove of the limitations of the duty to protect life. Besides, attitudes towards the right to a fair trial are positively ambivalent. Last but not the least, the right to protection of homosexuals from discrimination is viewed negatively by students. All in all, the results may not be entirely bad, but they do somewhat confirm some people's claims that Nigerians have an unimpressive culture of human rights (cf. Birnbaum, 1995; Dada, 2013; International Federation for Human Rights, 2010; Ojo, 2006; Onwuazombe, 2017). All the same, these findings need not be generalised.

In the next subheading we see how the students rated these human rights issues based on their religious affiliation. Did they evaluate the rights similarly or differently based on this social attribute?

6.2 Differences in Human Rights Evaluations by Religious Affiliation

The second question is whether the students evaluated the selected human rights differently because of their religious affiliation. Table 6.10 shows the results of the analyses of variance for one of the rights in question, namely the right to freedom of religion. The results show no statistically significant difference in the assessment of religious freedom between students, Christians (mean = 4.23, Sd = .67) and Muslims (mean = 4.28, Sd = .66) alike. The values of the mean and the standard deviation also show that they not only consider the right to be very important, but also seem to agree unanimously with it. And this, despite the alleged rivalry between the two religious groups in the country.

The same applies to their attitude towards gay rights, but in a reverse direction (see Table 6.11). The students did not differ significantly in their assessment of the said rights based on their religious affiliation (see Table 6.11). Both Christians (M = 2.16, Sd = 1.09) and Muslims (M = 2.09, Sd = 1.00) similarly disagreed that homosexuals should be protected from discrimination. The attitudes of these

Table 6.10 Freedom of religion and religious affiliation (t-test)

	N	Mean	Sd.	Df.	T-value
Christians	774	4.23	.67		
Muslims	403	4.28	.66	1175.00	−1.34

Note: four items are used for this scale. CA = .62. Scale for interpretation of means: 1.00–1.79 = total disagreement; 1.80–2.59 = disagreement; 2.60–2.99 = negative ambivalence; 3.00–3.39 = positive ambivalence; 3.40–4.19 = agreement; and 4.20–5.00 = full agreement

Table 6.11 Non-discrimination against homosexuals and religious affiliation (t-test)

	N	Mean	Sd.	Df.	T-value
Christians	774	2.16	1.09		
Muslims	403	2.09	1.00	1175.00	1.01

Note: two items are used for this scale. CA = .70. Scale for interpretation of means: 1.00–1.79 = total disagreement; 1.80–2.59 = disagreement; 2.60–2.99 = negative ambivalence; 3.00–3.39 = positive ambivalence; 3.40–4.19 = agreement; and 4.20–5.00 = full agreement

Table 6.12 Prohibition of the death penalty and religious affiliation (t-test)

	N	Mean	Sd.	Df.	T-value
Christians	774	3.36	.99		
Muslims	403	3.17	1.04	1175.00	3.06**

Note: two items are used for this scale. CA = .54. Scale for interpretation of means: 1.00–1.79 = total disagreement; 1.80–2.59 = disagreement; 2.60–2.99 = negative ambivalence; 3.00–3.39 = positive ambivalence; 3.40–4.19 = agreement;and 4.20–5.00 = full agreement

students reflect the general positions of their respective religions and the domestic laws on homosexuality in the Nigerian context. For such reasons, Nigerian Christians and Muslims were once described as having "largely hetero-patriarchal identities" (Izugbara, 2004: 12) and the country as a homophobic nation.

Table 6.12 displays a different picture than the previous table in the way the young Nigerian students evaluate the prohibition of the death penalty. There is a statistically significant positive difference between Christian and Muslim students' attitudes towards this practice. The Christian students (M = 3.36, Sd = .99) tend to be more open to the abolition of the death penalty than their Muslim fellow students (M = 3.17, Sd = 1.04). Of course, both Islam and Christianity have long supported the death penalty. But in the theoretical part we hinted at a remarkable orientation away from practice within Christianity in recent times. At the same time, we noticed a movement towards retentionism in Islam, particularly in relation to the reintroduction of the Sharia in Nigeria. However, these positions do not fully reflect the findings presented here, since the attitudes of students of both religious tradition towards the death penalty are positively ambivalent. This can be interpreted as a tendency on their part to support the abolition of this practice, although the Christians among them seem more open to the idea. There is also an interesting dimension to the attitudes of Muslim students, which seems to represent the ability to reflect on such

Table 6.13 Possibility of abortion and religious affiliation (t-test)

	N	Mean	Sd.	Df.	T-value
Christians	774	2.48	.89		
Muslims	403	2.42	.90	1175.00	1.26

Note: six items are used for this scale. CA = .75. Scale for interpretation of means: 1.00–1.79 = total disagreement; 1.80–2.59 = disagreement; 2.60–2.99 = negative ambivalence; 3.00–3.39 = positive ambivalence; 3.40–4.19 = agreement; and 4.20–5.00 = full agreement

Table 6.14 Possibility of euthanasia and religious affiliation (t-test)

	N	Mean	Sd.	Df.	T-value
Christians	774	2.94	1.26		
Muslims	403	2.50	1.31	1175.00	5.64***

Note: two items are used for this scale. CA = .81. Scale for interpretation of means: 1.00–1.79 = total disagreement; 1.80–2.59 = disagreement; 2.60–2.99 = negative ambivalence; 3.00–3.39 = positive ambivalence; 3.40–4.19 = agreement; and 4.20–5.00 = full agreement

issues independently of the official teaching of their religion. Accordingly, this development is due, among other things, to the cultural capital to which the school system exposes the learners.

Much like the students' attitudes towards the practice of the death penalty, the intricate differences between Christian and Islamic theological perspectives on the moral issue of abortion were not reflected in their assessments of the possibility of abortion (see Table 6.13). Both student subgroups disapprove of the possibility of abortion in no uncertain terms and, contrary to our expectation, there is no significant difference in their assessment of this right to life issue.

Table 6.14 shows the results of the t-test on the possibility of euthanasia, with the students' assessments of this bioethical issue differing significantly. The Muslim students assess the possibility of euthanasia negatively (M = 2.50, SD = 1.31), while their Christian fellow students do so with negative ambivalence (M = 2.94, SD = 1.26). This means that virtually all students opposed euthanasia, but Muslim students tended to disagree more with the practice than Christians.

Concerning the political rights, the results of the analysis of variance in Table 6.15 show that the students did not show any statistically significant differences in their evaluation of these rights. Both Muslims (M = 3.59, Sd = .59) and Christians (M = 3.66, Sd = .65) rate the cluster of rights in the political rights index positively and the quality of the standard deviations attest to the strength of their consensus, which can be described as great. This finding surprised us because, based on the theological perspectives of Islam and the Christian religion on democracy, political participation and the right to protest, we expected the students' attitudes towards political rights to differ significantly. While that is not the case here, it is still interesting to find that all students were positive about these rights, regardless of the teachings of their religions. Again, this suggests that these students can rise above certain denominational logics to support human rights.

Even though we expected students' attitudes towards political rights to differ significantly based on their religious affiliation, for the same reasons we never had

Table 6.15 Political rights index and religious affiliation(t-test)

	N	Mean	Sd.	Df.	T-value
Christians	774	3.66	.65		
Muslims	403	3.59	.59	1175.00	2.01

Note: six items are used for the index. CA = .60. Scale for interpretation of means: 1.00–1.79 = total disagreement; 1.80–2.59 = disagreement; 2.60–2.99 = negative ambivalence; 3.00–3.39 = positive ambivalence; 3.40–4.19 = agreement; and 4.20–5.00 = full agreement

Table 6.16 Right to a fair trial and religious affiliation (t-test)

	N	Mean	Sd.	Df.	T-value
Christians	774	2.94	.89		
Muslims	403	3.11	.87	1175.00	−3.15**

Note: four items are used for this scale. CA = .58. Scale for interpretation of means: 1.00–1.79 = total disagreement; 1.80–2.59 = disagreement; 2.60–2.99 = negative ambivalence; 3.00–3.39 = positive ambivalence; 3.40–4.19 = agreement; and 4.20–5.00 = full agreement

such an expectation regarding their evaluation of the right to a fair trial. However, according to Table 6.16, the Muslim and Christian students in our sample differ significantly in their assessment of this right. First, both have an ambivalent view of the right. Second, Muslims dissent less on the right than Christians. In fact, Muslim students were more likely to support the right to a fair trial (M = 3.11, SD = 0.87) compared to their Christian peers, who were more likely to oppose the right (M = 2.94, SD = 0.89). Therefore, this right seems to be more important to Muslim students than to their Christian counterparts.

Last but not the least, the results of the analysis of variance for socio-economic rights are presented in Table 6.17, and the students' attitudes towards the rights do not differ significantly. The Christian students (M = 4.37, Sd = .52) and their Muslim fellow students (M = 4.30, Sd = .56) rated the rights positively. It is believed that the high mean and low standard deviation values indicate both high and unanimous support for the rights.

In view of the second research question, the results of the variance analyses show that there are no statistically significant differences in the students' attitudes towards the right to freedom of religion, the right to non-discrimination against homosexuals, the possibility of abortion, political and socio-economic rights. However, Muslim and Christian students differed positively in their evaluation of the right to life issues of abolition of the death penalty and the possibility of euthanasia and negatively in relation to the right to a fair trial. Overall, the students differed less than might have been expected given the remarkable differences in the teachings of their religions on these human rights issues. This finding tends to underscore Norris and Inglehart's (2012) position that living in a particular country has a greater impact on people's belief systems than their specific type of belief, such that the core values of different belief systems within a country are sometimes closer together than they usually are. Norris and Inglehart attributed this primarily to the social function of educational institutions.

Table 6.17 Socio-economic rights index and religious affiliation (t-test)

	N	Mean	Sd.	Df.	T-value
Christians	774	4.37	.52		
Muslims	403	4.30	.56	1175.00	2.10

Note: twelve items are used for the index. CA = .83. Scale for interpretation of means: 1.00–1.79 = total disagreement; 1.80–2.59 = disagreement; 2.60–2.99 = negative ambivalence; 3.00–3.39 = positive ambivalence; 3.40–4.19 = agreement; and 4.20–5.00 = full agreement

6.3 Nexuses Between Human Rights Attitudes and Explanatory Factors

Table 6.18 contains the results of the correlation analyses between the explanatory factors and attitudes towards the selected human rights issues. Here the results are presented. We only report on all significant correlations but limit our comments to the moderately strong ($.15 \leq r < .30$) and strong associations ($r \geq .30$).

Column 1 contains five strongly or moderately significant connections between the concept of religion and the right to religious freedom. The belief that religions should play a social role is moderately strongly associated with support for religious freedom. The view that religion should play a spiritual role, the belief that religion is good for society's morality, the tendency to trust one's religious group, and individual religiosity all have strong positive associations with the right. From the table, students' religiosity has the highest positive relationships with religious freedom. Furthermore, correlations between the feeling of empathy and support for religious freedom are moderately strong. The same applies to preferences for values such as universalism, benevolence, achievement, self-direction, and conformity. The preference for security values is strongly related to the endorsement of the right of freedom of religion, while the basic values stimulation and tradition are only weakly related to the right. Agreement with the concept of dignity as merit and that of dignity as a moral standard have moderately strong and strong associations, respectively, with advocacy for religious freedom. Surprisingly, consent to the concept of inherent dignity does not correlate with this civil right at all. The surprise is due to the hypothetical relationship between the two. Regarding the contextual variables, the picture of correlation analysis changes a bit. The feelings of satisfaction with quality of life and society and the right to religious freedom are negatively associated, while respondents' perceptions of threats are positively correlated with the right. In both cases, however, the connection is only moderately strong. Apart from these, the other variables not mentioned have no significant correlations with freedom of religion.

Column 2 presents the results of the correlation analysis between homosexuals' right to protection from discrimination and the same explanatory factors. Here we see a long list of negative correlations. All variables of the concept of religion are significantly correlated with this right, to begin with. The belief that religions should play either a social or a spiritual function in society has a weak negative association with the LGBTI rights. The same applies to the view that religion is good for

Table 6.18 Correlations (Pearson's r) between the dependent and independent variables

	Civil rights:		*Right to life*			Political & judicial rights		Socio-economic rights
	Freedom of religion	Nondiscri- (homo-sexuals)	Prohibition death penalty	Possibility of Abortion	Possibility of Euthanasia	Political rights index	Right-to- a fair trial	Socio-economic rights index
Religion								
Function of religion								
Social religion	.28**	−.08**	.04	−.05	−.04	.15**	.05	.23**
Spiritual religion	.34**	−.10**	.06*	−.10**	−.02	.22**	.04	.42**
Cultural religion	−.04	.18**	.15**	.15**	.08**	.13**	.12**	.02
Rel. in contemp. Society								
Rel. good for morality	.35**	−.16**	.01	−.14**	−.08**	.17**	.01	.35**
Trust in religion								
Trust religious in-group	.31**	−.20**	−.03	−.22**	−.11**	.12**	−.07*	.32**
Trust rel. out-group	−.05	.16**	.08**	.16**	.15**	.06*	.19**	−.03
Interreligious interaction								
Pluralism	.00	.18**	.14**	.19**	.20**	.12**	.13**	.06*
Religiosity	.40**	−.19**	.01	−.22**	−.06*	.19**	−.03	.39**
Psychological dimension								
Empathy	.26**	−.11**	.07*	−.13**	−.01	.14**	.03	.34**
Values								
Value orientations:								
Universalism	.26**	−.11**	.07*	−.09**	−.01	.21**	−.03	.30**
Benevolence	.28**	−.14**	.06*	−.12**	−.02	.17**	.02	.35**
Power	.03	.04	.10**	.13**	.04	.06*	.06*	.03
Achievement	.27**	−.16**	.08**	−.11**	.05	.07*	−.12**	.27**

Hedonism	−.05	.19**	.02	.15**	.09**	−.00	.01	−.09**
Self-direction	.21**	−.05	.16**	−.04	.03	.13**	−.02	.27**
Stimulation	.07*	.00	.06*	.01	.02	−.02	−.03	.06*
Conformity	.28**	−.13**	.10**	−.15**	−.08**	.19**	−.01	.30**
Security	.32**	−.17**	.09**	−.09**	.02	.21**	−.04	.32**
Tradition	.14**	−.11**	−.07	−.02	−.07*	.04	−.03	.10**
Human dignity								
Dignity of merit	.18**	−.05	.04	−.01	−.05	.10**	.11**	.17**
Moral dignity	.30**	−.22**	.00	−.11**	−.07*	.17**	.02	.29**
Inherent dignity	.04	.11**	.07*	.04	.04	.13**	.08**	.14**
Socio-political context								
Satisfaction	−.17**	.15**	.14**	.19**	.13**	.03	.12**	−.14**
Perceived threats	.19**	−.06	.04	.03	−.01	.09**	−.02	.17**

Note: all correlations are significant at $p < .01$ (**) or $p < .05$ (*) level (2-tailed). Interpretation of correlations: weak ($r < .15$); moderately strong ($.15 \leq r < .30$); strong ($r \geq .30$) associations society's morality, the tendency to trust one's own religious group more and individual religiosity, but their associations with the right are comparatively moderately strong. Conversely, the position that religions should play a cultural role in society, i.e., should operate more with the zeitgeist, and the tendency to trust 'the religious other' and a pluralistic orientation towards religions are all somewhat strongly related in a positive way to the rights of homosexuals. The personality trait empathy as well as preferences for values such as universalism, benevolence, conformity, and tradition have weak negative correlations with gay rights. The basic values of achievement and security have a more robust negative association with the same rights compared to the above values. Of all basic values, only hedonistic value is positively related to LGBTI rights, and the association is moderately strong. Agreeing with the notion of moral dignity and the advocacy of gay rights have a fairly strong negative association, while inherent dignity and the same rights showed only weak positive correlations. However, the perceived quality of life is positive and somewhat strongly linked to the rights of homosexuals.

Column 3 concerns the students' evaluation of the prohibition of the mandatory death penalty. Most of the explanatory variables here only share weak associations with the question of the abolition of the practice. The religion-related variables of spiritual function of religion, trust in religious out-groups, and pluralistic orientations towards religions are positively related to the advocacy of the abolition of mandatory capital punishment. The same applies to the feeling of empathy, the preference for values of universalism, benevolence, power, achievement, stimulation, conformity and security, as well as the agreement with the concept of inherent dignity of every individual and the feeling of satisfaction with the perceived quality of life. However, the weight of the correlation coefficients indicates that these are only weak links. According to the results, only students who shared the view that religions should perform a cultural function in society and those who preferred the value of self-direction had a moderately strong positive relationship with the abolition of the practice.

Like advocacy for the rights of the LGBTI persons, the Nigerian students' evaluation of the legality of abortion and possible predictor variables shows a relatively long list of negative correlations (see column 4). Most of the religion-related variables showed varying degrees of correlation with the bioethical-moral issue of abortion. Belief in the spiritual role of religion and the mindset that religion is good for morality have weak negative relationships with the possibility of abortion. Trust in the religious in-group and individual religiosity have stronger negative correlations with support for abortion, meaning that students with higher trust in their own religious group and those with higher religiosity tend to be less willing to accept exceptions to the right to life in terms of abortion. But then, students who believe that religions should operate more with the zeitgeist, as well as those with higher trust in 'the religious other' and pluralistic worldviews relate positively to the advocacy of abortion. The propensity to feel compassion for others in unfortunate circumstances, as well as preferences for the values of universalism, benevolence, achievement, security, and agreement with the concept of moral dignity are negatively related to students' attitudes toward abortion, although the links are all weak. The correlations between the basic value of conformity and the possibility of abortion are moderately strong and naturally negative. A different picture emerges with regard to preferences for the values of power and hedonism as well as the perceived quality of life. While the advocacy of abortion showed significantly positive but weak correlations with preference for the basic value of power, its associations with hedonistic value orientation and the perceived quality of life are positive and moderately strong.

In the study we found some of the weakest correlations between the bioethical issue of euthanasia and our explanatory factors (see column 5). There are six significant correlations between support for the possibility of euthanasia and the concept of religion. The belief that religions should operate with the zeitgeist correlates positively with support for euthanasia. But the connection is less strong. Trust in the religious out-groups and, above all, a pluralistic attitude towards religions had moderately robust positive relationships with the right. The mentality that religion is good for societal morality, higher trust in religious in-groups, and higher individual religiosity are all negatively related to the bioethical-moral issue of euthanasia, and their correlations are weak. The same applies to the preference for the values of conformity and tradition and the agreement with the statement about moral dignity, which also have negative connections to the right. In contrast, the preference for the value of hedonism, and the feeling of satisfaction with the quality of life showed positive relationships.

Column 6 is about political rights. As you can see, contrary to the picture in column 5, there is here (in column 6) an impressive number of fairly strong significant correlations. All variables of the concept of religion showed varying degrees of positive correlations with political rights. In particular, positive evaluation of the statements that religion should focus on a spiritual function in society had the highest correlations with the endorsement of political rights in the study, and their correlations are somewhat strong. Also, the viewpoint that religion should be a social force in society, the mentality that religion is good for society's morality, and higher religiosity among students are also quite strongly associated with the political rights in the index, while the belief that religion should play a cultural role in society, the two variables of trust in religion and a pluralistic orientation towards religions are weakly connected with them. The same applies to empathy and value orientations of power, achievement and self-direction; they all also showed weak positive correlations. But preferences for the values of universalism, benevolence, conformity, and security have relatively strong correlations with support for political rights. For the first time in the study, all three forms of dignity and the dependent variable—and in this case the advocacy for political rights—are significantly related. Of the three forms, however, only agreement with the notion of moral dignity showed a fairly strong positive association with political rights. Connections to the other two are tenuous, as is the connection to the perceived threat construct.

Column 7 contains the weakest correlation results from the study. It is about the right to a fair trial. Consent to the cultural function of religion in society and consent to a pluralistic attitude towards religions have weak positive links to the right to a fair trial. The tendency to trust other religions is somewhat strongly related to support for this judicial right and actually posted the strongest correlations in the column, while a similar tendency to trust one's religion more is negatively but weakly related to the right. The preference for the value of achievement is also negatively related to the right to a fair trial, and the value orientation of power is positive. Consent to forms of merit and inherent dignity share positive relationships with the right too. Likewise, the concept of the perceived quality of life. Again, these are all slight correlations.

The last column contains the results of the correlation analysis between socio-economic rights and the predictor variables. In this column, the study found the highest number of significant correlations, with the strongest being between socio-economic rights and belief in the spiritual function of religion. Students who agree with the latter are strongly associated with the said rights. Agreement that religion is good for societal morality, higher trust in the religious in-group, and higher religiosity also have robust positive correlations with socio-economic rights. The position that religion should be more involved in society showed a moderately strong positive association with socio-economic rights, while agreement with a pluralistic worldview is also significantly and positively but weakly associated with the same rights. Column 8 also shows that there are robust positive associations between empathy and socio-economic rights. Understandably so, it is to be expected that higher levels of empathy will relate positively to the advocacy of labour rights, rights of women and children, and the rights of other more vulnerable members of society. Furthermore, students with preferences for the values of universalism, benevolence, conformity and security are also strongly related to the endorsement of these rights. The same can be said of those with preferences for the values of achievement and self-direction, although their relationships with the rights are weaker. The value orientations of stimulation and tradition correlate slightly positively with socio-economic rights, while the value of hedonism correlates with them in the same manner but negatively. Here, too, the three types of dignity recorded positive associations. Whereas students who agree with notions of merit and moral dignity appeared more open to socio-economic rights, those who agreed with the inherent dignity of all human beings showed only marginal positive associations with the same rights. The contextual variables are both negatively and positively associated with socio-economic rights. The perceived quality of life is negatively associated with the rights—albeit slightly, while threat perception showed a moderately strong positive association with them. This means that the students' advocacy of these rights positively associated with increased threat perceptions.

In view of the third research question, the overall results of the correlation analyses show that there are different forms of correlations between the selected human rights issues and the explanatory variables. In the study, the contextual variables show the fewest significant connections with human rights. First, the perceived threats construct showed a mix of weak and moderately strong significant correlations only with religious freedom, political and socio-economic rights. With the others it has no significant correlations. Second, perceived quality of life shows a similar picture; it had a mix of weak and relatively strong correlations with various human rights, except for political rights where it is not significant. Next is the psychological trait of empathy, which also registered few correlations with human rights. It is strongly linked to socio-economic rights, somewhat strongly related to religious freedom, and has weak relationships with the other rights, except for the issue of euthanasia and the right to a fair trial where it is not significant at all. Value systems are in third place. Overall, the concept of dignity posted only one strong correlation with human rights, namely in connection with freedom of religion. In addition, it shows some moderate and a series of weak correlations with other human rights issues. The basic human values have a comparatively better picture of connections with human rights, than the concept of dignity. There are strong correlations with freedom of religion and socio-economic rights, for example. However, there are also moderately strong, weak and, sometimes, no significant correlations with various rights. Finally, the concept of religion, the components of which, like basic human values, correlate to varying degrees with human rights. However, the concept of religion has slightly better correlation coefficients in most of its components and thus some of the highest correlations with human rights in this study. Based on this, is religion the main determinant or predictor of students' attitudes toward the selected human rights issues? What about the religiosity of the students, is it always the decisive religious factor? Are Nigerian students' human rights attitudes triggered by these explanatory factors with which they show significant correlations? It is important to note here that correlations do not usually imply causality. To answer these questions, therefore, further analysis is required, this time a regression analysis.

6.4 Predictors of Human Rights Attitudes of Students

It is necessary to conduct a series of regression models because the main aim of this study is to examine the factors that predict students' human rights attitudes. Here we are interested in all explanatory factors, and we focus more on the effects of religion-related variables, particularly religiosity, on the eight selected human rights issues. In order to achieve the best possible assessment of their effects, only explanatory factors with correlation coefficients of 0.10 and higher (Pearson's $r \leq .10$) are included in the models together with the control variables. And when reporting the regression analyses, we omitted any variables that did not show significant results in all models.

Predictors of Attitudes Towards the Right to Freedom of Religion

The right to religious freedom is one of the fundamental human rights that this study explores. What are the factors that predict the positive or negative evaluation of this right by the students?

The results in the first column of Table 6.19 show that 36% of the variance in attitudes towards the right to freedom of religion is explained by the model. Among the control variables, only the peer influence construct is statistically significant at 1% level but with a negligibly weak positive impact on students' evaluation of the right to freedom of religion, as indicated by the beta value ($\beta = .078$). The remainder of the value of the explained variance is contributed collectively by the concepts of religion, value systems, and social context variables. The relationship between the

Table 6.19 Regression analyses for human rights and the independent/control variables

	Civil rights:		*Right to life*			Political & judicial rights		Socio-economic rights
	Freedom of religion	Nondiscri- (homo-sexuals)	Prohibition death-penalty	Possibility of Abortion	Possibility of Euthanasia	Political rights index	Right-to- a fair trial	Socio-economic rights index
Religion								
Function of religion:								
Social religion	.107***							
Spiritual religion	.088**					.095**		.182***
Cultural religion		.090**	.086**			.098***		
Rel. in contemp. society:								
Religion_good for morality	.126***							.123***
Trust in religion:								
Trust rel. in-group		−.090**		−.093**	−.082**			
Trust rel. out-group		.090**			.099**		.134***	
Interreligious interaction:								
Pluralism				.107***	.105***			
Religiosity	.174***			−.104***		.101**		.171***
Psychological dimension								
Empathy								.081**
Values								
Value orientations:								
Universalism	.072**					.110***		.088***
Achievement	.133***	−.108***					−.122***	.088***
Hedonism		.099***						
Self-direction			.149***					

Security	.089**							
Human dignity:								
Dignity of merit							.102***	
Moral dignity	.079**	−.090**						.073**
Inherent dignity		.086**				.103***		.120***
Socio-political context								
Satisfaction	−.087**		.103***	.079**	.082**			
Population characteristics								
Age (*ref. younger students*) older students								−.077**
Religious socialisation:								
Rel. affiliation (*ref. Christians*) Muslims					−.133***		.098***	
Peers influence	.078**	−.076**		−.098***	−.101***			
Adj. R^2	.36	.17	.07	.16	.09	.13	.08	.41
F =	28.249***	11.051***	8.286***	11.114***	13.587***	8.908***	9.920***	33.681***
N = 1191								

Note: Standardised regression coefficients (ß) are significant at *p ≤. 05; **p ≤ .01; ***p ≤ .001. Reference categories: age = younger students; sex = male; religious affiliation = Christians concept of religion and attitudes towards religious freedom is statistically significant in four places. The conviction that religion should have a spiritual function in society positively affected students' assessment of the right to freedom of religion, at 1% level of significance—but the effects are of little importance. The picture looks a little better if one agrees that religion should be a social force and that religion is good for social morality. Both concepts are statistically significant ($\beta = .107$ and $\beta = .126$, respectively) at 0.1% level and had only a slight positive but considerable influence on the support for religious freedom. The picture improves even further in relation to the religiosity of the students; the latter as expected is the main predictor of attitudes towards religious freedom in this study and has a moderately strong positive influence on the evaluation of the right by the students ($\beta = .174$***). This means that the higher the religiosity of the students, the more likely they are to support freedom of religion.

The results also show that the basic value of achievement had a weakly positive influence on attitudes towards freedom of religion ($\beta = .133$***), meaning that students who prefer this value are more likely to support this right. The value orientations of universalism and security as well as the concept of moral dignity have a significantly positive connection with attitudes to the right to freedom of religion. The students' feeling of dissatisfaction with the quality of their lives is also significantly linked to their attitudes towards the right. However, its effect is negative. In general, these are rather meagre effects. The other variables, particularly the concept of inherent dignity and the construct of perceived threats, are not significant.

Predictors of Attitudes Towards Nondiscrimination Against Homosexuals

The students disagreed with the rights of homosexuals as defined in this study, and the results in column 2 show the factors on which their position is based. The results indicate that the predictor variables in model contribute about 17% of the explained variance on the homosexual non-discrimination scale. For the control variables, the influence of the peer group is once again statistically significant at the 1% level and with a minor impact on attitudes towards this right. Advocating the position that religion should operate with the zeitgeist and the students' evaluation of the item on trust in religious out-group have similar positive effects on their attitudes towards the rights of homosexuals, while higher trust in their own religion has a negative effect. Here, too, the effects are minor.

The basic values of hedonism and achievement are both statistically significant, but the latter appears to be the main driving force behind attitudes towards the rights of homosexuals here. Preference for the value of achievement had a negative impact ($\beta = -.108$***) and preference for the value of hedonism had a positive impact ($\beta = .099$***) on students' attitudes towards the rights of homosexuals. This implies that while students who prefer the value of achievement are less disposed to endorse the rights of LGBTI persons, those who are oriented towards hedonistic values appear willing to do so. Likewise, consent to the concept of moral dignity negatively affected students' attitudes towards the rights of LGBTI people, while agreement with the concept of inherent dignity is positively linked to attitudes towards the rights. These are generally weak effects though.

It is surprising that, contrary to our expectations, the individual religiosity of the students had no influence on their attitude towards LGBTI rights. Empathy does not matter either. We assumed that genuine empathy, as feeling compassion for those who are suffering should lead to advocacy of the rights of others. There is evidence in Table 5.1 that our respondents are empathetic people (M = 4.04, SD = 0.85), but this does not seem to help the cause of homosexuals here. One of the reasons for this could be, as Case et al. (2008: 31) aptly put it: "[s]ome empathic people may be unable to empathize with homosexuals because they view homosexuality as voluntarily immoral."

Predictors of Attitudes Towards the Prohibition of the Death Penalty
Column 3 displays the results of the hypothetical relationship between the explanatory factors and attitudes towards the prohibition of the death penalty. According to the results, the model explained nearly 7% of the variance in students' ratings of the anti-death penalty scale. The control variables had no impact on students' attitudes towards the global trend for this exception to the obligation to protect life. Their attitudes were mainly shaped by religion-related, basic value orientations and social context variables.

The belief that religion should play a more cultural role in society is statistically significant but with a slight positive effect on attitudes towards the prohibition of the death penalty. Students' feelings of dissatisfaction with the quality of their life impacted their attitudes slightly better; it is positive (β = .103) at 0.1% level of significance. The students' attitudes towards the prohibition of the death penalty were predominantly shaped by the value orientation of self-direction. The latter has a moderately strong positive beta value (β = .149***), which indicates that students who prefer this basic human value are more willing to accept the abolition of the practice of the mandatory death penalty.

Predictors of Attitudes Towards the Possibility of Abortion
The young Nigerian students evaluated the exception to the right to life through abortion clearly negatively. What factors explain their negative view of the abortion scale? Column 4 provides a summary of the net effects of the explanatory factors on the assessment of the abortion issue. For the control variables, only the interactions with their peer group members had a significant negative effect on the students' attitudes towards the possibility of abortions (β = −.098***). Apart from that, the students' attitudes towards this bioethical topic are significantly shaped by religious and social contextual variables.

A higher propensity to trust one's own religion is negatively related to attitudes toward abortion, at 1% level of significance. However, the negative assessment of the abortion scale by the students was largely determined by their religiosity. The results showed that the construct religiosity had a slightly more meaningful negative effect on attitudes towards abortion (β = −.104***), meaning that the more religious the students are, the less open they are to the question of abortion. This finding somewhat confirms the position of Norris and Inglehart (2004) on the social impact of religion, particularly on issues of private morality. A pluralistic orientation towards religions is also statistically significant (β = .107***). This has a positive impact on students' ratings of the abortion scale. It can be interpreted to mean that students with pluralistic orientations were more willing to adopt a permissive attitude towards abortion. The same is valid for the feeling of dissatisfaction with quality of life but for the strength of the impact of the variable, which is largely inconsequential. Overall, all the variables in this model contributed about 16% of the explained variance on the abortion scale.

Predictors of Attitudes Towards the Possibility of Euthanasia

Euthanasia is the last of the three exceptions to the obligation to protect life always explored in the study. What factors were responsible for the acceptance or rejection of the euthanasia scale? In column 5, the results also show that, in agreement with Norris and Inglehart (2004), students' bioethical attitudes were mainly shaped by religious factors, although religiosity is not significant. Higher levels of trust in one's own religion had a negative impact (at the 1% level of significance) on attitudes towards euthanasia, while higher trust in the religious out-group impacted the students' attitudes towards euthanasia positively ($\beta = .099^{**}$). It could be assumed on the strength of this finding that a change in the students' trust attitudes may lead to a positive change in their attitudes towards euthanasia. Agreement with the scale on religious pluralistic orientations is equally statistically significant. It also had a positive effect on attitudes towards euthanasia ($\beta = .105^{***}$), implying that students with a pluralistic orientation towards religions are more willing to modify their ideas about the inviolability of life in order to accommodate euthanasia. Students' dissatisfaction with quality of life and society is also significantly positive at the 1% level.

Of the control variables, being Muslim is significantly negatively associated with attitudes towards euthanasia ($\beta = -.133^{***}$). Muslim students tend to be less receptive to the moral issue of euthanasia, or in other words, they are more likely to disagree with the scale on euthanasia than their Christian peers. Once again, the influence of peers on the students on the issue of euthanasia is negative ($\beta = -.101^{***}$). Although they posted generally weak and, sometimes, irrelevant effects, the variables in this model accounted for 9% of the variance in the students' attitudes towards euthanasia.

Predictors of Attitudes Towards Political Rights

The students endorsed the political rights of all persons in Nigeria including non-citizens. The results in column 6 reveal that the endorsement of the index of political rights depended on the religion-related variables and the value systems of the students. Advocating a spiritual role for religion in society is statistically significant with a positive beta value ($\beta = .095^{***}$), as is preference for religion's cultural role in society ($\beta = .098^{***}$). The same applies to the religiosity construct ($\beta = .101^{***}$). In the study, however, the universalistic value orientation is the strongest predictor for attitudes towards political rights. It had a positive effect on attitudes towards political rights ($\beta = .110^{***}$). The result partially confirms the results of Gennerich and Ziebertz (2016) and Miloš and Novak (2018) in their studies, in which the value of universalism induced support for political rights. We interpret this to mean that students with preferences for universalistic values were more likely to support political rights than others in this study. In addition, student endorsement of political rights is related to agreement with the concept of inherent human dignity ($\beta = .103^{***}$). Again, the effects of the variables are not that strong. However, together they explained about 13% of the variance in the index of political rights.

Predictors of Attitudes Towards the Right to a Fair Trial

The right to a fair trial is one of the very important human rights that the students did not clearly endorse. They only rated the scale with positive ambivalence. We are interested in knowing the factors that influenced their assessment of this right. This information is provided by the research in column 7. The tendency to trust the religious out-group has a significantly positive impact on attitudes towards the right to a fair trial ($\beta = .134^{***}$). As it is, the construct 'trust in the religious out-group' is the most important variable here and the main driver of student attitudes. The more students tend to trust the religious other, the more they support the right to a fair trial. On the other hand, the preference for the performance value has a negative effect on the legal attitude ($\beta = -.122^{***}$), so that students with such a value orientation tend to support this judicial right less. Agreement with the concept of dignity as merit is also statistically significant and had a slightly positive impact on judicial rights attitudes ($\beta = .102^{***}$). Among the control variables, religious affiliation is positively related to students' attitudes towards the right to a fair trial ($\beta = 0.098^{***}$). The Muslim students are more likely to agree with this right. They consider it more important than their Christian counterparts. Overall, the regression model in column 7 explained circa 8% of the variance in attitudes toward the right to a fair trial.

Predictors of Attitudes Towards Socio-economic Rights

Socio-economic rights found the highest level of endorsement among the students. The last model in the table (column 8) displays the factors that predicted students' attitudes towards rights. The most important factor is the belief that religion should play a spiritual role in society, which the results found to be statistically significant. Agreement with this scale has a moderately positive impact on students' evaluation of the index of socio-economic rights ($\beta = .182^{***}$). The more students agree with this view, the more likely they are to support socio-economic rights. The same applies to the mindset that religion is good for public morality ($\beta = .123^{***}$) and the individual religiosity of the students ($\beta = .171^{***}$). As we can see, both are significantly positively associated with the rights mentioned, with the former having a slightly weaker influence. The feeling of empathy is statistically significant for the first time in the regression model. It had a slightly positive impact on attitudes towards socio-economic rights, as did the concept of moral dignity and preferences for the values of universalism and achievement. However, while value preferences are significant at the 0.1% level, empathy and the concept of moral dignity are significant at the 1% level. The concept of inherent dignity is also linked with a weakly positive but significant influence on attitudes towards socio-economic rights ($\beta = .120^{***}$). The more students agree with the idea of the inherent dignity of all human beings, the more willing they are to support socio-economic rights. Of the control variables, age is statistically significant with a marginally weak negative impact on students' attitudes towards socio-economic rights ($\beta = -.077^{**}$). The late adolescents tend to be less supportive of the socio-economic rights in the study than the middle adolescents. In short, the predictor variables in this model jointly explained 41% of the variance in students' attitudes toward socio-economic rights.

In summary, it can be said that apart from the construct 'perceived threat', the other variables, namely religion, empathy, basic human values, human dignity and perceived quality of life and society, all had different effects, ranging from marginally weak and weak effects to moderately strong effects on the students' attitudes towards the selected human rights issues. It is appropriate at this point, in the light of this awareness, to show whether we have made correct assumptions about students' human rights attitudes.

6.5 Are the Findings as Expected?

In the first hypothesis, we expected the students to evaluate freedom of religion and the right to a fair trial in strong positive terms (***hypothesis 1a***), the political and socio-economic rights with positive ambivalence (***hypothesis 1b***), but the protection of homosexuals from discrimination, the prohibition of the death penalty, and the possibility of abortion and euthanasia, negatively (***hypothesis 1c***). From the findings in Table 6.1, hypothesis 1a was only partially confirmed, since the right to freedom of religion was strongly positively evaluated by the students, but the right to a fair trial was not. In fact, it was evaluated with positive ambivalence. The hypothesis 1b, which expected the students to evaluate political and socio-economic rights with positive ambivalence, did not correspond to empirical facts, since both rights were clearly positively evaluated by the students. So, the expectation was not met. In hypothesis 1c, the expectation was only partially confirmed, since the LGBTI rights and the possibility of abortion were outrightly negatively evaluated by the students, while the possibility of euthanasia was evaluated with negative ambivalence. The prohibition of the death penalty by contrast was met with positive ambivalence.

In the second hypotheses, we expected the students to differ significantly in their attitudes regarding the permissibility of abortion and their willingness to support political rights based on the doctrinal orientations of their religions. This meant in concrete terms that Christian students were expected to have more unfavourable attitudes towards abortion than Muslims (***hypothesis 2a***), and Muslim students were expected to have less favourable attitudes towards political rights than Christians (***hypothesis 2b***). Both expectations were not met in the study, as the findings show that Nigerian students did not differ in their evaluation of the possibility of abortion (see Table 6.13) and their willingness to support political rights (see Table 6.15). In similar fashion, the students rejected the exception to the right to life through abortion and endorsed the political rights of citizens and non-citizens.

In hypothesis 3a, the religiosity of the students was expected to strongly predict their support for freedom of religion, and the right to a fair trial (***hypothesis 3a***), and to weakly predict the support for political and socio-economic rights (***hypothesis 3b***), but to strongly predict their rejection of the protection of homosexuals from discrimination, the prohibition of the death penalty and the possibility of abortion and euthanasia (***hypothesis 3c***). Furthermore, we expected: the students' feeling of empathy to impact their human rights attitudes in strong positive terms (***hypothesis 3d***); positive effects from the values of self-transcendence (universalism and benevolence) and openness to change (self-direction, stimulation, and hedonism) on the adolescents' human rights attitudes (***hypothesis 3e***); the agreement with the notion of inherent dignity to induce stronger support for human rights from the students (***hypothesis 3f***); that the more dissatisfied the students are with their lives and the functioning of their society is the stronger their advocacy for human rights will be (***hypothesis 3 g***); and that perceived threats by the students will lead to negative human rights attitudes (***hypothesis 3 h***). We do not confirm hypothesis 3a because, according to the findings in Table 6.19, religiosity had a moderately strong positive impact on freedom of religion but was not significant with respect to the right to a fair trial. Empirical facts only confirmed some parts of hypothesis 3b, as it had a weak effect on attitudes towards political rights, but its impact on attitudes towards socio-economic rights is somewhat strong. Then hypothesis 3c was not confirmed either. Religiosity had a weak negative influence on attitudes towards the possibility of abortion, and that was all; it had no significant effect on attitudes towards the protection of homosexuals from discrimination, the prohibition of the death penalty and the possibility of euthanasia. Furthermore, empathy had a minor impact on attitudes towards socio-economic rights and largely had no significant impact on other human rights issues. Therefore, the expectation 3d was not met. Concerning hypothesis 3e, the basic value of universalism had a positive effect on attitudes towards freedom of religion, political and socio-economic rights. It had no significant effects on other rights at all. Preference for the value of self-direction only impacted positively on attitudes towards the abolition of the death penalty, and the value orientation of hedonism is only positively related to attitudes towards non-discrimination against homosexuals. In relation to other rights, they had no significant impact on attitudes. The values of benevolence and stimulation by contrast had no significant effect on human rights attitudes at all. To that effect, the hypothesis was also partially confirmed. The hypothesis 3f, which postulated that the agreement with the notion of inherent dignity would induce stronger support for human rights by the students, was not confirmed as it did not correspond to empirical facts. The concept had weak positive impacts on attitudes towards LGBTI rights, political and socio-economic rights, but no significant effect on other human rights issues. In hypothesis 3 g, the perceived quality of life and society was expected to have positive impacts on attitudes towards human rights. The findings showed that this hypothesis was partially confirmed. Students' feeling of dissatisfaction with quality of life positively affected their attitudes towards the three instances of the right to life, although the impact was largely irrelevant. But it is negatively linked with attitudes towards the freedom of religion and had no significant impact on the rest. In the case of hypothesis 3f, the expectation did not correspond to empirical facts because the perception of threat did not predict students' attitudes towards any of the human rights issues in the study.

Then lastly, the students' religiosity was expected to be the main predictor of their human rights' attitudes (***hypothesis 4***). This much expected relationship was only partially confirmed, as religiosity was not the main predictor of the students' human rights' attitudes in all cases. In fact, this was the main factor on which their attitudes towards freedom of religion and abortion depended in this study. But the students' negative evaluation of the LGBTI rights depended primarily on something else, namely the preference for the value of achievement, just as their positively ambivalent evaluation of the prohibition of the death penalty was chiefly driven by the value orientation of self-direction. Furthermore, the propensity for higher trust in their religions can be considered the main predictor of the students' negative evaluation of the scale of euthanasia when the control variables are held constant. In the case of political rights that received positive evaluations by the students, it was due to their preference for universalistic values, whereas the positive ambivalent assessment that the right to a fair trial received tended to be based on trust in the 'religious other' as the main driving force. The students' massive endorsement of socio-economic rights was mainly triggered by a belief in the spiritual function of religion in society. The religiosity construct was equally an influential variable in relation to the socio-economic rights, but not as the main predictor of students' attitudes. In short, religiosity is an important predictor of attitudes towards human rights, but according to our results, it was not always the decisive religious factor. The beauty of empirical research is that it sometimes leads to surprising results. That seems to be the case here.

Summary

In this chapter, the empirical findings of the study were systematically presented and interpreted in four parts. First, the results of the descriptive analysis showed how the students evaluated the selected human rights issues. The right to freedom of religion was evaluated positively along with the political and socio-economic rights. The prohibition of the death penalty and the right to a fair trial were evaluated with positive ambivalence. The moral question of the possibility of euthanasia was met with negative ambivalence by the students, while the right to protection of homosexuals from discrimination and the possibility of abortion were evaluated negatively.

Second, the results of the variance analysis showed that the young Nigerian students did not differ in their evaluation of most rights based on their religious affiliation. In other words, they have similar attitudes towards the human rights issues, except for the prohibition of the death penalty, the possibility of euthanasia, and the right to a fair trial, where there are considerable differences in their evaluation.

Third, if the correlation analysis achieved anything in this study, it was to show that our explanatory factors, namely the concept of religion, empathy, basic human values, human dignity, perceived quality of life and perception of threat, all had varying degrees of relationships with the selected human rights issues. The correlations with individual rights were sometimes positive and at other times negative. But there were also non-significant correlations.

Fourth, since correlation does not necessarily imply causality, a regression analysis was conducted to determine the predictors of human rights attitudes of the students. The results showed that the concept of religion in general contributed the most to explaining human rights attitudes in this study, followed by basic human values, the concept of dignity and perceived quality of life, in that order. Empathy was significantly related to attitudes towards socio-economic rights, but its contribution was inconsequential, while the perception of threat did not contribute at all to explaining human rights attitudes.

References

A. Books and Journals

Birnbaum, M. (1995). *Nigeria: Fundamental rights denied: Report of the Trial of Ken Saro-Wiwa and Others*. University of Michigan.

Case, K. A., Fishbein, H. D., & Ritchey, P. N. (2008). Personality, prejudice, and discrimination against women and homosexuals. *Current Research in Social Psychology, 14*(2), 23–38.

Dada, J. A. (2013). The significance and limits of NGOs in human rights protection in Nigeria. *Journal of Law, Policy and Globalization, 19*, 82–91.

Gennerich, C., & Ziebertz, H.-G. (2016). Human rights and value priorities. In H.-G. Ziebertz & E. H. Ballin (Eds.), *Freedom of religion in the 21st century. A human rights perspective on the relation between politics and religion* (pp. 207–238). Brill.

Izugbara, C. O. (2004). *Patriarchal ideology and discourses of sexuality in Nigeria* (Understanding Human Sexuality Seminar Series, 2). Africa Regional Sexuality Resource Centre.

Miloš, D., & Novak, K. (2018). The role of value orientations and political preference on political and judicial human rights among the Croatian Youth. In C. Sterkens & H.-G. Ziebertz (Eds.), *Political and judicial rights through the prism of religious belief* (pp. 71–94). Springer.

Norris, P., & Inglehart, R. (2004). *Sacred and secular: Religion and politics worldwide*. Cambridge University Press.

Norris, P., & Inglehart, R. F. (2012). Muslim integration into western cultures: Between origins and destinations. *Political Studies, 60*, 228–251.

Nwafor, A. O. (2010). Comparative perspectives on Euthanasia in Nigeria and Ethiopia. *African Journal of International and Comparative Law, 18*(2), 170–191.

Ojo, E. O. (2006). Human rights and sustainable democracy in Nigeria (1999–2003). *Journal of Social Science, 13*(1), 15–29.

Onwuazombe, I. I. (2017). Human rights abuse and violations in Nigeria: A case study of the oil-producing communities in the Niger Delta region. *Annual Survey of International and Comparative Law, 22*(1/8), 115–160.

Van der Ven, J. A. (2016). On the brink of death: Euthanasia from the angle of law, morality and religion: A cross-cultural perspective. In H.-G. Ziebertz & E. H. Ballin (Eds.), *Freedom of religion in the 21st century. A human rights perspective on the relation between politics and religion* (pp. 257–299). Brill.

Ziebertz, H.-G. (2019). Human dignity, religious ethics or hedonism: what can predict young people's attitudes in Germany towards the right to life in the cases of euthanasia and abortion? In H.-G. Ziebertz & F. Zaccaria (Eds.), *Euthanasia, abortion, death penalty and religion – The right to life and its limitations* (pp. 83–104). Springer.

National Human Rights Instruments

International Federation for Human Rights. (2010, April). *Defending human rights – Not everywhere not every right: International factfinding mission report on Nigeria*. Available at: https://www.refworld.org/docid/4bed03412.html. Accessed 16 July 2014.

Other Internet Sources

Oniha, B. E., & Oniha, O. M. (2015). *Euthanasia and assisted suicide as basic constitutional rights under the 1999 constitution of Nigeria*. Available at: https://www.nigerianlawguru.com/articles/humanrightslaw/EuthanasiaandAssistedSuicide.Pdf. Accessed 01 Oct 2020.

Part III
Discussion of Salient Findings

Chapter 7
The Quest for an Authentic Culture of Human Rights

Contents

7.1 Determinants of Human Rights Attitudes in Nigeria 323
7.1.1 The Salience of Religion 323
7.1.2 The Significant Impact of Value Orientations 334
7.2 Significance of Study for Practical Theology 337
7.3 Significance of Study for the Pastoral Mission of the Church 339
7.4 Significance of Study for the Global Discourse on Human Rights 341
References 344

Introduction

The context of application of this study covers only one chapter, namely this chapter. It is a short chapter. The purpose of this chapter is simply to discuss key research findings and their relevance to promoting a culture of human rights. The major findings of the study are highlighted to begin with. These include the concept of religion, and value systems. They are described here as determinants of the human rights attitudes of the young people sampled in Nigeria. These so-called determinants of human rights attitudes are discussed in a little more detail in order to draw some preliminary but worthwhile conclusions for the academia, ecclesia, and society, in the quest for the formation and promotion of an authentic culture of human rights. The justification for this arises from the empirical-theological research design chosen for this study.

Practical theology is normative and pragmatic in approach (Osmer, 2008; Ziebertz, 2002). In his book, "*Practical theology: An introduction*", Osmer (2008) enumerated four tasks he sees as the core operations of practical theology as a discipline, namely the descriptive-empirical, interpretative, normative, and pragmatic tasks. These four tasks represent a paradigm of reflective practice. They are distinct but interdependent tasks that address four interrelated relevant questions. The first task is the descriptive-empirical. This is the phase of gathering information to better

M. C. Adimekwe, *The Impact of Religion, Personality, Values and Worldviews on Attitudes Towards Human Rights*, Religion and Human Rights 11,
https://doi.org/10.1007/978-3-031-65749-8_7

understand a particular context or experience. For this reason, this task asks the question "What is going on?" and attempts to arrive at a comprehensive description of an empirical phenomenon. This may entail collecting data about the actual research interest, and in this case the practical theologian may need to resort to social science methods such as participant observation, interviews, surveys, or a focus group to achieve this goal (Osmer, 2011; Carter, 2018). After an informed and thorough description of the actions and patterns taking place, the practical theologian embarks upon the task of interpreting them and explaining why they take place. This is where the task of interpretation begins. The question (s)he wants to answer here is: "Why is this going on?" Doing justice to the interpretative task entails entering into an intentional dialogue with certain theories to be able to correctly interpret the observed phenomenon (Osmer, 2011; Osmer, 2004; Carter, 2018). This is followed by the third normative task. At this stage, practical theology, incorporating the perspectives of theology, ethics, and other fields, raises a normative question such as "What ought to be going on?" (Osmer, 2011). This makes sense because after developing a grounded description of an observed phenomenon, the practical theologian brings the interpreted description into formal dialogue with a religious tradition of interest (Osmer, 2008). The target is not to develop a theological doctrine or write a scriptural commentary, but rather to construct ethical norms to guide practice (Carter, 2018). According to Osmer, a fourth task that closes the hermeneutic circle is the pragmatic one. The question that practical theology seeks to answer here is: "How might we respond to the particular context or experience?" or, more precisely, as Osmer later puts it: "How might this area of praxis be shaped to more fully embody the normative commitments of a religious tradition in this particular context or experience?" (Osmer, 2004: 151). In other words, the pragmatic task of practical theology is particularly concerned with the realistic approach to praxis (Carter, 2018). This implies attempting to create a specific plan of action and undertake specific responses aimed at shaping the context or experience in desirable directions. Attempts are made to develop 'practice theories' that could guide reflective practice (Osmer, 2011). All four tasks influence each other in a hermeneutic spiral that can be entered at any time. It is this interrelationship that enables practical theology to construct action-guiding theories of religious practice (Osmer, 2004).

From the foregoing analysis, it is clear that the efforts made in the last four chapters of this study have addressed the first two tasks of practical theology and they indeed fit perfectly into the research design. The normative and pragmatic tasks have not yet been applied. In the following subheadings, these dual aspects of a practical-theological method of reflection are applied to our interpretation of the observed human rights attitudes of a select group of young Nigerians in order to propose open-ended guidelines for future action. That is what this chapter is all about.

7.1 Determinants of Human Rights Attitudes in Nigeria

Research on human rights at various levels of analysis has revealed a number of variables as predictors of attitudes toward human rights. Some studies found that the concept of religion is a relevant predictor of attitudes towards human rights (Zaccaria et al., 2019; Francis et al., 2018; Ziebertz & Ziebertz, 2016; Van der Tuin & Fumbo, 2012; Francis et al., 2016). Others also point to psychological factors such as empathy as an explanatory factor for human rights attitudes (McFarland & Mathews, 2005; McFarland, 2015; Ziebertz et al., 2018; Ok et al., 2020; Case et al., 2008). Still others found that other factors, such as the concepts of human dignity (Ziebertz & Ziebertz, 2016), and value orientations (Doise et al., 1999; Gennerich & Ziebertz, 2016; McFarland, 2015; Miloš & Novak, 2018) are sometimes used to legitimise human rights attitudes. The research findings presented above (see Table 6.19) suggest that the human rights attitudes of the young people surveyed in Nigeria are determined by an array of explanatory factors such as the concept of religion, the psychological trait of empathy, value preferences and Human dignity, and perceived quality of life. However, of all these factors, only the concepts of religion and value orientations recorded a range of weak and moderately strong predictive values. The remaining three have predominantly weak or statistically irrelevant predictive outputs. Due to their low values, they are not discussed here in the same depth as the first pair of factors as determinants of the human rights attitudes of the sampled young Nigerians.

7.1.1 *The Salience of Religion*

The results of the study showed that religion is overall the most important predictor of the sampled students' attitudes towards the selected human rights provisions. This is the main outcome of the study. In some ways, this finding confirms the basic tenets of the secularisation models of Casanova (1994) and Norris and Inglehart (2004) when considered from a broader international perspective. At the heart of widespread opinion in the social sciences is the belief that traditional religions will terminally decline as societies modernise. A combined reading of Casanova and Norris and Inglehart's theses instead hypothesises the continued relevance of religion on both societal and personal levels. In fact, the results of this study indicate a significant influence of religion on young people's public and private lives.

More importantly, the findings lend credence to the assertion often made by African scholars about the salience of religion in the African context. On this point, Mbiti (1989: 1) had previously remarked: "[r]eligion permeates into all the department of life so fully that it is not easy or possible always to isolate it. … Religion is the strongest element in traditional background and exerts probably the greatest influence upon the thinking and living of the people concerned." Thorpe (1992: 3) agreed with Mbiti and suggested that for Africans, religion was "an integral part of life itself." Beyers (2010) sees it as the normal way Africans view and experience the world. This means that the religious factor cannot be ignored in any attempt to describe the African worldview. The latter can actually be described as religious. This was precisely the point that Amusan et al. (2019) made when they identified religion as one of the central factors that determine individuals' positions on certain societal issues in Africa. Recent quantitative studies seem to further confirm the thesis, as they provide evidence of the significant influence of religion on socio-political issues, particularly human rights issues (Dreyer & Aziz, 2021; see also van der Tuin & Fumbo, 2012; van der Ven et al., 2004).

The assertion that religion is a relevant societal actor has also been made by numerous social commentators at different times and in different circumstances in relation to Nigeria. For instance, Ezeanya (1980: 324) stressed some years ago that in Nigeria in particular and Africa as a whole, "life is religion, and religion is life". This point did not escape Uchem (2013: 544) in her recent essay on the need for reform of the National Christian Religious Studies (CRS) curriculum, in which she stated: "[r]eligion is a strong factor to reckon with in Nigeria." Some recent studies have also demonstrated this quantitatively. Admittedly, a direct comparison of data is very difficult due to differences in questions, contexts and profiles of the respondents. However, if one looks at the results of the respective 'religion' constructs in the Religions Monitor 2008 on Nigeria, the Odoeme Human Rights Survey 2011 and the International Survey on Religion and Human Rights 2014, some similarities can be observed.

In the said Religions Monitor, for example, about 99% of respondents described themselves as religious or very religious. The remaining 1% did not respond. When it comes to belief in God or a divine subject and belief in an afterlife, 97% of respondents reported that they have a moderate or high belief in this regard, while only 1% of them reported having a low belief in the same issues. Likewise, t when it comes to cultic or ritual participation, 98% of the respondents indicate that they moderately or highly participate in religious practices of their religious traditions, while 1% showed a low level of religious participation. Regarding prayer, all respondents (100%) affirm that prayer is moderately or highly important to them. They were also asked to indicate the importance of 'religiousness' in their lives, and 99% of them said it is moderately, fairly or very important to them in their lives. Only 1% noted that 'religiousness' is not important to them at all (see also Huber, 2008a). The young Nigerian respondents to Odeme's questionnaire in 2011 also evaluated religion-related variables highly. In the first place, all his respondents profess to be religious. When asked whether their religion or belief is important to them or not, around 93% of them said that their religion or belief is important to them, 1% said it is not important to them, while the rest 6.4% showed signs of ambivalence. The value here is slightly low compared to the Religion Monitor, but still high, and some respondents are ambivalent. The respondents here are all adolescents who, in contrast to those in the Religion Monitor, are probably going through puberty and so such a reaction was to be expected from them. In addition, their rating of the statement 'my religion or worldview has a great influence on my daily life' was very positive (Mean = 4.3). Approximately 92% indicate that their religion or worldview has a major influence on their life, around 4% answered "no" and around 5% were unsure. The belief in the immanence of God also got high endorsement from those sampled (Mean = 4.58) as did various theological perspectives on Jesus Christ and Mohammed. The Religion and Human Rights Survey—the dataset for this study—also recorded generally high scores for religion-related variables. About 99% of the research population identified themselves as believers. The remaining 1.2% did not respond to the item. This identification is accompanied by high levels of religious participation (Mean = 4.63) with circa 80% reporting that they attend religious services at least one or more times per week. The same applies to the importance of prayer, which was also rated highly by those surveyed (Mean = 4.53) with 71.2% indicating that they pray at least once or several times per day. Belief in God or something divine also remains high (Mean = 4.71). About 92% of them identify themselves as often or very often believing, 7% indicate that they believe occasionally, while only 1.3% identified as non-believing. The item on the importance of religion equally received a high rating (Mean = 4.10). Circa 82% say that their religion or worldview often or very often has a great influence on their daily life, around 14% are not sure whether their belief is an important issue for them, and 4.4% clearly say that religion is not relevant to them. Compared to the other two datasets, this shows a relatively new trend towards rejection of religion in the number of young people who think that religion is unimportant to them or are so unsure about the relevance of religion in their lives. The reasons are likely to be related to the spate of religious crises in the country, among many other factors. Nevertheless, we can attest that the respondents have a high level of religiosity (Mean value = 4.35).

Furthermore, it is well documented that religion shapes individual values and public policies in Nigeria (cf. Adegbite, 2012; Ayanleye, 2013; Okeke & Eze, 2013; Okpanachi, 2012). This claim appears to be supported by the results of this study. But there is an important side of the country's religious history that should not be overlooked, and that is that many Nigerians view religion as both a unifying force and a source of conflict in their society (Uzoma, 2004; see also Osaghae & Suberu, 2005). In pre-colonial Nigeria, religion largely functioned as a unifying force for the indigenous population, not necessarily due to the lack of religious diversity but rather the lack of sharp ideological differences between indigenous belief systems, among other things. Scholars of African history and traditional religion generally agree that the ATR was plural in form but inherently singular in terms of the philosophy that underlies religious life (Mbiti, 1990; see also Beyers, 2010; Krüger et al., 2009; Magesa, 2002). Thus, there existed in effect "a single 'universe of meaning'" that was shared by all members of society (Haralambos & Heald, 1985: 477; see also Uzoma, 2004). This remained so until the watershed came with the Arab and European expansion into Africa and since then 'the centre could no longer hold' as Achebe (1958) aptly put it in *Things Fall Apart*. Be that as it may, the results of this study seem to confirm the claim of an ambivalent role of religion in the Nigerian project, in the sense that the concept of religion is simultaneously a trigger for the acceptance of some selected human rights issues and a driving force for the rejection of others. For example, while the religion construct was used by the research population to endorse human rights such as freedom of religion, political and socio-economic rights, the 'trust in religious in-group' construct impacted negatively on the young people's attitude towards the right to non-discrimination based on sexual orientation. The good news here is that religion was largely the main or supporting factor on which students' positive evaluations of some human rights issues were based. This clearly shows, among other things, that religion can still be relied upon to cultivate and promote a human rights culture among the sampled students. It is therefore left to the relevant local authorities to find ways to harness this apparent religious capital of these young people—which includes their rich religious heritage and relatively high religiosity—to inculcate human-rights-friendly values in them.

7.1.1.1 The Teaching of Religion in Nigerian Schools

One way to achieve this is through appropriate teaching in religious education (hereinafter RE). As a matter of fact, the subject is currently taught in all schools in Nigeria. It is compulsory for pupils in primary schools and students in junior secondary school (hereinafter JSS) (Falade, 2016). It does not feature in the senior secondary school (hereinafter SSS) curriculum, although administrators of each school have the room to include it if desired (Asue & Kajo, 2018). Until recently, when ATR was incorporated into the national curriculum, RE was designed only for the country's two main religious traditions. The model is confessional, meaning that the subject is offered to students as a kind of introduction to religion according to their religious traditions. In general, the objective is to provide orientation on the specific religious traditions, but it is also about instilling in learners spiritual principles and moral values necessary for living together with others, in accordance with the educational philosophy of the country (cf. Federal Republic of Nigeria, 2014).

This confessional approach in the Nigerian context is in principle paired with a homegrown version of Skilbeck's (2005) process-based curriculum design known as the Comparative Educational Study and Adaptation Centre model. This so-called CESAC model (now NERDC) is the dominant model of curriculum development in the Nigerian school system (Ivowi, 1993; Owolabi et al., 2013). NERDC, the Nigerian Educational Research and Development Council, is the organ of the Federal Ministry of Education responsible for the content of the school curriculum, including the RE curriculum. This is usually done in collaboration with relevant actors in the education sector, namely teachers, students, parents, religious leaders and government professionals (cf. Ihedinma, 2004). The NERDC model of curriculum development is basically process-driven. It focuses on the process of learning and teaching (Ivowi, 1986) and is learner-centred, that is, it takes the learner's needs and interests into account. The aim is also continuous education for self-realisation and general development of society (Federal Republic of Nigeria, 2014). In order to implement this, RE teachers, like other teachers in the country, are usually trained in the course 'Education and Religious Studies' at universities, college of education or teacher training institute as part of their general teacher training for primary schools and as a stand-alone subject for secondary schools. When all is said and done, RE is expected to make a meaningful contribution to meeting the country's educational needs. These include, among other things, promoting mutual respect among citizens and helping to address issues of religious extremism and fundamentalism.

However, it does not appear that the status quo of RE, its general organisation and delivery in the country would do much to improve our respondents' attitudes towards human rights. The issue here revolves around two major considerations: model design and policy implementation. Firstly, RE in Nigeria is given a marginal status. This is a subject or course one can study without any real prospect of employment. Paradoxically, it has no place in Nigerian society because the country does not take it seriously. But a Nigeria where religion is a big issue and indeed 'a strong factor to be reckoned with in socio-political issue' needs to take RE seriously. Secondly, religion is treated as one of the subjects that anyone, even without training, can teach. Nevertheless, the important work that RE teachers or teachers in general do for society as implementers of the school curriculum should not be underestimated. NERDC's process-based curriculum model is a solid curriculum design developed by education experts. It has been further developed and continuously revised by the relevant bodies. However, to achieve the desired results, well-trained teachers are required for implementation. The Nigerian state has not yet done enough to train religious teachers, which is why there is a lack of competent RE teachers in the country (Falade, 2016, see also Ihedinma, 2004). One of the dire consequences of this is the danger that students will be indoctrinated by makeshift RE teachers, that is, RE teachers who are not formally trained in the subject. Another consequence of this is the unintentional recourse to the content-based curriculum approach by the school system. The latter emphasises the method of memorisation and was more or less the approach that the early missionaries and the colonial administration bequeathed to the country's education system. It has long been declared unsuitable because it no longer meets the educational needs of the country. If anything, the method has been criticised for its tendency to increase knowledge of a subject without necessarily developing the learner's mind (Walsh, 1997). Therefore, given their role as curriculum implementers, RE teachers need to be constantly trained in new teaching methods (cf. Asue & Kajo, 2018). The same reason for the dearth of competent RE teachers is also cited as one of the main reasons for the failure of the recent NERDC introduction of Religion and National Values as a unified religious subject for all (Falade, 2016). A Nigeria whose corporate existence is often threatened by religious conflicts and in which religious practices are sometimes used as a pretext for human rights violations cannot do without RE being appropriately taught in schools. In fact, the country needs an attitudinal shift in the way the subject is both perceived and taught.

Furthermore, given Nigeria's socio-political context, it is not clear to what extent the confessional RE that the country offers is the best form of religious formation for the young students in the sample to improve their human rights attitudes. This observation is based on the understanding that Nigeria is a multi-religious, multicultural society. Since the model aims at learning religious content and promoting specific religious traditions, it cannot prepare a school child for life in this context, as it is not suitable for familiarising school children with the diversity of their life-world. Civilised countries such as Germany, Austria, etc., which can be regarded as proponents of this model, are gradually moving towards some modified versions of the model due to the tendency of their societies becoming increasingly complex. The overarching objective is to give young people the skills to deal with this reality. There is no doubt that it is important that Nigerian school children receive an education that enables them to acquire the competence to engage with their own religious perspective. They also need to be helped to acquire the necessary competence to be able to deal constructively with other religious perspectives in their social context (cf. Olschewski & Schreiner, 2020). Therefore, based on the above analysis, this study suggests that apart from the above attitudinal change, a paradigm shift in RE is also required in the country.

7.1.1.2 Human Development Model: The Appropriate RE Approach for Nigerian Classrooms

Given a British context in which the study of religion in schools was dominated by the Christian instructional paradigm, Michael Grimmitt felt that the state should play a completely different role to the church in the discourse on religion in schools. He summarised this role in a single term *educating* as opposed to *instructing*. The reason was—and Grimmitt (1973) clearly admits this himself—that this approach was specifically aimed at leading the learner to faith and commitment to his or her religion (see also Engebretson, 2004).

It is a well-known fact that within the conventional pedagogy of instruction, the dominant pattern of teaching is the so-called Initiate-Response-Evaluation (IRE) (cf. Skrefsrud, 2022). In this teaching context, subject teachers convey the lesson content to learners, and these are only expected to dutifully memorise the information presented to them and then reproduce it afterwards without critically examining it. This learning approach is based on the pedagogical logic that perceives teachers as information providers and students as passive receptacles (Ziebertz, 2018; see also Shor & Freire, 1987). In keeping with this philosophical underpinning, learners in this traditional classroom are taught about world religions for the purpose of acquiring knowledge about them, as well as to acquire the sacred truth that their respective religions promise to offer (cf. Engebretson, 2004). Their engagement with the phenomenon of religion only reflects the curricular content. The model of religious instruction is geared towards the attainment of knowledge and is at best an instrument of recruitment and selection (Ziebertz, 2018). As such, it can rightly be described as "confessional" in conception, approach and goal (Grimmitt, 1973: 18; see also Engebretson, 2004; Skrefsrud, 2022).

Against this background, Grimmitt argued that the state as a separate entity needed to introduce a different pedagogical thinking to the study of religion in schools, particularly in the context of a rapidly diversifying British society. He called for a balance between teacher-centred teaching methods, in which teachers impart knowledge to learners about the phenomenon of religion, and student-centred methods that explore their existential situation of learners. For him, such pedagogical balance means that students' study of religion is more than just learning the various aspects of world religions, including their traditions, beliefs, rituals, symbols, aesthetics and histories. It is also about giving learners the opportunity to discuss ultimate questions and reflect on how these affect their own lives, and to help them explore what it means to be human (Grimmitt, 1973, 1987; Skrefsrud, 2022). Grimmitt was convinced that a non-denominational study of religion approached in the light of an experiential learning model can effectively achieve desired outcomes because it incorporates "a perspective of learning from in learning about [religion]" (Skrefsrud, 2022: 11). Consequently, he proposed a pedagogy for non-confessional RE in the British context, insisting that RE in public schools should educate learners about religion rather than instruct them for the purpose of strengthening their faith.

The term *'educate'*, which has just been introduced into the discourse here, is instructive. Grimmitt employes it in the sense that Peters (1966 cited in Engebretson, 2004: 8) used it to refer to a process by which learners are introduced to some "worthwhile ... specific modes of thought and awareness". Grimmitt expressed deep reservations about the view of most epistemologists that knowledge is intrinsically valuable. He stated categorically that education is valuable not because of its intrinsic worth but for its instrumental value, that is, for its contribution to the goals of education (Grimmitt, 1987). Education, as we know, aims to develop learners' skills and competencies towards full personal development. For Grimmitt, too, the fundamental goal of education is human development in both its personal and social dimensions (cf. Engebretson, 2004). Therefore, Grimmitt's reference to education in connection with school-based study of religion implies that RE should not only aim to provide learners with an understanding of world religions and worldviews, but rather that it should also focus on developing skills that are helpful to their personal development. In other words, the subject should be designed to help learners acquire competences for both pure and applied religion (Grimmitt, 1991). Suffice it to say, somewhat more technically, that he proposed the introduction of a critical element into religious education, since critical thinking is an essential part of education. This position is well supported in literature. Ziebertz (2018), for instance, is of the opinion that religious instruction in public schools should fundamentally have an informative and educational character. In this way, the RE subject provides learners valuable opportunities for exploring encounters between themselves and the subject content. And they will maximise the religious and educational privileges that the course content can offer them for their personal development. This dialectic between human experience and objective or received knowledge is key to the pedagogical shift that Grimmitt advocates (Grimmitt, 1987; Engebretson, 2004).

Having thus clarified the objectives of a pedagogy within RE, Grimmitt presented his preferred model for RE, the human development model, in his more recent writings (1987, 1991, 2000). It has a constructivist orientation and is based on the philosophical framework of phenomenology (Grimmitt, 1973, 1987, 2000). In this pedagogy, Grimmitt recognised as a starting point that students are spiritual beings and that this aspect of themselves also needs to be developed. To achieve this, he proposed treating the study of religion in public schools strictly as an educational enterprise, but with the proviso that the proposed RE subject must meet certain criteria to justify its inclusion as a useful subject in the curriculum. First, like other school subjects, it should incorporate a unique way of thinking that is valuable to a learner's personal development. Secondly, it should also contribute to his or her human development. And third, it should be taught in a way that promotes critical, independent scholarship (Grimmitt, 1973; see also Engebretson, 2004; Skrefsrud, 2022). In short, the three criteria rest on the subject's unique contribution to human development. Grimmitt sees RE as an essential part of the 'humanising' of people. By this he meant the process of becoming human (Grimmitt, 1987; Shackles, 1991). He locates the specific contribution of the subject to human development in the 'instrumental goods' that it offers to learners. These include a range of skills they acquire in the learning process, such as tolerance, empathy and reflective thinking, as well as other competences that help them develop their sense of identity, morals and values.[1] These skills facilitate their personal growth towards some model of being human (cf. Shackles, 1991). Grimmitt felt that these issues in an adolescent's life cannot be sufficiently addressed by the subjects in the curriculum.[2] Besides, he believes that learners need this aspect of knowledge about our world to form an overall picture of the human experience (cf. Shackles, 1991). With these, he considers RE to be a relevant discipline because of the unique form of knowledge it offers and is convinced that it deserves to be included in the curriculum as a distinct subject.

Accordingly, teaching and learning in a constructivist-humanist RE classroom lays emphasis on two main areas of interest, namely the religious lifeworld and the lifeworld of young people in the key areas of family, local community, larger society and global community (Engebretson, 2004). Grimmitt focused mostly on the latter but urges that commensurate attention be given to the former as well (Shackles, 1991). Lessons in this setting could, for example, follow a four-part schema of engagement, discovery, contextualisation and reflection (Grimmitt, 1991). To demonstrate this, students could "begin by sharing their spontaneous opinion (engagement) and then refine it picking on a certain point (discovery). Teachers then … provide some religious context to keep the debate on track and on topic (contextualisation) before the students take their refined points from earlier and apply their religious insight (reflection)."[3] The goal of this approach is to use discursive methods to leverage the religious and educational imports of a curricular content in a way that provides learners with maximum opportunities for spiritual and human flourishing.

Learning RE in this way is not abstract, as it does not detach itself from the everyday world of the learners, but rather attempts to relate facts to their lives.

---

[1] See Tutor Hunt International (2022). Examining Grimmitt's Human Pedagogy in Informing. Available at: https://www.tutorhunt.com/resource/26467/. Accessed 05 May 2023.

[2] Ibid.

[3] Ibid.

Therein lies the strength of the approach, namely its ability to respond directly to their existential situation. The expected learning outcome is not cognitive knowledge, but their personal development (Shackles, 1991). However, although the focus is more on human development, a non-confessional RE also provides learners with religious literacy. Here too, the focus is more on the learners' respective religious traditions, but the profiles of the religions in their environment are also presented to them in a neutral and objective manner. This creates an avenue through which they can learn to engage with different religions and philosophies (van der Tuin, 2009). In this way, it not only addresses their contexts, but also promotes their personal growth through a reflective engagement with a religious content. Constructivist pedagogy supports an open, active, free and engaging method of inquiry (Barry & Elliott, 2012). This reduces the risk of churning out students who are only proficient in the subject but lack the basic skills to manage diversity.

This brings us to some of the major concerns that some scholars have expressed about Grimmitt's pedagogical approach to RE. They criticise it as being pluralistic and theologically too demanding for theistic students and teachers.[4] They argue that the learning method that he proposes from a secular humanist perspective, risks deconstructing learners' religious beliefs and thereby producing non-religiously committed individuals. Kalve (1996) believes that this approach would be uncomfortable for most parents who wish to develop their children in their own traditions. Therefore, he assumes that its applicability in a strongly religious country will cause disagreement. These are legitimate concerns to begin with. Nevertheless, it is difficult to see how the skills that Grimmitt aims to develop with his pedagogical approach, such as reflective thinking, etc., could necessarily lead to learners denying the uniqueness of their religious beliefs rather than reinforcing them.[5] Furthermore, the model does not advocate that other actors in religious socialisation outsource their responsibility to cater for the interests of pious students to the school, since the school cannot do everything, but rather that the school should inter alia create room for a reflexive process, in which learners are encouraged to engage critically with what they are learning (cf. Skrefsrud, 2022). Be that as it may, the need for multicultural orientations in today's increasingly diverse society cannot simply be traded-off for a community's demand for a strong religious identity. The RE curriculum must respond to the urgent needs of twenty-first century global citizenship (Uchem, 2013). Regarding the claim that the approach places high demands on students and teachers, experts in the education sector see this differently. They argue instead that human development pedagogy provides a solid foundation for lesson planning and curriculum design. In addition, they believe that the emphasis on developing students' skills to promote their holistic development is consistent with the natural way students engage in classroom dialogue.[6]

---

[4] Ibid.

[5] Ibid.

[6] Ibid.; see also Engebretson (2004).

Given the strengths of the human development model, this study considers human-development-oriented RE as a more beneficial model for our research population than the confessional RE currently offered in the country. Our preference for the model is grounded on several factors, including the following. First, Grimmitt is particularly concerned with RE for young people (cf. Grimmitt, 1987; Shackles, 1991). Thus, the question of the suitability of this model for our research population does not arise, as the latter consists of secondary school students.

Second, there is no perfect model for RE. But due to his interest in human rights, the human development approach to RE seems to be the most promising way to religiously educate our research population, in view of the ultimate goal of this study, which is to explore factors that could promote the formation or improved maintenance of the culture of human rights in Nigeria. Of course, a human development pedagogy for RE is human rights friendly, as is attested in several human rights instruments, for example the Universal Declaration (article 26), the Convention against Discrimination in Education of 1960 [article 5(1)(a)], the ICESCR Act 1966 [article 13(1)]. All of these instruments advocate in their provisions RE and education in general, which aim at the full development of the human personality. The Toledo Guiding Principles (ODIHR, 2007) clearly state that education about religion can promote appreciation of the right to religious freedom, democratic citizenship and understanding of social diversity. Human rights scholars also agree that this is consistent with international human rights treaties (cf. Evans, 2008).

Thirdly, the preference for this model also considers the social context, that is, Nigerian society. Today, the importance of the so-called 'education in context' for the holistic development of individuals and nations cannot be overemphasised (see Zaccaria, Anthony & Sterkens, 2019). The human development model is consistent with the type of education that a pluralistic and multi-religious democratic society like Nigeria aspires to. Until now, the dominant model of RE in the country has been faith-oriented, with the subject being used to get learners to embrace Christianity or Islam. This approach tended to be overwhelmed by religious indoctrination and dogma, leaving learners only to cognitively learn facts from religious texts (Sampson, 2012). The human development approach is ad rem here in the sense that it engages students in developing and taking their affective learning skills seriously. It helps them to understand their religions and those of their peers, to reflect on their common values and to explore relevant topics that predispose to peaceful coexistence in their diverse society (Grimmitt, 2000). In this connection, it is important to mention the recently introduced subject Religion and National Values (RNV) for secondary schools. This study views the subject, which was incidentally removed from the curriculum, as a missed opportunity as these goals were part of what the subject sought to achieve. But it failed due to its implementation, which was marred by the usual primordial sentiments that have often veered the country off the developmental trajectory, such as ethnic, religious and political considerations, etc.

Lastly—and above all—the model advocates viewing RE *sensu strictu* as an educational enterprise. As already indicated in the earlier part, religious socialisation processes in the country also take place in informal settings, such as the family, religious communities, etc. These agents of religious socialisation primarily nurture learners in faith. In contrast, RE at school is intended to educate learners about religion. This basically means adding an element of critical reflection to what these other agents do. The model clearly delineates the goals of religious instruction and religious education. Education—from the Latin *'educare'* meaning 'to mould, form,' and '*educere*' meaning 'to lead out'—entails leading a malleable human being from the private spaces of his or her home into the public spaces of the larger society. In other words, it is a process through which an individual acquires the skills that enable him or her to function as a useful member of society. According to its philosophy, the school is a social institution. Through schools, states attempt to promote and develop their preferred values and national identities (Statham, 2016). In keeping with these etymological considerations, Grimmitt sees the aim of RE as helping "children mature in relation to their patterns of belief and behaviour through exploring religious beliefs and practices and related human experiences" (Grimmitt, 2000: 35). This aim is consistent with Nigeria's educational philosophy, which is "based on the development of the individual into a sound and effective citizen" (section 1, para. 4). Interestingly, Nigeria's national educational goals to which the philosophy is associated include, among other things, (i) "[t]he integration of the individual into the immediate community, the Nigerian society and the world" [section 1, para. 6(b)], and (ii) "[t]he development of appropriate skills, ... abilities and competences to empower the individual to live in and contribute positively to society" [section 1, para. 6(e)]. If the RE curriculum is to help learners achieve these goals, the following words from Denise Cush (2011: 82) must be taken seriously:

> ... whatever approach is taken to the place of religion in education, it must be agreed that in today's world it is an urgent necessity that our children and young people learn about the beliefs, values, practices and identities of the people that they will be interacting with, that they learn to respect but also to think critically about the various faiths and beliefs they will come across, and that they have access to ideas, values and customs that they can draw upon ... in transforming their own lives and those around them for the better.

In all, according to the 2014 National Policy on Education (hereinafter NPE, 2014), the quality of teaching must be oriented towards the teaching of values that promote the overall development of the child [section 1, para. 9(e)]. The important role of teachers in RE needs to be highlighted. The teacher is a massive factor. Almost everything depends on the teacher. Watson and Thompson (2013: 3) underscored this point when they said: "[t]he most fundamental factor in effective religious education, as in the effective teaching of any other subject, is the teacher." So, to treat religious studies in school as an educational enterprise simply means introducing a critical aspect to the teaching and learning of religion in Nigeria. From a policy perspective, this means that RE, like other school subjects, is viewed very strictly in line with the national educational philosophy enshrined in the 2014 NPE. Such a realignment would reposition the subject to focus on holistic development of the learner. This position has also been canvassed in a number of other studies, albeit from different perspectives (cf. Ajah, 2015; Ihedinma, 2004; Sampson, 2012; Uchem, 2013). In short, a paradigm and attitudinal shift in the perception of RE in Nigeria is necessary if the religious capital of the schoolchildren and youth in our sample can be harnessed to improve their human rights attitudes.

7.1.2 The Significant Impact of Value Orientations

The findings of this study also showed that values underlie human rights attitudes and that value preferences are the second main trigger for students' human rights attitudes behind the concept of religion. This is another interesting outcome of the research. It confirms the suitability of Schwartz's value theory for the study. Based on the scale used to rate the students' responses to the Portrait Values Questionnaire,[7] it can be seen that the single value types most frequently endorsed by them in Table 5.1 are security (M = 5.04; Sd = 1.19) and benevolence (M = 4.87; Sd = 1.21), achievement (M = 4.81; Sd = 1.37), conformity (M = 4.62; Sd = 1.40), self-direction (M = 4.38; Sd = 1.42), universalism (M = 4.30; Sd = 1.43) and tradition (M = 4.17; Sd = 1.50). Looking at this result, one can say that the value orientation of our respondents is somewhat diffuse. In the hypotheses, only the values of self-transcendence (i.e., universalism and benevolence) and openness to change (i.e., self-direction, stimulation, and hedonism) were expected to positively underlie the human rights attitudes of the students (see hypothesis 3e). However, the findings show that their human rights attitudes are located primarily in the basic values of self-direction and achievement. Self-direction shows a moderately strong connection with the prohibition of the death penalty It can be said that this core value motivates innovation. For this reason, it is assigned to the value area of openness to change (cf. Schwartz, 2012). Therefore, it is only logical that support for changing the practice of capital punishment is motivated by the preference for this basic value type. Achievement values are more about self-centred satisfaction (Potts, 2015). They are negatively related to the rights of homosexuals and the right to a fair trial. But they also relate positively to freedom of religion and socio-economic rights. The right to freedom of religion and the catalogue of selected political and socio-economic rights are anchored in the basic value of universalism. In contrast to the value of achievement, universalism includes the interests of others, which may sometimes conflict with self-interest. It is a prosocial value and as such contributes to positive social relationships (cf. Schwartz, 2012). Little wonder that a number of the human rights provisions under study are positioned in this value orientation, although not all of them as expected. Similarly, the rights of LGBTI persons are located in the hedonistic value preference, which also belongs to the value domain of openness to change, while freedom of religion is once again related to the value of security.

From this analysis, two patterns emerge regarding the relationship between students' value orientations and human rights attitudes that need to be highlighted. First, it can be observed that the above five basic values chosen by our respondents belong to the four different value domains that Schwartz and his associates sorted into two opposing dimensions as values competing for priority, namely self-transcendence (universalism) versus self-enhancement (achievement), and

[7] The rating scale was later elaborated to read as follows: 1 = not like me at all; 2 = not like me; 3 = a little like me; 4 = somewhat like me; 5 = like me; and 6 = very much like me.

openness to change (self-direction) versus conservation (security). The implication is that the human rights attitudes of the sampled students sometimes represent different values that conflict with one another. A typical example of this is the right to freedom of religion, which is located in the values of universalism and achievement belonging to two opposing camps in the value dimensions mentioned. This sounds quite strange, but it is not out of place. Schwartz (2012: 8) sees this as a possible development based on the character of values as "dynamic entities" in which people can pursue competing values in different situations, but "not in a single act". Gennerich and Ziebertz (2016) came to a similar conclusion in their study. Second, we remarked above that the single value types endorsed by the sampled students did not show a clear preference for a particular value domain. However, a closer look at the results reveals a general trend that tilts slightly towards the value domain of conservation (i.e., conformity, tradition, and security). By their nature, conservation values represent the motivation to preserve the status quo in order to achieve the greatest possible certainty. For this reason, the values denote resistance to change. Individuals with this value preference tend not to tolerate new and different ideas (Sagiv & Schwartz, 2000; Schwartz & Bardi, 2001; Sousa & Bradley, 2006). This trait could have serious human rights implications. Although this was not particularly the case in this study, the results nevertheless showed a series of largely negative correlations between the conservation value domain and human rights attitudes (see Table 6.18). The question then arises as to how we can convey human rights-friendly value orientations to our respondents, which could serve as a useful basis for promoting a culture of human rights among them. The good news is that values can be learned (see Schwartz, 2012). Some of the social agencies for the value upbringing of individuals are the family, school, religion, the media and peers. Here too, the study gives preference to school-based values education over these other social agencies, as these sometimes tend to narrow the lifeworlds to their needs. In contrast, the school tends to open the minds of learners to the vastness of lifeworlds (Lovat, 2005). More importantly, schools are the microcosms of their societies (Gulati & Pant, 2005). Over the years there have been repeated calls for the introduction of values education in Nigerian schools' curriculum (cf. Falade & Falade, 2013; Ikwumelu et al., 2015). Interestingly, the government responded to the demands by introducing values-related subjects such as social studies, security education, citizenship and civic education, and RE into the curriculum. These subjects are taught to pupils and students with the aim of providing them with the relevant skills, competences and attitudes for effective citizenship (NPE, 2014), among other things.

Values education does not mean "value imposition" (Gulati & Pant, 2005: 37); it is not a moral agenda handed to educators containing a list of values to be learnt (Kohlberg, 1981), nor are values developed by forcing people to memorise a list of values in order to pass exams. Here, teaching and learning are to be constructive or participatory (cf. NPE, 2014). Rorty (1990) highlights two main approaches to values education that we find interesting, namely socialisation and critical individuation. On the one hand, socialisation refers to a process through which an individual is introduced to the norms, values and traditions of his or her society. In this way, one takes on the identity of one's social group. Critical individuation, on the other hand, entails detaching people from their socialised or primary identities as private individuals to assume a secondary identity as citizens of the modern state (see also Solomons & Fataar 2011). The role of the school lies in the transition process between private and public life. The process of critical individuation practically repeats some of the points already made above. It requires a deliberative attitude that aims to provide learners with the necessary cognitive tools to make informed moral decisions and behave morally. The aim here is not to teach students values, but rather to teach them to think with specific reference to values. As Gulati and Pant (2005: 35) put it, it is "a process of inducing critical and reflective thinking, rationale choice and responsible behaviour". If students are taught how and not what to think, internalisation would take place and they would have been equipped for life.

As with RE, the role of the teacher in this entire process is very important, since values education is grounded on the power of 'productive pedagogy' that is, on the power of the teacher to put things into action (Lovat, 2005). A teacher's work goes beyond preparing students for exams (UNESCO, 1998)—a practice which is common in Nigerian schools. Rather, the focus is on developing the competences of students. This obliges the teacher to convey the lesson content to the learners in the most understandable way possible, so that learning can take place both communicatively and self-reflectively (Habermas, 1972). Besides, these lessons must be relevant to the learner's context. For the students in the sample, this implies inter alia: (i) they have to be taught to appreciate the diversity in their environment and develop respect for differences in identities; (ii) such a teaching has to enable them to imbibe social values, such as patriotism, tolerance, solidarity, justice, equality, freedom, and independence, etc.; (iii) it has to awaken in them a resolve to depart from practices characterised by micro-loyalties, lack of respect for diversity and human dignity. In short, a constructively designed and implemented school-based values education will furnish the students with relevant social standards for effective citizenship as well as better value orientations to promote human rights.

To recap, in the foregoing analyses we specified the main predictors of the human rights attitudes of the sampled students, namely the concept of religion, and value preferences. We highlighted some salient features of these predictors and, within the empirical-theological design with which the study was conducted, we made some recommendations on what can be done to achieve a better result, assuming that the human rights situation of the students were to be 'treated'. This is in line with the overall objective of the study to promote the formation of a culture of human rights among young Nigerians. To accomplish this objective, we put forward three results-oriented proposals. We proposed a non-confessional, human-development pedagogical approach to RE as better and more beneficial to the sampled students in view of human rights, as is a school-based values education. However, in order for students to understand the topic of human rights properly, it must be conveyed to them.

Having discussed the main findings of the study, we now look between the lines for its specific contributions to practical theology, the pastoral apostolate of the Church, and the larger society.

7.2 Significance of Study for Practical Theology

For the study's contribution to practical theology, we consider this in connection with the overall import of the religiosity of the sampled students.

Another remarkable finding of this study concerned the term religiosity. This should not be confused with another term, namely religion, which represents a broader construct in the way both terms are used in the study. While religiosity refers to the individual aspects of religion and belief, the construct of religion comprises a cluster of variables related to religious beliefs, conviction and practices, including religiosity itself. The latter is thus an integral part of the religion construct.

Religiosity was used in the study as conceptualised by Glock and Stark (1965) and operationalised by Huber (2008b). It is a complex concept and has been defined in these studies as having many dimensions covering different expressions of religion, such as knowledge of the belief system, acceptance of the belief system, subjective and emotional religious experience, the ethical consequences of faith in daily life and participation in religious activities. Religiosity was included in the study as a key component of the main independent variable, the concept of religion. Based on the basic assumption of the salience of religion in the country, as was held mostly by Nigerian theologians and religious scholars, it was hypothesised that religiosity would be the most important predictor of the attitudes of the sampled Nigerian adolescents towards human rights. This hypothesis has two notable sides: first, the construct 'religion' was expected to be the most important predictor of human attitudes in the models; and second, the religiosity component was expected to be the most potent religious variable determining the same attitudes.

From the research findings in Table 7.1, it appears that the claims about the level of religiosity among Nigerians are to some extent corroborated by the way the adolescents rated the items presented to them.

Apart from the items on the intellectual dimension of religiosity, to which about 26% of them reacted ambivalently and about 7% negatively, and the items on the experiential dimension, to which 19.1% and 6% reacted with ambivalent and negative attitudes, respectively, fewer than 15% of respondents rated the other dimensions (ideological, consequential, ritualistic) with ambivalence, while an even smaller number (less than 5%) rated the said dimensions with utter negativity. Conversely, two-thirds of respondents (67.1%) say they often or very often show interest in religious ideas, while significantly more (92%) say they accept that there is a God or a divine being. 75.1% of them affirm that they often or very often have emotional religious experiences, and 82% agree that their religious beliefs and convictions often or very often influence their lifestyle. We also found a high level of ritual participation among the sampled adolescents. Eighty six percent of them rated

Table 7.1 Religiosity (frequencies (%), means and standard deviation)

Items	Never	Rarely	Occasionally	Often	Very often	M	SD
How often do you think about religious issues?	.5	6.4	25.9	31.9	35.2	3.95	.96
To what extent do you believe that God or something divine exists?	.4	.9	7.0	10.3	81.4	4.71	.67
How often do you experience situations in which you have the feeling that God or something divine intervenes in your life?	.9	4.9	19.1	19.5	55.6	4.24	.98
What is your position on the statement: "My religion or worldview has great influence on my daily life"?	.5	3.9	13.8	48.3	33.5	4.10	.82
How often do you pray?	.0	3.6	10.6	14.6	71.2	4.53	.82
How often do you take part in religious services at a church or mosque or another place?	.7	2.7	9.4	7.5	79.7	4.63	.82

Legend: These items are used as one scale. They were recoded and then labelled to read henceforth: 'Religiosity'. Cronbach's Alpha = .64; mean = 4.35 and standard deviation = .52

regular prayer positively. 87.2% rated regular participation in religious activities equally positively. Overall, the results indicate a high level of religiosity among the students (Mean = 4.35; Sd = 0.52).

The research also shows that religion is largely the driving force behind the students' human rights attitudes across the models, although it was not strongly expressed nor had a sufficiently strong influence as expected. More interesting, however, is the finding that even in those human rights provisions where respondents' attitudes can be explained by or depended on the concept of religion, the construct of religiosity was not always the determinant religious variable. Whereas it mattered as the main predictor of attitudes towards the freedom of religion and the right to life issue of abortion, and as a supporting trigger in relation to political and socio-economic rights, it did not matter at all in the other cases. In other words, religiosity did not play a role in all models; it did in some, but not in others.

This finding has an interesting implication for practical theology as a discipline. It tends to support the current practice of demarcating the concept of religion into personal or individual religious orientation and the public aspect of the social phenomenon of religion, for the purpose of studies of similar interest. In the today's context of the preponderance of the "religious factor" in the public sphere and in social processes such as the human rights practice, this could be helpful in more easily identifying the source of influence on attitudes, whether it is from the supply or the demand side of religion. If the former is the case, then more attention would be paid to the way religious traditions convey their messages, their evangelisation strategies and proselytising methods, while in the latter case the focus would be on the way the religious message is received and what meaning is given to them by the individual, the "modus recipientis". This method of analysis offers practical theology, in its capacity as a reflection on a lived religion, experience and practice, a real path to greater knowledge.

7.3 Significance of Study for the Pastoral Mission of the Church

The significance of the study for the pastoral mission of the Catholic Church is viewed from two perspectives: one, from the perspective of the findings on the human rights attitudes of the sampled students in relation to their religious affiliation and, the other, from the perspective of the findings on their attitudes towards human rights vis-à-vis the construct of trust in religion.

In its Mission *'ad gentes'* (to the nations), the Catholic Church regards Christ's injunction to his Apostles to "[g]o … and preach the gospel to all creation" (Mark 16:15; Matthew 28:18–20) as its missionary mandate (Ad Gentes, hereinafter AG no. 1). The Church understood this assignment as a duty entrusted to it by virtue of its nature as a sacrament of Christ's presence in the world. In obedience to Christ, over the millennia it has diligently sought to fulfill this mission of spreading the gospel message to people of all nations, tribes, cultures and languages, as evidenced by the proportion of Christian believers worldwide and the presence of Christian churches in all corners of the world. The gospel is "a leaven of progress in human history, … a leaven of liberty, … of brotherhood, of unity and of peace" (AG no. 8). The Church believes that the gospel is a message for all peoples, but also that the missionary activity of proclaiming this gospel can be carried out differently according to circumstances, sometimes depending on the Church itself, sometimes depending on the people to whom the mission is directed (AG no. 6).

The world context in which the Christian message was first received and the basic tenets of the Christian doctrine were first formulated has changed significantly. The modern world is extremely complex and diverse. The Church apparently recognises this fact, as expressed in the document of the Second Vatican Council, Gaudium et Spes. This document addresses the role of the church in the modern world. It reflected the mood of the world at the time when it spoke of "[t]he present keener sense of human dignity … and attempts to bring about a politico-juridical order which will give better protection to the rights of the person" (GS no. 73). A number of human rights are recognised in the same place, such as the right to association, the right to freedom of expression, freedom of religion and political participation. Christians are enjoined, as a duty most appropriate to our times, to cooperate willingly and wholeheartedly in the creation of an international order that includes a genuine respect for all freedoms (GS no. 88, see also nos. 74 and 60). In fact, Gaudium et Spes has been evaluated as the Church's transition to its new globalised worldview or order. In a separate document, Pacem in Terris (no. 9), Pope John XXIII who convened the Vatican II council, which addressed multiculturalism in the modern Church, emphasised the importance of respect for human rights as an essential consequence of the Christian view of the human person. According to him, the rights arise from the nature of the human person as a being endowed with intelligence and free will. As such, they are universal, inviolable and inalienable.

The Catholic Church officially endorses an array of human rights. In addition to those already mentioned, these include the right to freedom of religion (GS no. 73; DH no. 2), freedom from discrimination (GS no.60), and freedom from 'unjust discrimination' based on sexual orientation (as it is called in CCC no. 2358), and the respect for the dignity of the human person (AG no.12; GS no. 60). Overall, the Church perceives the promotion of justice and peace as an integral part of its mission (Centesimus Annus nos. 53–59). With these, the Church sees itself as a promoter of human rights and does not doubt its commitment to the advancement of the course of human rights.

Against this backdrop, the findings of this study are as surprising to us as they are instructive. Religious affiliation is included in the study inter alia to enable us to gauge the human rights attitudes of the sampled students along denominational or broader religious lines. Of the 66% Christian subgroup, 37% are Catholics, circa 24% Protestants, and other smaller denominations constitute about 5%. Religious affiliation is used as a control variable. It is one of the independent variables in our model but is specifically used here as a control variable. From the results in Table 6.19, it appears that, contrary to the above claims about its commitment to the promotion of human rights, being Christian, or more specifically being Catholic, for the most part did not have a significant impact on students' attitudes towards the human rights provisions under study. For instance, it has no significant impact, positive or negative, on the right to freedom of religion and the right to freedom from discrimination based on sexual orientation, and this even though the CCC disapproves of 'unjust discrimination' against homosexuals. Other human rights provisions where religious affiliation did not matter include the right to life under the two instances of the prohibition of the death penalty and the moral question of abortion, as well as political and socio-economic rights. These findings are surprising to us because the Church's position on these human rights provisions is well known. If anything, the non-significant impact of students' religious affiliation on their attitude towards these human rights provisions tends to portray: (1) that religious people do not always act on the impulses of their religious beliefs. To put it more specifically, the human rights attitudes of the sampled Christian and Catholic students are not always determined by the teachings of their religion or denominations. Of course, this is not limited to them; it appears to be the general attitude of most religious adherents. In some cases, some other factors can also play a decisive role, such as value preferences, politics, social origin, culture and education. (2) It can also be said that the Church's claim to be committed to the promotion of human rights somehow does not reflect the attitude of its adherents towards human rights in this study. That sounds contradictory or looks like an accusation. In any case, it is more of an invitation for the church to look inward and examine its policies and methods of religious socialisation to determine how effective they are in promoting human rights.

Furthermore, the construct 'trust in religion' was also included in the model to enable us to ascertain the level of trust for religious in- and out-groups and as a possible predictor of attitudes towards human rights. Based on the research outcomes in Table 5.1, the sampled students have a high trust in the religious in-group members (Mean = 4.42; Sd = .81) and a low trust in out-groups, that is, members of other religious groups (Mean = 2.64; Sd = 1.23). This result lends credence to one of the findings of the PEW Survey on Religion and Public Life some years ago (2006), which reported widespread mutual distrust among adherents of different religious traditions in Nigeria. A combined analysis of the students' assessment of the two elements of trust also shows that around 58% of them have a high level of trust in their own religion and a low level of trust in other religions (cf. Adimekwe & Ziebertz, 2018). In the theoretical part of this study, we claimed that there is an atmosphere of rivalry between adherents of different religions in Nigeria. Mutual distrust could be one of the reasons for this. However, a more interesting finding is that these trust attitudes, particularly low trust in religious out-groups, influence the human rights attitudes of the sampled students. For example, the less trust they have in other religious communities, the less likely they are to support the right to freedom from discrimination based on sexual orientation. The same applies to the same trust item in relation to the right of every person to a fair trial (see Table 6.19).

Apart from the usual conflicts over limited resources, opportunities and the pursuit of political power, the struggle for members, the claim to majority status and the lack of respect for 'the other' are other factors responsible for the trust deficit and unhealthy interfaith rivalry in Nigeria. These are said to be the consequences of the missionary strategies of the country's dominant religious communities, and they do not promote a human rights-friendly environment. If the emergence of an appropriate human rights culture is to be expected in this context, then the Church must, for its part, take the path of review and re-education. In the spirit of constant renewal to which it often invites its adherents, the Church may need to review its mission strategies to ensure that they are human rights oriented. In its social teachings, it should evolve a comprehensive programme of re-education for adherents, especially young people and children. The programme would need to respond to the needs of twenty-first century global citizenship. Young people should be deliberately and properly informed about issues of human rights to prepare them for citizenship in today's increasingly complex world. Given the actual context of high level of religiosity and the high level of trust in the religious in-group among the sampled adolescents, the Church in Nigeria is in a good position to fulfill this task.

7.4 Significance of Study for the Global Discourse on Human Rights

We consider the implications of the study for society in connection with the concepts of human dignity and the perceived quality of life.

The study somehow confirms the relationship between human rights and the concept of dignity. Except for the right to life, the human rights attitudes of the students in the sample were also shaped by the three forms of dignity. In the mind of the students, the dignity of merit influenced their endorsement of the judicial right to a fair trial. The dignity of moral stature also had positive links with the right to freedom of religion and socio-economic rights but showed negative relations to the rights of the LGBTI persons, while the concept of inherent dignity of all persons shaped the students' acceptance of political and socio-economic rights, as well as the rights of LGBTI persons. The students' attitudes towards the right to life issues of capital punishment, abortion and euthanasia were not significantly related to their understanding of dignity.

Although these relationships were not always robust, the fact that the students used the three categories of dignity is an indication that they understood the general meaning of the concepts. What is worrying, however, is that most students did not seem to appreciate the notion of inherent dignity, and their understanding of dignity resides primarily in the contingent paradigms that refer to the forms of dignity that accrue to people because of their behaviour, social status, or personal achievements, in other words, the kinds of dignity that can be gained or lost. The results show that the concept of inherent dignity received the lowest rating from the students. It has the mean of 3.57 and standard deviation of 1.25 compared to merit dignity ($M = 3.80$; $Sd = 1.16$) and moral dignity ($M = 4.37$; $Sd = .90$). This makes it clear that the essential connection between the principle of human dignity and human rights, especially the right to life, is either not yet understood by the students or has been lost. From a policy perspective, this situation calls for a human rights education programme for students to provide them with useful information as a basis for human rights advocacy. Despite the controversy surrounding the general tenor of human dignity, it is the most fundamental principle of human rights within the framework of the UN. According to all human rights treaties, it is the basis of human rights. The inherent dignity of the human person is the fundamental logic of all human rights (Ziebertz & Ziebertz, 2016). Therefore, schoolchildren and adolescents should be helped to recognise this beginning from their primary education or as early as possible.

While many non-governmental human rights organisations in the country at various levels of society have been actively involved in this project, the role of the Nigerian state in this regard should not be downplayed. Ultimately, it is also the responsibility of the state to protect and promote the rights of its citizens. To date, Nigeria's approach to human rights has been largely driven by expediency. This undoubtedly reflects the historical context of human rights in the country, where the concept was deployed as a national rallying cry in the struggle for independence and then thereafter commitment to it became erratic and largely reactionary. This pattern of human rights practice appears to be the norm as there is no real visible proactive plan by the Nigerian State to deepen the human rights culture in the country. The students who responded to our questionnaire need a deliberate human rights education that would help them to acquire the core values for the formation and promotion of the culture of human rights. Education is a great tool for change. Any fundamental change in social and intellectual attitudes is possible through education.

On another note, the construct 'perceived quality of life', an emerging field of research, was included in the study to test its suitability for future research purposes. It also rightly served as a contextual variable. The perceived quality of life was operationalised with the subjective assessment of life satisfaction and the performance of formal institutions. Based on this definition, the students in the sample can be described as dissatisfied with the quality of their life (M = 2.55; Sd = .68) for unspecified reasons. In reference to human rights, the findings indicate a couple of significant relationships between the subjective perceptions of quality of life and students' attitudes towards human rights. First, the concept interacted negatively with students' attitudes towards the right to freedom of religion. It is not very clear what this particular outcome means, although it is inconsequential due to low score. Second, the students' attitudes towards the right-to-life issues such as the death penalty, abortion and euthanasia are positively related to their perceptions of their quality of life. Here, too, it is not entirely clear how the construct's connections to abortion and euthanasia could be interpreted.

Although the values in general are largely irrelevant, the results lend credence to the contemporary emphasis on the importance of social contexts to human rights issues, as noted in the theoretical perspectives. Human rights do not exist in a vacuum. Rather, they are practised in a context and as such can be shaped by it. Every human rights provision has a specific history. Human rights are not heaven-dictated precepts. Instead, they emerged in specific historical contexts and are products of experiences of dissatisfaction with injustice, oppression, slavery, genocide, etc. Students do not need to have these experiences themselves, nor do they have to be personally disaffected to become involved in the fight for human rights or before they can embrace the culture. But they need help to be able to recognise the authentic history of human rights in the context of people's struggles for a better life. On this basis, they can be encouraged to constructively view existing structures and instances of injustice, deprivation, and discontent, whether among themselves or with others, as opportunities to defend and promote human rights. This is yet another reason for the imperative of a deliberate human rights education for the sampled students, in line with the recommendation of the Universal Declaration.[8]

So far, we have highlighted the importance of study for the practical theological discipline, for the pastoral project of the Church and for society. The study's contribution to practical theology was considered in the context of the overall significance of students' religiosity, while its contribution to the pastoral mission of the Catholic Church was anchored in the relationship between students' human rights attitudes and individual constructs of religious affiliation and trust in religion. We see its importance for the larger society in terms of the relationship between attitudes toward human rights and the contextual variables of dignity and perceived quality of life. Having thus presented, interpreted and discussed the research findings, we would now like to succinctly itemise the tentative relevant conclusions that can be drawn from them for the development of an appropriate culture of human rights among Nigeria's youth.

---

[8] Cf. Preamble.

References

A. Books and Journals

Achebe, C. (1958). *Things Fall Apart*. Heinemann.

Adimekwe, M., & Ziebertz, H.-G. (2018). Attitudes towards Freedom of Religion among Nigerian Students. In H.-G. Ziebertz & C. Sterkens (Eds.), *Religion and Civil human rights in empirical perspectives* (pp. 177–214). Springer.

Ajah, M. (2015). Religious education and nation-building in Nigeria. *Stellenbosch Theological Journal, 1*(2), 263–282. https://doi.org/10.17570/stj.2015.v1n2.a12

Amusan, L., Saka, L., & Adekeye, M. O. (2019). Gay rights and the politics of anti-homosexual legislation in Africa: Insights from Uganda and Nigeria. *Journal of African Union Studies, 8*(2), 45–66.

Anthony, F. V., & Sterkens, C. (2019). Religion and the right to (dispose of) life: A study of the attitude of Christian, Muslim and Hindu students in India concerning death penalty, Euthanasia and Abortion. In H.-G. Ziebertz & F. Zaccaria (Eds.), *Euthanasia, abortion, death penalty and religion – The right to life and its limitations* (pp. 13–64). Springer.

Asue, D. U., & Kajo, D. (2018). Pedagogy of Christian religious education in Nigerian Schools. *Journal of Education and Practice, 9*(8), 37–49.

Ayanleye, O. A. (2013). Women and reproductive health rights in Nigeria. *OIDA International Journal of Sustainable Development, 6*(5), 127–140.

Barry, G., & Elliott, M. (2012). *Religious education approaches in contemporary religious education for Catholic Schools*. Catholic Education Archdiocese of Brisbane.

Beyers, J. (2010). What is religion? An African Understanding. *HTS Theological Studies, 66*(1), 1–8. https://doi.org/10.4102/hts.v66i1.341

Carter, E. C. (2018). The Hermeneutical promise of practical theology. *Andrews University Seminary Studies, 56*(2), 241–255.

Casanova, J. (1994). *Public religions in the modern world*. University of Chicago Press.

Case, K. A., Fishbein, H. D., & Ritchey, P. N. (2008). Personality, prejudice, and discrimination against women and homosexuals. *Current Research in Social Psychology, 14*(2), 23–38.

Cush, D. (2011). Without fear or favour: Forty years of non-confessional and multi-faith religious education in Scandinavia and the UK. In L. Franken & P. Loobuyck (Eds.), *Religious education in a plural, secularised society: A paradigm shift* (pp. 69–84). Münster.

Doise, W., Spini, D., & Clémence, A. (1999). Human rights studied as social representations in a cross-national context. *European Journal of Social Psychology, 29*, 1–29.

Dreyer, J. S., & Aziz, G. (2021). Religion and human rights attitudes of the youth of South Africa. In H.-G. Ziebertz & F. Zaccaria (Eds.), *The Ambivalent impact of religion on human rights* (pp. 199–223). Springer.

Engebretson, K. (2004). Learning about and Learning from Religion. The Pedagogical Theory of Michael Grimmitt. *Journal of Religious Education, 52*(3), 8–14.

Evans, C. (2008). Religious education in Public Schools: An international human rights perspective. *Human Rights Law Review, 8*(3), 449–473.

Ezeanya, S. N. (1980). The contributions of African traditional religion to nation building. In E. C. Amucheazi (Ed.), *Reading in social sciences*. Fourth Dimension.

Falade, D. A. (2016). Problems and prospects of teaching religion and national values in the Nigeria Upper Basic School. *Nigerian Journal of Social Studies, 29*(2), 41–49.

Falade, D. A., & Falade, M. (2013). Development of core values for national integration in Nigeria. *International Journal of Humanities and Social Science Invention, 2*(7), 57–63.

Francis, L. J., Robbins, M., & McKenna, U. (2016). Women's socio-economic rights and religion among Christian, Islamic and non-religiously affiliated students in England and Wales. In H.-G. Ziebertz & E. H. Ballin (Eds.), *Freedom of religion in the 21st century. A Human rights perspective on the relation between politics and religion* (pp. 239–256). Brill.

Francis, L. J., McKenna, U., & Robbins, M. (2018). Attitude toward political rights and religious affiliation, experience, saliency and openness: An empirical enquiry among students in England and Wales. In C. Sterkens & H.-G. Ziebertz (Eds.), *Political and Judicial rights through the prism of religious belief* (pp. 1–21). Springer.

Gennerich, C., & Ziebertz, H.-G. (2016). Human rights and value priorities. In H.-G. Ziebertz & E. H. Ballin (Eds.), *Freedom of religion in the 21*[st] *century. A human rights perspective on the relation between politics and religion* (pp. 207–238). Brill.

Glock, C. Y., & Stark, R. (1965). *Religion and society in tension*. Rand McNally & Co.

Grimmitt, M. (1973). *What can I do in religious education?* McCrimmon.

Grimmitt, M. (1987). *Religious education and human development*. McCrimmon.

Grimmitt, M. (1991). The use of religious phenomena in schools: Some theoretical and practical considerations. *British Journal of Religious Education, 13*(2), 77–88.

Grimmitt, M. (2000). Constructivist pedagogies of religious education project: Re-thinking knowledge, teaching and learning in religious education. In M. Grimmitt (Ed.), *Pedagogies of religious education* (pp. 189–207). McCrimmon.

Gulati, S., & Pant, D. (2005). *Education for values in schools – A framework*. National Council of Educational Research and Training.

Habermas, J. (1972). *Knowledge and Human Interests* (J. Shapiro, Trans.). Heinemann.

Haralambos, M., & Heald, R. M. (1985). *Sociology: Themes and perspectives*. University Tutorial Press.

Huber, S. (2008a). Aufbau und strukturierende Prinzipien des Religionsmonitors. In: Bertelsmann-Stiftung (Hrsg.), *Religionsmonitor 2008* (pp. 21–31). Gütersloher Verlagshaus.

Huber, S. (2008b). Kerndimensionen, Zentralität und Inhalt – Ein interdisziplinäres Modell der Religiosität. *Journal für Psychologie, 16*(3), 1–17.

Ihedinma, A. U. (2004). *Reconstructing the religious knowledge curriculum in Nigeria: A study of inclusive education and pedagogical reform*. Ph.D. dissertation, University of London, London.

Ikwumelu, S. N., Bassey, M. E., & Oyibe, O. A. (2015). Social studies education and the need for value-based education in Nigeria. *British Journal of Education, 3*(11), 63–74.

Ivowi, U. M. O. (1986). *Comparative education study and adaptation centre: Theoretical basis and operations of a curriculum development centre*. CESAC.

Ivowi, U. M. O. (1993). *Curriculum development in nigeria*. Sam Bookman Services.

Kalve, P. (1996). Some aspects of the work of Michael Grimmitt. *British Journal of Religious Education, 8*(3), 181–190.

Kohlberg, L. (1981). *Essays on moral development: Moral stages and the idea of Justice*. Harper and Row.

Krüger, J. S., Lubbe, G. J. A., & Steyn, H. C. (2009). *The human search for meaning: A multireligion introduction to the religions of humankind*. Van Schaik Publishers.

Lovat, T. J. (2005). *Values education and teachers' work: A quality teaching perspective*. Australian Government Department of Education Science and Training.

Magesa, L. (2002). *African religion: The moral traditions of abundant life*. Orbis Books.

Mbiti, J. S. (1989). *African religions and philosophy*. Heinemann Educational Publishers.

Mbiti, J. S. (1990). *African religions and philosophy*. Heinemann Educational Publishers.

McFarland, S. (2015). Culture, individual differences, and support for human rights: A general review. *Peace and Conflict: Journal of Peace Psychology, 21*(1), 10–27.

McFarland, S., & Mathews, M. (2005). Who cares about human rights? *Political Psychology, 26*(3), 365–385.

Miloš, D., & Novak, K. (2018). The role of value orientations and political preference on political and judicial human rights among the Croatian Youth. In C. Sterkens & H.-G. Ziebertz (Eds.), *Political and judicial rights through the prism of religious belief* (pp. 71–94). Springer.

Norris, P., & Inglehart, R. (2004). *Sacred and secular: Religion and politics worldwide*. Cambridge University Press.

Odoeme, P. C. (2011). *Human rights and the mission of the Church in Nigeria*. Lit Verlag.

Ok, Ü., Gören, A. B., Akbulut, S., & Getir, S. D. (2020). Religion and attitude to economic deprivation among Muslims: Checking the roles of value preference and empathy. In H.-G. Ziebertz (Ed.), *International empirical studies on religion and socio-economic human rights* (pp. 277–298). Springer.

Okeke, G. N., & Eze, G. E. (2013). The Ambivalence of the 1999 Nigerian constitution in matters relating to Secularism: A case for a constitutional review. *International Journal of Humanities and Social Science Invention, 2*(3), 65–69.

Okpanachi, E. (2012). *Ethno-religious identity and conflict in Northern Nigeria: Understanding the dynamics of Sharia in Kaduna and Kebbi States*. French Institute for Research in Africa.

Osaghae, E., & Suberu, T. (2005). *A history of identities, violence, and stability in Nigeria*. University of Oxford.

Osmer, R. R. (2004). Johannes Van der Ven's contribution to the new consensus in practical theology. In C. A. M. Hermans & M. E. Moore (Eds.), *Hermeneutics and empirical research in practical theology* (pp. 149–167). Brill.

Osmer, R. R. (2008). *Practical theology: An introduction*. William B. Eerdmans.

Osmer, R. R. (2011). Practical theology. A current international perspective. *HTS Teologiese studies/Theological Studies, 67*(2), 156–162.

Owolabi, A., Akindoju, O., & Onafowokan, B. (2013). Science curriculum development in Nigeria: A psychological perspectives. In R. O. Okuneye (Ed.), *Education, a multi-disciplinary approach to improving quality of life* (pp. 231–238). Lagos State University.

Rorty, R. (1990). Education without Dogma. *Dialogue, 88*(2), 44–47.

Sagiv, L., & Schwartz, S. H. (2000). Value priorities and subjective well-being: Direct relations and congruity effects. *European Journal of Social Psychology, 30*(2), 177–198.

Sampson, I. T. (2012). Religious violence in Nigeria: Causal diagnoses and strategic recommendations to the state and religious communities. *African Journal on Conflict Resolution, 12*(1), 103–134.

Schwartz, S. H. (2012). An overview of the Schwartz Theory of basic values. *Online Readings in Psychology and Culture, 2*(1), 1–20.

Schwartz, S. H., & Bardi, A. (2001). Value hierarchies across cultures: Taking a similarities perspective. *Journal of Cross-Cultural Psychology, 32*(3), 268–290.

Shackles, T. A. (1991). *The interface of adventure education and religious education: A study of curriculum interrelations*. B.Ed. thesis. Murdoch University, Australia.

Shor, I., & Freire, P. (1987). *A pedagogy for liberation: Dialogues on transforming education*. Bergin and Garvey.

Skilbeck, M. (2005). School-based curriculum development. In A. Lieberman (Ed.), *The roots of educational change* (pp. 109–132). Springer.

Skrefsrud, T.-A. (2022). A proposal to incorporate experiential education in non-confessional, intercultural religious education: Reflections from and on the Norwegian context. *Religions, 13*(727), 1–13.

Solomons, I., & Fataar, A. (2011). A conceptual exploration of values education in the context of schooling in South Africa. *South African Journal of Education, 31*, 224–232.

Sousa, C. M. P., & Bradley, F. (2006). Cultural distance and psychic distance: Two peas in a pod? *Journal of International Marketing, 14*(1), 49–70.

Statham, P. (2016). How ordinary people view Muslim group rights in Britain, The Netherlands, France and Germany: Significant 'Gaps' between majorities and Muslims? *Journal of Ethnic and Migration Studies, 42*(2), 217–236.

Thorpe, S. A. (1992). *Primal religions worldwide: An introductory descriptive review*. University of South Africa.

Uchem, R. (2013). The National Christian religious studies curriculum and the imperative for change in an era of globalization. *Asian Academic Research Journal of Multidisciplinary, 1*(16), 534–546.

Uzoma, R. C. (2004). Religious pluralism, cultural differences, and social stability in Nigeria. *Brigham Young University Law Review, 7*(3), 651–664.

Van der Tuin, L. (2009). Religious education in Europe: Do pupils get the RE they want? In H.-G. Ziebertz, W. K. Kay, & U. Riegel (Eds.), *Youth in Europe III: An international empirical study about the impact of religion on life orientation* (Vol. 10, pp. 105–117). Lit Verlag.

Van der Tuin, L. W. J. M., & Fumbo, C. D. (2012). Women rights and religion among Christian and Islamic students in Tanzania. In J. A. van der Ven & H.-G. Ziebertz (Eds.), *Tensions within and between religions and human rights* (pp. 203–222). Brill.

Van der Ven, J. A., Dreyer, J. S., & Pieterse, H. J. C. (2004). *Is there a God of human rights? The complex relationship between human rights and religion: A South African case*. Brill.

Walsh, P. (1997). *The curriculum: Context, design and development*. University of London.

Watson, B., & Thompson, P. (2013). *The effective teaching of religious education* (2nd ed.). Routledge.

Zaccaria, F., Anthony, F. V., & Sterkens, C. (2019). The impact of religion on attitudes towards abortion and Euthanasia. An empirical study among Italian students. In H.-G. Ziebertz & F. Zaccaria (Eds.), *Euthanasia, abortion, death penalty and religion – The right to life and its limitations* (pp. 105–138). Springer.

Ziebertz, H.-G. (2002). Normativity and empirical research in practical theology. *Journal of Empirical Theology, 15*(1), 5–18.

Ziebertz, H.-G. (2018). Religion und Erziehung. In D. Pollack, V. Krech, O. Müller, & M. Hero (Hrsg.), *Handbuch Religionssoziologie* (pp. 809–831). Springer.

Ziebertz, H.-G., & Ziebertz, C. M. (2016). Labour rights and the impact of human dignity, Religious belief and perception of society. An empirical study among youth in Germany. *Journal of Empirical Theology, 29*(1), 45–77. https://doi.org/10.1163/15709256-12341337

Ziebertz, H.-G., Döhnert, S., & Unser, A. (2018). Predictors of attitudes towards human dignity. An Empirical Analysis among Youth in Germany. In H.-G. Ziebertz & C. Sterkens (Eds.), *Religion and Civil Human Rights in Empirical Perspective* (pp. 17–60). Springer.

Dailies

Adegbite, K. (2012). Is Nigeria a Secular or Non-Secular State? *The Newjurist*, 28th May 2012. Available at: http://www. newjurist.com/. Accessed 01 Oct 2014.

Policy Documents (Ecclesiastical Documents)

Catechism of the Catholic Church. (1997). II Edition. Libreria Editrice Vaticana.

John Paul II. (1991). *Centesimus Annus: Encyclical Letter on the Hundreth Anniversary of Rerum Novarum*. Available at: https://www.vatican.va/content/john-paul-ii/en/encyclicals/documents/hf_jp-ii_enc_01051991_centesimus-annus.html. Accessed 01 July 2015.

John XXIII. (1963). *Pacem in Terris: Encyclical Letter on Establishing Universal Peace*. Available at: https://www.vatican.va/content/john-xxiii/en/encyclicals/documents/hf_j-xxiii_enc_11041963_pacem.html. Accessed 01 Feb 2019.

The Holy Bible. (2011). New International Version. Zondervan.

Vatican II Council. (1965a). *Gaudium et Spes: Pastoral Constitution on the Church in the Modern World*. Available at: https://www.vatican.va/archive/hist_councils/ii_vatican_council/index.htm. Accessed 7 July 2018.

Vatican II Council. (1965b). *Ad gentes: Decree on the Church's Missionary Activity*. Available at: https://www.vatican.va/archive/hist_councils/ii_vatican_council/index.htm. Accessed 07 July 2018.

Vatican II Council. (1965c). *Gravissimum Educationis: Declaration on Christian Education*. Available at: https://www.vatican.va/archive/hist_councils/ii_vatican_council/index.htm. Accessed 7 July 2018.

Vatican II Council. (1965d). *Dignitatis Humanae: Declaration on religious freedom*. Available at: https://www.vatican.va/archive/hist_councils/ii_vatican_council/documents/vat-ii_decl_19651207_dignitatis-humanae_en.html. Accessed 08 Jan 2019.

International Human Rights Instruments

Office for Democratic Institutions and Human Rights (ODIHR). (2007). *Toledo guiding principles on teaching about religions and beliefs in public schools*. Organization for Security and Co-operation in Europe (OSCE). Available at; https://www.osce.org/odihr/29154. Retrieved 01 Sept 2020.

National Human Rights Instruments

Federal Republic of Nigeria. (2014). *National policy on education*. NERDC.

PEW Research Center. (2006). *Report of the survey on religion and public life*. Available at: https://www.pewresearch.org/politics/2006/08/24/section-i-religion-and-public-life/. Accessed 03 May 2015.

Other Internet Sources

Olschewski, J., & Schreiner, P. (Eds.). (2020). Case studies on religious education. *Intellectual Output* 3. READY-Erasmus+. Available at: http://hv.diva-portal.org/smash/get/diva2:1244662/. Accessed 02 May 2020.

Potts, D. (2015). *The Schwartz theory of basic values and some implications for political philosophy*. Available at: https://irfankhawajaphilosopher.com/2015/08/12/the-schwartz-theory-of-basic-values-and-some-implications-for-political-philosophy/. Accessed 10 Nov 2021.

Tutor Hunt International. (2022). *Examining Grimmitt's human pedagogy in informing*. Available at: https://www.tutorhunt.com/resource/26467/. Accessed 05 May 2023.

UNESCO. (1998). *Learning to live together in peace and harmony. Values education for peace, human rights, democracy and sustainable development for the Asia-Pacific region: A UNESCO-APNIEVE sourcebook for teacher education and tertiary level education*. UNESCO-PROAP.

General Conclusion

The study was designed to explore the human rights attitudes of a select group of Nigerian students and the predictors of their attitudes. A total of 1191 students aged 14–22 from 18 secondary schools in the country's capital, Abuja, and six other States took part in the study. After a series of analyses, a number of conclusions emerged, the most important of which are presented here.

First, the human rights attitudes of the students fell short of expectations. Of the human rights issues selected for study, only the right to religious freedom, political and socio-economic rights received outright positive ratings. The right to life received just a slight positive endorsement when the outcomes of the right to life issues of the death penalty, abortion and euthanasia are considered together. The right to non-discrimination against homosexuals was evaluated negatively, while the right to a fair trial was rated with ambivalence. All these human rights issues were operationalised using scales with different numbers of items.

Second, the student subgroups differed less in their assessment of human rights issues based on their religious affiliation. The human rights attitudes of 774 students who self-identified as Christians were compared to those of 403 others who self-identified as Muslims. Incidentally, their proportion here did not represent the proportion of religious affiliation in Nigeria; it is just the characteristic of the dataset used. The expectation was that the evaluation of the questionnaire by Muslim and Christian students would conform to the general principles of their religious traditions. However, among the human rights issues mentioned above, young Muslims and Christians differed positively in their evaluation of the right to life issues of the abolition of the death penalty and the permissibility of euthanasia and negatively in relation to the right to a fair trial. Their stance on the remaining human rights issues did not differ at all. To get a clearer picture of subgroup differences in human rights attitudes, future studies may need to consider denominational differences in each of these religious traditions.

M. C. Adimekwe, *The Impact of Religion, Personality, Values and Worldviews on Attitudes Towards Human Rights*, Religion and Human Rights 11,
https://doi.org/10.1007/978-3-031-65749-8

Third, the selected human rights issues showed a mix of weak, moderately strong and robust correlations with religion, empathy, basic human values, human dignity, perceived quality of life, and perceived threat. There were also cases of non-significant correlations. Of these six explanatory factors, only four shaped the students' human rights attitudes. The concept of religion was the main predictor of human rights attitudes in the study. As an important aspect of the concept of religion, the religiosity of the students was sometimes the determining religious factor for their human rights attitudes, sometimes not. Next in the order of importance are basic human values, followed by the concept of dignity and perceived quality of life. Surprisingly, the personality trait empathy was not a significant predictor of human rights attitudes in this study. To confirm this finding, further studies may expand on the Empathic Concern Scale used to assess empathy or try a different Davis' Interpersonal Reactivity Index Scale, such as the Personal Distress Scale or the Perspective-Taking Scale. Threat perception also did not help to explain students' attitudes towards human rights. However, the operationalisation of this concept in the study omitted the experience of conflict and tension, unlike Doise and colleagues (1999) did in their study, and it yielded significant results. It is therefore recommended that further studies include both the perception of threats and the experience side of the concept to be able to determine the actual impact of this concept. More importantly, a closer look at the set of explained variances reveals a collection of low values. The implication is that our model did not explain much of the students' attitudes towards the selected human rights issues, particularly the right to life issues of the death penalty and euthanasia, and the right to a fair trial. Future studies can compensate for this by adding other factors that may help to better explain these youth's human rights attitudes. Examples of such factors are peer pressure, social media, migration and globalisation processes, etc.

Fourth, the following social science paradigms used for this study proved to be suitable for the study: the theories of the social significance of religion, basic human values, human dignity and perceived quality of life. Their use corresponds to the empirical-theological research design chosen for the study. The application of empirical method in theological research may be viewed as speculative or ambitious since the scientific nature of theology and/or its connection with the term "science" is still very controversial. However, the choice was justified by our understanding of theology as a reflection on the past that has transformative implications for the present. Thus, if theology is to be relevant in the present, that is, if it has to contribute meaningfully to explain contemporary realities, then it cannot be isolated; it has to be in dialogical relationship with other disciplines, including science in general. Accordingly, practical theology supports the interdisciplinary approach, which consists in the sharing of methods and useful insights with other disciplines. That said, the application of the empirical research method here has been insightful and enriching, but also difficult.

The study has additional difficulties in terms of limitations. The first issue concerns the reliability of some scales, which is reflected in the low values of most Cronbach's alphas. This is an indication of the low internal consistencies of the concerned scales and could have negatively influenced the research results.

Therefore, future studies would also have to consider how the quality of the measurement scales can be improved. The second concerns the questionnaire used for data collection. We mentioned earlier that students complained about the length, which they found to be too long, and the grammar, which they sometimes found difficult to understand. In such circumstances, it is possible that some of them responded to the questionnaire just to please us. It is also possible that they did not understand some points well enough and still responded to them. All of this can affect the research results. As language raises real questions about the comprehension of the items and ultimately the quality of the responses, future studies in the Nigerian context may need to consider diversifying the language of the instrument, including for example translation also into Pidgin English and/or even into vernacular. Not only would this result in an optimal output or response, but it would also cover semi-educated or out-of-school youth. The third limitation concerns the study data, which is not representative. Data collection was not carried out using the random sampling method and therefore we cannot make generalisations to all young people in Nigeria. While the results of the study provide useful insights into the topic under study in the Nigerian context, they must be interpreted with caution. The last of the limitations concerns the lack of quantitative studies on human rights attitudes of young people in Nigeria. For this reason, we lack relevant literature to verify most of our claims. Nevertheless, this study can be regarded as one of the few attempts to venture into this largely untapped field of research and aims to generate interest in the topic as such.

Appendices

Results of Correlation Analyses (Tables 1, 2, 3, 4, 5, 6, 7, and 8)

Table 1 Correlations (Pearson's r) between religion and psychological dimension

	Psychological dimension
Religion	Empathy
Function of religion:	
Social religion	.131**
Spiritual religion	.313**
Cultural religion	−.044
Rel. in contemporary society:	
Religion_good for morality	.212**
Trust in religion:	
Trust in-group	.205**
Trust out-group	−.020
Interreligious interaction:	
Pluralism	.009
Religiosity	.210**

All correlations are significant at $p<.01$ (**) or $p<.05$ (*) level (2-tailed). Interpretation of correlations: weak ($r < .15$), moderately strong ($.15 \leq r < .30$); strong ($r \geq .30$) associations

M. C. Adimekwe, *The Impact of Religion, Personality, Values and Worldviews on Attitudes Towards Human Rights*, Religion and Human Rights 11,
https://doi.org/10.1007/978-3-031-65749-8

Table 2 Correlations (Pearson's r) between religion and individual value orientations

	Value orientations									
Religion	1	2	3	4	5	6	7	8	9	10
Function of religion:										
Social religion	.111**	.004	.108**	.052	.102**	.047	.054	.133**	.111**	.161**
Spiritual religion	.146**	.010	.223**	–.051	.265**	.095**	.008	.165**	.110**	.120**
Cultural religion	.054	.128**	–.006	.122**	.034	.002	.025	.044	.098**	.020
Rel. in contp. Society:										
Rel._good for morality	.139**	.006	.234**	–.122**	.182**	.128**	.026	.232**	.138**	.098**
Trust in religion:										
Trust in-group	.100**	–.009	.189**	–.116**	.186**	.122**	.016	.218**	.128**	.124**
Trust out-group	–.015	.062*	–.017	.073*	–.021	–021	.029	–.030	.046	–.010
Interrel. Interaction:										
Pluralism	.105**	.059*	.034	.083**	.015	.066*	.055	.060*	.146**	–.073*
Religiosity	.164**	–.073*	.179**	–.092**	.249**	.114**	–.015	.218**	.185**	.133**

All correlations are significant at $p<.01$ (**) or $p<.05$ (*) level (2-tailed). Interpretation of correlations: weak ($r < .15$), moderately strong ($.15 \le r < .30$); strong ($r \ge .30$) associations. Value codes: 1 = self-direction; 2 = power; 3 = security; 4 = hedonism; 5 = benevolence; 6 = achievement; 7 = stimulation; 8 = conformity; 9 = universalism; and 10 = tradition

Table 3 Correlations (Pearson's r) between religion and human dignity

	Human dignity		
Religion	Dignity of merit	Moral dignity	Inherent dignity
Function of religion:			
Social religion	.109**	.128**	.065*
Spiritual religion	.111**	.228**	.072*
Cultural religion	.056	−.050	.083**
Rel. in contemporary society:			
Religion_good for morality	.162**	.216**	.055
Trust in religion:			
Trust in-group	.118**	.162**	−.004
Trust out-group	.073*	−.029	.090**
Interreligious interaction:			
Pluralism	.056	−.013	.147**
Religiosity	.131**	.177**	.005

All correlations are significant at p<.01 (**) or p<.05 (*) level (2-tailed). Interpretation of correlations: weak ($r < .15$), moderately strong ($.15 \leq r < .30$); strong ($r \geq .30$) associations

Table 4 Correlations (Pearson's r) between religion and socio-political context

	Socio-political context	
Religion	Satisfaction	Perceived threats
Function of religion:		
Social religion	.026	.183**
Spiritual religion	−144**	.179**
Cultural religion	.254**	.037
Religion in contemporary society:		
Religion_good for morality	−.097**	.128**
Trust in religion:		
Trust in-group	−.078**	.067*
Trust out-group	.229**	−.081**
Interreligious interaction:		
Pluralism	.203**	.017
Religiosity	−.168**	.125**

All correlations are significant at p<.01 (**) or p<.05 (*) level (2-tailed). Interpretation of correlations: weak ($r < .15$), moderately strong ($.15 \leq r < .30$); strong ($r \geq .30$) associations

Table 5 Correlations (Pearson's r) between values and psychological dimension

	Psychological dimension
Values	Empathy
Value orientations:	
Self–direction	.153**
Power	−.020
Security	.201**
Hedonism	−.098**
Benevolence	.564**
Achievement	.190**
Stimulation	.026
Conformity	.307**
Universalism	.160**
Tradition	.086**
Human dignity:	
Dignity of merit	.147**
Moral dignity	.174**
Inherent dignity	.103**

All correlations are significant at $p<.01$ (**) or $p<.05$ (*) level (2-tailed). Interpretation of correlations: weak ($r < .15$), moderately strong ($.15 \leq r < .30$); strong ($r \geq .30$) associations

Table 6 Correlations (Pearson's r) between psychological dimension and socio-political context

	Socio-political context	
Psychological dimension	Satisfaction	Perceived threats
Empathy	−.068*	.203**

All correlations are significant at $p<.01$ (**) or $p<.05$ (*) level (2-tailed). Interpretation of correlations: weak ($r < .15$), moderately strong ($.15 \leq r < .30$); strong ($r \geq .30$) associations

Table 7 Correlations (Pearson's r) between values and socio-political context

	Socio-political context	
Values	Satisfaction	Perceived threats
Value orientations:		
Self–direction	–.039	.081**
Power	.114**	.106**
Security	–.053	.171**
Hedonism	.120**	–.011
Benevolence	–.056	.162**
Achievement	–.030	.143**
Stimulation	.036	.017
Conformity	–.041	.112**
Universalism	.014	.060*
Tradition	–.048	.113**
Human dignity:		
Dignity of merit	.020	.151**
Moral dignity	–.096**	.172**
Inherent dignity	.053	.035

All correlations are significant at $p<.01$ (**) or $p<.05$ (*) level (2-tailed). Interpretation of correlations: weak ($r < .15$), moderately strong ($.15 \leq r < .30$); strong ($r \geq .30$) associations

Table 8 Correlations (Pearson's r) between the dependent and background variables

	Civil rights:		Right to life			Political & judicial rights		Socio-economic rights
	Freedom of rel.	Nondiscri- (homosexuals)	Prohibition—the death penalty	Poss. of Abortion	Poss. of Euthanasia	Political rights index	Right to a fair trial	Socio-economic rights index
Population characteristics								
Age	−.065*	−.007	−.019	.048	−.057*	−.020	.041	−.116**
Sex	−.080**	−.040	−.059*	.073*	.034	−.021	.036	−.073*
Rel. socialisation:								
Rel. affiliation	.039	−.029	−.089**	−.037	−.162**	−.059*	.091**	−.061*
Peers influence	.166**	−.122**	−.020	−.137**	−.103**	.010	−.046	.107**

All correlations are significant at p<.01 (**) or p<.05 (*) level (2-tailed). Interpretation of correlations: weak ($r < .15$), moderately strong ($.15 \leq r < .30$); strong ($r \geq .30$) associations

References

A. Books and Journals

Ajah, M. (2015). Religious education and nation-building in Nigeria. *Stellenbosch Theological Journal, 1*(2), 263–282. https://doi.org/10.17570/stj.2015.v1n2.a12

Augustin. (n.d.). Epistle CLXXXV (J. R. King, Trans.) In P. Schaff (Ed.) (1887). *Nicene and Post-Nicene Fathers* (Vol. 4, pp. 633–651). Christian Literature Co.

Campbell, J. (2014). Boko Haram: Origins, challenges and responses. *Norwegian Peacebuilding Resource Centre Policy Brief*, 1–4.

Cush, D. (2011). Without fear or favour: Forty years of non-confessional and multi-faith religious education in Scandinavia and the UK. In L. Franken & P. Loobuyck (Eds.), *Religious education in a plural, secularised society: A paradigm shift* (pp. 69–84). Münster.

Krüger, J. S., Lubbe, G. J. A., & Steyn, H. C. (2009). *The human search for meaning: A multireligion introduction to the religions of humankind*. Van Schaik Publishers.

Lucius Lactantius. (n.d.). Divine Institutes (W. Fletcher, Trans.). In A. Roberts, J. Donaldson, & A. C. Coxe (Eds.) (1886). *Ante-Nicene Fathers* (Vol. 7, pp. 9–328). Christian Literature Co.

Murray, S., & Will, R. (Eds.). (1998). *Boy-wives and female husbands: Studies of African homosexualities*. Macmillan.

wa Mutua, M. (1999). Limitations on religious rights: Problematizing religious freedom in the African Context. *Buffalo Human Rights Law Review, 5*(2), 75–105.

Ogunbode, T. O., Ayodele, I.-O. A., Oyebamiji, V. O., & Faboro, O. O. (2023). A review of farmers/herders clashes in Nigerian environment: Consequences and the way forward. *Journal of African Conflicts and Peace Studies, 5*(1), 120.

Onwubiko, E. (2017). *A minister's bigoted agenda*. Available at: http://huriwa.blogspot.com/2017/06/a-ministers-bigotedagenda-by-emmanuel.html. Accessed 12 Feb 2020.

Schwartz, S. H., & Bardi, A. (2001). Value hierarchies across cultures: Taking a similarities perspective. *Journal of Cross-Cultural Psychology, 32*(3), 268–290.

Skrefsrud, T.-A. (2022). A proposal to incorporate experiential education in non-confessional, intercultural religious education: Reflections from and on the Norwegian context. *Religions, 13*(727), 1–13.

Shor, I., & Freire, P. (1987). *A pedagogy for liberation: Dialogues on transforming education*. Bergin and Garvey.

M. C. Adimekwe, *The Impact of Religion, Personality, Values and Worldviews on Attitudes Towards Human Rights*, Religion and Human Rights 11,
https://doi.org/10.1007/978-3-031-65749-8

Watson, B., & Thompson, P. (2013). *The effective teaching of religious education* (2nd ed.). Routledge.
Ziebertz, H.-G. (2002). Normativity and empirical research in practical theology. *Journal of Empirical Theology, 15*(1), 5–18.

B. Online Sources:

Dailies

Still on Hijab-for-School Controversy. *The Guardian Newspaper*, 7th February 2019. Available at: https://guardian.ng/opinion/still-on-hijab-for-school-controversy/. Accessed 12 Feb 2020.

Policy Documents (Ecclesiastical Documents)

Catechism of the Catholic Church. (1997). *II Edition*. Libreria Editrice Vaticana.
CDF. (1980). *Declaration on Euthanasia*. Available at. https://www.vatican.va/roman_curia/congregations/cfaith/documents/rc_con_cfaith_doc_19800505_euthanasia_en.html. Accessed 3 May 2018.
CDF. (1987). *Donum Vitae: Instruction on respect for human life in its origin and on the dignity of procreation*. Libreria Editrice Vaticana.
CDF. (2021). *Responsum to a Dubium regarding the Blessing of the unions of persons of the same sex* (Bollettino No. 210315b). Holy See Press Office.
Francis. (2015). *Laudato Si': Encyclical letter on care for our common home*. Available at: https://www.vatican.va/content/francesco/en/encyclicals/documents/papa-francesco_20150524_enciclica-laudato-si.html. Accessed 01 Feb 2019.
Francis. (2017). *Address to participants in the International Forum on "Migration and Peace", 21st February 2017*. Available at: https://www.vatican.va/content/francesco/en/speeches/2017/february/documents/papa-francesco_20170221_forum-migrazioni-pace.html. Accessed 01 Apr 2017.
Gregory XVI. (1832). *Mirari Vos: Encyclical Letter on Liberalism and Religious Indifferentism*. Available at: https://www.papalencyclicals.net/greg16/g16mirar.htm. Accessed 08 Jan 2019.
John XXIII. (1963). *Pacem in Terris: Encyclical Letter on Establishing Universal Peace*. Available at: https://www.vatican.va/content/john-xxiii/en/encyclicals/documents/hf_j-xxiii_enc_11041963_pacem.html. Accessed 01 Feb 2019.
John Paul II. (1987). *Sollicitudo Rei Socialis (SRS): Papal Encyclical on Social Concern*. Available at: https://www.vatican.va/content/john-paul-ii/en/encyclicals/documents/hf_jp-ii_enc_30121987_sollicitudo-rei-socialis.html. Accessed 01 July 2015.
John Paul II. (1988). *Mulieris Dignitatem: Apostolic Letter on the Dignity and Vocation of Women*. Available at: https://www.vatican.va/content/john-paul-ii/en/apost_letters/1988/documents/hf_jp-ii_apl_19880815_mulieris-dignitatem.html. Accessed 01 Feb 2021.
John Paul II. (1991). *Centesimus Annus: Encyclical Letter on the Hundreth Anniversary of Rerum Novarum*. Available at: https://www.vatican.va/content/john-paul-ii/en/encyclicals/documents/hf_jp-ii_enc_01051991_centesimus-annus.html. Accessed 01 July 2015.
John Paul II. (1993). *Veritatis Splendor: Papal Encyclical on the Splendor of the Truth*. Available at: https://www.vatican.va/content/john-paul-ii/en/encyclicals/documents/hf_jp-ii_enc_06081993_veritatis-splendor.html. Accessed 01 July 2015.

Pius IX. (1864a). *Quanta Cura: Encyclical Letter Condemning Current Errors*. Available at: https://www.papalencyclicals.net/pius09/p9quanta.htm. Accessed 08 Jan 2019.

Pius IX. (1864b). *Syllabus of Errors: Issued as an Annex to the Encyclical Quantum Cura*. Available at: https://www.papalencyclicals.net/pius09/p9syll.htm. Accessed 08 Jan 2019.

Pius VI. (1791). *Quod Aliquantum: Encyclical Letter issued in Condemnation of the Civil Constitution of the Clergy*. Available: https://www.vatican.va/content/pius-vi/it/documents/breve-quod-aliquantum-10-marzo-1791.html. Accessed 08 Jan 2019.

Pius X. (1906). *Vehementer Nos: Encyclical Letter on the French Law of Separation*. Available at: https://www.vatican.va/content/pius-x/en/encyclicals/documents/hf_p-x_enc_11021906_vehementer-nos.html. Accessed 08 Jan 2019.

Pius XI. (1930). *Casti Connubii: Encyclical Letter on Christian Marriage*. Available at https://www.vatican.va/content/pius-xi/en/encyclicals/documents/hf_p-xi_enc_19301231_casti-connubii.html. Accessed 01 July 2015.

Pontifical Council for Justice and Peace. (2006). *Compendium of the Social Doctrine of the Church*. Libreria Editrice Vaticana.

Pontifical Council for the Pastoral Care of Migrants and Itinerant People. (2004). *Erga Migrantes Caritas Christi (EMCC): Instruction on people on the move*. Available at: http://www.vatican.va/roman_curia/pontifical_councils/migrants/documents/rc_pc_migrants_doc_20040514_erga-migrantes-caritas-christi_en.html. Accessed 01 Jan 2021.

Pontificia Commissio Justitia et Pax. (1975). *The Church and human rights*. Vatican Publishing House.

The Holy Bible. (2011). New International Version. Zondervan.

Vatican II Council. (1965a). *Gaudium et Spes: Pastoral Constitution on the Church in the Modern World*. Available at: https://www.vatican.va/archive/hist_councils/ii_vatican_council/index.htm. Accessed 7 July 2018.

Vatican II Council. (1965b). *Ad gentes: Decree on the Church's Missionary Activity*. Available at: https://www.vatican.va/archive/hist_councils/ii_vatican_council/index.htm. Accessed 07 July 2018.

Vatican II Council. (1965c). *Gravissimum Educationis: Declaration on Christian Education*. Available at: https://www.vatican.va/archive/hist_councils/ii_vatican_council/index.htm. Accessed 7 July 2018.

Vatican II Council. (1965d). *Dignitatis Humanae: Declaration on religious freedom*. Available at: https://www.vatican.va/archive/hist_councils/ii_vatican_council/documents/vat-ii_decl_19651207_dignitatis-humanae_en.html. Accessed 08 Jan 2019.

Policy Documents (Islamic Documents)

Islamic Council of Europe. (1981). *Universal Islamic Declaration of Human Rights (UIDHR)*. Available at: http://www.alhewar.com/ISLAMDECL.html. Accessed 01 Feb 2017.

League of Arab States. (1994). *Arab Charter on Human Rights, 15th September 1994*. Available at: https://www.refworld.org/legal/agreements/las/1994/en/10672. Accessed 04 Mar 2017.

League of Arab States. (2004). *Arab Charter on Human Rights, 22nd May 2004*. Available at: https://www.refworld.org/legal/constinstr/las/2004/en/123762. Accessed 04 May 2017.

Organization of the Islamic Conference (OIC). (1990). *Cairo Declaration on Human Rights in Islam*. Available at: https://www.refworld.org/docid/3ae6b3822c.html. Accessed 03 Feb 2021.

Sharia Penal Code Law Zamfara State of Nigeria. (2000). Available at: https://www.f-law.net/law/threads/37487-Shari-ah-Penal-Code-Law-Zamfara-State-Of-Nigeria-January-2000. Accessed 01 July 2019.

The Quran, with Surah Introductions and Appendices. (2013). Saheeh International Translation. Edited by A.B. al-Mehri. Maktabah Booksellers and Publishers.

International Human Rights Instruments

Council of Europe. (1950). *European convention for the protection of Human Rights and fundamental freedoms, as amended by protocols Nos. 11 and 14*, ETS 5, 4th November 1950. Available at: https://www.refworld.org/legal/agreements/coe/1950/en/18688. Accessed 04 Feb 2014.

Human Rights Council. (2012). *Human rights, democracy and the Rule of Law, UN Doc A/HRC/RES/19/36 19th April 2012*. Available at: https://www.right-docs.org/doc/a-hrc-res-19-36/. Accessed 01 July 2017.

Human Rights Council. (2015). *Human rights, democracy and the Rule of Law, UN Doc A/HRC/RES/28/14, 9th April 2015*. Available at: https://ap.ohchr.org/documents/dpage_e.aspx?si=A/HRC/RES/28/14. Accessed 01 July 2017.

Human Rights Council. (2016). *The promotion and protection of human rights in the context of peaceful protests, UN Doc. A/HRC/RES/31/37, 24th March 2016*. Available at: https://www.right-docs.org/doc/a-hrc-res-31-37/. Accessed 01 Dec 2020.

Human Rights Watch. (2016). *Tell me where i can be safe: The impact of Nigeria's same sex marriage (prohibition) act*. Available at. https://www.hrw.org/report/2016/10/20/tell-me-where-i-can-be-safe/impact-nigerias-same-sex-marriageprohibition-act. Accessed 1 Jan 2020.

ILO. (1944a). *Declaration of Philadelphia*. Available at: http://blue.lim.ilo.org/cariblex/pdfs/ILO_dec_philadelphia.pdf. Accessed 10 Oct 2017.

ILO. (1944b). *Income Security Recommendation* (No. R067). Available at: https://www.ilo.org/dyn/normlex/en/f?p=NORMLEXPUB:12100:0::NO::P12100_ILO_CODE:R067. Accessed 01 Feb 2017.

ILO. (1944c). *Medical Care Recommendation (No. R069)*. Available at: https://www.ilo.org/dyn/normlex/en/f?p=NORMLEXPUB:12100:0::NO:12100:P12100_INSTRUMENT_ID:312407:NO. Accessed 01 Feb 2017.

ILO. (1958). *Discrimination (Employment and Occupation) Convention* (No. C111). Available at: https://www.refworld.org/docid/3ddb680f4.html. Accessed 15 June 2021.

ILO. (1973). *Minimum Age Convention* (No. C138). Available at: https://www.refworld.org/docid/421216a34.html. Accessed 02 Aug 2021.

ILO. (1998). *Declaration on fundamental principles and rights at work and its follow-up*. International Labour Office.

ILO. (1999a). *Worst Forms of Child Labour Convention* (No. C182). Available at: https://www.refworld.org/docid/3ddb6e0c4.html. Accessed 02 Aug 2021.

ILO. (1999b). *Worst Forms of Child Labour Recommendation* (No. R190). Available at: https://www.ilo.org/dyn/normlex/en/f?p=NORMLEXPUB:12100:0::NO:12100:P12100_INSTRUMENT_ID:312528:NO. Accessed 01 Feb 2017.

ILO (2012). *Recommendation Concerning National Floors of Social Protection* (No. R202). Available at: https://www.refworld.org/docid/5c77a49f7.html. Accessed 02 Aug 2021.

International Commission of Jurists (ICJ). (1997). *Maastricht guidelines on violations of economic, social and cultural rights*. Available at: https://www.refworld.org/docid/48abd5730.html. Accessed 03 May 2021.

ILO and NBS. (2001). *Nigeria National Child Labour Survey (NCLS) report 2000/2001. International Programme on the Elimination of Child Labour (IPEC)*. Available at: https://www.ilo.org/ipecinfo/product/download.do?type=document&id=8671. Accessed 1 Jan 2014.

ILO and UNICEF. (2021). *Child labour: Global estimates 2020, trends and the road forward*. ILO and UNICEF.

International Criminal Tribunal for Rwanda. (1994). *Rules of Procedure and Evidence, UN. Doc. ITR/3/REV.1, 8th November 1994*. Available at: https://unictr.irmct.org/sites/unictr.org/files/legal-library/950629-rpe-en.pdf. Accessed 01 Mar 2021.

International Criminal Tribunal for the former Yugoslavia. (1993). *Rules of Procedure and Evidence, UN Doc. IT/32/Rev.50, 25th May 1993*. Available at: https://www.icty.org/en/documents/rules-procedure-evidence. Accessed 01 Mar 2021.

Nowak, M. (2005). *Human rights: A handbook for parliamentarians*, No. 8. OHCHR.
OHCHR. (1992). *CCPR General Comment No. 20: Article 7 (Prohibition of Torture, or Other Cruel, Inhuman or Degrading Treatment or Punishment), CCPR/C/GC/20, 10th March 1992*. Available at: https://www.refworld.org/docid/453883fb0.html. Accessed 30 Apr 2020.
OHCHR. (2014). *Women's rights are human rights, UN Doc. HR/PUB/14/2, 2014*. Available at: https://www.refworld.org/docid/5566cfd14.html. Accessed 07 June 2021.
OHCHR. (n.d.). *Status of Ratification of 18 International Human Rights Treaties*. Available at: http://indicators.ohchr.org/. Accessed 01 July 2019.
Organization of American States (OAS). (1969). *American Convention on Human Rights, 22nd November 1969*. Available at: https://www.refworld.org/legal/agreements/oas/1969/en/20081. Accessed 04 Apr 2017.
UN CEDAW. (1992). *General Recommendation No. 19: Violence against Women, UN Doc. A/47/38, 1992*. Available at: https://www.refworld.org/docid/52d920c54.html. Accessed 15 June 2021.
UN Commission on Human Rights. (1984). *The Siracusa Principles on the Limitation and Derogation Provisions in the ICCPR, UN Doc. E/CN.4/1985/4, 28th September 1984*. Available at: https://www.refworld.org/legal/resolution/unchr/1984/en/57200. Accessed 29 Feb 2017.
UN Committee on the Elimination of Discrimination against Women (UN CEDAW). (1989). *General Recommendation No. 12: Violence against Women, UN Doc. A/44/38, 1989*. Available at: https://www.refworld.org/docid/52d927444.html. Accessed 16 June 2021.
UN Department of Economic and Social Affairs (UNDESA) Population Division. (2019). *World population prospects 2019 – Special aggregates*. Available at: https://population.un.org/wpp/Download/SpecialAggregates/EconomicTrading/. Accessed 2 Mar 2020.
UN Economic and Social Council (ECOSOC). (1985). *Implementation of the International Covenant on Economic, Social and Cultural Rights, UN Doc. E/Res/1985/17, 28th May 1985*. Available at: https://ap.ohchr.org/documents/alldocs.aspx?doc_id=8704. Accessed 01 Feb 2017.
UN ECOSOC. (1990). *CESCR General Comment No. 3: The Nature of States Parties' Obligations (Art. 2, Para. 1, of the Covenant), UN Doc. E/1991/23, 14th December 1990*. Available at: https://www.refworld.org/legal/general/cescr/1990/en/5613. Accessed 27 Sept 2021.
UN ECOSOC. (1999). *CESCR General Comment No. 12: The Right to Adequate Food (Art. 11 of the Covenant), UN Doc. E/C.12/1999/5, 12th May 1999*. Available at: https://www.refworld.org/docid/4538838c11.html. Accessed 03 May 2021.
UN ECOSOC. (2000). CESCR *General Comment No. 14: The Right to the Highest Attainable Standard of Health (Art. 12 of the Covenant), UN Doc. E/C.12/2000/4, 11th August 2000*. Available at: https://www.refworld.org/docid/4538838d0.html. Accessed 03 May 2020.
UN ECOSOC. (2002). *Further measures to promote and consolidate democracy, UN Doc. E/CN.4/RES/2002/46, 23rd April 2002*. Available at: https://digitallibrary.un.org/record/481906. Accessed 01.0.2017.
UN ECOSOC. (2016). *CESCR General Comment No. 22: The Right to Sexual and Reproductive Health (Article 12 of the International Covenant), UN. Doc. E/C.12/GC/22, 2nd May 2016*. Available at: https://digitallibrary.un.org/record/832961?ln=zh_CN. Accessed 01 July 2020.
UN ECOSOC. (2018). *List of non-governmental organizations in consultative status as of 1st September 2018, UN Doc. E/2018/INF/5, 31st October 2018*. Available at: https://documents.un.org/doc/undoc/gen/n18/352/55/pdf/n1835255.pdf. Accessed 1 Dec 2018.
UN General Assembly. (1965). *International Convention on the Elimination of All Forms of Racial Discrimination (ICERD), 21st December 1965*. United Nations Treaty Series (UNTS), 660, p. 195. Available at: http://www.refworld.org/docid/3ae6b3940.html. Accessed 10 Oct 2017.
UN General Assembly. (1979a). *Code of Conduct for Law Enforcement Officials, UN Doc. A/RES/34/169, 17th December 1979*. Available at: https://www.refworld.org/docid/48abd572e.html. Accessed 31 Dec 2020.
UN General Assembly. (1979b). *Convention on the Elimination of All Forms of Discrimination against Women (CEDAW), UN Doc. A/RES/34/180, 18th December 1979*. UNTS, 1249, p. 13. Available at: https://www.refworld.org/docid/3b00f2244.html. Accessed 11 Sept 2017.

UN General Assembly. (1981). *Declaration on the elimination of all forms of intolerance and of discrimination based on religion or belief, UN Doc. A/RES/36/55, 25th November 1981.* Available at: https://www.refworld.org/legal/resolution/unga/1981/en/5952. Accessed 04 Mar 2017.

UN General Assembly. (1989). *Convention on the Rights of the Child (CRC), 20th November 1989.* UNTS, vol. 1577, p. 3. Available at: http://www.refworld.org/docid/3ae6b38f0.html. Accessed 10 Oct 2017.

UN General Assembly. (1990). *International Convention on the Protection of the Rights of All Migrant Workers and Members of their Families, UN Doc. A/RES/45/158, 18th December 1990.* Available at: https://www.refworld.org/legal/agreements/unga/1990/en/27627. Accessed 8 Feb 2016.

UN General Assembly. (1993a). *Declaration on the Elimination of Violence against Women, UN Doc. A/RES/48/104, 20th December 1993.* Available at: https://www.refworld.org/docid/3b00f25d2c.html. Accessed 16 June 2021.

UN General Assembly. (1993b). *National institutions for the Promotion and Protection of Human Rights, UN Doc. A/RES/48/134, 20th December 1993.* Available at: https://www.refworld.org/docid/3b00f25e14.html. Accessed 05 Dec 2019.

UN General Assembly. (1993c). *The World Conference on Human Rights: Vienna Declaration and Programme of Action, A/CONF.157/23, 12 July 1993.* Available at: https://www.refworld.org/legal/resolution/unga/1993/en/14730. Accessed 01 Aug 2018.

UN General Assembly. (1998). *Rome Statute of the International Criminal Court (Last Amended 2010), UN Doc. A/CONF.183/9, 17th July 1998.* Available at: https://www.refworld.org/docid/3ae6b3a84.html. Accessed 24 Mar 2021.

UN General Assembly. (2005a). *Enhancing the role of regional, subregional and other organizations and arrangements in promoting and consolidating democracy, UN Doc. A/RES/59/201, 23rd March 2005.* Available at: https://www.refworld.org/docid/43f3122f6.html. Accessed 28 Nov 2019.

UN General Assembly. (2005b). *World Summit Outcome: Resolution, UN Doc. A/RES/60/1, 24th October 2005.* Available at: https://www.refworld.org/docid/44168a910.html. Accessed 19 Nov 2019.

UN General Assembly. (2006). *Human Rights Council: Resolution, UN Doc. A/RES/60/251, 3rd April 2006.* Available at: https://www.refworld.org/docid/4537814814.html. Accessed 05 Dec 2019.

UN General Assembly. (2015). *Transforming our world: The 2030 Agenda for sustainable development, UN Doc. A/RES/70/1, 21st October 2015.* Available at: http://www.refworld.org/docid/57b6e3e44.html. Accessed 10 Oct 2017.

UN General Assembly. (2019). *Moratorium on the Use of the Death Penalty, UN Doc. A/RES/73/175, 17th December 2018.* Available at https://undocs.org/pdf?symbol=en/A/RES/73/175. Accessed 02 Feb 2020.

UNHCR (2010). *Convention and protocol relating to the status of refugees.* UNHCR Communications and Public Information Service. Available at: https://www.unhcr.org/protect/PROTECTION/3b66c2aa10.pdf. Accessed 01 Feb 2021.

UN HRC. (1992). *CCPR General Comment No. 20 on Article 7 (Prohibition of Torture, or Other Cruel, Inhuman or Degrading Treatment or Punishment), CCPR/C/GC/20, 10th March 1992.* Available at: https://www.refworld.org/docid/453883fb0.html. Accessed 30 Apr 2015.

UN HRC. (1993). *CCPR General Comment No. 22: Article 18 (Freedom of Thought, Conscience or Religion),* CCPR/C/21/Rev.1/Add.4, 30th July 1993. Available at: https://www.refworld.org/docid/453883fb22.html. Accessed 18 Dec 2015.

UN HRC. (1994). *Toonen v. Australia, Communication No. 488/1992, UN. Doc CCPR/C/50/D/488/1992, 31st March 1994.* Available at: http://hrlibrary.umn.edu/undocs/html/vws488.htm. Accessed 01 Mar 2016.

UN HRC. (2007). *General Comment No. 32: Article 14 (Right to Equality Before Courts and Tribunals and to Fair Trial), CCPR/C/GC/32, 23rd August 2007.* Available at: https://www.refworld.org/docid/478b2b2f2.html. Accessed 27 Feb 2021.

UN HRC. (2011). *CCPR General Comment No. 34 on Article 19 (Freedoms of Opinion and Expression), CCPR/C/GC/34, 12th September 2011*. Available at: https://www.refworld.org/docid/4ed34b562.html. Accessed 01 Dec 2020.

UN HRC. (2018). *CCPR General Comment No. 36 on Article 6 (Right to Life), CCPR/C/GC/36, 30th October 2018*. Available at: https://www.ohchr.org/EN/HRBodies/CCPR/Pages/GC36-Article6Righttolife.aspx. Accessed 23 June 2020.

UN Human Rights Council. (2007). *A resolution on Moratorium on the Use of the Death Penalty, UN Doc. A/RES/62/149, 18th December 2007*. Available at: https://documents.un.org/doc/undoc/gen/n07/472/71/pdf/n0747271.pdf?token=j2TD1excZ4BWQo3cgF&fe=true. Accessed 02 Dec 2019.

UN Human Rights Council. (2012a). *Report of the special Rapporteur on the Rights to Freedom of Peaceful Assembly and of Association, UN Doc. A/HRC/20/27, 21st May 2012*. Available at: https://www.refworld.org/docid/525fad894.html. Accessed 21 Dec 2020.

UN Human Rights Council. (2012b). *The protection of human rights and fundamental freedoms while countering terrorism, UN Doc. A/HRC/22/26, 17th December 2012*. Available at: https://www.refworld.org/docid/5118eb762.html. Accessed 27 Feb 2021.

UN Human Rights Council. (2013). *Report on effective measures and best practices to ensure the promotion and protection of human rights in the context of peaceful protests, UN Doc. A/HRC/22/28, 21st January 2013*. Available at: https://www.refworld.org/docid/5118f0612.html. Accessed 21 Dec 2020.

UN Security Council. (1993). *Statute of the International Criminal Tribunal for the Former Yugoslavia (ICTY), 25th May 1993 (Last Amended on 17th May 2002)*. Available at: https://www.refworld.org/docid/3dda28414.html. Accessed 24 Mar 2021.

UN Security Council. (1994). *Statute of the International Criminal Tribunal for Rwanda* (ICTR), *8th November 1994 (Last Amended on 13th October 2006)*. Available at: https://www.refworld.org/docid/3ae6b3952c.html. Accessed 24 Mar 2021.

WEF Global Gender Gap Report. (2020). Available at: https://www.weforum.org/reports/gender-gap-2020-report-100-years-pay-equality. Accessed 01 May 2021.

Regional Human Rights Instruments

African Commission. (2014a). *General Comment No. 2 on Article 14.1(a), (b), (c) and (f) and Article 14. 2(a) and (c) of the Protocol to the ACHPR on the Rights of Women in Africa, 28th November 2014*. Available at: https://www.achpr.org/legalinstruments/detail?id=13. Accessed 11 Sept 2020.

African Commission. (2014b). *Resolution on Protection against Violence and Other Human Rights Violations against Persons on the Basis of their Real or Imputed Sexual Orientation or Gender Identity, ACHPR/Res.275 (LV), 28th April – 12th May 2014*. Available at: https://www.achpr.org/adoptedresolution. Accessed 01 July 2014.

African Commission. (2015). *General comment No. 3 of the African charter on human and peoples' rights: The right to life (Article 4), 4th to 18th November 2015*. Available at: https://www.achpr.org/legalinstruments/. Accessed 01 July 2014.

African Commission on Human and Peoples' Rights (African Commission). (2003). *Principles and Guidelines on the Right to a Fair Trial and Legal Assistance in Africa, 29th May 2003*. Available at https://www.achpr.org/legalinstruments/detail?id=38. Accessed 01 July 2014.

OAU. (1982). *African Charter on human and peoples' rights ("Banjul Charter"), CAB/LEG/67/3 rev. 5, 21 I.L.M. 58, 27th June 1981*. Available at: https://www.refworld.org/docid/3ae6b3630.html. Accessed 24 Mar 2021.

OAU. (1990). *African Charter on the Rights and Welfare of the Child, CAB/LEG/24.9/49 (1990), 11th July 1990*. Available at: https://www.refworld.org/legal/agreements/oau/1990/en/13798. Accessed 05 Nov 2018.

Organization of African Unity (OAU). (1969). *Convention governing the specific aspects of refugee problems in Africa ("OAU Convention"), 10th September 1969*. 1001 UNTS, 45. Available at: https://www.refworld.org/docid/3ae6b36018.html. Accessed 16 Jan 2021.

National Human Rights Instruments

Abuja: *Penal Code Act, Cap. 53 Laws of Federation of Nigeria (LFN) 1960*. Available at: http://oceansbeyondpiracy.org/sites/default/files/Nigeria_Penal_Code_Act_1960.pdf. Accessed 01 Jan 2020.

Amnesty International Nigeria. (2017). *NGO Bill Threatens Freedoms in Nigeria* (Index No.: AFR 44/7590/2017). Amnesty International Publications.

Amnesty International Nigeria. (2019). *Human rights agenda*. Index No.: AFR 44/0431/2019. Amnesty International Publications.

Eze, E.O. (2005). *Religion and state in Nigeria*. Available at: http://iheu.org/ReligionandStateinNigeria_InternationalHumanistandEthicalUnion.htm. Accessed 2 Nov 2015

Federal Republic of Nigeria. (2014). *National policy on education*. NERDC.

Federal Republic of Nigeria. (2018). *National guidelines on safe termination of pregnancy for legal indications*. Federal Ministry of Health.

Federal Republic of Nigeria. (n.d.). *National Action Plan (NAP) for the promotion and protection of human rights in Nigeria 2009–2013*. Available at: https://www.ohchr.org/sites/default/files/Documents/Issues/Education/Training/actionsplans/Excerpts/Nigeria09_13.pdf. Accessed 1 May 2015

Human Rights Council. (2018a). *National report submitted in Accordance with Paragraph 5 of the Annex to HRC Resolution 16/21: Nigeria, UN Doc. A/HRC/WG.6/31/NGA/1, 27th August 2018*. Available at: https://documents-dds-ny.un.org/doc/UNDOC/GEN/182/589/9X/PDF/1825899.pdf?OpenElement. Accessed 01 Oct 2019.

Human Rights Council. (2018b). *Report of the Working Group on the Universal Periodic Review – Nigeria, UN Doc. A/HRC/40/7, 26th December 2018*. Available at: https://www.ecoi.net/en/file/local/1457455/1930_1549370422_g1844665.pdf. Accessed 01 June 2019.

International Federation for Human Rights. (2008). *Nigeria: NGO coalition shadow report to the CEDAW committee, 31st July 2008*. Available at: https://www.refworld.org/docid/48a0007a2.html. Accessed 16 July 2014.

International Federation for Human Rights. (2010, April). *Defending human rights – Not everywhere not every right: International fact-finding mission report on Nigeria*. Available at: https://www.refworld.org/docid/4bed03412.html. Accessed 16 July 2014.

International Labour Organization (ILO) and Federal Office of Statistics of Nigeria. (2001). *Nigeria National Child Labour (NCL) Survey Report 2000/2001. International Programme on the Elimination of Child Labour (IPEC)*. Available at: https://www.ilo.org/ipecinfo/product/download.do?type=document&id=8671. Accessed 01 Jan 2014.

National Bureau of Statistics (NBS). (2020). *Nigeria Living Standards (NLS) Survey 2018/2019*. Proshare.

Nigeria: *Constitution of the Federal Republic of Nigeria (CFRN)*. (1999). *Updated with the First, Second and Third Alterations (2010) and the Fourth Alteration (2017)*. Federal Ministry of Justice.

Nigeria. (2004a). *The Compulsory, Free Universal Basic Education Act 2004. Compendium of Education Sector Laws in Nigeria* (Vol. 1, 3rd ed.). Federal Ministry of Education.

Nigeria. (2004b). *UN Convention on the Rights of the Child: Second country periodic report*. Federal Ministry of Women Affairs.

Nigeria. (2006). *National Gender Policy*. Federal Ministry of Women Affairs and Social Development.

Nigeria. (2017). *6th periodic country report 2015–2016 on the implementation of the African Charter on human and peoples' rights in Nigeria*. Federal Ministry of Justice

Nigeria: *Administration of Criminal Justice Act (ACJA), Cap C40 LFN 2015*. Available at: http://lawsofnigeria.placng.org/laws/C23.pdf. Accessed 01 Jan 2016.

Nigeria: *Armed Forces Act, Cap. A20 LFN 2004*. Available at: https://laws.lawnigeria.com/2018/04/19/lfn-armed-forces-act/. Accessed 01 Feb 2020.

Nigeria: *Children and Young Persons Act, Cap 32 LFN 1958*. Available at: https://laws.lawnigeria.com/2020/06/19/index-lfn-laws-of-the-federation-of-nigeria-3/. Accessed 01 Jan 2020.

Nigeria: *Child's Rights Act (CRA) 2003, 31st July 2003*. Available at: https://www.refworld.org/docid/5568201f4.html. Accessed 01 June 2016.

Nigeria: *Criminal Code Act, Cap C38 LFN 2004*. Available at: https://www.refworld.org/docid/49997ade1a.html. Accessed 10 June 2020.

Nigeria: *Employee's Compensation Act 2010*. Available at: https://laws.lawnigeria.com/2020/06/19/index-lfn-laws-of-the-federation-of-nigeria-3/. Accessed 01 Jan 2020.

Nigeria: *Factories Act 2004*. Available at: https://laws.lawnigeria.com/2020/06/19/index-lfn-laws-of-the-federation-of-nigeria-3/. Accessed 01 Jan 2020.

Nigeria: *Labour Act, Cap. L1 LFN 2004*. Available at: https://laws.lawnigeria.com/2020/06/19/index-lfn-laws-of-the-federation-of-nigeria-3/. Accessed 01 Jan 2020.

Nigeria: *National Commission for Refugees Act, Cap N21 LFN 2004*. Available at: https://www.refworld.org/docid/3ae6b522e.html. Accessed 16 Jan 2021.

Nigeria: *National Minimum Wage Act 2011*. Available at: https://laws.lawnigeria.com/2020/06/19/index-lfn-laws-of-the-federation-of-nigeria-3/. Accessed 01 Jan 2020.

Nigeria: *Penal Code Act Cap 53 LFN (Abuja)*. Available at: http://oceansbeyondpiracy.org/sites/default/files/Nigeria_Penal_Code_Act_1960.pdf. Accessed 01 Jan 2015.

Nigeria: *Pensions Reform Act 2014*. Available at: https://laws.lawnigeria.com/2020/06/19/index-lfn-laws-of-the-federation-of-nigeria-3/. Accessed 01 Jan 2020.

Nigeria: *Same Sex Marriage (Prohibition) Act, 17th December 2013*. Available at: https://www.refworld.org/docid/52f4d9cc4.html Accessed 23 Apr 2015.

Nigeria: *Shari'ah Penal Code Law 2000, Zamfara State of Nigeria*. Available at: https://www.f-law.net/law/threads/37487-Shari-ah-Penal-Code-Law-Zamfara-State-Of-Nigeria-January-2000. Accessed 01 Feb 2015.

Nigeria: *Trade Disputes Act, Cap. T8 LFN 2004*. Available at: https://laws.lawnigeria.com/2020/06/19/index-lfn-laws-of-the-federation-of-nigeria-3/. Accessed 01 Jan 2020.

Nigeria: *Trade Union Act, Cap. T14 LFN 2004*. Available at: https://laws.lawnigeria.com/2020/06/19/index-lfn-laws-of-the-federation-of-nigeria-3/. Accessed 01 Jan 2020.

Nigeria: *Trafficking in persons (prohibition) enforcement and administration (NAPTIP) Act 2015*. Available at: https://laws.lawnigeria.com/2020/06/19/index-lfn-laws-of-the-federation-of-nigeria-3/. Accessed 01 Jan 2020.

Nigeria: *Violence Against Persons (Prohibition) Act, 2015 (VAPP), 25th May 2015*. Available at: https://www.refworld.org/docid/556d5eb14.html. Accessed 30 Apr 2016.

Nigeria Civil Society Situation Room. (2019). *Report of Nigeria's 2019 general elections*. Available at: https://www.placng.org/situation_room/sr/wp-content/uploads/2019/09/Report-on-Nigerias-2019-General-Elections.pdf. Accessed 01 Dec 2020.

OHCHR. (2006). *National Action Plan (NAP) for the promotion and protection of human rights in Nigeria 2006*. Federal Republic of Nigeria. Available at: https://www.ohchr.org/sites/default/files/Documents/Issues/NHRA/nigeria.pdf. Accessed 02 July 2015.

OHCHR. (2018). *UN Human Rights Report 2017*. Available at: https://www2.ohchr.org/english/OHCHRreport2017/allegati/Downloads/1_Whole_Report_2017.pdf. Accessed 1 July 2019.

Pew Research Center. (2007). *Nigeria's Presidential election: The Christian-Muslim divide*. Available at: https://www.pewresearch.org/religion/2007/03/21/nigerias-presidential-election-the-christian-muslim-divide/. Accessed 02 July 2015.

Stakeholder Democracy Network (SDN). (2020). *Women's political participation and representation in the Niger Delta.* Available at: http://www.stakeholderdemocracy.org/wp-content/uploads/2020/02/More-women-in-governance.-Report.-2019.-DIGITAL.pdf. Accessed 1 Dec 2020.

The World Factbook. (2021). *Nigeria: People and society.* Available at: https://www.cia.gov/the-world-factbook/countries/nigeria/#people-and-society. Accessed 23 Jan 2022.

UBEC Annual Report. (2010). *National framework for the development and integration of Almajiri education into UBE Programme.* Universal Basic Education Commission.

US Department of State. (2014). *Nigeria: Human Rights Report 2013.* Available at: https://2009-2017.state.gov/documents/organization/220358.pdf. Accessed 03 May 2015.

Other Internet Sources

Aquinas, T. (n.d.). *On The Law: Summa Theologiae* (A. J. Fredosso, Trans.). St. Thomas Education Project (STEP). Available at: http://www.thomasinternational.org/projects/step/treatiseonlaw/delege000.htm. Accessed 01 Feb 2021.

Christianity and Capital Punishment. (2009). Available at http://www.bbc.co.uk/religion/religions/christianity/christianethics/capitalpunishment_1.shtml. Accessed 08 Aug 2020.

Democracy. (n.d.). Available at: https://www.un.org/en/sections/issues-depth/democracy/index.html. Accessed 01 Nov 2019.

Democracy and the United Nations. The Youth Café. (n.d.). Available at https://www.theyouthcafe.com/un-democracy-day-information-kit/2019/9/democracy-and-the-united-nations-the-youth-cafe. Accessed 09 Sept 2019.

Democracy Web. (n.d.). Available at: https://democracyweb.org/freedom-of-religion-history. Accessed 01 Feb 2020.

Dickson, P.C. (2014). Homophobia unites Muslims and Christians in Nigeria. *GlobalPost.* Available at: https://www.pri.org/stories/2014-02-13/homophobia-unites-muslims-and-christians-nigeria. Accessed 01 Jan 2020.

Miranda Rights in Nigerian Criminal Jurisprudence. (n.d.). Available at: https://www.lawyard.ng/wp-content/uploads/2020/07/Miranda-in-Nigerian-Criminal-Jurisprudence.pdf. Accessed 01 Feb 2021.

Nigeria: *World Prison Brief Data.* Birkbeck: University of London. Available at: https://www.prisonstudies.org/country/nigeria. Accessed 01 Apr 2021.

Nigeria: *Voter Education Handbook (VEH).* (n.d.). ACE Project 1998–2020. Available at: http://aceproject.org/ero-en/regions/africa/NG/voter-education-handbook.pdf/view. Accessed 01 Dec 2020.

Political Protest. (n.d.). *Governments of the world: A global guide to citizens' rights and responsibilities.* Available at: https://www.encyclopedia.com/international/legal-and-political-magazines/political-protest. Accessed 19 Dec 2020.

Roser, M. (n.d.). *Democracy.* Available at: https://ourworldindata.org/democracy. Accessed 01 Nov 2019.

Symbolum Quicunque: The Athanasian Creed. Creeds of Christendom, II. (n.d.). Available at: https://www.ccel.org/ccel/schaff/creeds2.iv.i.iv.html. Accessed 08 Aug 2014.

Tutor Hunt International. (2022). *Examining Grimmitt's human pedagogy in informing.* Available at: https://www.tutorhunt.com/resource/26467/. Accessed 05 May 2023.

What are Contractual Rights? (n.d.). Available at https://www.legalmatch.com/law-library/article/what-are-contractual-rights.html. Accessed 14 Sept 2019.

When is Civil Disobedience Allowed for a Christian? (n.d.). Available at: https://www.gotquestions.org/civil-disobedience.html. Accessed 01 Feb 2021.

The manufacturer's authorised representative in the EU is Springer
Nature Customer Service Centre GmbH, Europaplatz 3, 69115 Heidelberg,
Germany. If you have any concerns regarding our products, please
contact ProductSafety@springernature.com

Printed and bound by CPI Group (UK) Ltd, Croydon, CR0 4YY
01/10/2026
02225897-0015